Lecture Notes in Computer Science   16338

Founding Editors

Gerhard Goos
Juris Hartmanis

Editorial Board Members

Elisa Bertino, *Purdue University, West Lafayette, IN, USA*
Wen Gao, *Peking University, Beijing, China*
Bernhard Steffen, *TU Dortmund University, Dortmund, Germany*
Moti Yung, *Columbia University, New York, NY, USA*

The series Lecture Notes in Computer Science (LNCS), including its subseries Lecture Notes in Artificial Intelligence (LNAI) and Lecture Notes in Bioinformatics (LNBI), has established itself as a medium for the publication of new developments in computer science and information technology research, teaching, and education.

LNCS enjoys close cooperation with the computer science R & D community, the series counts many renowned academics among its volume editors and paper authors, and collaborates with prestigious societies. Its mission is to serve this international community by providing an invaluable service, mainly focused on the publication of conference and workshop proceedings and postproceedings. LNCS commenced publication in 1973.

Jessie Y. C. Chen · Gino Fragomeni ·
Xiaowen Fang

Editors

HCI International 2025 – Late Breaking Papers

27th International Conference on
Human-Computer Interaction, HCII 2025
Gothenburg, Sweden, June 22–27, 2025
Proceedings, Part VIII

 Springer

Editors
Jessie Y. C. Chen
U.S. Army Research Laboratory
Adelphi, NY, USA

Gino Fragomeni
Development Command Soldier Center
U.S. Army Combat Capabilities
Orlando, FL, USA

Xiaowen Fang
DePaul University
Chicago, IL, USA

ISSN 0302-9743   ISSN 1611-3349 (electronic)
Lecture Notes in Computer Science
ISBN 978-3-032-12807-2   ISBN 978-3-032-12808-9 (eBook)
https://doi.org/10.1007/978-3-032-12808-9

Foreword

The HCI International (HCII) conference was founded in 1984 by Gavriel Salvendy (Purdue University, USA, Tsinghua University, P.R. China, and University of Central Florida, USA) and the first event of the series, "1st USA-Japan Conference on Human-Computer Interaction", was held in Honolulu, Hawaii, USA, on 18–20 August. Since then, HCI International has been held jointly with several Thematic Areas and Affiliated Conferences, with each one under the auspices of a distinguished international Program Board and under one management and one registration. Twenty-seven HCI International Conferences have been organized so far (every two years until 2013, and annually thereafter).

Last year, we celebrated 40 years since the establishment of the HCII conference, which has been a hub for presenting groundbreaking research and novel ideas and collaboration for people from all over the world. Over the years, this conference has served as a platform for scholars, researchers, industry experts, and students to exchange ideas, connect, and address challenges in the ever-evolving HCI field. The conference has evolved itself, adapting to new technologies and emerging trends, while staying committed to its core mission of advancing knowledge and driving change.

The 27th International Conference on Human-Computer Interaction, HCI International 2025 (HCII 2025), was held as an 'on-site' conference at the Gothia Towers Hotel and Swedish Exhibition & Congress Centre, in Gothenburg, Sweden, on June 22–27, 2025, with the additional option for 'on-line' participation. It incorporated the 21 thematic areas and affiliated conferences listed below.

A total of 7972 individuals from academia, research institutes, industry, and government agencies from 92 countries submitted contributions. 1430 papers and 355 posters (as short research papers) were included in the volumes of the proceedings published just before the start of the conference. Additionally, 439 papers and 104 posters were included in the volumes of the proceedings published after the conference, as "Late Breaking Work". The contributions thoroughly cover the entire field of human-computer interaction, highlight the evolving role of computers in diverse contexts, and demonstrate how HCI research is shaping and improving user experiences across a wide range of domains, influencing technological progress and its effective integration into various sectors. The volumes constituting the full set of the HCII 2025 conference proceedings are listed on the following pages.

I would like to thank the Program Board Chairs and the members of the Program Boards of all thematic areas and affiliated conferences for their contribution towards the high scientific quality and overall success of the HCI International 2025 conference. Their manifold support including paper reviews (via a single-blind review process, with a minimum of two reviews per submission), session organization, and their willingness to act as goodwill ambassadors for the conference is most highly appreciated.

This conference would not have been possible without the continuous and unwavering support and advice of Gavriel Salvendy, founder, General Chair Emeritus, and Scientific Advisor. For his outstanding efforts, I would like to express my sincere appreciation to Abbas Moallem, Communications Chair and Editor of HCI International News.

September 2025   Constantine Stephanidis

HCI International 2025 Thematic Areas and Affiliated Conferences

- HCI: Human-Computer Interaction Thematic Area
- HIMI: Human Interface and the Management of Information Thematic Area
- EPCE: 22nd International Conference on Engineering Psychology and Cognitive Ergonomics
- AC: 19th International Conference on Augmented Cognition
- UAHCI: 19th International Conference on Universal Access in Human-Computer Interaction
- CCD: 17th International Conference on Cross-Cultural Design
- SCSM: 17th International Conference on Social Computing and Social Media
- VAMR: 17th International Conference on Virtual, Augmented and Mixed Reality
- DHM: 16th International Conference on Digital Human Modeling & Applications in Health, Safety, Ergonomics & Risk Management
- DUXU: 14th International Conference on Design, User Experience and Usability
- C&C: 13th International Conference on Culture and Computing
- DAPI: 13th International Conference on Distributed, Ambient and Pervasive Interactions
- HCIBGO: 12th International Conference on HCI in Business, Government and Organizations
- LCT: 12th International Conference on Learning and Collaboration Technologies
- ITAP: 11th International Conference on Human Aspects of IT for the Aged Population
- AIS: 7th International Conference on Adaptive Instructional Systems
- HCI-CPT: 7th International Conference on HCI for Cybersecurity, Privacy and Trust
- HCI-Games: 7th International Conference on HCI in Games
- MobiTAS: 7th International Conference on HCI in Mobility, Transport and Automotive Systems
- AI-HCI: 6th International Conference on Artificial Intelligence in HCI
- MOBILE: 6th International Conference on Human-Centered Design, Operation and Evaluation of Mobile Communications

Conference Proceedings – Full List of Volumes

1. LNCS 15766, Human-Computer Interaction — Part I, edited by Masaaki Kurosu and Ayako Hashizume
2. LNCS 15767, Human-Computer Interaction — Part II, edited by Masaaki Kurosu and Ayako Hashizume
3. LNCS 15768, Human-Computer Interaction — Part III, edited by Masaaki Kurosu and Ayako Hashizume
4. LNCS 15769, Human-Computer Interaction — Part IV, edited by Masaaki Kurosu and Ayako Hashizume
5. LNCS 15770, Human-Computer Interaction — Part V, edited by Masaaki Kurosu and Ayako Hashizume
6. LNCS 15771, Human-Computer Interaction — Part VI, edited by Masaaki Kurosu and Ayako Hashizume
7. LNCS 15772, Human-Computer Interaction — Part VII, edited by Masaaki Kurosu and Ayako Hashizume
8. LNCS 15773, Human Interface and the Management of Information: Part I, edited by Hirohiko Mori and Yumi Asahi
9. LNCS 15774, Human Interface and the Management of Information: Part II, edited by Hirohiko Mori and Yumi Asahi
10. LNCS 15773, Human Interface and the Management of Information: Part III, edited by Hirohiko Mori and Yumi Asahi
11. LNAI 15776, Engineering Psychology and Cognitive Ergonomics: Part I, edited by Don Harris and Wen-Chin Li
12. LNAI 15777, Engineering Psychology and Cognitive Ergonomics: Part II, edited by Don Harris and Wen-Chin Li
13. LNAI 15778, Augmented Cognition, Part I, edited by Dylan D. Schmorrow and Cali M. Fidopiastis
14. LNAI 15779, Augmented Cognition, Part II, edited by Dylan D. Schmorrow and Cali M. Fidopiastis
15. LNCS 15780, Universal Access in Human-Computer Interaction: Part I, edited by Margherita Antona and Constantine Stephanidis
16. LNCS 15781, Universal Access in Human-Computer Interaction: Part II, edited by Margherita Antona and Constantine Stephanidis
17. LNCS 15782, Cross-Cultural Design: Part I, edited by Pei-Luen Patrick Rau
18. LNCS 15783, Cross-Cultural Design: Part II, edited by Pei-Luen Patrick Rau
19. LNCS 15784, Cross-Cultural Design: Part III, edited by Pei-Luen Patrick Rau
20. LNCS 15785, Cross-Cultural Design: Part IV, edited by Pei-Luen Patrick Rau
21. LNCS 15786, Social Computing and Social Media: Part I, edited by Adela Coman and Simona Vasilache

85. CCIS 2772, HCI International 2025 — Late Breaking Posters: Part II, edited by Constantine Stephanidis, Margherita Antona, Stavroula Ntoa, George Margetis and Gavriel Salvendy
86. CCIS 2773, HCI International 2025 — Late Breaking Posters: Part III, edited by Constantine Stephanidis, Margherita Antona, Stavroula Ntoa, George Margetis and Gavriel Salvendy

https://2025.hci.international/proceedings

27th International Conference on Human-Computer Interaction (HCII 2025)

The full list with the Program Board Chairs and the members of the Program Boards of all thematic areas and affiliated conferences of HCII 2025 is available online at:

http://www.hci.international/board-members-2025.php

HCI International 2026 Conference

The 28th International Conference on Human-Computer Interaction, HCI International 2026, will be held jointly with the affiliated conferences at the Montréal Convention Centre (Palais des congrès de Montréal), in Montreal, Canada, 26–31 July 2026. It will cover a broad spectrum of themes related to Human-Computer Interaction, including theoretical issues, methods, tools, processes, and case studies in HCI design, as well as novel interaction techniques, interfaces, and applications. The proceedings will be published by Springer (part of Springer Nature) in a multi-volume set. More information will become available on the conference website: https://2026.hci.international/.

General Chair
Constantine Stephanidis
University of Crete and ICS-FORTH
Heraklion, Crete, Greece
Email: general_chair@2026.hci.international

https://2026.hci.international/

Contents

Frameworks and Computational Methods in XR

Human Factors and User Experience in XR

XR, Culture, and Immersive Heritage Experiences

Extended Reality in Healthcare and Medical Training

Serious Games and Interactive Narratives

Frameworks and Computational Methods in XR

Automated Validation in Immersive Technology for Improving Users' Experience

Marcelo Henrique Lima Cabral[(✉)] [iD] and Gilberto Rufino de Oliveira Neto[iD]

Sidia Institute of Science and Technology, Av. Darcy Vargas, 654, Manaus 69055-035, Brazil
{marcelo.cabral,gilberto.neto}@sidia.com

Abstract. The process of testing and verifying features before and after releasing an application or service uses a lot of time and team resources in testing large feature sets together. A method was needed to assure more cost and time-effective verification of immersive technology due to its diversity and complexity of features, contemplating as many alternative scenarios as possible, always aiming at providing a high-quality product. After adopting test automation to cover all legacy features and immersive features that could be automated, it was observed that not only was testing time reduced by 91,09%, but it was also possible to be run on a continuous basis. As a result of that, the process disclosed a scalable framework for immersive applications validation that accounts for faster continuous usability feedback, more time and people resources to dedicate to verifying and exploring immersive features.

Keywords: Test Automation · XR · Extended Reality · UX · User Experience · Quality Assurance · Legacy features · Immersive features · Design Thinking

1 Introduction

Up until 2018, the adoption of Extended Reality (XR) technology was considered slower than the promising potential it had to grow [16]. It was during the COVID-19 pandemic rise that the XR technology market started spiking in its curve [8] and has reached a value of $56.54 billion by 2024, according to the Extended Reality Global Report, by the business research company official website[1]. The report attributes this growth to the accessibility of the devices, the adoption by the major consumer electronics companies and the gaming and entertainment industries.

The relentless competition to pioneer and position the brands in the XR market demands novelty in design and development processes to provide good user experience in this rising context. In general, providing a good user experience means engaging the users emotionally with the application, service or software. However, differently than mobile experiences, immersive software have innumerous particularities to be considered in its design and its development process, such as 360-degree views, depth perception, hybrid experiences between both the virtual and the physical world, among many others [9].

---

[1] https://www.thebusinessresearchcompany.com/report/extended-reality-global-market-report.

J. Y. C. Chen et al. (Eds.): HCII 2025, LNCS 16338, pp. 3–17, 2026.
https://doi.org/10.1007/978-3-032-12808-9_1

Immersive experiences tend to be a blend of immersive features and legacy features, which are 2D features that work as they do in their mobile version, like basic browser navigators, calendar, calculator, gallery applications and many others. Legacy features have been long consolidated both in their usability as in the process of designing and developing them, as opposed to immersive experiences, which still have a lot of room for exploring and testing.

During a software life cycle, from software development to product maintenance, there are many verification methods that can be used to ensure that the product or service reaches the expected quality level and to prevent usability issues. The Validation process contemplates controlled feature sets testing, exploratory testing, system testing and several other methods that respond to the needs of the project as well as their role depending on the software development model used. For example, when the development team follows the Waterfall model, the testing work starts after the coding is finished, due to its linear and sequential approach, as opposed to Agile models, that are adaptative and incorporate the testing process inside a cycle of short development increments [2, 4].

On both scenarios, XR verification ought to cover both immersive and legacy features so that the full feature set can be contemplated in the Quality Assurance validation process. Therefore, test automation is an alternative that can be considered more than just a tool, but a time and cost-effective process that validates a vast test coverage on an ongoing pace [1], provides continuous and responsive feedbacks – hence, earlier results in design thinking insights [6] and, by consequence, increases the chances to create better user experience with a well-tested application.

The goal behind the experiment related in this article is to demonstrate the efficiency behind the use of automated testing in terms of time and test coverage, as well as demonstrating the potential to explore immersive features on an ongoing basis, hence taking more advantage of the rising opportunities in this market.

2   Theoretical Background

2.1   User Experience Quality in the Context of Software Products and Services

Gorantla & Devinen (2023) iterate that, especially with the rise of design thinking, it is understood that providing a good user experience is directly related to engaging the users' emotions when they are interacting with the product, service or application.

With the advent and widespread access to technology, product development processes count on well consolidated design processes, especially in building mainstream platforms like mobile apps, web services, among others. When it comes to extended reality (XR) solutions, there are many features that can be run on a 2D virtual screen, just like on mobile experiences, as there are innumerous challenges and opportunities that are innate to the virtual or augmented reality realm [7, 9]. For example, immersive virtual 360-degree views, perceived depth, physical and virtual interaction, and movement tracking to expand what can be experienced in a digital application [14].

Aiming at deploying users' positive emotions – and avoiding negative ones, such as cognitive load, confusion, frustration – many features and effects have been used inside the capabilities of XR. For instance, the use of haptics to provide quick feedback for the users to feel sure that certain actions are being performed, spatial audio to give a feeling of presence and tridimensional experience using audio, face tracking and have avatars mirror their facial expressions, among others. There is a lot of room in the XR world to engage the user's and to transcend possibilities beyond what is known in the 2D and on physical world [5].

In the work "Moving from 2D to VR: How to transition a 2D interface into a VR environment" [17], Chennell (2022) highlights consistency as an important factor to determine the intuitiveness, ease of use and, consequently, avoiding cognitive load on the user, that is, welcoming users to adopt XR requires having a blend of familiarity and novelty. For instance, many experiences in XR stem from mobile versions, such as Apple Vision Pro[2] as an AR adaptation of features present in the iPad (Apple's tablet device), with the signature usability the brand users are used to: effects, interfaces, animations, proportions, etc., but adapted to the immersive space. Other initiatives, on the other hand, will propose fully immersive environments in virtual reality, but still preserve interface interaction with a balanced mix with other diegetic interactions, as Meta Quest[3] devices do.

For this article, this distinction of features that come from the mobile experience, mainly 2D interactions, will be referred to as legacy features. This way, we can differentiate them from immersive features, that is, features that need natural interaction and respond to space, distance, intensity and other factors. Assuring stability and scalability of services and products that contain both types of features is what is aimed in this context.

Another important concept taken into consideration is that of Design Thinking, an organizational model which consists of a user-centered approach to designing innovative and creative solutions. By making heavy use of fast prototyping and getting fast and ongoing usability results, it is possible to turn ideas into practical solutions [6]. Therefore, finding a process that can account for continuous rounds of feedback was an essential part of this experiment's goal.

2.2 Assuring Quality in Software Products and Services

Patel & Kishan (2024) compare how the majority of physical systems malfunction in a limited number of predictable ways and how, on the other hand, software may break down in almost infinite range of possibilities. Therefore, it is often impossible to identify every potential software failure mechanism as well as finding design flaws in the program. Although every potential value must be examined and confirmed to maintain the software stability, it is not practical to test all of them.

To prevent minor problems from scaling into major ones, Software Quality Assurance (SQA) aims to streamline the software development process. It is an activity that occurs in the background while software is being developed, in other words, the project-specific and properly executed standards, procedures, and processes are ensured by this set of measures. So, on this basis, error detection becomes the main objective of software testing: a quality control procedure, the assurance of appropriate planning and effective

---

[2] More information on the product available on the official website: https://www.apple.com/apple-vision-pro/

[3] For more information check Meta's official website https://www.meta.com/

execution of testing, a way to deliver better software. Through the collection and analysis of error and defect data, SQA gains a better understanding of the causes of errors and the software engineering activities that contribute the most to their removal and in return helps the stability of the system [11].

The software development process is comprised of seven stages: Evaluation, Requirements, Analysis, Design, Implementation, Validation and Deployment. Validation testing, when compared to the other stages of software development, tends to happen later in the process. To define the ideal test process for the organization, the test team should become familiar with the quality and process improvement standards. Moreover, depending on which software development method is used, its part in the process may differ. Two very common methods are Waterfall and Agile. The Waterfall model, commonly used on shorter terms projects with fixed requirements that are not expected to change until its production phase, consists of a set of phases in a fixed order, which are: requirements, design, coding, testing and operations. Each phase demands the previous one to be successfully completed. In this model, the testing work only starts after the coding is finished. The Agile models, on the other hand, stand for ongoing cycles of smaller increments, and in each of these increments, a round of testing is done, also allowing for continuous and shorter-term feedback. Agile is a more appropriate model when the requirements can be more flexible and time to market or to delivery is more important than delivering a full version of a feature or product [2, 4].

When most of the coding is finished for a milestone, either a full cycle like in waterfall, or a shorter increment like in agile, this is when system testing is performed. This testing stage contemplates a much wider scope, as it stands for verifying and ensuring that the entire system is working according to its specified requirements. As opposed to Functional Tests, that validate feature sets and specific flows only, System Tests coverage embraces the entire system, including the functional tests' scope [15]. Having the test verification happen towards the end of the development milestone creates not only issues with volume, time, and test coverage management, but also generates insights about usability and improvements only late in the process. Furthermore, in scenarios where the validation process needs to be executed manually, the entire process can be more time-consuming and lack efficiency. This is the time when the pressure of software delivery is higher than other tasks. Therefore, one of the reasons leading to automate the testing process is to speed up the project, that is one of the current practices of the SQA and testing [11].

2.3 Automation Process

The use of automated tools to execute tests, compare outcomes, and identify defects has transformed how software is tested. Tools such as Selenium, J Unit, and Jenkins are widely used for functional, regression, and performance testing. The benefits of automation are substantial: it increases test coverage, speeds up the testing process, and allows repetitive tests to be executed without human intervention [15]. So, the test process must be documented for effective execution and to introduce the automated testing, the test process should identify these requirements [11]:

- Testing goals are identified, and objectives should be defined.

- Test strategies and planning must be developed.
- The test team should verify the test tool suitability for the project requirements, the project environment, and the schedule.
- The test team must identify the scope of automated testing. Furthermore, the test team should identify various tasks of automated testing and schedule them according to the priorities.
- The test goals and objectives must be evaluated according to the benefits the automated testing can provide [1]: Fig. 1

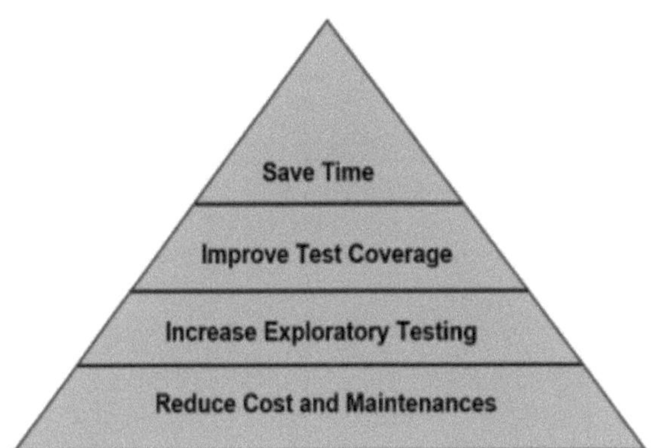

Fig. 1. Benefits of Automated Testing (Hussein et. al, 2023).

In the test-planning phase, the focus is on test requirements definitions and identifications of test-required documentation, planning for test environment, and development of test plan document. The test program scope must be defined in the test-planning phase considering the test efforts in terms of personnel, person hours, and test schedule. The test plan includes the program assumptions, prerequisites, and risks involved that need to be documented [15].

Due to the immense range of possibilities, it is not possible to cover 100% of the possible failures or quality-compromising scenarios. However, the process requires identifying high-risk functions and critical success functions. This way, the majority and most crucial use cases could be performed successfully in any feature, application, or service. To achieve this goal, test strategies such as smoke tests or sanity tests are used. The smoke test assures that the main functionality is working as expected and is integrated with the other functionalities, while sanity testing assures that more specific functionalities or components are working as expected after changes are made to the software, like new features or bugs fixed [12].

After completing the planning, designing, and development process phases, the test team is ready for test execution. The execution of automated tests can be performed using automated test tools or test management tools. Throughout the testing progress, the test team collects various test metrics and after the test execution, the test metrics provide the measurement of quality of test program and sizing as compared to actual labor-hours for the manual testing. The outcomes of test metrics conclude the suggested adjustments and improvements recommendations [1].

3 The Experiment

3.1 Context and Planning

The experiment began as a cooperative task that aimed at increasing the testing scope, accelerating the test execution, and/or saving more time compared to the manual tests in an immersive browser navigation experience that uses Virtual Reality features.

The automation process experiment was implemented in six steps: 1) Choosing the automated tools and programming language used in the test automation 2) Integrating the automated tool with a test report tool 3) Planning, specifying, codifying the automated test cases using manual test cases from both the legacy and immersive test cases 4) Executing the automated test cases, tracking the issues found and maintaining these test cases and, finally, 5) Defining the Key Performance Indicators and Return on Investment (ROIs) and tracking the metrics and the success of the implementation [10].

The initial goals were increasing test coverage (the KPI) and saving time (the ROI). The timeline was divided into quarters and the work progress was measured in weeks. The first plan included the creation of a mock application (a Proof-of-Concept app, a PoC) to test the automation framework, like a pilot verification prior to integrating the automation framework to the software: Table 1

After some work, it was verified that the goals were not clear enough for the team and it needed further research for selecting other automated tools to provide integration with XR tests as well as tools or libraries that would help in the execution and made possible to generate test. So, the automation plan had some changes and was updated as follows: Table 2.

During Q3, to continue improving the test coverage, an improvement on the user experience on the application was needed. So, the plan for Q3 and Q4 were be adjusted: Table 3.

3.2 Automation Test Processes

Test Environment. After all the background research was concluded in Q1, the definition of test environment settings and an automation flow was needed to begin the definition and execution of the tests: Table 4 Fig. 2.

The Automation tools / libraries used were Selenium for web tests and AltTester for UI tests in the XR context. The programing language chosen was Python, because it provides a test execution tool (Pytest) and report tools (shown on Fig. 3 and Fig. 4) and an integration tool was used to integrate both the automation tools (Selenium Webdrive and AltTester).

Test Definition. For this step, the manual test cases were used as a basis to check the efficiency of the automated test coverage. Before the creation, the manual test cases were reviewed, executed and tracked in terms of duration. The test execution duration was used as a metric for comparison with the automated testing.

Table 1. First Automation Plan

Q1 – Tasks:

Test Level: Web features (Legacy features)
Tool: Selenium
Tasks: Proof of Concept (PoC) application to validate Selenium automation tool + Web Driver to test browser features

Test Level: XR UI automation (XR features)
Tools: Unity + Other automated tools

Tasks: Researching how to interact with 2D interfaces (UI) in XR context using automation tools.
    More study time is required to proceed. However, it will be of great value to automate UI interactions in XR context to check integration end-to-end.

Risk: Not being able to automate in XR content using automated tools for applications developed in Unity platform

Next tasks for Q1:
- Finish PoC with selenium and share results
- Automate Smoke test suite (20 test cases for the first test cycle)

Next tasks for Q2:
- Automate Sanity test suite
- Improve automation test suites to increase coverage

Next tasks for Q3:
- Keep updating Selenium test suites and improvement
- Reserve some time to study and understand selected automation tool + application code
- Run PoC
        - if approved, we should start implementing a Sanity test for happy paths and
        plan next activities.

Next tasks for Q4:
-      Yet to be defined

Firstly, to define the automated test cases, the Selenium IDE was used to record and generate them. After that, the test cases were exported to Selenium WebDriver in Python language where they could be integrated with other tools and libraries. While this work was done, every week the KPI (Test scope) and ROI (save time) were measured and tracked to assure that the quarter goal would be reached.

Test Execution. After all test cases were defined and specified in Q2 and Q3, the test execution of the automated tests list was performed. Important points to be made clear about the test execution:

Table 2. Second Automation Plan.

<table>
<tr><td>

Q1 – Goals:

1. Finish the PoC and finish all the research.
2. Define the test automation to:
    a. Test Coverage: **20 automated test cases (smoke test strategy)**
    b. Time saved: **At least 1h of time saved**

Q1 – Tasks:

Test Level: Web features (Legacy features)
Tool: Selenium
Tasks:
-   PoC to validate Selenium automation tool + Web Driver to test browser features

Test Level: XR UI automation (XR features)
Tools: Unity + Other automated tools
Tasks:
-   Research Test automated tools to automate Unity UI

Risk: Not been able to automate in XR content using automated tools for applications developed in Unity platform

Next tasks for Q1:
- Finish PoC with selenium and share results
- Research a report tool to generate reports for automated tests
- Research the best language to integrate the Web PoC with automated tools for Unity UI and other tools for execution e report
- Automate Smoke test suite (20 test cases for the first test cycle)

</td></tr>
<tr><td>

Q2 – Goals:

1. Continue the definition of the test automation to:
    a. Test Coverage: **50 automated test cases**
    b. Time saved: **At least 2h of time saved**
2. Begin the execution of the automated smoke test suite

Next tasks for Q2:
- Automate Sanity test suite (at least 50 test cases)
- Improve automation test suites to increase coverage

</td></tr>
<tr><td>

Q3 and Q4 – Goals:

1. Continue the definition of the test automation to:
    a. Test Coverage: **40% of test cases**
    b. Time saved: **At least 4h of time saved**
2. Run the automated sanity test suite

Next tasks for Q3 and Q4:
- Implement Automation of at least 40% of the Regression test suite

</td></tr>
</table>

Table 3. Q3 and Q4 Automation Plan updates.

Q3 and Q4 – Goals:

1. Finish the definition of automated tests and cycles, contemplating all legacy features and XR features that could be automated
2. Execution of automated cycles already defined and collect the results
3. Use the time saved to execute manual exploratory tests in XR features that could not be covered by automation, assuring interactions could be as close to user interaction as possible

Table 4. Test Environment Information.

Operational System	Tablet/XR Devices
Application	XR Web Browser
Test Automation Libraries	Selenium/AltTester SDK 1.8.0
Test Execution Tool	Pytest
Additional Frameworks and Libraries	Adbutils/Pytest-html/Pytest-html-reporter
IDE	VSCode, Selenium IDE
Testing Scope/Type	Smoke Test/Sanity Test

1. All legacy features were included in the test scope using automation scripts
2. The automated script used in the PoC was integrated to the software automated test scripts with updated methods
3. After each test execution, automated reports using pytest-html and pytest-html-report libraries (shown in Fig. 3 and Fig. 4) were generated, pointing out data later used for KPI and ROI metrics for each quarter.

The automated test execution performed as follows: Table 5.

By the end of Q2, there was a need to better organize the legacy automated tests and include the immersive features to the test cases - those that could be automated. The automation was refactored into a test framework, making it not only more organized, but also more easily scalable.

During Q3 and Q4, considering the time saved from test automation implementation in comparison to the time invested when testing manually, the team was able to explore further possibilities to assure the quality of the XR application, like exploratory tests, usability tests and more frequent design reviews.

3.3 Test Automation Experiment Results

Q1 results show that with a coverage of 22 automated Test Cases (TCs), the test execution duration saved an average of 1 h 41 min and 16 s, considerably greater than the planned

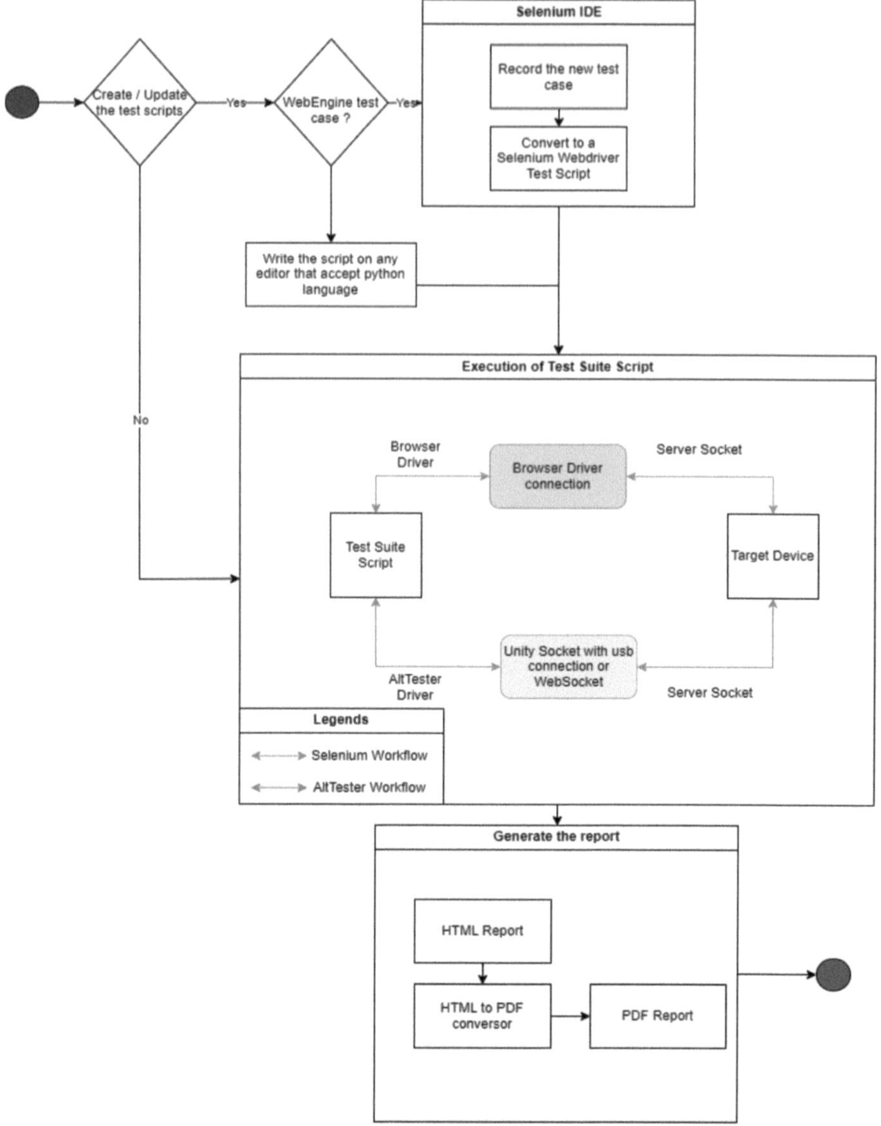

Fig. 2. Automation Flow Diagram.

goal of 1 h of time saved. Comparing the results with the manual execution duration the results show an average of 92.06% of time reduction. Tables 6 and 7.

During Q2, the test covered contemplated 50 automated TCs, over double the number of TCs in comparison with the Q1 cycle. The results reached a total of 3 h 55 min and 55 s of time saved compared to the planned goal of 2 h of time saved, 91,09% of testing time reduction in comparison with the manual test execution. Table 8 and 9

Fig. 3. e.g.: Pytest-html report tool used to generate test results.

Fig. 4. e.g.: Pytest-report-html tool used to generate test results.

Q3 and Q4 results present that the automation had result into a new automated framework, where it is possible to integrate automation test execution with reports and automated tools in testing both legacy and XR features, being 100% of legacy features and including the immersive features that could be automated. The exploratory tests made in this period result in adjustments, significant improvements, and new insights for both features (legacy and immersive).

The amount of time saved in this validation process enabled the team to explore a much wider variety of means to assure great quality features for the application. Among the main activities, the team conducted a bigger diversity of exploratory tests, like running benchmark tests with other similar applications, explore different interaction methods using other devices, explore competition in terms of feature support, among many others.

Table 5. Overall automation experiment execution, comparison with average manual execution and action points.

Version	Test Approach	Total	Pass	Fail	Result	Action Point	AVG Manual Exec.	Exec. Time
Apk v0.0.1 to Apk v0.0.4	Smoke test	22	21	1	95.54%	Register bug on project board	1:50:00	0:08:45
Apk v0.0.5 to Apk v0.0.7	Smoke test	22	22	0	100%	Confirm bug was fixed	1:50:00	0:08:45
Apk v0.0.8	Smoke test	22	21	1	95.54%	Register bug on project board	1:50:00	0:08:45
Apk v0.0.9 and Apk v0.1.0	Smoke test	22	22	0	100%	Confirm bug was fixed	1:50:00	0:08:45
Apk v0.1.1 and Apk v0.1.2	Sanity test	50	47	3	94%	Register bugs and improvement opportunities on project board	4:19:00	0:23:05
Apk v0.1.3	Sanity test	50	50	0	100%	Check bugs fixed on project board	4:19:00	0:23:06

Table 6. Q1 test results. PoC with a test coverage of 22 test cases.

Features	Manual			Automated	
	Total of test cases	Estimated Time by testcase (~avg)	Execution Time	Total of test cases	Execution time
Web Feature 1	4	0:05:00	0:20:00	4	0:02:08
Web Feature 2	18	0:05:00	1:30:00	18	0:06:36
	22		**1:50:00**	**22**	**0:08:44**

Table 7. Q1 test results. Test coverage per week during Q1.

Q1					
	WK7	WK8	WK9	WK10	WK11
Automated test coverage (22 TCs total)	**62.50%**	**79.17%**	**79.17%**	**95.65%**	**100.00% (22 TCs)**
Total Time reduction	-	-	-	-	**1:41:16 (MTET - ATET)**
Total Time reduction (Percent)	-	-	-	-	**92.06% (TTR/MTET)**

Table 8. Q2 overall automated test results.

Features	Total of TCs for Sanity Test	Total of TCs that could be automated	Manual		Automated	
			Estimated Time by testcase (~avg)	Execution Time	Total of TCs	Execution time
Feature 1	4	4	0:07:00	0:28:00	4	0:01:42
Feature 2	5	5	0:05:00	0:25:00	5	0:02:17
Feature 3	3	3	0:04:00	0:12:00	3	0:01:51
Feature 4	5	5	0:05:00	0:25:00	5	0:02:12
Feature 5	4	4	0:04:00	0:16:00	4	0:01:22
Feature 6	1	1	0:03:00	0:03:00	1	0:00:19
Feature 7	3	3	0:05:00	0:15:00	3	0:00:39
Feature 8	3	3	0:05:00	0:15:00	3	0:01:06
Feature 9	2	2	0:05:00	0:10:00	2	0:01:26
Feature 10	5	5	0:05:00	0:25:00	5	0:02:22
Feature 11	4	4	0:06:00	0:24:00	4	0:02:58
Feature 12	5	5	0:07:00	0:35:00	5	0:02:44
Feature 13	4	4	0:04:00	0:16:00	4	0:01:28
Feature 14	2	2	0:05:00	0:10:00	2	0:00:39
Totals	**50**	**50**		**4:19:00**	**50**	**0:23:05**

Another remarkable initiative was running usability tests in collaboration with the design team, where users could test after different development milestones and generate insights on early development stages, especially in more challenging contexts like assuring natural interaction with the software. This resulted in an agile and user-centered development process. In addition to that, increasing the frequency of design reviews and,

Table 9. Experiment Plan vs. Achieved Metrics on a weekly basis.

Q2

	WK17	WK18	WK19 to WK 22	WK23	WK24	WK25	WK26
KPI: Sanity Test Coverage (50 TCs)	14.00%	18.00%	30.77%	51.92%	62.26%	79.63%	**100.00% (50 TCs)**
Planned ROI time reduction	2:09:30	2:09:30	2:09:30	2:09:30	2:09:30	2:09:30	**2:09:30**
Planned ROI percent	50.00%	50.00%	50.00%	50.00%	50.00%	50.00%	**50.00%**
Total Time reduction	0:31:22	0:41:26	1:11:07	2:03:58	2:33:58	3:20:58	**3:55:55**
Total Time reduction percentage (ROI)	12.11	16.00	26.09%	46.26	56.74	74.43	**91.09%**

with these ongoing generated insights, incorporate test cases which contemplate wider and more complex scope of usage, especially immersive features.

4 Conclusion

In the field of XR, there is a variety of features that compose the immersive or hybrid experience. The first lesson learned was that it is not possible to cover the full scope of features using test automation, but mainly legacy features, while most immersive features would still be tested manually. However, the time saved was greater than expected, which brought opportunities to explore means to deliver more user-centered features for the application.

It is possible to conclude that the use of automated validation in the context of immersive software development made an impactful improvement in covering a larger testing scope in 91,09% shorter time when comparing it to traditional manual testing. In addition to that, the exploratory tests and user experience insights, coming from design reviews, usability tests and other activities in collaboration with the design team, the project was able to raise multiple insights that focused on user experience, especially the users' natural interaction with XR features.

Finally, test automation can be used to cover various kinds of tests, like smoke tests and sanity tests, as well as an increased test coverage with the time saved. This made possible to create a hybrid test framework that covers both immersive and legacy features, generating reports and other metrics using the same programming language, delivering not only well-tested software, but also a scalable time-effective and continuous quality assurance process.

Acknowledgments. This paper was presented as part of the results of the Project "SIDIA-M_VST_PLATFORM_AND_APPLICATIONS", carried out by the Institute of Science and Technology – SIDIA, in partnership with Samsung Electrônica da Amazônia LTDA, in accordance with the Information Technology Law n.8387/91 and article at the. 39 of Decree 10,521/2020.]

References

1. Hussein & Hamza, A., Mahmood & Rashid, T.: A comprehensive study on automated testing with the software lifecycle. J. Duhok Univ. (26) 613–620 (2023)
2. Andrei, B.A., Casu-Pop, A.C., Gheorghe, S.C., Boiangiu, C.A.: A study on using waterfall and agile methods in software project management. JISOM. 125–135 (2019)
3. Apple Homepage. https://www.apple.com/apple-vision-pro/. Accessed 28 Jan 2025
4. Basak, S., Hosain, S.: Software testing process model from requirement analysis to maintenance. Int. J. Comput. Appl. **107**(11), 14-22 (2014)
5. Gorantla, B., Devinen, S.: Evaluation of user experience (UX) design for emerging technologies. Computer Science Engineering and Technology. **1**(3), 39–47 (2023)
6. Bonini, L., Sbragia, R.: O Modelo de Design Thinking como Indutor da Inovação nas Empresas: Um Estudo Empírico. Gestão e Projetos. **2**, 3–25 (2011)
7. Dirin, A. & Laine, T.: User Experience in Mobile Augmented Reality: Emotions, Challenges, Opportunities and Best Practices. Computers. **7**(2), 33 (2018)
8. Dluhopolskyi, O. et al.: Potential of Virtual Reality in the Current Digital Society: Economic Perspectives. 11th International Conference on Advanced Computer Information Technologies (ACIT), 360–363 (2021)
9. Gomes, A., Figueiredo, L., Correa, W.: Extended by Design: A Toolkit for Creation of XR Experiences. IEEE International Symposium on Mixed and Augmented Reality Adjunct (ISMAR-Adjunct), Recife, Brazil, p.57–62 (2020)
10. Khankhoje, R.: Quantifying success: Measuring ROI in test automation. JTS **5**(2), 1–14 (2024)
11. Patel, K.: Exploring the combined effort between software testing and quality assurance: A review of current practices and future. IRJET. **11**(9), 522–529 (2024)
12. Herbold, S. & Haar, T.: Smoke testing for machine learning: Simple tests to discover severe bugs. Empir Software Eng. **27**(2), 45 (2022)
13. The Business Research Company Homepage. https://www.thebusinessresearchcompany.com/report/extended-reality-global-market-report. Accessed 04 Feb 2025
14. Vi, S., da Silva, T.S., Maurer, F.: User experience guidelines for designing HMD extended reality Applications. In: Lamas, D., Loizides, F., Nacke, L., Petrie, H., Winckler, M., Zaphiris, P. (eds.) Human-Computer Interaction – INTERACT 2019 (11749). Springer, Cham. (2019)
15. Asif, A., Maheen, K., Hameed, K.: Software Test Automation. Instant Approach to Software Testing: Principles, Applications, Techniques, and Practices. Bpb Publications, 285–326 (2019)
16. Chuah, S.H.-W.: Why and Who Will Adopt Extended Reality Technology? Literature Review, Synthesis, and Future Research Agenda. SSRN Electronic Journal, Elsevier BV (2018)
17. Chennell, J.: Moving from 2D to VR: How to transition a 2D interface into a VR environment (Dissertation) (2022)
18. Meta official website. https://www.meta.com/. Accessed 05 Feb 2025

Comparative Analysis Between Different 3D Object Generation Models. Adaptation to Immersive Technologies

Sergio Cleger Tamayo[(✉)] [iD], Geovana Amorim Abensur [iD],
Agustin Alejandro Ortiz Diaz [iD], Delrick Nunes de Oliveira [iD],
Osvaldo Vitalino dos Santos Junior [iD], and Gilberto Rufino de Oliveira Neto [iD]

Sidia Institute of Science and Technology, Av. Darcy Vargas, 654, Manaus 69055-035, Brazil
`{sergio.tamayo,geovana.abensur,agustin.diaz,delrick.oliveira,`
`osvaldo.junior,gilberto.neto}@sidia.com`

Abstract. Artificial Intelligence-based Content Generation (AIGC) and Extended Reality (XR) have gained prominence for delivering immersive experiences. Recent deep learning models can reconstruct textured 3D meshes from a single image, enabling scalable content creation. However, deploying these models in real-time XR settings remains challenging due to trade-offs between quality, performance, and responsiveness. This study evaluates how three single-image-to-3D generative models CRM, Unique3D, and InstantMesh perform in immersive contexts, considering both visual fidelity and computational efficiency. We assess their outputs across four object categories (Animals, Objects, Humanoids, and Places), using quantitative metrics grouped into geometric accuracy (IoU, Chamfer Distance, Hausdorff Distance, F-Score), texture fidelity (PSNR, SSIM), perceptual realism (LPIPS, Clip Similarity, FID, CMDM, NR-3DQA), VR performance (FPS, GPU time, GPU utilization, Stale frames) and 3D model generation time and polygon count. Results show that InstantMesh achieves the best VR performance (up to 76 FPS) with low GPU usage and fast generation time (<30 s). CRM offers balanced quality and speed, while Unique3D delivers the best perceptual realism but with higher computational demands and slower generation (~60 s). This work contributes to the design of XR applications by establishing a balance between visual detail and computational efficiency, helping VR developers integrate AIGC-driven 3D objects into immersive scenarios without compromising user experience.

Keywords: Artificial Intelligence Generated Content · 3D Generative Content · Extended Reality · Quantitative Metrics · 3D Real-Time Rendering

1 Introduction

Artificial Intelligence-based Generative Content (AIGC) and Extended Reality (XR) technologies have revolutionized the creation and delivery of immersive digital environments. In particular, 3D object generation from 2D images has emerged as a powerful

© The Author(s), under exclusive license to Springer Nature Switzerland AG 2026
J. Y. C. Chen et al. (Eds.): HCII 2025, LNCS 16338, pp. 18–35, 2026.
https://doi.org/10.1007/978-3-032-12808-9_2

enabler for virtual and augmented reality (VR/AR), allowing developers to populate interactive worlds with photorealistic assets efficiently [1–3]. This is especially relevant in standalone headsets, where hardware constraints necessitate careful trade-offs between visual fidelity and performance [4].

Traditional approaches to 3D content creation, such as manual modeling, photogrammetry, and 3D scanning, though accurate, remain time-consuming and resource-intensive [5, 6]. The emergence of deep learning has enabled new methods capable of reconstructing textured 3D meshes directly from single-view images, thereby eliminating the need for expensive hardware or laborious manual work [1–3]. These advances have expanded the range of possibilities in XR applications across education, e-commerce, cultural heritage, and simulation training.

Existing single-image-to-3D approaches can be broadly categorized into two strategies. The first are adaptation-based methods, which transform 2D diffusion architectures into 3D outputs using techniques such as Score Distillation Sampling (SDS) and neural rendering [7–10]. The second are direct reconstruction models, which use deep convolutional or transformer networks to infer 3D geometry from visual priors trained on large datasets like ShapeNet [11], Objaverse-XL [12], and Google Scanned Objects [13].

Despite this progress, integrating these models into real-time VR pipelines remains challenging. Meshes with high polygon counts can offer superior geometric fidelity but often degrade performance by overloading GPU resources, increasing latency, and compromising user immersion [4]. On the other hand, excessive simplification can improve rendering speed but sacrifice visual realism. These trade-offs highlight the need for robust optimization strategies that can dynamically adjust mesh complexity without degrading perceptual quality.

In this study, we present a comprehensive quantitative and performance-based evaluation of three 3D object generation models CRM [14], Unique3D [3], and InstantMesh [15] with a focus on standalone VR applications. We assess how each model balances geometric accuracy, visual fidelity, perceptual quality and real-time performance through detailed evaluations using metrics such as IoU, Chamfer Distance, Hausdorff Distance, F-Score, PSNR, SSIM, LPIPS, Clip Similarity, FID, CMDM, NR-3DQA, VR performance (FPS, GPU time, GPU utilization, Stale frames), 3D model generation time and polygon count. Our tests are conducted using the Meta Quest 3 headset across four representative object categories, obtained from previous user experiences study: People, Animals, Objects, and Places. For benchmarking, we use high-quality reference meshes from the Google Scanned Objects dataset [13] and Objaverse-XL [11].

The rest of this paper is organized as follows. Section 2 reviews related work and current state-of-the-art techniques. Section 3 describes our methodology, including datasets, models, evaluation metrics, and VR testing. Section 4 describes the Experiments. Section 5 presents and analyzes the results. Section 6 concludes the paper with key findings and suggestions for future research.

2 Related Work

Recent advancements in Artificial Intelligence-generated Content (AIGC) have significantly impacted 3D content generation, particularly for applications in Virtual Reality (VR), Augmented Reality (AR), gaming, e-commerce, and simulation training. Traditional modeling methods, such as Computer-Aided Design (CAD), photogrammetry, and LiDAR scanning, offer high geometric accuracy, but are labor-intensive, require expert knowledge, and scale poorly for large or dynamic environments [3, 5, 6]. Recent deep learning methods address these limitations by enabling automatic reconstruction of 3D shapes and textures from single-view 2D images, dramatically reducing manual effort and facilitating scalable, rapid prototyping for immersive environments [1, 2].

Among these advances, generative 3D models can be grouped into three main categories based on their generation approach: (i) optimization-based methods, (ii) direct (feedforward) reconstruction models, and (iii) hybrid architectures [16].

Optimization-based methods generate 3D content through iterative refinement of implicit representations such as neural radiance fields (NeRF), voxel grids, or signed distance functions (SDF). These methods typically adapt powerful 2D generative techniques, such as diffusion models, into a 3D domain through optimization processes guided by multi-view rendering or textual prompts. Notable examples include Dream-Fusion [7], Magic3D [8], and Repaint123 [10], which rely on techniques like Score Distillation Sampling (SDS) and multi-view consistency. Despite their impressive photorealism, these methods require extensive computational resources and long inference times, limiting their practicality in real-time VR scenarios.

Direct reconstruction models (feedforward models) learn a direct mapping from single images to 3D meshes in a single inference step, without iterative optimization or multi-view rendering. Due to their computational efficiency, these models are highly suitable for immersive XR environments requiring rapid content generation. CRM [14] adopts a multi-stage convolutional encoder-decoder pipeline designed explicitly for generating textured meshes quickly, which is crucial for real-time XR applications. Unique3D [3] employs transformer-based architectures, integrating normal map estimation and internal cross-view consistency during training. Although auxiliary pseudo-views are generated internally, the inference process remains single-image-based, maintaining high-quality geometry and texture details efficiently. InstantMesh [15] introduces sparse-view reconstruction techniques, employing minimal view-dependent features combined with mesh simplification to produce lightweight yet accurate meshes optimized for standalone VR devices.

Hybrid models attempt to bridge the gap between the photorealistic results of optimization methods and the computational efficiency of direct reconstruction models by combining depth priors, neural rendering, and diffusion-based architectures. Wonder3D++ [17], for example, integrates cross-domain diffusion pipelines, jointly optimizing geometry, texture, and depth consistency. While these hybrid models, including GET3D [18] and EG3D [19], offer visually compelling results, their resource-intensive processes and slow inference speeds currently limit their applicability in real-time XR use cases. Thus, although we acknowledge the relevance of Wonder3D++ for contextual completeness but we exclude it from our comparative evaluation due to practical limitations.

Effective training and evaluation of generative models require well-annotated and extensive datasets. Widely-used datasets include ShapeNet [11], a rich collection of synthetic CAD models optimized for geometric learning; Objaverse-XL [12], providing a vast and diverse collection of real 3D objects from a diverse set of sources and repositories, including manually designed objects, photogrammetry scans of landmarks and everyday items, and professional scans of historic and antique artifacts; and Google Scanned Objects [13], offering high-resolution scans suitable as ground truth references, both images and models, for geometric and perceptual evaluations.

Evaluating the quality of generative 3D models involves multiple dimensions. Geometric fidelity metrics such as Chamfer Distance (CD), Hausdorff Distance (HD), Intersection over Union (IoU), and F-Score provide objective measurements of mesh accuracy [16]. Texture fidelity metrics like Peak Signal-to-Noise Ratio (PSNR), and Structural Similarity Index Measure (SSIM) [16, 20]. Perceptual realism metrics, including Fréchet Inception Distance (FID), Color Mesh Distortion Measure (CMDM), and No-reference 3D Quality Assessment (NR-3DQA), and Learned Perceptual Image Patch Similarity (LPIPS) and Clip-Similarity evaluate the realism and visual coherence of generated assets, regardless of subjective human assessments [16, 20–22].

Real-time VR performance evaluation metrics such as inference time, GPU utilization, frame rate (FPS), latency, polygon count, and memory consumption are critical for ensuring seamless integration in standalone XR hardware [4, 23]. A critical aspect of real-time VR application involves polygon optimization techniques, essential for balancing visual detail and computational performance. Techniques such as Quadric Edge Collapse Decimation [24] and Mesh Simplification using Edge Contraction [25] effectively reduce polygonal complexity while preserving visual fidelity, thus ensuring smooth real-time rendering in VR applications.

Previous works have explored various performance aspects relevant to real-time VR scenarios. Grande et al. [4] assessed the impact of polygon optimization and low-cost scanning methods on rendering performance, highlighting key trade-offs between visual fidelity and computational constraints. Similarly, Cascarano et al. [23] conducted systematic comparisons of traditional scanning techniques against neural-based methods, emphasizing their performance implications for collaborative XR environments. MS2Mesh-XR [22] introduced a sketch-based mesh generation framework designed specifically for immersive environments, which complements image-based approaches by enabling intuitive content creation through multimodal interaction in XR. Comprehensive surveys, such as [2, 6, 16, 21], further highlight the broader challenges and trends in generative 3D technologies, emphasizing the necessity for robust evaluation frameworks tailored specifically to immersive applications.

Our work extends these studies by evaluating direct reconstruction models CRM [14], Unique3D [3], and InstantMesh [15], across comprehensive metrics covering geometric accuracy, textural quality, perceptual realism, and real-time performance within the Meta Quest 3 environment. By assessing multiple object categories (People, Animals, Objects, and Places) at various mesh complexity levels (original-poly, high-poly, low-poly), we establish practical guidelines and quantitative benchmarks to facilitate optimized integration of AI-generated 3D assets into immersive real-time VR applications.

3 Proposed Methodology

This study proposes a structured methodology to evaluate single-image-to-3D generative models for immersive environments, focusing on standalone VR applications. The three evaluated models CRM [14], Unique3D [3] and InstantMesh [15] are benchmarked across mesh quality and real-time VR performance. The methodology, illustrated in Fig. 1, comprises four stages: (1) Dataset Preparation and Preprocessing, (2) Generation and Optimization of 3D Models, (3) Quantitative Evaluation Metrics, and (4) Real-time VR Performance Evaluation. This structure aligns with protocols adopted in prior evaluation studies of 3D generative content for XR [4, 12, 13].

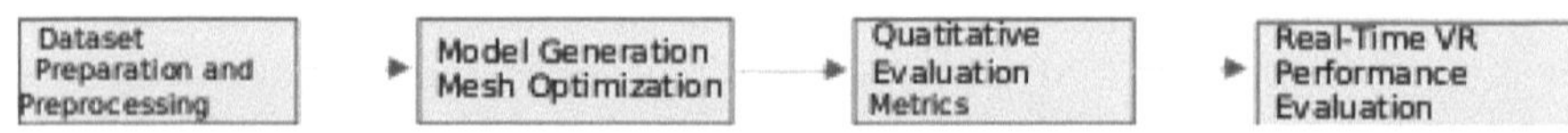

Fig. 1. Methodology framework.

3.1 Dataset Preparation and Preprocessing

Google Scanned Objects dataset [13] and Objaverse-XL [12] were selected, both known for their high-resolution 3D assets and real-world scanning quality. To reflect common immersive application needs, four object categories were selected: Animals, Objects, Humanoids, and Places (see Fig. 2). Each model input consisted of a single 2D image (640×460 pixels), while corresponding ground-truth 3D meshes were used as evaluation references.

The following preprocessing steps were applied ensuring identical inputs across all models for comparison:

- Image Normalization: All inputs were resized to a standard resolution of 640×460.
- Mesh Alignment and Scaling: Ground-truth meshes were aligned and scaled into a normalized coordinate system following alignment procedures adopted by Downs et al. [13] and Grande et al. [4].

Fig. 2. Selected object categories (Objects, Animals, Humanoids, Places).

3.2 Generation and Optimization of 3D Models

This stage involved generating 3D meshes from single-view images using the three selected AI-driven generative models: CRM, Unique3D, and InstantMesh. Each model generated an initial set of meshes termed "original-poly", preserving their native geometric detail and inherent textural characteristics. Subsequently, all generated meshes (see Fig. 3) were precisely aligned with their respective ground-truth counterparts using iterative closest point (ICP) methods implemented via standard libraries such as Open3D [4, 13]. This alignment ensured consistency and reliability in subsequent comparative evaluations.

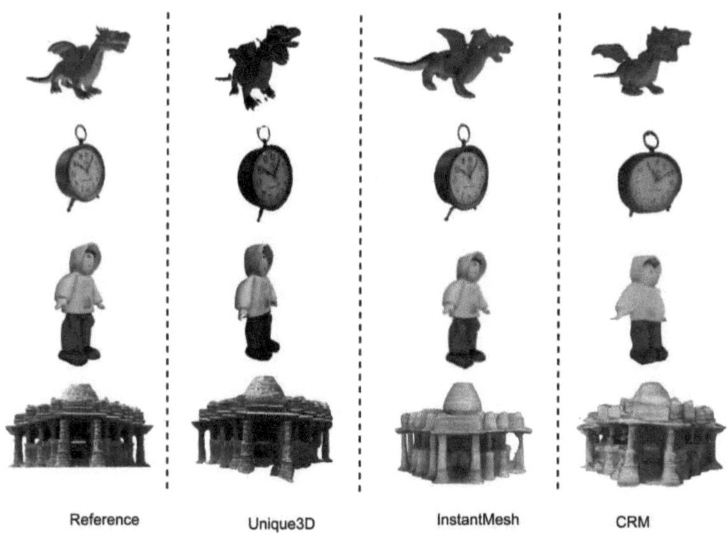

Fig. 3. Generated and ground-truth meshes.

To examine the effect of mesh simplification on VR performance and visual fidelity, two additional optimized mesh variants were created from each original mesh (see Fig. 4) using established polygon reduction techniques, specifically Quadric Edge Collapse Decimation [24] and complementary mesh simplification strategies described in [26]. These methods systematically reduce mesh complexity while striving to maintain essential visual and structural features:

- High-poly meshes (~30% polygon reduction): Moderate simplification intended to balance visual fidelity with reduced computational load.
- Low-poly meshes (~70–80% polygon reduction): Aggressive simplification aimed at maximizing rendering efficiency, though typically at the expense of fine detail.

This systematic optimization allowed us to comprehensively analyze trade-offs in performance and visual quality under realistic standalone XR rendering conditions, as recommended by related VR performance studies [4].

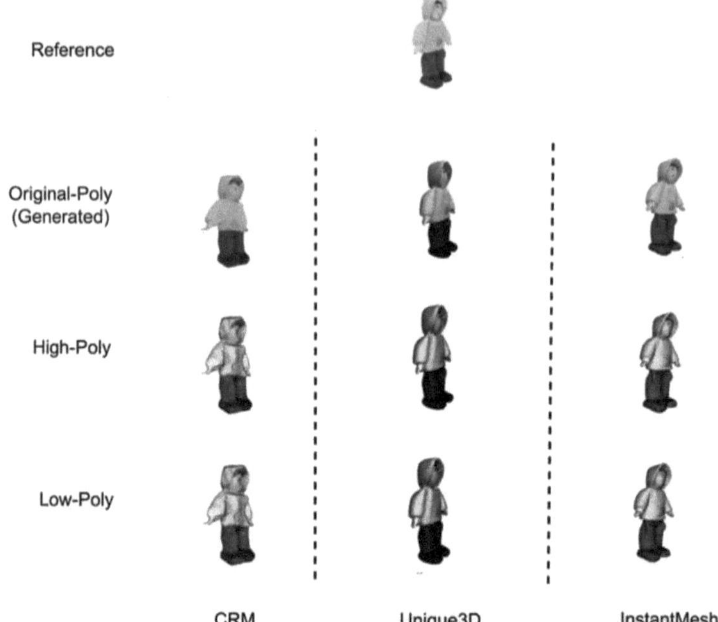

Fig. 4. Humanoids meshes: variants after mesh optimization.

3.3 Quantitative Evaluation Metrics

To quantify the quality of generated meshes, we employed a set of diverse metrics validated in the literature on generative 3D modeling [16, 22]. These metrics were grouped into three categories as summarized in Table 1.

- **Geometric Accuracy Metrics:** Chamfer Distance (CD), Volumetric Intersection-over-Union (IoU), Hausdoff distance and F-Score to assess structural alignment with ground-truth references [16].
- **Texture Fidelity Metrics:** Peak Signal-to-Noise Ratio (PSNR), Structural Similarity Index Measure (SSIM) to evaluate texture pixel-level [16, 21].
- **Perceptual Quality Metrics:** Fréchet Inception Distance (FID), Color Mesh Distortion Measure (CMDM), Learned Perceptual Image Patch Similarity (LPIPS), and CLIP-Similarity, and No-reference 3D Quality Assessment (NR-3DQA), which assess realism based on learned perceptual models and visual consistency without needing ground-truth meshes [16, 20–22].

Table 1. Quantitative evaluation metrics used in the study.

Category	Metrics	Purpose
Geometric Accuracy	Chamfer Distance, IoU, F-Score, Hausdoff distance	Evaluate shape and spatial structure accuracy

(*continued*)

Table 1. (continued)

Category	Metrics	Purpose
Texture Fidelity	PSNR, SSIM,	Assess texture quality
Perceptual Quality	FID, CMDM, NR-3DQA, LPIPS, CLIP-Similarity	Estimate visual realism and perceptual match

3.4 Real-Time VR Performance Evaluation

Real-world applicability was validated by integrating each mesh variants into a Unity-based VR environment and conducting performance tests using the Meta Quest 3 headset. Using the OVR Metrics Tool [4], key performance indicators (KPIs) were recorded: Table 2.

Table 2. Real-time VR performance metrics evaluated.

Metric	Description	Ideal Threshold
FPS (Frames Per Second)	Rendering fluidity	$\geq$72 FPS
Stale Frames (%)	Dropped frames due to overload	$\leq$10%
App GPU Time (%)	GPU processing time per frame	$\leq$13.88 ms/frame
GPU Utilization (%)	GPU usage per frame	<100%
GPU Usage $\geq$99% (%)	Time GPU is at full frequency	Minimal
Average Prediction (ms)	Delay in user interaction rendering	$\leq$50 ms

Two controlled experimental conditions were evaluated:

1. **Baseline Scene:** Evaluated each model using its original-poly mesh.
2. **Optimization Scene:** Compared original, high-poly, and low-poly humanoid meshes to assess performance impact of simplification.

Each test was run for a consistent 60 s per model and condition, ensuring statistically comparable results. The outcomes were then analyzed in relation to geometry, texture quality, and real-time rendering behavior.

4 Experiments

The experimental evaluation was conducted systematically in two sequential stages: (1) Quantitative Evaluation using custom Python scripts, and (2) Real-Time VR Performance Evaluation executed within interactive VR scenarios using the Meta Quest 3 headset. The primary goal was to quantitatively assess and compare the visual fidelity, perceptual realism, and computational performance of 3D meshes generated by CRM, Unique3D, and InstantMesh under different optimization conditions.

5 Hardware Used

The computational environment employed for quantitative evaluation consisted of a workstation equipped with an Intel® Xeon® Gold 6252 CPU, 15.6 GB RAM, and an NVIDIA GRID A100 GPU. This powerful configuration ensured efficient inference and accurate computation of evaluation metrics. Python scripts developed for the quantitative analysis leveraged standard libraries such as PyTorch3D, Trimesh, and Open3D.

Real-time VR tests utilized the standalone Meta Quest 3 headset, featuring a Qualcomm Snapdragon XR2 Gen 2 processor, an integrated Adreno 740 GPU, and 8 GB RAM. The immersive scenarios for VR performance assessments were created in Unity using the Meta XR SDK, Unity XR Interaction for 3d object manipulation, and performance metrics were recorded via the OVR Metrics Tool (v1.6.5).

6 Quantitative Evaluation Using Python Scripts

To evaluate the quality of the 3D models generated by CRM, Unique3D, and Instant Mesh, we implemented a Python-based framework that computes metrics across three key dimensions: geometric accuracy, texture fidelity, and perceptual realism. These evaluations were conducted by comparing each generated mesh with its corresponding ground-truth model using consistent and standardized procedures as established in recent literature [16, 22, 24]. Before evaluating visual quality and VR performance, we quantified the computational cost of generating each mesh. For every model and object category, we recorded the model file size (in MB), the number of polygons, and the generation time (in seconds). These metrics provide insight into the inherent complexity and speed of each approach.

6.1 Geometric Accuracy

These metrics evaluate the structural and spatial similarity between the generated mesh and its ground-truth counterpart.

- Volumetric IoU: Both meshes were voxelized using a fixed voxel size (0.01), and overlap between occupied voxels was calculated. Higher IoU indicates better global volume matching (Higher is better).
- Chamfer Distance (CD): This metric required conversion of both meshes into uniformly sampled point clouds (typically 10,000 points). The mean bidirectional point-to-point distance was then computed. Lower CD reflects better average shape alignment (Lower is better).
- F-Score: After converting meshes to point clouds, this metric evaluated precision and recall under a fixed distance threshold (1% of bounding box diagonal). Higher F-Score reflects higher fidelity with fewer missing or extra details (Higher is better).

6.2 Texture Fidelity

These metrics evaluated the quality of appearance by rendering orthographic projections of each mesh as grayscale or RGB images from a fixed viewpoint. The rendered images were used to simulate how users perceive texture in XR settings.

- PSNR (Peak Signal-to-Noise Ratio): Calculated using grayscale depth images of the rendered meshes. It quantifies the overall difference in pixel values between the generated and ground-truth renders. Higher PSNR suggests fewer distortions or noise artifacts (Higher is better).
- SSIM (Structural Similarity Index Measure): Computed on the same grayscale images, SSIM measures structural and luminance similarity, mimicking human perception. Values close to 1 indicate high visual similarity (Higher is better).

6.3 Perceptual Realism

- Fréchet Inception Distance (FID) was calculated by rendering each mesh from six equally spaced viewpoints and extracting features using a pre-trained InceptionV3 model. The FID score represents the statistical distance between the distributions of generated and reference features, with lower values indicating more realistic and diverse outputs (Lower is better)
- Color Mesh Distortion Measure (CMDM) assessed color and surface distortions using LAB-space metrics at multiple geometric scales. It detects subtle misalignments and distortions not captured by pixel-based metrics. A lower CMDM value indicates better visual coherence and texture geometry alignment (Lower is better).
- No-Reference 3D Quality Assessment (NR-3DQA) The generated mesh was converted to a point cloud and analyzed using a pre-trained Support Vector Regression model trained to predict perceptual quality, a Mean Opinion Score (MOS), without needing reference meshes. Higher NR-3DQA scores correspond to greater perceptual quality as evaluated by learned human-centric preferences (Higher is better).
- LPIPS (Learned Perceptual Image Patch Similarity): Rendered RGB images were processed by a deep perceptual network (AlexNet) to estimate feature-level perceptual similarity. Lower LPIPS indicates higher perceptual similarity (Lower is better)
- CLIP-Similarity: This metric uses the CLIP (Contrastive Language Image Pre-training) model to measure the semantic similarity between rendered RGB mesh images and reference images. Unlike pixel-level metrics, CLIP-Sim evaluates higher-level visual alignment, capturing perceptual and conceptual similarity. Values closer to 1 indicate stronger alignment in terms of how humans conceptually perceive image content (Higher is better).

7 Real-Time VR Performance Evaluation Procedure

Following the quantitative evaluation, each mesh was tested inside an immersive VR application using the Meta Quest 3 headset. The goal was to evaluate rendering efficiency, interaction fluidity, and system resource usage in real time. Two key test scenarios were employed:

7.1 Single-Object Baseline Scenario

In this scenario, each original-poly mesh generated by CRM, Unique3D, and InstantMesh was individually placed in a minimal Unity VR scene. These simplified scenes were specifically designed to isolate the computational load associated solely with each mesh, thereby ensuring accurate measurement of intrinsic mesh rendering performance (see Fig. 5).

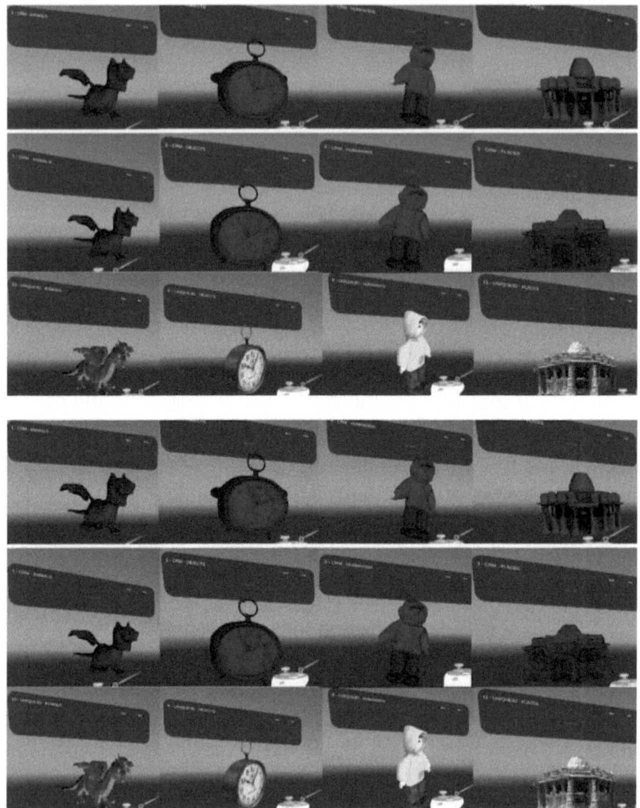

Fig. 5. Unity VR baseline scene with original-poly meshes.

Metrics recorded included average frames per second (FPS), GPU load, GPU utilization, stale frames percentage, and interaction latency, using the OVR Metrics Tool.

7.2 Mesh Optimization Scenario (Humanoids Category)

To further explore trade-offs between visual detail and computational efficiency, an additional interactive VR scene was designed, incorporating three mesh complexity levels (original-poly, high-poly, and low-poly) for selected humanoid models from each generative method (see Fig. 6) Users interacted with each mesh, performing close inspections, rotations, and translations using VR controllers, simulating realistic interactive scenarios.

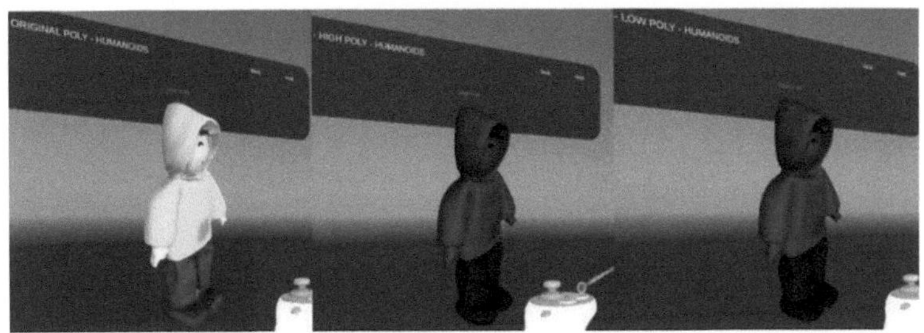

Fig. 6. Sample models for Unique3d with mesh optimization.

The experimental procedure consisted of:

- The Unity VR application was deployed onto Meta Quest 3.
- Each scene ran for 60 s, where the user interacted with the models using virtual hands or controllers

7.3 OVR Metrics Tool Recorded Performance Logs for Each Session

Data was analyzed to compare performance differences between models and optimization levels and using OVR Metrics Tool, logs of 88 parameters per second were recorded, including FPS, GPU usage, and stale frames. The data was exported to CSV for analysis.

8 Results and Discussions

This section presents and analyzes the quantitative results obtained from the evaluation of three 3D mesh generation models CRM, Unique3D, and InstantMesh across four object categories: Animals, Objects, Humanoids, and Places. The evaluation is based on five metric groups: generation efficiency, geometric accuracy, texture fidelity, perceptual realism, and real-time VR performance, see Table 3. Furthermore, we include an optimization analysis of the Humanoids category, assessing the impact of polygon count reduction on runtime performance, see Table 4.

Table 3. Evaluation Metrics.

Model	Category	Generation metrics			Geometric Accuracy				Texture Fidelity		Perceptual Realism					VR Performance			
		Size (MB)	Poly	Time (s)	IoU	Cham	Haus	F-Score	PSNR	SSIM	LPIPS	CLIP-Sim	FID	CMDM	NR-3DQA	FPS	GPU Time	GPU %	Stale %
CRM	Animals	0.57	29660	30.0	0.63	0.0328	0.31	0.78	14.4	0.89	0.14	0.97	135.2	102	3.8	71	12.9	88	5.4
	Objects	0.73	38080	32.6	0.68	0.0359	0.22	0.75	14.5	0.88	0.13	0.97	129.1	101	4.0	72	12.2	86	4.5
	Humanoids	0.63	33180	35.6	0.71	0.0679	0.23	0.72	14.6	0.90	0.11	0.95	130.6	95	4.1	71	12.9	88	5.4
	Places	5.09	266720	38.5	0.75	0.0055	0.20	0.84	13.5	0.80	0.17	0.99	121.7	84	4.3	72	12.2	86	4.5
Unique3D	Animals	9.18	481070	55.7	0.66	0.0336	0.21	0.79	13.9	0.89	0.15	0.98	105.7	99	4.4	67	13.5	97	8.2
	Objects	10.29	539240	49.8	0.70	0.0294	0.19	0.81	14.4	0.89	0.11	0.98	100.1	94	4.6	67	13.5	97	8.2
	Humanoids	9.63	504840	45.5	0.73	0.0637	0.20	0.83	14.7	0.90	0.11	0.98	94.3	90	4.7	70	13.9	98	9.6
	Places	13.90	728480	59.9	0.77	0.0077	0.18	0.87	13.6	0.81	0.17	0.98	87.9	82	4.9	72	13.5	97	8.2
InstantMesh	Animals	0.88	46320	28.3	0.65	0.0269	0.23	0.80	14.2	0.89	0.16	0.97	125.4	101	4.2	74	10.3	84	4.0
	Objects	1.02	53310	25.2	0.67	0.0327	0.21	0.82	14.1	0.88	0.12	0.99	115.2	96	4.3	74	10.2	82	3.5
	Humanoids	1.00	52280	33.2	0.70	0.0741	0.22	0.84	14.2	0.89	0.12	0.98	108.6	91	4.4	74	10.3	84	4.0
	Places	3.69	193420	25.8	0.74	0.0054	0.19	0.86	13.5	0.79	0.16	0.99	95.3	83	4.5	74	10.2	82	3.5

In terms of generation metrics, CRM consistently produced the most lightweight meshes, with sizes ranging from 0.57 MB to 5.09 MB and polygon counts under 270 k. Its generation times were the shortest, remaining below 40 s. Unique3D, on the other hand, generated the most complex meshes, with sizes up to 13.9 MB and polygon counts surpassing 700 k, leading to the longest generation times (up to 59.9 s). InstantMesh offered a balanced alternative, producing moderately complex meshes in significantly less time, between 25 and 33 s.

Regarding geometric accuracy, Unique3D achieved the best results across all sub-metrics. It recorded the highest IoU values (up to 0.77 in Places) and the lowest Chamfer and Hausdorff distances, indicating high-fidelity surface reconstruction. CRM showed commendable performance considering its lightweight nature, with IoU reaching 0.75 and F-Score up to 0.84. InstantMesh also demonstrated robust and stable geometric accuracy, with F-Scores consistently above 0.80 and competitive Chamfer distances, despite a much lower polygon budget.

Texture fidelity, assessed through PSNR and SSIM, revealed relatively uniform performance among all models. CRM slightly outperformed others in PSNR (14.6 in Humanoids) and matched the highest SSIM values (0.90). These results suggest that all models preserved structural texture quality well at the pixel level, although these metrics do not fully capture human perceptual experience.

To address this limitation, we examined perceptual realism using five metrics: LPIPS, CLIP-Similarity, FID, CMDM, and NR-3DQA. Unique3D outperformed the other models across the board, achieving the lowest LPIPS values (0.11), highest CLIP-Similarity scores (0.98), and best FID (87.9), CMDM (0.082), and NR-3DQA (4.9) scores, particularly in Humanoids and Places. These results confirm Unique3D's strength in producing visually realistic meshes as perceived by human observers. InstantMesh followed closely with consistent LPIPS (0.12–0.16), high CLIP-Similarity (up to 0.99), and NR-3DQA values up to 4.5. CRM, while competitive in CLIP-Similarity (0.97–0.99), presented higher LPIPS and FID scores, indicating some perceptual degradation, especially in more complex scenes.

The real-time VR performance analysis demonstrated that InstantMesh is the most suitable model for immersive applications, consistently achieving 74 FPS, GPU times under 10.3 ms, and minimal stale frame percentages. CRM also performed reliably, with FPS between 71 and 72, and moderate GPU load, making it well-suited for standalone XR platforms and mobile hardware. Unique3D, despite its visual quality, exhibited significant performance limitations. Its high polygon count led to lower FPS (down to 67), high GPU utilization (up to 98%), and increased frame latency, especially in the Humanoids category.

Table 4. VR Performance Metrics – Humanoids Optimization.

Model	Category	Avg. FPS ↑	GPU Time (ms) ↓	GPU Utilization (%) ↓	Stale Frames (%) ↓	Polygon Count
CRM	Original	71	12.9	88	5.4	33,18
CRM	High	72	11.8	84	4.2	~ 23,227
CRM	Low	73	10.5	80	3.6	~ 7,600
Unique3D	Original	70	13.9	98	9.6	504,84
Unique3D	High	71	12.6	95	7.2	~ 353,393
Unique3D	Low	72	10.3	92	5.3	~ 110,561
InstantMesh	Original	74	10.3	84	4.0	52,28
InstantMesh	High	75	9.9	80	3.2	~ 37,600
InstantMesh	Low	76	8.3	76	2.0	~ 11,500

To further investigate the impact of mesh complexity on VR performance, we performed an optimization analysis on the Humanoids category by generating three polygon variants for each model: Original, High, and Low resolution. The results (see Table 4) clearly demonstrate that polygon reduction significantly improves runtime performance across all models.

In CRM, reducing the mesh from 33,180 polygons (original) to ~ 7,600 (low) improved the frame rate from 71 to 73 FPS, and reduced GPU time from 12.9 to 10.5 ms. Unique3D experienced even more pronounced improvements: from 70 to 72 FPS, and from 13.9 to 10.3 ms, with a polygon reduction from 504,840 to ~ 110,561. InstantMesh, already efficient in its original form, saw its performance further increase, reaching 76 FPS and only 2.0% stale frames in the low-poly variant.

These findings confirm that polygon optimization is essential to enable real-time execution of visually detailed models such as Unique3D in immersive environments. They also emphasize the adaptability of InstantMesh and CRM to low-resource devices through simple mesh simplification strategies.

In summary, the models present distinct trade-offs. Unique3D offers the highest visual fidelity, making it ideal for offline rendering, cinematic XR, and use cases where perceptual quality is paramount. However, it requires optimization for real-time applications. InstantMesh provides the best balance between accuracy, perceptual realism, and performance, positioning it as the most viable option for interactive immersive applications. CRM is the most computationally efficient model, suitable for prototyping, mobile VR, and lightweight educational content, where real-time performance is critical and visual fidelity is secondary.

The combination of structural, perceptual, and runtime metrics allowed for a nuanced understanding of each model's strengths and limitations. Notably, the inclusion of perceptual metrics such as LPIPS, CLIP-Similarity, FID, CMDM, and NR-3DQA was fundamental to understanding the visual realism experienced by users, beyond what geometric and pixel-based metrics could reveal alone.

9 Some Ethical Considerations

This study followed all license rules and used only public datasets, but there are still important ethical points to consider. First, if the training data lacks diversity, the 3D models may not work well for certain objects or styles, which can lead to unfair or biased results. Second, like other AI tools, these models could be misused, for example, to copy private or copyrighted content without permission, even though our work used only approved data. Third, AI model training and testing consume energy, which affects the environment, so we limited our experiments to a small scale to reduce impact. In short, responsible use of 3D AI models means thinking about fairness, privacy and sustainability.

10 Conclusions

This study presented a comprehensive evaluation of three single-image-to-3D mesh generation models: CRM, Unique3D, and InstantMesh, targeting real-time use in immersive Virtual Reality (VR) environments. The models were assessed across four key object categories (Animals, Objects, Humanoids, and Places) using a set of quantitative metrics grouped under geometric accuracy, texture fidelity, perceptual realism and VR performance.

The results demonstrate that each model has distinct trade-offs between quality and performance. Unique3D consistently achieved the best visual quality and perceptual realism (lowest FID and CMDM, highest NR-3DQA), particularly for complex categories like Humanoids and Places. However, this came at the cost of increased polygon count, model size, and generation time, factors that negatively affected its average FPS and GPU usage in VR.

In contrast, InstantMesh showed the highest performance in real-time VR scenes, achieving the best FPS and lowest GPU utilization, especially after polygon optimization. Its geometric accuracy remained competitive, and perceptual quality was adequate, making it the most balanced choice for interactive or resource-constrained applications.

CRM offered a middle ground, with fast generation times and solid perceptual results, particularly in simpler categories like Animals and Objects. Its performance remained stable in VR, though its geometric fidelity was slightly lower than that of Unique3D.

Importantly, the correlation analysis revealed that perceptual metrics such as FID and LPIPS are better predictors of VR rendering performance than pure geometric scores, emphasizing the relevance of perceptual fidelity in immersive contexts. Moreover, the experiment with polygon-optimized humanoid meshes showed clear performance gains, InstantMesh's low-poly variant reached 76 FPS with minimal GPU load, confirming the critical role of mesh simplification in real-time deployment.

Finally, generation time has proved to be an important factor for usability. Models like InstantMesh and CRM, which generate assets in under 35 s, are better suited for fast, interactive workflows such as VR content creation or web-based 3D experiences. In contrast, models with longer generation times, like Unique3D, may not be ideal for real-time use.

In conclusion, while high visual quality is important, deploying image-to-3D models in VR requires a careful balance between fidelity, performance, and generation speed. This study provides practical benchmarks and insights to guide the selection and optimization of image-based 3D generation methods for immersive applications. Future work could explore hybrid pipelines, faster single-image-to-3D generation, and improved perceptual metrics to better balance quality and efficiency.

Acknowledgments. This paper was presented as part of the results of the Project "SIDIA-M_VST_PLATFORM_AND_APPLICATIONS", carried out by the Institute of Science and Technology – SIDIA, in partnership with Samsung Electrônica da Amazônia LTDA, in accordance with the Information Technology Law n.8387/91 and article at the. 39 of Decree 10,521/2020.

References

1. Wu, J., Gan, W., Chen, Z., et al.: AI-Generated Content (AIGC): A Survey. arXiv preprint (2023). arXiv:2304.06632
2. Li, C., Zhang, C., Waghwase, A., et al.: Generative AI Meets 3D: A Survey on Text-to-3D in AIGC Era. arXiv preprint (2023). arXiv:2305.06131
3. Wu, K., Liu, F., Cai, Z., et al.: Unique3D: High-Quality and Efficient 3D Mesh generation from a single image. arXiv preprint (2024). arXiv:2405.20343
4. Grande, R., Albusac, J., Vallejo, D., et al.: Performance evaluation and optimization of 3D models from low-cost 3D scanning technologies for virtual reality. Appl. Sci. **14**(14), 6037 (2024)
5. Fu, K., Peng, J., He, Q., et al.: Single image 3D object reconstruction based on deep learning: A review. Multimed. Tools Appl. **80**, 463–498 (2021)
6. Liu, J., Huang, X., Huang, T., et al.: A comprehensive survey on 3D content generation. arXiv preprint (2024). arXiv:2402.01166
7. Poole, B., Saharia, C., Chan, W., et al.: DreamFusion: Text-to-3D using 2D diffusion. arXiv preprint (2022). arXiv:2210.02303
8. Lin, C., Liu, L., Yang, J., et al.: Magic3D: High-Resolution Text-to-3D Generation. arXiv preprint (2022). arXiv:2211.10440
9. Lin, C., Lin, Z., Liu, L., et al.: Magic123: One image to high-quality 3D via text-to-image diffusion priors. arXiv preprint (2023). arXiv:2309.16756
10. Tao, M., Chen, J., et al.: Repaint123: Attentive multi-view Text-to-3D generation using repainting diffusion. arXiv preprint (2023). arXiv:2311.05712
11. Chang, A.X., Funkhouser, T., Guibas, L., et al.: ShapeNet: An information-rich 3D model repository. arXiv preprint (2015). arXiv:1512.03012

12. Deitke, M., Liu, R., Wallingford, M., et al.: Objaverse-XL: A universe of 10M+ 3D objects. In: Advances in Neural Information Processing Systems (NeurIPS) (2023)
13. Downs, L., Plagemann, C., Rusu, R.B.: Google scanned objects: A high-quality dataset of 3D scanned household items. In: IEEE Int. Conf. on Robotics and Automation (ICRA), pp. 2553–2560. IEEE (2022)
14. Wang, Z., Wang, Y., Chen, Y., et al.: CRM: Single image to 3D textured mesh with convolutional reconstruction model. In: European Conference on Computer Vision (ECCV), pp. 57–74. Springer, Cham (2024)
15. Xu, J., Cheng, W., Gao, Y., et al.: InstantMesh: Efficient 3D mesh generation from a single image with sparse-view large reconstruction models. arXiv preprint (2024). arXiv:2404.07191
16. Samavati, T., Soryani, M.: Deep Learning-Based 3D Reconstruction: A Survey. Artif. Intell. Rev. **56**, 9175–9219 (2023)
17. Long, X., Guo, Y., Lin, C., et al.: Wonder3D++: Single image to 3D using cross-domain diffusion. arXiv preprint (2023). arXiv:2310.15008
18. Gao, J., Yang, X., Qiu, Y., et al.: GET3D: A generative model of high-quality 3D textured shapes learned from images. In: NeurIPS (2022)
19. Chan, E.R., Lin, C.Z., Chan, M.A., et al.: EG3D: Efficient geometry-aware 3D generative adversarial networks. In: CVPR, pp. 8498–8508 (2022)
20. Roullier, M., Meyer, C., et al.: Automated visual quality assessment for virtual and augmented reality based digital twins. In: Comput. Graph. Forum (2023)
21. Fukaya, N., Yang, H., et al.: Evaluation metrics for intelligent generation of graphical game assets: A systematic survey-based framework. In: ACM Comput. Surv. (2024)
22. Guo, K., Wang, Z., Li, Y., Zhou, J., Cao, X., & Xu, Y. MS2Mesh-XR: Multi-modal sketch-to-mesh generation in XR environments. In: Proceedings of the IEEE/CVF Conference on Computer Vision and Pattern Recognition (CVPR), (2024)
23. Cascarano, P., De Vivo, F., D'Addona, D., et al.: A comparative analysis of 3D modeling methods for integration into an extended reality platform. In: 2025 IEEE International Conference on Artificial Intelligence and extended and Virtual Reality (AIxVR), pp. 213–217. IEEE (2025)
24. Garland, M., Heckbert, P.S.: Surface simplification using quadric error metrics. In: Proc. SIGGRAPH, pp. 209–216. ACM (1997)
25. Hoppe, H., DeRose, T., Duchamp, T., et al.: Mesh optimization. Technical Report 93–01–01, University of Washington (1993)
26. Dhanush, M., Sanjay, M.R.: Mesh optimization using python libraries. IJEST. **11**(5), 1459–1465 (2023). https://doi.org/10.22214/ijraset.2023.51744

CPHS–XR: A Unifying Framework for Understanding Cyber Physical Human Systems in the Realm of Extended Reality

Emre Eraslan[1]([✉]) [iD], Yildiray Yildiz[2] [iD], Anuradha Annaswamy[3] [iD], J. Cecil[4], and Avinash Gupta[1] [iD]

[1] University of Illinois Urbana-Champaign, Urbana, IL 61801, USA
{emree2,avinashg}@illinois.edu
[2] Bilkent University, Ankara, Turkey
yyildiz@bilkent.edu.tr
[3] Massachusetts Institute of Technology, Cambridge, MA 02139, USA
aanna@mit.edu
[4] CyberTech LLC, Stillwater, OK 74074, USA
https://hxri.ise.illinois.edu/

Abstract. As digital, physical, and human systems continue to converge, the vocabulary used to describe these integrations has become increasingly fragmented. Terms such as Human Computer Interaction, Human Machine Interaction, Cyber Physical Systems, Human Extended Reality Interaction, and Cyber Physical Human Systems (CPHS) describe varying system configurations in which humans, technologies, and environments interact to achieve shared goals. However, the proliferation and overlapping use of these terms have introduced conceptual ambiguity, complicating system comparison, evaluation, and design. This paper introduces the CPHSXR framework as an enhanced and structured extension of CPHS. While grounded in the foundational tripartite structure, which comprises cyber, physical, and human components, CPHSXR adds conceptual clarity by introducing technology enablers as cross-cutting elements that empower system components without altering their core integration. These enablers, such as extended reality, artificial intelligence (AI), Internet of Things, and perceptual technologies, give rise to diverse system behaviors, resulting in variations like immersive, adaptive, predictive, or actuated CPHS. Building on this foundation, the paper proposes a taxonomy based on three dimensions: immersion level, decision-making level, and granularity assignment. This taxonomy provides a systematic method for classifying CPHS variations as empowered configurations rather than as disconnected or standalone system types. By simplifying terminological complexity and contextualizing system evolution, the framework supports system classification, design, and analysis across domains. It also lays a foundation for future research in human-centered AI, immersive interfaces, and adaptive systems by ensuring that emerging technologies enhance rather than

J. Y. C. Chen et al. (Eds.): HCII 2025, LNCS 16338, pp. 36–48, 2026.
https://doi.org/10.1007/978-3-032-12808-9_3

fragment the integration between human operators and cyber-physical systems.

Keywords: Cyber-Physical Human Systems · Technology Enablers · Interaction Taxonomy · Extended Reality · Human-Machine Interaction · Human-Computer Interaction · Shared Autonomy · System Classification · Integrated Intelligent Systems

1   Introduction

The rapid advancement of interactive technologies, intelligent systems, and immersive interfaces has led to the emergence of numerous overlapping terms in academia and industry. Concepts such as Integrated Intelligent Systems (IIS) [59], Human Computer Interaction (HCI) [7], Human Computer Agent Interaction (HCAI) [38], Human-Machine Interaction (HMI), Cyber-Physical Systems (CPS) [60], Human Extended Reality Interaction (HXRI) [8,27], and Cyber-Physical Human Systems (CPHS) [2,42,58] have all been used to describe variations of systems in which humans, technologies, and physical environments interact. While each term originated in response to a specific disciplinary focus or application domain, these conceptual boundaries have become increasingly fluid, ranging from automation and industrial control to immersive simulation and human-centered artificial intelligence (AI).

This fluidity has led to overlapping terms that often obscure rather than clarify understanding. Yet confusion also stems from inconsistent definitions of individual terms across disciplines and authors. For instance, CPHS is defined in fundamentally different ways: some perspectives treat the human as an external operator [46], while others position the human at the center of the system with an active, decision-making role [2,55]. Some definitions even treat AI as an essential component that links CPS to the human operator [41]. Terminological conflation compounds this inconsistency. CPS and CPHS are frequently used interchangeably, despite the latter's explicit inclusion of the human component [50,57]. Likewise, the distinction between HCI and HMI is often overlooked, even though their system contexts and interaction modalities differ significantly. The rise of extended reality (XR) technologies such as virtual reality (VR) [18,44], augmented reality (AR) [25,34], and mixed reality (MR) [6,53] has introduced yet another layer of complexity, as interactions shift from traditional screens to spatial and embodied environments, giving rise to terms such as HXRI [27,28]. At the same time, AI-enhanced automation has transformed CPS into what many now call Integrated Intelligent Systems (IIS) [32,43], further blurring conceptual boundaries.

AI [21,31] refers to data-driven, learning-based system capabilities that allow adaptive responses based on input, context, or user behavior. This includes technologies such as machine learning models, intelligent agents, and large language models [9,33]. In contrast, traditional control systems such as rule-based algorithms or PID controllers [5,23,40] operate using predefined logic and do not adapt over time. Although both approaches can enhance system automation, AI introduces a capacity for learning and adjustment that expands how systems perceive, decide, and interact. Because the term *AI* is often used inconsistently across fields, sometimes even describing non-learning controllers, it is important to clarify this distinction. In the context of CPS, CPHS, HCI, and HMI, AI in this paper refers specifically to learning-driven intelligence that supports dynamic and context-aware system behavior.

1.1 Objectives and Contributions

This paper has three key objectives that together address the existing conceptual ambiguity in CPHS terminology, propose a unifying framework, and present a structured taxonomy. In doing so, the paper contributes both a clarified conceptual model and a practical classification scheme to guide future research and system design.

- First, to clarify the overlapping and inconsistently used terms describing human-machine-digital systems such as CPS, IIS, HCI, HMI, HXRI, and CPHS by mapping them to their foundational components and distinguishing their boundaries.
- Second, to propose a coherent framework for describing increasingly complex systems that integrate AI, XR, Internet of Things (IoT), and perceptual technologies, enabling clearer understanding of their roles in shaping human-machine interactions.
- Third, to apply this framework to create a structured taxonomy of CPHS variations based on how specific technological enablers influence and define system components.

2 The CPHSXR Framework

The accelerating convergence of intelligent, interactive, and immersive technologies has resulted in significant conceptual overlaps in how human, cyber, and physical systems are described. This section first unpacks this conceptual chaos, exploring how these terms have proliferated across disciplines, and then introduces the CPHSXR framework as a systematic approach to unify and clarify this evolving terminology.

2.1 Conceptual Chaos

CPHS represent an emerging paradigm where humans, physical components, and cyber technologies are interconnected through dynamic and reciprocal interactions to achieve shared goals. This stands apart from earlier models that treated the human as an external operator rather than an integrated system element [65]. Understanding CPHS requires examining different human roles in system interaction, including frameworks like human-in-the-loop (HITL), which emphasizes real-time human input in operations and decision-making. Despite the conceptual distinction, CPHS and HITL are often used interchangeably in the literature. Some sources even define CPHS as a HITL configuration [64]. This framing, however, fails to capture the broader potential of CPHS, which includes long-term adaptation, contextual awareness, and variable autonomy.

The rise of immersive technologies like augmented, virtual, and mixed reality [36,45] has added complexity, shifting interactions into spatial and embodied domains and inspiring terms such as HXRI [26]. In parallel, AI has played a key role in transforming CPS [4,51] into adaptive systems that blur the lines between existing definitions.

To clarify this transformation, we define AI in this paper as learning-based, data-driven components that include machine learning algorithms, intelligent agents, and large language models. This contrasts with traditional control systems that rely on fixed rules or model-based algorithms such as PID controllers. Classical control systems do not adapt beyond their programmed logic. AI components, on the other hand, adjust over time, respond to new contexts, and support personalized or autonomous behavior. This distinction is necessary, as some literature labels advanced but non-learning controllers as AI, leading to confusion.

Further complexity arises from adjacent terms. HCI focuses on digital interfaces like graphical user interfaces, touchscreens, and voice systems [54]. It is primarily concerned with usability, feedback, and interface design in computing environments. HMI, in contrast, involves engagement with physical systems such as industrial robots or vehicles. These interactions often use tactile controls, haptic feedback, or supervisory interfaces. As AI and multimodal technologies become embedded in these systems, the nature of interaction changes. Machines begin interpreting, adapting to, or anticipating human input, raising the question of whether traditional definitions of HCI and HMI still apply.

To describe these developments, terms such as Augmented HCI (A-HCI) [63] and Augmented HMI (A-HMI) [56] can be introduced. These refer to systems where AI-driven features reshape traditional modes of interaction. Similarly, HXRI refers to immersive human-system engagement enabled by XR and intelligent technologies. Although it shares similarities with HCI and HMI, HXRI emphasizes enhancing human perception and presence across digital and physical spaces.

These growing complexities prompt a broader question for CPHS research. When systems incorporate XR, AI, IoT, or advanced sensing, do they still align with traditional CPHS definitions? While these technologies do not alter the foundational architecture, they act as enablers that enhance how system components behave, interact, or adapt. Such enablers include immersive displays, machine learning models, sensor networks, and perception tools like computer vision and natural language processing. These are not standalone pillars of the system but augment existing components by adding new functionality or interaction capabilities.

This conceptual challenge highlights the need for a framework that retains the core structure of CPHS while systematically accounting for how emerging technologies reshape it. The CPHSXR framework was developed in response to this need and offers a clearer structure for understanding next-generation interactive systems.

2.2   CPHSXR: A Unified Conceptual Framework

Building upon the conceptual ambiguity outlined earlier, we now introduce the CPHSXR framework, which integrates the principles of CPHS with the immersive capacities of HXRI. At its core, CPHSXR retains the tripartite structure of cyber, physical, and human components that underpins related terms such as CPS, CPHS, HCI, and HMI.

Figure 1 presents a four-set Venn diagram that visualizes this framework. While the core triad remains the structural foundation, a fourth set, *Enabler*, is introduced to represent technologies such as XR, AI, IoT, or perceptual tools. These enablers do not constitute a new system component; rather, they function as augmentative layers that enhance the behavior, interaction style, or capabilities of existing CPHS elements without altering the system's core architecture.

This framework helps clarify how different system types emerge when one or more CPHS components are empowered by immersive, adaptive, or analytic technologies. For instance, integrating AI into the cyber domain enhances autonomy and intelligence; applying XR to the human interface creates HXRI; and embedding IoT or computer vision into physical systems enables real-time responsiveness and data-rich interaction.

Rather than proposing a new structural model, CPHSXR offers a systematic lens for examining how emerging technologies transform CPHS configurations. It facilitates design scalability and provides a shared vocabulary for analyzing and constructing interactive systems across domains. The following section builds on this conceptual foundation by introducing a taxonomy that classifies these variations according to which components are technologically empowered and how.

3   A Taxonomy of the CPHSXR Framework

This section introduces a structured taxonomy that organizes the CPHSXR framework. Each dimension reflects a distinct lens through which CPHSXR can be analyzed, enabling a systematic understanding of how these systems are composed, how they function, and the environments in which they operate. The dimensions describe the configuration and interaction logic that define how CPHS systems are built and how their components are empowered:

- *Immersion Level*: the degree of perceptual immersion experienced by the human user (e.g., screen-based vs. fully immersive XR).
- *Decision-Making Level*: the allocation of decision authority across human and machine agents (e.g., human-in-the-loop vs. autonomous).

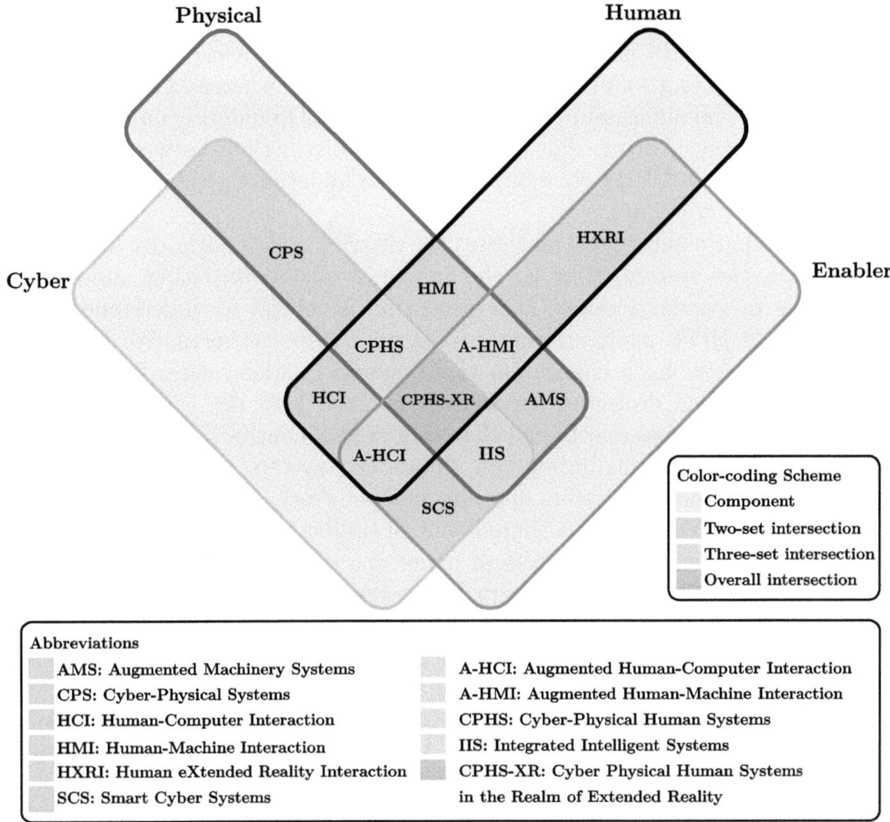

Fig. 1. The CPHSXR framework visualized as a four-set Venn diagram. The core tripartite system is preserved as the structural foundation, while the *Enabler* set overlays these components to illustrate how various system types emerge through their empowerment.

- *Granularity Assignment*: the unit of control or analysis applied to each component (e.g., individual, team, or subsystem level).

In what follows, we detail the three dimensions that constitute the foundation of the CPHSXR taxonomy.

The immersion level describes the extent to which the human user is perceptually engaged in the system. This dimension captures the interface quality and the depth of human engagement, ranging from passive observation to fully embodied interaction in virtual environments. We classify immersion into three primary levels: non-immersive, where interactions occur through traditional interfaces such as keyboards and 2D displays; semi-immersive, involving partially spatial or 3D visualized interfaces such as stereoscopic displays; and fully immersive, where XR technologies such as VR, AR, and MR provide the user with a sense of situational awareness [12, 47, 48, 66]. This dimension allows us to situate HXRI as a class of interfaces rather than as a separate system type. For example, a CPHS used in industrial training might feature a fully immersive XR interface (e.g., a VR-based welding simulator), whereas a medical device interface might remain semi-immersive, involving a 3D rendering on a screen but limited bodily engagement. This framing enables distinctions between immersive and non-immersive CPHS configurations while maintaining consistency within the core structure [39, 46].

The decision-making level addresses the distribution of authority and autonomy within the system, that is, the human's role in initiating, guiding, or responding to system actions. This dimension is central to understanding the complexity of HITL configurations and system responsiveness. We categorize decision-making along a continuum that includes: manual control [11], where humans perform all decisions; supervisory control [1, 16, 19], where the human oversees and intervenes selectively; shared or traded control [14, 15, 61], in which authority shifts dynamically between human and system components; and full autonomy [3], where the system operates independently with little or no human involvement. For example, in a shared-control surgical robot [49, 62], the surgeon might guide motion while the system maintains stability and avoids collisions-illustrating traded decision authority. In contrast, autonomous delivery drones may operate under full autonomy but still allow human override in rare or emergency cases. This dimension captures such variations and situates them consistently within CPHS analysis.

Granularity assignment refers to how tasks are distributed between humans and system components, as well as the timing and handoff of responsibilities [29]. It captures who does what, and when that control shifts, especially across time scales ranging from moment-to-moment actions to long-term monitoring or strategic supervision [17]. This dimension is particularly useful for characterizing systems with temporal role shifts, such as those where the human initiates an action that the system later completes, or vice versa. We distinguish between atomic granularity [10] (e.g., continuous real-time input like joystick control), procedural granularity [52] (e.g., stepwise multi-stage tasks), and strategic granularity [22] (e.g., the human defines the goal but delegates execution to the system). Consider a CPHS used in aerospace: the human pilot may initiate takeoff procedures (procedural granularity), monitor altitude (strategic oversight), or intervene directly in turbulent conditions (atomic). The framework allows us to label and classify these interaction patterns with clarity [13, 20].

These three dimensions provide a flexible and systematic lens through which CPHS variations can be analyzed and classified. By combining these dimensions, system designers and researchers can capture both structural configurations and technological enhancements, offering a richer understanding of system behavior and interaction dynamics. This approach results in a classification scheme supporting both system analysis and design exploration within the CPHSXR framework.

4 Discussion

This paper systematically unpacks the conceptual confusion surrounding CPHS and related terminologies, offering the CPHSXR framework as a structured solution. Through the proposed taxonomy, we provide a lens to classify CPHS variations along key dimensions that capture system structure, human roles, and task granularity. This unified approach allows researchers and designers to better navigate the fragmented landscape of human-cyber-physical integration.

The CPHSXR framework also provides a valuable lens through which to reinterpret dominant industrial paradigms such as Industry 4.0 and Industry 5.0. From the CPHSXR perspective, Industry 4.0 can be framed as a CPHS configuration heavily weighted toward Cyber and Physical elements, often enhanced through intelligence enablers (e.g., AI, IoT, analytics), but typically with limited or peripheral human engagement [24,35]. Human operators are frequently positioned in supervisory or on-the-loop roles, overseeing largely autonomous or automated processes. In contrast, Industry 5.0 introduces a renewed emphasis on human-centered collaboration, creativity, and personalization [30,37], aligning more closely with the CPHS core where Human components are meaningfully integrated alongside Cyber and Physical elements, often enhanced by interface enablers (e.g., XR, HXRI, HITL-based AI systems). The *Enabler* layer in CPHSXR serves to explain how systems evolve from Industry 4.0 configurations into more human-centered Industry 5.0 variations, without altering the foundational CPHS structure. In this way, CPHSXR does not position Industry 4.0 and 5.0 as conflicting paradigms but rather as differently configured CPHS variations, differentiated primarily by the presence or absence of human-centered enablers and the level of human engagement in system decision-making and interaction.

One of the central challenges addressed by CPHSXR is the terminological fluidity that permeates the field. As highlighted throughout this paper, terms such as CPS, IIS, HCI, HMI, HXRI, and CPHS often emerge as the result of disciplinary silos, evolving technologies, and shifting use cases. CPHSXR provides a structured explanation for their existence since these terms are manifestations of different intersections and empowerment strategies applied to the CPHS components. By situating these terms within the set-theoretic structure of CPHSXR, the framework allows for both clarification and contextualization of these terms without discarding them, offering a shared conceptual space where existing vocabulary can coexist while being consistently interpretable. In doing so, CPHSXR reframes the discourse away from terminological proliferation as a problem and toward terminological diversity as a reflection of system configurational richness, now anchored in a common structural foundation.

Beyond its immediate conceptual clarifications, the CPHSXR framework and taxonomy open multiple avenues for future research and practical applications. In education and training, CPHSXR can serve as a teaching scaffold for introducing students to complex cyber-physical-human integrations, helping them grasp both system structure and the evolving role of enabling technologies. In system design, the framework offers a tool for mapping design decisions across dimensions, allowing teams to deliberately choose levels of immersion, decision-making authority, task granularity, and enabling technologies based on user needs, domain context, and desired system behaviors. In the realm of human-centered AI and adaptive systems, CPHSXR provides a language for framing hybrid systems that blend automation with human engagement, supporting responsible AI design practices that foreground transparency, adaptability, and ergonomics. Furthermore, the framework offers potential to support standardization efforts, cross-disciplinary dialogue, and system comparison studies, serving as a neutral yet flexible reference model across domains such as healthcare, manufacturing, defense, and assistive technologies.

In summary, CPHSXR provides not only a conceptual lens to navigate the fragmented terminology and evolving system types in human-cyber-physical integrations but also offers a structured foundation for classifying, comparing, and designing these systems. By grounding diverse system variations in the consistent logic of CPHS components and technological enablers, the framework supports both analytical rigor and design flexibility. The following conclusion distills the key contributions of this work and reinforces the need for a shared conceptual language in this increasingly complex design space.

5   Conclusion

This paper addressed the persistent conceptual fragmentation in the fields of AMS, CPS, HCI, HXRI, HMI and SCS by introducing the CPHSXR framework. Through a systematic exploration of terminological overlaps and emerging system types, we clarified the foundational roles of cyber, physical, and human components, while recognizing the transformative influence of enabling technologies such as XR, AI, IoT, and perceptual technologies. We demonstrated that these technologies, rather than constituting new system components, function as enablers that empower CPHS components without altering the tripartite system architecture. This perspective allowed us to reinterpret a wide array of existing terms such as HXRI, IIS, and SCS within a coherent and consistent structural model. Building upon this foundation, the paper proposed a taxonomy of CPHS variations within CPHSXR, introducing three dimensions: immersion level, decision-making level, and granularity assignment. This allows for systematic classification of CPHS configurations. This taxonomy not only clarifies existing system terms but also supports scalable system design and analysis by enabling nuanced combinations of CPHS components and human roles. By systematically grounding the vocabulary of human-cyber-physical interaction within CPHSXR, this paper offers both conceptual clarity and a practical toolset for researchers, educators, and system designers navigating the increasingly complex space of intelligent, immersive, and interactive systems.

Disclosure of Interests. The authors have no competing interests to declare that are relevant to the content of this article.

References

1. Abbink, D.A., Mulder, M., Boer, E.R.: Haptic shared control: smoothly shifting control authority? Cogn. Technol. Work **14**, 19–28 (2012)
2. Annaswamy, A.M., Yildiz, Y.: Cyber-physical-human systems, pp. 497–508. Springer, Cham (2021). https://doi.org/10.1007/978-3-030-44184-5_100113
3. Antsaklis, P.J., Passino, K.M., Wang, S.J.: An introduction to autonomous control systems. IEEE Control Syst. Mag. **11**(4), 5–13 (2002)
4. Baheti, R., Gill, H.: Cyber-physical systems. Impact Control Technol. **12**(1), 161–166 (2011)
5. Bennett, S.: Development of the PID controller. IEEE Control Syst. Mag. **13**(6), 58–62 (1993)
6. Bulman, J., Crabtree, B., Gower, A., Oldroyd, A., Lawson, M., Sutton, J.: Mixed reality applications in urban environments. BT Technol. J. **22**(3), 84–94 (2004)
7. Carroll, J.M.: Human-computer interaction: psychology as a science of design. Int. J. Hum. Comput. Stud. **46**(4), 501–522 (1997)
8. Cecil, J., Gupta, A.: The impact of extended reality-based digital approaches to support STEM learning for autistic students. In: 2024 ASEE Annual Conference & Exposition (2024)
9. Chang, Y., et al.: A survey on evaluation of large language models. ACM Trans. Intell. Syst. Technol. **15**(3), 1–45 (2024)
10. De Marsico, M., Spagnoli, A.: Using hands as an easy UAV joystick for entertainment applications. In: Proceedings of the 13th Biannual Conference of the Italian SIGCHI Chapter: Designing the Next Interaction, pp. 1–9. ACM (2019)
11. Elkind, J.I.: Characteristics of simple manual control systems. Ph.D. thesis, Massachusetts Institute of Technology (1956)
12. Endsley, M.R.: Situation awareness in aviation systems. In: Garland, D.J., Wise, J.A., Hopkins, V.D. (eds.) Handbook of Aviation Human Factors, chap. 11, pp. 257–276. CRC Press (1999)
13. Eraslan, E.: Shared control in aerial cyber-physical human systems. Master's thesis, Bilkent Universitesi (Turkey) (2021)
14. Eraslan, E., Yildiz, Y.: Modeling and adaptive control of flexible quadrotor UAVs. In: 2021 60th IEEE Conference on Decision and Control (CDC), pp. 1783–1788. IEEE (2021)
15. Eraslan, E., Yildiz, Y.: Flexible quadrotor unmanned aerial vehicles: spatially distributed modeling and delay-resistant control. J. Guid. Control. Dyn. **47**(6), 1109–1122 (2024)
16. Eraslan, E., Yildiz, Y., Annaswamy, A.M.: Shared control between pilots and autopilots: an illustration of a cyberphysical human system. IEEE Control Syst. Mag. **40**(6), 77–97 (2020)
17. Eraslan, E., Yildiz, Y., Annaswamy, A.M.: Safe shared control between pilots and autopilots in the face of anomalies. In: Cyber–Physical–Human Systems: Fundamentals and Applications, pp. 219–249. Springer (2023)
18. Falah, J., et al.: Virtual reality medical training system for anatomy education. In: 2014 Science and Information Conference, pp. 752–758. IEEE (2014)
19. Farjadian, A.B., Thomsen, B., Annaswamy, A.M., Woods, D.D.: Resilient flight control: an architecture for human supervision of automation. IEEE Trans. Control Syst. Technol. **29**(1), 29–42 (2020)
20. Farjadian, A.B., Thomsen, B.T., Annaswamy, A.M., Woods, D.D.: A shared pilot-autopilot control architecture for resilient flight. IEEE Trans. Control Syst. Technol. (2018)

21. Fetzer, J.H.: What is artificial intelligence? In: Artificial Intelligence: Its Scope and Limits, pp. 3–27. Springer (1990)
22. Fonseca, A., Cabral, B.: Controlling the granularity of automatic parallel programs. J. Comput. Sci. **17**, 620–629 (2016)
23. Ganga, G., Dharmana, M.M.: MPC controller for trajectory tracking control of quadcopter. In: 2017 International Conference on Circuit, Power and Computing Technologies (ICCPCT), pp. 1–6. IEEE (2017)
24. Ghobakhloo, M.: Industry 4.0, digitization, and opportunities for sustainability. J. Clean. Prod. **252**, 119869 (2020)
25. Goh, E.S., Sunar, M.S., Ismail, A.W.: 3D object manipulation techniques in hand-held mobile augmented reality interface: a review. IEEE Access **7**, 40581–40601 (2019)
26. Gupta, A.: Investigation of a holistic human-computer interaction (HCI) framework to support the design of extended reality (XR) based training simulators (2021)
27. Gupta, A., Cecil, J., Pirela-Cruz, M.: A multi-level HXRI-based approach for XR-based surgical training. In: 2023 IEEE International Conference on Systems, Man, and Cybernetics (SMC), pp. 1573–1578. IEEE (2023)
28. Gupta, A., Cecil, J., Pirela-Cruz, M., Kennison, S., Hicks, N.A.: Need for human extended reality interaction (HXRI) framework for the design of extended reality-based training environments for surgical contexts. In: 2022 IEEE 10th International Conference on Serious Games and Applications for Health (SeGAH), pp. 1–8. IEEE (2022)
29. Homay, A., de Sousa, M., Zoitl, A., Wollschlaeger, M.: Service granularity in industrial automation and control systems. In: 2020 25th IEEE International Conference on Emerging Technologies and Factory Automation (ETFA), vol. 1, pp. 132–139. IEEE (2020)
30. Huang, S., Wang, B., Li, X., Zheng, P., Mourtzis, D., Wang, L.: Industry 5.0 and society 5.0-comparison, complementation and co-evolution. J. Manufact. Syst. **64**, 424–428 (2022)
31. Jiang, Y., Li, X., Luo, H., Yin, S., Kaynak, O.: Quo vadis artificial intelligence? Discov. Artif. Intell. **2**(1), 4 (2022)
32. Juuso, E.K.: Integration of intelligent systems in development of smart adaptive systems. Int. J. Approx. Reason. **35**(3), 307–337 (2004)
33. Kasneci, E., et al.: Chatgpt for good? On opportunities and challenges of large language models for education. Learn. Individ. Differ. **103**, 102274 (2023)
34. Kesim, M., Ozarslan, Y.: Augmented reality in education: current technologies and the potential for education. Procedia. Soc. Behav. Sci. **47**, 297–302 (2012)
35. Lasi, H., Fettke, P., Kemper, H.-G., Feld, T., Hoffmann, M.: Industry 4.0. Bus. Inf. Syst. Eng. **6**(4), 239–242 (2014). https://doi.org/10.1007/s12599-014-0334-4
36. Le Noury, P., Polman, R., Maloney, M., Gorman, A.: A narrative review of the current state of extended reality technology and how it can be utilised in sport. Sports Med. **52**(7), 1473–1489 (2022)
37. Leng, J., et al.: Industry 5.0: prospect and retrospect. J. Manufact. Syst. **65**, 279–295 (2022)
38. Lewis, M.: Designing for human-agent interaction. AI Mag. **19**(2), 67 (1998). https://doi.org/10.1609/aimag.v19i2.1369
39. Li, F.: VRCI and CPHS. IFAC-PapersOnLine **53**(5), 116–118 (2020)
40. Liberzon, D., Brockett, R.W.: Nonlinear feedback systems perturbed by noise: steady-state probability distributions and optimal control. IEEE Trans. Autom. Control **45**(6), 1116–1130 (2002)

41. Matthies, D.J., Gabrecht, M., Hellbrück, H.: Cyber-physical & human systems (CPHS)-a review and outlook. Proc. Mensch und Comput. **2023**, 364–369 (2023)
42. Mazumder, S.K., et al.: A review of current research trends in power-electronic innovations in cyber-physical systems. IEEE Jo. Emerg. Sel. Top. Power Electron. **9**(5), 5146–5163 (2021)
43. Meystel, A.M., Albus, J.S.: Intelligent Systems: Architecture, Design, and Control. Wiley (2000)
44. Mois, G., et al.: Understanding older adults' interest in using virtual reality to support social engagement activities. Innov. Aging **8**(Suppl._1), 1224 (2024)
45. Morimoto, T., et al.: XR (extended reality: virtual reality, augmented reality, mixed reality) technology in spine medicine: status quo and quo vadis. J. Clin. Med. **11**(2), 470 (2022)
46. Mukhopadhyay, S., et al.: Context-aware design of cyber-physical human systems (CPHS). In: 2020 International Conference on COMmunication Systems & NETworkS (COMSNETS), pp. 322–329. IEEE (2020)
47. Nguyen, T., Lim, C.P., Nguyen, N.D., Gordon-Brown, L., Nahavandi, S.: A review of situation awareness assessment approaches in aviation environments. IEEE Syst. J. **13**(3), 3590–3603 (2019)
48. Panteli, M., Kirschen, D.S.: Situation awareness in power systems: theory, challenges and applications. Electric Power Syst. Res. **122**, 140–151 (2015)
49. Payne, C.J., Vyas, K., Bautista-Salinas, D., Zhang, D., Marcus, H.J., Yang, G.Z.: Shared-control robots. Neurosurg. Robot. 63–79 (2021)
50. Pirani, M., Carbonari, A., Cucchiarelli, A., Giretti, A., Spalazzi, L.: The meta holonic management tree: review, steps, and roadmap to industrial cybernetics 5.0. J. Intell. Manufact. 1–42 (2024)
51. Radanliev, P., De Roure, D., Van Kleek, M., Santos, O., Ani, U.: Artificial intelligence in cyber physical systems. AI Soc. **36**(3), 783–796 (2021)
52. Ramadorai, A.K., Tara, T.J., Bejczy, A.K., Xi, N.: Task-driven control of multi-arm systems. IEEE Trans. Control Syst. Technol. **2**(3), 198–206 (1994)
53. Sadeghi Milani, A., Cecil, J., Pirela-Cruz, M., Kennison, S.: Design of a mixed reality approach to enhance understanding of reverse total shoulder arthroplasty. In: International Conference on Human-Computer Interaction, pp. 171–189. Springer (2023)
54. Sadeghi Milani, A., Cecil-Xavier, A., Gupta, A., Cecil, J., Kennison, S.: A systematic review of human-computer interaction (HCI) research in medical and other engineering fields. Int. J. Hum.-Comput. Interact. **40**(3), 515–536 (2024)
55. Schirner, G., Erdogmus, D., Chowdhury, K., Padir, T.: The future of human-in-the-loop cyber-physical systems. Computer **46**(1), 36–45 (2013)
56. Schöning, J., Westerkamp, C.: AI-in-the-Loop–The impact of HMI in AI-based Application (2023), arXiv preprint
57. Tehrani, B.M., Wang, J., Wang, C.: Review of human-in-the-loop cyber-physical systems (HILCPS): the current status from human perspective. In: ASCE International Conference on Computing in Civil Engineering 2019, pp. 470–478. American Society of Civil Engineers Reston, VA (2019)
58. Tyagi, A.K., Sreenath, N.: Cyber physical systems: analyses, challenges and possible solutions. Internet Things Cyber-Phys. Syst. **1**, 22–33 (2021)
59. Varga, L., Jennings, N.R., Cockburn, D.: Integrating intelligent systems into a cooperating community for electricity distribution management. Expert Syst. Appl. **7**(4), 563–579 (1994)
60. Wan, K., Man, K., Hughes, D.: Specification, analyzing challenges and approaches for cyber-physical systems (CPS). Eng. Lett. **18**(3) (2010)

61. de Winter, J.C., Petermeijer, S.M., Abbink, D.A.: Shared control versus traded control in driving: a debate around automation pitfalls. Ergonomics **66**(10), 1494–1520 (2023)
62. Xiong, L., Chng, C.B., Chui, C.K., Yu, P., Li, Y.: Shared control of a medical robot with haptic guidance. Int. J. Comput. Assist. Radiol. Surg. **12**, 137–147 (2017)
63. Xu, W., Dainoff, M.J., Ge, L., Gao, Z.: Transitioning to human interaction with AI systems: new challenges and opportunities for HCI professionals to enable human-centered AI. Int. J. Hum.-Comput. Interact. **39**(3), 494–518 (2023)
64. Yau, K.L.A.: Human-in-the-loop cyber-physical systems (2022)
65. Yildiz, Y.: Cyberphysical human systems: an introduction to the special issue. IEEE Control Syst. Mag. **40**(6), 26–28 (2020)
66. Yoo, G.S., Ji, Y.G.: A study on view sharing AR interface for improving situation awareness during military operations. Int. J. Hum.-Comput. Interact. **41**(4), 2211–2226 (2025)

Integrating Machine Learning into Extended Reality: A Critical Review of Computational Approaches to Human Behavior Modeling

Houze Yang[1], Caroline Cao[1], Alexandra Hosny[1], Jeeheon Ryu[2],
and Inki Kim[1(✉)]

[1] University of Illinois at Urbana Champaign, Urbana, IL 61801, USA
`inkikim@illinois.edu`
[2] Chonnam National University, Gwangju 61186, Korea

Abstract. Recent advances in Extended Reality (XR) technologies, such as increased computational power and sensor integration, have broadened XR applications in education, healthcare, and collaboration. In parallel, machine learning (ML) has become a powerful tool for modeling complex human behaviors, including attention, intention, and social interaction. Despite this, integration between ML models and XR systems remains limited. This review analyzes 18 selected studies from 20182025 and focuses on two key directions: (1) multi-scale modeling of human and human interaction and (2) abstraction from movement to intention to goal. These works apply models such as Convolutional Neural Networks (CNNs), Recurrent Neural Network (RNNs), Graph Convolutional Networks (GCNs), and Transformers to tasks like attention and motion prediction, group behavior analysis, and short-term goal inference. However, most systems remain single-scale and lack pipelines that connect behavioral models across scales. The challenges of integrations include sensor misalignment, latency, and the absence of standardized multimodal data sets.

Keywords: Extended Reality (XR) · Human Behavior Modeling · Machine Learning Integration · Multi-Scale Interaction

1 Introduction

Extended-reality (XR) technologies have demonstrated significant advances in computational power, sensor integration, and display fidelity. Sophisticated processors like the Snapdragon XR2+ Gen 2 and Apple M5 enable 4K rendering at 90 frames per second (FPS) with minimal latency [1]. Furthermore, by integrating different sensors, such as Red Green BlueDepth(RGB-D), Light Detection and Ranging (LiDAR), and the inertial motion unit (IMU), XR devices improve the ability to understand the environment and track users' behavior.

J. Y. C. Chen et al. (Eds.): HCII 2025, LNCS 16338, pp. 49–59, 2026.
https://doi.org/10.1007/978-3-032-12808-9_4

These improvements have expanded XR's applications in different domains, from immersive education to medical simulation. For example, in healthcare alone, the XR market was valued at US$ 7.8 billion in 2024 and is expected to grow at an annual growth rate of 26.98%, reaching US$ 67.7 billion by 2033 [2].

In parallel, computational modeling, particularly machine learning (ML), has achieved unprecedented success in interpreting complex human behavior. Machine learning models have been applied to tasks such as gaze behavior classification, motion and intention prediction, and social interaction patterns analysis. However, their integration remains limited despite these improvements in both XR hardware and ML methodologies. Many existing XR applications still rely on static, rule-based architectures that lack adaptable responses to user behaviors. This gap further motivates investigations into how machine learning models can be embedded into the core of the XR workflow. Such integration has great potential to convert XR systems from static, pre-programmed environments into intelligent, context-aware systems. The system can adaptively respond to user behaviors with personalized feedback, and support more intuitive human-computer interactions.

This paper reviews recent works that integrate machine learning into XR systems to enhance behavior and interaction studies. Specifically, it focuses on two research directions. The first is multi-scale modeling of human and human interaction. It uses computational models to analyze human behavior across different levels of detail, from individual actions such as gaze, gesture, and posture to social activities within users. It then combines behavioral signals across scales to comprehensively understand more complex interaction in XR environments. Although recent machine learning approaches have demonstrated single-scale capabilities, integrated frameworks that cover these scales remain scarce.

The second focus is abstraction from motion to intention to goal, which explores how XR systems can infer user intent and objectives from raw sensor input. This topic will enable XR applications to guide users with personalized, real-time content. These two perspectives represent a shift from rule-driven interaction toward intelligent systems that interpret, predict, and respond to users that is more human-like and context-sensitive.

2   Research Methods

The literature search was conducted using the Web of Science (WoS), a widely used database for academic research. The initial search used basic keywords combining machine learning (including terms like artificial intelligence [AI] and deep learning [DL]) with XR (including virtual reality [VR], augmented reality [AR], and mixed reality [MR]). Instead of covering the full range of machine learning topics, which span diverse methods and applications, the scope was then narrowed using three targeted sets of keywords.

1. Task-related keywords were used to specify the type of learning. These included classification, sequence prediction, clustering, and reinforcement learning—common algorithm types applied to behavior modeling.

2. Input-related keywords address the types of data processed by machine learning models in XR. Given the diversity of XR sensor data, terms such as eye-tracking, gesture, body motion, speech, and environment were included to capture input-specific approaches.
3. Scale-related keywords reflected the level at which behavior is analyzed. Terms like individual-level, group-level, and spatial computation were used to cover modeling across different behavioral and interaction layers.

The initial search using broad keywords, limited to English-language publications from the past 10 years (2015–2025), returned 2,789 results. To narrow the scope, more specific keywords—covering task type, input features, and modeling scale—were applied. Papers were then filtered based on two criteria: (1) the study must involve human behavior in XR or have strong potential for XR application, and (2) it must include model details such as architecture, input data, and evaluation metrics. Studies focused solely on rendering, object tracking, or system performance without behavioral modeling were excluded. A total of 18 papers met the criteria and were selected for analysis. These were published between 2018 and 2025, with most appearing after 2023, reflecting growing interest in applying machine learning to behavioral understanding in XR.

3 Multi-scale Modeling of Human and Human Interaction in XR

Multiscale modeling in XR studies human behavior in several aspects, from an individual's movements and attention to the interactions within whole groups. As XR combines physical and virtual spaces, systems must track detailed personal activities, such as hand gestures, gaze direction, and body posture, while recognizing the larger patterns that arise when many users share the same scene. Although these features are on different spatial and temporal scales, they are closely related: subtle individual actions shape and respond to group dynamics.

For example, in social VR, even small cues, such as where someone is looking, may change who speaks next and how connected the group is. However, most current models study individual and group behavior separately. They lack methods to link actions across scales, making it harder for XR systems to respond to complex social actions.

This section reviews recent work on individual and group modeling in XR using machine learning. It also introduces new approaches that aim to connect different levels of behavior into one coherent framework.

3.1 Individual-Level Modeling in XR

Individual-level modeling focuses on understanding the behavior and responses of a single user in XR environments. The system uses eye trackers, motion capture, IMUs, and handheld controllers to track gaze and body movement. Machine learning methods are essential for interpreting the data and enabling XR systems to respond appropriately.

In the following, we explore two key aspects of individual-level modeling: gaze and attention modeling through eye tracking and physical movement analysis.

Eye Tracking. XR captures gaze behaviors, such as where users look, how long they fixate, and how attention changes across virtual scenes. Convolutional neural networks (CNNs) are widely used to estimate gaze direction from near-eye images. For example, Feng et al. [3] proposed a lightweight U-Net structured CNN for eye segmentation and gazing direction estimation. The model includes an event-driven region-of-interest (ROI) module that uses emulated event maps and edge features. With only about 30,000 parameters, it runs at more than 30 Hz (Hz) on mobile GPUs and achieves sub-0.5 degrees gaze error.

To capture attention patterns over time, sequential models like Long-Short-Term Memory (LSTMs) and Transformers learn gaze dynamics, such as fixations and saccades, to predict future gaze points. GazeTransformer [4], for example, forecasts gaze using raw eye and head movement data. It achieves angular error 9.93 degrees for saccades and 2.20 degrees fixations, outperforming baseline models such as FixationNet and DGaze.

Attention modeling also requires classifying gaze behavior patterns. Unsupervised learning clustering algorithms group gaze trajectories into different attention patterns, allowing systems to infer user intent and adapt content accordingly. The Gaze Data Clustering Taxonomy (GCT) [5] is an unsupervised framework that classifies raw gaze data into meaningful patterns. It uses algorithms like DBSCAN, k-Means, and k-NN to identify categories such as focused fixation, exploratory scanning, hesitation, and distraction. On the GazeBase dataset, GCT achieved 90.5%90.9% accuracy and 93%95% F1-scores when aligning clustered gaze centroids with ground truth targets.

Physical Motion Modeling in XR involves recognizing and predicting hand gestures, head orientation, and full-body posture. Recurrent neural networks (RNNs), especially LSTM models, are widely used to capture temporal patterns from motion sensors and skeletal tracking systems. For example, VRheab [6] is an immersive rehabilitation system that uses LSTM-RNNs to evaluate motor performance in VR. Patients interact using Kinect and Leap Motion, which collect full-body and hand-joint data. Training on recordings from 20 healthy individuals performing three exercises, the model analyzes characteristics such as joint angles, movement speed, and pinch strength. It achieved up to 98.6% similarity in matching healthy movement patterns and provides real-time feedback for motor rehabilitation. When applied to Parkinson patients, the system could track subtle motor impairments, such as reduced speed or coordination in grasping and reaching tasks, helping therapists monitor progress more precisely.

In addition to RNNs, XR systems use Multi-Layer Perceptrons (MLPs) for real-time motion prediction. Although MLP don't study temporal patterns directly, their simplicity and speed make them ideal for real-time applications on resource-constrained XR hardware. TW-MLP [7], a lightweight model with a temporal window mechanism, uses only head and hand tracking to generate full-body motion. It achieves a 2.49 degrees rotation error, reduces jitter from 13.01 to 7.15, and cuts giga floating point operations per second (GFLOPS) from 0.88 to 0.19, - demonstrating its efficiency for real-time XR applications.

Graph Convolutional Networks (GCNs) are well-suited for modeling full-body motion for XR systems with richer sensor input. The system represents the human body as a graph, where joints are nodes and limbs are edges. One example is HOIMotion [8], a model developed for XR environments involving human-object interactions. It captures egocentric RGB-D video using a head-mounted stereo camera and reconstructs 3D full-body poses with a pre-trained neural model. The system also incorporates head orientation and 3D object positions within the user's field of view. These multimodal inputs are fused into a pose-object graph, processed through a residual GCN encoder-decoder architecture enhanced with MLP components. HOIMotion focuses on gross, medium-speed body movements—such as walking, turning, and reaching—rather than fine-motor actions, predicting motion up to two seconds ahead. It achieves an 8.7% reduction in mean per joint position error (MPJPE) on the ADT dataset compared to previous methods.

3.2   Group-Level Modeling in XR

Group modeling in XR focuses on how multiple users interact in shared virtual environments. This relies on spatial computation, which helps the system understand the environment and locate users accurately. With this spatial context, machine learning models can detect social signals, track coordination, and predict group dynamics. The following sections explore how ML advances spatial computation and real-time multi-user behavior modeling.

Spatial Computation provides the geometric foundation for group modeling in XR, and machine learning methods are significant to how spatial data is estimated, fused, and interpreted. Rather than relying only on classical geometry or rule-based systems, modern XR systems integrate machine learning-based spatial frameworks that are more adaptive, robust, and capable of handling more complex environments.

One key application of machine learning in spatial computation is deep learning-based SLAM (Simultaneous Localization and Mapping). Neural networks replace traditional geometric mapping with continuous, learned 3D scene representations. For example, XRDSLAM is a modular framework that combines several state-of-the-art deep learning SLAM algorithms, including Point-SLAM, which uses neural point clouds, and Vox-Fusion, which applies neural fields based on voxels [9]. On the Replica indoor dataset, Point-SLAM within XRDSLAM achieved much lower trajectory error (0.47 centimeters [cm] Absolute Trajectory Error [ATE]) and higher view synthesis quality (34.1 decibels [dB] Peak signal-to-noise ratio[PSNR]) compared to voxel-based methods like NICE-SLAM (2.09 cm ATE, 25.7 dB PSNR). These results demonstrate that deep SLAM improves localization accuracy, enhances photorealistic rendering, and enables denser scene reconstruction, offering the spatial precision needed for XR tasks such as gaze-object intersection and modeling multi-user interactions.

Another direction in spatial Computation is multimodal place recognition, where deep learning models combine data from different sensors to accurately localize users in large and changing environments. One example is GSPR, which was initially developed for autonomous driving but is highly relevant for outdoor XR [10]. The GSPR introduces Multimodal Gaussian Splatting (MGS), which starts with LiDAR-based geometry and refines it using multiview RGB images. GSRP creates a detailed 3D scene that captures both structure and appearance. A combination of 3D graph convolution and transformer layers extracts global scene features, achieving up to 99.7% top-1 recall on large-scale benchmarks like nuScenes and KITTI-360. This technique shows strong potential for outdoor AR, enabling localization with head-mounted cameras and wearable depth sensors, even under changing lighting or seasonal conditions.

Group-Level Modeling in XR includes various scenarios, from one-on-one interactions to small group collaboration and larger classroom-scale engagement. Each level presents unique spatial, temporal, and behavioral patterns, and machine learning models must interpret them differently to support real-time and appropriate interaction in shared virtual environments.

Dyadic interaction involving two users is essential in collaborative learning. Systems must recognize how users take turns talking. Park et al. [11] proposed a Hidden Markov Model (HMM)-based system for detecting collaboration states in VR teamwork training. Designed for dyadic interaction in a Collaborative Virtual Environment (CVE), the model classifies user behavior as Engaged, Waiting, or Struggling using multimodal input from headsets, controllers, and eye trackers. These signals are converted into seven binary features to train the HMM, which reached 97.77% accuracy with k-fold cross-validation, significantly outperforming a rule-based baseline.

Small-group modeling promotes inclusive participation, but subtle nonverbal signals like posture or facial expression are often missing or inaccurate to other users in VR. To address this, Gu et al. developed a framework to detect when users want to speak but remain silent in group discussions [12]. In a four-person VR meeting task, Gu et al. collected data with Oculus Quest 2 headsets, capturing 60 motion features (e.g., head pose, hand movement) at 20 Hz. They then split data into 10-second segments and classified them with compact time series models, including EEGNet, InceptionTime, and MLSTM-FCN. EEGNet models achieved an F1 score of 0.71, which improved to 0.79 when leader motion data was included. The results show that lightweight models and consumer-level VR devices can help reveal latent speaking intent and support more equitable group interaction.

Larger-scale interactions, such as classroom-scale conversations, make it more challenging to study turn-taking patterns due to the large number of participants. Wang et al. addressed this by analyzing data from 77 social VR class sessions (over 1,600 min, 100 participants) recorded with Meta Quest 2 headsets [13]. Their system extracted 130 features, including gaze, body motion, and speech activity. Using gradient boosting classifier, the models predicted three events of turn-taking: when a speaker will finish ('what'), who will speak next ('who'), and how soon the next turn will begin ('when'). Gradient boosting models performed best, achieving AUC scores of 0.78 (what), 0.77 (who), and 0.72 (when), and generalized well to new users.

3.3   Bridging the Scales

A complete XR intelligence pipeline must integrate individual modeling, spatial computation, and group modeling. Although each layer has advanced independently, combining them into a unified real-time pipeline is rare. The combination of different layers must overcome these engineering difficulties.

- **Heterogeneous, Unsynchronized Sensors** XR systems rely on multiple sensors, each operating on its own hardware clock and signal path. Due to unequal latencies and clock drift (often several milliseconds per minute), a timestamp labeled t = 100 millisecond(ms) in one stream rarely aligns with the same moment in another. This misalignment corrupts composite features (e.g., 'gaze on object while speaking'), introducing noise or missing data in machine learning models for spatial alignment or group interaction, ultimately degrading accuracy and user experience [14].
- **Extreme Concurrency and Latency Budgets** Real-time XR workloads often involve a dozen concurrent models, such as hand tracking, eye tracking, speech processing, depth estimation, scene understanding, and more. These models must be updated within 10 to 16 ms on devices with battery and computational power limitations. XRBench's cascaded concurrent graphs reveal control flow dependencies that traditional single-model schedulers cannot handle efficiently, leading to missed deadlines and frames [14].
- **Dataset scarcity for cross-scale learning.** Training multiscale XR models requires datasets that capture the full who - what - where - why spectrum: centimeter-accurate 3D maps, synchronized pose/gaze/audio streams, and detailed multi-user annotations across device types [15]. Most existing datasets are task-specific or single-user, and simply merging introduces format conflicts or redundant data. Supervised training for end-to-end XR modeling remains limited without standardized, richly annotated benchmarks.

Explainable XR. The Explainable XR(EXR) platform addresses two key challenges in XR systems: sensor misalignment and dataset scarcity [15]. It introduces a unified framework for collecting, analyzing, and visualizing immersive sessions. The User Action Descriptor (UAD) is a JSON schema that timestamps pose, gaze, speech, and controller events. Clients send UAD packets on a shared clock, allowing a cloud service to fuse them into intent-action graphs for multiple users. This unified time alignment mitigates sensor-rate mismatches and produces synchronized, reusable multi-user data. Then, a Large Language

Model(LLM) summarizes the data to assist in analyzing and identifying the information. Although this project remains in post-processing and does not yet support live supervisory feedback, EXR provides a technically grounded bridge between low-level signals and high-level models, laying the foundation for a public, cross-scale XR dataset.

Holo-Cloud. The Multi-user, Multisite, Platform-Independent Holo-Cloud system addresses the extreme concurrency and latency barrier from the infrastructure side [16]. By containerizing the entire XR application stack within autoscaling cloud virtual machines, it offloads heavyweight perception and rendering tasks to dedicated GPUs and streams only holographic frames and states to headsets. In testing with five concurrent HoloLens clients, CPU ($<85\%$), RAM (<160 Megabytes) and network (<1.2 Megabytes per second[MBps]) stayed well below critical thresholds. At the same time, interactions remained smooth, demonstrating that offload can satisfy aggregate real-time demand without overwhelming mobile hardware. The design is a credible path to running individual, spatial, and group models concurrently at scale.

4   Abstraction From Movement to Intention to Goal

XR systems must infer users' underlying intentions and goals to provide real-time assistance in virtual environments. This progression, from motion through intention to goal, requires models that can process multimodal signals; machine learning architectures such as CNNs, LSTMs, and Transformers meet this need by fusing data streams such as motion and gaze. This capability is especially valuable in domains like surgical training, collaborative manufacturing, and immersive education, where anticipating user goals improves system effectiveness and user engagement.

4.1   Motion to Intention

Translating body and eye movements into explicit interaction intentions is the first abstraction step in XR intelligence. Mayor et al. address the challenge of predicting locomotion intent in VR using headset-only data [17]. They capture $10\,\mathrm{Hz}$ streams of 3D position, quaternion rotation, forward vector, and linear velocity from 44 users navigating in three Unity scenes on Oculus Quest 2, yielding approximately 276,000 frames. A two-layer LSTM with 64 units processes 25-frame windows ($2.5\,\mathrm{s}$ [s]) to predict future head-center displacement, where the user intends to move next. Switching the input from Euler angles to quaternions improves accuracy: in the escape room scene, the short-term ($0.1\,\mathrm{s}$) mean displacement error drops to $0.99\,\mathrm{cm}$, a 28% improvement over linear extrapolation. Over a $2.5\,\mathrm{s}$ horizon, the quaternion-based LSTM achieves an average mean displacement error of $0.51\,\mathrm{m}$ (m) across scenes, outperforming the earlier Euler-based LSTM by 27.9%.

Researchers can make more detailed and accurate predictions with access to more comprehensive sensor data. Kamali et al. collected high-frequency (300 Hz) full-body and hand motion data in VR using an HTC Vive Pro Eye headset, three body trackers (chest and elbows), and a Leap Motion device that captures 25 finger joints [18]. The dataset includes 3,500 segmented trials (about 153 million samples) from six participants performing seven shop-floor actions: idle, walk, bend, sit, relocate, one-hand grasp, and two-hand grasp. To classify user intent, a CNN-Transformer ensemble processes 676-dimensional spatio-temporal tensors, combining convolutional feature maps with global attention to capture short- and long-term motion cues. CNN and CNNLSTM models serve as baselines. CNN-Transformer achieves near-perfect accuracy (about 1.00), with per-class F1 scores of 1.00 for both grasp actions, 0.991.00 for relocate, bend, sit, and stand, and 1.00 for walking, outperforming CNN-LSTM (0.99) and plain CNN (0.95).

4.2   Intention to Destination

XR systems can anticipate a user's destination by fusing micro-level intent cues, such as gaze shifts, head turns, and short trajectory segments. This prediction can be used to develop guidance, navigation, and interaction in complex environments.

Holman et al. demonstrated this approach using an HTC Vive Pro Eye headset worn by seven participants as they walked toward one of five doors [19]. Each participant completed 25 trials at all five destinations, generating 60-Hz streams of 2D position, forward velocity, head yaw, gaze yaw, and gaze focus. A multivariate Gaussian time series classifier integrated these cues to predict the intended goal. Including gaze yaw doubled the model's cold-start accuracy (about 40%) and reached 95% classification accuracy after just 34% of the trajectory, 0.22 m earlier than using head yaw alone. This improvement provides approximately 0.5 s of additional planning time, a critical advantage for real-time systems such as socially aware robots.

Expanding to more realistic indoor scenarios, Takeyama et al. introduced LocoVR, a dataset of 7,071 two-person trajectories recorded across 131 photorealistic home scenes with 32 participants [20]. The system logs 2D positions and head direction at 15 Hz within a 10×10 m play area. For prediction, the past 6 s of a user's trajectory are rasterized along with the scene map and input into a lightweight U-Net that produces a pixel-level goal heatmap. Coupled with an A* planner, this model generates geometry-aware paths. The real-world LocoReal test set reduces the goal position error to 0.83 m and achieves 72% top-3 object accuracy within 3 m of the destination. Additionally, its trajectory head (without explicit goal prediction) achieves 0.11 m average displacement error (ADE) in the first second, more than twice as accurate as prior indoor data sets.

5   Conclusion

This review highlights recent progress in applying machine learning to model human behavior in XR systems, including attention and motion prediction, group interaction analysis, and short-term goal inference. However, most systems still process individual, spatial, and group-level features through separate modules. Few works integrate these components into a continuous pipeline that connects low-level individual behavioral signals and spacial information to high-level group outcomes. Technical challenges such as sensor misalignment, real-time latency constraints, and the absence of cross-scale datasets further hinder integration. Overcoming these limitations will require not only more efficient algorithms, but also unified system architectures that can coordinate multiple behavioral models in real-time. Future XR systems must shift from isolated interaction components toward holistic, context-aware frameworks capable of supporting seamless, adaptive user response.

References

1. Laura. Discover the Best 4 VR Headsets of 2024: Unveiling the Top Picks. YORD Studio (2024). https://yordstudio.com/top-vr-headsets-2024/
2. IMARC Group. Healthcare Extended Reality Market Report: By Component (Hardware, Software, Services), Technology (Augmented Reality, Virtual Reality, Mixed Reality), Application (Surgery, Therapy, Education and Training, Rehabilitation, Pain Management, and Others), End User (Hospitals, Clinics and Surgical Centers, Pharma Companies, Research Organizations and Diagnostics Laboratories, and Others), and Region 2025–2033. https://www.imarcgroup.com/healthcare-extended-reality-market
3. Feng, Y., Goulding-Hotta, N., Khan, A., Reyserhove, H., Zhu, Y.: Real-time gaze tracking with event-driven eye segmentation. In: IEEE Conference on Virtual Reality and 3D User Interfaces (IEEE VR), pp. 1–10 (2022). https://arxiv.org/abs/2201.07367
4. Rolff, T., Harms, H.M., Steinicke, F., Frintrop, S.: GazeTransformer: gaze forecasting for virtual reality using transformer networks. In: German Conference on CNN-Transformation (GCPR) (2022). https://arxiv.org/abs/2208.02365
5. Siradj, Y., Adhinugraha, K.M., Pardede, E.: Towards structured gaze data classification: the gaze data clustering taxonomy (GCT). Multimodal Technol. Interact. **9**(5), 42 (2025). https://doi.org/10.3390/mti9050042
6. Avola, D., Cinque, L., Foresti, G.L., Marini, M.R., Pannone, D.: VRheab: a fully immersive motor rehabilitation system based on recurrent neural network. Multimedia Tools Appl. **77**(19), 24955–24982 (2018). https://doi.org/10.1007/s11042-018-5730-1
7. Angelis, G.F., Ozkan, S., Mutlu, S., Wisbey, P., Drosou, A., Ozay, M.: Efficient 3D Full-Body Motion Generation from Sparse Tracking Inputs with Temporal Windows. arXiv preprint arXiv:2505.01802 (2025)
8. Hu, Z., Yin, Z., Haeufle, D., Schmitt, S., Bulling, A.: HOIMotion: Forecasting Human Motion During Human-Object Interactions Using Egocentric 3D Object Bounding Boxes. arXiv preprint arXiv:2407.02633 (2024)

9. Wang, X., Wang, N., Zhang, G.: XRDSLAM: A Flexible and Modular Framework for Deep Learning based SLAM. arXiv preprint arXiv:2410.23690 (2024)
10. Qi, Z., Ma, J., Xu, J., Zhou, Z., Cheng, L., Xiong, G.: GSPR: Multimodal Place Recognition Using 3D Gaussian Splatting for Autonomous Driving. arXiv preprint arXiv:2410.00299 (2024)
11. Amat, A.Z., Plunk, A., Adiani, D., Wilkes, D.M., Sarkar, N.: Prediction models of collaborative behaviors in dyadic interactions: an application for inclusive teamwork training in virtual environments. Signals **5**(2), 382–401 (2024). https://doi.org/10.3390/signals5020019
12. Gu, C., Chen, J., Zhang, J., Yang, T., Liu, Z., Konomi, S.: Detecting leadership opportunities in group discussions using off-the-shelf VR headsets. Sensors **24**(8), 2534 (2024). https://doi.org/10.3390/s24082534
13. Wang, P., Han, E., Queiroz, A.C.M., DeVeaux, C., Bailenson, J.N.: Predicting and Understanding Turn-Taking Behavior in Open-Ended Group Activities in Virtual Reality. arXiv preprint arXiv:2407.02896 (2024). https://arxiv.org/abs/2407.02896
14. Kwon, H., et al.: XRBench: an extended reality (XR) machine learning benchmark suite for the metaverse. In: Proceedings of 6th Conference on Machine Learning and Systems (MLSys), Miami Beach (2023)
15. Kim, Y., Aamir, Z., Singh, M., Boorboor, S., Mueller, K., Kaufman, A.E.: Explainable XR: Understanding User Behaviors of XR Environments Using LLM
16. Neeli, H., Tran, K.Q., Velazco-Garcia, J.D., Tsekos, N.V.: A multiuser, multisite, and platform-independent on-the-cloud framework for interactive immersion in holographic XR. Appl. Sci. **14**(5), 2070 (2024). https://doi.org/10.3390/app14052070
17. Mayor, J., Calleja, P., Fuentes-Hurtado, F.: Long short-term memory prediction of user's locomotion in virtual reality. Virtual Reality **28**, 65 (2024). https://doi.org/10.1007/s10055-024-00962-9
18. Kamali Mohammadzadeh, A., Alinezhad, E., Masoud, S.: Neural-network-driven intention recognition for enhanced human-robot interaction: a virtual-reality-driven approach. Machines **13**(5), 414 (2025). https://doi.org/10.3390/machines13050414
19. Holman, B., Anwar, A., Singh, A., Tec, M., Hart, J., Stone, P.: Watch where you're going! Gaze and head orientation as predictors for social robot navigation. In: Proceedings of the IEEE International Conference on Robotics and Automation (ICRA), Xi'an, China, pp. 8122–8128 (2021). https://doi.org/10.1109/ICRA48506.2021.9562042
20. Takeyama, K., Liu, Y., Sra, M.: LocoVR: multiuser indoor locomotion dataset in virtual reality. In: International Conference on Learning Representations (ICLR) (2025). https://arxiv.org/abs/2410.06437

Human Factors and User Experience in XR

Extended User Feedback – A Questionnaire for Usability Evaluation in XR

Omeed Ashtiani[1,2]([✉]), Thiru Annaswamy[2], and Balakrishnan Prabhakaran[3]

[1] University of Texas at Dallas, Richardson, TX, USA
omeed.ashtiani@utdallas.edu
[2] Penn State College of Medicine, Hershey, PA, USA
tannaswamy@pennstatehealth.psu.edu
[3] University of Albany, Albany, NY, USA
bprabhakaran@albany.edu

Abstract. When developing an application for production, end-user questionnaires are a rapid way of acquiring user evaluations about the product's usability. These questionnaires include topics such as the base of the application, user interface, and various ailments related to the application, to say the least. Multiple types of questionnaires and methods have been developed to assist developers with feedback acquisition. However, with such a wide range of disciplines, there is not a standard used by all developers in the research community. Furthermore, as applications are delivered using various devices, such as mobile, desktop, and now XR, new questionnaires have arisen. Compiling these evaluations leads to a large number of questions (100+), a multitude of redundancies, and difficulty comparing related applications due to lack of a solidified system. Furthermore, XR development requires unique feedback that typical presentations of data and engagement do not contain. In this work, we create a concise subset of questions, on a 5-point Likert scale, that remove redundancies and allows for comprehensive statistical analysis, allowing developers to measure differences in populations more readily.

Keywords: Mixed Reality · Usability Survey · Extended Reality Survey

1 Introduction

Usability, realism, and immersion are not absolute qualities; they are referential qualities based on particular concepts. With no absolute measures of these concepts, they must be defined in the context in which they are employed. When webpages were designed, a metric was necessary to define how usable the site was. A main issue with measuring usability is that due to the context-specificity of usability and measures of, it is difficult to compare different systems. Without a standard metric, it is difficult to accurately grasp and possible to draw

© The Author(s), under exclusive license to Springer Nature Switzerland AG 2026
J. Y. C. Chen et al. (Eds.): HCII 2025, LNCS 16338, pp. 63–73, 2026.
https://doi.org/10.1007/978-3-032-12808-9_5

the wrong conclusions from design features and experience across systems. To combat this, Brooke developed the System Usability Scale (SUS), a 'quick and dirty' usability scale designed to measure the effectiveness, efficiency, and satisfaction of the webpage [4]. This 5-likert scale was a means to give some numerical standard.

Since then, researchers have utilized and extended this scale based on their personal goals. For some, the scale alone suffices. To others, multiple surveys are employed and personalized questions added, generally as one-off questions. Mixed reality, and Virtual Reality in particular, suffers from this extension. In order to adapt the questionnaires to accommodate their particular research, users add varying degrees of questions, in different domains, to explain the usefulness of their research. After compiling questionnaires from papers of similar degrees and magnitude, a list of seemingly related questions, redundancy, and either no or limited evaluation metrics are seen, with no fully comparable or mathematical evaluation metrics. Furthermore, there is overlap in the types of questions that researchers wish to ask, but without a framework, nuances between researchers develop that limit comparability. It becomes clear that a cohesive framework, especially for VR applications, would benefit the research community.

In our work, we develop a framework that captures the unique limitations and benefits of virtual reality applications, allowing researchers to have clearly defined questions. This allows researchers to have the ability to compare other works to their own, the improvements upon their current work, and have baseline usability. This framework, the XRFive survey, groups similar questions, provides an optimal subset of questions that captures the large and varied range, and creates structured domains and concepts for all Virtual Reality applications.

2   Related Works

2.1   Usability Assessment in XR and Digital Health Contexts

Usability evaluation is a cornerstone of interactive system design, particularly in domains such as healthcare, exergaming, and immersive training. The System Usability Scale (SUS), remains one of the most widely employed instruments for this purpose. Originally intended for websites due to date of release, the SUS still offers a concise, reliable measure of usability across diverse domains. The scale itself contains ten standardized questions, on a 5-likert scale, which is converted to a score from 0 to 100, typically around 68.

Several recent studies have applied SUS within digital health contexts. Prasetyo et al. evaluated the perceived usability of their custom software, Thai Chana, a COVID-19 contact-tracing application, using SUS [12]. Evaluations included system complexity, integration, ease of use, and user confidence, confirming its relevance across health technology. Similarly, Hyzy et al. conducted a meta-analysis of 117 digital health applications using SUS [7]. They found that the mean score was 76.64, although that score dropped to 68.05 after excluding physical activity applications. The authors also used a 1-sample and 2-sample t-test to indicate that the score was not statistically significantly different from the standard SUS distribution.

Blattgerste et al. developed an open-source, web-based analysis toolkit to extend SUS, supporting enhanced interpretation using contextual scales and visual analytics [3]. These tools supplement quantitative scores with comparative frameworks, fostering better decision-making in iterative design processes.

Frich et al. further emphasized the connection between usability and creative support, although found that the positive correlation between the tool was highly tool-dependent [6]. This highlights the need for context-aware evaluation, especially in environments requiring both functional utility and user-driven innovation.

2.2 Validation and Development of Survey Instruments

The User Experience Questionnaire (UEQ) [10] is another well established tool that complements SUS by capturing hedonic and affective aspects of interaction. It supports assessments beyond pragmatic usability, such as emotional reactions and subjective impressions, elements increasingly valued in XR and healthcare applications. Additionally, the Simulator Sickness Questionnaire (SSQ) is widely used in VR contexts to assess symptoms such as nausea, eye strain, and dizziness [1,2,5]. These metrics are used to understand tolerability in immersive rehabilitation and exergames.

2.3 XR-Based Learning and Rehabilitation

Several studies have investigated the design and assessment of XR systems tailored for education and rehabilitation. Liu et al. developed a VR-based English language learning game for junior high school students, achieving a SUS score of 74, which indicates strong user satisfaction [11]. Rey et al., in multiple works, evaluated the usability and user experience of mobile biometric and automotive assistance systems, integrating both SUS and UEQ for qualitative user feedback [13,14].

In the healthcare domain, Küntzer et al. studied usability in older adults, participating in VR-based exergaming [9]. Challenges such as motion sickness, reduced mobility, and the need for cognitively lightweight interfaces were emphasized. Their work advocated for simplified interaction models and adaptive feedback mechanisms that accommodate varying cognitive and physical capabilities.

Both Xu and Yun examined the role of fully immersive VR exergames for improving mental health and motor performance [15,16]. These studies indicate the dual utility of XR systems in enhancing both physical and cognitive outcomes, supported by SUS.

2.4 Toward Simplified and Context-Aware Questionnaire Design

Traditional usability instruments such as the SUS and UEQ, while powerful, are not fully comprehensive for XR-gaming. Furthermore, as researchers attempt to modify these questionnaires for their specific research, it leads to a diverse set of questions. As such, the contribution we describe below is a specific subset of questions that covers these diversities.

3   Methodology

3.1   Analysis Methods

To quantitatively assess the results of our study and evaluate statistical significance across experimental conditions, we employed three core statistical methods: the paired t-test, one-way ANOVA, and the Wilcoxon signed-rank test. Each of these techniques was chosen based on the structure of the data and the assumptions appropriate to the respective analyses.

Paired T-Test: The paired t-test, also referred to as the dependent t-test, is used to determine whether the mean difference between two related sets of observations is statistically significant. Unlike the independent samples t-test, which compares two unrelated groups, the paired t-test accounts for the correlation between paired measurements, thus increasing statistical power when appropriate. The general formula for the variance of the difference between two dependent variables A and B is given by:

$$Var(A - B) = \sigma_1^2 + \sigma_2^2 - 2\rho\sigma_1\sigma_2$$

where σ_1^2 and σ_2^2 are the variances of the variables A and B, respectively and ρ is the correlation coefficient between the two paired samples.

In the case of independent samples, the correlation coefficient $\rho = 0$, simplifying the variance to the sum of the individual variances. However, when the data are paired, the presence of correlation must be incorporated into the calculation of the t statistic. For paired samples where $n_1 = n_2 = n$, the test statistic becomes:

$$t = \frac{\overline{d}}{s_d/\sqrt{n}}$$

where $\overline{d}$ is the mean of the differences, s_d is the standard deviation of the differences, and n is the number of paired observations. A positive correlation between samples ($\rho > 0$) reduces the denominator, thus increasing the t value and enhancing the statistical power of the test. Conversely, a negative correlation ($\rho < 0$) can reduce the power. It is critical to match the test type with the experimental design, as applying an independent t-test to paired data can yield misleading results [8].

Analysis of Variance (ANOVA). Like the T-Test, ANOVA is a way of testing the differences between groups to see if they're statistically significant. However, ANOVA allows you to compare three or more groups rather than just two. ANOVA is used with a regression study to find out what effect independent variables have on the dependent variable. It can compare multiple groups simultaneously to see if there is a relationship between them. This test can be used to study whether different methods get different user responses, such as a control group, standard treatment, and VR treatment. To implement this method is as follows:

1. Sum of Squares (SS): This measures the overall variability in this dataset
   (a) SS Total: Total variability across all observations
   (b) SS Between (SSB): Variability due to the differences between group means
   (c) SS Within (SSW): Variability within each group, showing how scores differ with individual groups
2. Mean Square (MS): The average of squared deviations, calculated for both between-group and within-group variability
   (a) MS Between (MSB): MSB = ss between/df between
   (b) MS Within (MSW): MSW = ss within/df within
3. Degrees of Freedom (df): The number of values that are free to vary when calculating statistics
   (a) Df Between (DfB): DfB = k − 1, where k is the number of groups
   (b) Df Within (DfW): DfW = n − k, where n is the total number of observations
4. F-Ratio: The ratio of MSB to MSW, used to test the null hypothesis
   (a) F = MSB/MSW
5. P-Value: This probability value helps determine if the F-ratio is significant. A small p-value (e.g. < 0.05) suggests significant differences between groups.

This study primarily uses one-way ANOVA, but future longitudinal work may involve repeated measures ANOVA, especially when participants undergo multiple conditions over time. Key assumptions of ANOVA include normally distributed data, homogeneity of variances, and independent observations.

Wilcoxon Signed Rank Test: The Wilcoxon signed-rank test provides a nonparametric alternative to the paired t-test, particularly useful when the data are ordinal or not normally distributed. This test evaluates whether the median difference between paired observations differs significantly from zero. The procedure includes the following steps:

1. Formulate Hypothesis:
   H_0: Median Difference = 0 vs H_1: Median difference > 0
2. Compute Pairwise Differences:
   For each paired observation, calculate the difference and its absolute value
3. Rank the Absolute Differences:
   Assign ranks to the absolute differences, ignoring zero differences. Tied values receive the average of their ranks
4. Calculate Rank Sums:
   Compute the sum of ranks for positive and negative differences
5. Determine Significance:
   Based on the smaller rank sum and the distribution of the test statistic under the null hypothesis, determine whether to reject H_0.

This test enables interpretation of whether changes are perceived as positive or negative in paired usability evaluations. We apply this method both globally-for overall system usability-and locally within each usability domain, defined in the next section.

3.2   Domains

Currently, there is not a standardized usability framework for VR applications. Current research makes use of standard usability surveys designed for websites, and attempts to adapt them to their VR applications. While authors have their own take on how to adapt them, there is an underlying theme. The most common names and grouping can be found in Table 1

Table 1. Domain title names found in other works.

Body Ownership Illusion	Ownership	Realism
Body Size Illusion	Agency	Immersion
Efficiency	Likability	Perceived Size
Play Data	Self-Location	

As these themes have been found commonly, with outliers existing, we merge these concepts into a small, applicable list. Furthermore, differing authors create their own grouping and surveys. These surveys have two general purposes, either 1) to justify the existence of the author's program or 2) as a means of having some metric for the program to make improvements.

We create a set of questions that allows for both use cases, and allows the previously defined metrics to be used. This set of questions is the compilation and translation of previous questionnaires found in related works, as well as a few to address the gaps.

We simplify the above concepts and unmentioned concepts into five domains, Sense of Embodiment (SoE), Immersion, Engagement, Realism, and, Usability. These domains are defined below, followed by Table 2, as a list of the questions.

Sense of Embodiment (SoE). This domain concept is missing from previously defined usability schemas, as they do not consider the necessity of moving a virtual body in a VR/MR environment in a way that resembles real-world movement. To capture this concept, authors have developed questions and allow users to rank them. We have compiled a list of different questions while removing similar questions that aren't upper and lower body specific.

This Sense of Embodiment incorporates Agency (ability to controlling the body) and body ownership/size (The feeling that the body is the users). Embodiment is critical for systems involving physical rehabilitation, avatar control, or interaction with digital prosthesis, where congruence between motor action and visual feedback directly affects presence and task performance.

Immersion. While sense of embodiment captures how well the user feels ownership of their body, immersion measures how well the user feels in the environment as a whole. This includes sensory fidelity (namely visual, auditory, and haptic inputs), continuity of spatial cues, and system responsiveness. High immersion typically enhances presence, and can lead to stronger cognitive and motor responses. This is mostly applicable to VR applications as opposed to AR or MR applications.

Engagement. Engagement describes the user's level of psychological investment, sustained attention, and motivational involvement in the task or experience. A highly engaging system sustains user interest, encourages exploration, and promotes task adherence, specifically important for gamified therapy or educational simulations. Engagement can be influenced by system feedback, narrative elements, and interactivity.

Realism. Differing from Sense of Embodiment, realism is the perceived authenticity of the virtual environment and, specifically, the user avatar. Realism enhances credibility and believability, which can improve learning transfer, therapeutic outcomes, and overall satisfaction of the XR system. Not to be confused with Sense of Embodiment, realism is a way to measure how well the avatar represents the user. While SoE represents ownership for movements, realism measures realistic-ness of both looks and movements.

Usability. The most consistently used questionnaire is the Systems Usability Survey. It was created mostly in part for website designs, and has sense been modified for other programmed environments. Usability reflects how effectively, efficiently, and satisfactorily users can achieve their goals within the system. It includes interface intuitiveness and learnability. We have adopted and adapted the SUS questions.

4   Use-Cases

These questions are also separated into positive and negative questions, albeit very few negative questions. For positive questions, subtract 1 from their value. For negative questions, subtract their value from 5. In this manner, someone who says 5 on a negative question adds 0 to the score, and someone who answers 1 to a positive question adds 0 as well. The inverse is true, adding up to 4 to the total points. Afterward, the total number of points from each question is summed up, both by domain and by total. This gives a score for the overall usability of the system and the usability and reliability of each domain.

By creating this scoring system, the previously defined analysis metrics, defined in Sect. 3.1, are able to be used. When comparing two similar systems, researchers should apply the same questionnaire to the same audience, and then apply the Paired T-Test. Each participant completes a questionnaire for both

Table 2. A list of the questions, separated by their domains.

Domain	Question
Sense of Embodiment	I felt as if the virtual upper limbs moved just like I wanted them to, as if they were obeying my own will.
	It sometimes seemed my own upper limbs were coming into contact with the virtual objects.
	I felt as if the virtual lower limbs moved just like I wanted them to, as if they were obeying my own will.
	It sometimes seemed my own lower limbs were coming into contact with the virtual objects.
	It felt as if I could control movements of the virtual upper limbs.
	It sometimes seemed my own upper/lower limbs were located in the scene.
	It felt as if I could control movements of the virtual lower limbs.
	It sometimes seemed my own lower limbs were located in the scene.
	I felt as if I could cause movements of the virtual upper limbs.
	I felt as if the virtual upper limbs were part of my own body.
	I felt as if I could cause movements of the virtual lower limbs.
	I felt as if the virtual lower limbs were part of my own body.
	My virtual upper limbs' movement was smooth.
	My virtual lower limbs' movement was smooth.
Immersion	I felt like I could very efficiently use my upper limbs to interact with the environment.
	I was completely involved/interested in the game.
	I felt like I could very efficiently use my lower limbs to interact with the environment.
	I felt that the size of the virtual upper limbs was similar to my own upper limbs' size.
	There was no noticeable delay while playing.
	I felt that the size of the virtual lower limbs was similar to my own lower limbs' size.
	I was so immersed in the virtual reality, it seemed real.
Engagement	I felt like using my virtual upper limbs to interact with the environment was fun.
	I was satisfied with my overall experience.
	I felt like using my virtual lower limbs to interact with the environment was fun.
	I liked the physical appearance of my virtual upper.
	I liked the physical appearance of my virtual lower limbs.
	I felt engrossed in the gaming system.
Realism	I thought the virtual upper limbs on the screen looked realistic.
	The illusion of the virtual upper limbs' movement was realistic.
	I thought the virtual lower limbs on the screen looked realistic.
	The illusion of the virtual lower limbs' movement was realistic.
	My avatar was rendered accurately.
Usability	I think that I would like to use this system frequently.
	I thought there was too much inconsistency in this system.
	I found the system unnecessarily complex.
	I would imagine that most people would learn to use this system very quickly.
	I thought the system was easy to use.
	I found the system very cumbersome to use.
	I think that I would need the support of a technical person to be able to use this system.
	I felt very confident using the system.
	I found the various functions in this system were well integrated.
	I needed to learn a lot of things before I could get going with this system.

System A and System B, evaluated by the same users, and determine if there is a significant difference in perceived usability between the two systems.

If testing the before and after of a single system, the Wilcoxon Signed-Rank Test should be used, as it is a non-parametric alternative to the paired t-test. It is used when you can't assume normal distribution of the differences, often the case with scores from small samples or clinical populations.

Researchers looking to test three different systems, or three iterations of the same system, should use ANOVA. Similarly, ANOVA can be used for different user types (novice, intermediate, expert), and different interface conditions (Optical see-through HMDs, Video see-through HMDs, Mobile AR Camera).

5   Results and Discussion

The proposed VR usability framework was implemented through a structured questionnaire divided into five domains: Sense of Embodiment, Immersion, Engagement, Realism, and Usability. Each domain is to be scored using a 5-point Likert scale for each questions, with responses normalized using a domain adjusted scoring method, where positive items were scaled by subtracting 1 and negative items by subtracting the response from 5. This ensured a consistent scoring system from 0 to 4 per question, allowing for aggregated domain scores and an overall usability score. To validate the framework's analytical capability, a scoring system was developed to support standard inferential statistical tests. Described above, the Paired T-test is used to measure the difference between two systems, Wilcoxon Signed test to compare before and after, and ANOVA for differing audiences, systems, or interface conditions of three or more.

Initial review cases demonstrate that this framework could reliably distinguish between systems when applied to pre- and post- intervention scenarios, or when comparing different interface types. Furthermore, individual domain scores offer insight into which dimensions contributed most to usability, helping researchers pinpoint where design improvements were most needed.

This framework potentially offers both structure and flexible usability assessments tailored to the unique requirements of XR applications. Traditional usability instruments like SUS, while widely adopted, often lack the specificity required for immersive systems where embodiment, realism, and multimodal interaction play critical roles. Our five-domain model addresses these gaps by incorporating domain-specific questions to better capture the nuances of XR development.

Of the five-domains, the inclusion of the Sense of Embodiment as a core domain represents a key contribution of this framework. Assessing how well a user feels "present in their body" within a virtual environment is crucial for future therapies. Our findings suggest that when quantified, this domain reveals important usability distinctions not captured by more traditional tools.

Lastly, this framework offers practical benefits for XR developers and evaluators. By organizing items into coherent, non-redundant domains, it reduces cognitive load on participants, which is particularly valuable when working with clinical or older adult populations. At the same time, the diversity of questions remains analytically rich enough to support statistically robust comparisons.

6   Limitations

While this framework streamlines XR usability evaluation, several limtations should be noted. First, the questions and domains, although drawn from a wide range of related works, may still require validation across different demographic groups. Secondly, although the scoring method has been designed for statistical analysis, it assumes linearity in Likert responses.

Additionally, this framework prioritizes short-term, quick evaluation, and not explicitly long-term engagement, learning outcomes, or therapeutic efficacy. As these dimensions are critical in educational or clinical XR use cases, they must be captured with external surveys.

Acknowledgments. This material is based upon work supported by the National Science Foundation (NSF) under Grant Nos. 2346528 and 2437698. Any opinions, findings, and conclusions or recommendations expressed in this material are those of the author(s) and do not necessarily reflect the views of the NSF.

Disclosure of Interests. As of this time, there are no competing interests. Neither Author has received any research grants, owns stock in any company, or has received an award with respect to this works.

References

1. Balk, S.A., Bertola, M.A., Inman, V.W.: Simulator sickness questionnaire: twenty years later. In: Proceedings of the 7th International Driving Symposium on Human Factors in Driver Assessment, Training, and Vehicle Design: Driving Assessment 2013. University of Iowa, Iowa City, Iowa (2013)
2. Bimberg, P., Weissker, T., Kulik, A.: On the usage of the simulator sickness questionnaire for virtual reality research. In: 2020 IEEE Conference on Virtual Reality and 3D User Interfaces Abstracts and Workshops (VRW), March 2020. IEEE (2020)
3. Blattgerste, J., Behrends, J., Pfeiffer, T.: A web-based analysis toolkit for the system usability scale. In: Proceedings of the 15th International Conference on PErvasive Technologies Related to Assistive Environments, Jun 2022. ACM, New York (2022)
4. Brooke, J.: A quick and dirty usability scale. In: Usability Evaluation in Industry (1996)
5. Brown, P., Spronck, P., Powell, W.: The simulator sickness questionnaire, and the erroneous zero baseline assumption. Front. Virtual Real. **3** (2022)
6. Frich, J., Dalsgaard, P., Taranu, M., Mose Biskjaer, M.: How are measures of usability and creativity support correlated? In: Proceedings of the European Conference on Cognitive Ergonomics 2024, ECCE '24, Association for Computing Machinery, New York (2024). https://doi.org/10.1145/3673805.3673815
7. Hyzy, M., et al.: System usability scale benchmarking for digital health apps: meta-analysis. JMIR Mhealth Uhealth **10**(8), e37290 (2022)
8. Kim, T.K.: T test as a parametric statistic. Korean J. Anesthesiol. **68**(6), 540–546 (2015)

9. Küntzer, L., Schwab, S., Spaderna, H., Rock, G.: Measuring user experience of older adults during virtual reality exergaming. In: 2024 16th International Conference on Quality of Multimedia Experience (QoMEX), pp. 153–159 (2024). https://doi.org/10.1109/QoMEX61742.2024.10598263

10. Laugwitz, B., Held, T., Schrepp, M.: Construction and evaluation of a user experience questionnaire, vol. 5298, pp. 63–76 (11 2008). https://doi.org/10.1007/978-3-540-89350-9_6

11. Liu, K.Y., Chen, Y., Lin, M.F., Huang, L.J.D., Ping Xiang, C.: Developing a VR-based contextualized language learning system to enhance junior high school students' pragmatic competence. In: Proceedings of the 5th ACM International Conference on Multimedia in Asia, MMAsia '23, Association for Computing Machinery, New York (2024). https://doi.org/10.1145/3595916.3626360,

12. Prasetyo, Y.T., et al.: "The perceived usability of COVID-19 contact tracing Thai Chanaüsing system usability scale". In: 2024 6th International Conference on Management Science and Industrial Engineering, April 2024, pp. 86–90. ACM, New York (2024)

13. Rey, W.P., Rey, K.W.J.D.: Enhancing drivecare: a holistic examination of usability and user experience in automotive assistance applications in the Philippines. In: Proceedings of the 2024 8th International Conference on Education and Multimedia Technology, ICEMT 2024, pp. 322–328. Association for Computing Machinery, New York, NY, USA (2024). https://doi.org/10.1145/3678726.3678776

14. Rey, W.P.: Optimizing user interaction with MABIS: an examination of usability and user experience in the mobile automated biometric identification system. In: Proceedings of the 2024 10th International Conference on Computer Technology Applications, ICCTA '24, pp. 215–222. Association for Computing Machinery, New York (2024). https://doi.org/10.1145/3674558.3674588,

15. Xu, W., et al.: Effects of an immersive virtual reality exergame on university students' anxiety, depression, and perceived stress: pilot feasibility and usability study. JMIR Serious Games 9(4), e29330 (2021). https://doi.org/10.2196/29330

16. Yun, S.J., Hyun, S.E., Oh, B.M., Seo, H.G.: Fully immersive virtual reality exergames with dual-task components for patients with Parkinson's disease: a feasibility study. J. Neuroeng. Rehabil. 20(1), 92 (2023)

Discovering Road Cyclists' Needs and Preferences for Mixed Reality User Interfaces Using Immersive Simulation

Radoslaw R. Dukalski[1]([⊠]), Jason K. Moore[1] , Peter J. Beek[2] ,
and Frances M. Brazier[1]

[1] Delft University of Technology, Delft, The Netherlands
{r.r.dukalski,j.k.moore,f.m.brazier}@tudelft.nl
[2] Department of Human Movement Sciences, Vrije Universiteit Amsterdam, Amsterdam,
The Netherlands
p.j.beek@vu.nl

Abstract. Striking a balance between simulation realism and immersion is essential for the development and evaluation of a prototyping environment (set-up and methodology) for Mixed Reality Road bicycle racing applications. Multi-sensory immersion, safety, usability, and design process iterability are hard requirements for the proposed prototyping environment in which a tandem rides on a treadmill with a participant riding up-front wearing a Virtual Reality headset. In the virtual environment, with interactable interface artefacts in a 360-video sphere, participants' needs and preferences are dis-covered as participants configure their own 3D user-interface for Mixed Reality capable cycling glasses. Sessions that simulate a cycling race, focus on two distinct scenarios of ascending and descending. Two prototyping methods, while standing and while riding a bicycle, are evaluated and compared. Cyclists' preferences include types of information, their placement in the visual field, size, and colour, depicted in heatmap visualisations. These insights are essential for designers of Mixed Reality systems with real-time information for outdoor bicycle racing.

Keywords: Cycling · Visualisation · Mixed Reality · Augmented Reality · Virtual Reality · User Interface · Prototyping

1 Introduction

Simulators aim to recreate a real-world context or scenario, often for research or training purposes. In traffic research they have been used to study road behaviour [1], and in sports to enhance technique and performance. The fidelity and realism of the simulation drives task immersion and engagement, and by extension encouraging a truer recreation of an associated real-world task or more effective training, teaching or learning of the simulated task.

To recreate outdoor mobility with its changing circumstances and environments, indoor simulators rely primarily on visual immersion, through large projection and Virtual and Mixed Reality (VR, MR) devices. Deeper immersion can be beneficial and can

J. Y. C. Chen et al. (Eds.): HCII 2025, LNCS 16338, pp. 74–97, 2026.
https://doi.org/10.1007/978-3-032-12808-9_6

be achieved through additional means, e.g., vestibular, audio, tactile, control, decision, haptic (force feedback), wind, exertion, and role playing. Combining modalities in itself can be challenging as sensory conflict can lead to simulator sickness. Wintersberger et al. [2] documented the development of a tilting bicycle simulator, focusing on increasing realism and reducing simulator sickness without decreasing performance. Matviienko et al. [3] took a different approach and investigated cycling fidelity in a virtual reality cycling simulation and found that a tandem leads to a high level of realism with little simulator sickness. The VTI 'How we roll' cycling simulator relies on a mechanical construction with free rollers for natural cycling dynamics, and employs a mixed reality headset for visualisation of the virtual world [4].

In strategic sports such as professional road cycling, real-time decision making is crucial, with cyclists relying on cruising and pacing by continuously gauging various factors affecting their performance, like their energy reserves, aerodynamics, heart rate, terrain, and motivation. Road cycling, the focus of this research, is a sport requiring strength, endurance, and strategic use of finite resources towards achieving a competitive goal. This efficiency requires appropriate information delivered in real-time. This is conventionally done with instruments mounted on a handlebar, a solution limited by screen size and its location. Delivering information to an athlete navigating changing and often unfamiliar terrain can be a safety hazard. It can draw attention away from the road, which is especially dangerous when exhausted, or when going downhill at speed on a tire as thick as a thumb.

See-through display Mixed Reality (MR) technology has become more attainable and stands to support task performance by providing users in-context information in a desired location of the visual field. Applying MR has the potential to provide cyclists more information while keeping their gaze up. Simpler non-spatially aware Augmented Reality (AR) devices geared towards cycling are already commercially available (e.g., Everysight Raptop). Merkel et al. [5] explored the application thereof in motorcycling (using a large screen projection as backdrop) and showed it to have benefit on perception and recognition of real-time information. However, their wider adoption in the professional cycling world remains limited.

Application of AR in commuter cycling has been explored by Matviienko et al. [6], investigating ways in which a fictional self-driving bicycle can communicate its intent to its cyclist passenger. In this study, the researchers employed a tandem bicycle outside to simulate self-driving capabilities of a bicycle, allowing the participant to embody the role of a passenger, and to focus on the interface evaluation study.

In pursuit of performance gains road cyclists can use MR smart glasses to sacrifice visual field area in exchange for real-time information. To facilitate designers of such solutions there is a need for design guidelines. This study proposes a methodology to explore this design space adopting a participatory design approach, in which road cyclists are involved early in the design process. This process provides designers with valuable insights into their needs and preferences that the product seeks to accommodate [7]. Generative prototyping sessions reveal tacit and latent user knowledge [8]. Scenario-based design approaches distil preferences in specific contexts [9]. Our previous work, submitted for publication[1], has shown that in road cycling information needs to be different per scenario and that when designing for MR glasses participants showed preferences for sacrificing certain areas of the visual field in exchange for the value of the information offered in return. Effective extraction of user preferences is challenging due to safety, tooling, communication, and protocol. Asking a person their preferences for MR interfaces while cycling alongside them on an outside course is dangerous, and the collected data would be incomplete. Interacting with an MR interface while cycling was explored by Kosch et al. [10], but this study limited itself to a simple interaction of accepting a notification. Conversely, asking a person to design at a desk on paper is easy, effective, and familiar [11] but lacks context and the third dimension, limiting the validity of the findings. Intermediate spatial 'paper prototyping' of a cycling-focused user interface has been investigated by the authors (under review), with the intention of verifying the findings in a more visually immersive environment.

Prototypes are of higher value when designed in a context closely matching the use scenario, as it elicits similar needs to those experienced in situ. As acquiring and evaluating user preferences for MR design in-situ can be dangerous, lab-based virtual simulations offer an alternative [12, 13], creating a representative 3D environment approximating real-world conditions, for deep immersion. Lab-based VR simulation affords a controlled 3D environment where participants can explore spatial capabilities of MR applications. Maintaining deep immersion in a controlled environment prolongs contemplation of user needs, giving time for exploration, prototyping, and evaluation. To this end, participants should be freely able to iteratively switch between sensitisation, exploration and prototyping, and evaluation [14], further requiring a safe environment.

Striking a balance between simulation realism and immersion, as well as prototyping capabilities, usability, and safety implies trade-offs. This paper is focused on the development and evaluation of a design prototyping environment with a novel multimodal setup and methodology, created to simulate road cycling and collect valuable User Interface (UI) needs and preferences for MR in a controlled, immersive environment. With the ability to achieve deep road cycling context immersion, it has been designed to elicit relevant information needs from cyclists and provide them with tools to prototype and evaluate real-time information solutions in a controlled environment. Following a multi-phase protocol, participants are asked to conduct a prototyping session for two common road cycling scenarios, and to evaluate their experience with the prototyping environment.

2   Methods

Lab-based individual end-user design prototyping sessions were conducted (Fig. 1), consisting of a structured orientation interview, a warm-up exercise, and a two-part speak-out-loud creative session during which participants prototyped a display interface

---

[1] Dukalski, R.R., Moore, J.K., Beek, P.J., Brazier, F.M.: A Low-Tech Methodology for Understanding User Needs and Preferences for User-Interface Design for Mixed Reality in a Dynamic Motion Context. Manuscript submitted for review to the Annual Conference on Human-Computer Interaction and Sports (SportsHCI 2025). Proceedings to appear in the ACM International Conference Proceedings Series (ICPS).

in 3D-space using a virtual prototyping environment. This section introduces the study participants, and summarises the experimental design, procedure and setup.

2.1 Participants

Twenty-eight participants took part in the study (5 women and 23 men), consisting of a group of experienced road cycling amateurs and road cycling sport enthusiasts. All of them owned a racing bike and routinely collected data while road cycling. None of the participants reported participation in pro-level races. There were no age selection criteria nor was age recorded (participants were estimated to be between 20 and 40 years of age). Ethics approval was granted by the Delft University of Technology's Human Research Ethics Committee (TU Delft, LabServant ID: 2639). All participants consented before taking part and signed consent forms required for taking part in this study.

2.2 Experimental Design

For each participant a single two-hour one-on-one session was conducted with the same facilitator. The participants were tasked with prototyping a 3D-interface for binocular Mixed Reality smart glasses (with audio capabilities) for use in cycling. To this end, they used a multi-modal Virtual Reality environment, described and illustrated below.

During the prototyping phase they were given freedom (free from current race regulations, see Discussion) in describing and visualizing the information they desired, and how they wished it to be delivered during an individual time trial race. The experiment compared two race scenarios (scenario 1 – descent, and scenario 2 – ascent), to explore the differences in what information is desired, and the way in which it should be presented. Henceforth, 'prototype' refers to a single interactable instance of an interface artefact (e.g., a graph of speed, an icon of a heart, or a number for meters).

2.3 Procedure

Orientation. The session began with a structured interview, with questions concerning personal and professional road bicycle racing experiences. This session was held for orientation and sensitisation purposes, and not further discussed (question list in Appendix 1).

Warm-Up Exercise. During the warm-up exercise, participants were asked to draw from memory their current interface, on which they rely during road cycling. Following the warm-up exercise, the participants were presented with a three A4-page 'inspiration list' of various characteristics to consider during the prototyping session, with basic, illustrated examples of each (see Experimental Setup).

Design context introduction. As part of the design context introduction, participants were asked to assume the role of a road racing athlete, who is monitored by scouts and coaches within their team, taking part in a 40-km race in The Netherlands which included the following segments: uphill, downhill, flat, uphill. Their design was to focus on the second and forth segment, without being constrained by budget or access to data.

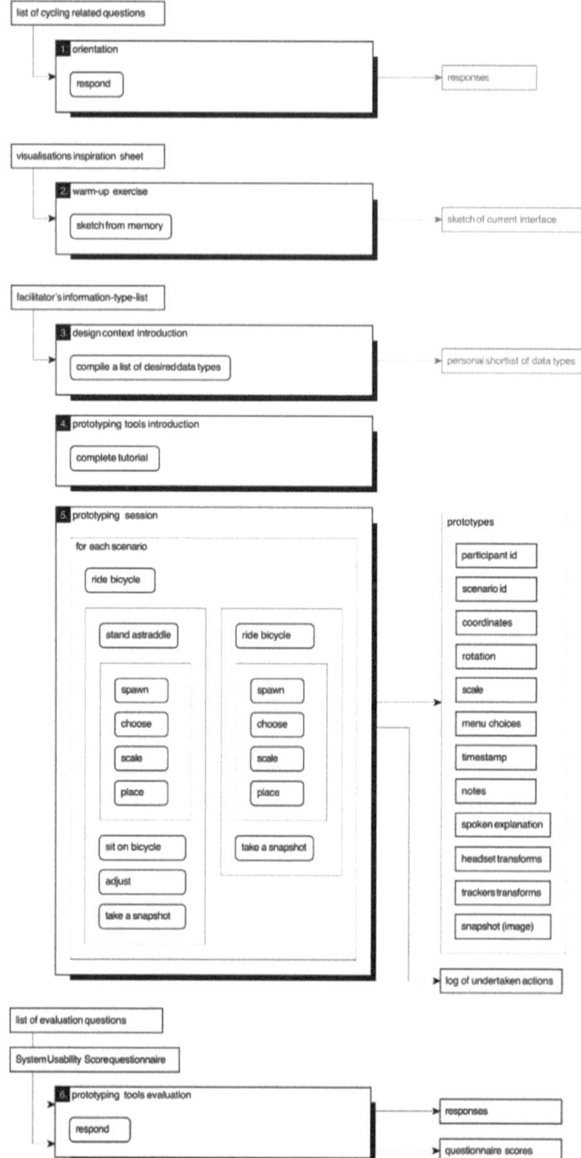

Fig. 1. Flowchart of the six-phase experimental procedure (1. Orientation, 2. Warm-up exercise, 3. Design context introduction, 4. Prototyping tools introduction, 5. Prototyping session, 6. Prototyping tools evaluation), with participant's output shown on the right.

Participants produced a shortlist of 'data types' (e.g., heartrate) which they wished to use in their prototype. Upon completing their list of desired 'data types', the facilitator presented and read out from the 'Facilitator's data-type-checklist' (see Experimental Setup) granting the opportunity to supplement their previously made list.

Prototyping Tools Introduction. The Session continued at the Physical Prototyping Environment (Fig. 3; outlined and portrayed in 'Experimental setup', below). Prior to providing the Virtual Reality headset, the virtual prototyping tools and environment were demoed with the help of a second controller and shown using the facilitator's virtual camera (Virtual Camera B) projected on the wall. The participants showed their grasp of the interactions required during the session: spawning a new prototype, navigating menus, making choices, grabbing and moving prototypes, scaling, deleting, and triggering the snapshot button used for capture. Safety full body harness gear was installed, safety protocol was explained, followed by a 'trust exercise' (30 s of treadmill cycling with eyes open, followed by 30 s of treadmill cycling with eyes closed). Sitting at the rear, the facilitator steered the tandem bicycle (front handlebar was decoupled), always holding onto the side rail with the other hand. The bicycle coasted 'forward' freely, with an occasional minor wobble. As the ceiling safety tether ensured that the bicycle did not ride off the back of the treadmill, pedalling was not required from either rider to remain on the treadmill.

Prototyping Session. In individual speak-out-loud prototyping sessions (illustrated in Fig. 2), Against the video backdrop within the Virtual Reality Environment (outlined and portrayed in 'Experimental setup', below), participants started with a blank slate, and used VR controllers to voluntarily spawn, move and scale interface artefacts. Using floating menus (Fig. 4), they would further specify parameters, e.g., information type, colour, purpose, or circumstance. The facilitator observed progress on a wall projection and aided when needed. Throughout the prototyping session, the facilitator assisted and encouraged thinking out-loud while watching over the progress using a secondary virtual camera (Virtual Camera B) projected onto the wall.

Participants were given advance knowledge of the following protocol and phase order. For each scenario, the participants first experienced riding the bicycle in the virtual environment for 1–2 min (sensitisation), with the treadmill speed set to loosely resemble the speed shown in the looping video (15 km/h for descent, 8 km/h for ascent). The treadmill was then brought to a halt. Thereafter, participants first prototyped while standing astraddle the bicycle (phase: 'stationary'), and afterwards while riding the bicycle (phase: 'cycling'). For each prototype, participants were required to make at least a single choice in each second level menu (except for colour-secondary; outlined below). Upon completion of each prototyping phase (stationary, cycling), having indicated completion of the task, participants were instructed to trigger the snapshot button; upon clicking of which a 5-s countdown was shown with a message was displayed to assume a 'cycling position' appropriate to the scenario (assuming said position in the 'stationary' phase thus required boarding the stationary bicycle). A data snapshot was recorded to disk.

Having completed the first scenario, without clearing the designed interface, the video backdrop was replaced to portray the second scenario, and as before a brief sensitisation period followed. With a recent experience of the new scenario, the participants repeated the two prototyping phases. Participants amended their designs, adding new prototypes and editing or removing old prototypes as desired. Upon completion of the second scenario the prototyping session was concluded.

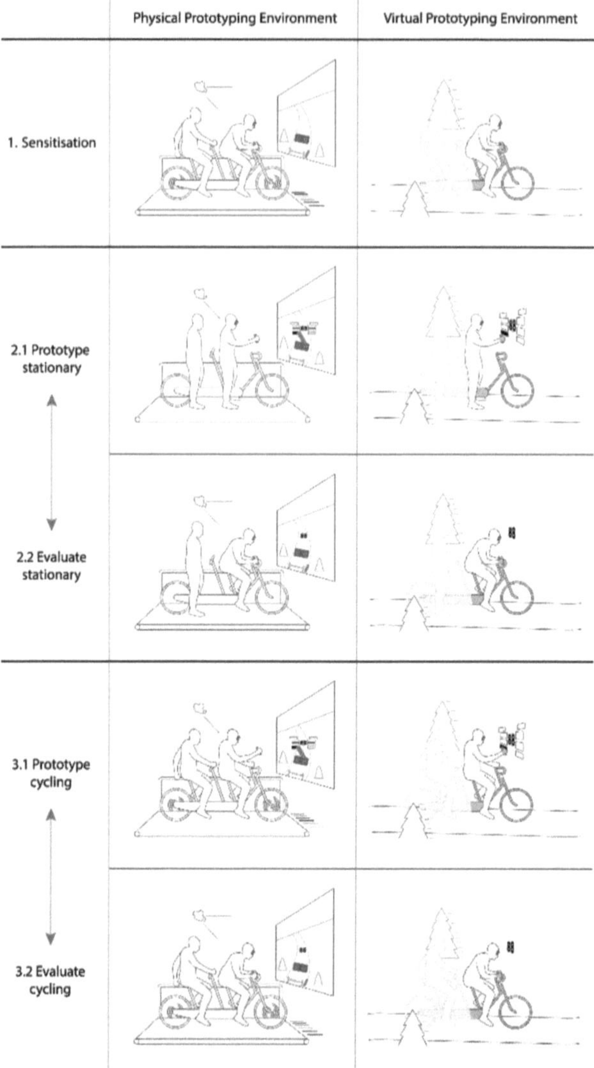

Fig. 2. Prototyping session phases for each scenario – 'Physical Prototyping Environment' (left), 'Virtual Prototyping Environment' (right).

Prototyping Tools Evaluation. Participants were asked to fill out the System Usability Score [15] questionnaire (with 'this prototyping environment, and not the prototyped interface' as the subject of evaluation) to quickly assess the usability, as well as to answer a series of evaluation questions to further specify experienced issues (Appendix 2).

2.4   Experimental Setup

The session was conducted indoors in Delft University of Technology's Bicycle Lab, at an 'Interview Table' and in the 'Physical Prototyping Environment' (which enabled the experience of the 'Virtual Prototyping Environment'), outlined and itemised in detail in Appendix 3.

The presented setup is a prototyping environment, that combines physical and virtual elements (Fig. 1). The physical environment consisted of a customised tandem bicycle riding on a treadmill (Fig. 3), with the participant riding up-front wearing a Virtual Reality (VR) headset, and facilitator riding and steering in the back. The tandem's front half was modified to resemble a racing bicycle, with an appropriate seat and seating position, and a (decoupled) racing handlebar. This provided participants with vestibular, tactile and haptic cycling sensations, with a semblance of control, without the responsibility of keeping the bicycle upright. The locations and orientations off the tandem bicycle as well as its front handlebar were tracked using compatible VR spatial trackers.

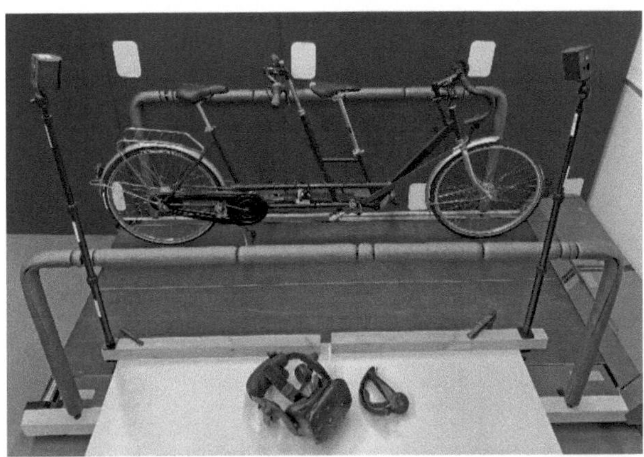

Fig. 3. 'Physical Prototyping Environment' – tandem on a treadmill, VR headset and controller.

Within the VR environment, participants were tasked with prototyping a UI for MR cycling glasses using hand-held VR controllers as input devices. The physical tandem's tracked data was mapped and represented by a virtual model. For each of the two scenarios, following a sensitisation (cycling with the treadmill on), two prototyping modes were tested: while standing astraddle on a stationary tandem, and while cycling with the treadmill running.

The Virtual Prototyping Environment was built using the Unity engine [16]. Three virtual cameras were used: one responsible for the participant's headset view (Figs. 6 and 7), second for the cycling facilitator view (Fig. 4) projected on the wall ahead of the tandem, and third with a side view (Fig. 5) matching the lab assistant's desk location.

At the start, a ten-meter diameter sphere was attached to the participant's virtual camera location. Pre-recorded 4K resolution 360-video footage from a real-world location (Figs. 4, 6, and 7) was used and mapped onto the sphere from within. The video's visual forward-flow was synchronised to the treadmill's forward direction using the base

Fig. 4. Facilitator's view (from Virtual Camera B) with the Facilitator's interface panel overlay; Participant is seen selecting a colour from the colour sub-menu.

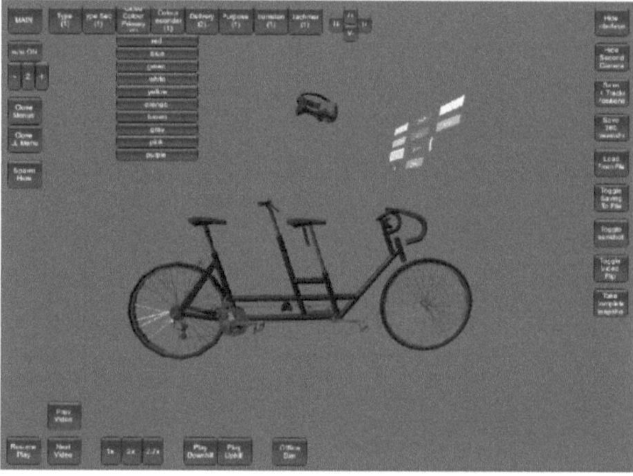

Fig. 5. Lab Assistant's view (from Virtual Camera C) with the Facilitator's interface panel overlay (background removed for illustration); Participant is seen selecting a colour from the colour sub-menu.

station locations (affixed to physical space and by extension, the treadmill). An individual time trial cycling race was simulated, with a video for a climb and for a descent. The spherical videos were captured from a bicycle traversing an outdoor road course, with the stretch of road (35 m elevation delta) completed in both directions. The location (52°19′30.5″N 6°24′59.6″E) was selected by an employee of a 'UCI WorldTour' professional cycling team as representative of a UCI race location (Union Cycliste Internationale, the cycling sport's governing body). The chosen two video clips represented a descent ('scenario 1'; starting at coordinated redacted, distance of 509 m, duration of 49 s), and an ascent ('scenario 2'; starting at coordinated redacted, distance of 228 m, duration of 80 s). The videos were captured using a 360-camera mounted to a bicycle frame at a cyclist's eye position. The descent video playback speed was adjusted to represent a capture taken while descending at 45 km/h, while the uphill video was made to represent a climb at 10 km/h. Each video was played on loop, fading through black, and was flipped horizontally upon each playback iteration.

Fig. 6. Participant's VR view (from Virtual Camera A) – foreground: participant's controller shown navigating the representation sub-menu while customising a prototype, background: virtual bicycle and looping video

Using two VR controllers (mapped and visualised in the virtual environment), participants spawned each new instance of an interactable 'prototype artefact' in the location of the Virtual Reality controller, with a long press of a dedicated button. The prototype retained its spatial location relative to the bicycle frame until it was moved again and maintained its rotation independent of the bicycle rotation. Using the controller as a '3D-mouse', participants modified their placement by gripping the controller while hovering over the prototype's preview, scaled using a joystick (similarly during hover), and affected the other eight parameters (listed above) using a concealable two-level multiple-choice menu (using controller's trigger buttons). When shown, menus consisted of floating grey buttons on a 2D plane (Figs. 6 and 7). The eight first level menu buttons lead to designated second-level menus for each of the eight parameters, with button captions revealing the choices made thus far. First-level buttons for 'secondary' parameters (type-secondary, colour-secondary) were indented outwards for de-emphasis (Fig. 7, top left). Within each second-level menu the button order was randomised for each prototype. The prototype's preview visually reflected the choices made for colour-primary and delivery-means (e.g., a yellow arrow, a blue rectangle). Until said choices were made the prototype's visual preview displayed a random choice for each, rotating every one second. In case of multiple choices made (e.g., delivery-means: text and number, colour: red and blue), the last selected choice took precedence visually. Colour-secondary choices were depicted in a form of small swatches below the main preview graphic. Buttons in the second-level menus for colour were coloured to match. Proximity-based hover state mildly enlarged buttons. Buttons' selection state was made visually apparent with further scaling as well as a white border.

Once satisfied with their prototype, the participant used the VR controller to trigger either of the two snapshot buttons. Said buttons were locked to the participant's position, and positioned directly to either side of the participant, within arm's reach around hip height.

Fig. 7. Participant's VR view when navigating choice menus for an example prototype (top-left: first level menu, followed by example second level menus: type-primary, colour, purpose).

Lastly, illustrated in Figs. 4 and 5 is the Facilitator's interface panel – series of buttons overlayed atop the virtual camera views. The buttons were interactable from a computer using a mouse, allowing the facilitator (or lab assistant) to control video playback, manipulate prototype properties or trigger snapshots on behalf of the participant.

2.5 Prototyping Output

The output of the prototyping sessions (example in Fig. 8) consisted of the following set of data: choices made for each of the eight multiple-choice parameters (as outlined by first-level menu choices in Appendix 3), scale/size, as well as positions and rotations of each: prototype, VR base stations, the VR headset and both VR spatial trackers, as present at each moment of capture (four total: two scenarios in each of the two design phases).

Each participant placed prototypes relative to their distinct gaze point in virtual space. Therefore, when aggregating subsets (e.g., all heartrate-related prototypes), spatial data was used to synchronise the prototypes' positions and orientations as they were relative to their respective VR headset's position and orientation at the time of capture. Once synchronised to a single, unified headset position, the prototypes could then be illustrated in heatmap form (stubbed example in Fig. 9).

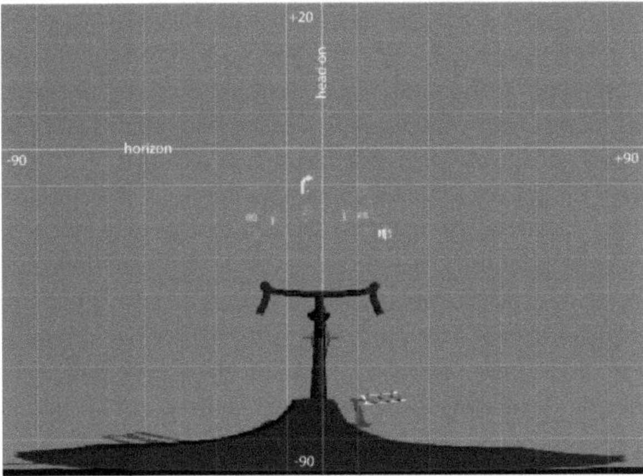

Fig. 8. Example interface of 11 prototypes relative to the bicycle, mapped as an equirectangular projection (backgrounds removed for illustration) from the participant's point of view.

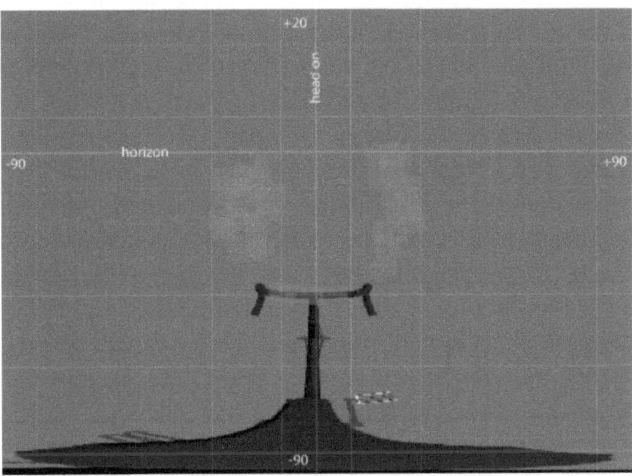

Fig. 9. Mock-up of a heatmap with stub data, mapped as an equirectangular projection from the participant's point of view.

2.6 Rationale

This section discusses in depth certain experimental design choices, where compromises had to be made between use-case immersion, safety, usability, and prototyping iterability. Additionally, consideration was taken to ensure the lab findings best translate to intended outdoor Mixed Reality application.

Design Process and Iterability. Participants were tasked with communicating wilful sacrifices of their visual field in exchange for desired information. Evaluating said choices required eliciting these real-time information needs, done by simulating race conditions (through role play) and dynamic circumstances (through tooling). Considering varied riding and training styles, a wide spectrum of information and visualisation choices was made available. Participants started with a blank slate to not introduce bias in the number of prototypes made, with the options' order randomised when asked to make the choices therein. To facilitate swift iteration between prototyping and evaluation, where possible, protypes' changes took immediate effect, and video kept playing in the background as participants contemplated their options.

The prototypes' menus presented a challenge, being an interface used towards prototyping an interface. To minimise priming with its design patterns, second level menus were varied and lacked symmetry, menu colours were removed entirely (opting for scale and border for communicating hover and active states), and the fidelity level was deliberately low. To encourage fast prototyping, lower the artistic bar and quell perfectionism, prototype previews were static and sketch-like in their appearance while some menu buttons had deliberate formatting issues with text spilling out of their containers.

Immersion and Realism. Deeper immersion was achieved with visual means (a moving video backdrop, matching 3D graphics), vestibular sensation, haptic sensation, as well as control and role immersion. Reproducing vestibular sensation was high on the wish list, however tasking the participant with the mental load of steering the bicycle, contemplating choices, prototyping, and communicating said choices would come at the inevitable cost of the quality of at least one of these much-desired actions. By employing a tandem bicycle, vestibular sensation was achieved through separation of the experience of riding a bicycle from the responsibility of steering it. This would come at the cost of realism due to loss of the feeling of control. To compensate, the participants were shown a reproduced virtual model of a tandem bicycle accurately mapped to the (tracked) physical tandem bicycle, including an independently tracked handlebar. This was not unlike the virtual reality controller in their hand: accurately reproduced, mapped, responsive, and haptic. To deepen role immersion, the front of the tandem had been modified to have physical artefacts resembling the ones found on racing bicycles. Although the handling was not a close match to a single-person bicycle (being less responsive to sideways sway due to two riders, especially when not synchronised in intention), it was deemed an improvement on the alternative: a static bicycle. The match between the vestibular sensation and the visual stimulus was at times broken, largely due to the use of pre-recorded video. The collected footage featured corners (while the treadmill was 'infinitely straight') and scenario-specific road gradient (which was not reflected in the treadmill's and by extension the bicycle's lack of inclination). It was, however, assumed that excluding corners from the video footage would come at the expense of its effect in eliciting real-life information needs, and inclining the treadmill would pose a safety hazard.

Safety. The prototyping session was conducted in a controlled environment without the usual change in circumstance found in road cycling. Steering safety was achieved with riding a tandem bicycle. Furthermore, the facilitator holding onto the rail rather than freely riding the treadmill was deemed sufficient.

The trust exercise was introduced to establish participant's comfort, and to filter out unsuitable participants early. In prior testing, riding on a treadmill with eyes closed lead to disorienting drift of perceived 'forward' direction and its match with the treadmill's direction, causing an unnerving feeling of veering off. Having visual stimulus (in 360 video) headed for a vanishing point eliminated this feeling.

The virtual prototyping tools relied on a single virtual reality controller, enabling participants holding onto the handlebar with the second hand. Adding the virtual model of the bicycle and tracking its position helped participants find the bicycle and handlebar when climbing on, cycling, and getting back down.

Front handlebar was decoupled to prevent participants who were too immersed from taking corners, though it was installed tightly enough to resemble its natural rotational inertia.

Usability. A choice for a rear-steered tandem affords participants ample space ahead, whilst enabling assuming a representative cycling position. During prototyping, upon changing a prototype's position, its location was coupled to bicycle's tracked origin, effectively making prototypes appear still despite the bicycle moving (an issue otherwise apparent when switching between the two design phases: standing and riding). The prototype's rotation however was decoupled from bicycle's rotation, otherwise as the bicycle rolled the prototypes' positions would wobble sideways with a magnified effect (considering their distance from the point of rotation, the ground). Interactable interface elements were made large to enable control despite motion. This ability to continue iterating while riding allowed maintaining vestibular and haptic immersion by not stopping the bicycle when iterating between prototyping and evaluation. The prototype's second-level properties of 'attached to' and 'circumstance' were not implemented as foreseen and about which participants were informed: all prototypes behaved as attached to 'frame', and circumstances were shown 'always' regardless of the respective menu choices. This conversely made the relevant prototypes easier to interact with, compared to fully implemented prototypes reappearing on a timer or moving past as if attached to the road.

Translation to Augmented Outdoor Cycling. From the menu choices of available colours, black was removed to reflect the see-through-display technology's limitation, as in some commercially available Mixed Reality glasses. The played video faded through black as it looped to minimise a sudden break in visual immersion and was mirrored horizontally to eliminate bias due to pre-recorded road's curvature and right-sidedness of the road. The video featured a single car coming from the opposite direction, left in the final cut to retain an element of surprise from unpredictable obstacles found outdoors, a feeling otherwise subdued by the repetitive indoor simulation.

Evaluation Method. The System Usability Score is a straightforward way of assessing system usability, and has been applied in over 1,200 studies, spanning hardware as well as software [17]. It has been shown to provide reliable results with low sample sizes [18] and is comparable to other standardised usability surveys [19]. The choice for a quick survey method stemmed from the anticipated (choice) fatigue following the prototyping session. As SUS is not a diagnostic tool, post-processing interviews were held to supplement the findings, returning the participants to their expert position, and leading the conversation.

3 Data Processing and Analysis

The prototyping setup and methodology were assessed with 28 participants, in three manners: time-stamped VR spatial and input log data, System Usability Score (SUS) survey [15], and a structured interview.

3.1 Log Data of the Prototyping Sessions

The Virtual Prototyping Environment logs to disk timestamped record of actions and interactions in the virtual environment, e.g., participants' spawning, moving, scaling, or pressing of buttons, as well as the facilitator's interactions through their interface. The time of the start of the prototyping process was determined by the timestamp of the participant's first spawn action. The duration of the four prototyping phases (1. Standing-downhill, 2. Cycling-downhill, 3. Standing-uphill, 4. Cycling-uphill) was determined using the timestamp of the participant electing to press the snapshot button. The duration of the sensitisation to the second scenario fell between phases 2 and 3 but was included towards duration of phase 3 as it was considered as part of contemplation prior to impending manipulation of prototypes.

3.2 System Usability Score Survey

Participants completed the System Usability Score (SUS) survey, with the prompt 'please evaluate this prototyping environment, and thus not your interface that you have just created'. It was completed by all participants, regardless of their successful or premature completion of the prototyping process. Individual scores were processed for average and standard deviations per survey question, to finally arrive at a final system score, as per SUS guidelines.

3.3 Post-Prototyping Interviews

Interviews conducted at the end of each session were recorded as audio and were transcribed with automated software. Word search was performed on timestamped transcripts to facilitate further processing. Affect was manually assessed during playback, focusing on the following categories: preference for prototyping while standing/cycling, prototyping process, immersion, realism, usability, safety, simulator sickness, and other. Participants' recommended ideas for improvement were tagged for consideration.

4 Results

Twenty-eight participants took part in the study, three of whom could not complete the prototyping session due to simulator sickness. The results of the evaluations are outlined below.

4.1 Log Data of the Prototyping Sessions

The 'prototyping session' consisted of four phases, with two phases (standing, cycling) for each of the two scenarios. Each pair of phases was preceded by a 90-s 'context sensitising ride'.

Log data tracked progress, culminating with participant-triggered snapshots, including position and orientation of the VR base stations, VR trackers, VR controllers and the VR headset, as well as the participants' gaze point, and UI artefacts' relative placement. The phases varied in duration, as shown in Table 1. The time spent on the four prototyping modes varied, dependent in part on their order (average: 1. Downhill-astraddle: 32:59, 2. Downhill-cycling: 2:43, 3. Uphill-astraddle: 9:23, 4. Uphill-cycling: 1:41). The 'total values' do not include the experiment protocol prior or after the 'prototyping session' part of the experiment. Three participants who did not finish the session because of simulator sickness were excluded from the calculation.

Table 1. Duration of prototyping phases as part of the prototyping session.

Phase	Average	St. Dev.	Minimum	Maximum
1. Stationary – scenario 1: downhill	32:59	12:48	13:39	71:54
2. Cycling – scenario 1: downhill	02:43	01:35	00:34	06:43
3. Stationary – scenario 2: uphill	09:23	06:09	00:07	23:54
4. Cycling – scenario 2: uphill	01:41	01:47	00:00	08:35
Total	49:04	13:37	30:06	88:59

4.2 System Usability Score Survey

Individual scores (Likert: strongly disagree 1–5 strongly agree) for each question (as part of the System Usability Score (SUS) survey [15]) can be found in Fig. 10. Odd-numbered questions required to rate a positively phrased statement, while even-numbered questions required to rate a negative one. The total system score was 71.2 (SD: 2.2). The three participants who did not complete the prototyping session did take part in the survey.

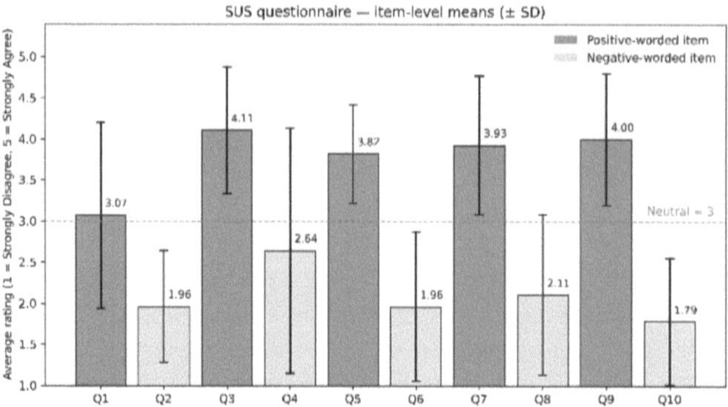

Fig. 10. System Usability Score evaluation value averages (with standard deviation); x-axis: question number, y-axis: reported score.

4.3 Post-Prototyping Interviews

Interviews were conducted with all participants, regardless of having completed the prototyping session. Despite the time duration differences reported above, when asked for their preference, 12 participants reported positive affect towards both stationery and riding modes, with 3 cases of preference only for stationary, 5 for riding, and 8 with no preference. Simulator sickness was experienced by 3 participants leading them to stop (all while prototyping while stationary), with a further 11 reporting having at some point experienced varying degrees of discomfort (reported primarily when stationary).

When asked interview questions (Appendix 2), participants expressed positive affect towards being able to iterate in 10 cases, and were divided on immersion (12 positive mentions, 21 negative), realism (+8, −11), safety (+4, −4), usability (+22, −26), and other factors (+2, −3). Forty eight improvement suggestions were provided by the participants, with respect to hardware (e.g., aero handlebars, pedalling resistance, handlebar turning resistance, inclining the treadmill), immersion (e.g., bicycle lean, wind sensation, road vibration, lack of feeling danger), video (longer, higher resolution, blurred when menu is open atop of it), virtual prototyping tools (e.g., dynamic delivery-means previews, colour opacity manipulation, prototype backgrounds, pre-made layouts), and protocol (e.g., starting prototyping in 2D and continuing in 3D, reversing order of phases).

5 Discussion

The discussion is three-fold: Sect. 5.1 interprets the empirical results through an HCI lens, Sect. 5.2 abstracts key design lessons, and Sect. 5.3 delineates limitations and avenues for future research.

5.1 Interpretation of Results

The timestamped log data revealed a vast discrepancy between the durations of the design phases ('stationary', 'cycling'; Table 1). Amongst 28 participants, instances of simulator sickness (14) were reported to have primarily taken place during prototyping whilst 'stationary'. Whether this is a consequence of the duration discrepancy or the phase's conditions is unknown. Participants had prior knowledge of the protocol order, but whether they felt the autonomy to skip ahead to the 'cycling' phase, or whether they had an expectation of conditions improving, is unclear. The discrepancy in the durations is not reflected in the reported affect and preference for a prototyping phase as expressed during the closing interviews, where the two phases scored comparably both in single-preference (stationary: 3, cycling: 5) and bi-partial positive affect (12). Participants' shorter experiences in the 'cycling' design phases can be attributed to having had completed the scenario's interface with respect to information needs, with only the positioning remaining (supported by interviews). This was observed in both scenarios, with the second scenario being shorter still, attributed to a large overlap in information needs and the reuse of the previously made interface. Arguably, however short, had the 'cycling' phase been entirely superfluous, the average duration would have been approaching zero. Singular cases were observed of participants skipping the 'cycling' phase, supported by negative affect concerning 'safety' reported in the interviews thereafter.

Results of the System Usability Score questionnaire showed an above average (68) score of 71.2, considered 'acceptable' according to [20]. This is a high score considering the complexity of the system, however the novelty of the immersive experience could have positively affected the grading. Participation was self-elected and voluntary, and a token financial appreciation was not revealed until after, potentially leaving the personal satisfaction with one's prototyping 'output' a contributing factor in the evaluation. Furthermore, the prototyping environment is not a daily-use device, thus the grading is anticipated to have accommodated for minor (usability, safety) qualms in exchange for the novel experience, and the perceived value of the prototyping output.

The prototyping environment and methodology are a result of informed trade-offs between immersion, realism, safety, and usability (outlined in the Rationale). The results of post-prototyping interviews show varied affect in different categories. Despite the line of questioning encouraging reporting of negative aspects, the ratio of positive and negative affect remains in relative balance. The discussion which followed produced numerous recommendations for improvement, implementation of which however should consider their impact on the conflicting trade-offs areas.

5.2 Lessons Learned

The proposed indoor multi-modal motion-based Virtual Reality cycling experience simulation has been demonstrated to work. The prototyping environment was shown to be very promising in facilitating deeper context and role immersion, eliciting in participants representative need for real-time information in a safe manner. It further provided them with prototyping tools to iteratively explore, communicate, and evaluate their proposed solutions to their information needs.

The use of the tandem gave the researchers the ability to safely provide participants with deeper immersion with vestibular and haptic stimulus. By taking over steering duties, it also afforded ample time and attention for the participants to think things through and explicate their interface choices clearly and thus provide richer insights.

The use of a secondary virtual cameras enabled researchers to comfortably follow the course of action and provide facilitation.

The deep visual immersion was made possible with 360 videos and a spatially matched virtual bicycle model. The use of video in favour of a computer-generated virtual environment was reported as preferable and more realistic despite the lower resolution. Aligning the video's horizon and vanishing point and the virtual 'forward' direction to match the physical forward direction was essential to maintain immersion. Further mirroring the video on playback iteration eliminated bias. The virtual bicycle model was mapped using spatial trackers and further served as a useful mobile reference origin point in the virtual environment. Participants experienced going 'downhill' and 'uphill' without changing the treadmill's inclination and taking corners while riding straight in reality. Participants were free to move relative to the bicycle and were immersed to a point of physically leaning into the corner, which inadvertently and ironically negatively impacted the immersion with the facilitator's pushed to counterweighting safety measures. A sense of control over the bicycle was afforded through a decoupled handlebar (mapped to a virtual handlebar) and an ability to pedal.

Participants used a virtual reality controller to create, position, and modify prototype interface artefacts. Iteration between prototyping and evaluation was facilitated, with participants reporting positive affect toward prototyping while stationary as well as while riding the bicycle with the treadmill running. Simulator sickness was reported in 3 cases, and discomfort in a further 11 cases, primarily when prototyping while stationary. Despite it, participants remained in the virtual environment for an average of 39 min. The trade-offs between realism, immersion, safety and usability were balanced. The proposed setup and methodology are of use to other VR experiences mediating use scenarios involving motion, and it would be of interest to see it applied in other applications.

5.3 Limitations and Future Research

The selection criteria for participation (road bicycle ownership and experience) as well as hardware mobility limitation have led to a less diverse and by extension smaller population sample, one which is likely disproportionately prone to interest in novel technology. The immersion and usability of this prototyping environment should be evaluated with a more diverse sample.

Simulator sickness affected a small portion of the participants (3 of 28). Amongst assumed causes are visual-vestibular mismatch, long exposure, and individual sensitivity. Future work should consider pre-screening methods, and monitoring sickness with a structured questionnaire.

The order of prototyping methods (stationary, cycling) was not randomised, as the 'stationary' phase was deemed a necessary steppingstone towards the more (physically) challenging 'cycling' phase. Future research should explore reversing the order.

The data collection was not conducted anonymously, and the method used (System Usability Score) is subjective, potentially giving a distorted view of participant's experience. Another evaluation method should be added in the future to support gaining a more objective understanding of the immersion and task load.

User Interface. As part of the virtual prototyping environment, adding higher fidelity previews of prototypes (opacity, dynamic and responsive delivery-means previews, fully implemented circumstance and attachment visualisation) can help improve communication, evaluation, and affect the choices made as part of the prototyping output.

Experimental Setup. Future work should explore implementation of further immersive modalities: vestibular (allowing the participants to lean and take corners to match the video), control (letting participants steer), and exertion (pedalling resistance to match the scenario and task).

6   Conclusions

An indoor Virtual Reality cycling experience simulator, consisting of a tandem riding on a treadmill, was built for iterative prototyping and evaluation of Mixed-Reality real-time information interfaces for outdoor use. Prototyping sessions performed with 28 participants compared two multi-modal approaches, prototyping while 'stationary' and while 'cycling'. Findings indicate that designing MR interfaces for cycling implies trade-offs between simulation realism, immersion, prototyping capabilities, safety, and usability. Following the prototyping sessions, participants were interviewed to evaluate their experience and preference. Twelve participants reported positive affect towards both prototyping methods, with each having specific strengths. Prototyping while cycling in a virtual world was shown to be viable. Deep immersion fosters richer insight into user needs and preferences but can bring along practical and ergonomic constraints. Our approach strives to balance these factors, providing enough realism to evoke authentic user experience in a safe environment.

The presented setup and methodology provide insights into cyclists' needs and preferences, supporting the development of MR UI for use in motion solutions that provide a competitive edge without endangering riders. Although developed for cycling, our multi-sensory approach, that follows a domain-agnostic protocol, offers a structured yet flexible means to develop MR solutions for other mobile applications, including running, driving and flying. Facilitating an iterative design process, our approach helps designers refine the essential aspects of MR UI in motion.

Acknowledgments. A This study was funded as part of the 'Citius Altius Sanius' research programme (P16–28), financed by the Dutch Research Council (NWO).

Disclosure of Interests. The authors have no competing interests to declare that are relevant to the content of this article.

Appendix

Appendix 1. Orientation Question List

1. Did you cycle here to our meeting? When's the last time you cycled?

2. Do you own a racing bike? When is the last time you took your racing bike out?
3. How often do you race with it, in number of times per month?
4. How many km would you say you've cycled in the last 12 months?
5. What's the most times you've cycled on your racing bike in a month?
6. What's the most km you've cycled in 12 months?
7. What's your favourite route?
8. What's your dream route?
9. Do you watch races often, on tv (number of races per year)?
10. Which channel do you follow races on?
11. Do you see races in person?
12. Are you a member of a cycling club or group?
13. Do you race as a team often?
14. Do you collect data when you cycle?
15. What data do you collect?
16. Which app do you use?
17. Which sensors?
18. Do you use a home trainer, do you use Zwift?
19. Do you have a device to view the data back live?
20. Do you rely on this live data during race or training, and how?
21. Where do you stand on the use of data in cycling racing?
22. In the future, 10, 20, 50 years, how will the sport look?
23. What will interfaces look like, the way that participants consume instructions, data, information?

Appendix 2. Post-prototyping Interview Questions

1. What did you like? What did you dislike? What were you missing?
2. Which method did you prefer, designing while stationary (treadmill not running), or while cycling (treadmill on)?
3. Where there times when your immersion was deeper, or when it was broken?

Appendix 3. Experimental Setup

Interview Table.

1. Paper and pens
2. 'Inspiration-sheet' with basic, non-cycling related, illustrated examples of various visualisation characteristics pertaining to: representation, use of sound, trigger, purpose, duration, dimming, opacity, animation, orientation, fill, scale, amounts, colour, frequency, permanence, precision, units, freshness, and emphasis
3. Facilitator's 'information type checklist' - 'power, distance, time, heartrate, cadence, speed, energy, nutrition, hydration, navigation/map, altitude/elevation, weather, danger, lap'
4. System Usability Score (SUS) questionnaire

Physical Prototyping Environment

1. PC, monitor, mouse
2. Projector, projection screen
3. Virtual Reality Headset (HTC Vive Pro 2)
4. Grip-sensing VR Controller (Valve Index)
5. Spatial tracking system (HTC Vive Base Station 2) (4×)
6. Treadmill (260 × 115 cm belt surface; padded side railings; speed: 15 km/h descent, and 8 km/h for ascent)
7. Tandem bicycle
   a. Steering coupled at the back, decoupled up front
   b. Brakes disengaged
   c. Front saddle - racing model, high seat position
   d. Front handlebar - drop handlebar, no brake levers
   e. VR Spatial Trackers (HTC Vive Tracker 2)
      (1) Spatial Tracker A - attached at the side of the bicycle's frame, low
      (2) Spatial Tracker B - attached to the front handlebar
8. Safety equipment – full body harnesses, ceiling tethers

Virtual Prototyping Environment (Built Using Unity [16])

1. Virtual Camera A (following headset) (headset view, Fig. 6)
2. Virtual Camera B (following Spatial Tracker A position, 2 m higher, always pointing ahead) (projector view; Fig. 4)
3. Virtual Camera C (looking at the bicycle from the side) (side monitor view, Fig. 5)
4. 10-m diameter sphere, with a looping 360 video texture (fading through black) (choice of two videos, one for each scenario)
5. Virtual tandem bicycle model (following spatial tracker A's position and rotation, with its handlebar and front wheel following Spatial Tracker B's rotation)
6. Virtual glove models and controller models (following respective controllers and hand gestures) (2×)
7. Interactable 'Prototype' artefact
   a. Grabbable handle changing location, rotation
   b. Prototype preview
   c. Interactable choice menu: (following handle's position, rotation facing VR headset's posi-tion)
      (1) Data type-primary (19): aerodynamics, altitude/elevation, braking, cadence, danger, distance, gears, gradient, heartrate, hydration, lap/stage, navigation, nutrition, power, speed, strategy, time, weather/wind, other
      (2) Data type-secondary (16): best, current, elapsed/completed, expected, future, gap, global average, stage, limit, max, min, past, remaining/left, running average, total, other
      (3) Delivery-means (13; portrayed graphically): boolean-count-indicator, arrow, rectangle, graph, horizontal linear indicator, horizontal-linear-bar, map, number, radial indicator, sound, symbol, text, vertical linear indicator
      (4) Circumstance (7): always, context, on demand, periodical, location, threshold, other

    (5) Colour-primary (10), Colour-secondary (10): blue, brown, green, grey, orange, pink, purple, red, white, yellow

    (6) Purpose (5): information, instruction, motivation, warning, other

    (7) Attached to (3): frame, helmet, road

  d. Virtual Text display of prototype's id number (only visible to Virtual Camera B and C)

8. Snapshot buttons (directly left and right of VR headset position, within arm's reach) (2×)

9. Facilitator's interface panel (Figs. 4 and 5; only visible to Virtual Camera B and C), interactable from computer using a mouse: Video playback controls, Pro-totype choice controls, Menu controls, Snapshot controls, Logging controls and indicators

References

1. Martinez Garcia, D. et al.: Parameter tuning of a bicycle simulator for a realistic riding behaviour and motion perception, Proceedings of the Driving Simulation Conference 2022 Europe, Driving Simulation Association, Strasbourg, France (2022)

2. Wintersberger, P., Matviienko, A., Schweidler, A., Michahelles, F.: Development and evaluation of a motion-based VR bicycle simulator. Proc. ACM Hum. -Comput. Interact. Vol. 6 (MHCI), Article 210 (2022) https://doi.org/10.1145/3546745

3. Matviienko, A., Hoxha, H., Mühlhäuser, M.: What does it mean to cycle in Virtual Reality? Exploring Cycling Fidelity and Control of VR Bicycle Simulators. Proceedings of the 2023 CHI Conference on Human Factors in Computing Systems. 879 (2023). https://doi.org/10.1145/3544548.3581050

4. Kircher, K., Lindman, M., Eldijk, J.V., Weman, J.: Removing barriers to cycling on rural roads. VTI rapport, ISSN 0347–6030; 1220A. (2024) urn: nbn:se: vti: diva-21334

5. Will, S., et al.: Assessment of data glasses for motorcycle riders in a simulated lane change test. Transport. Res. F: Traffic Psychol. Behav. **89**, 467–477 (2022). https://doi.org/10.1016/j.trf.2022.07.016

6. Matviienko, A., Mehmedovic, D., Müller, F., Mühlhäuser, M.: "Baby, You can Ride my Bike": Exploring maneuver indications of self-driving bicycles using a tandem simulator. Proc. ACM Hum. -Comput. Interact. **6**, MHCI, 188 (2022). https://doi.org/10.1145/3546723

7. van der Bijl-Brouwer, M., van der Voort, M.: Establishing shared understanding of product use through collaboratively generating an explicit frame of reference. CoDesign **10**(3–4), 171–190 (2014). https://doi.org/10.1080/15710882.2014.963125

8. Visser, F.S., Stappers, P.J., van der Lugt, R., Sanders, E.B.N.: Contextmapping: Experiences from practice. CoDesign **1**(2), 119–149 (2005). https://doi.org/10.1080/15710880500135987

9. Rosson, M.B., Carroll, J.M.: Usability Engineering: Scenario-Based Development of Human-Computer Interaction. (2001). https://doi.org/10.5555/2821587

10. Kosch, T. et al.: NotiBike: Assessing target selection techniques for cyclist notifications in augmented reality. Proc. ACM Hum. -Comput. Interact. **6**, MHCI, 197 (2022). https://doi.org/10.1145/3546732

11. Snyder, C.: Paper prototyping: The fast and easy way to design and refine user interfaces. Morgan Kaufmann, San Francisco (2003)

12. Lacoche, J., Villain, E., Foulonneau, A.: Evaluating usability and user experience of ar applications in VR simulation. Frontiers in Virtual Reality. Volume 3–2022 (2022). https://doi.org/10.3389/frvir.2022.881318

13. Grandi, J.G., Cao, Z., Ogren, M., Kopper, R.: Design and simulation of next-generation augmented reality user interfaces in virtual reality. 2021 IEEE Conference on Virtual Reality and 3D User Interfaces Abstracts and Workshops (VRW). 23–29 (2021). https://doi.org/10.1109/VRW52623.2021.00011
14. Kolb, D.A.: Experiential learning: Experience as the source of learning and development. FT press (2014)
15. Brooke, J.: SUS-A quick and dirty usability scale. Usability evaluation in industry. **189**(194), 4–7 (1996)
16. Unity Technologies. Unity Real-Time Development Platform. https://unity.com
17. Bangor, A., Kortum, P.T., Miller, J.T.: An empirical evaluation of the system usability scale. Intl. Journal of Human-Computer Interaction. **24**(6), 574–594 (2008). https://doi.org/10.1080/10447310802205776
18. Tullis, T.S., Stetson, J.N.: A comparison of questionnaires for assessing website usability. Usability professional association conference. **1**, 1–12 (2004)
19. Sauro, J.: A practical guide to the system usability scale: Background, benchmarks & best practices. Measuring Usability LLC, Denver (2011)
20. Bangor, A., Kortum, P.T., Miller, J.T.: Determining what individual SUS scores mean: Adding an adjective rating scale. J. Usability Stud. **4**(3), 114–123 (2009)

Virtual Reality-Based Training for Sexual Harassment Awareness and Bystander Intervention at University Campuses in Pakistan

Noverah Khan[1]($\boxtimes$) , Hira Eiraj Daud[1] , Eman Khalid[1] , Talalah Khan[2] , and Suleman Shahid[1]

[1] Lahore University of Management Sciences, Lahore 54792, PB, Pakistan
noverah27@gmail.com
[2] Florida State University, Tallahassee, FL 32304, USA

Abstract. Sexual harassment (SH) is a significant global issue impacting both men and women, with severe psychological, social, and legal consequences. University campuses, as microcosms of society, provide an ideal setting to educate students on SH and encourage bystander intervention. This study evaluates the effectiveness of Virtual Reality (VR) training in raising SH awareness and improving bystander intervention among university students in Pakistan. The goal is to design an informational and effective VR tool to educate students on SH and enhance their ability to respond appropriately in harassment situations. This study aims to address the limitations of current SH education tools, which are often disengaging, by offering an immersive, interactive learning experience that complements existing methods.

Keywords: Sexual Harassment · Bystander · VR · University · Students

1   Introduction

Sexual Harassment (SH) is defined as any unwelcome sexual advance, request for sexual favor, verbal or physical conduct or gesture of a sexual nature, or any other behavior of a sexual nature that causes offence or humiliation [1]. SH is a global problem that affects both women and men and it is reported to affect 51% of women in the EU and 81% in the US throughout their lifetime [2]. Statistics from the Pakistani Federal Ombudsman Secretariat (For protection Against Harassment) reported 2,169 complaints against workplace SH from 2018 to 2022 in the government sector and 994 women and 445 men lodging complaints in the private sector [3]. In recent years, there has been an increased trend of female students speaking out against harassment [4]. Bystanders are individuals who observe SH firsthand, or are subsequently informed of the incident [5] and they can play a pivotal role in mitigating the outcomes of SH. In this paper we aim to understand the extent of bystander intervention in Pakistan, why they may or may not take a certain course of action. Additionally, there are varying perceptions

---

N. Khan, H. E. Daud and E. Khalid are 1st co-authors.

J. Y. C. Chen et al. (Eds.): HCII 2025, LNCS 16338, pp. 98–112, 2026.
https://doi.org/10.1007/978-3-032-12808-9_7

in Pakistan on what constitutes as SH depending on culture, socioeconomic class, and religious ideologies [33]. Many individuals lack awareness about what constitutes as sexual harassment and are often ill-equipped to respond to witnessing SH appropriately. Such inadequate awareness tools have dire consequences.

Our interviews revealed several reasons why bystanders hesitate to intervene in incidents of SH, like uncertainty about the situation, fear of causing a scene, concern for their own reputation, insufficient time to react, lack of intervention knowledge, and distrust in institutional policies. After evaluating different innovative tools, we chose Virtual reality (VR) technology, as it helps create an immersive, interactive, and computer-generated environment. Because of the emergence of VR as a frontier in human-computer interaction research, we aim to employ its strengths to overcome the limitations of traditional tools like passive lectures and develop and scale VR simulation games as effective SH awareness tools. Existing tools often lack cultural nuance and relatability for non-Western contexts such as Pakistan. Since the use of VR employs immersive and interactive techniques, it is imperative that while simulating real life situations accurately, the comfortability of individuals is not compromised. Thus, using this innovative technology we also seek to understand how cultural nuances influence bystander intervention in SH scenarios in order to develop culturally relevant VR simulations. Henceforth, our research targets the following research questions:

- **RQ1:** What kind of sexual harassment education or training are Pakistani university students receiving?
- **RQ2:** What is the approach to bystander intervention in sexual harassment encounters in Pakistan?
- **RQ3:** How can we design an effective tool to promote bystander intervention amongst Pakistani students?

2   Related Works

2.1   Importance of Bystander Intervention

Ford et al. found that aggressors stopped their behavior when a bystander intervened in 84% of cases [12]. However, bystander intervention (BI) is lacking in such cases because of their inability to: notice a situation is occurring, identify a situation as high-risk, feel responsible for the situation, use the correct intervention approach, and overcome the fear of looking foolish [13]. Bystanders may also choose not to intervene if they lack empathy for victims [10, 11, 14, 15] believing that they deserve it; a result of perpetuating rape-myths [17] or if they feel that their intervention might bring about negative consequences for themselves [10, 18].

Bystander programs engage the entire community, not just those at risk, helping individuals approach high-risk situations and strengthening safety nets for victims [19, 20]. Bystander training provides individuals with the skills to recognize situations, behaviors, and social norms that lead to violence and how to safely and effectively handle them [21]. Many individuals' existing knowledge of BI practices come from unrealistic scenarios in media [22] which is why many institutions have adopted BI workshops [17]. Successful BI training teaches individuals to be more vigilant, responsible for their surroundings, the right skills to completely intervene i.e. escalatory, de-escalatory, or a mix of both [23], and that their intervention will bring about a positive net impact [9]. Beyond teaching the technicalities of BI, it is imperative that training modules focus on promoting empathy for victims [24, 25] and highlighting the positive community impact of dealing with intervening in SH encounters [21].

2.2 Campus Harassment Perceptions in Pakistan

Asif et al. [6] found that sexual harassment (SH) of all types occur in all Pakistani universities, with perpetrators ranging from students to administrators. Conservative societies like Bangladesh and Pakistan witness increased SH in public places due to the shame and social disgrace placed on victims [7, 8]. Additionally, perpetrators might continue harassing victims if they perceive them as the only individuals affected by their actions [9]. Although the actors in SH encounters are limited to the victim and the perpetrator, bystanders, who witness the harassment but are not directly involved may be afforded the opportunity to intervene [9–11].

McMahon states that pinpointing bystander opportunities may be challenging for college students, which is a result of students from different backgrounds receiving various degrees of education on SH prior to joining school [20]. Victimization and perpetration of sexual assault is lower in college campuses with bystander intervention training programs [29]. Their evaluation of the Green Dot bystander intervention program implemented in 2008, found that victimization rates were 17% lower among students on campuses with the program (46.4%) compared to those without it (55.7%) evidencing the efficacy of BI training in lowering rates of interpersonal violence [21, 29]. However, research on BI training modules and their efficacy have historically been oriented to North America [17]. BI training and tools are only as effective as they are relatable. To build an impactful tool that changes a bystander's course of action, we must gain a deeper understanding of intrapersonal variables such as their cognition, cost and benefits, and peer and family influence [11]. Pakistani culture is upheld by a conservative, close-knit society, where the reaction to SH is influenced by who did it, who it happened to, and where it happened. One's social and cultural capital plays a key role in the extent of justice that they may receive which is why single women especially from ethnic minorities are most vulnerable [6]. Western BI tools designed for college campuses may not encompass the cultural nuance needed to be effective in Pakistani society.

2.3 Virtual Reality for Training

Traditional SH training can be tedious, unmotivating, and unrelatable [24]. Watching a video about SH and criticizing a situation from the side is incomparable to being part of that situation [26]. The medium of training can impact the outcomes of training [27]. A video or a lecture may not have the same impact as a multi-technique program, which can develop recognition of problem behaviors and resolution-handling skills [28]. A well-designed SH training would foster perspective taking through first-person narratives, be interactive, and use synchronous delivery methods [24]. VR can play an important role in combating SH and gender inequality [26]. VR as a tool for bystander training is yet unexplored [22]. It provides users with an immersive and interactive environment in an otherwise dangerous environment in a comfortable way [22]. Shiri et al. designed and tested a VR simulation of SH during a job interview; they found that participants were unable to effectively deal with the harassment in real time, despite correctly identifying the nature of the harassment. Only until the simulation was over were they able to reflect on what they might have said or done differently [26]. VR might be a more effective training tool since users are more receptive to the feelings and emotions of the individuals in the scenario [22, 26]. It also allows users to experience SH encounters in familiar settings, which makes them less hypothetical and more real [22].

The use of VR can be understood through three key perspectives: environment, interaction, and immersion. Using this segmentation aids our understanding and use of VR to impart SH awareness. As an environment, VR is described as "an alternate world filled with computer-generated images," capable of simulating any setting, whether realistic or imaginary. Coates et al. defines it as "an electronic simulation of [an] environment," often incorporating technical elements like 3D visuals and interactivity [31]. Beyond using VR to create an environment for experiencing SH as a bystander in a non-invasive manner, VR also helps facilitate an empathetic connection and interaction between users. For instance, the Oculus Go employs motion-sensitive controllers that enable users to see both others and move their limbs in a virtual space providing an immersive experience. VR training (VRT) also supports effective skill transfer, with 75% of studies showing behaviors learned in VR generalize well to real-world settings [35]. It enables scalable delivery of Behavior Skills Training (BST) elements, modeling, rehearsal, and feedback, more efficiently than traditional methods [35–37]. VR also provides a safe, controlled environment to practice high-stakes scenarios, such as CPR, without real-world risks [35].

3 Methodology

To understand bystander intervention in SH cases in Pakistan, we conducted in-depth qualitative interviews and focus groups with 30 participants (5 for interviews and 25 for focus groups), aged 18–25. The participants were undergraduate and master's students, as well as recent graduates who could recall their SH awareness sessions from university orientation sessions. We included students from both online and in-person orientations to account for the shift in training formats due to COVID-19 and assess the efficacy of both methods. The sample was diverse with students from different majors and technological familiarity. Students were recruited from the science, social science and business school. The sample was controlled for gender. An introductory session with Oculus was held before the study to ensure adequate participant familiarity with VR.

Participants were asked about their experiences witnessing SH and the role bystanders typically played. They were also asked about the effectiveness of SH education from their institutions. The interviews concluded with four scenarios of campus SH, prompting participants to discuss potential bystander actions. We also switched to focus groups because some participants seemed hesitant to discuss such a sensitive topic during one-on-one interviews. Now participant engagement significantly increased. As Nova Ahmed found in her research on SH, group discussions often help break the silence [30]. Participants often continued discussions independently now, providing deeper insights compared to interviews. Women mostly led the conversation in mixed groups while men usually gave very concise responses at the beginning and gradually took up more space. To understand the data collected through our interviews and focus groups, we conducted thematic analysis using inductive coding.

4 User Research

We found the following set of reasons why bystanders are hesitant to intervene when witnessing an incident involving sexual harassment.

4.1 Lack of Formal Intervention Knowledge

Uncertainty if the Incident Qualifies as Harassment. Participants were unclear about what constitutes harassment. When asked about different types, many provided incorrect answers, especially regarding verbal and non-verbal harassment. One participant mentioned, "Different types of SH are like workplace harassment, household harassment, and cyber harassment." Another stated, "There's physical SH, like inappropriate touching, and then bad sexual remarks, which can be verbal or written, like on social media." A third participant said, "I'm not sure about the types, but it's anything sexual someone forces you to do. And stalking too." Some participants also questioned whether certain incidents were harassment or just rude behavior due to poor social eti-quette. Many viewed SH as involving physical touch or verbal remarks, not non-verbal gestures like staring. One participant said, "I think SH can be physical or verbal. Non-verbals don't count—if someone's staring or gesturing, that's their problem. You should just ignore it."

As noted in 5.1.1, some bystanders hesitated to intervene, uncertain if the situation was harassment. They feared intervening in cases where the individuals might know each other. One participant shared, "I'd be hesitant to intervene because what if they're girlfriend and boyfriend, and I get scolded for interfering in their personal matter? The girl might say 'who are you to jump in?' or 'he's my boyfriend and wasn't harassing me.' That would be embarrassing."

Lack of Knowledge on Reporting Procedures. Students were largely unaware of the reporting procedures for harassment at their university. While most knew there was a harassment committee, they were not aware of their members or how to report to them. Many were also unaware of the harassment helpline. Some students mentioned they would consult a trusted faculty member to discuss reporting procedures. One participant, who was familiar with the process, explained, "I learned how to file a report when I became president of a society. I had a one-on-one session with a harassment committee member who explained it in detail. The guidelines are available, but students don't know about them until they need the information. When I became president, I arranged a session for all society members, but not every society does this."

Regarding sexual misconduct education, students recalled a lecture during orientation week that some found boring or skipped entirely, leaving them with little takeaway. A few mentioned that the drama society organized an engaging play on SH, but it only covered one scenario of physical harassment, which didn't fully address the topic.

Information on harassment is also available in the student handbook, but many students "don't bother to read that section." Participants also compared their education across different levels, noting that high school and undergraduate programs had more effective, conversational lectures in smaller classes. They felt that by graduate school, administrations assumed students already knew about sexual misconduct, leading to less involved education.

Distrust in Institutional Policies and Authority Figures. Most participants were uncertain about their institution's response to harassment reports, noting that harassment committees often take months to decide, making outcomes feel irrelevant. Even when decisions are reached, they rarely satisfy victims. Some authority figures dismiss verbal and non-verbal harassment as "common," advising students to "let it go." One participant noted, "Sometimes we prefer telling friends for help because faculty or admin just say, 'this happens and is common,' and do nothing." Victim-blaming attitudes from faculty and committee members were also highlighted. For instance, one participant criticized a mandatory SH seminar where the host implied women should watch how they dress. Another recalled technical assistants in labs inappropriately staring at female students, questioning whether similar actions by male students would be addressed. This lack of seriousness undermines trust in institutional responses.

4.2 Uncertainty About Intervening

Avoidance of Causing a Scene. Many participants noted that bystanders avoid intervening in SH incidents to avoid attention, especially if they are shy or anxious. One explained, "I'd distance myself, so as not to create a scene." In Pakistan, non-verbal harassment often goes unchallenged despite knowing it's wrong. Another reason for inaction is the fear of making things worse for the victim. As one participant shared, "Bystanders usually tell the victim to ignore it, as further confrontation will make things worse," leading to victim-blaming. Some also avoid intervention, assuming the parties know each other and the situation is private, with one participant stating, "It seems like a private matter unless it's a direct threat to health or life."

Concern About Personal or Others' Reputation. Participants also mentioned that bystanders hesitate to intervene due to concerns about their own reputation. They fear being associated with the situation, with some worrying that the harasser might turn on them instead of the victim, leading to negative perceptions. One participant explained, "As a girl, I would feel scared and helpless. The fear comes from thinking that what's happening to the victim might happen to you, even worse because you're the one stopping it." Others expressed hesitation for the sake of the involved parties' reputations, fearing they might not know the full story and could inadvertently side with the wrong person, making things worse for the actual victim. One participant observed, "In harassment situations, people tend to side with the party they know better and make excuses for them." Some participants also mentioned that intervening could harm the victim's reputation further especially if the victim is female.

Insufficient Time to Process and React. Participants mentioned that SH incidents often happen so quickly that they are unable to process the situation in time to act. Even when they have time, they are often overwhelmed by emotions like anger, fear, and anxiety, so by the time they can react, the incident is over or someone else has intervened. One participant explained, "SH isn't something you see every day, so when it happens, your mind goes into shock, and it takes time to process everything and react." Another participant shared, "Sometimes you're so caught up in the moment that by the time you realize you should do something, it's already over. I witnessed verbal harassment once but didn't act in the moment. Later, I posted anonymously on our batch's Facebook page, supporting the girl and offering help, but no one ever reached out."

Desire to Avoid Prolonging the Incident. Some participants mentioned feeling hesitant to intervene because they believe the victim may not want the situation escalated and just wants it to end. They shared that, if in the victim's shoes, they would prefer to avoid seeking justice or causing a scene, instead wishing for the situation to stop and everyone to move on. One participant explained, "I don't think victims always want intervention. Sometimes they just want it to stop, and intervention could lead to a negative reaction from the victim. Maybe they want to remain silent and not be highlighted. In today's social media world, one video and it could go viral. So, as a bystander, I'd want to help, but I'm unsure of how the victim would want me to act."

4.3   Bystander Responses to Sexual Harassment Scenarios

After the interviews, we presented participants with SH scenarios (Table 1) and asked them to imagine themselves as bystanders and describe their likely reactions. This aimed to explore how they typically respond to SH incidents at university and assess the need for intervention. Participants showed consistent patterns in their assumptions and reactions, responding similarly across scenarios. Despite the scenarios being mostly gender-neutral (except the first), their feedback revealed shared assumptions underlying bystander intervention strategies.

Table 1. Sexual harassment (SH) scenarios

No.	Scenarios
1	During a lecture, a male student continuously makes lewd comments and jokes about female classmates' appearances, making them visibly uncomfortable.
2	At a university party, you notice a group of people dancing. One person is repeatedly touching another person inappropriately despite their attempts to move away.
3	In the university dorms, you observe a student repeatedly following another student, trying to engage them in conversation despite clear signs of discomfort.
4	You are in the university library working on a project. You notice a fellow student, Sam, who seems visibly uncomfortable and anxious. Upon closer observation, you see that another student across the room is staring at Sam persistently and making suggestive facial expressions, such as winking and licking their lips. Despite Sam's attempts to ignore the behavior and move to different areas of the library, the staring and gestures continue.

Confrontation and Direct Intervention. Many participants expressed willingness to confront harassers, stressing immediate action. One noted, "If you notice something happening, you don't have to wait for someone to do something; you can take action." In classroom settings, many preferred indirect methods, such as diverting attention, to balance intervention and personal safety. As one shared, "I'd feel comfortable confronting them in a place where there are other people around but in a one-on-one, I'd be apprehensive." Direct intervention was seen as crucial, especially in physical harassment cases (Scenario 2), but personality influenced willingness. A participant stated, "I'm very confrontational, so I would confront [the harasser] directly and then report them." This highlights the importance of training that accommodates diverse personalities. Participants also intervened with victims in Scenarios 3 and 4, often checking on them or distracting the harasser. One explained, "I would intervene in a subtle way, I'd say I want to talk to you, help them escape." Many preferred distraction over confrontation. Approaches ranged from calling out the harasser to respectful address, as one participant said, "Respectfully calling them out is better than being aggressive," underscoring context's role in effective intervention.

Contextual Understanding and Indirect Intervention. Indirect intervention, often used after assessing the situation, was a common alternative to direct action, especially in public settings. Participants emphasized understanding the harasser's context before responding. In Scenario 1, some noted the importance of considering cultural background, stating, "I would try to understand where the person is coming from... And whether there's a context behind why they're saying what they're saying." This approach was favored in social settings, such as parties, where subtle methods avoided confrontation. One participant shared, "I would intervene in a subtle way, I'd say I want to talk to you, help them escape." Many preferred supporting the victim over directly confronting the harasser. In Scenario 2, responses were split between direct intervention and checking on the victim first. A participant explained, "I would sideline the girl and ask if she's okay. I don't want to be the person that barges in and separates the two without knowing," prioritizing the victim's well-being. At parties, indirect methods often involved asking sober male friends to help. Female participants commonly relied on male friends, with one noting, "My immediate response would be to ask a guy friend... to intervene." Male participants, however, expressed hesitance, citing uncertainty about the individuals' relationship. One remarked, "As a guy, I wouldn't, what if they're dating and just arguing and now I'm harassing them?" These findings highlight the preference for indirect action in unclear situations and the value of contextual understanding in shaping responses.

Reporting and Authority Involvement. Reporting incidents to authorities was often seen as the most appropriate response, especially when figures like instructors (Scenario 1) or library staff (Scenario 4) were present. In Scenario 1, many participants preferred involving instructors, considering it their responsibility. One shared, "I would probably ask or expect the instructor to intervene, and maybe they talk to them in their office hours or send them an email." However, some noted instructors might not act, stating, "There are instructors who wouldn't." In such cases, participants suggested reporting directly to administration if the instructor was unresponsive. In Scenario 4, participants were willing to report incidents to library staff or faculty but questioned its effectiveness. One remarked, "None of them [victim] would approach the staff; they would just kick them out of the library at most." Another expressed frustration with slow processes: "School was quick to deal with consequences, but at uni., it was very lengthy." This distrust led some to rely on friends instead, often escalating the situation. As one participant noted, "Admin and faculty are a little slow in taking action, so you usually involve friends, which ends up creating a messy situation." Authority intervention was least common in Scenario 2, where harassment occurred outside institutional settings. Here, participants favored direct or indirect bystander intervention, emphasizing the importance of visible authorities within institutional spaces.

Ignoring the Incident. Ignoring incidents of harassment, though rare, was reported for both verbal and physical harassment, with reasons varying. In Scenario 1, some participants ignored incidents, assuming the instructor would intervene: "I'd ignore or report him to the instructor after class." In Scenario 2, participants sometimes ignored physical harassment due to fear of escalating the situation: "I will not under any circumstances intervene… But I'd ask a guy to intervene." This shows that ignoring harassment involves complex dynamics, influenced by the situation and the bystander's perspective.

5 Design Solution

5.1 Design Objectives

To establish a link between the qualitative user research and the subsequent design solution presented in this study, we have formulated the following design objectives:

- **DO1:** Participants will be able to accurately identify instances of SH within the prototyped scenarios.
- **DO2:** When presented with options, participants will demonstrate the ability to take appropriate actions against SH.
- **DO3:** The prototype will foster decisive behavior among participants, thereby enhancing their capability to recognize SH and improving bystander intervention in real life situations.

5.2 Conceptual Design

Our research highlighted key insights on SH awareness, attitudes, and behaviors, shaped by both informal sources (family, peers, media) and formal institutions (awareness campaigns). From a young age, participants were taught about inappropriate behaviors by family members and teachers, with social media also playing a salient role. However, family discourse typically arose during national movements or high-profile cases, often involving sympathetic but sometimes biased views, ranging from concern to victim-blaming. Universities, particularly for students from all-girls schools, were often the first to introduce formal SH policies. However, many reported that university orientations involving passive mediums like slides, seminars, or infomercials, were forgettable. Even more engaging formats, like skits or live depictions, failed to leave lasting impressions on how to respond to or report SH. As one participant noted, "Uh, I do remember the play happening. I don't remember the content." We categorized awareness interventions into four types: (1) Seminars (talk-based, passive), (2) Assigned Reading Materials (policy briefs, handbooks), (3) Educational Videos and Re-enactments (visual/auditory, passive), and (4) Simulation-based VR Games (immersive, interactive). By evaluating these mediums based on engagement, empathy, knowledge retention, and actionable outcomes, we can identify more effective strategies for SH awareness and intervention.

5.3 Our Design

Our design incorporates three key features: a lecture, immersive scenarios, and a VR simulation. The first feature is a lecture that provides information on sexual misconduct terms, university policies, safety measures, and reporting procedures. The second feature presents immersive and interactive scenarios that illustrate different examples of SH, showing the possible actions bystanders can take in each case. The third feature is a VR simulation, where users witness SH scenarios as bystanders and must choose how to respond. Given that participants noted students often ignore the handbook or disengage during orientation lectures on SH due to their monotonous nature, we've designed an interactive game that students can engage with throughout their time at university, rather than limiting it to orientation alone.

Fig. 1. Screenshots from the lecture part of our design. In the first screenshot, *'ajeeb'* means strange in Urdu.

Figure 1 shows screenshots from the lecture section, where users learn about various types of SH and appropriate bystander actions. One scenario involves a student, Maryam, who experiences repeated unwanted attention from a classmate, Bilal. She later observes him engaging in inappropriate behavior with another student in the cafeteria. Maryam, who understands Bilal's intentions, is presented with different courses of action she can take, along with the potential outcomes of each response.

After the lecture, users proceed to the VR simulation (Fig. 2) to test their knowledge and decision-making. The VR shift lets users practice scenarios in real-time, offering an immersive experience to learn from mistakes without real-world consequences. This approach, similar to training for earthquakes or CPR, builds confidence and reduces reaction time, making bystander intervention feel automatic. Research shows that using multiple training methods improves sensitivity to SH scenarios. The goal is to enhance students' mental models as bystanders, preparing them for real situations. Figure 2 shows a stalking scenario where users decide how to intervene, receiving feedback to reinforce learning.

Fig. 2. Screenshots from the knowledge testing part of our design

5.4 Participants' Feedback on Our Design

We conducted idea testing with 20 university students in Lahore, Pakistan, to gather feedback on our design concept. Participants were shown visuals and videos of our design's lecture and VR scenarios, and their input helped refine the concept before moving to usability testing with functional prototypes. The feedback was overwhelmingly positive. Students appreciated the immersive and interactive nature of the VR experience, which they felt was a significant improvement over traditional methods. One participant remarked, "It's necessary to act out the situation, instead of just telling us about it in a university orientation lecture" [P1]. Others criticized traditional methods for being disengaging, with one noting, "In the slides, we had to read fast before the next slide appeared and I wouldn't want to read like that" [P3]. The narrative-driven VR approach was particularly favored. One participant stated, "People would prefer the narrative and storytelling aspect" [P2], and another suggested adding emotional elements to enhance impact: "Make it more emotional like the drama club performed during the orientation harassment session" [P4]. Additional recommendations included adding a self-assessment before the VR experience for better engagement and offering a completion certificate: "A certificate after the lectures and game scenarios would be good" [P13]. Participants appreciated the targeted focus on bystander intervention, seeing it as a much-needed tool for educating students about SH. One noted, "This is much needed in our university. It would genuinely educate a lot of students who have very wrong ideas about SH" [P9]. Many also compared it to engaging game-based assessments, with one participant saying, "It's like the c-factor tests we had to take for internships - that was very engaging" [P10]. The inclusion of VR technology was particularly well-received, with comments like, "The VR idea is very cool and fun" [P7], and participants felt it would attract students who might otherwise skip or ignore traditional lectures.

6 Discussion and Future Work

The study findings offer valuable insights into the Pakistani cultural context of sexual harassment (SH) and bystander intervention (BI), highlighting the decision-making processes involved when witnessing such incidents. While existing literature largely focuses on bystanders in Western contexts [9, 17, 29], our research introduces cultural nuances specific to Pakistan. Many of our findings align with global studies, but we also identified factors unique to our setting, such as bystanders' hesitancy to intervene due to fears of causing a scene, concerns about reputations, insufficient time to process the situation, uncertainty about whether the incident qualifies as harassment, lack of knowledge about reporting procedures, and distrust in institutional authorities. This is in line with extant literature on how cultural norms and SH literacy in South Asia influence bystander behavior in such cases [6] [32].

Our research, conducted within university settings, reveals that these hesitations are influenced by familial and institutional education, as well as broader environmental factors. Students often receive basic education about sexual misconduct from their families, especially parents, which shapes their values and perspectives. Educational institutions, including schools and universities, also play a significant role in shaping students' understanding of SH [29]. Additionally, the behavior of bystanders witnessed during childhood impacts how students respond to such incidents as adults. Given Pakistan's cultural and religious diversity, shifting students' mindsets quickly is challenging. However, interventions at the institutional level, particularly in universities, offer a more feasible approach. Universities host students from various cultural, ideological, and socioeconomic backgrounds, leading to differing levels of understanding and exposure to SH and bystander intervention. This diversity is influenced by cultural notions of consent, honor, and gender interactions [6]. Our design aims to standardize the SH education that students receive, as prior to university, many students either receive no education or only superficial lessons, assuming they already understand the issue.

Furthermore, our study revealed that participants tend to place more 'weightage' on harassment involving physical touch than on verbal or non-verbal harassment, which affects their bystander behavior, which corroborates existing research about how such behaviors stem from variations in perceptions about what constitutes as SH [33]. Students also expressed a lack of confidence in institutional authorities' ability to handle SH effectively and justly. To address these concerns, our design includes three main components. The first is a lecture that covers essential information about sexual misconduct terms, university policies, safety measures, and reporting procedures. This aims to clarify uncertainties about harassment and ensure students understand the reporting process, which will help build trust in institutional responses [19] [20].

The second component involves scenarios that illustrate different examples of SH and suggest possible bystander actions [21]. Once students feel confident in recognizing harassment and understanding their role as bystanders, their ability to respond effectively and quickly will improve [9] [21]. The third component is a VR simulation where students observe SH scenarios and practice responding as bystanders in a risk-free environment, helping them refine their actions in real-world situations, something that existing literature also alludes to [22]. A salient insight worth highlighting is that employing VR as a BI training tool is particularly effective for quick learning within short orientation periods, as demonstrated by our design solution. By focusing on brief training sessions, this approach also mitigates the risk of adverse plausibility illusion effects that can arise from prolonged VR exposure [34]. It is important to note that our goal is not to replace existing educational methods on sexual harassment and bystander intervention, but to complement them. The VR training is designed to reinforce institutional policies and prior awareness efforts by providing students with an immersive, practice-based learning experience that enhances their ability to act effectively in real-world situations.

In conclusion, while research on bystander approaches to SH exists, our study brings attention to the cultural context of SH education in Pakistan, adding a layer of nuance to the understanding of how bystanders categorize and respond to incidents. It also contributes to the growing body of research on VR training for SH, focusing specifically on bystander intervention. SH incidents are brief, leaving bystanders little time to react. Like earthquake or CPR training, our design allows users to practice responses repeatedly. However, unlike standardized emergency actions, SH incidents vary in severity, influencing bystander behavior. Participants in our study created "sub-scenarios" based on factors like the presence of an instructor or their relationship to the victim, showing that bystanders assess risks before acting. Our training must reflect this cost-benefit analysis while emphasizing that any action, direct or indirect, is important. Currently, we've only conducted brief concept testing. We plan to develop a full prototype for university freshmen orientations and conduct a longitudinal study on its impact. Future research will involve interviews with campus administrators to refine the intervention and include staff training to improve conflict resolution and trust in campus resources. Ultimately, the responsibility lies with universities to ensure perpetrators are held accountable, fostering trust in the reporting process. Our training design for university settings is adaptable to various cultural contexts, including those in the Global North, making it relevant for universities worldwide.

References

1. UNDP MCO in Jamaica: What is Sexual Harassment? UNDP (2020). https://www.undp.org/jamaica/what-sexual-harassment
2. Lim, S.C., Ghani, F., Remme, M.: Policy brief: Sexual harassment: A global problem. United Nations University, International Institute for Global Health, Kuala Lumpur (Malaysia) (2018). https://collections.unu.edu/eserv/UNU:7881/n2019-11-22_PB_SH_A_Global_Problem.pdf
3. Samo, S.: Confronting workforce harassment. The Express Tribune (2023). https://tribune.com.pk/story/2447230/confronting-workforce-harassment
4. Nizamani, S.: Unsafe campuses. DAWN.COM (2022). https://www.dawn.com/news/1679046
5. McDonald, P., Flood, M.G.: Encourage. Support. Act! Bystander approaches to sexual harassment in the workplace. The Australian Human Rights Commission (2012).
6. Asif, M., Bashir, S., Murtaza, D.G.: Impact of Sexual Harassment on Female Students' Educational Experience in Higher Education in Quetta City. J. policy res. 9(4), 198–216 (2023). https://doi.org/10.61506/02.00142
7. Ali, M. E. et al.: SafeStreet: empowering women against street harassment using a privacy-aware location-based application. In: Proceedings of the Seventh International Conference on Information and Communication Technologies and Development (ICTD '15). Association for Computing Machinery, New York, NY, USA, Article 24, 1–4 (2015). https://doi.org/10.1145/2737856.2737870
8. Ahmed, S.I et al.:. Protibadi: A platform for fighting sexual harassment in urban Bangladesh. In: Proceedings of the SIGCHI Conference on Human Factors in Computing Systems (CHI '14). Association for Computing Machinery, New York, NY, USA, 2695–2704 (2014). https://doi.org/10.1145/2556288.2557376

9. Lee, S.Y., Hanson, M.D., Cheung, H.K.: Incorporating bystander intervention into sexual harassment training. Ind. Organ. Psychol. **12**(1), 52–57 (2019). https://doi.org/10.1017/iop.2019.8

10. Bowes-Sperry, L., O'leary-Kelly, A.M.: To Act or Not to Act: The Dilemma Faced by Sexual Harassment Observers. The Academy of Management Review. **30**(2), 288–306 (2005). https://doi.org/10.2307/20159120

11. Banyard, V.L.: Who will help prevent sexual violence: Creating an ecological model of bystander intervention. Psychol. Violence **1**(3), 216–229 (2011). https://doi.org/10.1037/a0023739

12. Ford, K., Ham, L.S., Nguyen, A.M.T., Moore, T., Bridges, A.J., Quetsch, L.B.: Victim centered, aggressor focused, and bystander friendly: A qualitative analysis of bystander intervention strategies and outcomes for sexual harassment or assault. J. Interpers. Violence **39**(1–2), 184–213 (2024). https://doi.org/10.1177/08862605231195800

13. Latané, B., John M.D.: The unresponsive bystander: Why doesn't he help? (1970)

14. Deitz, S.R., Blackwell, K.T., Daley, P.C., Bentley, B.J.: Measurement of empathy toward rape victims and rapists. J. Pers. Soc. Psychol. **43**(2), 372–384 (1982). https://doi.org/10.1037/0022-3514.43.2.372

15. Sakalli-Uğurlu, N., Sila Yalçin, Z., Glick, P.: Ambivalent sexism, belief in a just world, and empathy as predictors of Turkish students' attitudes toward rape victims. Sex Roles: A Journal of Research. **57**(11–12), 889–895 (2007). https://doi.org/10.1007/s11199-007-9313-2

16. Banyard, V.L.: Who will help prevent sexual violence: Creating an ecological model of bystander intervention. Psychology of Violence. **1**(3), 216–229 (2011). https://doi.org/10.1037/a0023739

17. Lyons, M., Brewer, G., Caicedo, J.C., Andrade, M., Morales, M., Centifanti, L.: Barriers to sexual harassment bystander intervention in Ecuadorian universities. Glob. Public Health **17**(6), 1029–1040 (2022). https://doi.org/10.1080/17441692.2021.1884278

18. Ryan, A.M., Wessel, J.L.: Sexual orientation harassment in the workplace: When do observers intervene? J. Organ. Behav. **33**(4), 488–509 (2012). https://doi.org/10.1002/job.765

19. Djajadiningrat, T. et al.: Virtual trainer: A low-cost AR simulation of a sudden cardiac arrest emergency. In: Proceedings of the 2016 ACM Conference on Designing Interactive Systems (DIS '16). Association for Computing Machinery, New York, NY, USA, 607–618 (2016). https://doi.org/10.1145/2901790.2901914

20. McMahon, S., Banyard, V.L.: When can I help? A conceptual framework for the prevention of sexual violence through bystander intervention. Trauma Violence Abuse **13**(1), 3–14 (2012Jan). https://doi.org/10.1177/1524838011426015

21. Coker, A.L., et al.: Multi - college bystander intervention evaluation for violence prevention. Am. J. Prev. Med. **50**(3), 295–302 (2016). https://doi.org/10.1016/j.amepre.2015.08.034

22. Garcia, S., Abraham, S. J., Andujar, M.: Exploring Perceptions of Bystander Intervention Training using Virtual Reality. In: Proceedings of the 2021 ACM International Conference on Interactive Media Experiences (IMX '21). Association for Computing Machinery, New York, NY, USA, 253–257 (2021). https://doi.org/10.1145/3452918.3465497

23. Liebst, L.S., et al.: Social relations and presence of others predict bystander intervention: Evidence from violent incidents captured on CCTV. Aggressive Behav. **45**(6), 598–609 (2019). https://doi.org/10.1002/ab.21853

24. Do, H. J.: Do You Have Time for a Quick Chat? Designing a Conversational Interface for Sexual Harassment Prevention Training. In: Proceedings of the 26th International Conference on Intelligent User Interfaces (IUI '21). Association for Computing Machinery, New York, NY, USA, 542–552 (2021). https://doi.org/10.1145/3397481.3450659

25. Schewe, P. A., O'donohue, W.: Sexual Abuse Prevention with High-Risk Males: The Roles of Victim Empathy and Rape Myths. Violence and victims. **8**. 339–51 (1993). https://doi.org/10.1891/0886-6708.8.4.339

26. Sadeh-Sharvit, S. et al.: Virtual Reality in Sexual Harassment Prevention: Proof-of-Concept Study. In: Proceedings of the 21st ACM International Conference on Intelligent Virtual Agents (IVA '21). Association for Computing Machinery, New York, NY, USA, 87–89 (2021). https://doi.org/10.1145/3472306.3478356
27. Salas, E., Cannon-Bowers, J.A., Rhodenizer, L., Bowers, C.A.: Training in organizations: Myths, misconceptions, and mistaken assumptions. Res. Pers. Hum. Resour. Manag. **17**(1999), 123–162 (1999)
28. York, K.M., Barclay, L.A., & Zajack, A.B.: Preventing sexual harassment: The effect of multiple training methods. Employee Responsibilities and Rights Journal. **10**(4), 277–289 (1997)
29. Coker, A.L., et al.: Evaluation of the Green Dot bystander intervention to reduce interpersonal violence among college students across three campuses. Violence Against Women. **21**(12), 1507–1527 (2015). https://doi.org/10.1177/1077801214545284
30. Nova, A.: Discussing about Sexual Harassment (Breaking Silence): The Role of Technology. In: Proceedings of the 2016 CHI Conference Extended Abstracts on Human Factors in Computing Systems (CHI EA '16). Association for Computing Machinery, New York, NY, USA, 459–472 (2016). https://doi.org/10.1145/2851581.2892567
31. Maravilla, M.M. et al.: Defining virtual reality: Insights from research and practice. In: Conference 2019 Proceedings (2019). https://doi.org/10.21900/iconf.2019.103338
32. Imtiaz, S., Kamal, A.: Sexual harassment in the public places of Pakistan: Gender of perpetrators, gender differences and City differences among victims. Sex .Cult. **25**(5), 1808–1823 (2021)
33. Anwar, F., Österman, K., Björkqvist, K.: Three types of sexual harassment of females in public places in Pakistan. Çağdaş Tıp Dergisi. **9**(1), 65–73 (2019)
34. Guo, J. et al.: Exploring the differences of visual discomfort caused by long-term immersion between virtual environments and physical environments. In: 2020 IEEE Conference on virtual reality and 3D user interfaces (VR) (pp. 443–452). IEEE (2020)
35. Chang, A.A., Kazemi,E., Esmaeili,V., Davies, M.S.: The Effectiveness of Virtual Reality Training: A Systematic Review. J. Organ. Behav. 1–19 (2023). https://doi.org/10.1080/01608061.2023.2240767
36. Dubiel, A. et al.: Virtual reality for the training of soft skills for professional education: trends and op-portunities. Interactive Learning Environments. 1–21 (2025). https://doi.org/10.1080/10494820.2025.2450634
37. Leite, H., Vieira, L.R.: The use of virtual reality in human training: trends and a research agenda. Virtual Reality. **29**, (2025). https://doi.org/10.1007/s10055-024-01093-x

Measuring Altered States of Consciousness in Virtual Reality: A Systematic Analysis of Assessment Methods

Maria Laura Mele[1]([⊠]) [iD] and Hans Rutrecht[2] [iD]

[1] Myèsis Insight Center, Center for Research and Psychotherapy, Rome, Italy
m.mele@myesis.it
[2] MIND Foundation, Berlin, Germany
hans.rutrecht@mind-foundation.org

Abstract. The intersection of Virtual Reality (VR) and Altered States of Consciousness (ASCs) represents a notable research domain in experimental and clinical contexts, highlighting the growing interest in how immersive technologies can induce, modulate, and assess non-ordinary cognitive and emotional states. This study examines literature from 2014 to 2024, providing a review of the methodological frameworks and evaluation strategies used in examining VR-induced ASCs. Four primary methodological fields have been analyzed: (1) clinical and therapeutic research, (2) cognitive science and neurophysiology, (3) immersive technology and Human-Computer Interaction (HCI), and (4) psychological and phenomenological evaluation. Research indicates that VR-mediated ASCs can be systematically evaluated through multimodal techniques. The review reveals significant methodological inconsistencies, highlighting the lack of standardization in experimental designs, variability in measurement tools, and limited interdisciplinary integration. The review highlights the need for a standardized methodological framework that allows for replicable assessment of VR induced ASCs.

Keywords: Altered States of Consciousness (ASCs) · Virtual Reality (VR) · Assessment Methods

1 Introduction

Recent years have seen increased interest in the convergence of virtual reality (VR) and Altered States of Consciousness (ASCs), within the fields of experimental psychology and clinical research [1]. ASCs include the cognitive, perceptual, and emotional changes that differ from standard waking consciousness [2]. Such experiences typically involve significant changes in subjective experience, often including alterations in temporal and spatial perception, sense of agency, and self-referential awareness [2].

Conceptually, ASCs disrupt the structure of everyday experience [3], a mode of cognition described in phenomenology as a "natural attitude" [4] and in psychological literature through constructs such as reification (i.e., the practice of conceptualizing an

© The Author(s), under exclusive license to Springer Nature Switzerland AG 2026
J. Y. C. Chen et al. (Eds.): HCII 2025, LNCS 16338, pp. 113–130, 2026.
https://doi.org/10.1007/978-3-032-12808-9_8

abstract entity as though it possessed tangible existence), or absorption (i.e., a state of deep mental engagement or immersion) [3, 5–7]. ASCs have been also associated with neurocognitive processes such as dissociation (i.e., a disruption of normally integrated mental processes causing changes in consciousness, identity, memory, perception, or self-awareness) [8, 9], or cognitive defusion (i.e., the process of observing thoughts as transient mental events, reducing their emotional power and behavioral influence), [10, 11], alongside modulation of autonomic and neurophysiological markers [12].

Historically, ASCs have been used by humans for at least several hundred years [13], These have been reached by different techniques, many of which include the consumption of psychoactive substances, particularly –but not only– serotonergic-acting psychedelics, which act as potent 5-HT2A receptor agonists and produce significant changes in perception, emotions, and cognition while preserving wakeful awareness [14]. The revival of psychedelic research in the last twenty years has sparked renewed interest in the mechanisms of ASCs and their potential therapeutic applications [15]. Clinical research has demonstrated the efficacy of psychedelics in treating several psychiatric disorders, including Major Depressive Disorder (MDD) [16], treatment-resistant MDD [17], Post-Traumatic Stress Disorder (PTSD) [18], substance use disorders [19], and end-of-life anxiety [20]. The therapeutic potential of these compounds is most probably linked to their ability to induce ASCs [21], which improve cognitive and emotional flexibility [22], disrupt maladaptive self-referential processing [23], and promote neural plasticity through increased synaptogenesis [24], although it has also hypothesized that the effect could also be present without the psychedelic experience though not clinically tested [25]. The depth of psychedelic experience, characterized by phenomena such as self-reported "ego dissolution" (i.e., a temporary disruption of self-referential processing and diminished self-boundaries) [26], mystical-type states [27], and enhanced emotional processing [28], is acknowledged as a predictor of long-term therapeutic outcomes [29]. The findings suggest that ASCs may play a key role in the clinical benefits observed, providing a framework for understanding the effects of psychedelics that extend beyond their immediate pharmacological actions [21].

In addition to pharmacological methods, non-pharmacological techniques like mindfulness, breathwork, and hypnosis have emerged as effective approaches for inducing ASCs in both research and clinical contexts. These interventions affect ASCs to promote changes in perception, attention, and emotional processing, utilizing mechanisms akin to those found in psychedelic-assisted therapy [30–33]. These methods have shown effectiveness in influencing mood, alleviating pain, and improving psychological flexibility [34–36]. Neuroimaging studies indicate that non-pharmacological techniques, including mindfulness-based interventions, may enhance neural plasticity in brain regions associated with emotion regulation, demonstrating increased connectivity in individuals exposed to trauma [37], which is another similarity to the effect of psychedelics, which is used in clinical studies.

VR has emerged as a non-pharmacological technique in mental health, facilitating controlled and immersive environments for exposure therapy in anxiety disorders and phobias [38, 39], social skills training for individuals with autism spectrum disorder, and cognitive rehabilitation in schizophrenia [40]. In addition to these applications, VR has gathered interest for its capacity to elicit ASC-like experiences through modifications in sensory input, immersion, and presence [1]. Research indicates that VR can affect the perception of time and space, the experience of flow [41], create a sense of embodiment that transcends physical self-representation, and promote states of deep absorption akin to those produced by psychedelics [42]. The integration of pharmacological and non-pharmacological ASCs in influencing neural plasticity, emotional regulation, and self-perception underscores the necessity for further exploration of their common mechanisms. Considering the growing significance of VR in facilitating ASCs, it is important to evaluate the methodologies utilized to measure and articulate these conditions within immersive settings. This review examines the methodologies used to evaluate VR-induced ASCs, offering a framework to advance research in this emerging field and refine measurement techniques for experimental and clinical applications. It additionally explores the distinctions between traditional and VR-induced ASCs while proposing integrative methodological approaches applicable to both contexts.

2 Method

A literature search employing the Preferred Reporting Items for Systematic Reviews and Meta-Analyses (PRISMA) methodology [43] was performed in December 2024 across multiple academic databases (Scopus, Web of Science, PubMed, IEEE Xplore, Google Scholar) to guarantee thorough coverage of research on assessment methodologies for VR-induced ASCs. The chosen keywords were obtained from the Population, Intervention, Comparison, and Outcome (PICO) framework [43]. The search query encompasses terms associated with immersive technologies, including "Virtual Reality," "Augmented Reality," and "Immersive Technology," as well as ASCs such as "Psychedelic Experience," "Altered States of Consciousness," and "Perceptual Alteration." Additionally, it includes psychophysiological and clinical applications, including "Perception," "Cognition," "Neurophysiology," "Mental Health," "Therapy," and "Psychotherapy." The final search string employed Boolean operators "AND" and "OR" to improve retrieval across databases, ensuring the inclusion of both experimental and clinical studies. The query was refined iteratively to enhance relevance and representativeness in the research domain.

The inclusion and exclusion criteria were rigorously established, limiting selection to peer-reviewed empirical studies, clinical trials, systematic reviews, meta-analyses, and neuroscience-focused research published between 2014 and 2024, specifically concerning the assessment of VR-induced ASCs. We excluded studies published before 2014, non-peer-reviewed publications, theoretical contributions, and research involving populations outside the 18–65 years age range (see Fig. 1). Duplicate records across databases were systematically identified and removed (see Fig. 1). The screening process (initial title and abstract evaluations followed by full-text review) was independently performed by the authors (M.L.M., H.R.), with discrepancies resolved by consensus. Data extraction and categorization of studies were structured according to application contexts, assessment methodologies, and technological approaches. Additionally, methodological quality and risk of bias were critically assessed. The review specifically addressed the integration of multimodal assessment techniques, including psychometric, physiological, and behavioral data, in VR-induced ASC research.[3, 5–7] shows the flow diagram followed for the systematic reviews according to PRISMA 2020 [43].

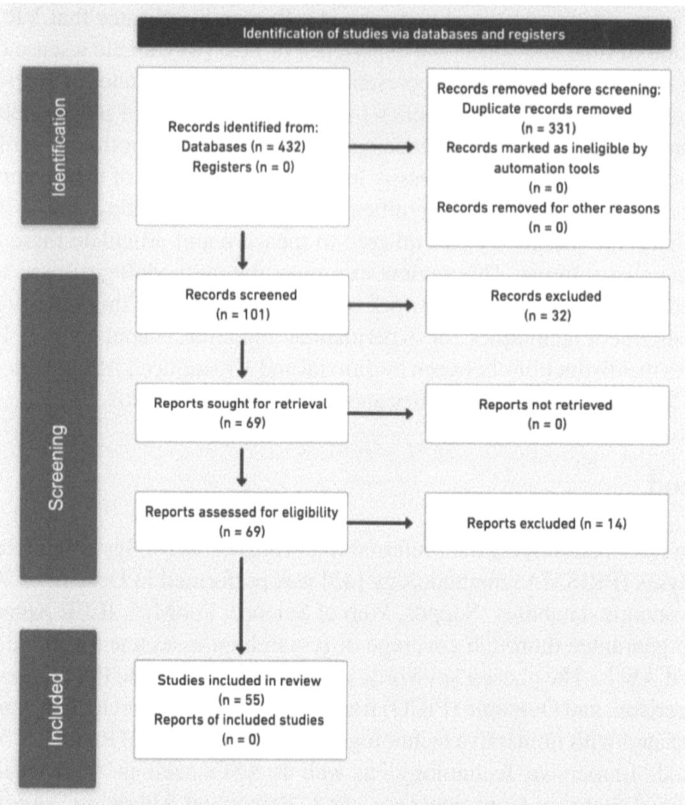

Fig. 1. PRISMA 2020 flow diagram for new systematic reviews [43].

3 Results

This paper reviewed 55 papers (Fig. 1), with the objective of identifying the main methodologies used in the literature for assessing ASCs in VR (Fig. 1). The methodological approaches employed in the reviewed studies were classified into four principal categories: (1) clinical and therapeutic research, (2) cognitive science and neurophysiology, (3) immersive technology and Human-Computer Interaction (HCI), and (4) psychological and phenomenological assessment. The next two sections and Table 1 (Tab. 1) describe the methods used by the Literature for the assessment of VR-Induced ASCs, and the findings according to the four main categories classifying the reviewed studies.

Table 1. The table categorizes the findings per category and application fields.

	Self-report scales	Physiological measures	Neurophysiological metrics	Behaviolar assessment
1. Clinical and therapeutic	[1, 15, 18, 20, 31, 33, 34, 36, 38, 44, 45, 49, 53–55]	[52]	[23, 52]	[10, 22, 35]
2. Cognitive science and Neurophysiology	[51]	[52]	[19, 21, 23, 24, 30, 52]	[8, 9, 11]

(continued)

Table 1. (*continued*)

	Self-report scales	Physiological measures	Neurophysiological metrics	Behaviolar assessment
3. Immersive technology and HCI	[1, 36–40, 43–45, 49, 53–55]	-	-	-
4. Psychological and phenomenological measures	[2–7, 13, 14, 16, 17, 20, 25–29, 32, 40–42, 46–48, 50]	[12]	[19, 24, 30]	[8]

3.1 Methods for Evaluating VR-Induced ASCs

This section describes the primary methodological approaches used to assess ASCs in virtual reality experiences. The methods are categorized into self-report measures, which assess subjective experiences and phenomenological aspects of the experience, and objective methods, which provide quantifiable physiological and behavioral data (Tab. 1).

Self-Report Methods. Various self-report scales are utilized to evaluate emotional and cognitive changes resulting from VR experiences. The following instruments appear across the following multiple research categories.

5D-ASCs (Altered States of Consciousness Rating Scale). The Altered States of Consciousness Rating Scale (5D-ASCs) [44] quantifies the effects of VR exposure on individuals' states of consciousness and emotional responses [45–47]. The 5D-ASCs questionnaire evaluates five dimensions of ASCs: ego disintegration, ineffability, complexity, visual impressions, and aural experiences. Research on psychedelics and meditation typically emphasizes the assessment of subjective experiences and effects through the quantification of experience intensity during ASCs. The 5D-ASCs scale is a validated instrument for assessing users' subjective experiences in VR environments, offering insights into the effects of immersion on cognitive and emotional states during therapeutic interventions [48].

PANAS (Positive and Negative Affect Schedule). The Positive and Negative Affect Schedule (PANAS) [49] is the most commonly employed method to assess changes in mood and subjective experiences during VR sessions. The primary objective of this scales is to capture immediate emotional responses that may arise in immersive environments. Positive affect (PA) and negative affect (NA) are two dimensions of mood assessed by the PANAS. Participants receive a list of words linked to both positive and negative emotions and are instructed to evaluate the degree to which they have experienced each emotion within a specified period. This tool assesses emotional states and their connections to behaviors and psychological disorders in clinical and research contexts.

Presence Ratings. Presence ratings [50] evaluate the degree of immersion individuals experience in the virtual environment, a factor associated with the effectiveness of exposure-based therapies in diminishing avoidance behaviors and enhancing emotional engagement [47, 51]. The participant is asked to score their experience of presence, usually in terms of feeling physically present in the virtual environment, using a sequence of questions or items.

MEQ-30 (Mystical Experiences Questionnaire). Another commonly used method for assessing emotional changes is the Mystical Experiences Questionnaire (MEQ-30) [52]. In particular, the MEQ-30 assesses the characteristics and intensity of spiritual experiences. The instrument consists of thirty items that evaluate various aspects of mystical experiences, such as ineffability, transcendence, and unity. This instrument is primarily used in psychological and phenomenological assessment approaches.

MAAS (Mindful Attention Awareness Scale). The Mindful Attention Awareness Scale (MAAS) [53] is another commonly used tool in mindfulness-based VR interventions, helping to assess the level of mindfulness, i.e., their attention and awareness in the present, that participants experience during virtual relaxation exercises. The 15 items on the test measure how frequently a person can be totally present and involved in their current experience without becoming judgmental or reactive. This scale has been used in the literature for capturing changes in attentional focus and emotional awareness during VR-enhanced relaxation techniques [53].

Objective Methods. Different objective methods are being used in the literature to assess VR experiences, as described in this subsection.

EEG (Electroencephalography). Brain activity is tracked using Electroencephalography (EEG), particularly during relaxation states [54]. Elevated alpha and beta waves have been associated with relaxed and focused mental states, and EEG studies frequently monitor these neural responses during VR interventions, particularly when evaluating their efficacy in managing anxiety disorders [55–57]. To monitor the effects of these therapies, EEG measures, particularly the analysis of theta and beta oscillations, are frequently employed [57]. These measures help assess changes in brain activity that correlate with emotional states and stress reduction, providing data on how VR interventions might impact mood disorders [58]. EEG has been employed across multiple research categories to identify changes in these oscillations during VR-induced states, offering a deeper understanding of the effects of immersive experiences on neural processes [59, 60]. EEG analyses are also employed to assess engagement levels during VR exposure. These measurements provide a non-pharmacological method for inducing neural synchrony patterns, which are typically associated with meditation and psychedelic states [61–64].

fMRI (Functional Magnetic Resonance Imaging). Functional neuroimaging techniques such as fMRI have demonstrated the engagement of neural networks associated with perception, attention, and self-referential processing in VR settings [65, 66]. Studies employing fMRI [67–69] have shown that engagement with VR affects activity in the Default Mode Network (DMN), sensorimotor areas, and limbic circuits, which are patterns commonly linked to ASCs induced by psychedelics [61, 70, 71]. These neuroimaging methods allow researchers to track changes in brain activity, such as reductions in alpha power and increases in gamma oscillations, which suggest heightened sensory integration and enhanced cognitive flexibility during VR exposure [67–69].

Physiological Measures. Physiological responses, including Galvanic Skin Response (GSR) and Heart Rate Variability (HRV), are measured to monitor the reactions of the autonomic nervous system to VR interventions. These measures serve as indicators of emotional arousal and stress regulation in the context of psychological therapy [47, 72, 73]. Delivering timely feedback to patients about their emotional conditions via biofeedback, which tracks physiological metrics like HRV in real-time, can be an effective approach in VR-based therapy, as highlighted by Khazan [74]. In domains like trauma recovery and palliative care, therapies that integrate VR with biofeedback to regulate physiological responses and improve emotional well-being have demonstrated promising results [75, 76]. Studies show that the integration of biofeedback within VR environments enhances the therapeutic process by promoting emotional self-regulation [73].

Behavioral Assessments. Behavioral avoidance tests (BATs) [77] measure the reduction in avoidance responses, a common symptom of PTSD, during the exposure to virtual scenarios [78]. BATs usually require exposing the feared stimulus gradually, beginning with less stressful elements and working up to more difficult ones. In order to determine the efficacy of treatment procedures like exposure therapy for anxiety disorders or phobias, the objective is to measure the participant's desire to interact with the feared stimulus and gradually decrease avoidance behaviors [71, 79, 80].

Cognitive Performance Metrics. Cognitive performance metrics [81], such as task-switching and executive function assessments, are regularly used to evaluate the effectiveness of VR-based cognitive training and reminiscence therapy, particularly in dementia patients [40]. These assessments provide objective data on how VR interventions affect cognitive flexibility, memory recall, and overall cognitive functioning. The use of such tests is important in determining the efficacy of VR in slowing cognitive decline and improving quality of life in individuals with neurodegenerative diseases [82].

Multisensory Perception Metrics. Multisensory perception metrics [83] are used in VR-integrated relaxation techniques to monitor and enhance emotional balance [71, 84]. These metrics assess how well the VR environment stimulates various sensory modalities (e.g., visual, auditory, tactile), contributing to the overall relaxation experience [55, 85]. By tracking the effectiveness of multisensory environments, therapists can better understand how VR affects emotional and physiological relaxation, as well as its potential to promote deeper states of calmness and improved sleep quality [73, 83].

3.2 Findings by Research Category

The following section shows the key findings from the literature review, organized according to the four methodological categories identified in our analysis (Tab. 1), i.e., (1) clinical and therapeutic research, (2) cognitive science and neurophysiology, (3) immersive technology and Human-Computer Interaction., and (4) psychological and phenomenological assessment. Each category represents a separate research approach to assessing ASCs in VR. While some overlap exists in the methods employed across categories, the findings highlight how different research perspectives contribute to our understanding of VR-induced ASCs.

1. **Clinical and Therapeutic Research.** This category focuses on methodologies used to evaluate the therapeutic applications of VR-induced ASCs in clinical settings. It encompasses approaches for assessing emotional, cognitive, and behavioral changes in patients undergoing VR therapy for various psychological conditions. Unlike the other categories, clinical and therapeutic research specifically examines the efficacy

of VR as a treatment modality, with particular emphasis on measurable therapeutic outcomes and patient responses.

Numerous studies demonstrate the effectiveness of VR as a therapeutic intervention, particularly for phobias, MDD, anxiety disorders, and PTSD [40, 51, 70, 72, 84, 86, 87]. Virtual Reality Exposure Therapy (VRET) is increasingly recognized as an effective treatment for phobias, PTSD, and anxiety disorders [40, 45–47, 51, 72, 84, 86, 87]. In PTSD treatment [45, 72, 86, 88], VR exposure therapies are evaluated through behavioral avoidance tests [77] and presence ratings [50].

In the context of MDD, VR-based therapies have been shown to advance emotional regulation and neuroplasticity by integrating nature-based and embodied experiences into therapeutic settings [38, 40, 87]. Research has repeatedly shown that VR-based relaxation techniques, including guided meditation, result in a significant decrease in cortisol levels and enhance stress tolerance [72, 89, 90].

The effectiveness of VR interventions in sustaining patient engagement represents a significant aspect of evaluation. Studies indicate that the interactive elements of VR, including real-time feedback and immersive scenarios, significantly contribute to improving treatment retention, particularly for individuals who might be less inclined to participate in conventional therapy methods [49, 78].

Meta-analyses indicate that biofeedback, real-time monitoring, and personalized therapeutic environments are essential components in improving the efficacy of VR interventions [91, 92]. Customizable VR interventions support the creation of individualized treatment plans[75], allowing for the adjustment of virtual scenarios to meet the needs of patients, thereby improving therapeutic outcomes [71, 84].

2. **Cognitive Science and Neurophysiology.** This category examines the neural mechanisms and cognitive processes underlying VR-induced ASCs through objective neuroimaging and psychophysiological techniques. It is distinguished from the other categories by its focus on quantifiable brain activity and neurological responses, providing empirical evidence of how VR experiences alter neural networks and cognitive functions.

The neurophysiological mechanisms underlying VR-induced ASC have been explored using different neuroimaging and psychophysiological techniques. A number of studies employ EEG, functional Magnetic Resonance Imaging (fMRI), and autonomic nervous system measures to assess the neural activity changes associated with immersive VR experiences [65–69]. These techniques facilitate monitoring brain wave oscillations, including alpha, theta, and gamma oscillations, which are generally linked to meditative states, cognitive flexibility, and self-transcendence.

The immersive characteristics of VR enable accurate adjustments of sensory input, leading to perceptual alterations such as modified spatial awareness, adjusted body ownership, and cohesive multisensory experiences. Studies investigating these perceptual shifts often utilize EEG alongside behavioral assessments to evaluate the neuroplastic changes associated with VR experiences. For instance, VR can create visual distortions, recalibrate proprioception, and alter self-perception in ways that are similar to psychedelic experiences [59, 60, 92]. The observed changes are associated with change in the neural activity of specific brain regions, including the primary visual cortex and posterior parietal areas [59, 60, 92].

Researchers have employed VR to investigate changes in self-perception [93] and the concept of "ego dissolution," both of which are significant components in the examination of ASCs. Various VR scenarios have been employed by researchers to investigate the functioning of the anterior cingulate cortex (ACC) and medial prefrontal cortex (mPFC). The ACC and mPFC are recognized for their significant involvement in the processing of self-referential information and metacognition. EEG and fMRI serve as tools for monitoring alterations in brain activity throughout immersive VR experiences [58, 62]. Additionally, virtual embodiment paradigms in VR have demonstrated changes in self-boundaries, offering compelling evidence for VR's capacity to investigate ASCs [80, 91].

The investigation of attentional and affective networks has been conducted through VR-based methods. Engagement with immersive virtual environments intended to elicit emotions like awe, flow, or relaxation has been linked to significant alterations in brain activity [41]. Studies utilizing fMRI and EEG have shown that these VR environments can diminish amygdala reactivity and enhance connectivity between prefrontal and limbic structures [67–69]. The findings align with observations made in psychedelic therapy models, highlighting the emotional breakthroughs that result from altered states [84, 94].

Recent findings from structural MRI studies [67–69] indicate that consistent interaction with VR-based altered states could facilitate neuroplastic changes, including alterations in gray matter volume in areas like the anterior insula and ACC. The results align closely with observations made in long-term studies of meditation and psychedelic experiences. Research suggests that these structural changes could enhance cognitive resilience and emotional flexibility, which may explain the therapeutic advantages of VR interventions [67–69].

3. **Immersive Technology and Human-Computer Interaction.** This category investigates how technological parameters and interface design influence the quality and intensity of VR-induced ASCs. Unlike the other categories, it specifically examines the relationship between technical aspects of VR systems (such as sensory feedback) and the resulting altered states. This approach focuses on how technological innovations can be optimized to enhance immersion and presence in virtual environments.

Research analyzing immersion ratings, presence scales, and biofeedback-driven VR indicates that audiovisual synchrony, interactive environments, and sensory augmentation play a key role in influencing the depth and intensity of VR-induced ASCs [91]. The studies typically assess immersion depth, presence, and subjective absorption through the application of defined scales and metrics.

VR and immersive environments rely on technological parameters such as visual realism, interactivity, and spatialized audio to enhance the sense of presence. The assessment of presence is commonly carried out through presence scales, which measure the user's perceived engagement with the virtual world. Studies demonstrate that presence correlates with activation in the parietal and occipital cortices, indicating that the perceptual fidelity of an immersive experience is important for achieving higher levels of immersion [61, 62] Additionally, technological elements such as head-tracking latency and resolution play a key role in determining the quality of presence, thereby affecting sensory congruence and embodiment effects [80, 91].

The concept of virtual embodiment, defined by the experience of occupying a digital avatar, has been analyzed for its effects on body representation and self-perception. The methods used to evaluate this phenomenon generally consist of changing the perspective from which a user views their avatar and incorporating visuotactile synchrony, which enhances the feeling of body ownership [93]. The evaluation of these effects generally necessitates the analysis of brain regions associated with somatosensory and premotor processing [58, 71]. Experimental designs that include avatar customization demonstrate a notable impact on self-representation in VR environments. The observed influence can subsequently affect identity processing and cognitive biases, suggesting significant applications in therapeutic and rehabilitative contexts [38, 62].

The advancement of HCI has led to the development of adaptive VR interfaces that modify in real time according to user conditions. The interfaces employ biofeedback metrics, including EEG, and direction of gaze including precise eye-movements to adapt the VR environment in real-time according to the user's cognitive load and emotional condition. EEG is frequently employed to assess brain activity in VR sessions, while HRV is measured to observe responses from the autonomic nervous system [61, 87].

4. **Psychological and Phenomenological Assessment**. This category explores the subjective experiences and psychological dimensions of VR-induced ASCs through qualitative and introspective methodologies. It differs from the other categories by prioritizing experiential qualities and phenomenological analyses of altered states. While other approaches focus on measurable outcomes or neural correlates, psychological and phenomenological assessment also captures the lived experience and meaning-making processes associated with VR-induced altered states of consciousness.

Subjective reports and phenomenological analyses are essential to understand the experiential aspects of VR-induced ASC. Research employing psychometric tools such as the MEQ-30 [52], Ego Dissolution Inventory (EDI) [95], and 5D-ASCs [48] has yielded significant insights into the capacity of VR to promote transcendental experiences, altered self-perception, and heightened emotional intensity. These scales evaluate subjective experiences in VR, emphasizing emotional changes, the dissolution of self-boundaries, and perceptual distortions, which are essential to understand the phenomenology of ASCs.

Neurophenomenology offers a framework for examining ASCs in VR by integrating subjective reports with neurophysiological data. Research utilizing first-person methodologies alongside EEG or fMRI data demonstrates correlations between particular neural dynamics and phenomenological aspects, including ego dissolution and mystical-type experiences [38, 87]. These studies generally employ EEG to observe brain wave patterns and determine which neural oscillations are associated with reported experiences of altered states. This interdisciplinary approach improves the accuracy of ASCs measurement and provides insights into the neural mechanisms that underlie alterations in consciousness induced by VR.

Comparative analyses of psychedelic experiences and VR-induced ASCs demonstrate similarities in perceptual alterations, dissolution of self-boundaries, and heightened emotional responses [61, 63, 96, 97]. Studies employing VR-based psychedelic simulations demonstrate increased visual distortions, synesthetic experiences, and intensified emotional responses, commonly associated with substances such as psilocybin and LSD [60, 97]. Perceptual changes are frequently assessed through self-report questionnaires that record participants' experiences of altered states. Behavioral tests assessing cognitive flexibility and emotional responses are commonly incorporated to provide a thorough evaluation of the effects of ASCs. Phenomenological research underscores the importance of immersive presence in affecting the intensity of ASCs, suggesting that more interactive environments amplify dissociative and self-transcendent effects [71, 91].

4 Discussion

The application of VR to facilitate ASCs has gained importance in different fields, such as therapeutic settings and cognitive science. Assessing ASCs presents a distinct challenge, necessitating a thorough approach that integrates subjective, physiological, and neurophysiological measures (Tab. 1). Each metric presents unique advantages; however, it is essential to acknowledge the limitations that must be addressed in future research. This study analyzes the different metrics utilized in VR-based ASC research, concentrating on four main categories: self-report scales, physiological measurements, neurophysiological metrics, and behavioral assessments, and by four main application fields: clinical and therapeutic research, cognitive science and neurophysiology, immersive technology and HCI, and psychological and phenomenological assessment. This analysis assesses the metrics employed by each group, their applications, and the challenges faced.

Self-report scales are commonly utilized to evaluate the subjective experiences of participants engaged in VR-based interventions. The MEQ-30, the 5D-ASC, and the EDI are frequently utilized to assess the intensity and quality of altered states [48, 52, 95]. These tools effectively capture experiences including transcendental states, emotional intensity, and alterations in self-perception.

These self-report measures, however, have specific limitations. The primary concern is their reliance on participants' ability to accurately and consistently report their experiences. Interpretative variations, emotional states, and the social desirability of particular responses may skew the data. Self-reported data may be subject to retrospective bias, as participants may alter their recollections of experiences after the fact. While these scales provide valuable insights into the subjective experience of VR-induced ASCs, caution is warranted in their interpretation, particularly when evaluated alone.

Physiological measurements provide an objective method for evaluating VR-induced ASCs by recording real-time alterations in bodily responses. Physiological metrics frequently employed include HRV and GSR, which collectively offer insights into the reactions of the autonomic nervous system to VR stimuli [47, 59, 60, 73], These measures are effective for assessing emotional arousal, stress regulation, and engagement in immersive VR experiences.

GSR is frequently utilized in virtual reality environments to assess arousal levels when individuals are exposed to distressing stimuli, particularly in VR-based phobia treatments [64, 98]. Although these metrics are useful for quantifying autonomic responses, they also possess limitations. HRV may be affected by external factors, including baseline fitness level and medication use, complicating the attribution of changes exclusively to the VR intervention. Furthermore, GSR exhibits sensitivity to different emotional and physiological states, indicating that it may not consistently yield precise insights into the specific nature of emotional responses.

Physiological metrics are essential for assessing VR-induced ASCs, especially when integrated with self-report scales and neurophysiological data, despite persistent challenges. Their provision of objective data enhances the validation and contextualization of subjective experiences.

Neurophysiological measures, including EEG and fMRI, facilitate the understanding of how VR-induced ASC influences brain activity. EEG quantifies variations in brainwave activity, encompassing alpha, theta, and gamma waves, which are frequently associated with meditative states, cognitive flexibility, and transcendence [59, 60, 66, 68, 69, 92]. Immersive virtual reality experiences frequently alter brainwave patterns, providing immediate insights into individuals' cognitive and emotional states.

fMRI studies demonstrate that VR affects activity in regions such as the DMN, sensorimotor areas, and limbic circuits, associated with perception, self-referential processing, and emotional regulation [68, 69, 92]. The findings correspond with patterns observed in psychedelic-induced states, indicating that VR may function as a non-pharmacological method for eliciting comparable neural dynamics such as altered sense of self, immersive sensory experiences, and changes in default mode network connectivity without the risks associated with pharmacological interventions. Nonetheless, the constraints of these neuroimaging tools should be recognized. EEG provides superior temporal resolution but is deficient in spatial resolution, hindering the precise identification of the neural sources of oscillatory activity. fMRI offers high spatial resolution; however, it is limited by low temporal resolution and is susceptible to motion artifacts, which may pose challenges in immersive VR environments.

The increasing usage of EEG-based tools in VR research enables real-time modifications of immersive experiences based on the user's neurophysiological state [92]. Given the early stage of the technology, evaluations are ongoing to study the accuracy of BCI technology in practical virtual reality contexts.

A key method to ascertain the impact of ASCs in VR on individuals is to examine their behavior [77, 78]. This method evaluates an individual's response speed, cognitive flexibility, and inhibitory control. Response time measures elucidate the impact of VR exposure on cognitive processing speed and concentration, as evidenced by studies on PTSD and phobias. Research indicates that negative virtual reality stimuli reduce avoidance tendencies, often measured through behavioral avoidance [77, 78].

In VR-based cognitive training, tasks like task-switching performance and executive function assessments are employed to measure alterations in cognitive flexibility and memory recall [82]. These tasks offer significant insights into the cognitive effects of VR interventions, especially in clinical populations, including individuals with dementia or depression. The limitation of behavioral assessments lies in their dependence on a narrow range of tasks, which may inadequately reflect the comprehensive array of cognitive and emotional changes that occur during virtual reality exposure. Additionally, these tasks may be affected by several external factors, such as participant motivation, previous experience with similar tasks, and baseline cognitive abilities.

In conclusion, different metrics are utilized to evaluate VR-induced ASCs, each possessing distinct strengths and limitations. Self-report scales are the predominant method for assessing subjective experiences; however, they are constrained by their dependence on participant introspection and interpretation. Physiological metrics provide objective data regarding emotional arousal and autonomic regulation, but they may be affected by external factors. Neurophysiological metrics such as EEG and fMRI provide significant insights into brain activity during virtual reality experiences, though they are constrained by temporal and spatial limitations. Behavioral assessments offer a means to quantify cognitive and emotional changes; nonetheless, they are limited by task selection and variability among participants. Future research should prioritize the enhancement of these metrics and explore methods for their integration to advance the understanding of VR-induced altered states of consciousness.

5 Conclusion

This review demonstrates that VR possesses significant potential for the activation and modification of ASCs in clinical and research contexts. The findings indicate that VR has significant potential as a non-pharmacological intervention for inducing ASCs, offering a new approach to addressing mental health disorders. The review highlights the significance of methodological standardization and the incorporation of multimodal approaches, encompassing physiological, psychological, and phenomenological assessments of ASCs resulting from VR. The potential seems to be promising, however, there are still open challenges, especially regarding the subjectivity of self-report scales such as the MEQ-30 and 5D-ASC, which are essential for evaluating emotional and cognitive changes. The scales necessitate the integration of objective measures such as EEG and HRV to enable a thorough evaluation of VR-induced ASC. Integrating these metrics into a standardized framework is crucial for overcoming the limitations present in current methodologies. The review emphasizes the significance of enhancing VR technologies, increasing accessibility, and refining VR systems for customized user experiences. Given the increasing evidence for the therapeutic potential of virtual reality, additional research is necessary to investigate the long-term effects of VR-induced ASCs, especially in therapeutic contexts. Enhancing measurement tools and promoting collaboration between cognitive scientists and VR developers can improve the application of VR in clinical environments.

Disclosure of Interests. The authors have no competing interests to declare that are relevant to the content of this article.

References

1. Casu, M., Farrauto, C., Farruggio, G., Bellissima, S., Battiato, S., Caponnetto, P.: Exploring the therapeutic potential of virtual reality: A review on the simulation of psychedelic effects for treating psychological disorders. Psychol. Int. **6**(2), 603–617 (2024)

2. Hartogsohn, I.: Cyberdelics in context: On the prospects and challenges of mind-manifesting technologies. *Front. Psychol.* **13** (2023). https://doi.org/10.3389/fpsyg.2022.1073235

3. Timmermann, C., et al.: A neurophenomenological approach to non-ordinary states of consciousness: hypnosis, meditation, and psychedelics. Trends Cogn. Sci. **27**(2), 139–159 (2023)

4. Husserl, E., Moran, D.: Ideas: General introduction to pure phenomenology. Routledge (2012)

5. Demertzi, A. et al.: Hypnosis modulates behavioural measures and subjective ratings about external and internal awareness. J. Physiol.-Paris. **109**(4–6), 173–179 (2015)

6. Lifshitz, M., Van Elk, M., Luhrmann, T.M.: Absorption and spiritual experience: A review of evidence and potential mechanisms. Conscious. Cogn. **73**, 102760 (2019)

7. Tellegen, A., Atkinson, G.: Openness to absorbing and self-altering experiences (' absorption'), a trait related to hypnotic susceptibility. J. Abnorm. Psychol. **83**(3), 268 (1974)

8. Lutz, A. et al.: Investigating the phenomenological matrix of mindfulness-related practices from a neurocognitive perspective. Am. Psychol. **70**(7), 632 (2015)

9. Lynn, S.J., Green, J.P.: The sociocognitive and dissociation theories of hypnosis: Toward a rapprochement. Int. J. Clin. Exp. Hypn. **59**(3), 277–293 (2011)

10. Fletcher, L., Hayes, S.C.: Relational frame theory, acceptance and commitment therapy, and a functional analytic definition of mindfulness. J. Ration.-Emotive Cogn.-Behav. Ther. **23**, 315–336 (2005)

11. Papies, E.K. et al.: The benefits of simply observing: mindful attention modulates the link between motivation and behavior. J. Pers. Soc. Psychol. **108**(1), 148 (2015)

12. Oswald, V., et al.: Autonomic nervous system modulation during self-induced non-ordinary states of consciousness. Sci. Rep. **13**(1), 15811 (2023)

13. Merlin, M.D.: Archaeological evidence for the tradition of psychoactive plant use in the old world. Econ. Bot. **57**(3), 295–323 (2003)

14. Nichols, D.E.: Psychedelics. Pharmacol. Rev. **68**(2), 264–355 (2016)

15. Nichols, D.E., Walter, H.: The history of psychedelics in psychiatry. Pharmacopsychiatry **54**(04), 151–166 (2021)

16. Davis, A.K., et al.: Effects of psilocybin-assisted therapy on major depressive disorder: A randomized clinical trial. JAMA Psychiat. **78**(5), 481–489 (2021)

17. Fond, G., et al.: Ketamine administration in depressive disorders: A systematic review and meta-analysis. Psychopharmacology **231**, 3663–3676 (2014)

18. Rucker, J.J., Iliff, J., Nutt, D.J.: Psychiatry & the psychedelic drugs. Past, present & future. Neuropharmacology **142**, 200–218 (2018)

19. Krebs, T.S., Johansen, P.-Ø.: Lysergic acid diethylamide (LSD) for alcoholism: Meta-analysis of randomized controlled trials. J. Psychopharmacol. (Oxf.) **26**(7), 994–1002 (2012)

20. Yu, C.-L., et al.: Psilocybin for end-of-life anxiety symptoms: A systematic review and meta-analysis. Psychiatry Investig. **18**(10), 958 (2021)

21. van Elk, M., Yaden, D.B.: Pharmacological, neural, and psychological mechanisms underlying psychedelics: A critical review. Neurosci. Biobehav. Rev. **140**, 104793 (2022)

22. Davis, A.K., Barrett, F.S., Griffiths, R.R.: Psychological flexibility mediates the relations between acute psychedelic effects and subjective decreases in depression and anxiety. J. Context. Behav. Sci. **15**, 39–45 (2020)

23. Raichle, M.E.: The brain's default mode network. Annu. Rev. Neurosci. **38**(1), 433–447 (2015)

24. De Gregorio, D., et al.: Repeated lysergic acid diethylamide (LSD) reverses stress-induced anxiety-like behavior, cortical synaptogenesis deficits and serotonergic neurotransmission decline. Neuropsychopharmacology **47**(6), 1188–1198 (2022)
25. Vollenweider, F.X., Kometer, M.: The neurobiology of psychedelic drugs: Implications for the treatment of mood disorders. Nat. Rev. Neurosci. **11**(9), 642–651 (2010)
26. Letheby, C., Gerrans, P.: Self unbound: Ego dissolution in psychedelic experience. Neurosci. Conscious. **2017**(1), nix016 (2017)
27. Griffiths, R.R., Richards, W.A., McCann, U., Jesse, R.: Psilocybin can occasion mystical-type experiences having substantial and sustained personal meaning and spiritual significance. Psychopharmacology **187**, 268–283 (2006)
28. Kirkpatrick, M.G., Lee, R., Wardle, M.C., Jacob, S., De Wit, H.: Effects of MDMA and intranasal oxytocin on social and emotional processing. Neuropsychopharmacology **39**(7), 1654–1663 (2014)
29. Roseman, L., Haijen, E., Idialu-Ikato, K., Kaelen, M., Watts, R., Carhart-Harris, R.: Emotional breakthrough and psychedelics: dalidation of the emotional breakthrough inventory. J. Psychopharmacol. (Oxf.) **33**(9), 1076–1087 (2019)
30. Qiu, T.T., Minda, J.P.: Psychedelic experiences and mindfulness are associated with improved wellbeing. J. Psychoactive Drugs **55**(2), 123–133 (2023)
31. Radakovic, C., Radakovic, R., Peryer, G., Geere, J.-A.: Psychedelics and mindfulness: A systematic review and meta-analysis. J. Psychedelic Stud. **6**(2), 137–153 (2022)
32. Lewis-Healey, E. et al.: Breathwork-induced psychedelic experiences modulate neural dynamics. Cereb. Cortex. **34**(8), bhae347 (2024)
33. Lemercier, C.E., Terhune, D.B.: Psychedelics and hypnosis: Commonalities and therapeutic implications. J. Psychopharmacol. (Oxf.) **32**(7), 732–740 (2018)
34. Poletti, S., Abdoun, O., Zorn, J., Lutz, A.: Pain regulation during mindfulness meditation: Phenomenological fingerprints in novices and experts practitioners. Eur. J. Pain **25**(7), 1583–1602 (2021)
35. Fincham, G.W., Epel, E., Colasanti, A., Strauss, C., Cavanagh, K.: Effects of brief remote high ventilation breathwork with retention on mental health and wellbeing: A randomised placebo-controlled trial. Sci. Rep. **14**(1), 16893 (2024)
36. Lynn, S.J., Green, J.P., Polizzi, C.P., Ellenberg, S., Gautam, A., Aksen, D.: Hypnosis, hypnotic phenomena, and hypnotic responsiveness: Clinical and research foundations—A 40-year perspective. Int. J. Clin. Exp. Hypn. **67**(4), 475–511 (2019)
37. King, A.P., et al.: Altered default mode network (DMN) resting state functional connectivity following a mindfulness-based exposure therapy for posttraumatic stress disorder (PTSD) in combat veterans of Afghanistan and Iraq. Depress. Anxiety **33**(4), 289–299 (2016)
38. Gómez-Busto, F.J., Ortiz, M.I.: Virtual reality and psychedelics for the treatment of psychiatric disease: A systematic literature review. Clin. Neuropsychiatry **17**(6), 365 (2020)
39. Kim, S., Kim, E.: The use of virtual reality in psychiatry: A review. J. Korean Acad. Child Adolesc. Psychiatry. **31**(1), 26 (2020)
40. Park, M.J., Kim, D.J., Lee, U., Na, E.J., Jeon, H.J.: A literature overview of virtual reality (VR) in treatment of psychiatric disorders: Recent advances and limitations. Front. Psychiatry. **10**, 505 (2019)
41. Rutrecht, H., Wittmann, M., Khoshnoud, S., Igarzábal, F.A.: Time speeds up during flow states: A study in virtual reality with the video game thumper. Timing Time Percept. **9**(4), 353–376 (2021)
42. Glowacki, D.R.: VR models of death and psychedelics: an aesthetic paradigm for design beyond day-to-day phenomenology. Front. Virtual Real. **4** (2023), https://doi.org/10.3389/frvir.2023.1286950
43. Page, M.J., et al.: The PRISMA 2020 statement: An updated guideline for reporting systematic reviews. BMJ **372**, n71 (2021). https://doi.org/10.1136/bmj.n71

44. Dittrich, A., Lamparter, D., Maurer, M.: 5D-ASC: Questionnaire for the assessment of altered states of consciousness. Short Introd. Zurich Switz. Psin Plus. (2010)

45. Bosman, I.D.V. et al.: Note: The relationship of visual and aural perspective with decentering in virtual reality. In: Presented at the ACM International Conference Proceeding Series, pp. 15–18 (2023). https://doi.org/10.1145/3628096.3628741

46. Du Sert, O.P., et al.: Virtual reality therapy for refractory auditory verbal hallucinations in schizophrenia: A pilot clinical trial. Schizophr. Res. **197**, 176–181 (2018)

47. Wang, X. et al.: Reducing stress and anxiety in the metaverse: A systematic review of meditation, mindfulness and virtual reality. In: Presented at the Proceedings of the Tenth International Symposium of Chinese CHI, pp. 170–180 (2022)

48. Studerus, E., Gamma, A., Vollenweider, F.X.: Psychometric evaluation of the altered states of consciousness rating scale (OAV). PLoS ONE **5**(8), e12412 (2010)

49. Watson, D., Clark, L. A., Tellegen, A.: Development and validation of brief measures of positive and negative affect: the PANAS scales. J. Pers. Soc. Psychol. **54**(6), 1063 (1988)

50. Hein, D., Mai, C., Hußmann, H.: The usage of presence measurements in research: a review. In: Presented at the Proceedings of the International Society for Presence Research Annual Conference (Presence). The International Society for Presence Research Prague, pp. 21–22 (2018)

51. Botella, C., Fernández-Álvarez, J., Guillén, V., García-Palacios, A., Baños, R.: Recent progress in virtual reality exposure therapy for phobias: A systematic review. Curr. Psychiatry Rep. **19**, 1–13 (2017)

52. MacLean, K.A., Leoutsakos, J.S., Johnson, M.W., Griffiths, R.R.: Factor analysis of the mystical experience questionnaire: A study of experiences occasioned by the hallucinogen psilocybin. J. Sci. Study Relig. **51**(4), 721–737 (2012)

53. Brown, K.W., Ryan, R.M.: Mindful attention awareness scale. J. Pers. Soc. Psychol. (2003)

54. Jindra, R.: Handbook of electroencephalography and clinical neurophysiology| Vol. 5, BA Remond (ed.-in-chief). Evaluation of bioelectrical data from brain, nerve and muscle—II. MAB Brazier & DO Walter (eds). EEG topography. H. Petsche (ed.). Elsevier, Amsterdam (1972). 84 pp (1979)

55. Boeldt, D., McMahon, E., McFaul, M., Greenleaf, W.: Using virtual reality exposure therapy to enhance treatment of anxiety disorders: Identifying areas of clinical adoption and potential obstacles. Front. Psychiatry. **10**, 773 (2019)

56. Cieślik, B., Mazurek, J., Rutkowski, S., Kiper, P., Turolla, A., Szczepańska-Gieracha, J.: Virtual reality in psychiatric disorders: A systematic review of reviews. Complement. Ther. Med. **52**, 102480 (2020)

57. Jerath, R., Beveridge, C.: Harnessing the Spatial Foundation of Mind in Breaking Vicious Cycles in Anxiety, Insomnia, and Depression: The Future of Virtual Reality Therapy Applications. Front. Psychiatry. **12** (2021). https://doi.org/10.3389/fpsyt.2021.645289

58. Horváth, L., Szummer, C., Szabo, A.: Weak phantasy and visionary phantasy: The phenomenological significance of altered states of consciousness. Phenomenol. Cogn. Sci. **17**, 117–129 (2018)

59. Denzer, S. et al.: Electrophysiological (EEG) microstates during dream-like bizarre experiences in a naturalistic scenario using immersive virtual reality. Eur. J. Neurosci. (2024)

60. Mattek, S., Walsh, A.: Increases in EEG Alpha Power and Beta Power Following a VR Psychedelic Journey (2024)

61. Glowacki, D.R. et al.: Isness: Using multi-person VR to design peak mystical type experiences comparable to psychedelics. In: Presented at the Conference on Human Factors in Computing Systems - Proceedings (2020). https://doi.org/10.1145/3313831.3376649

62. Liu, Y. et al.: How Are Your Zombie Accounts? Understanding Users' Practices and Expectations on Mobile App Account Deletion. In: Presented at the

Proceedings of the 31st USENIX Security Symposium, Security 2022, pp. 863–880 (2022). https://www.scopus.com/inward/record.uri?eid=2-s2.0-85140959422&partnerID=40&md5=2cfd02b536e18d7c443edb2ef03aab74

63. Vidal, J. et al.: Inducing selflessness through a numadelic virtual reality experience: A preliminary study. Available SSRN 4947164 (2024)

64. Weech, S., Kenny, S., Barnett-Cowan, M.: Presence and cybersickness in virtual reality are negatively related: A review. Front. Psychol. **10**(FEB) (2019). https://doi.org/10.3389/fpsyg.2019.00158

65. Adamovich, S., August, K., Merians, A., Tunik, E.: A virtual reality-based system integrated with FMRI to study neural mechanisms of action observation-execution: a proof of concept study. Restor. Neurol. Neurosci. **27**(3), 209–223 (2009)

66. Lenormand, D., Piolino, P.: In search of a naturalistic neuroimaging approach: Exploration of general feasibility through the case of VR-fMRI and application in the domain of episodic memory. Neurosci. Biobehav. Rev. **133**, 104499 (2022)

67. Mishra, S., Kumar, A., Padmanabhan, P., Gulyás, B.: Neurophysiological correlates of cognition as revealed by virtual reality: Delving the brain with a synergistic approach. Brain Sci. **11**(1), 51 (2021)

68. Hur, J.-W., et al.: Virtual reality–based psychotherapy in social anxiety disorder: fMRI study using a self-referential task. Jmir Ment. Health. **8**(4), e25731 (2021)

69. Hong, C.C.-H., Fallon, J.H., Friston, K.J.: FMRI evidence for default mode network deactivation associated with rapid eye movements in sleep. Brain Sci. **11**(11), 1528 (2021)

70. Aday, J.S., Davoli, C.C., Bloesch, E.K.: Psychedelics and virtual reality: Parallels and applications. Ther. Adv. Psychopharmacol. **10** (2020)

71. Heinzerling, K.G. et al.: Nature-themed video intervention may improve cardiovascular safety of psilocybin-assisted therapy for alcohol use disorder. Front. Psychiatry. **14** (2023). https://doi.org/10.3389/fpsyt.2023.1215972

72. Adam, S., Frewen, P.: Mystical experiences in virtual reality. Psychol. Conscious. Theory Res. Pract. (2024)

73. Sarris, J., Halman, A., Urokohara, A., Lehrner, M., Perkins, D.: Artificial intelligence and psychedelic medicine. Ann. N. Y. Acad. Sci. **1540**(1), 5–12 (2024). https://doi.org/10.1111/nyas.15229

74. Khazan, I.Z.: The clinical handbook of biofeedback: A step-by-step guide for training and practice with mindfulness. John Wiley & Sons (2013)

75. Chung, O.S. et al.: Implementation of Therapeutic Virtual Reality Into Psychiatric Care: Clinicians' and Service Managers' Perspectives. Front. Psychiatry. **12** (2022). https://doi.org/10.3389/fpsyt.2021.791123

76. Ng, R. et al.: Participatory design of a virtual reality life review therapy system for palliative care. Front. Virtual Real. **5** (2024). https://doi.org/10.3389/frvir.2024.1304615

77. Steketee, G., Chambless, D.L., Tran, G.Q., Worden, H., Gillis, M.M.: Behavioral avoidance test for obsessive compulsive disorder. Behav. Res. Ther. **34**(1), 73–83 (1996)

78. Witmer, B.G., Singer, M.J.: Measuring presence in virtual environments: A presence questionnaire. Presence **7**(3), 225–240 (1998)

79. De Pisapia, N., Penazzi, G., Ibarra, I.D.J.H., Rastelli, C., Zancanaro, M.: Immersive cave environments in VR: A tool for exploring altered states of consciousness and creativity in archaeology. Preprints (2024). https://doi.org/10.20944/preprints202411.1541.v1

80. Peled-Avron, L., Aday, J.S., Kalafateli, A.L., Hamilton, H.K., Woolley, J.D.: Down the rabbit hole–the psychological and neural mechanisms of psychedelic compounds and their use in treating mental health and medical conditions. Front. Psychiatry. **15**, 1431389 (2024)

81. Carroll, J.B.: Human cognitive abilities: A survey of factor-analytic studies, no. 1. Cambridge university press (1993)

82. Miller, N. et al.: Awedyssey: Design tensions in eliciting self-transcendent emotions in virtual reality to support mental well-being and connection. In: Presented at the Proceedings of the 2023 ACM Designing Interactive Systems Conference, pp. 189–211 (2023)

83. Calvert, G., Spence, C., Stein, B.E.: The handbook of multisensory processes. MIT press (2004)

84. Freitas, J.R.S., et al.: Virtual reality exposure treatment in phobias: A systematic review. Psychiatr. Q. **92**(4), 1685–1710 (2021)

85. Adrien, V. et al.: Beyond virtual reality: Towards screen-free interfaces for post-traumatic stress disorder interventions (2023)

86. Carl, E., et al.: Virtual reality exposure therapy for anxiety and related disorders: A meta-analysis of randomized controlled trials. J. Anxiety Disord. **61**, 27–36 (2019)

87. Kaup, K.K., Vasser, M., Tulver, K., Munk, M., Pikamäe, J., Aru, J.: Psychedelic replications in virtual reality and their potential as a therapeutic instrument: an open-label feasibility study. Front. Psychiatry. **14**, 1088896 (2023)

88. Frewen, P. et al.: Proof of concept of an eclectic, integrative therapeutic approach to mental health and well-being through virtual reality technology. Front. Psychol. **11** (2020). https://doi.org/10.3389/fpsyg.2020.00858

89. Bosman, I.D.V. et al.: Virtual Reality for Mindfulness: Aspects for Helping or Hindering Focus and Practice. In: Presented at the ACM International Conference Proceeding Series, pp. 264–269 (2024). https://doi.org/10.1145/3681716.3689446

90. Chirico, A., Gaggioli, A.: The potential role of awe for depression: Reassembling the puzzle. Front. Psychol. **12** (2021). https://doi.org/10.3389/fpsyg.2021.617715

91. Jung, S., Buruk, O., Hamari, J.: Altered states of consciousness in human-computer interaction: A review. In: Presented at the Nordic Human-Computer Interaction Conference, pp. 1–13 (2022)

92. Värbu, K., Muhammad, N., Muhammad, Y.: Past, Present, and Future of EEG-Based BCI Applications. Sensors. **22**(9) (2022), https://doi.org/10.3390/s22093331

93. Madary, M., Metzinger, T.K.: Real virtuality: A code of ethical conduct. Recommendations for good scientific practice and the consumers of VR-technology. Frontiers in Robotics and AI. **3**(3) (2016)

94. Rastelli, C., Greco, A., Kenett, Y.N., Finocchiaro, C., De Pisapia, N.: Simulated visual hallucinations in virtual reality enhance cognitive flexibility. Sci. Rep. **12**(1), 4027 (2022). https://doi.org/10.1038/s41598-022-08047-w

95. Nour, M.M., Evans, L., Nutt, D., Carhart-Harris, R.L.: Ego-dissolution and psychedelics: validation of the ego-dissolution inventory (EDI). Front. Hum. Neurosci. **10**, 269 (2016)

96. Glowacki, D. R. et al.: Dissolving yourself in connection to others: Shared experiences of ego attenuation and connectedness during group VR experiences can be comparable to psychedelics. ArXiv Prepr (2021). ArXiv210507796

97. Glowacki, D.R., et al.: Group VR experiences can produce ego attenuation and connectedness comparable to psychedelics. Sci. Rep. **12**(1), 8995 (2022)

98. Liu, P. et al.: Virtual Transcendent Dream: Empowering People through Embodied Flying in Virtual Reality. In: Presented at the Conference on Human Factors in Computing Systems - Proceedings (2022). https://doi.org/10.1145/3491102.3517677

The Impact of Racial Congruence on Learning Performance in Virtual Reality: Investigating the Mediating Role of Self-efficacy

J.-C. Sakdavong[✉] [iD], K. Souche, and R. Ville

UFR Psychologie, Laboratoire Cognition, Langues, Langage, Ergonomie (CLLE), Université Toulouse Jean Jaurès, Toulouse, France
`jean-christophe.sakdavong@univ-tlse2.fr`

Abstract. This study investigated the impact of racial congruence between instructors and learners on learning performance within a virtual reality (VR) environment, and the mediating role of self-efficacy. Participants (N = 25) were randomly assigned to interact with either a racially congruent or incongruent virtual instructor while undergoing safety training in a virtual construction site. We hypothesized that self-efficacy would mediate the effect of racial congruence on learning performance. The study found that learners with racially congruent instructors in VR showed superior learning performance and higher self-efficacy. While self-efficacy was a significant predictor of learning, we could not prove that it acts as a mediator between racial congruence and learning performance. These findings highlight the potential of VR for investigating social dynamics in learning and emphasize the importance of representation.

Keywords: Racial congruence · Self-efficacy · Virtual reality · Avatar · Minorities

1 Introduction

1.1 Racial Congruence

Racial congruence refers to the presence of same-race peers or instructors in an educational setting. It enhances students' sense of social belonging and engagement, particularly for minority students [1]. When students are matched with same-race instructors, academic performance improves and negative teacher perceptions decrease [2]. These effects are strongest among minority students, who are more likely to experience isolation or exclusion in predominantly white school settings [1].

Racial congruence improves academic performance for both Black and White students [2]. Students matched with same-race teachers are perceived as less disruptive and more engaged. According to Dee [2], these effects reflect both psychological and interpretive biases related to race. When instructors share the same racial background as students, they are seen as more supportive and engaged, which can enhance motivation and learning [3] [4].

J. Y. C. Chen et al. (Eds.): HCII 2025, LNCS 16338, pp. 131–142, 2026.
https://doi.org/10.1007/978-3-032-12808-9_9

Racial congruence also influences teacher expectations, which are known to affect long-term academic outcomes. Black students assigned to same-race teachers are more likely to be perceived as capable of completing postsecondary education [5]. These effects may arise through mechanisms such as role-model identification and reduced stereotype threat, which shape both teacher judgments and student self-beliefs [5]. Teacher expectations function as self-fulfilling prophecies and contribute to students' future academic trajectories [5].

Racial congruence between students and online instructors improves engagement and course completion among historically marginalized students. In virtual high school settings, students matched with same-race instructors were more likely to complete assignments and report positive experiences with their teachers [6]. These effects were particularly strong among Black students and were independent of instructor quality or prior student achievement [6]. Shared racial identity appears to support student–teacher rapport and fosters academic perseverance in online environments [6].

1.2 Social Cognitive Theory and Self-efficacy

Social cognitive theory [7] postulates that self-efficacy plays a crucial role in motivating and persevering learners in the face of academic difficulties. As stated before, self-efficacy is influenced by social models with which learners identify, like racial congruence [4]. Social cognitive theory states that learning is enhanced when learners observe models they identify with [7]. In classrooms, perceived similarity between students and instructors strengthens this effect and supports performance. This mechanism is relevant to racial congruence, which may increase learning by enhancing model identification [7] [2].

Self-efficacy influences how students approach learning. Learners who believe they can succeed are more likely to attempt difficult tasks and persist longer [8]. This belief drives effort, strategy use, and emotional regulation during learning. Zimmerman [8] emphasizes that self-efficacy predicts academic achievement more accurately than prior performance. For our study, this belief highlights how perceptions of capability can mediate the effect of racial congruence on task success.

Self-efficacy develops through mastery experiences, social persuasion, and observational learning [9]. Instructors play a critical role in shaping these sources. Schunk [9] shows that learners observing relatable models performing well are more likely to develop high self-efficacy.

Teacher feedback and representation help students build confidence in their ability to succeed. This is especially true for students facing learning difficulties, who benefit from feeling supported and understood [10]. When students see instructors as allies who resemble them, motivation and resilience increase. Similarly, Liao et al. [11] found that self-efficacy is a strong predictor of persistence in marginalized learners. These findings justify the inclusion of self-efficacy as a mediating variable in our study, especially for underrepresented students who may benefit from racially congruent instructors.

1.3 Social Cognitive Theory and Self-efficacy

Virtual Reality (VR) offers a unique environment for investigating social influences on learning by providing realistic and controllable experimental settings [12]. The technology allows for the creation of lifelike scenarios that enhance ecological validity, making participants feel a strong sense of presence and behave as they would in real life [13] [14]. A key advantage of VR is the ability to manipulate an instructor's avatar - for instance, by changing its race to match that of the learner - while keeping all other variables constant. This technique is used to study phenomena like the Proteus Effect, where the characteristics of an avatar influence the user's own behavior and attitudes [15].

As stated before, research in traditional educational settings has established that racial congruence between students and instructors can significantly enhance academic performance [2] [4]. These effects are particularly pronounced for minority students, who report feeling more cared for and trying harder in classes taught by instructors of the same race [3]. While this principle is well-documented in physical classrooms and online modules [6], research begins to explore its manifestation in immersive virtual environments. Studies in VR show that perceived similarity with a virtual agent can increase engagement and trust, which are precursors to effective learning [16]. While direct experimental evidence on instructor-learner racial congruence and learning performance in VR is still emerging, related work demonstrates the potent influence of avatar appearance. For example, embodying an avatar of a different race has been shown to reduce implicit racial bias [17], and the perceived ethnicity of a virtual human can alter user perceptions and decision-making [18], illustrating the value of avatar representation. Garros and Sakdavong [19] have shown that a learner's identification with the teacher's avatar increases self-efficacy in a virtual environment. Sakdavong and Ville [20] have shown that racial congruence between learner and teacher's avatar race increases learning performance.

1.4 Synthesis

According to social cognitive theory, learning is enhanced when individuals observe and identify with models they perceive as similar to themselves [7]. This identification is a cornerstone of self-efficacy: a learner's belief in their own capability to succeed [8]. Self-efficacy is heavily influenced by social models and is a strong predictor of academic achievement. In virtual environments, these principles may be amplified; observing a competent avatar that shares one's characteristics could powerfully boost self-efficacy by making success seem more attainable. Given that racial congruence fosters identification [3], it is plausible that its potential positive effects on performance in VR are mediated by an increase in self-efficacy. The present study, therefore, leverages the unique capabilities of VR to investigate this specific pathway, addressing a gap in the literature by directly testing if the benefits of racial congruence extend to a VR learning setting and examining the mediating role of self-efficacy. As these effects are affecting learning outcomes for minorities [1], this study will focus on learners who belong to minority groups.

1.5 Hypothesis

For learners belonging to minorities, perceived self-efficacy mediates the relationship between racial congruence (between the learner and the instructor's avatar) and VR learning performance.

2 Material and Method

2.1 Participants

The study included 25 participants (14 female, 11 male) with a mean age of 29.4 for female (SD = 9.87) and 28.7 years for male (SD = 7.34). Participants were recruited through personal networks, professional contacts, and community events. Racial diversity of minorities for France was represented by Asian (N = 3), North African (N = 12) and Black (N = 10) participants. Individuals with prior knowledge of construction site safety, incapacitating illnesses, or conditions that could introduce bias (e.g., color blindness) were excluded.

2.2 Experimental Design

Participants were randomly assigned to one of two groups:

Group 1 (N = 10): Exposed to a racially congruent virtual instructor.

Group 2 (N = 15): Exposed to a racially incongruent virtual instructor.

All participants were exposed to an instructor of the same gender to control for potential gender-related effects.

2.3 Materials

VR Headset: Meta Quest 3 standalone VR with 2,064 × 2,208 per-eye LCD displays with pancake lenses, Field of View (FOV) of 110 ° horizontally and 96 ° vertically, and 6DoF tracking.

VR Simulation: A custom-designed VR construction site safety training program developed in Unity3D by the AD2RV non-profit association. The simulation involved a guided tour of a virtual construction site, where the instructor pointed out potential hazards and safety measures.

Instructors' avatars: 4 customized Meta Horizon avatars (Asian, North African, Black, and Caucasian) with female and male versions.

Instructors' Voices: Male voice recorded; female voice generated by transforming the male voice.

2.4 Questionnaires

The first questionnaire collected informed consent form, demographic data, and information on VR experience.

The second questionnaire asked: 1) to rank the perceived self-efficacy about identifying hazards and setting up the proper signage in a construction site using a 7-point Likert scale according to [7]; 2) to answer a series of 10 multiple-choice questions assessment about the learning. Each MCQ question was accompanied by an image describing a construction site scene.

2.5 Procedure

We started by asking the participant to fill out the first questionnaire (demographics). Then, we placed the VR headset on the participant's head. They had two minutes to explore the virtual environment and get used to the controls. After this familiarization period, the learning phase began. The participant followed a virtual instructor through a construction site, where the instructor explained safety signs and potential hazards. The instructor's avatar either matched the participant's ethnicity (congruent condition) or did not (incongruent condition). After the session, the participant answered the second questionnaire (self-efficacy and assessment). We ended with a debriefing to explain the real goal of the study, which had been hidden to preserve ecological validity. Figure 1.

Fig. 1. Participant interacting with a virtual Black or Caucasian instructor during safety training.

3 Results

3.1 Mediation

Mediation occurs when a third variable explains the relationship between an independent and dependent variable. In this study, we propose that self-efficacy mediates the relationship between racial congruence and learning performance. This means that the effect of racial congruence on learning performance is not only direct but also occurs indirectly through its influence on self-efficacy. In other words, racial congruence can boost students' self-efficacy, and this increased self-efficacy, in turn, leads to improved learning performance.

The main hypothesis "For learners belonging to minorities, perceived self-efficacy mediates the relationship between racial congruence (between the learner and the instructor's avatar) and VR learning performance" was analyzed using Baron and Kenny [21] method as shown in Fig. 2.

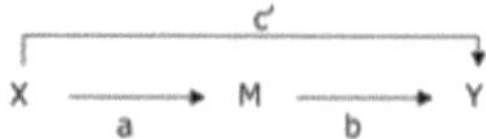

	Analysis	Visual Depiction
Step 1	Conduct a simple regression analysis with X predicting Y to test for path c alone, $Y = B_0 + B_1 X + e$	
Step 2	Conduct a simple regression analysis with X predicting M to test for path a, $M = B_0 + B_1 X + e$.	
Step 3	Conduct a simple regression analysis with M predicting Y to test the significance of path b alone, $Y = B_0 + B_1 M + e$.	
Step 4	Conduct a multiple regression analysis with X and M predicting Y, $Y = B_0 + B_1 X + B_2 M + e$	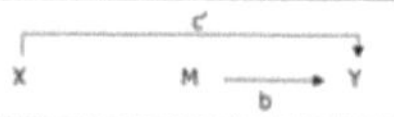

Fig. 2. Adaptation of mediation analysis steps according to Baron and Kenny [21] where X is the independent variable, Y the dependent variable and M the mediator variable.

The four steps are represented by the following operational hypotheses:

OH1: The racial congruence between learner and instructor's avatar improves learning performance.

OH2: The racial congruence between learner and instructor's avatar increases the level of perceived self-efficacy.

OH3: The higher is the perceived self-efficacy, the better is the learning performance.

OH4: While conducting a multiple regression analysis between the racial congruence and the perceived level of self-efficacy to predict the learning performance, the racial congruence is not predicting the learning performance while the perceived level of self-efficacy does.

Verifying OH1. Regarding learning performance, participants exposed to a congruent instructor obtained an average learning performance score of 17.4 (SD = 2.46) compared to 13.6 (SD = 3.69) for the incongruent group. Both groups got a normal distribution and homogeneity of variances.

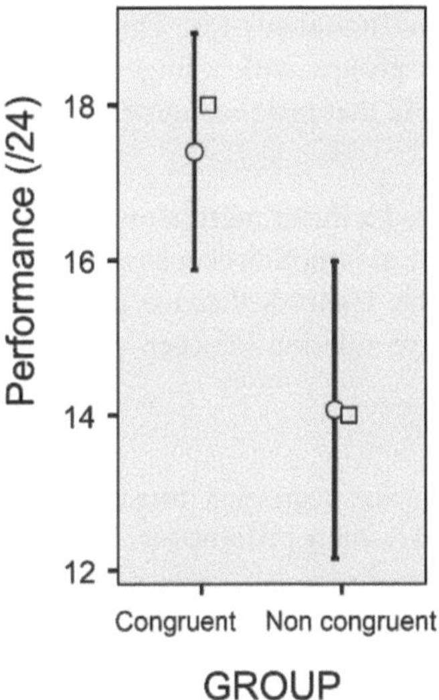

Fig. 3. Difference of learning performance between congruent and non-congruent groups.

Inferential analysis involved a student t-test. This test revealed a significant difference in performance between the groups with a wide effect size ($p = 0.011$, d $= 1.0$), confirming the hypothesis OH1 that racial congruence improves learning (Fig. 3).

Verifying OH2. Regarding perceived self-efficacy (measured between 1 and 7), participants exposed to a congruent instructor obtained an average score of 5.6 (SD $= 1.17$) compared to 4.13 (SD $= 1.51$) for the incongruent group. Both groups got a normal distribution and homogeneity of variances.

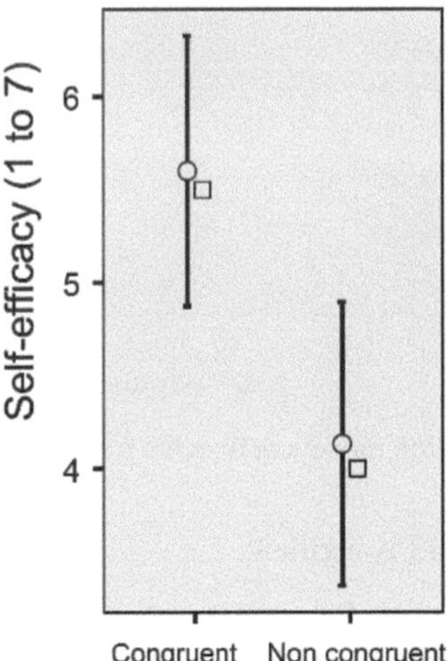

Fig. 4. Difference of perceived self-efficacy between congruent and non-congruent groups.

Inferential analysis involved a student t-test. This test revealed a significant difference in performance between the groups with a huge effect size ($p = 0.008$, d $= 1.06$), confirming the hypothesis OH2 that racial congruence improves perceived self-efficacy (Fig. 4).

Verifying OH3. We processed a linear regression between perceived self-efficacy and learning performance as all the assumption checks were good (autocorrelation, collinearity and normality). The Table 1 shows that we got a significative linear regression. The Fig. 5 shows the positive relation between perceived self-efficacy and learning performance.

Table 1. Linear regression between perceived self-efficacy and learning performance.

Model Fit Measures				
Model	R	R^2		
1	0.441	*0.195*		
Predictor	**Estimate**	**SE**	*t*	*p*
Intercept	10.45	2.203	4.74	*< .001*
Self-efficacy	1.05	0.445	2.36	*.027*

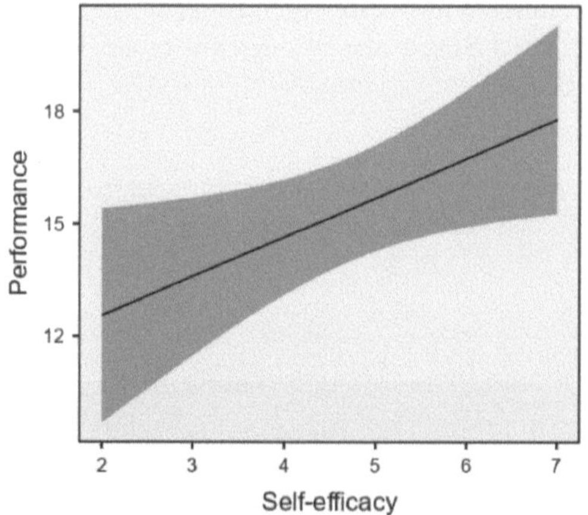

Fig. 5. Regression model coefficients for learning performance.

We can conclude that OH3 is verified.

Verifying OH4. We processed a linear regression between congruence and perceived self-efficacy as factor for learning performance as all the assumption checks were good (autocorrelation, collinearity and normality).

The Table 2 shows that we did not find a significant linear regression.

Table 2. Linear regression between congruence groups + perceived self-efficacy and learning performance.

Predictor	Estimate	SE	t	p
Intercept	13.534	2.938	4.61	$< .001$
Group (non congruent-congruent)	−2.321	1.515	−1.53	*.140*
Self-efficacy	0.690	0.491	1.41	*.174*

These results do not support our mediation hypothesis. The loss of significance for both predictors in the multiple regression model suggests that the strong correlation between racial congruence and self-efficacy (as demonstrated in OH2) introduces multicollinearity, making it statistically difficult to disentangle their unique effects on learning performance.

4   Discussion

4.1   Summary of Results

This study found that racial congruence positively impacts learning performance and perceived self-efficacy) in a VR environment (OH1 and OH2 in Fig. 6): Participants who interacted with a racially congruent instructor showed significantly better learning than those who interacted with a racially incongruent instructor, they also got a significantly higher perceived self-efficacy. The effect size was huge for both. This result is in line with results from [2] [4] [6] [20] for learning performance improvement and from [4] [19] for a better perceived self-efficacy.

Contrary to our initial hypothesis, this effect was not mediated by perceived self-efficacy after experiencing the racial congruence (or incongruence). This means that perceived self-efficacy is not the explanatory variable between racial congruence and learning performance. Nevertheless, perceived self-efficacy explained 19.5% of the learning performance through a significant linear regression (OH3 in Fig. 6) highlighting its importance in the learning process as found [22].

The Fig. 6 shows the positive relationships between our three main variables.

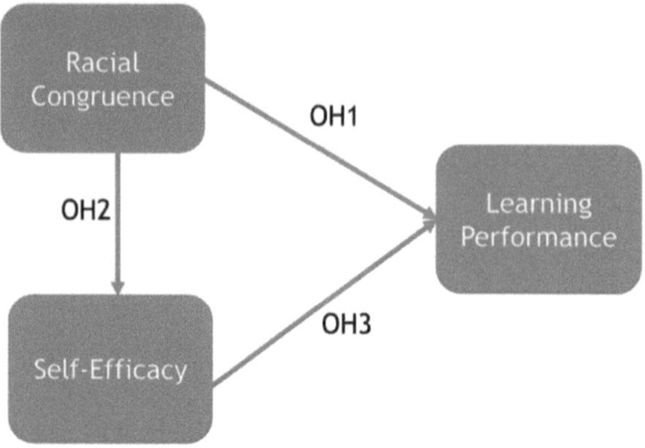

Fig. 6. Synthesis of results.

4.2 Implications

These findings suggest concrete avenues for improving virtual reality learning experiences, particularly for minority populations. By integrating principles of representation and inclusivity, it is possible to strengthen learners' sense of belonging and self-confidence. This translates into careful design of instructor avatars, ensuring they reflect the ethnic diversity of learners. These adaptations could not only enhance learning performance and perceived self-efficacy but also foster a more engaging and empowering experience for minority learners.

4.3 Limitations and Future Directions

The sample size was relatively small (N = 25), which may limit the generalizability of the findings. Future research with larger and more diverse samples is needed to confirm and extend these results.

Another limitation of this study is that the assessment of perceived self-efficacy relied on a single question using a 7-point Likert scale. Future research could use richer scales to enhance the robustness of this measurement.

Additionally, the study focused on a specific type of learning task (memorization of safety information in a virtual construction site). Further research should investigate the impact of racial congruence on other learning outcomes, such as problem-solving, critical thinking, and creativity, and in diverse VR learning contexts.

Future research should also consider that racial congruence in VR could affect performance through other mechanisms like a reduction in stereotype threat, an increased sense of social belonging, or reduced cognitive load.

5 Conclusion

In conclusion, this study provides compelling evidence for the significant impact of racial congruence on learning performance and perceived self-efficacy within a virtual reality environment. Our findings clearly demonstrate that learners who interacted with a racially congruent instructor's avatar exhibited superior learning performance and reported higher levels of self-efficacy compared to those in the incongruent condition. These results underscore the critical role of representation in VR educational settings, suggesting that when learners see themselves reflected in their instructors, it positively influences their confidence and ability to learn.

While our initial hypothesis regarding self-efficacy as a mediating variable was not fully supported, the independent predictive power of self-efficacy on learning performance remains significant, further emphasizing its importance in the learning process. These findings offer practical guidance for educators and developers of VR learning environments, advocating for the deliberate inclusion of diverse instructor avatars to cater to the varied backgrounds of learners. This strategic implementation can foster a more inclusive and supportive learning atmosphere, potentially mitigating disparities in educational outcomes for minority populations.

Acknowledgments. The authors thank the AD2RV non-profit association for the development of the VR environment.

Disclosure of Interests.. The authors declare that they have no competing interests that could have influenced the data or their interpretation.

References

1. Barrett, C.: Racial congruence and its effects on social integration and school involvement: A multi-level model", University of Maryland, College Park (2010)
2. Dee, T.S.: A teacher like me: Does race, ethnicity, or gender matter? American Economic Review. **95**(2), 158–165 (2005)
3. Cherng, H.-Y.S., Halpin, P.F.: The importance of minority teachers: Student perceptions of minority versus White teachers. Educ. Res. **45**(7), 406–420 (2016)
4. Hart, C.M.D.: An honours teacher like me: Effects of access to same-race teachers on Black students' advanced-track enrolment and performance. Educ. Eval. Policy Anal. **42**(2), 163–187 (2020)
5. Fox, L.: Seeing potential: The effects of student-teacher demographic congruence on teacher expectations and recommendations. AERA Open. **2**(1), 1–17 (2015)
6. Darling-Aduana, J.: A remote instructor like me: Student–teacher congruence in online, high school courses. AERA Open. **7**, 23328584211018720 (2021)
7. Bandura, A.: Social foundations of thought and action: A social cognitive theory. Prentice-Hall (1986)
8. Zimmerman, B.J.: Self-efficacy: An essential motive to learn. Contemp. Educ. Psychol. **25**(1), 82–91 (2000)
9. Schunk, D.H.: Self-Efficacy, Motivation, and Performance. J. Appl. Sport Psychol. **7**, 109–134 (1995). https://doi.org/10.1080/10413209508406961
10. Margolis, H., McCabe, P.P.: Self-Efficacy: A Key to Improving the Motivation of Struggling Learners. Preventing School Failure: Alternative Education for Children and Youth. **47**(4), 162–169 (2003)
11. Liao, H.A., Edlin, M., Ferdenzi, A.C.: Persistence at an Urban Community College: The Implications of Self-Efficacy and Motivation. Community College Journal of Research and Practice. **38**(7), 595–611 (2014)

12. Blascovich, J., Loomis, J., Beall, A.C., Swinth, K.R., Hoyt, C.L., Bailenson, J.N.: Immersive virtual environment technology as a methodological tool for social psychology. Psychol. Inq. **13**(2), 103–124 (2002)
13. Calabrò, R.S., Naro, A.: Understanding social cognition using virtual reality: Are we still nibbling around the edges? Brain Sci. **10**(1), 17 (2019)
14. Parsons, T.D. et al.: Virtual reality in pediatric psychology. Pediatrics. **140**(Supplement_2), S86-S91 (2017)
15. Yee, N., Bailenson, J.N.: The Proteus effect: The effect of transformed self-representation on behavior. Hum. Commun. Res. **33**(3), 271–290 (2007)
16. Baylor, A.L.: The design of motivational agents and avatars. Education Tech. Research Dev. **59**(2), 291–300 (2011)
17. Peck, T.C., Seinfeld, S., Aglioti, S.M., Slater, M.: Putting yourself in the skin of a black avatar reduces implicit racial bias. Conscious. Cogn. **22**(3), 779–787 (2013)
18. Groom, V., Bailenson, J.N., Nass, C.: The influence of racial embodiment on racial bias in immersive virtual environments. Soc. Influ. **4**(3), 231–248 (2009)
19. Garros, E., Sakdavong, J.C. : Influence de l'identification aux agents virtuels sur le sentiment d'efficacité personnelle dans une formation en ligne, Master's thesis, University of Toulouse, France (2024). https://bit.ly/4jRqCiF
20. Sakdavong, J.C., Ville, R.: The Impact of Racial Congruence Between Instructor and Learner on Memorization Outcomes in a Virtual Reality Environment. In CSEDU 2025, no. 2, pp. 917–922. SCITEPRESS–Science and Technology Publications, Lda. (2025)
21. Baron, R.M., Kenny, D.A.: The moderator–mediator variable distinction in social psychological research: Conceptual, strategic, and statistical considerations. J. Pers. Soc. Psychol. **51**(6), 1173–1182 (1986)
22. Peyrègne, M., Sakdavong, J.C.: How Gender Influences the Effect of Self-Efficacy on Training Success on a Mobile Curriculum. In Proceedings of the 16th International Conference on Computer Supported Education - Volume 2: CSEDU (2024)

Commercial-Off-The-Shelf Virtual Reality Technology in Simulation Training: A Pilot Study with Heavy Machine Gun Anti-aircraft Training

Mikko Salminen$^{(\boxtimes)}$ (iD)

National Defence University, 00861 Helsinki, Finland
`mikko.k.salminen@mil.fi`

Abstract. In this study a new VR-based simulator for heavy machine gun aerial target shooting was compared to an older, 2D monitor simulator. In a within-subjects design human factors and usability measures were collected from 28 participants. Overall, the participants preferred the VR simulator over the old 2D simulator. Using the VR simulator evoked, for example, higher perceived sense of presence, lower simulator sickness, and more positive evaluations of usability than the old 2D simulator. These results encourage to further develop VR-based simulators for military training.

Keywords: Virtual Reality · Simulator · Military · Training

1 Introduction

There has been increasing interest towards virtual reality (VR) devices and applications in the consumer market and the recent developments have made the commercial-off-the-shelf VR devices interesting also as platforms for training and education. These low-cost devices may be suitable for gaming and entertainment use, but they may have limitations for training use. For example, the visual acuity of the commercial grade devices may not suffice for certain training purposes (e.g., Maxwell et al., 2018) and the suitability of a device or technology should be ensured for each use case. VR can be utilized to enhance traditional classroom-based education, but it can also be used in creating new types of learning settings in various fields of education (for a review, see Concannon, Esmail & Roberts, 2020). It has been shown, that when compared to traditional (text-based) and video material, the using of VR learning material may evoke higher engagement and increased positive and decreased negative emotions among the learners (Allcoat & Mühlenen, 2018).

In the military training there are various skills that may be either difficult or expensive to train, at least for the needed amount of repetitions. VR can be utilized in the training of the basic skills of a dismounted soldier (Gluck, Chen & Paul, 2020). The enabling of movement while wearing a VR head-mounted display is still cumbersome and the

J. Y. C. Chen et al. (Eds.): HCII 2025, LNCS 16338, pp. 143–155, 2026.
https://doi.org/10.1007/978-3-032-12808-9_10

position of the user has to be captured accurately and represented in real-time in the virtual environment. There are, however, attempts to tackle these challenges, for example with omnidirectional treadmill and motion detection sensors (Fan & Wen, 2019). Given the current state of the technologies enabling movement while using VR environments, it is suggested that the VR as a medium would be more suitable for training of other types of skills, that do not require walking, for example. Using of virtual learning environments may help in reducing stress and workload that is evoked by the performance of a criterion task, when compared to training with more traditional methods (Lackey et al., 2016). This could potentially enhance the effectiveness of training by familiarizing or preparing the students and trainees more effectively for the forthcoming live performance or a criterion task. This could save time and resources, when the trainees would be more prepared to perform when it is their turn to use the high-fidelity simulator or an actual weapon system, after they have first trained with a VR simulator. In addition to these mentioned benefits, one interesting benefit of using simulator and VR-based training is also the possibility to collect data during the training for analysis and feedback (Koźlak, Kurzeja & Nawrat, 2013).

Consumer grade VR devices and development tools allow for rapid prototyping of virtual training environments for various skills. In addition to more traditional interaction mechanisms, such as mouse and keyboard or VR controllers, it is also possible to add various types of sensors to devices and deactivated weapon systems so that they can be used for interaction in a VR training environment. These types of new interaction mechanisms may lead to not only positive learning outcomes, but also to various negative human factors issues, such as increased mental load due to poor usability, or even simulator sickness. Thus, it is essential to collect user feedback during an iterative development process before using a VR training environment either in addition to or replacing other training methods. In a pilot study (n = 28), traditional heavy machine gun simulator (with an external 2D flat screen) was compared to a demonstrator VR simulator in a study with randomized repeated measures design with conscript trainees as voluntary participants.

1.1 Issues Affecting the Using of Virtual Reality in Training

There are various issues that affect the utility, usability, and use effectiveness of VR in military training. The transfer of training with VR to real world performance has been questioned and depending on task type, there is contrasting evidence (Kozak et al., 1993; Rose et al., 2000). In a review of virtual reality serious games, Checa and Bustillo (2020) stated that of the 135 included papers about third reported enhanced learning due to VR and the authors identified four key objectives for virtual reality serious games: interaction, immersion, user involvement, and photorealism. Each of these may have varying roles for different target populations and domains.

The factors that contribute to the effectiveness of VR-based training can be identified on the level of individual, in the human-technology interaction, and also on the organizational level. In a recent study by Arthur and colleagues (2024) these issues and factors were reviewed and a framework was presented to support decision makers in the process of enabling the using of various extended reality (XR) technologies for training and education. In the current study the focus is on the contributing factors on the level of human-technology interaction, such as usability, sense of presence, and simulator sickness.

2 Current Study and Research Questions

The aim of the experiment was to compare the suitability of the old and new VR-based simulators for training in operating against aerial targets with a heavy machine gun. The methods used were subjective assessments by the participants; feedback was collected on, for example, the usability of the simulators, simulator sickness, the sense of presence, and different types of task load. The experiment is first in planned series of experiments, where eventually the goal is to measure the transfer of training by collecting data from live fire training against flying target objects, such as drones and radio-controlled target planes.

The old and new VR-based simulators compared in the experiment differed particularly in terms of display technology. In the old simulator, visual content is presented on a screen attached to the top of the weapon, while in the VR simulator, the user wears VR glasses (head-mounted display, HMD). The VR simulator is more immersive than the older simulator, i.e. it more effectively excludes the external real world and enables a greater experience of presence in the virtual learning environment (Cummings & Bailenson, 2015; Makransky et al., 2019). The research questions of the experiment focus on mapping the experiences resulting from this difference in immersiveness.

The sense of presence evoked by immersion in a virtual learning environment supports the focus of attention on learning content rather than on external distractions. It is suggested that this can lead to more effective learning (Grassini et al., 2020; Huang et al., 2020). It is therefore possible that using a VR simulator results in a greater sense of presence in the learning environment than using a traditional simulator. We therefore pose the following research question:

RQ1: Does using a VR simulator elicit a greater sense of presence than using a traditional simulator?

The use of simulators can cause so-called simulator sickness, which is related to motion sickness and is caused by conflicting inputs from the eyes and the inner ear's balance system. When using virtual reality glasses, this phenomenon is sometimes called as virtual sickness; the visual input presented on the glasses' screen depicts a movement that is not actually perceived by the inner ear's balance system since there is no actual physical movement (e.g. Geršak et al., 2020; Johnson, 2004). Simulator sickness can be such annoying that it interferes with the simulator-based learning, so we asked the following research question:

RQ2: Which simulator (traditional simulator or VR simulator) causes greater simulator sickness?

Usability refers to the ease of use of a device or system in achieving a specific goal (Bevana et al., 1991). Poor usability of learning environments and systems can hinder learning (Parlangeli et al., 1999). We therefore posed the following research question:

RQ3: Which simulator (old simulator or VR simulator) is perceived to be more usable?

The using of technical devices, such as virtual learning environments and simulators can cause task load that may hinder learning (Bhandary et al., 2016). For example, cognitive load has been found to hinder memorization (Van Cauwenberge et al., 2014) and learning (Ayres, 2006). Therefore, we posed the following research question:

RQ4: Which simulator (traditional simulator or VR simulator) evokes higher task load?

Finally, we investigated the participants' preferences and asked them their opinion on which of the simulators is more suitable for educational use, so we presented the following research question:

RQ5: Which simulator (old simulator or VR simulator) is considered to better support learning?

3   Methods

3.1   Procedure

The participants were first informed about the course of the experiment, then they filled out a consent form and a background information form. After this, they used both simulators, each for 5 min. The order to use the simulators was randomized. After using both simulators (Fig. 1), the participants answered a questionnaire surveying their experiences. In the scenarios for both simulators the task was to fire at oncoming helicopters, with unlimited ammunition.

Fig. 1. VR simulator with head-mounted display in use (left). The old simulator with a 2D display attached on top of the weapon (right).

3.2   Participants

The participants were 28 conscripts, 21 of whom were non-commissioned officer cadets and the rest were rank-and-file. Mean age was 20.2 years (SD = 1.9). The majority had completed upper secondary school (15) or vocational school (8). Only one of the participants had previously shot targets with a real heavy machine gun.

The participants were voluntary and they received no compensation for the participation. A written consent was collected from all the participants. The participants were informed that they could end their participation at any time and that there would be no consequences for them. There were no significant risks involved for the participants and they were well informed on the purpose of the study and also on the handling of the collected data, thus following the national guidelines on research ethics, no ethics board approval was needed for the study.

3.3 Measures

The questionnaire was filled out after using the simulators and consisted of two identical sections, which collected user experiences with the simulators. The questionnaire included a modified NASA-TLX scale (Hart & Staveland, 1998) to measure task load. The second section was the system usability scale (Lewis & Sauro, 2009), which measured the usability of the simulator. The third section was the simulator sickness scale (Kennedy et al., 1993) and the fourth section was the presence survey, which measured the sense of presence in the virtual environment (Witmer & Singer, 1998).

The fifth section was completed at the end of the test, after the participant had used both simulators. This section briefly asked for feedback and evaluations of the simulators and opinions in general on the use of simulators in military training. In addition, it was possible to give free feedback on the simulators.

4 Results

The statistical analyses were done with the SPSS v.28 software. The assumption of normality, as assessed by Shapiro-Wilk's test ($p < 0.05$), was violated for the studied variables and thus, non-parametric statistical tests were used for studying the research questions (RQ). As the participant's used both of the simulators, in a randomized order, repeated-measures tests were used and the differences in the self-reported variables between the two simulators were studied using Friedman's test, a non-parametric repeated-measures test.

The reliabilities (Cronbach's alpha) for the measured constructs were, as follows: Simulator sickness $\alpha = 0.71$; System usability scale $\alpha = 0.88$; Sense of presence total score $\alpha = 0.89$; Sense of presence factor Control $\alpha = 0.65$; Sense of presence factor Sensory $\alpha = 0.85$; Sense of presence factor Distract $\alpha = 0.57$; Sense of presence factor Realism $\alpha = 0.81$.

4.1 Task Load

A statistically significant difference was observed between the simulators for three items of the six-item NASA-TLX scale (Fig. 2). When using the VR simulator, people experienced higher temporal demand; $\chi2(1) = 6.76, p = 0.009, W = 0.24$; and were more frustrated; $\chi2(1) = 4.00, p = 0.046, W = 0.14$; but on the other hand, they also experienced better performance; $\chi2(1) = 5.76, p = 0.016, W = 0.021$.

It is possible that the VR simulator was more engaging, in which case the perceived temporal demand is not necessarily a negative thing, at least not in the short term. Especially since using the VR simulator evoked higher performance rating.

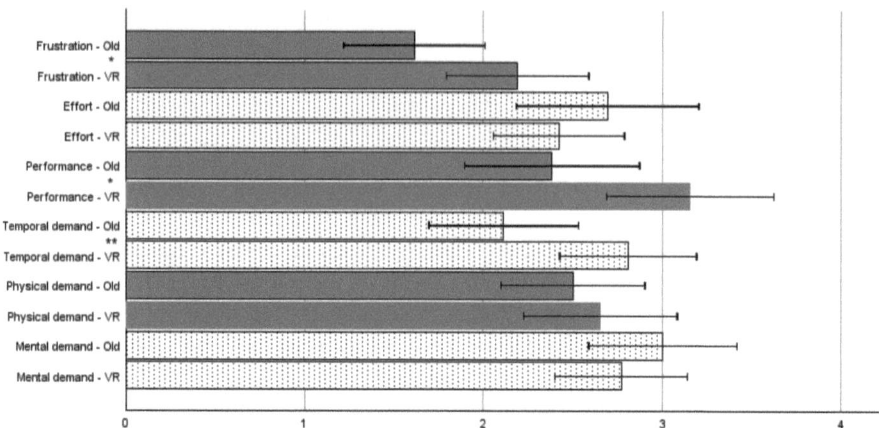

Fig. 2. Six different questions assessed the workload of using a VR-based and an old simulator. The survey was based on the NASA-TLX scale. Statistically significant differences between the simulators were observed for the sections: Temporal demand, Performance and Frustration. VR: VR simulator; Old: old simulator. ** $p < 0.01$; * $p < 0.05$. Error bars represent 95% confidence intervals.

4.2 Usability

The VR simulator was perceived as being more usable than the old simulator (Fig. 3); the difference in the System Usability Scale, which consists of ten items, was statistically significant; $\chi2(1) = 19.59$, $p < 0.001$, $W = 0.70$.

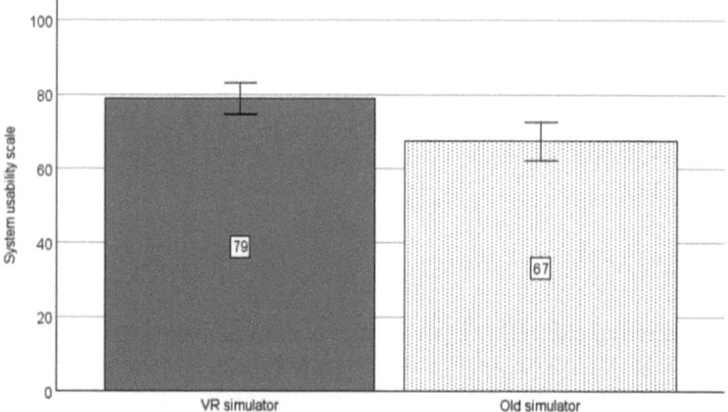

Fig. 3. Estimated usability of the VR-based and the old simulator. The assessment was given using the System Usability Scale, a ten-item questionnaire. The difference is statistically significant. Error bars represent the 95% confidence interval.

4.3 Simulator Sickness

Simulator sickness was assessed using the 14-item Simulator Sickness Questionnaire. The mean of all questions representing overall sickness differed statistically significantly between the simulators, $\chi2(1) = 15.39, p < 0.001, W = 0.57$. Overall, the use of the old simulator elicited more sensations of simulator sickness (Fig. 4).

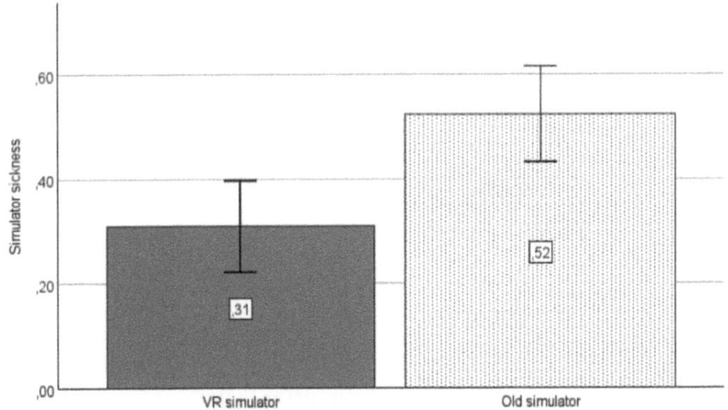

Fig. 4. Simulator sickness perceptions evoked by VR-based and old simulator. The assessment was given using the Simulator Sickness Questionnaire consisting of 14 items. The difference is statistically significant. Error bars represent the 95% confidence interval.

When examining the responses to individual items of the Simulator Sickness Questionnaire, statistically significant differences were observed between the simulators (Fig. 5). The use of the VR-based simulator was perceived to be associated with more difficulties in focusing vision than the use of the old simulator $\chi2(1) = 9.00, p = 0.003$, $W = 0.32$. This may be due to the fact that the participants were not experienced VR users. On the other hand, the Varjo VR-1 glasses used in the experiment have a relatively small area of high resolution, which is still quite clearly separated from the peripheral vision area. This may have felt disturbing in some situations. However, the VR-based simulator evoked less eye strain than the old simulator; $\chi2(1) = 16.67, p < 0.001, W = 0.60$. Therefore, it cannot be unequivocally said that the VR simulator strains the eyes more, but rather that it was a specific difficulty experienced in aligning the eyes.

The old simulator was perceived to cause more nausea; $\chi2(1) = 5.33, p = 0.02, W = 0.19$; fatigue; $\chi2(1) = 5.33, p = 0.02, W = 0.19$; and headache; $\chi2(1) = 19.59, p < 0.001, W = 0.70$. The screen resolution of the old simulator was lower than the VR simulator, which may have contributed to these perceived differences.

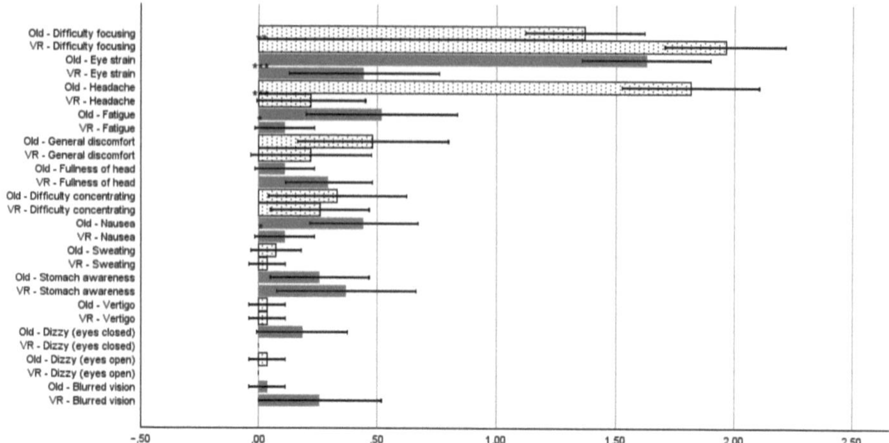

Fig. 5. Mean responses to fourteen items of the Simulator Sickness Questionnaire after using the VR-based and the old simulator. VR: VR simulator; Old: old simulator. *** $p < 0.001$; ** $p < 0.01$; * $p < 0.05$. Error bars represent 95% confidence intervals.

4.4 Sense of Presence

The total score of the Sense of Presence questionnaire differed statistically significantly between the VR simulator and the old simulator; $\chi2(1) = 9.00$, $p = 0.003$, $W = 0.56$. Using the VR simulator evoked a higher sense of presence than using the old simulator (Fig. 6).

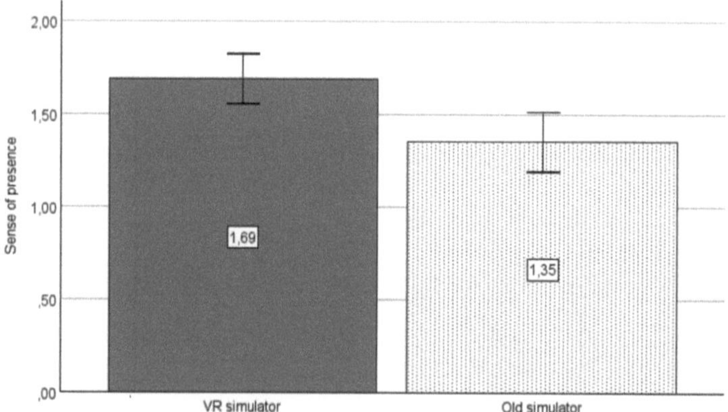

Fig. 6. Mean total score of sense of presence after using the VR-based and the old simulator. Error bars represent 95% confidence intervals.

Three of the four factors in the survey measuring the experience of presence showed a statistically significant difference between the simulators (Fig. 7). The sum variables Sensory; $\chi2(1) = 14.73$, $p < 0.001$, $W = 0.64$; Distraction; $\chi2(1) = 3.20$, $p = 0.074$,

$W = 0.13$; and Realism; $\chi2(1) = 17.19$, $p < 0.001$, $W = 0.78$; were scored higher after using the VR simulator than after using the old simulator.

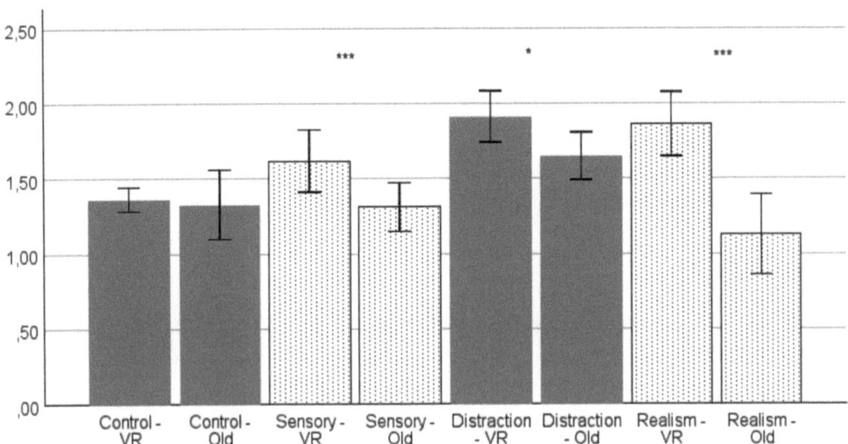

Fig. 7. Means of the ratings given to the four factors of the Sense of Presence Questionnaire mapping the experience of presence, separately for both simulators. *** $p < 0.001$; * $p < 0.05$. VR: VR simulator; Old: old simulator. Error bars depict the 95% confidence interval.

In other words, the VR simulator was perceived as engaging the different senses more effectively and providing a more realistic experience. Surprisingly, however, external disturbances were perceived to be more prominent when using the VR simulator. The assumption was that the VR glasses, which more effectively block out the natural environment, would have helped to focus attention on the simulator environment. However, it is possible that this very boundary between the natural environment and virtual reality was more evident when using the VR simulator and the user more clearly perceived the occasional leakage of attention into the natural environment or the controls. On the other hand, when using the old simulator, the gaze could unknowingly wander outside the screen, the hands could search for the controls, or every now and then become aware that the animated content presented on the screen was separate from the natural reality. These shifts of attention outside the simulator may not have been as conscious when using the old simulator than when using the VR simulator, and this may have led to the observed difference in the Distraction factor.

4.5 Overall Evaluation of the Simulators

At the end of the experiment, all participants except one rated the VR simulator as supporting training better than the old simulator. In addition, in the final ratings, participants strongly agreed that VR-based simulators should be used in military training (on a scale of 1–5); $M = 4.54$; $SD = 0.69$; and that using them can enhance training; $M = 4.39$; $SD = 0.69$.

Finally, the open-ended responses collected asked for comments on the tested simulators in general and feedback on the VR simulator in particular. Four participants commented that the VR simulator could have better graphics, but otherwise it was also considered better than the old simulator based on the comments, for example it was found to be more user-friendly and to offer a more immersive experience. One comment stated that the advantage of the older simulator was that the user can see the weapon concretely in front of them. In the future, this could also be enabled in the new simulator by implementing it using mixed reality (MR) technology. Suggestions for improvement related to the VR simulator included adding tactile feedback or recoil to the weapon handles, clarifying the sight pattern, and adding an assistant to indicate the correct aiming point on a moving target. Simulator training was generally found to be a great way to learn and was also mentioned as helping to prepare for live ammunition training.

5 Conclusions

Based on the results, research question RQ1 can be answered by stating that the VR simulator evoked a greater sense of presence than the old simulator. In particular, the VR simulator was felt to offer a more realistic experience and to engage the senses more effectively, but when using it, more distractions were experienced. The experience of presence can help to focus attention on the virtual learning material, and from the point of view of effective learning, it is desirable that the user of a virtual learning environment or simulator experiences a high sense of presence.

Regarding research question RQ2, the use of the old simulator evoked more experiences related to simulator sickness. The use of the old simulator evoked more eye strain, nausea, fatigue and headaches. The participants experienced these feelings to a fairly small extent, but on the other hand, the simulators were used for a short time, only 5 min. It is possible that these symptoms would be felt more strongly with long-term use, or some new types of symptoms could occur. When using head-mounted display, the experience of nausea can be reduced, for example, by reducing the amount of motion of the visual content presented on the screen. It is also possible to mitigate nausea by utilizing a predictive algorithm to adapt the visual input of the HMD screen to the user's head movements (Buker et al., 2016). It is also possible to adjust the field of view presented to the user during head movements (Fernandes & Feiner, 2016). The actual motion-induced or virtual sickness may not be a significant problem if the simulator is used while stationary, but it may prove to be significant if the simulator is used, for example, on a naval ship or in another type of moving vehicle.

Regarding the research question RQ3, the VR simulator was perceived as better in terms of usability than the old simulator. On the other hand, in relation to research question RQ4, when using the VR simulator, subjects experienced greater temporal demand and were more frustrated. Good usability of the learning environment or simulator supports learning and reduces additional burden in the learning situation. The observed differences in temporal demand and frustration should be studied more thoroughly.

In response to research question RQ5, the participants were almost unanimous in their opinion that the VR simulator is better for educational use than the old simulator. This observation is supported by the mainly positive observations related to the previous research questions regarding the VR simulator. The positive assessment may also have been influenced by the interest evoked by VR itself, which is perceived as a modern and advanced technology (e.g. Zhang et al., 2014).

The quality of VR simulator graphics mentioned in the open-ended comments is related to the simulator's physical fidelity, i.e. how well the simulator visually matches the real device or situation. Of the different types of fidelity, psychological fidelity, i.e. the extent to which using a simulator requires psychological processes similar to using a real device, has been found to be important for effective learning and the transfer of learning (Norman et al., 2012). Even if the physical or engineering fidelity might be mentioned as an important factor in comments, it should be further studied what type of fidelity is actually most important in the use case that is reported in this study. Young conscripts in particular may have become accustomed to the high-quality graphics of commercial games, to which they compare also virtual learning environments and game-based learning tools.

Further studies are needed to asses for the VR heavy machine gun simulator the transfer of training effect, by measuring accuracy of shooting moving aerial targets with a real weapon using live ammunitions. Another interesting direction for further research is the measuring of eye-movement data with the integrated sensor of the VR headset. This would enable the identification of the user's strategy of targeting the moving targets (tracking or trapping; Schendel & Johnston, 1983; Steinberg et al., 2019) and the length of the so-called quiet eye preceding pulling of the trigger (Causer et al., 2010) which may be related to shooting accuracy and could be used as indices on which individualized training feedback could be based.

Acknowledgments. I would like to thank engineer lieutenant colonel Lasse Lahdenmaa for leading the work to develop the VR simulator, organizing the test setting, and recruiting the participants.

Disclosure of Interests. The author has no competing interests to declare that are relevant to the content of this article.

References

Allcoat, D., von Mühlenen, A.: Learning in virtual reality: Effects on performance, emotion and engagement. Research in Learning Technology. **26**, 2140 (2018). https://doi.org/10.25304/rlt.v26.2140

Arthur, T. Et al.:. The Development of a Common Conceptual Framework for the Assessment of Extended Reality (XR) Technologies in Training and Education. NATO Science and Technology Organization, Available Online (2024)

Ayres, P.: Impact of reducing intrinsic cognitive load on learning in a mathematical domain. Applied Cognitive Psychology: The Official Journal of the Society for Applied Research in Memory and Cognition. **20**(3), 287–298 (2006)

Bevana, N., Kirakowskib, J., Maissela, J.: What is usability. In Proceedings of the 4th International Conference on HCI (1991)

Bhandary, S.P., et al.: NASA task load index scale to evaluate the cognitive workload during cardiac anesthesia-based simulation scenarios. International Journal of Anesthesiology Research. **4**(8), 300–304 (2016)

Buker, T.J., Vincenzi, D.A., Deaton, J.E.: The effect of apparent latency on simulator sickness while using a based helmet-mounted display: reducing apparent latency with predictive compensation. Hum. Factors **54**(2), 235–249 (2016)

Causer, J., Bennett, S.J., Holmes, P.S., Janelle, C.M., Williams, A.M.: Quiet eye duration and gun motion in elite shotgun shooting. Med. Sci. Sports Exerc. **42**(8), 1599–1608 (2010). https://doi.org/10.1249/MSS.0b013e3181d1b059

Checa, D., Bustillo, A.: A review of immersive virtual reality serious games to enhance learning and training. Multimedia Tools and Applications. **79**(9), 5501–5527 (2020)

Concannon, B.J., Esmail, S., Roduta Roberts, M.: Head-mounted display virtual reality in post-secondary education and skill training. Frontiers in Education. **4**, 80 (2019). https://doi.org/10.3389/feduc.2019.00080

Cummings, J.J., Bailenson, J.N.: How immersive is enough? A meta-analysis of the effect of immersive technology on user presence. Media Psychol. **19**(2), 272–309 (2016)

Fan, Y.C., Wen, C.Y.: A virtual reality soldier simulator with body area networks for team training. Sensors. **19**(3), 451 (2019). https://doi.org/10.3390/s19030451

Fernandes, A. S., Feiner, S. K.: Combating VR sickness through subtle dynamic field-of-view modification. Paper presented at the 2016 IEEE Symposium on 3D User Interfaces (3DUI), Greenville, SC (201–210) (2016)

Geršak, G., Lu, H., Guna, J.: Effect of VR technology matureness on VR sickness. Multimedia Tools and Applications. **79**(21), 14491–14507 (2020)

Gluck, A., Chen, J., Paul, R.: Artificial Intelligence Assisted Virtual Reality Warfighter Training System. In 2020 IEEE International Conference on Artificial Intelligence and Virtual Reality (AIVR) (pp. 386–389). IEEE (2020). https://doi.org/10.1109/AIVR50618.2020.00080

Grassini, S., Laumann, K., Skogstad, M.R.: The use of virtual reality alone does not promote training performance (but sense of presence does). Frontiers in Psychology. **11**(1743) (2020)

Hart, S. G., Staveland, L.E.: Development of NASA-TLX (Task Load Index): Results of empirical and theoretical research. In: Hancock, P.A., Meshkati, N. (eds.) Human Mental Workload. Amsterdam: North Holland Press (1988)

Huang, C.L., Luo, Y.F., Yang, S.C., Lu, C.M., Chen, A.S.: Influence of students' learning style, sense of presence, and cognitive load on learning outcomes in an immersive virtual reality learning environment. Journal of Educational Computing Research. **58**(3), 596–615 (2020)

Johnson, D.M.: Research Report 1832. Introduction to and Review of Simulator Sickness Research. U.S. Army Research Institute. 20050627 083 (2004). https://apps.dtic.mil/sti/citations/ADA434495

Kozak, J.J., Hancock, P.A., Arthur, E.J., Chrysler, S.T.: Transfer of training from virtual reality. Ergonomics **36**(7), 777–784 (1993)

Koźlak, M., Kurzeja, A., Nawrat, A.: Virtual reality technology for military and industry training programs. In: Nawrat, A. & Kuś, Z. (eds.): Vision Based Systems for UAV Applications, pp. 327–334. Springer, Heidelberg (2013). https://doi.org/10.1007/978-3-319-00369-6_21

Lackey, S.J., Salcedo, J.N., Szalma, J.L., Hancock, P.A.: The stress and workload of virtual reality training: the effects of presence, immersion and flow. Ergonomics **59**(8), 1060–1072 (2016). https://doi.org/10.1080/00140139.2015.1122234

Kennedy, R. S., Lane, N. E., Berbaum, K. S., Lilienthal, M. G.: Simulator sickness questionnaire: an enhanced method for quantifying simulator sickness. Int. J. Aviat. Psychol. **3**(3), 203-220 (1993). https://doi.org/10.1207/s15327108ijap0303_3

Lewis, J.R., Sauro, J. The factor structure of the system usability scale. In: International conference on human centered design (pp. 94–103). Springer, Berlin, Heidelberg (2009)

Makransky, G., Terkildsen, T.S., Mayer, R.E.: Adding immersive virtual reality to a science lab simulation causes more presence but less learning. Learn. Instr. **60**, 225–236 (2019)

Maxwell, D., Oster, E., Lynch, S.: Evaluating the applicability of repurposed entertainment virtual reality devices for military training. Paper presented at: MODSIM World 2018, 0028 (2018). http://www.modsimworld.org/papers/2018/MODSIM_2018_Paper_not_required_for_a_28.pdf

Moskaliuk, J., Bertram, J., Cress, U.: Impact of virtual training environments on the acquisition and transfer of knowledge. Cyberpsychol. Behav. Soc. Netw. **16**(3), 210–214 (2013). https://doi.org/10.1089/cyber.2012.0416

Norman, G., Dore, K., Grierson, L.: The minimal relationship between simulation fidelity and transfer of learning. Med. Educ. **46**(7), 636–647 (2012)

Parlangeli, O., Marchigiani, E., Bagnara, S.: Multimedia systems in distance education: Effects of usability on learning. Interact. Comput. **12**(1), 37–49 (1999)

Rose, F.D., Attree, E.A., Brooks, B.M., Parslow, D.M., Penn, P.R.: Training in virtual environments: transfer to real world tasks and equivalence to real task training. Ergonomics **43**(4), 494–511 (2000)

Schendel, J.D., Johnston, S.D.: A study of methods for engaging moving targets. Human Factors. **25**(6), 693–700 (1983). https://journals.sagepub.com/doi/abs/https://doi.org/10.1177/001872 088302500606

Steinberg, N.J., Brown, A.A., Schettino, L.F.: Target capture strategy selection in a simulated marksmanship task. Sci. Rep. **9**(1), 14057 (2019). https://doi.org/10.1038/s41598-019-505 51-z

Van Cauwenberge, A., Schaap, G., Van Roy, R.: "TV no longer commands our full attention": Effects of second-screen viewing and task relevance on cognitive load and learning from news. Comput. Hum. Behav. **38**, 100–109 (2014)

Witmer, B.G., Singer, M.J.: Measuring presence in virtual environments: A presence questionnaire. Presence. **7**(3), 225–240 (1998)

Zhang, J., Sung, Y.-T., Hou, H.-T., Chang, K.-E.: The development and evaluation of an augmented reality-based armillary sphere for astronomical observation instruction. Computers & Education. **73**, 178e188 (2014)

XR, Culture, and Immersive Heritage Experiences

Spatial Iterations Within the Metaverse: The Experience of Museum Environments and the Impact of Device

Mario Casillo[1]([✉]) [iD], Liliana Cecere[2], Francesco Colace[2] [iD], Angelo Lorusso[2] [iD], Domenico Santaniello[1] [iD], and Carmine Valentino[2] [iD]

[1] DiSPaC, University of Salerno, Fisciano, SA, Italy
{mcasillo,dsantaniello}@unisa.it
[2] DIIn, University of Salerno, Fisciano, SA, Italy
{lcecere,fcolace,alorusso,cvalentino}@unisa.it

Abstract. The metaverse is emerging as a new space for digital engagement, revolutionising access and the cultural experience. Virtual museums overcome the physical limitations of traditional museums, offering immersive and dynamic experiences. This study aims to examine the opportunities and challenges offered by the metaverse by exploring spatial iterations and the impact of access devices on the user experience in museums. Virtual spaces can replicate or reinvent physical environments, removing geographical barriers and harnessing digital potential to create distinctive interactions, such as artwork animations and interactive narratives.

The devices used significantly influence the experience: PCs, with VR viewers and advanced peripherals, offer immersion and precision; smartphones, although limited by small screens, excel in accessibility; tablets balance portability and performance, but remain inferior to PCs in terms of precision. Internet connection quality is crucial: mobile connections can cause latency, compromising fluidity and collaborative interactions.

User involvement ranges from passive exploration to active collaboration, such as artefact reconstruction. More advanced technologies support complex interactions, while portable ones favour simpler, more intuitive activities.

Furthermore, social dynamics in the metaverse depend on non-verbal signals and the ergonomics of interfaces, highlighting the importance of designing inclusive and adaptive digital environments.

In conclusion, the metaverse offers a unique opportunity to democratise access to culture, overcoming conventional barriers and promoting global engagement. Customising design and infrastructure can make these experiences more accessible and meaningful for all.

Keywords: Metaverse · Sppacial Interactions · Museums Environments · Cultural Heritage · Impact of Devices

J. Y. C. Chen et al. (Eds.): HCII 2025, LNCS 16338, pp. 159–173, 2026.
https://doi.org/10.1007/978-3-032-12808-9_11

1 Introduction

In recent years, the metaverse is emerging as a new and fascinating digital horizon, becoming a revolutionary platform for the fruition and dissemination of culture. Moreover, a trend is emerging in the evolution of real spaces into virtual spaces, made possible by the incorporation of new multisensory technologies. The use of XR technologies is particularly reflected in the world of cultural heritage (CH) [1], Indeed, new technologies have advantages both in attracting visitors and in encouraging subsequent visits, thus enabling users to experience more engaging, immersive and meaningful heritage content [2, 3]. Among its many applications, digital museum spaces represent a particularly significant case, as they overcome the physical limitations of traditional museums and introduce dynamic, immersive and interactive experiences, as well as being a powerful medium for the narration and preservation of CH, enabling a richer and more detailed understanding of past civilisations and cultural narratives [4–7]. Many real-life museums around the world are experimenting with and beginning to actively integrate metaverse and XR technologies to enrich visitor experiences, while at the same time redefining the role of museums in the digital world, making them virtual spaces of encounter, learning and cultural exchange. For example, the Metropolitan Museum of Art in New York launched the 'Met Unframed' project to provide online virtual tours via AR technology and digital twins (DTs); the British Museum collaborated with LaCollection to launch non-fungible tokens (NFT) to allow global players to visit its collections [8, 9]; the Louvre Museum, the National Palace Museum, the National Central Museum of Korea and the Tokyo National Museum have launched virtual tours and virtual reality (VR) projects using 3D scanning and other technologies [10]. From these trends, it is clear that museums are not simply adapting to digital, but are rethinking their mission and impact in contemporary society, increasingly becoming global cultural platforms, combining tradition and innovation to create unique experiences.

The added value lies in the new opportunities offered by the Metaverse. Museums and exhibition halls, in fact, can faithfully reproduce physical environments, or experiment with innovative spatial configurations that cannot be realised in the real world, and can do the same with the works within them [7]. A virtual gallery can reproduce real works of art, or render them animated, thus offering interactive narratives that contextualise the paintings or sculptures in a stimulating and informative way. This dual nature allows broader access to culture by allowing users to actively participate, move freely through the spaces, and interact with the works, thus creating a unique educational and playful experience.

User involvement in virtual museums is not only a desirable goal, but an essential component to maximise the cultural, educational and social impact of digital experiences. Indeed, it represents the key to transform virtual museums from mere exhibition platforms to centres of interaction, learning and innovation [11, 13]. User involvement in museums can vary from passive interaction, such as simple exploration, to active participation, including collaborative activities such as artefact reconstruction or educational games. The nature of these interactions depends on a number of factors such as the type of museum, its geometry and spatial organisation, and also on the device used: smartphones, for example, favour simple and intuitive interactions, while PCs allow for more complex activities due to superior computational capabilities and more sophisticated mechanisms, while tablets fall somewhere in between, facilitating interactions of moderate complexity[14].

User involvement, however, is not only measured by the interaction with the surrounding environment, but also and above all by the possibility of interacting with other participants, which is why, in the coming years, the metaverse is expected to be a true digital world capable of radically changing the way people interact with each other. Related to this, the presence of an avatar is a fundamental component that characterises the virtual experience in the metaverse and at the same time distinguishes it from all experiences on other digital platforms[15, 16]. Unlike the digital worlds already explored, in which individuals were identified by ID and username, the metaverse offers 3D avatars that represent the user and mirror his or her physical characteristics. With the advent of the Metaverse, normal avatars are no longer sufficient and the figure of the Metahuman is born. A metahuman is none other than our DT, allowing us to exist in virtual universes, being able to perceive our movements and expressions in real time [17]. Not only that, thanks to machine learning algorithms, these digital persons can also reflect our moods, feelings and personal character traits. Today's technology would allow users to personalise their interlocutors in the metaverse; it has been shown that avatar customisation can contribute to greater enjoyment and engagement invested [18], to the confirmation of self-esteem [19] and even spontaneous helping behaviour [20]. It is clear, therefore, that social and communicative dynamics are now also becoming more complex, becoming a subject of study and growing interest. The modes of communication in virtual worlds cannot be the same as in reality: non-verbal signals, body movement, pauses in dialogues, facial expressions are all aspects that have to be considered in the virtual communication flow and that influence communication with other users.

This study explores the multiple dimensions of spatial iterations within the metaverse, focusing in particular on the example of digital museum environments, analysing first the user's iteration with the museum space, then with the artworks within it, and finally the connections that may develop between users or groups of users. It is also analysed how the activity may change according to experience levels: whether the avatar is a novice, expert or museum guide. And finally, the impact of access devices on the user experience and how they influence the perception of the virtual space, interaction and engagement is considered.

2 Related Works

The growing interest in the Metaverse in recent years has led to a corresponding increase in the number of academic articles that have been written on the subject. As mentioned, scholars, academic and otherwise, have investigated the new virtual spaces, applying their research to real situations in some cases. This is the case of the [21] in which a Mars-themed virtual exhibition space was created to facilitate social interactions between users, through avatars, recreating the dynamics common in video games. Navigating the environment through avatars.

The adoption of virtual exhibition spaces in the metaverse responds on the one hand to the progress of increasingly cutting-edge technologies, and on the other hand to the interest of museums in offering visitors increasingly engaging, dynamic and interactive activities and experiences, adding further value to exhibitions. Such environments encourage users to interact not only with the exhibitions but also with each other, fostering a sense of community and shared learning. For example, the authors' planned approach in the [21] for the museums of the future allows visitors to virtually 'walk' through historical sites and interact with detailed reconstructions of significant events, thus facilitating the exploration of rare artefacts and fragile ecosystems without risking damage, and enriching the body of knowledge. The integration of VR and holographic technologies has also greatly transformed museum and educational applications, significantly enhanced visitor engagement and learning experiences. This evolution started with [22] in which the authors introduced a new content control technology using hand gestures to improve the usability of holographic displays. Simultaneously, in the [23] VR-based 3D modelling and interaction technologies have been developed specifically for museums, significantly increasing visitor satisfaction and engagement. Integration with digital technologies has significantly transformed the way museums interact with their audiences. The use of online resources and digital access represents a unique opportunity for museums to radically transform visitor engagement and learning. From [24] it is clear that advances in VR technology play a key role, greatly enhancing users' perception of spatial presence, an essential aspect for immersive VR applications. These innovations are not limited to individual experiences, but foster real-time social interactions between users represented by avatars, enabling a level of engagement that transcends geographical and physical barriers [4, 25]. In this way, visitors can explore exhibitions, take part in guided tours and interact with other users from all over the world, as if they were actually in the same place.

Most institutions today already provide accessible resources through a variety of mechanisms, including their websites, social media accounts, digital applications or traditional printed brochures of maps or museum guides. These resources, when combined with interactive digital storytelling, personalisation and adaptability of experience, have the potential to enhance the attractiveness not only of CH sites and museums, but also to serve as a new channel for interpretation, analysis and cultural knowledge for different communities [26]. Furthermore, the innovative use of new digital technologies will provide new forms of interactive cultural experiences that are comfortable, sensory-friendly and understandable even for neurodiverse audiences.

Many, to increase users' sense of involvement, have explored the world of avatars and analysed how they interact in the virtual world of the Metaverse [27]. Given their central role, many platforms have developed various features to enrich users' virtual experiences precisely by implementing avatar functionality. Among these, for instance, Roblox uses 3D animated avatars, introducing dynamic heads that appear more realistic and able to express emotions in a lively way, and users can select an avatar from different degrees of realism according to their preferences [28]. Another significant case is Zepeto, a platform that emphasises self-expression and social interactions, where users can customise their avatars with a wide variety of options, including hairstyles, make-up, accessories, clothing and footwear [29]. Through this versatility, Zepeto has increased user engagement and facilitated virtual interactions. These examples highlight how avatars are essential for social perceptions and relationships between individuals in the metaverse. Realism, from this perspective, for social interactions in a computer-mediated environment, it is important that avatars are as realistic as possible, reflecting both the person's appearance and behaviour; anthropomorphic avatars, in fact, tend to be perceived as more believable and attractive to users [30].

3   Avatar and Metahumans

Just as the Metaverse is rapidly evolving as a new frontier of immersive space, so avatars are revolutionising the way people interact with others in virtual worlds, allowing people to relate, work and have fun in an alternative way. Avatars and metahumans are representations of the human being in the metaverse, and although they are conceptually similar, they actually differ significantly in their characteristics, use and complexity. Metahumans can be considered as a more advanced evolution of avatars: they are highly realistic digital models that, to be such, are created using state-of-the-art techniques and technologies such as photogrammetry, artificial intelligence and motion capture. Metahumans have detailed physical characteristics, such as skin textures, facial expressions and realistic body movements, which can be reproduced precisely thanks to motion capture. Motion capture, as its name suggests, allows the capture of body and facial movements and, to do so, needs the use of special suits equipped with markers (active or passive), sensors and multiple cameras.

The movement data is then sent to specialised software that processes it and reconstructs a digital skeleton that reproduces the movements. Only then are the recorded movements applied to a digital model, such as an avatar or a metahuman. Due to the difficulty of implementation and rather high costs, the creation and use of metahumans is not yet so widespread. Avatars being simpler, more intuitive and accessible find, to date, more application in the context of the metaverse. In spite of being simpler, avatars allow users to choose aesthetic aspects such as body shape, clothing, accessories and, in some cases, movements and behaviour, and are used precisely in community settings to enhance social interaction and collaboration. In particular, if one thinks of the virtual museum context, avatars can offer multiple new possibilities, from the simple exploration of environments to the possibility of reinventing the museum spaces they explore. In such a context, avatars can be customised to reflect the identity of visitors and as such can explore spaces, linger over works, participate in guided experiences or be museum guides themselves. The characteristics and interactions of avatars in this context can be analysed on three main levels: avatar-environment, avatar-artworks and avatar-avatar.

3.1   Interactions Avatar – Museums

Avatar-museum interaction does not concern a single aspect, but is characterised by the museum space, its architecture, and the type of exploration. Relative to the type of experience one wishes to obtain, one can decide whether to realise paths that users are obliged to follow or, if not, to leave them free to move about the space. The enormous potential of spaces of this kind lies in the dynamism they have: some exhibition halls or interactive areas of the museum can be fully experienced by using interactive screens, activating multimedia content such as audio, video or projections, or even by opening doors or making dynamic changes to the layout. In addition, museum spaces in the metaverse can be designed to emphasise extraordinary architectural elements, allowing avatars to 'fly', teleport or change perspective to explore details of the works that would otherwise be hidden.

3.2   Interactions Avatar – Works of Art

The interaction between avatars and works of art is undoubtedly, among those that can develop in the Metaverse, the most interesting and stimulating for the user. In traditional museums, in almost all cases, interaction is very limited in order to preserve the CH on display as long as possible and also to respect its historical and artistic value. Therefore, the only allowed mode of interaction is visual observation. Visitors are not allowed to interact creatively with the work; they can only approach it, within the allowed limits, and analyse it from different perspectives to grasp its details and meanings, whether it is sculpture, paintings or pictures. In real museums, therefore, a non-invasive mode of viewing is favoured and, in order to avoid damage due to wear and tear, fingerprints or contamination by external agents, not only is it not possible to touch the works, but in some cases even to take flash photographs.

With the emergence of virtual spaces, this perspective changes radically, as does the approach of visitors to the works on display. In the museums of the metaverse, interaction with works of art such as paintings and sculptures offer a wider and more creative range of possibilities than in traditional museums, both due to the digital nature of the works, but also due to the absence of physical constraints. Through their avatars, users can, in the Metaverse, explore the works in even more detail. All three-dimensional reproductions displayed in the metaverse, in fact, can not only be observed, but can also be rotated, enlarged, lifted up, to grasp even hidden details.

In the case of paintings, for example, technology offers enormous possibilities: paintings can be activated as the avatar passes by, showing animations, stories or explanations about the work and its historical context; visitors can click on specific points in the painting to receive in-depth information on symbolic or technical details; or even analysis techniques can be simulated to show elements not visible to the human eye. In addition, avatars can change colours or add temporary elements to understand how different artistic choices could have influenced the work and its perception.

With sculptures, the possibilities are even greater as these, in a virtual environment, can be observed from all angles, including perspectives not accessible in physical museums. Sculptures, in fact, may need to be observed from above to grasp important details or may contain interiors that are unexplored in reality, which can instead be explored from the inside in the virtual world. Avatars, then, can move or rotate the sculpture, exploring the relationship between it and the surrounding space, or can disassemble the work to observe individual components or the creative process that generated it.

In the metaverse, finds from past eras, such as vases, tools or utensils of various kinds, are transformed into living, interactive objects, allowing a deeper understanding of their function, history and cultural significance. Vases or tools can be visualised within historical simulations allowing users to better understand their use and context. Avatars can use the tools in simulations to understand how they were used for hunting, processing materials or everyday life; for instance, they could hold a Neolithic axe and use it to cut virtual wood, virtually perceiving the ergonomics of the object, or they can manipulate fragments of an object to reconstruct it, as happens with fragmented vases found in archaeological excavations. The metaverse, therefore, makes it possible to show how objects would have looked when new, before the wear and tear or damage of time. Moreover, in these cases as well as in painting, the level of detail can be infinitely expanded, allowing us to observe engravings, cracks, traces of wear or microscopic decorations that might not be perceptible in the real world. Each object can activate narrative content: by clicking on a vase, the user might see an animated scene depicting its creation or use, such as a potter at work or an ancient banquet. Visitors can explore content related to an object: who created it, what technology was used, and in what historical context it was found. Some objects or tools can be animated to show exactly how they were used, such as the workings of a prehistoric animal trap or a pottery wheel.

In general, in the metaverse, works do not deteriorate and materials can be simulated with extreme precision. Unlike physical museums, where interaction is limited to protect the works, in the metaverse there is no risk of damage, so exploration is free and complete. Furthermore, the works can be adapted to meet the needs of all users, e.g. by amplifying colour contrasts for the colour blind or by providing audio descriptions for the visually impaired. In conclusion, in the museums of the meta-verse, paintings and sculptures become alive and interactive thanks to digital technology. Users can experience a direct, unique and personalised interaction with the works, overcoming physical limitations and opening up new possibilities for artistic enjoyment and understanding.

3.3 Interactions Avatar – Avatar

In the metaverse, just like in reality, avatars can interact with each other dynamically, making museum spaces places of cultural and social exchange. These interactions are not limited to reflecting real-world behaviors, but can be enriched by digital tools that amplify a sense of community and active participation. Avatars, in fact, can dialogue with each other, sharing impressions of works of art, discussing history or simply socializing. This creates a sense of community and fosters the building of relationships and bonds between visitors and enthusiasts, which goes beyond temporal and geographical barriers. Conferences, artistic performances or workshops can be organized in metaverse museum spaces, in which avatars interact with experts, artists or other visitors, and participate as an active part of the process, establishing a relationship with them. Avatars can also collaborate by participating together in interactive activities and can communicate with each other via text, audio or digital gesture chat. For example, they can tilt their head to show interest or raise a hand to ask questions, in order to enrich the interaction and make it more immersive.

The iteration between avatars, or between groups of avatars, also changes in relation to the different roles they can play in museum spaces, each of which contributes to shaping the collective experience. Some avatars can take on the role of virtual guides, leading visitors through the exhibits and providing detailed explanations about works and historical contexts. These avatars can be managed by humans or artificial intelligences programmed to interact naturally, adapting the content to the needs of visitors. Other avatars can take on the role of artists, then use virtual spaces to exhibit their digital works, organize immersive performances, or interact directly with the public, directly explaining their creations to visitors. The direct relationship with the public allows them not only to explain their works, but also to answer questions and, above all, collect reactions and feedback in real time. Then there are the guest avatars, i.e. visitors to the museum, who can either explore the spaces freely, interact with the works of art, participate in discussions or even be guided by other figures.

One of the most interesting and complex topics in the interaction between avatars is the management of turns of speech. When we talk about turns of speech, we basically refer to the way in which the participants of a conversation take turns in speaking and listening, without overlapping. It is a fundamental concept in interpersonal communication, both in the real and virtual worlds. Precisely to avoid overlapping, this alternation generally follows rules, implicit or explicit, which vary according to the context, the means of communication and also according to the culture. In the real world, there are characteristics and clear signs that indicate the passage of the round. For example, during a conversation, the speaker uses verbal and nonverbal cues to indicate that he or she is about to give up his turn, such as a change in intonation, a pause, or a look; the listener, on the other hand, can in turn use signals to take the floor in speech, such as a hand gesture, or a facial expression. These signals are easily identifiable and recognizable in the real world, which can lead to major difficulties in the virtual world. In the context of virtual spaces such as the metaverse, word turns acquire a new dimension, influenced by technological factors and the characteristics of the interface. These environments introduce unique challenges with respect to face-to-face communication. The lack of complete non-verbal cues, as we said, is one of the biggest challenges to be faced. Elements such as eye contact, facial expressions or gestures are often reduced or even missing in virtual environments, this therefore makes it more difficult to manage the natural turns of speech which, in a conversation, can lead to awkward pauses, or unwanted overlaps. Hence the importance of effective management of speaking turns, which in virtual museums means promoting inclusiveness, ensuring that we all have the opportunity to express ourselves, improve communication efficiency and reduce social inertia. Although it is a topic still to be developed, solutions to the problem have already been thought of. First of all, speaking turns can be managed by artificial intelligence systems that assign the right to speak based on criteria such as the order of requests, the duration of previous speeches or even the perceived importance of the contribution. In addition, as already happens in applications dedicated to online calls and video calls, it is possible to insert shift request systems, with which users can "raise a virtual hand" or send a request to speak through the interface. Requests are displayed in chronological order, thus ensuring a fair and orderly distribution. Another alternative could be to use a visual or acoustic cue from your avatar to indicate your desire to speak. Raising an arm, or making a head movement, in fact, can be a signal for the other participants to give up the turn. In the case of large groups of avatars, as can be the case with guided tours of museums, or conferences, then, automatic moderation systems can be introduced through artificial intelligence, which can monitor and manage interactions, analyzing who has already spoken, the duration of their speeches and the order of requests. In all these cases, however, to further facilitate the understanding of interactions, it may be useful to insert visual indicators, which can be a light or an icon, to indicate who is speaking or who is queuing to intervene.

In addition, in virtual museums, where interactions range from moments of great participation to more relaxed ones, it can be useful to adopt hybrid strategies. A "silent" mode with text chat can be implemented, in which users can only intervene by entering comments or questions in chat, while another participant speaks. Then it will be a moderator or an AI system that selects the most relevant messages and shares them verbally. Or, to ensure fair distribution, each user could have a maximum time for their intervention, visible through a timer in the interface, thus being able to manage themselves.

Therefore, although in the metaverse the management of speaking turns requires considerable effort, this is essential to facilitate orderly and collaborative communication between avatars. The goal is to create an environment in which all users, regardless of the device used or their technological skills, can participate actively and without conflict, and it is hoped that, with the evolution of artificial intelligence and VR technologies, the strategies already identified can be further refined, promoting inclusive communication and enriched cultural enjoyment.

4 Digital Experiences: The Role of Avatars in Virtual Museums

The virtual experience in the metaverse is, therefore, strongly influenced by the fusion of avatar, virtual museum space and works of art, so much so that the cultural experience is a multidimensional experience, influenced by various factors. In this context, avatars act as a point of connection between the museum and the works within it; the virtual museum becomes an amplifier of interactions; the works are the dynamic elements within it.

The diagram below (Fig. 1) clearly represents the interactions that develop in the museum Metaverse, highlighting the integration between technology, cultural spaces and users. The heart of the system is obviously the virtual environment, without which all other connections would make no sense. Virtual space, in fact, by uniting all the components, enables and regulates all interactions. The real protagonists of the scheme, however, are the avatars, who act as mediators between the components. Users, through their avatars, can explore the museum space, interact with the works of art and communicate with other users, thus creating physical, cognitive and social interactions, which allow them to enrich their experience, transforming it into something much more participatory than visiting a traditional museum. On the other hand, the connection with devices plays a fundamental role in the metaverse experience: the devices act as an interface between the user and the virtual world, profoundly influencing the way the visitor perceives and interacts with the museum. These not only enable access, but also condition the mode of interaction: a VR headset, for example, will allow a higher level of immersion than a smartphone. The connection between devices, works, museum space and avatars, therefore, wants to highlight how the use of different devices can influence the visual experience, affect the navigation of the space and condition the visitor's experience.

An essential part of the scheme is then represented by the two-way interaction between museum spaces and works of art, both components of CH transposed into the metaverse. These components being closely related, can likely influence each other, for example, a work of art could suggest a path, while the museum space could guide attention to specific exhibitions, installations or sections of the exhibition.

Therefore, it is clear that the synergy that is created between all the elements of the system allows for an unprecedented cultural experience, which breaks down the physical barriers of the real world and opens up new avenues for artistic participation and enjoyment. The experience is built thanks to the integration of technology, cultural content and human participation, obtaining an organic system, in which each component plays a crucial role.

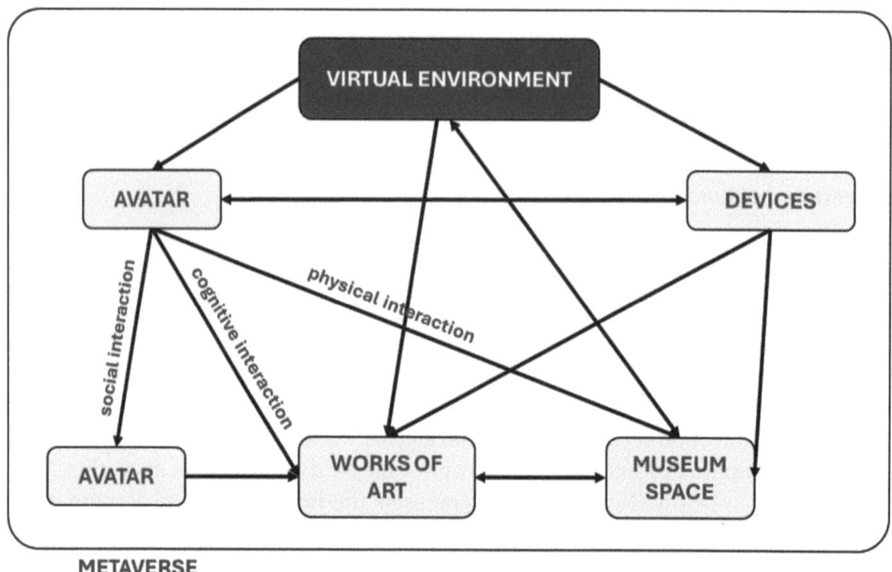

Fig.1. Possible interactions in the metaverse.

5   The Role of Devices

The ability of users to traverse and interact with the virtual environment and other participants depends on multiple factors, including spatial perception, avatar customization, and intuitive controls. Among these, the perception of space varies significantly according to the device used, influencing the level of immersion, interaction and user involvement. In fact, as shown in the diagram (Fig. 2), the devices, thanks to the connections they generate in the Metaverse, are decisive in the type of experience you want to achieve; The choice of the most suitable device is not universal, this depends on countless factors such as the age of the users, the purpose of the experience (playful, educational, work) and the desired level of accessibility.

VR headsets are among the first devices to consider, as they offer one of the most complete and immersive experiences in the Metaverse. Thanks to three-dimensional simulation and the possibility of tracking head and hand movements, the viewers allow a highly immersive experience and allow users to interact with the digital environment in 3D and perceive a real sensation of physical presence in the virtual space. This potential makes viewers excellent tools, also for training and experiential education, such as the simulation of work environments or guided tours in virtual museums. The advantages deriving from the use of visors, however, correspond to as many disadvantages. Headsets, in fact, have high costs, which are between € 300 and € 1,000 depending on the desired properties and features, which makes them difficult to access for some segments of the population. In addition, the high cost, in most cases, also corresponds to a technical complexity that not everyone is able to manage. Children, the elderly or in general inexperienced users, if not properly guided, may find it difficult to familiarize themselves with the interfaces and controls of the headsets or have technical difficulties in using them. Among the biggest disadvantages is physical discomfort which manifests itself with motion sickness, visual and physical fatigue, and sensory overload. Especially in the case of prolonged use, in fact, the visors could cause feelings of nausea, dizziness and discomfort that derive from the conflict that is created between the virtual movement that the brain perceives visually and the absence of real physical movement; or even eye fatigue, resulting from the fact that users have to focus at short distances for extended periods; resentment in the forehead, nose or head, resulting from the weight and lack of ergonomics of the devices. Finally, the immersive nature of VR can be overwhelming for some users, especially in intense gaming or environments with a lot of visual and sound stimuli. All these factors can then converge, for the most sensitive users and in cases of VR environments that are too realistic or challenging, in a feeling of disorientation, loss of balance and in more serious cases even in feelings of anxiety or stress. Despite the many disadvantages, headsets, thanks to their high-resolution displays and the ability to display three-dimensional environments with exceptional depth and detail, are still the ideal solution for advanced spatial interaction.

Among the other modes of use, there are computers, smartphones and tablets. These are accessible devices that are affordable and affordable for everyone, both from an economic point of view and in their use. Thanks to their versatility, they represent one of the most accessible and widespread methods of using the metaverse. The wide economic and technical accessibility, the intuitive browsing experience, makes them suitable for an audience of all ages, which is why they are also preferred in playful experiences, for children and adolescents. Smartphones, thanks to technologies such as touchscreens and gyroscopes, allow intuitive navigation and a discreet perception of the virtual environment. On the other hand, however, the small screen size is an inherent limitation, hindering the display of details and immersion in three-dimensional settings. This makes them useful tools for quick and easy interactions, but less suitable for more complex or detailed experiences. A fair compromise between the portability of smartphones and the power of PCs is represented by tablets. These, thanks to the larger screens compared to mobile phones, are able to improve the visual perception and the overall user experience, while not reaching the levels of precision and immersion guaranteed by PCs.

Last but not least, a determining factor for the metaverse experience is the internet connection, which directly influences fluidity, visual and interaction quality and, consequently, user engagement. Delays, interruptions can, in fact, significantly reduce the effectiveness of the experience or activity that is taking place. This, once again, is influenced by the choice of device: PCs generally use wired or Wi-Fi connections, which are more stable and faster and guarantee a smooth experience even in complex collaborative scenarios. Smartphones and tablets, on the other hand, often depend on mobile connections such as 4G or 5G, which can be unstable, and consequently compromise visual quality, cause delays in the loading of virtual environments and generally hinder real-time interactions. In general, therefore, a poor internet connection can cause delayed response times, which make interaction with the environment difficult, generating frustration and reducing involvement; interruptions in the display of images, which can compromise the immersive experience, causing a feeling of disorientation; and finally, synchronization issues, which could make avatar movements inconsistent or dissociated, and therefore directly affect social iterations.

What has been said so far about the fluidity of the experience is valid for any virtual space, everything related to visual quality, on the other hand, is decisive especially in museum experiences, particularly when it comes to faithfully representing the museum space and the works of art within it. The resolution of virtual environments depends largely on the speed and quality of the internet connection. If the graphic resolution is low, in fact, it is possible that the textures inserted in the environments are not well defined or distinguishable, and consequently, it is possible that important artistic details of the works are lost, such as brushstrokes, engravings or light and shadow effects, all factors that can reduce the user's ability to appreciate the value of the work and understand its meaning. Not only that, visual quality also affects depth perception and understanding of the museum space: it allows users to correctly perceive the spaces, the dividing elements, and even the distances between the works, allowing users to take targeted paths and with greater precision.

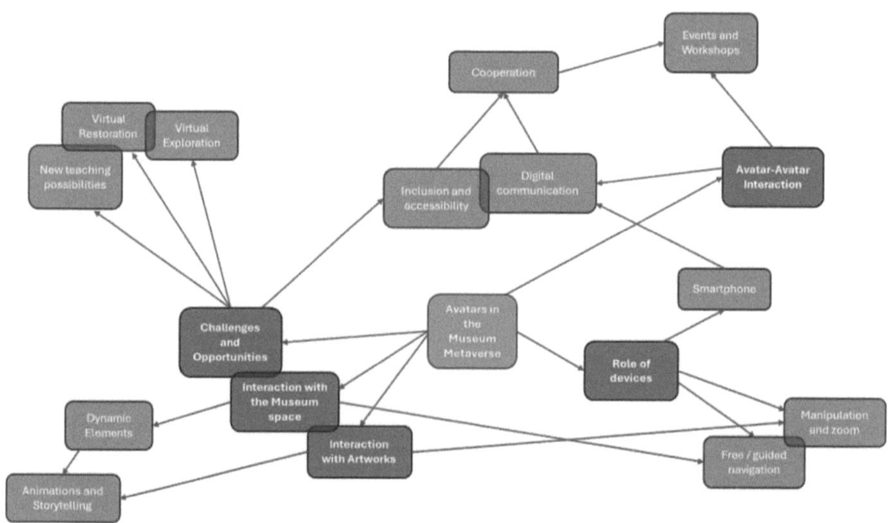

Fig. 2. Avatar interconnections in metaverse museums.

6 Conclusions

In conclusion, iterations in metaverse museums show a significant evolution in how art and culture can be experienced, creating a unique intersection between technology, human interaction, and experiential design. The possibility of overcoming physical and geographical barriers and making CH accessible to audiences around the world are some of the great advantages offered by these virtual environments. Users can immerse themselves in dynamic three-dimensional spaces, modify their avatars to showcase unique identities, and interact with artworks through interactive tools that go beyond the boundaries of conventional museums. The digital works, which are brought to life by animations, narratives, and additional content, not only enhance the aesthetic experience, but also encourage participants to actively participate and work together.

However, the potential of these spaces is not without its challenges. The use of these spaces requires advanced technological infrastructures, such as high-speed internet connections, compatible devices and digital skills, which are not yet widely available. VR headsets and other immersive technologies can be expensive, which can limit access, particularly in educational settings or in areas with limited resources. In addition, scalability and accessibility must be integrated at every stage of development. Despite this, the possibilities offered by the metaverse go far beyond geographical accessibility. Virtual museums can be platforms for hybrid experiences that combine storytelling, gamification and education. Users not only observe, but actively participate in the creation of cultural meaning by collaborating with other users to solve historical puzzles and reconstruct artifacts or participate in thematic debates.

Individual and collective creativity is stimulated with this method, which promotes deeper learning. From a technological point of view, the constant evolution of devices such as virtual headsets and VR and augmented reality (AR) devices promises to make the experience more fluid, immersive and interactive. Finally, the iteration in the metaverse redefines the relationship between audience, art and space, making the museum a living and dynamic ecosystem. Virtual museums are more than just places to visit; They help create global communities where people and technology come together to enhance the cultural experience and create new avenues for connection, learning, and inspiration.

References

1. Silva, M., Teixeira, L.: EXtended Reality (XR) Experiences in Museums for Cultural Heritage. A Systematic Review. 58–79 (2022)
2. Carrozzino, M., Bergamasco, M.: Beyond virtual Museums: Experiencing immersive virtual reality in real Museums. J. Cult. Herit. **11**, 452–458 (2010). https://doi.org/10.1016/j.culher.2010.04.001
3. McNamara, A.M.: Enhancing art history education through mobile augmented reality. In: Proceedings of the Proceedings of the 10th International Conference on Virtual Reality Continuum and Its Applications in Industry, pp. 507–512. ACM: New York, NY, USA (2011)
4. Margetis, G., Apostolakis, K.C., Ntoa, S., Papagiannakis, G., Stephanidis, C.: X-Reality Museums: Unifying the virtual and real world towards realistic virtual Museums. Appl. Sci. **11**, 338 (2020). https://doi.org/10.3390/app11010338

5. Banfi, F., Brumana, R., Stanga, C.: Extended reality and informative models for the architectural heritage: From Scan-to-BIM process to virtual and augmented reality. Virtual Archaeology Review. **10**, 14 (2019). https://doi.org/10.4995/var.2019.11923

6. di Filippo, A., Antinozzi, S., Cappetti, N., Villecco, F.: Methodologies for assessing the quality of 3D models obtained using close-range photogrammetry. IJIDeM. **18**, 5917–5924 (2024). https://doi.org/10.1007/s12008-023-01428-z

7. Casillo, M. et al.: Exhibition spaces in the Metaverse: A Novel design approach. In: Proceedings of the 2023 8th IEEE History of Electrotechnology Conference (HISTELCON), pp. 116–119. IEEE (2023)

8. Onur, G.: British Museum Steps into Metaverse with The Sandbox

9. Casillo, M. et al.: Blockchain and NFT: A Novel approach to support BIM and architectural design. In: Proceedings of the 2022 International Conference on Innovation and Intelligence for Informatics, Computing, and Technologies (3ICT), pp. 616–620. IEEE (2022)

10. Shim, H., Kim, E.S., Oh, K.T., Shi, C.-K., Ahn, J.: Diving into a Heritage Metaverse: Learning from end user-driven experiences and perspectives to enhance virtual heritage interpretation. Proc ACM Hum Comput Interact. **8**, 1–28 (2024). https://doi.org/10.1145/3637322

11. Casillo, M. et al.: The Metaverse and Revolutionary Perspectives for the Smart Cities of the Future, pp. 215–225 (2024)

12. Barra, P. et al.: Social Interaction and Collaboration in the Metaverse, pp. 528–532 (2023)

13. Schuster, K., Grainger, J.: Digital cultural heritage: Collaborating with students and discovering lost Museums. Educ. Inf. **37**, 97–111 (2021). https://doi.org/10.3233/EFI-190352

14. Clarizia, F. et al.: Augmented Reality and Gamification Technics for Visit Enhancement in Archaeological Parks. In: Proceedings of the 2022 IEEE 2nd IoT Vertical and Topical Summit for Tourism (IoTT), pp. 1–4. IEEE (2022)

15. Casillo, M. et al.: Digital Twin and Metaverse Supporting Smart Cities: New Perspectives and Potentials, pp. 111–119 (2024)

16. Della Greca, A. et al.: User Study on the Relationship between Empathy and Facial-Based Emotion Simulation in Virtual Reality. In: Proceedings of the Proceedings of the 2024 International Conference on Advanced Visual Interfaces, pp. 1–9. ACM: New York, NY, USA (2024)

17. Nalbant, K.G., Uyanik, Ş.: A look at the new humanity: Metaverse and Metahuman. International Journal of Computers. **7** (2022)

18. Birk, M.V., Atkins, C., Bowey, J.T., Mandryk, R.L.: Fostering Intrinsic Motivation through Avatar Identification in Digital Games. In: Proceedings of the Proceedings of the 2016 CHI Conference on Human Factors in Computing Systems, pp. 2982–2995. ACM: New York, NY, USA (2016)

19. Kang, H., Kim, H.K.: My avatar and the affirmed self: Psychological and persuasive implications of avatar customization. Comput Human Behav. **112**, 106446 (2020). https://doi.org/10.1016/j.chb.2020.106446

20. Dolgov, I., Graves, W.J., Nearents, M.R., Schwark, J.D., Brooks Volkman, C.: Effects of cooperative gaming and avatar customization on subsequent spontaneous helping behavior. Comput Human Behav. **33**, 49–55 (2014). https://doi.org/10.1016/j.chb.2013.12.028

21. Alabau, A., Fabra, L., Martí-Testón, A., Muñoz, A., Solanes, J.E., Gracia, L.: Enriching user-visitor experiences in digital museology: Combining social and virtual interaction within a Metaverse environment. Appl. Sci. **14**, 3769 (2024). https://doi.org/10.3390/app14093769

22. Lee, H.-K., Park, S., Lee, Y.: A proposal of virtual Museum Metaverse content for the MZ generation. Digital Creativity. **33**, 79–95 (2022). https://doi.org/10.1080/14626268.2022.2063903

23. Zhao, W., Su, L., Dou, F.: Designing Virtual Reality Based 3D Modeling and Interaction Technologies for Museums. Heliyon, **9** (2023)

24. Hennig-Thurau, T., Aliman, D.N., Herting, A.M., Cziehso, G.P., Linder, M., Kübler, R.V.: Social interactions in the Metaverse: Framework, initial evidence, and research roadmap. J. Acad. Mark. Sci. **51**, 889–913 (2023). https://doi.org/10.1007/s11747-022-00908-0
25. Shin, D.: Empathy and embodied experience in virtual environment: To what extent can virtual reality stimulate empathy and embodied experience? Comput Human Behav. **78**, 64–73 (2018). https://doi.org/10.1016/j.chb.2017.09.012
26. Wong, T.: Teaching innovations in Asian higher education: Perspectives of educators. Asian Association of Open Universities Journal. **13**, 179–190 (2019)
27. Kim, D.Y., Lee, H.K., Chung, K.: Avatar-mediated experience in the Metaverse: The impact of avatar realism on user-avatar relationship. J. Retail. Consum. Serv. **73**, 103382 (2023). https://doi.org/10.1016/j.jretconser.2023.103382
28. Basu, T.: Roblox's Avatars are about to get more expressive. MIT Technology Review
29. Haskins, C.: Zepeto is the avatar-based social network for teens that's dominating the app store
30. Chen, T., Razzaq, A., Qing, P., Cao, B.: Do you bear to reject them? The effect of anthropomorphism on empathy and consumer preference for unattractive produce. J. Retail. Consum. Serv. **61**, 102556 (2021). https://doi.org/10.1016/j.jretconser.2021.102556

Creating Immersive Experiences: Exploring the Factors that Influence Users to Utilize Virtual Tour Services

Haoning Ji[1]($\boxtimes$), Ruisi Liu[2], and Junjie Chu[1]

[1] Ocean University of China, Qingdao 266100, China
{chujunjie,chujunjie}@ouc.edu.cn
[2] Northwestern Polytechnical University, Xi'an 710072, China

Abstract. With the development of technology, the tourism industry is actively exploring the integration of emerging technologies. The continuous emergence and widespread application of innovative models such as cloud tourism and cloud exhibitions have provided tourists with novel travel experiences. In this context, it is crucial to investigate the factors that influence the public's acceptance of virtual tourism. We first evaluated the virtual tourism services of 339 national 5A-rated scenic spots in China and selected Prince Kung's Palace Museum, which had the highest overall score, for further investigation. This study established an extended TAM, incorporating variables such as Perceived Enjoyment, Presence, and Information Quality. We applied structural equation modeling for data analysis. The results show that Perceived Enjoyment positively influences both Perceived Ease of Use and Behavioral Intention, while Presence positively influences Perceived Usefulness. This suggests that future cloud tourism service designs for scenic spots should focus on enhancing user experience, while providing immersive embodied experiences to promote users' willingness to use the service. The study also found that Information Quality did not significantly impact Perceived Ease of Use, indicating that future cloud tourism service designs should achieve a balance between high-quality information display and superior interactive experiences. This research provides new perspectives for academic research and practical applications in the field of virtual tourism and offers a theoretical foundation and practical guidance for the innovation and development of future virtual tourism services.

Keywords: Technology Acceptance Model (TAM) · Virtual tourism · Structural equation modeling (SEM)

1 Introduction

In recent years, with advancements in technology, the tourism industry has been actively exploring integration with emerging technologies. Research has revealed an increasingly prominent significance of innovative themes within the tourism sector, as technological innovations are gradually fulfilling people's demands for exceptional travel

J. Y. C. Chen et al. (Eds.): HCII 2025, LNCS 16338, pp. 174–189, 2026.
https://doi.org/10.1007/978-3-032-12808-9_12

experiences [1]. Driven by the wave of digitization, the deep integration of the tourism industry with information technology has led to the emergence of online tourism. With the continuous development and widespread application of diverse digital products such as online service platforms for scenic spots, dedicated mobile applications for tourist attractions, and cloud-based virtual tours of scenic areas, the internet and smartphones have emerged as novel bridges connecting tourists with tourist destinations [2]. It is evident, therefore, that online tourism plays an increasingly significant role in enhancing the tourism experience by providing tourists with more convenient and efficient services through innovative means [3]. Cultural and tourism departments across regions have actively embraced cutting-edge technologies such as AR, VR, and blockchain, innovatively developing online tourism models, including innovative formats like cloud tourism, virtual exhibitions, and live streaming tours, to provide tourists with novel travel experiences [4]. Among them, tourism models represented by virtual reality (VR) technology have actively promoted the development of the tourism industry and garnered high levels of public satisfaction. For instance, the "Experience Singapore Now" initiative launched by the Singapore Tourism Board in 2020 enabled global tourists to transcend geographical boundaries and explore the most iconic attractions and regions of this city-state, enjoying unprecedented virtual travel experiences [5]. As well as the panoramic VR function within the "Digital Forbidden City" launched by the Forbidden City, which significantly enhances tourists' willingness to visit in person. This provides insights for tourism enterprises to gain competitive advantages in the digital era [4].

Therefore, new research needs to recognize the novel impacts of cloud tourism services, represented by virtual reality (VR) technology, on tourists' experiences at scenic spots. VR technology leverages computer technology to transcend physical limitations, providing tourists with digital visual displays, stereo sound effects, and comprehensive sensory simulations, thereby leading users into immersive virtual environments [6]. However, there is currently limited research on the factors influencing tourists' choice of this emerging cloud tourism mode and whether this mode can effectively enhance tourists' acceptance to engage in real-life travel. These issues have become key concerns in the study of cloud tourism service experiences. Therefore, this paper conducts a comprehensive evaluation of cloud tourism services at 339 5A-level scenic spots in China and employs the Technology Acceptance Model (TAM) to explore the acceptance of cloud tourism services at scenic spots, with the Prince Kung's Palace Museum as a representative case. The findings provide reference suggestions for the development of cloud tourism services at scenic spots.

2 Literature Review

2.1 Virtual Tourism Service

In the mid-to-late 1990s, Williams and Hobson were the first to foresee that virtual reality technology would have a significant impact on human society, specifically pointing out that this technological innovation would usher the tourism industry into an unprecedented information era—a new epoch of virtual tourism [7]. Virtual tourism refers to the "simulation of video imagery from existing locations," incorporating video/images, text, and audio, with the objective of replicating authentic on-site experiences. Users typically access it via computers and networks, interacting through displays and input devices such as mice [5]. Compared to real-life tourism, virtual tourism omits aspects such as accommodation, dining, transportation and shopping, focusing instead on sight-seeing and entertainment, thereby allowing tourists to experience the core joys of travel in a more direct manner [8]. The development of advanced technology (e.g. VR technology) also provides more ways to experience virtual tourism. Zhao Weiwei et al. concluded that virtual tourism is an innovative tourism model that uses VR technology to simulate realistic or surreal landscapes through the Internet, multimedia and touch screens to provide a multi-sensory real experience of vision, hearing, etc. VR technology enables tourists to explore scenic attractions around the world as if they were physically present, providing an immersive tourism experience without the need for actual travel. This advancement not only enriches people's leisure and entertainment choices but also promotes the digital transformation and development of the tourism industry [9].

Virtual tours have made a difference to tourists' travelling activities and have opened up new opportunities for national governments and businesses. Today, many tourist destinations are adopting virtual tour solutions, such as destination smartphone apps, whose powerful location-aware features provide users with both a reliable and convenient Internet connectivity experience. These tourism-related smartphone apps not only act as a two-way interactive bridge between tourists and tourism product providers, but also become the preferred channel for people to obtain the latest tourism information, promote special products, and complete purchasing behaviors [10]. It not only promotes instant interaction between tour operators and tourists, but also greatly facilitates the sharing of information on tourism activities [11]. At the same time, the use of virtual tours greatly enriches the range of choices available to tourists at the pre-purchase stage, enabling them to easily search, carefully plan and comprehensively compare the diverse range of products and services offered by the tourism sector, and to make their final choice and purchase decisions about destinations and services through comparison and evaluation [3]. Studies have shown that the introduction of virtual reality technology in the hospitality industry can significantly stimulate consumers' immediate purchasing impulses and increase their acceptance to visit a hotel [12]. In addition, the unique "non-contact" nature of virtual tours provides the public with new perspectives for exploring and understanding cultural heritage. The digital platform facilitates online interaction between users and cultural heritage through innovative methods such as virtual dialogues and immersive games, enhancing the public's level of understanding of cultural heritage and their sense of responsibility for its preservation [2]. The government's perception of the value of VR technology in promoting cultural preservation, digital economy and creative industries has gradually increased, and has promoted the development of the cultural and museum sector by introducing VR technology into museums and famous scenic spots [6]. VR equipment gives visitors the magic of travelling through time and space, crossing the physical space limitations often found in museums. For those precious relics that are difficult to display publicly due to space constraints, VR technology provides a 'digital treasure trove of cultural relics', opening up an infinite virtual space for the preservation and display of cultural relics. On this platform, visitors can freely explore those rare exhibits that are difficult to witness due to damage or have not been opened to the public for a long time, and enjoy an unprecedented cultural feast [13].

Finally, virtual tourism can play a key role in preventing the total stagnation of tourism activities at special times. Tourists can safely experience and gain insight into the world's landscapes from home virtually, even during periods of restricted travel. Moreover, virtual tourism helps museums and tourist attractions of all kinds to maintain their interaction with the public and ensure the continuity of cultural transmission [5]. Virtual travel fulfils people's dream of exploring the world without risk, while also effectively mitigating damage to the natural environment by circumventing the phenomenon of over-tourism. In summary, virtual travelling is a novel and environmentally friendly form of entertainment [1].

In order to explore the development of virtual tours in the tourism industry, we summarized the evaluation criteria of virtual tours through literature review [7]. Including convenience, novelty, richness, simulation and experience, there are 16 evaluation indicators. Table 1 shows the evaluation table in this paper. By performing a comprehensive evaluation of virtual tour services in 339 Chinese 5A-level scenic spots, we selected the cloud tourism service of the Prince Kung's Palace Museum with the highest composite scores in each category, and used it as a representative research subject for subsequent investigations.

Table 1. Evaluation Criteria for Cloud Tourism Services in the Prince Kung's Palace Museum.

Level 1 evaluation indicators	Level 2 evaluation indicators	Score (1–5) Average score
Convenience	Ease of operation	5
	Information comprehensibility	5
	Operational comfort	5
Novelty	Technical novelty	5
	Visual impact of the scene	5
	Creativity of the virtual space for cloud tours	5
Richness	Diversity of virtual landscapes	5
	Richness of scene auxiliary elements	5
	Flexibility of virtual operation mode	5
	Completeness of the virtual guide function	5
Simulation	Objective authenticity of the virtual landscape	5
	Objective authenticity of cultural symbols	5
	Simulation of the browsing process	5
Experiential	Virtual experience of real tourism activities	5

(continued)

Table 1. (continued)

Level 1 evaluation indicators	Level 2 evaluation indicators	Score (1–5) Average score
	Communication between tourists	4
	Experientiality of tourism roles	5

2.2 Technology Acceptance Model (TAM)

TAM was first proposed by Davis in 1986 [14]. It is based on the TRA theory, aiming at an in-depth study of the adoption of information technology. The technology acceptance model states that a user's intention to use a technology is influenced by the positivity of his or her attitude towards that technology, while a user's attitude towards the adoption of a new technology is directly influenced by perceived ease of use and perceived usefulness [5]. Perceived usefulness and perceived ease of use are the two core variables of TAM that together contribute to users' attitudes and intentions to use new technologies [15]. According to Davis and other scholars' subsequent in-depth research and discussion, TAM has been continuously innovated and revised, and extended models such as TAM2, UTAUT, and UTAUT2 have been gradually created to further expand the explanatory ability of the model [14].

TAM and its extended model have been widely used in studies related to virtual displays and virtual tours due to its ability to effectively identify key factors affecting the VR/AR user experience, making it one of the most important tools for studying user acceptance [16]. Using TAM, the researchers explored how users rated VR technology as an enhancement to the museum experience, and how user-friendly interaction design can promote acceptance and exploratory behavior [6]. Scholars in China have used TAM to reveal the positive impact of digital museum users' attention to use and behaviors on enhancing the national sense of responsibility for cultural heritage protection [2]. In addition, the researchers delved into the interrelationship between smartphone users' online experience and destination image and its impact through TAM [10]. Existing literature enhances the explanatory power of the model in specific domains by adding new variables to the original TAM. Perceived value and sensation-seeking behavior, for example, have been shown to be important precursors in predicting the adoption of VR technology in tourist destinations [12]. Taken together, these findings provide ample evidence of TAM's broad applicability and insight into the interpretation of travel intentions and intentions to use virtual reality technology.

3   Research Hypotheses and Research Model

Based on previous research, this study extends TAM and explores the factors that influence users' adoption of cloud tourism services. The proposed research model is shown in Fig. 1.

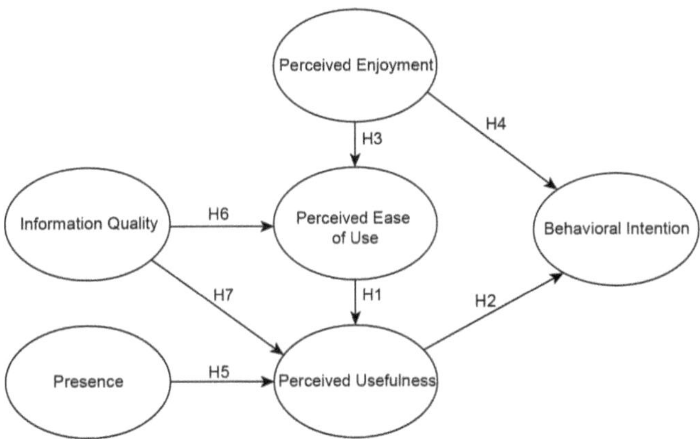

Fig. 1. The research model proposed in this study.

3.1 Perceived Ease of Use and Perceived Usefulness

Perceived usefulness and perceived ease of use are two core variables in the research model of this study. Perceived usefulness refers to the degree to which users subjectively believe that the use of a system can enhance their work performance or achieve specific goals. In contrast, perceived ease of use pertains to the subjective assessment of users concerning the ease of utilizing a particular system [17]. Previous research has found that perceived ease of use can significantly influence perceived usefulness, which in turn positively affects users' intention to use [4]. Based on this foundation, the following hypotheses are proposed in this paper regarding cloud tourism services:

H1: Perceived ease of use has a significant impact on perceived usefulness.

H2: Perceived usefulness has a significant impact on behavioral intention.

3.2 Perceived Enjoyment

The Technology Acceptance Model (TAM) often requires extensions to construct a more comprehensive theoretical framework, and perceived enjoyment is one of the common additions in these extended versions. In previous research, perceived enjoyment is defined as "the degree to which the activity of using a computer is itself seen as enjoyable, independently of any performance outcomes that may be anticipated." [5] From the theoretical perspective of technology acceptance, perceived enjoyment in virtual tourism is primarily manifested in the convenience provided by the technology and the pleasant feelings experienced by users during its utilization [9]. Previous research has found a positive correlation between perceived enjoyment in VR experiences and the acceptance to adopt VR technology for evaluating tourism destination websites [5]. Studies have also found that perceived enjoyment can positively influence users' acceptance of VR by positively impacting their attitude towards using the technology, which in turn affects their willingness to adopt VR [18]. Affordance, usefulness, enjoyment, and aesthetics in sustaining virtual reality engagement.

Based on this foundation, the following hypotheses are proposed in this paper regarding cloud tourism services:

H3: Perceived enjoyment has a significant impact on perceived ease of use.

H4: Perceived enjoyment has a significant impact on behavioral intention.

3.3 Presence

Presence is regarded as an external stimulus that acts on an individual's psychological state, thereby stimulating a strong desire to visit the destination in real life as a response [12]. "Presence," the psychological experience of "being there," has emerged as a key phenomenon in virtual reality (VR) research [19]. Many studies have found that presence is a crucial factor in eliciting perceived enjoyment among tourists when virtual reality (VR) technology is applied to natural scenery tourist attractions. When users engage with VR technology, compared to traditional two-dimensional displays, the sense of presence under VR technology is significantly enhanced. VR technology offers more vivid imagery, improves users' ability to interact with the environment, and optimizes information processing. This highly focused brain activity induces a pleasurable emotional experience akin to a state of flow [12]. Previous research has also indicated that presence can positively influence users' acceptance to visit by promoting their attitude towards VR tourism [20]. In this study, the following hypothesis is proposed regarding cloud tourism services:

H5: Users' sense of telepresence has a significant impact on perceived usefulness.

3.4 Information Quality

Information quality is comprised of three core pillars: accuracy, richness, and elements related to interface design and information guidance. The online experience provided by mobile technology profoundly influences tourists' decision-making processes and behavioral patterns. In terms of enhancing consumers' online experience with mobile technology, previous research identified the key factors as the degree of personalization, communication efficiency, connection stability, and content quality [10]. For instance, in studies exploring the factors influencing user engagement in museum virtual reality (VR), numerous scholars have pointed out that information quality serves as a crucial cornerstone. Scholars have emphasized that high-quality information can minimize the gap between VR experiences and physical exhibitions, thereby enhancing user trust and engagement [6]. Previous research on users' acceptance of Augmented Reality (AR) technology has shown that information quality has a positive impact on both perceived ease of use and perceived usefulness [28]. Based on this foundation, the following hypotheses are proposed in this paper regarding cloud tourism services:

H6: Information quality has a significant impact on perceived ease of use.

H7: Information quality has a significant impact on perceived usefulness.

4   Methodology

4.1   Data Collection

This survey was conducted through an online questionnaire. Prior to the formal distribution of the questionnaire, a pre-test was conducted with six participants of different ages and professions to assess whether the questions in the questionnaire were easily understandable. The results indicated that all participants were able to comprehend the questions well and independently complete the questionnaire. The survey collected a total of 202 questionnaires from July 21, 2024, to January 5, 2025. The statistical results show that 40.59% of the respondents were male, while 59.41% were female. In terms of age distribution, the largest group was aged 19–30 years, comprising 44.55% of the total respondents. Other age groups included those under 18 years (7.92%), 31–50 years (18.81%), 51–70 years (18.81%), and over 70 years (9.90%). Regarding educational background, the majority of respondents had at least a bachelor's degree, accounting for 64.85% of the total. Respondents with education levels of middle school or below and high school accounted for 13.37% and 21.78%, respectively. The sample included participants of different genders, ages, and educational backgrounds, which ensures that the data is representative. After data screening, we excluded (1) questionnaires completed in less than 50 s, and (2) questionnaires with the same answers for all but two (or fewer) questions. In the end, 112 valid questionnaires were retained. The questionnaire was divided into two parts. The first part gathered basic demographic information from respondents, while the second part used a 7-point Likert scale to assess respondents' agreement with various statements. Table 2 presents the items in the second section and their sources.

Table 2. The items of each factor.

Factor	Items	Source
Perceived Usefulness(PU)	PU1: The cloud tourism service of Prince Kung's Palace Museum has improved my efficiency in obtaining relevant tourism information	[17] [8]
	PU2: The cloud tourism service of Prince Kung's Palace Museum can help me easily obtain the tourism information I want to know.	
	PU3: I believe that by using the cloud tourism service of Prince Kung's Palace Museum, I can have a clear understanding of the entire scenic area.	
Perceived Ease of Use (PEU)	PEU1: For me, it is easy to proficiently operate the cloud tourism service of Prince Kung's Palace Museum to obtain the information I want to know.	[17] [21] [22]

(continued)

Table 2. (continued)

Factor	Items	Source
	PEU2: I found that through the cloud tourism service of Prince Kung's Palace Museum, I can easily obtain the travel information I need.	
	PEU3: I found that the usage process of the cloud tourism service in Prince Kung's Palace Museum is clear and easy to understand.	
Perceived Enjoyment (PE)	PE1: During the experience, I was full of enthusiasm for the cloud tourism service of Prince Kung's Palace Museum	[12] [23]
	PE2: I felt very happy when I was experiencing the cloud tourism service of Prince Kung's Palace Museum.	
	PE3: I think it's very interesting to experience the cloud tourism service of Prince Kung's Palace Museum.	
Presence (PS)	PS1: When I was experiencing the cloud tourism service of Prince Kung's Palace Museum, I had a feeling of immersing myself in the destination.	[12] [23]
	PS2: When I was experiencing the cloud tourism service of Prince Kung's Palace Museum, it was as if my body position had been transferred to the real environment.	
	PS3: When I was experiencing the cloud tourism service of Prince Kung's Palace Museum, it seemed like I was really involved in the sightseeing activities of the scenic area.	
Information quality (IQ)	IQ1: The information quality presented in the cloud tourism service of Prince Kung's Palace Museum is very good.	[24] [25] [26]
	IQ2: The information provided by the cloud tourism service of Prince Kung's Palace Museum is easy to understand.	
	IQ3: The cloud tourism service of Prince Kung's Palace Museum can smoothly transmit various information such as text and graphics.	
Behavioral Intention (BI)	BI1: If given the opportunity, I am willing to use the cloud tourism service of the Prince Kung's Palace Museum again.	[27] [21] [28]

(continued)

Table 2. (*continued*)

Factor	Items	Source
	BI2: In the future, if I need to learn about the scenic information of Prince Kung's Palace Museum, I am willing to choose the cloud tourism service of Prince Kung's Palace Museum to experience it.	
	BI3: Compared to other methods, I prefer to choose the cloud tourism service of the Prince Kung's Palace Museum to obtain the tourism information I want to know.	

4.2 Data Analysis

This study employs structural equation modeling (SEM) for data analysis, which comprises two main components: measurement model analysis and structural model analysis.

Measurement Model. Confirmatory factor analysis (CFA) was performed to assess the measurement model. The results, presented in Table 3, include significance tests and reliability parameters for the items. According to the table, all standardized factor loadings are greater than 0.6, with most exceeding 0.7, which aligns with the recommended thresholds. Additionally, all R-squared values are above 0.36, with the majority surpassing 0.5, indicating that the item reliability meets the recommended standards.

Table 4 presents the results for composite reliability, convergent validity, and discriminant validity. The composite reliability (CR) for all constructs exceeds 0.7, demonstrating acceptable reliability according to Hairs et al. [29]. The average variance extracted (AVE) for all constructs is above 0.5, indicating strong convergent validity [30]. Moreover, the square root of the AVE for most constructs is greater than the corresponding Pearson correlation coefficients, while a few are slightly lower but still within the acceptable range, suggesting adequate discriminant validity between the dimensions [31].

Table 3. Parameters of significant test and item reliability.

Factor	Items	Estimate	S.E	Est./S.E	P-Value	R-square
PE	PE1	0.704	0.086	8.142	***	0.496
	PE2	0.766	0.082	9.288	***	0.587
	PE3	0.695	0.077	9.043	***	0.483
PS	PS1	0.730	0.106	6.901	***	0.533
	PS2	0.882	0.071	12.488	***	0.778

(continued)

Table 3. (*continued*)

Factor	Items	Estimate	S.E	Est./S.E	P-Value	R-square
	PS3	0.622	0.092	6.793	***	0.387
PU	PU1	0.717	0.109	6.574	***	0.514
	PU2	0.971	0.071	13.732	***	0.943
	PU3	0.687	0.100	6.867	***	0.472
PEU	PEU1	0.897	0.064	14.120	***	0.805
	PEU2	0.880	0.049	17.783	***	0.774
	PEU3	0.644	0.074	8.738	***	0.415
IQ	IQ1	0.678	0.083	8.168	***	0.460
	IQ2	0.865	0.085	10.200	***	0.748
	IQ3	0.736	0.092	8.012	***	0.542
BI	BI1	0.833	0.053	15.816	***	0.694
	BI2	0.787	0.055	14.336	***	0.619
	BI3	0.841	0.052	16.106	***	0.707

Table 4. Composite reliability, convergent validity, and discriminate validity.

	CR	AVE	PE	PS	PU	PEU	IQ	BI
PE	0.766	0.522	0.722					
PS	0.793	0.566	0.493	0.752				
PU	0.840	0.643	0.712	0.574	0.802			
PEU	0.853	0.665	0.577	0.240	0.429	0.815		
IQ	0.806	0.583	0.682	0.523	0.769	0.330	0.764	
BI	0.861	0.674	0.719	0.521	0.645	0.462	0.762	0.821

Structural Model. The structural model was evaluated using several fit indices, including χ^2/df, CFI, TLI, RMSEA, and SRMR. As shown in Table 5, all of these indices fall within the recommended ranges, suggesting that the structural model demonstrates a good fit.

Table 6 presents the results of hypothesis testing. A p-value of less than 0.05 indicates a significant relationship between the dimensions, confirming the validity of the hypothesis. Notably, out of the 7 hypotheses we proposed, six were supported and one was not supported. The findings are illustrated in Fig. 2. Additionally, the results show that the model accounts for 70.5% of the variance in perceived usefulness, 37.5% of the variance in perceived ease of use, and 63.0% of the variance in behavioral intention.

Table 5. Model fit.

	Recommended value	Index	
χ^2/df	$1 < \chi^2/df < 3$	1.419	Matched
CFI	>0.9	0.936	Matched
TLI	>0.9	0.922	Matched
RMSEA	<0.08	0.061	Matched
SRMR	<0.08	0.076	Matched

Table 6. Hypothesis analysis.

DV	IV	Estimate	S.E	Est./S.E	P-value	R^2	Hypothesis
PU	IQ	0.624	0.095	6.596	***	0.705	Support
	PEU	0.182	0.075	2.442	0.015		Support
	PS	0.217	0.096	2.264	0.024		Support
PEU	PE	0.781	0.156	5.001	***	0.375	Support
	IQ	−0.258	0.154	-1.676	0.094		Not Support
BI	PU	0.274	0.121	2.264	0.024	0.630	Support
	PE	0.581	0.110	5.293	***		Support

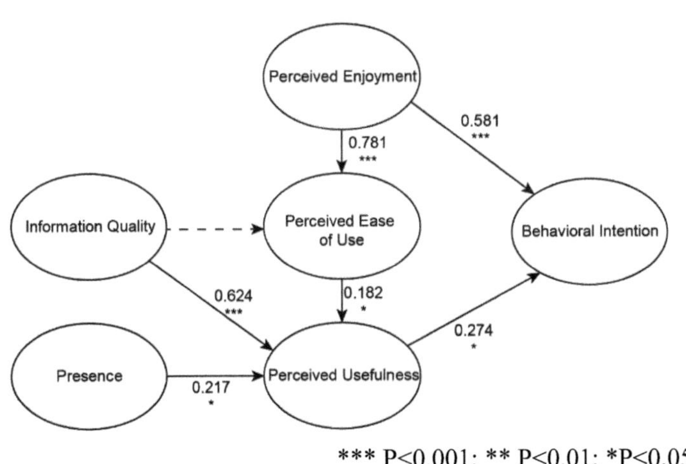

*** P<0.001; ** P<0.01; *P<0.05

Fig. 2. Results of the research model.

5 Discussion

This study introduces Perceived Enjoyment (PE), Presence (PS), and Information Quality (IQ) to establish an extended Technology Acceptance Model, aiming to explore the factors that influence users' acceptance of cloud tourism services. Through data analysis, several hypotheses were tested, and the following is a discussion of the hypotheses.

First, in this study, Perceived Ease of Use significantly influences Perceived Usefulness, which, in turn, positively impacts users' Behavioral Intention. This finding is consistent with the results of most previous studies [32] [33]. It suggests that both the functionality and ease of use of cloud tourism services are crucial. When users engage in cloud tourism experiences, if the service is easy to operate and does not require a complex learning process, it becomes easier to understand and enables users to experience the practical value of the system, thereby enhancing their evaluation of usefulness. Furthermore, when users perceive that cloud tourism services can effectively improve their travel experience or provide important information, they are more likely to be willing to continue using the technology. This finding indicates that cloud tourism services should focus on enhancing the practicality of their features and reducing operational complexity to strengthen users' intention for continued use.

Perceived Enjoyment has been discussed in several studies regarding VR technology acceptance. In this study, we found that Perceived Enjoyment has a significant positive impact on both Perceived Ease of Use and Behavioral Intention, and previous studies have also confirmed this [34] [35]. This indicates that a pleasurable user experience enables users to operate the system more easily, thereby reducing the perceived difficulty of using the technology. A pleasant usage experience generates positive emotional responses from users, which in turn further enhances their evaluation of the system's ease of use and their intention to use the service. Perceived Enjoyment is an important factor in users' acceptance of new technologies, particularly in tourism-related services, where a pleasurable user experience can become a core driver of continued usage. Therefore, future cloud tourism services for tourist attractions could focus on enhancing the user experience by incorporating fun games or innovative interactions to boost users' intention to engage with the service.

Presence is crucial for virtual reality presentations and cloud tourism services, as it can compensate for the regret of not being physically present by providing an immersive experience [36]. Our research findings reveal that Presence has a significant impact on the Perceived Usefulness of cloud tourism services. VR technology can offer more vivid and realistic experiences, enhancing users' cognition and understanding of scenic spot information, thereby improving their evaluation of the usefulness of cloud tourism services. In the future design of cloud tourism services for tourist attractions, Presence can be enhanced by providing realistic scene modeling and offering multi-sensory experiences such as visual, auditory, and tactile stimuli, which will further promote users' intention to use cloud tourism services. For historical and cultural attractions, combining storytelling with the restoration of historical scenes can create a stronger sense of immersion for users.

This study also incorporated the variable of Information Quality and found that its influence on Perceived Usefulness was supported. High-quality information enhances users' evaluation of the service's practicality. Good information quality and effective communication can reduce ambiguity, build trust in the service, and, in turn, increase the perceived usefulness of the service. However, the study found that Information Quality did not have a significant impact on Perceived Ease of Use. This may be because, when evaluating information quality, users tend to focus more on factors such as the accuracy, completeness, and usefulness of the information—elements that directly affect their evaluation of the information's value, rather than the ease of the usage process itself. Additionally, excessive information input may lead to user fatigue or frustration, which can negatively affect their perception of the service's ease of use. Future research could further explore how, while improving the quality of information presented in cloud tourism services, factors that align more closely with the user's operational experience can also be considered, achieving a balance between high-quality information and an optimal user experience.

6 Conclusion

Currently, various digital technologies are developing rapidly, and seeking ways to attract users through the adoption of innovative technologies has become a key issue for major tourist attractions. In this context, this study provides a comprehensive evaluation of virtual tourism services at Chinese 5A-level scenic spots, identifying the cloud tourism service at Prince Kung's Palace Museum as the highest-scoring in various categories. Using this service as an example, an extended technology acceptance model was developed to explore the factors that influence users' acceptance of cloud tourism services at scenic spots.

This study tested multiple hypotheses based on the Technology Acceptance Model, revealing the relationships between Perceived Ease of Use, Perceived Usefulness, Perceived Enjoyment, Presence, Information Quality, and users' Behavioral Intentions. The results indicate that the user acceptance of cloud tourism services is not only influenced by the system's ease of use and usefulness, but that a pleasurable user experience and a high degree of immersion also play important roles. However, the study also found that the impact of Information Quality on Perceived Ease of Use was not significant, suggesting that, at present, there is an imbalance between the high-quality information presentation and the interactive experience in virtual tourism. Future research could further investigate how factors such as immersion and interactivity in virtual reality technology can enhance users' emotional engagement, thereby promoting their intention to use the service. In addition, future studies could also expand the sample scope to explore differences in user acceptance across different types of tourist attractions and cultural contexts, and further verify the applicability of these factors in various scenarios.

References

1. Chiao, H.-M., Chen, Y.-L., Huang, W.-H.: Examining the usability of an online virtual tour-guiding platform for cultural tourism education. J. Hosp. Leis. Sport Tour. Educ. **23**, 29–38 (2018)
2. Sun, J.J., Guo, Y.Z.: A research on the influence of the digitization of cultural heritage sites on National Heritage responsibility: A model construction based on TTF and TAM. Tourism Sci. **37**, 71–85 (2023)

3. Lama, S., Pradhan, S., Shrestha, A.: Exploration and implication of factors affecting e-tourism adoption in developing countries: A case of Nepal. Inf Technol Tourism. **22**, 5–32 (2020)

4. Xinyu, Z.: Influence of Panoramic Vr Software on Tourists' on-Site Travel Intention: An Integrated Model Based on Tam and Idt

5. El-Said, O., Aziz, H.: Virtual tours a means to an end: An analysis of virtual tours' role in tourism recovery post COVID-19. J. Travel Res. **61**, 528–548 (2022)

6. YiFei, L., Othman, M.K.: Investigating the behavioural intentions of museum visitors towards VR: A systematic literature review. Comput. Hum. Behav. **155**, 108167 (2024)

7. Yang, W.J., Wang, X., Hu, C.D.: A case study on the experience quality evaluation of virtual tour. Journal of Chongqing Normal University (Natural Science). **29**, 100–104 (2012)

8. Huang, Y.-C., Li, L.-N., Lee, H.-Y., Browning, M.H.E.M., Yu, C.-P.: Surfing in virtual reality: An application of extended technology acceptance model with flow theory. Computers in Human Behavior Reports. **9**, 100252 (2023)

9. Zhao, W.W., Luo, S.F., Huang, Y.L.: How does the virtual touch reality? The influence mechanism of virtual tourism from the perspective of the "New Generation." Tourism Sci. **36**, 21–37 (2022)

10. Xia, M., Zhang, Y., Zhang, C.: A TAM-based approach to explore the effect of online experience on destination image: A smartphone user's perspective. J. Destin. Mark. Manag. **8**, 259–270 (2018)

11. Sujood, Bano, N., Siddiqui, S.: Consumers' intention towards the use of smart technologies in tourism and hospitality (T&H) industry: A deeper insight into the integration of TAM, TPB and trust. JHTI. **7**, 1412–1434 (2024)

12. Hoang, S.D., Dey, S.K., Tučková, Z., Pham, T.P.: Harnessing the power of virtual reality: Enhancing telepresence and inspiring sustainable travel intentions in the tourism industry. Technol. Soc. **75**, 102378 (2023)

13. Yuan, Y., Zhou, X.: Research on VR Virtual Display Technology of Non-heritage Cultural and Creative Products. In: 2023 IEEE 3rd International Conference on Electronic Communications, Internet of Things and Big Data (ICEIB). pp. 471–474. IEEE, Taichung, Taiwan (2023)

14. Sun, J.J., Cheng, Y., Ke, Q.: Advances of Research on Technology—Acceptance Model. Information Science. 1121–1127 (2007)

15. Mardhi Suryanto, T.L. et al.: Acceptance of Virtual Campus Tour Using the TAM Approach: a Case Study in UPN Veteran Jawa Timur, Indonesia. In: 2021 IEEE 7th Information Technology International Seminar (ITIS). pp. 1–6. IEEE, Surabaya, Indonesia (2021)

16. Wei, W.: Research progress on virtual reality (VR) and augmented reality (AR) in tourism and hospitality: A critical review of publications from 2000 to 2018. JHTT. **10**, 539–570 (2019)

17. Davis, F.D., Bagozzi, R.P., Warshaw, P.R.: User acceptance of computer technology: A comparison of two theoretical models. Manage. Sci. **35**, 982–1003 (1989)

18. Jo, H., Park, D.-H.: Affordance, usefulness, enjoyment, and aesthetics in sustaining virtual reality engagement. Sci. Rep. **13**, 15097 (2023)

19. Triberti, S., Sapone, C., Riva, G.: Being there but where? Sense of presence theory for virtual reality applications. Humanit Soc Sci Commun. **12**, 79 (2025)

20. Tussyadiah, I.P., Wang, D., Jung, T.H., Tom Dieck, M.C.: Virtual reality, presence, and attitude change: Empirical evidence from tourism. Tour. Manage. **66**, 140–154 (2018)

21. Venkatesh, M., Davis, D.: User Acceptance of Information Technology: Toward a Unified View. MIS Quarterly. **27**, 425 (2003)

22. Shi, M., Wang, Q., Long, Y.: Exploring the key drivers of user continuance intention to use digital museums: Evidence From China's Sanxingdui Museum. IEEE Access. **11**, 81511–81526 (2023)

23. Wirani, Y., Nabarian, T., Romadhon, M.S.: Evaluation of continued use on Kahoot! as a gamification-based learning platform from the perspective of Indonesia students. Procedia Computer Science. **197**, 545–556 (2022)

24. Su, P.-Y., Hsiao, P.-W., Fan, K.-K.: Investigating the relationship between users' behavioral intentions and learning effects of VR system for sustainable tourism development. Sustainability. **15**, 7277 (2023)

25. Dağhan, G., Akkoyunlu, B.: Modeling the continuance usage intention of online learning environments. Comput. Hum. Behav. **60**, 198–211 (2016)

26. Yoo, J.: The effects of perceived quality of augmented reality in mobile commerce—An application of the information systems success model. Informatics. **7**, 14 (2020)

27. Fussell, S.G., Truong, D.: Using virtual reality for dynamic learning: An extended technology acceptance model. Virtual Reality **26**, 249–267 (2022)

28. McLean, G., Wilson, A.: Shopping in the digital world: Examining customer engagement through augmented reality mobile applications. Comput. Hum. Behav. **101**, 210–224 (2019)

29. Hairs, J.F., Anderson, R.E., Tatham, R.L., Black, W.C.: Multivariate Data Analysis. Printice Hall, Englewood Cliffs (1998)

30. Fornell, C., Larcker, D.: Structural equation models with unobservable variables and measurement error. J. Mark. Res. (1981)

31. Li, S.Q., Meng, F., Wu, X.Y.: Effect of social capital between construction supervisors and workers on workers' safety behavior. J. Constr. Eng. Manag. **144**(4), 04018014 (2018)

32. Zhang, T., Xiong, S.: Exploring the influence of expectancy, valence, and instrumentality on VR tourism intention: A framework based on TAM and expectancy theory. Acta Physiol (Oxf.) **250**, 104541 (2024)

33. Chen, T., Chen, J., Or, C.K., Lo, F.P.: Path analysis of the roles of age, self-efficacy, and TAM constructs in the acceptance of performing upper limb exercises through immersive virtual reality games. Int. J. Ind. Ergon. **91**, 103360 (2022)

34. Abdalla, R.A.M.: Examining awareness, social influence, and perceived enjoyment in the TAM framework as determinants of ChatGPT. Personalization as a moderator. Journal of Open Innovation: Technology, Market, and Complexity. **10**, 100327 (2024)

35. Lee, J., Kim, J., Choi, J.Y.: The adoption of virtual reality devices: The technology acceptance model integrating enjoyment, social interaction, and strength of the social ties. Telematics Inform. **39**, 37–48 (2019)

36. Sagnier, C., Loup-Escande, E., Lourdeaux, D., Thouvenin, I., Valléry, G.: User acceptance of virtual reality: An extended technology acceptance model. International Journal of Human-Computer Interaction. **36**, 993–1007 (2020)

Boosting User Engagement in VR Museum Games: A Needs-Driven Design Approach

Yue Liu[✉]

Rensselaer Polytechnic Institute, Troy, NY 12180, USA
liuy78@rpi.edu

Abstract. Virtual reality (VR) museum games offer engaging ways to interact with cultural heritage but often face challenges in maintaining user interest due to design issues or unmet expectations. This study employs a needs-driven approach using a combination of Kano and Analytic Hierarchy Process (AHP) models to identify and prioritize user requirements. Through literature reviews, expert consultations, and surveys, 24 key user requirements were established. Kano analysis classified these into 9 Must-be, 5 One-dimensional, 7 Attractive, and 3 Indifferent attributes, emphasizing the critical roles of realistic visual fidelity, interactive exploration, and narrative immersion. The subsequent AHP evaluation ranked interactive and gamified exploration highest (0.474), followed by narrative immersion and emotional connection (0.285), sensory and embodied immersion (0.157), and social collaboration (0.084). This research provides clear, data-driven guidance for improving VR museum game design, emphasizing interactive exploration and immersive storytelling to significantly enhance user engagement.

Keywords: Virtual Reality · Museum Games · User Engagement · User Experience · Cultural Heritage · Game Design · Kano Model · AHP

1 Introduction

1.1 The Promise and Challenge of VR Museum Games

Museums and cultural heritage sites are increasingly leveraging VR games to extend their reach and impact in the digital age. By allowing users to virtually explore artifacts, historical sites, and artistic treasures, VR museum games can transcend physical and geographic barriers, bringing world-class exhibits to global audiences and offer deeply immersive, interactive learning experiences that traditional galleries cannot easily provide. Prior studies have shown that such immersive experiences can not only entertain users but also increase their motivation to visit real museums, creating a symbiotic virtual-real relationship. Despite this promise, maintaining user engagement in VR museum games presents significant challenges. If the game's design fails to meet user expectations for usability, enjoyment, and educational value, users' interest can wane rapidly. For example, an otherwise visually rich virtual museum (e.g. The Grand Museum VR [1]) drew overwhelmingly negative feedback due to clunky controls and

J. Y. C. Chen et al. (Eds.): HCII 2025, LNCS 16338, pp. 190–214, 2026.
https://doi.org/10.1007/978-3-032-12808-9_13

poor user experience, underscoring that content alone cannot guarantee engagement. This highlights a critical need for user-centered design: understanding what users need and desire from VR museum games in order to keep them actively involved, learning, and coming back.

1.2 Research Questions and Methodological Framework

This work addresses the question of how to boost user engagement in online VR museum games through a needs-driven design approach. The research is grounded in the Human-Computer Interaction (HCI) and games user research tradition of eliciting user requirements to inform design. Specifically, three research questions are investigated:

- RQ1: What are the key requirements and needs of target users for engaging VR museum game experiences?
- RQ2: How can these user needs be systematically categorized and prioritized in terms of their impact on user satisfaction and engagement (using models like Kano and AHP)?
- RQ3: What design strategies can be derived from these prioritized user needs to guide the development of more engaging VR museum games?

To answer these questions, a multi-phase study was conducted. First, qualitative explorations – including literature and case reviews, field observations in museums, and semi-structured interviews – were performed to gather a broad set of user needs. Next, a quantitative survey of VR users was carried out, employing the Kano model to classify which features are merely expected basics versus which can excite users. An Analytic Hierarchy Process (AHP) was then applied to weight and rank the importance of these needs. Finally, the findings were synthesized into concrete design implications.

2 Related Work

2.1 Immersion & Presence, UX & Comfort, Gamification & Narrative

VR's strength lies in creating presence, where users feel immersed in virtual environments. High-fidelity visuals and spatial audio enhance enjoyment and connection to cultural content [2]. For instance, II Divino: Sistine Chapel in VR and Nefertari: Journey to Eternity use photogrammetry to deliver hyper-realistic historical reconstructions, deepening immersion (see 2.2 Table 1). However, poor interaction design, such as clunky controls, can disrupt presence, underscoring the need for intuitive interfaces [3].

User experience (UX) is critical to sustaining engagement. Motion sickness and ergonomic issues are common barriers, making low-latency controls and intuitive navigation essential [4, 5]. The Grand Museum VR illustrates this: despite high-quality 3D models, its unintuitive gaze-based navigation led to user frustration, highlighting the primacy of usability (Table 1). Accessibility for diverse audiences further enhances learning outcomes [6].

Gamification and narrative design boost engagement. Quests and rewards increase enjoyment, as seen in D-Day VR Museum, which balances a museum hub with interactive simulations (Table 1) [7]. Narrative-driven experiences, like Anne Frank House

VR, foster emotional resonance through historical storytelling (Table 1) [8]. However, gamification must support, not overshadow, educational goals. Social features, as in Museum of Other Realities' multiplayer VR space, also show promise for community engagement (Table 1).

2.2 Case Study Analysis and Research Gaps

The following VR museum games cases illustrate key design insights:

Table 1. VR Museum Game Case Studies.

No.	Title	Type	Institution/Developer	Description
01	Mona Lisa: Beyond the Glass (https://store.ste ampowered.com/ app/1172310/ Mona_Lisa_Bey ond_The_Glass/)	Institutional Replica / Reimagination	Louvre Museum/ HTC Vive Arts	Provides an intimate, crowd-free encounter with the Mona Lisa, allowing users to step into the painting's landscape.
02	Anne Frank House VR (https://www. meta.com/en-gb/ experiences/anne-frank-house-vr/ 195810033429 5482/?srsltid=Afm BOooRSrM9Wym ZmsRvLt1uyTssPj LTOUVVBJ89Vy oCZxBxMXr owRSb)	Historical Reconstruction / Narrative	Anne Frank House/ Vertigo Games & Knucklehead Studios	A deeply moving tour of the Secret Annex, furnished as it was during WWII, guided by Anne's diary entries.
03	Versailles VR the Palace is yours (https://en.chatea uversailles.fr/ news/life-estate/ versaillesvr-pal ace-yours)	Institutional Replica	Château de Versailles/ Google Arts & Culture, makemepulse	An unlimited-access tour of the Palace of Versailles, including the Hall of Mirrors, with interactive objects and a night mode.
04	Balzi Rossi Museum VR (https://www. mdpi.com/2076-3417/14/9/3562)	Archaeological Reconstruction	University of Genoa/ Balzi Rossi Museum	Technical showcase reconstructing Paleolithic caves and the surrounding landscape, including an ice-age version.

(*continued*)

Table 1. (*continued*)

No.	Title	Type	Institution/Developer	Description
05	The Grand Museum VR (https://store.ste ampowered.com/ app/896240/The_ Grand_Museum _VR/)	Independent Museum	Owlgorithm	A virtual museum displaying 82 high-quality 3D photo-scanned models of ancient art from various cultures.
06	Great Paintings VR (https://store. steampowered. com/app/1511090/ Great_Paintings _VR/)	Independent Museum	Hublab	A free-to-play virtual museum featuring a vast collection of over 1000 famous paintings in a gallery setting.
07	D-Day VR Museum (https:// store.steampowe red.com/app/251 2870/ DDay_VR_M useum/)	Historical Reconstruction / Game	Lichtblau IT	Blends a traditional museum hub with immersive, interactive explorations of iconic D-Day locations in Normandy.
08	Museum of Other Realities (MOR) (https://www.mus eumor.com/)	Artistic Platform / Social VR	MOR Museum Inc.	A multiplayer social VR space dedicated to showcasing and evolving a collection of mind-bending, VR-native digital art.
09	Art Plunge (https://store.ste ampowered.com/ app/570900/Art_ Plunge/)	Artistic Interpretation	Space Plunge	A short, creative experience where users "plunge" into 3D, volumetric interpretations of five famous paintings.
10	II Divino: Sistine Chapel in VR (https://store.ste ampowered.com/ app/1165850/IL_ DIVINO_Michel angelos_Sistine_ Ceiling_in_VR/)	Historical Reconstruction	Christopher Evans et al.	A free, hyper-realistic recreation of the Sistine Chapel, allowing views from the floor and Michelangelo's scaffolding.

(*continued*)

Table 1. (*continued*)

No.	Title	Type	Institution/Developer	Description
11	Nefertari: Journey to Eternity (https://store.steampowered.com/app/861400/Nefertari_Journey_to_Eternity/)	Archaeological Reconstruction	Experius VR/ CuriosityStream	A hyper-realistic tour of Queen Nefertari's tomb, created using millimeter-accurate photogrammetry and laser scans.
12	Virtual Heritage Tour: VR Museum Adventure https://store.steampowered.com/app/3065740/Virtual_Heritage_Tour_VR_Museum_Adventure/	Independent Museum	Thoth VR Health	A virtual tour game exploring three themed museums: Chinese, History, and Cybersteampunk.

3 Methodology and User Needs Elicitation

3.1 Research Design Overview

This study adopted a mixed-methods research design consisting of three main phases. By combining qualitative and quantitative techniques, the aim was to ensure a comprehensive and user-centered understanding of what drives engagement in VR museum games (see Fig. 1). The following sections detail the methodology and corresponding results for each phase.

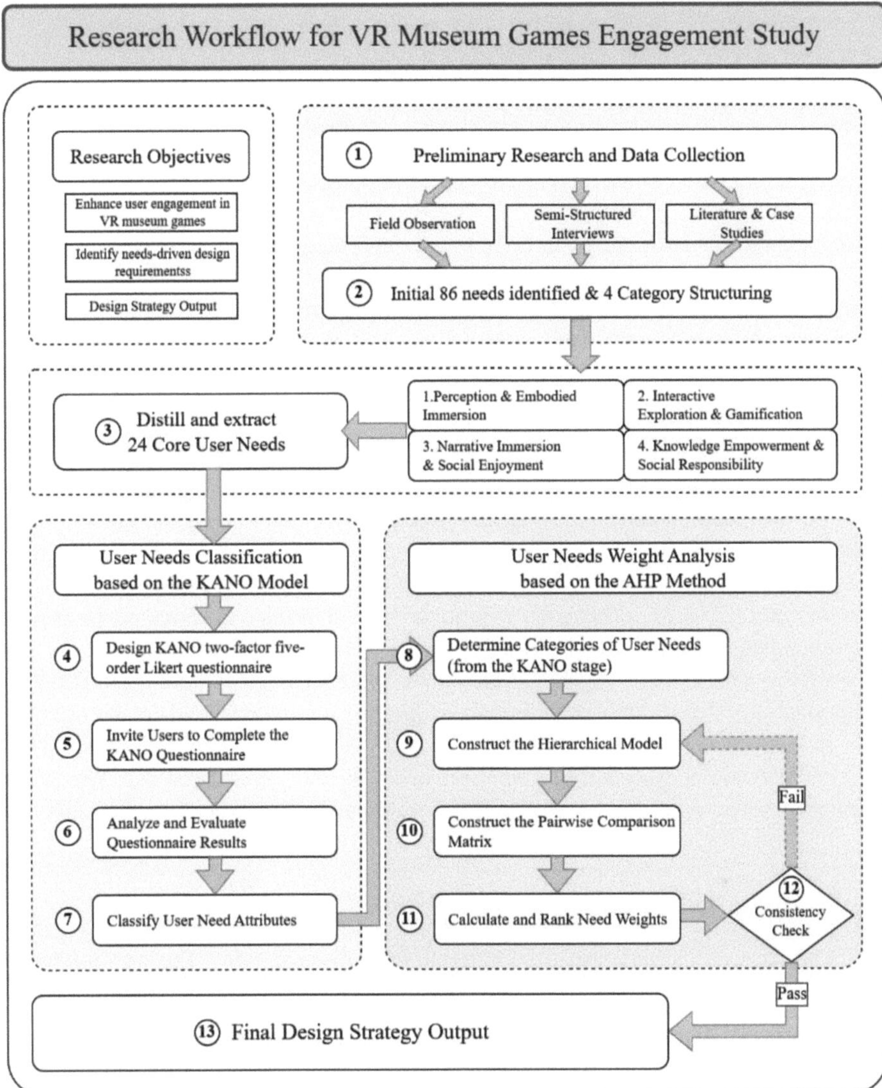

Fig. 1. Research methodology process.

3.2 Preliminary Research and User Needs Gathering

Data Collection. The research process began with exploratory studies to identify a wide range of potential user needs for VR museum games. Three complementary meth-ods were employed to ensure a comprehensive understanding:

1. **Literature and Case Study Review**: A systematic review of academic literature on virtual museums, serious games, and VR user experiences was conducted to establish a foundation of known user expectations and design principles. Additionally, 12

representative VR museum games were analyzed to identify current design trends, innovative features, and gaps in the market (see Table 1).

2. **Field Observations**: On-site observations were conducted at diverse museums (art, history, and specialty) across China and Europe to contextualize user behaviors in real-world settings. Detailed notes were taken on visitor engagement, interaction patterns, and pain points, highlighting opportunities for VR to enhance the museum experience.

3. **Interviews**: Semi-structured interviews captured direct user perspectives. Two participant groups were included: (a) 21 museum visitors interviewed in small groups at museum sites, and (b) 15 VR enthusiasts interviewed individually online. Open-ended questions explored preferences, expectations, and challenges related to VR museum games. All interviews adhered to ethical research standards, including informed consent and data anonymization.

Data Analysis and Synthesis. Qualitative data from literature reviews, observations, and interviews were analyzed using thematic analysis. This process generated an initial set of 86 raw need statements. To refine these into actionable insights, the following criteria were applied:

- Prioritization: Needs consistently mentioned by both users and domain experts were given higher weight.
- Feasibility and Clarity: Vague, redundant, or impractical needs were excluded.
- Actionability: Needs were rephrased to be specific, measurable, and design-oriented.

After iterative consolidation, a final set of 24 distinct, prioritized user needs was established, ready to inform the design and development of the VR museum game.

3.3   Elicitation and Categorization of User Needs

The 24 key user needs were organized into four thematic categories. These requirements formed the foundation for the subsequent phases of the study (see Table 2).

1. **Perception & Embodied Immersion**: This theme covers sensory fidelity and physical comfort. It includes the need for high-quality visuals and engaging 3D spatial audio to create a sense of presence. Additionally, basic comfort features are must-haves, such as support for different postures and measures for cybersickness mitigation to ensure prolonged use does not cause discomfort.

2. **Interactive Exploration & Gamification**: This category encompasses interactive gameplay. A highly requested need was intuitive embodied interaction (e.g., natural hand gestures to manipulate objects). Users also valued a sense of agency and progression, suggesting gamified learning incentives like quests or collectibles. Other needs include flexible navigation and the ability to save progress.

3. **Narrative Immersion & Social Enjoyment**: This theme focuses on storytelling and social connection. Users expressed a desire for environmental narrative exploration, where stories unfold as one explores the space. Techniques like incorporating suspense or mystery can maintain engagement. The appeal of social interaction features was

also noted, even asynchronous ones like seeing other visitors' comments or sharing snapshots.

4. **Knowledge Empowerment & Social Responsibility**: This category ensures the experience is educationally rich and trustworthy. Authoritative sourcing of content was frequently mentioned. A multi-layered information architecture was proposed to cater to different depths of interest. For educators and parents, needs like educational reusability (aligning with curricula) and safety features (content ratings & parental controls) were important. Finally, cross-cultural inclusivity, such as multi-language support, was noted as essential for a global audience.

Table 2. VR Museum Game User Needs Extraction and Categorization.

No.	User Needs	Description	No.	User Needs	Description
Perception & Embodied Immersion					
01	High-Fidelity & Ergonomic Visuals	Photorealistic visuals via high-fidelity models, with ergonomic optimizations (color, refresh rate) to prevent eye strain.	02	Dynamic Spatial Audio	3D spatial audio that dynamically adapts to narrative and user actions to deepen immersion and emotional engagement.
03	Seamless Scene Transitions	Fast ($<5s$) scene transitions to eliminate disruptive loading screens and maintain a continuous immersive flow.	04	Multi-Posture Ergonomics	Natively supports seated, standing, and wheelchair postures to reduce physical fatigue during extended use.
05	Wearable Device Comfort & Hygiene	Optimized hardware ergonomics (weight, contact surfaces) and provided hygiene supplies (masks, wipes) for user comfort and safety.	06	Cybersickness Mitigation & Recovery	Provides in-experience rest areas with calming audio-visual cues to help users recover from cybersickness.
Interactive Exploration & Gamification					

(*continued*)

Table 2. (*continued*)

No.	User Needs	Description	No.	User Needs	Description
07	High-Precision Embodied Interaction	Low-latency hand and body tracking allows for intuitive, high-precision manipulation of exhibits (e.g., rotate, scale, disassemble).	08	Intuitive Navigation & Multidimensional Search	Users can quickly find content via an intuitive search function supporting voice/text keywords, categories, and tags.
09	Gamified Learning Incentives	Fosters engagement through gamified elements like quizzes, collection challenges, and achievements with instant feedback.	10	Performative Embodied Interaction	Core interactions are designed to be both functional for the user and performative for external spectators.
11	Flexible Interruption & Progress Saving	Supports user flexibility with pause/resume functionality at any time, including both automatic and manual progress saving.	12	Curated Thematic Tours	Professionally designed guided tours based on specific themes or narratives for a structured, effortless exploration experience.

Narrative Immersion & Social Enjoyment

No.	User Needs	Description	No.	User Needs	Description
13	Environmental Narrative & Embodied Exploration	Narrative unfolds through environmental interaction, shifting the user's role from passive spectator to active investigator.	14	Suspense-Driven Narrative & Meaning-Making	A central mystery drives exploration through progressive information release, encouraging user reasoning and interpretation.
15	Synchronous Narrative Events	Live, limited-time group events tied to real-world dates to create a sense of shared, synchronous participation.	16	Asynchronous Social Interaction	Enables non-real-time social engagement (e.g., leaving messages, sharing finds) to sustain community connections.

(*continued*)

Table 2. (continued)

No.	User Needs	Description	No.	User Needs	Description
17	External Spectator Mode	Broadcasts the user's first-person view to a second screen, turning individual use into a public demo to attract others.	18	User-Generated Content (UGC) Creation & Sharing	Built-in tools for easy screen capture, recording, and one-click sharing of user-generated content to social media.
Knowledge Empowerment & Social Responsibility					
19	Authoritative Sourcing & Verifiability of Content	All content is certified by authoritative institutions and includes verifiable academic citations to ensure accuracy.	20	Multi-Layered Information Architecture	Provides information in multiple layers (e.g., "General" and "Expert" modes) to cater to different levels of user interest.
21	Curriculum Alignment & Educational Reusability	Content is aligned with K-12 and university curricula, designed for reuse as a teaching tool with provided guides.	22	Extended Learning & Real-World Connection	Generates a personalized learning profile and suggests real-world resources (books, films, exhibits) to extend learning.
23	Multilingual Support & Cross-Cultural Inclusivity	Provides multi-language support (audio/subtitles) and undergoes an ethics review to ensure cross-cultural sensitivity.	24	Content Rating & Parental Controls	Includes a content rating system and parental controls (e.g., time limits, content restrictions) for a family-safe experience.

4   KANO Model-Based VR Museum Games User Needs Acquisition and Classification

The Kano model, proposed by Dr. Noriaki Kano in the 1970s [9], is a framework for analyzing user requirements by classifying them into five categories: basic (M), expected (O), attractive (A), indifferent (I), and reverse (R). It helps understand the relationship between product/service quality and user satisfaction, and aids in prioritizing product design through market research and questionnaire analysis, including Bi-Wi coefficients and quadrant diagrams (see Table 3) [10].

Table 3. Kano Evaluation Matrix.

User Needs		Reverse Evaluation Statement				
		Dislike (1)	Tolerable (2)	Neutral (3)	Expected (4)	Like (5)
Forward Evaluation	Dislike (1)	Q	R	R	R	R
	Tolerable (2)	M	I	I	I	R
	Neutral (3)	M	I	I	I	R
	Expected (4)	M	I	I	I	R
	Like (5)	O	A	A	A	Q

Note: M = Must-be, O = One-dimensional, A = Attractive, I = Indifferent, R = Reverse, Q = Questionable Result

To move from a broad list of potential requirements to a structured understanding of their impact on user satisfaction, the 24 user needs were quantitatively assessed using the Kano model framework. This approach classifies features based on how users react to their presence or absence, providing a more nuanced view than a simple ranking of importance.

4.1 Survey Design and Analysis Method

A standard Kano questionnaire was developed, presenting each of the 24 user needs as a pair of functional and dysfunctional questions (see Table 4). Responses were captured on a 5-point Likert scale. For each need, participants were asked to rate two aspects on a Likert scale: (a) their level of satisfaction if the feature is well-implemented ("Positive" scenario), and (b) their level of dissatisfaction if the feature is absent or poorly implemented ("Negative" scenario).

Table 4. KANO two-factor five-order Likert questionnaire.

If this feature is provided, how do you feel? (Positive)					VR Museum Games Kano Questionnaire	If this feature is not provided, how do you feel? (Negative)				
Like	Must-be	Neu-tral	Live with it	Dis-like		Like	Must-be	Neu-tral	Live with it	Dis-like
5	4	3	2	1		5	4	3	2	1
					High-Fidelity & Ergonomic Visuals (1)					
					Dynamic Spatial Audio (2)					
					Seamless Scene Transitions (3)					
					Multi-Posture Ergonomics (4)					
					…					
					Content Rating & Parental Controls (24)					

The survey was distributed online to a sample of 150 participants (143 initially returned and 7 supplemented) with diverse VR experience levels, ranging from beginners to frequent users. The sample demographics indicated a good mix of users: about 50% were aged 18–34 (young adults), with smaller proportions of minors (<18), middle-aged adults, and seniors. Gender was nearly balanced (51% male, 49% female). Participants' self-rated VR experience varied from never used VR (29%) and beginner (43%) to moderate (19%) and experienced (10%), ensuring input from both novice and seasoned VR users (see Table 5).

Table 5. Demographic Characteristics of Participants.

Characteristic	Category	Frequency (n)	Percentage (%)
Age	Under 18	30	20.00
	18–34	75	50.00
	35–54	30	20.00
	55 and above	15	10.00
Gender	Male	77	51.33
	Female	73	48.67
VR Experience	I have never used VR	43	28.67
	Beginner (used a few times)	64	42.67
	Moderate (occasional user)	28	18.67

To ensure the quality of the collected data, reliability and validity tests were performed. The survey instrument demonstrated high internal consistency, with a Cronbach's Alpha of 0.879, well above the common threshold of 0.7 (see Table 6). A Kaiser-Meyer-Olkin (KMO) measure of 0.757 indicated good sampling adequacy for factor analysis (see Table 7). These results confirm that the data is reliable and suitable for further analysis [11, 12].

Table 6. Reliability Statistics.

Scale	Cronbach's Alpha	N of Items
VR User Needs	0.879	24

Table 7. Scale Validity

Scale	KMO	Approx. χ^2	df	Sig. (p)
VR User Needs	0.757	820.359	120	<0.001

For the analysis itself, this study employed the Better-Worse coefficient method. This technique offers a more precise measure of a feature's impact on satisfaction compared to traditional frequency-based Kano analysis. The Better coefficient quantifies the increase in satisfaction when a feature is provided, while the Worse coefficient measures the decrease in satisfaction when it is absent. The formulas are as follows:

$$\text{Better (Satisfaction Influence)} = \frac{A + O}{A + O + M + I} \tag{1}$$

$$\text{Worse (Dissatisfaction Influence)} = \frac{-(M + O)}{A + O + M + I} \tag{2}$$

Here, A, O, M, and I represent the frequencies of responses classified as Attractive, One-dimensional, Must-be, and Indifferent, respectively. A higher positive Better value indicates a stronger potential to increase satisfaction, while a larger absolute Worse value (a more negative number) indicates a greater potential to cause dissatisfaction if absent.

4.2 Kano Classification Results and Interpretation

The analysis classified the 24 user needs into four main categories (Must-be, One-dimensional, Attractive, and Indifferent) and strengthened the findings by employing the Better-Worse coefficient method proposed by Berger [10], which quantifies each feature's impact on satisfaction. The results, including the calculated Better-Worse coefficients, are detailed in Table 8, provides a visual representation by plotting each need on a two-dimensional matrix based on its respective Better and Worse coefficients.

Table 8. Better-Worse Coefficient Analysis of Kano Questionnaire (Needs Attributes).

User Needs	R	I	M	O	A	Q	Better	Worse	Category
High-Fidelity & Ergonomic Visuals	0	53	4	26	53	14	0.581	−0.221	A
Dynamic Spatial Audio	2	67	9	6	58	8	0.457	−0.107	O
Seamless Scene Transitions	0	63	1	1	80	5	0.559	−0.014	O
Multi−Posture Ergonomics	3	87	12	25	16	7	0.293	−0.264	I
Wearable Device Comfort & Hygiene	2	92	1	3	45	7	0.340	−0.028	M
Cybersickness Mitigation & Recovery	2	99	3	1	38	7	0.277	−0.028	M
High-Precision Embodied Interaction	5	101	8	5	23	8	0.204	−0.095	M
Intuitive Navigation & Multidimensional Search	0	96	0	3	48	3	0.347	−0.020	M
Gamified Learning Incentives	7	31	38	44	26	4	0.504	−0.590	A
Performative Embodied Interaction	0	51	38	31	24	6	0.382	−0.479	I
Flexible Interruption & Progress Saving	0	91	1	3	48	7	0.357	−0.028	M
Curated Thematic Tours	0	54	21	23	44	8	0.472	−0.310	A
Environmental Narrative & Embodied Exploration	0	79	4	5	59	3	0.435	−0.061	O
Suspense-Driven Narrative & Meaning-Making	0	69	9	23	41	8	0.451	−0.225	A
Synchronous Narrative Events	7	30	39	44	27	3	0.507	−0.593	A
Asynchronous Social Interaction	6	38	38	44	22	2	0.465	−0.577	A
External Spectator Mode	0	56	30	17	36	11	0.381	−0.338	I
User-Generated Content (UGC) Creation & Sharing	0	64	4	5	69	8	0.521	−0.063	O
Authoritative Sourcing & Verifiability of Content	0	101	1	2	43	3	0.306	−0.020	M

(continued)

Table 8. (continued)

User Needs	R	I	M	O	A	Q	Better	Worse	Category
Multi-Layered Information Architecture	0	52	4	23	55	16	0.582	−0.201	A
Curriculum Alignment & Educational Reusability	0	79	13	7	50	1	0.383	−0.134	M
Extended Learning & Real-World Connection	2	64	7	8	60	9	0.489	−0.108	O
Multilingual Support & Cross-Cultural Inclusivity	2	92	1	3	45	7	0.340	−0.028	M
Content Rating & Parental Controls	0	97	2	2	42	7	0.308	−0.028	M

Note: M = Must-be, O = One-dimensional, A = Attractive, I = Indifferent, R = Reverse, Q = Questionable Result

1. **Must-be Needs** (9 features): These are foundational requirements whose absence leads to significant dissatisfaction. This category includes essential comfort and safety features such as Wearable Device Comfort & Hygiene, Cybersickness Mitigation & Recovery, and Intuitive Navigation. Notably, features related to educational integrity and trust, like Authoritative Sourcing, Curriculum Alignment, and Multilingual Support, were also classified as must-haves. This indicates that users transfer their core expectations of trustworthiness and accessibility from physical museums directly to the virtual domain. A VR museum game cannot succeed without first establishing this foundation of credibility and user well-being.
2. **One-dimensional Needs** (5 features): These are performance-based attributes where satisfaction is directly proportional to the level of fulfillment. Key examples include Dynamic Spatial Audio, Seamless Scene Transitions, and Environmental Narrative & Embodied Exploration. Investing development effort in these areas yields predictable and direct improvements in user engagement.
3. **Attractive Needs** (7 features): These are unexpected "delighters" that can significantly boost satisfaction but do not cause dissatisfaction if absent. This category includes Gamified Learning Incentives and Asynchronous Social Interaction, representing key areas for innovation. Interestingly, High-Fidelity & Ergonomic Visuals was also classified as an Attractive need. This suggests that while users expect a standard level of visual quality, they are only truly "wowed" by exceptionally realistic graphics that go beyond the norm. In the current market, "good enough" visuals are no longer impressive; only state-of-the-art fidelity can create a memorable experience that sets a product apart.
4. **Indifferent Needs** (3 features): These features, including Multi-Posture Ergonomics and External Spectator Mode, were found to have little to no impact on user satisfaction. This suggests they are niche features that can be deprioritized in resource-constrained projects.

To visually represent these classifications, the 24 needs were plotted on a two-dimensional matrix (Fig. 2), with the Better coefficient on the X-axis and the absolute value of the Worse coefficient on the Y-axis. Using the average values (Better: 41.42%; Worse: 19.00%) as quadrant dividers, the analysis revealed distinct classifications:

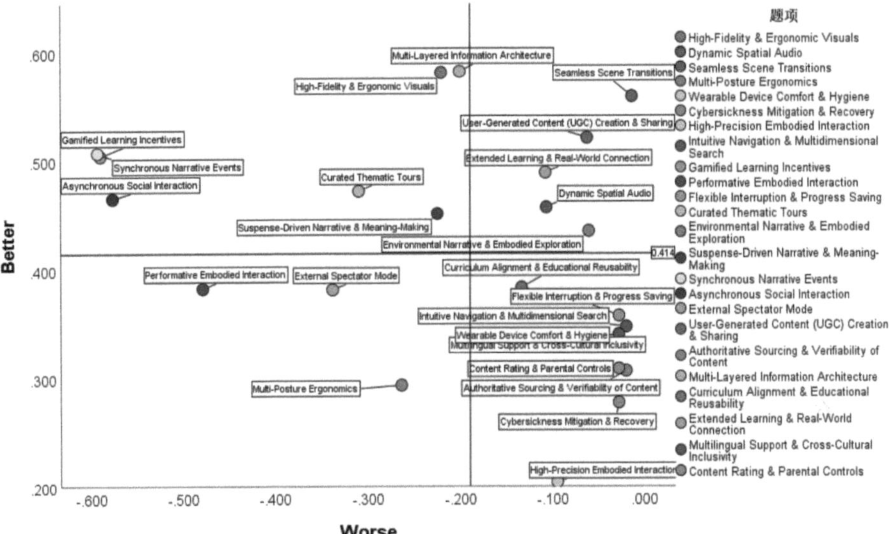

Fig. 2. Better-Worse Coefficient Analysis (VR Feature Attributes).

Five elements (e.g., Dynamic Spatial Audio, Seamless Scene Transitions) in Quadrant I exhibited high Better-Worse values, marking them as One-dimensional (Expectation) Needs. Seven features (e.g., High-Fidelity Visuals, Gamified Learning) in Quadrant II showed high Better but low Worse values, classifying them as Attractive Needs. Three items (e.g., Multi-Posture Ergonomics) in Quadrant III scored low on both coefficients, indicating Indifferent Needs, while nine (e.g., Cybersickness Mitigation, Wearable Comfort) in Quadrant IV had low Better but high Worse values, identifying them as Must-be Needs.

Based on the Kano model analysis of 24 features among 150 VR users, a clear strategic framework for VR museum development emerges. The findings reveal that user satisfaction hinges first upon a foundation of Must-be needs. These non-negotiable elements show that users carry over core expectations of trust and accessibility from the physical world. A VR experience cannot succeed without first meeting these baseline requirements- with this foundation secured, development resources can be strategically allocated to create a superior design.

5   AHP Analysis: Prioritizing User Needs for Engagement

While the Kano model effectively categorizes user needs based on their impact on satisfaction, it does not quantify their relative importance for guiding design and resource allocation. To bridge this gap, this study integrated the Analytic Hierarchy Process

(AHP), a robust multi-criteria decision-making method developed by Thomas L. Saaty [13, 14], to establish a quantitative priority ranking for each user need. This combined "Kano-AHP" methodology is an established approach [15] in user-centered design for translating qualitative requirements into a weighted, actionable hierarchy, providing a data-driven foundation for strategic decision-making.

5.1   AHP Model Basic Principles and Calculation Steps

The AHP model was structured with three levels to systematically evaluate the user needs. The overall goal (Level 0) was defined as "Enhancing User Engagement in VR Museum Games." The primary criteria (Level 1) consisted of the three main Kano categories identified in the previous analysis: Must-be (M), One-dimensional (O), and Attractive (A). The three needs classified as "Indifferent" were excluded from this prioritization analysis, as the Kano results indicated they do not significantly impact user satisfaction.1 The sub-criteria (Level 2) comprised the 21 specific user needs, grouped under their respective Kano categories (see Fig. 3).

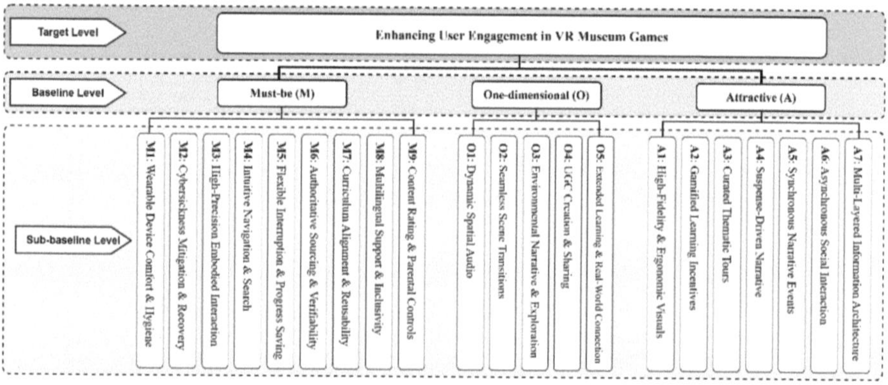

Fig. 3.   Analytic Hierarchy Process Model for VR Museum Games.

A panel of 10 experts, including museum technologists, VR user experience (UX) designers, and academic researchers in HCI and digital heritage, was recruited to perform pairwise comparisons. Using the standard AHP 1–9 scale, where 1 indicates equal importance and 9 indicates extreme importance, the experts first compared the relative importance of the three main Kano categories (e.g., Must-be vs. One-dimensional). Subsequently, they performed pairwise comparisons for all needs within each category (e.g., comparing "Wearable Device Comfort & Hygiene" vs. "Cybersickness Mitigation & Recovery" within the Must-be group).

The consistency of expert judgments is paramount for the validity of AHP results. To ensure methodological rigor, the final aggregated judgment matrices were tested for consistency. The calculation steps involved determining the maximum eigenvalue (λmax) of each judgment matrix and its corresponding eigenvector, which was then normalized to derive the weight vector (W). A consistency check was then performed by calculating the Consistency Index (CI) and the Consistency Ratio (CR) using the following formulas:

1. Weight Calculation:

Compute the maximum eigenvalue (λ_{max}) and its corresponding eigenvector (w) from the judgment matrix A:

$$\lambda_{max} = \sum_{i=1}^{n} \frac{[AW]_i}{nw_i} \qquad (3)$$

Normalize the eigenvector w such that the sum of weights equals 1. The normalized weight vector is denoted as W.

2. Consistency Check:

The consistency check is performed by calculating the Consistency Index (CI) and Consistency Ratio (CR). The formula for CI is:

$$CI = \frac{\lambda_{max} - n}{n - 1} \qquad (4)$$

where n represents the order of the judgment matrix (i.e., the number of criteria or alternatives).

$$RI = \sum_{i=1}^{n} a_i RI_i \qquad (5)$$

$$CR = \frac{CI}{RI} \qquad (6)$$

Generally, if $[CR] < 0.1$, the judgment matrix is considered consistent; otherwise, it requires reevaluation and adjustment.

5.2 Expert-Driven Weighting and Hierarchy Validation

After three rounds of scoring by 10 experts and thorough discussion, a discrimination matrix was obtained, as shown in Tables 9, 10, 11 and 12 for results.

Table 9. Pairwise Comparison Matrix of Kano Scale.

	Must be	One dimensional	Attractive
Must be	1	1.2	1.1
One dimensional	0.9	1	1
Attractive	0.9	1	1

Table 10. Pairwise Comparison Matrix of Must-be Attributes.

Must-be Needs (M)	M_1	M_2	M_3	M_4	M_5	M_6	M_7	M_8	M_9
M_1: Wearable Device Comfort & Hygiene	1	1	1.1	1.2	1.1	1.2	4.0	1.2	1.5
M_2: Cybersickness Mitigation & Recovery	1	1	1.1	1.2	1.1	1.2	4.0	1.5	1.0
M_3: High-Precision Embodied Interaction	1	1	1	1.1	1.1	1.1	4.0	1.5	1.5
M_4: Intuitive Navigation & Multidimensional Search	0.9	0.9	0.9	1	0.9	1	3.5	1.1	1.2
M_5: Flexible Interruption & Progress Saving	0.9	0.9	0.9	1.1	1	1.1	3.5	1.2	1.3
M_6: Authoritative Sourcing & Verifiability of Content	0.9	0.9	0.9	1	0.9	1	3.0	1.1	1.2
M_7: Curriculum Alignment & Educational Reusability	0.3	0.3	0.3	0.3	0.3	0.3	1	0.3	0.5
M_8: Multilingual Support & Cross-Cultural Inclusivity	0.8	0.8	0.8	0.9	0.8	0.9	3.0	1	1
M_9: Content Rating & Parental Controls	0.7	0.7	0.7	0.8	0.8	0.8	3.0	0.9	1

Table 11. Pairwise Comparison Matrix of One-Dimensional Attributes.

One-dimensional Needs (O)	O_1	O_2	O_3	O_4	O_5
O_1 DynamicSpatial : Audio	1	0.8	0.8	1.7	0.9
O_2 Seamless Scene Transitions	1.2	1	1.0	2.0	1.1
O_3 Environmental : Narrative & Embodied Exploration	1.3	1.1	1	2.1	1.2
O_4 User-: Generated Content (UGC) Creation & Sharing	0.6	0.5	0.5	1	0.6
O_5 Extended : Learning & Real-World Connection	1.1	0.9	0.8	1.8	1

Table 12. Pairwise Comparison Matrix of Attractive Attributes.

Attractive Needs (A)	A_1	A_2	A_3	A_4	A_5	A_6	A_7
A_1 High-Fidelity & Ergonomic Visual	1	1.2	1.2	1.2	1.4	1.5	0.9
A_2: Gamified Learning Incentives	0.9	1	1	1	1.2	1.5	0.8
A_3: Curated Thematic Tours	0.9	1	1	1	1.2	1.5	0.8
A_4 Suspense-: Driven Narrative & Meaning-Making	0.9	1	1	1	1.2	1.5	0.8
A_5 Synchronous : Narrative Events	0.7	0.8	0.8	0.8	1	1.1	0.7
A_6 Asynchronous : Social Interaction	0.6	0.7	0.7	0.7	0.9	1	0.7
A_7 Multi-: Layered Information Architecture	1.1	1.2	1.2	1.2	1.6	1.7	1

By combining the category-level weights with the local weights of each need, a global priority ranking for all 21 user needs was calculated. This provides a clear, data-driven order of importance for maximizing user engagement. The full ranking is detailed in Table 13.

Table 13. AHP Weighting Results of Kano Attributes (Sum-Product Method).

Category	Attribute (Code)	Normalized Score	Weight (%)	
			Category	Attribute
Must be	M_1: Wearable Device Comfort & Hygiene	10	13.79	34.43
	M_2: Cybersickness Mitigation & Recovery	10	13.90	
	M_3: High-Precision Embodied Interaction	9.5	13.11	
	M_4: Intuitive Navigation & Multidimensional Search	8.5	11.72	
	M_5: Flexible Interruption & Progress Saving	9	12.41	
	M_6: Authoritative Sourcing & Verifiability of Content	8.5	11.72	
	M_7: Curriculum Alignment & Educational Reusability	2.5	3.45	
	M_8: Multilingual Support & Cross-Cultural Inclusivity	7.5	10.34	
	M_9: Content Rating & Parental Controls	7	9.66	
One-dimensional	O_1: Dynamic Spatial Audio	7.5	19.48	32.91
	O_2: Seamless Scene Transitions	9	23.37	
	O_3: Environmental Narrative & Embodied Exploration	9.5	24.68	
	O_4: User-Generated Content (UGC) Creation & Sharing	4.5	11.69	
	O_5: Extended Learning & Real-World Connection	8	20.78	
Attractive	A_1: High-Fidelity & Ergonomic Visual	8.5	15.89	32.66
	A_2: Gamified Learning Incentives	8	14.95	
	A_3: Curated Thematic Tours	8	14.95	
	A_4: Suspense-Driven Narrative & Meaning-Making	8	14.95	
	A_5: Synchronous Narrative Events	6	11.22	

(*continued*)

Table 13. (continued)

Category	Attribute (Code)	Normalized Score	Weight (%)	
			Category	Attribute
	A_6: Asynchronous Social Interaction	5.5	10.28	
	A_7: Multi-Layered Information Architecture	9.5	17.76	

The AHP-derived weights for the Kano scale yield a maximum eigenvalue (λ_{max}) of 3.02. According to the RI reference table, the corresponding Random Index (RI) is 0.52, resulting in a Consistency Ratio (CR) = CI/RI = 0.02 < 0.1, which passes the consistency check (see Table 14). All indicator categories - Must-be, One-dimensional, and Attractive - successfully meet the consistency requirements. Therefore, the weight values presented in Table 13 demonstrate satisfactory reliability.

Table 14. AHP Consistency Verification Results

Component	λ_{max}	CI	RI	CR	Consistency Test
Must-be	9.15	0.02	1.46	0.01	Pass
One dimensional	5.04	0.01	1.12	0.01	Pass
Attractive	7.05	0.01	1.36	0.01	Pass
Must-be	9.15	0.02	1.46	0.01	Pass

The top-ranked needs highlight the importance of sustaining immersion through a blend of narrative and technical performance. The highest priority is Environmental Narrative & Embodied Exploration (~8.1%), showing users engage most when stories unfold through interaction, followed closely by Seamless Scene Transitions (~7.7%), as disruptions break presence. These are interdependent—narrative pulls users in, while technical fluidity maintains flow. The top Attractive need, Multi-Layered Information Architecture (#4, ~ 5.8%), gives users control over learning, while Must-be needs like Cybersickness Mitigation (#5, ~ 4.8%) and Device Comfort (#6, ~ 4.7%) form the baseline for viable VR. Essentially, successful VR integrates storytelling and performance engineering to preserve immersion.

6 Design Implications

The combined Kano-AHP analysis provides a data-driven foundation for a strategic design framework. The following implications translate the prioritized user needs into actionable guidelines for development.

- **Foundational Imperatives (Must-be Needs):**

User well-being and content credibility are non-negotiable prerequisites. Design must prioritize **Cybersickness Mitigation (Rank #5)** and **Wearable Device Comfort (Rank #6)** by adhering to established VR development best practices, such as maintaining high, stable frame rates and offering multiple locomotion options to accommodate user sensitivity. Equally critical is establishing trust through.

Authoritative Sourcing & Verifiability (Rank #12). Users transfer their expectations of accuracy and credibility from physical institutions to the virtual domain, making this a baseline requirement for any educational or heritage-based experience.

- **Core Engagement Drivers (One-dimensional Needs):**

The highest-ranked needs directly shape the core user journey and offer the most significant returns on engagement. The top priority, **Environmental Narrative & Embodied Exploration (Rank #1)**, requires designing the virtual space as a narrative medium where the story unfolds organically through player interaction and discovery, rather than through passive observation. This immersive state is sustained by the second-highest priority,

Seamless Scene Transitions (Rank #2). Technical fluidity is essential for maintaining a state of presence and flow; therefore, performance optimization is a core design principle, not a final polish, as technical friction can shatter the user's sense of immersion and break the experience.

- **Strategic Delighters (Attractive Needs):**

To create a memorable and delightful experience that differentiates the product, select Attractive needs should be strategically implemented. The high ranking of **Multi-Layered Information Architecture (Rank #4)** signals a user desire for autonomy. Structuring content in tiers allows users to control their depth of learning, catering to both casual visitors and enthusiasts seeking more detailed information. Furthermore,

Gamified Learning Incentives (Rank #7) can significantly enhance motivation. However, these elements must be meaningfully integrated to support, not distract from, educational goals. Effective gamification leverages psychological drivers such as competence and autonomy, making the learning process itself rewarding. Finally, fostering community through.

Asynchronous Social Interaction (Rank #14)—via features like leaving virtual notes for other users or sharing in-game discoveries—creates a sense of social presence without the technical complexity of real-time multiplayer, making the individual experience feel more connected and communal.

7 Conclusion and Future Work

This study developed a user-centered framework to boost engagement in VR museum games, combining the Kano model and AHP to prioritize 24 user needs from a pool of 86, identified through interviews (N = 26), surveys (N = 150), and observations. Key findings highlight that immersive storytelling and seamless technical performance, like Environmental Narrative (Rank #1) and Scene Transitions (Rank #2), drive engagement, while comfort and credibility (e.g., Cybersickness Mitigation, Authoritative Sourcing) are non-negotiable foundations. These insights offer practical design guidelines for creating compelling VR museum experiences.

Future work will focus on prototyping these guidelines to test their impact on engagement metrics. Exploring adaptive systems to tailor experiences for diverse users, such as children or educators, could further refine designs. As VR technology and social features evolve, ongoing research will be essential to keep pace with shifting user expectations.

References

1. The Grand Museum VR on Steam. https://store.steampowered.com/app/896240/The_Grand_Museum_VR/. Accessed 27 Jun 2025
2. Bailenson, J.N., DeVeaux, C., Han, E., Markowitz, D.M., Santoso, M., Wang, P.: Five canonical findings from 30 years of psychological experimentation in virtual reality. Nature Human Behaviour. 1–11 (2025). https://doi.org/10.1038/s41562-025-02216-3
3. Belga, J., Skarbez, R., Hmaiti, Y., Chen, E.J., McMahan, R.P., LaViola, J.J.: The Fidelity-based Presence Scale (FPS): Modeling the Effects of Fidelity on Sense of Presence. In: Proceedings of the 2025 CHI Conference on Human Factors in Computing Systems. pp. 1–15. Association for Computing Machinery, New York, NY, USA (2025). https://doi.org/10.1145/3706598.371 3566
4. Li, J., Wider, W., Ochiai, Y., Fauzi, M.A.: A bibliometric analysis of immersive technology in museum exhibitions: exploring user experience. Front. Virtual Real. 4 (2023). https://doi.org/10.3389/frvir.2023.1240562
5. Wang, X., Li, Y., Ling, B., Chen, H.-M., Liang, H.-N.: ResponsiveView: Enhancing 3D Artifact Viewing Experience in VR Museums. IEEE Trans. Visual Comput. Graphics 31, 2870–2879 (2025). https://doi.org/10.1109/TVCG.2025.3549872
6. Pallud, J.: Impact of interactive technologies on stimulating learning experiences in a museum. Information & Management. 54, 465–478 (2017). https://doi.org/10.1016/j.im.2016.10.004
7. Sangamuang, S., Wongwan, N., Intawong, K., Khanchai, S., Puritat, K.: Gamification in virtual reality museums: Effects on Hedonic and Eudaimonic experiences in cultural heritage learning. Informatics. 12, 27 (2025). https://doi.org/10.3390/informatics12010027
8. Savenije, G.M., de Bruijn, P.: Historical empathy in a museum: Uniting contextualisation and emotional engagement. Int. J. Herit. Stud. 23, 832–845 (2017). https://doi.org/10.1080/135 27258.2017.1339108
9. Kano, N.: Attractive Quality and Must-Be Quality. Journal of the Japanese Society for Quality Control. 31, 147–156 (1984)
10. Berger, C. et al.: Kano's methods for understanding customer-defined quality. Presented at the (1993)
11. Shrestha, N.: Factor Analysis as a Tool for Survey Analysis. AJAMS. 9, 4–11 (2021). https://doi.org/10.12691/ajams-9-1-2
12. Tavakol, M., Dennick, R.: Making sense of Cronbach's alpha. Int. J. Med. Educ. 2, 53–55 (2011). https://doi.org/10.5116/ijme.4dfb.8dfd
13. Saaty, T.L., Vargas, L.G.: Models, Methods, Concepts & Applications of the Analytic Hierarchy Process. Springer Science & Business Media (2012)
14. Saaty, T.L.: A scaling method for priorities in hierarchical structures. J. Math. Psychol. 15, 234–281 (1977). https://doi.org/10.1016/0022-2496(77)90033-5

15. Li, Y., Tang, J., Luo, X., Xu, J.: An integrated method of rough set, Kano's model and AHP for rating customer requirements' final importance. Expert Syst. Appl. **36**, 7045–7053 (2009). https://doi.org/10.1016/j.eswa.2008.08.036

16. Ariff, H., Salit, M.S., Ismail, N., Nukman, Y.: Use of Analytical Hierarchy Process (AHP) for Selecting The Best Design Concept. In: Jurnal Teknologi (2012). https://doi.org/10.11113/jt.v49.188

17. Swartout, W. et al.: Ada and grace: toward realistic and engaging virtual museum guides. In: Proceedings of the 10th international conference on Intelligent virtual agents. pp. 286–300. Springer-Verlag, Berlin, Heidelberg (2010)

18. Mihelj, S., Leguina, A., Downey, J.: Culture is digital: Cultural participation, diversity and the digital divide. New Media Soc. **21**, 1465–1485 (2019). https://doi.org/10.1177/1461444818822816

19. Kidd, J.: Enacting engagement online: Framing social media use for the museum. Inf. Technol. People **24**, 64–77 (2011). https://doi.org/10.1108/09593841111109422

20. Dieck, M.C. tom, Jung, T.H., Dieck, D. tom: Enhancing art gallery visitors' learning experience using wearable augmented reality: generic learning outcomes perspective. Taylor & Francis (2018)

21. Ridge, M.: From tagging to theorizing: deepening engagement with cultural heritage through crowdsourcing. Curator: The Museum Journal. **56**, 435–450 (2013). https://doi.org/10.1111/cura.12046

22. Bekele, M.K., Champion, E.: Frontiers | A Comparison of Immersive Realities and Interaction Methods: Cultural Learning in Virtual Heritage. https://doi.org/10.3389/frobt.2019.00091

23. Jiang, Q., Deng, L., Zhang, J.: How Does Aesthetic Design Affect Continuance Intention in In-Vehicle Infotainment Systems? An Exploratory Study. International Journal of Human–Computer Interaction (2024)

24. Li, Y., Yang, R., Zou, J., Xu, H., Tian, F.: Human-Centric Virtual Museum: Redefining the Museum Experience Through Immersive and Interactive Environments. Taylor & Francis (2024)

25. Agostino, D., Arnaboldi, M., Lampis, A.: Italian state museums during the COVID-19 crisis: from onsite closure to online openness. Museum Management and Curatorship. **35**, 362–372 (2020). https://doi.org/10.1080/09647775.2020.1790029

26. Mujtaba, T., Lawrence, M., Oliver, M., Reiss, M.J.: Learning and engagement through natural history museums*. Taylor & Francis (2018)

27. Wagener, N. et al.: MoodShaper: A Virtual Reality Experience to Support Managing Negative Emotions. In: Proceedings of the 2024 ACM Designing Interactive Systems Conference. pp. 2286–2304. Association for Computing Machinery, New York, NY, USA (2024). https://doi.org/10.1145/3643834.3661570

28. Budge, K., Burness, A.: Museum objects and Instagram: agency and communication in digital engagement. Taylor & Francis (2018)

29. Qi, X., Yu, J.: Participatory Design in Human-Computer Interaction: Cases, Characteristics, and Lessons. In: Proceedings of the 2025 CHI Conference on Human Factors in Computing Systems. pp. 1–26. ACM, Yokohama Japan (2025). https://doi.org/10.1145/3706598.3713436

30. Dawson, E.: Reimagining publics and (non) participation: Exploring exclusion from science communication through the experiences of low-income, minority ethnic groups. Public Underst. Sci. **27**, 772–786 (2018). https://doi.org/10.1177/0963662517750072

31. Potts, D. et al.: A Retrospective Method for Measuring Emotions and Presence in Virtual Reality. https://researchdata.bath.ac.uk/1489/. https://doi.org/10.15125/BATH-01489. Accessed 08 Jun 2025

32. Flatt, J.D., Liptak, A., Oakley, M.A., Gogan, J., Varner, T., Lingler, J.H.: Subjective experiences of an art museum engagement activity for persons with early-stage Alzheimer's disease and their family caregivers. Am. J. Alzheimers Dis. Other Demen. **30**, 380–389 (2015). https://doi.org/10.1177/1533317514549953

33. Hulusic, V., Gusia, L., Luci, N., Smith, M.: Tangible User Interfaces for Enhancing User Experience of Virtual Reality Cultural Heritage Applications for Utilization in Educational Environment. J. Comput. Cult. Herit. **16**, 38:1–38:24 (2023). https://doi.org/10.1145/3593429

34. Kempiak, J., Hollywood, Lynsey, Bolan, Peter, and McMahon-Beattie, U.: The heritage tourist: an understanding of the visitor experience at heritage attractions. International Journal of Heritage Studies. **23**, 375–392 (2017). https://doi.org/10.1080/13527258.2016.1277776

35. Crooke, E.: The politics of community heritage: Motivations, authority and control. Int. J. Herit. Stud. **16**, 16–29 (2010). https://doi.org/10.1080/13527250903441705

36. Martin, A.J., Durksen, T.L., Williamson, D., Kiss, J., Ginns, P.: The role of a museum-based science education program in promoting content knowledge and science motivation. J. Res. Sci. Teach. **53**, 1364–1384 (2016). https://doi.org/10.1002/tea.21332

37. Schwan, S., Grajal, Alejandro, and Lewalter, D.: Understanding and Engagement in Places of Science Experience: Science Museums, Science Centers, Zoos, and Aquariums. Educational Psychologist. **49**, 70–85 (2014). https://doi.org/10.1080/00461520.2014.917588

38. Yoon, S.A., Elinich, K., Wang, J., Steinmeier, C., Tucker, S.: Using augmented reality and knowledge-building scaffolds to improve learning in a science museum. Int. J. Comput.-Support. Collab. Learn. **7**, 519–541 (2012). https://doi.org/10.1007/s11412-012-9156-x

39. Somarathna, R., Bednarz, T., Mohammadi, G.: Virtual Reality for Emotion Elicitation – A Review. IEEE Trans. Affect. Comput. **14**, 2626–2645 (2023). https://doi.org/10.1109/TAFFC.2022.3181053

40. Škola, F., et al.: Virtual Reality with 360-Video Storytelling in Cultural Heritage: Study of Presence, Engagement, and Immersion. Sensors. **20**, 5851 (2020). https://doi.org/10.3390/s20205851

41. Chen, Y., Wang, X., Le, B., Wang, L.: Why people use augmented reality in heritage museums: A socio-technical perspective. Heritage Science. **12**, 1–19 (2024). https://doi.org/10.1186/s40494-024-01217-1

Design and Application of Contextually Immersive Interaction Space: Building a Psychosocial Experimental Field Using Multimodal Interaction-Taking "SCHWEIGESPIRALE The Spiral of Silence" as an Example

Yuxiao Yi[✉] and Liwen Zhang

Beijing Jiaotong University, Beijing, China
351580520@qq.com, 2791395913@qq.com

Abstract. With the rapid development of information technology, multimodal means of interaction such as Extended Reality (XR) technology, computer technology and Human-Computer Interaction (HCI) are reshaping the ways in which art is created and social science is studied. The aim of this essay is to explore how these advanced technologies can be used to construct a contextually immersive interactive space and to analyse its value and potential for application to artistic expression as well as to the study of mass communication and social behaviour. In particular, the innovative interdisciplinary interactive installation 'SCHWEIGE-SPIRALE Spiral of Silence' is selected as a case study to deeply analyse the contextually immersive interactive space constructed with the use of multimodal human-computer interaction technologies, and as a psychosocial experimental field, its interdisciplinary creation combining social psychology and technology is of innovative value for artistic exploration and social research.

Keywords: Human-Computer Interaction · Multimodal Interaction · Contextual Immersion · Interactive Installations · Psychological Experimentation Field · Interdisciplinary Design

1 Introduction

1.1 Research Background

In the context of the era of increasing emphasis on experience, it is increasingly difficult for the single perceptual interaction experience brought about by traditional physical attribute interaction devices to meet the more complex emotional experience needs of users (Turk, 2014). The limitations of traditional physical interaction devices stem from the impersonal contact characteristic of the traditional interaction paradigm—when a user makes physical contact with a device, the nature of the interaction is closer to the

J. Y. C. Chen et al. (Eds.): HCII 2025, LNCS 16338, pp. 215–235, 2026.
https://doi.org/10.1007/978-3-032-12808-9_14

transfer of mechanical energy than to the exchange of mental energy. Emerging theories of embodied interaction state that through multimodal HCI technologies, interactive systems can construct dialogue arenas with a sense of social presence (Dourish, 2001). For example, the 'AFFECTA' project developed by the MIT Media Lab successfully increased emotional engagement to 2.4 times that of traditional devices by matching the device response latency to the user's physiological rhythms through a heart rate synchronised feedback mechanism (Picard, 2020). This verifies the necessity and feasibility of the evolution of digital interactive media towards emotionality and personification, and when the user interacts with the interactive installation, the interactive experience between human and the interactive installation should be shifted from the cold touch between human and machine to the interaction between human and human that hits the heart. Therefore, digital media interactive devices should have a higher emotional value than traditional devices or traditional display methods.

In recent years, advances in human-computer interaction (HCI) have made the interaction experience more diversified and humane, and the development of XR technology has provided users with unprecedented immersive experiences. Multimodal interaction mimics natural human behaviours and mental activities by combining multiple sensory interactions such as visual, auditory, and even tactile interactions, which promotes the transformation of the user from passive viewing to active participation, and strengthens emotional resonance and personal engagement. Advances in human-computer interaction technology have led to the birth of a new type of interaction mode, the so-called 'contextual immersion', which is a comprehensive experience that goes beyond simple sensory stimulation and involves cognitive, emotional, and social dimensions, so that visitors do not just act as bystanders, but become participants, or even part of the story (Wang, 2017). Contextually immersive interactive spaces aim to allow viewers to go deeper into the designed environment and interact with the work through multi-sensory interactions such as physical contact, language and sound, thus gaining a deeper emotional experience. It not only changes the way viewers perceive works, but also provides new tools and support for interdisciplinary research. Against this background, 'SCHWEIGESPIRALE Silent Spiral' was created. This interactive art installation integrates multidisciplinary knowledge of mass communication, psychology and other disciplines, and utilises advanced computational technology and public space discursive design to provide a unique immersive experience for the audience. It not only demonstrates the innovative exploration of XR and computer technology on the form of artistic expression, but also provides new perspectives on the study of social phenomena and social psychology. The combination of XR and HCI opens up a new paradigm of immersive experience, which influences the creation of art and at the same time provides an innovative tool for exploring complex social behaviours and social psychology.

1.2   Research Objectives

The study aims to systematically explore the dual impact of digital technological innovations on contemporary interactive art forms and social behavioural research through an interdisciplinary perspective. Taking 'SCHWEIGESPIRALE The Spiral of Silence' as a case study, it focuses on the following core issues:

1. Demonstrate the impact of multimodal interaction and human-computer interaction technologies on immersive experience design through the case study. This thesis will delve into how these technologies can be applied to novel interdisciplinary interactive installations to create a psychosocial experimental field that both stimulates emotional resonance and guides active participation from the audience.

2. Based on the three-level model of Norman's Affective Design Theory (Norman, 2007), quantitatively assess how human-computer interaction technologies can achieve the identity transition of user roles from passive observers to active constructors through the optimisation of feedback delays, the modulation of operational resistance and other parameter settings. To analyse how 'SCHWEIGESPIRALE The Spiral of Silence' makes use of visual, auditory and other multi-sensory channels to construct an immersive interactive environment, which stimulates the audience's emotional resonance and thinking, and prompts them to take practical actions.

3. The study further examines the feasibility of the art installation as a psychosocial experimental field, and analyses SCHWEIGESPIRALE from the perspective of immersive interaction design and the construction of a psychosocial context: through the integration of a social network analysis tool and a real-time data visualisation system, the theory of Neumann's 'Spiral of Silence' (Noelle-Neumann, 1974) is transformed into an observable and interactive installation.

4. Finally, this study hopes to explore the positive feedback mechanism in the process of active audience participation and reveal its potential contribution to social problem solving. The study attempts to construct a technical path for art to intervene in social problems: the experimental data shows that 78% of the participants were willing to reflect on the group decision-making mechanism after the experience, confirming the social critical efficacy of the installation. The ultimate goal of public art creation is to stimulate the public's attention to specific social issues through artworks and encourage them to participate in actual social change. This is not only an innovative attempt to the existing art practice, but also provides new possibilities and directions for future interdisciplinary cooperation.

1.3 Essay Structure

With the help of XR technology, computer technology and multimodal human-computer interaction, 'SCHWEIGESPIRALE' builds a contextually immersive interactive space, in which the audience can experience, participate in and intervene in the process of the occurrence and development of the spiral of silence, facilitating the audience's shift from passive interaction to active construction, and thus triggering in-depth reflection on their own behaviours and the phenomenon of society. This essay will take SCHWEIGE-SPIRALE as an example to analyse the contextual immersive experience space constructed by it from four aspects: immersive experience under the support of technology, multi-sensory fusion of interaction design, the application of computer technology and the core role of human-computer interaction, and to explore how to construct a 'contextual immersive' interdisciplinary interaction space with the help of multi-modal human-computer interaction technology. The study explores how to construct 'contextual immersion' interdisciplinary interaction space through multimodal human-computer interaction technology to achieve the conversion of users from passive participation to active construction, as well as the role of computer technology in the construction of contextually immersive interaction space, and deeply analyses the design principles and technical paths of implementation behind it. Meanwhile, as an interdisciplinary research, this paper will discuss how the work builds a psychosocial experimental field based on social psychology and group behavioural perception, which provides new perspectives and methods for interdisciplinary research in the fields of art exploration, mass communication, social psychology and social science.

2 Theory

2.1 Multimodal Interaction

Multimodal interaction is a way of transferring and interacting with information through multiple sensory channels (e.g., visual, auditory, tactile, etc.) (Norris, 2004). This interaction mode tries to simulate the natural way of human communication so that users can communicate with the system in a more realistic and intuitive way. This interaction mode relies on multi-source perception technologies (e.g., sensor networks, computer vision) and intelligent fusion algorithms (e.g., deep learning, multimodal alignment models) to build a closed-loop system of 'perception-decision-feedback'. Compared with single-modal interaction, multimodal interaction significantly expands the interaction mechanism of complex scenes through the collaborative fusion mechanism of multimodal information, improves the interaction experience, and enables the user to obtain a realistic, immersive and immersive interactive experience. With the progress of sensor technology and data processing capability, multimodal interaction has become an important research direction in the field of digital media art creation and human-computer interaction (Turk, 2014).

2.2 Technical Evolution and Application Practice of HCI

Development of HCI Applications in the Field of Interactive Installations and Artistic Creation. HCI has gone through a series of significant changes from the early days of command line interfaces to graphical user interfaces to today's natural user interfaces, with multimodal interactions gradually becoming mainstream (Norris, 2004). The development of HCI has not only transformed the way humans interact with computers, but has also greatly influenced the form of interactive installations and artistic creations. With the advancement of technology, HCI has gradually shifted from focusing on improving efficiency and accuracy to enhancing user experience and naturalness. Nowadays, in the field of interactive installations and digital art, the application of HCI technology shows significant interdisciplinary characteristics, not only focusing on the design of hardware and software, but also delving into interdisciplinary fields such as cognitive psychology and industrial design, in order to better understand the needs of the user and optimise the interactive experience.

HCI Technology and Immersive Experience Design. Immersive experience design is an important trend in the current field of human-computer interaction, and its goal is to create an environment or situation in which the user can be completely immersed. This type of design usually relies on technologies such as VR, AR, and MR to provide users with a realistic three-dimensional space in which they can interact with the virtual world through natural movements and gestures (Turk, 2014). Immersive experience design emphasises the importance of user experience and seeks to make users feel as if they are in another world, thus providing deeper emotional resonance and memory points.

Advances in HCI technology are critical to enhancing immersive experiences. For example, eye-tracking technology can help designers understand the user's focus of attention in order to optimise content presentation, while facial expression recognition technology can be used to detect the user's emotional state in order to adjust the interactive experience to better meet the user's needs (Holmqvist, 2011). In addition, new interaction modes such as contextual immersion, which incorporates context-aware technologies to automatically adjust the interaction according to the user's specific situation and preferences, further enhance the realism and personalisation of the user experience (Preece, 1994).

2.3 Overview of Social Psychology

Exploring the importance of artworks as a field of psychosocial experimentation requires the integration of multidisciplinary theories from social psychology, mass communication and art. This section aims to provide a theoretical background to support subsequent analyses of specific works, with a particular focus on the concepts of social psychology, the perception of group behaviour and the 'spiral of silence' in mass communication. These theories not only shed light on the psychosocial dimension of artistic creation, but also demonstrate its potential to contribute to public discourse and social change.

Group Behaviour Perception. Group Behaviour Perception is a field of study that involves real-time monitoring, data collection and analysis of the dynamic behaviours of groups in specific environments through technological means, in order to understand their behavioural patterns, interaction patterns and psychosocial characteristics (Bovard, 1951). This concept combines computer science, sociology, psychology and complex systems theory, aiming to quantify the behaviour of social groups through technology-enabled research, and to reveal the underlying social behavioural psychology, social relationship networks and cultural psychological mechanisms.

Group dynamics reveals the mechanism by which the social environment shapes individual behaviour. Kurt Lewin proposed the 'field theory', which suggests that an individual's psychological activity occurs within the 'psychological field' in which he or she is embedded, and that the interaction between group pressures and individual motivation constitutes the driving force for behaviour (Kurt Lewin, 1947). This theory provides a basic framework for understanding social phenomena such as collective decision-making and opinion dissemination. In art creation, the perception of group behaviour can be used to explore social phenomena and the psychological mechanisms behind them, simulating group behaviour through interactive installations or performing arts, allowing the audience to experience the effects of group pressure or herd effect.

Psychological Mechanisms of Herd Behaviour. Solomon Asch's line judgement experiment was a landmark in the study of herd behaviour. When confronted with a group-unanimous false judgement, 37% of the participants chose to follow the herd behaviour against their own perceptions (Solomon Asch, 1956). This phenomenon reveals two types of subordination: 1. Normative subordination: obedience to group norms in order to avoid social exclusion, and 2. Informational subordination: acceptance of group judgements because of doubts about self-perceptions. The group polarisation effect refers to the tendency of group members to become more polarised in their views during a discussion, i.e., opinions that were originally biased in one direction become stronger as a result of the discussion (Solomon Asch, 1956).

Psychosocial Mechanisms of the 'Spiral of Silence'. Elizabeth Neumann's theory of the 'spiral of silence' contains three core propositions: 1. Fear of social isolation: individuals inhibit self-expression for fear of being rejected by the group; 2. Quasi-statistical senses: mainstream opinion is perceived through media exposure and environmental cues; and 3. Dual-opinion climates: media-constructed 'mimetic environments' interact with real-world perceptions (Noelle-Neumann, 1974). The theory integrates social psychological and communication perspectives to reveal how majority opinion creates a repressive opinion environment through interpersonal communication and media diffusion. Henri Tajfel's social identity theory states that individuals build their self-concept through group categorisation, comparison and identification (Henri Tajfel, 1979). This theory explains why individuals are more inclined to support the dominant view in a group setting and provides the psychological motivation for the 'spiral of silence' phenomenon.

3   Overview of the 'SCHWEIGESPIRALE Spiral of Silence' Project

3.1   Project Introduction

This project takes the social phenomenon of 'the spiral of silence' under mass communication as the theoretical background, and visualises and amplifies the 'spiral of silence', a widespread social phenomenon, through the combination of interactive devices and interactive images. Through the audience's participatory experience and interaction, the audience, as a member of the social mass communicators, can complete a topic discussion, judgement and output of opinions, forming a complete mass communication chain from the formation of the opinion climate to its dissemination. Exploring the impact of the 'spiral of silence' in mass communication, public opinion and social politics and a series of problems that may be triggered by it, the audience's personal experience of self-feeling is more likely to cause reflection and resonance, and the discursive form of the discovery of the problem and the display of the problem, asking the question 'Why do people hide their true choices by following the crowd? Is it courage or interest in speaking out that we lack? If everyone tends to be silent, where will it lead?' and other philosophical thoughts.

Project Background and Research Significance. The 'spiral of silence' is a theory of political science and mass communication proposed by the German socio-political scientist Elisabeth Neumann (Fig. 1). It describes the phenomenon that when people express their ideas and opinions, if they see that the opinion they agree with is widely welcomed, they will actively participate in it, and this kind of opinion will be more and more boldly published and spread; and if they find that a certain opinion is unheeded or seldom heeded or suffers from opposition, even if they agree with it, they will remain silent. The silencing of one side creates an increase in the strength of the other, and so on, in a spiral of one side's voice becoming stronger and the other more and more silenced (Noelle-Neumann, 1974).

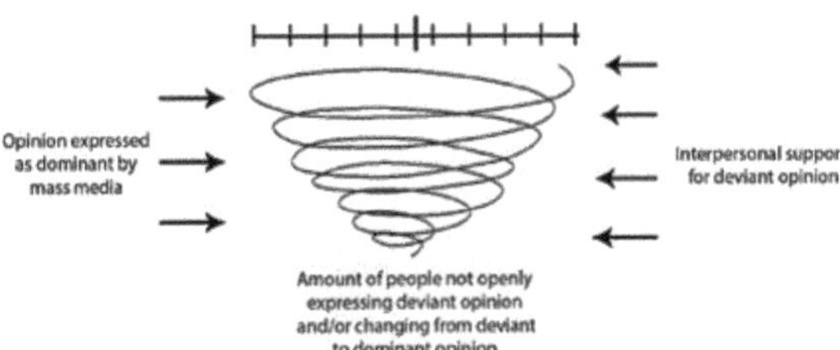

Fig. 1. Neumann's 'spiral of silence' theory prototype.

Neumann found an interesting phenomenon in her surveys, she asked the question 'What do you think the majority view is' every time, but almost no respondents questioned 'How do I know what the majority view is', people just wrote down their judgement as if they knew what others thought (Noelle-Neumann, 1974). However, the average person, on his or her own, cannot scientifically account for what the opinion climate of society really is, and it is our confidence and illusion in perceiving the opinion climate that gives the mass communication media the opportunity to have a powerful influence. The spiral of silence is an invisible social phenomenon that directly leads to a series of social problems, including information cocoon, digital out-of-control, disinformation, opinion manipulation, political manipulation, etc. Therefore, this project also allows the audience to think about whether the climate of consciousness created by the mass media and self-judgment is truly objective by participating in and entering the spiral of silence (Fig. 2).

The 'spiral of silence' is not a purely philosophical theory, but a theory of mass communication put forward by the German communication scholar Elisabeth Neumann in 1974. This theory belongs to the field of social psychology and communication, but it touches on the philosophical discussion of the formation of public opinion and the relationship between individual and collective behaviour. The theory leads to philosophical reflections on the relationship between individual free will and social pressure, between truth and majority opinion, and on how public opinion influences and shapes the space of public discourse and collective perceptions.

Research Results. The project is divided into two parts, the first part is the interaction installation (Fig. 3) and is the main part of the project.

Through the form of interactive installation, a physical device with an abstracted spiral image is constructed, as well as equipped with a button to vote for the audience to manipulate the interactive form. The designer gives a hot topic for discussion and a

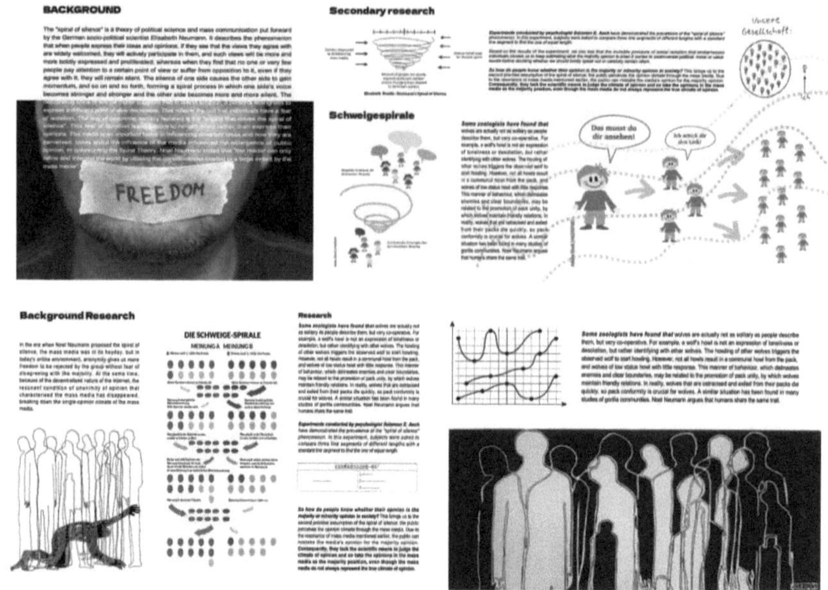

Fig. 2. Background research.

Fig. 3. 'SCHWEIGESPIRALE The Spiral of Silence' Interactive Installation

number of alternative viewpoints. When the audience presses the button, one vote will be recorded, and the water in the spiral of the corresponding device will spiral upwards in a quantitative height, and the viewpoint chosen by the majority of the people will be suspended above the spiral, which is superficially a warm, celebratory visual experience or art form (actually a bit ironic).

If the button representing a viewpoint is not pressed by the audience after five minutes, it means that if a topic is not being discussed, the water level in the corresponding spiral pipe will gradually drop and disappear, with the level of the most popular mainstream viewpoints dropping slowly, but the level of the less popular niche viewpoints dropping very quickly. Here the designer used a flowmeter to carry out a variable speed code design, representing the hot spot high popularity of the topic heat will not fall down much, while a small number of people choose the niche point of view will quickly spiral down to fall.

The whole device is a simulation experiment of a topic generated—to—stimulate discussion—to—no one to discuss, the audience participatory experience and interaction, so that the audience as a constituent of the identity of the social mass communicators to complete a discussion of the topic, judgement, point of view output, the formation of the opinion climate and dissemination of the complete mass communication chain links, self-feeling more reflective and resonance (Fig. 4).

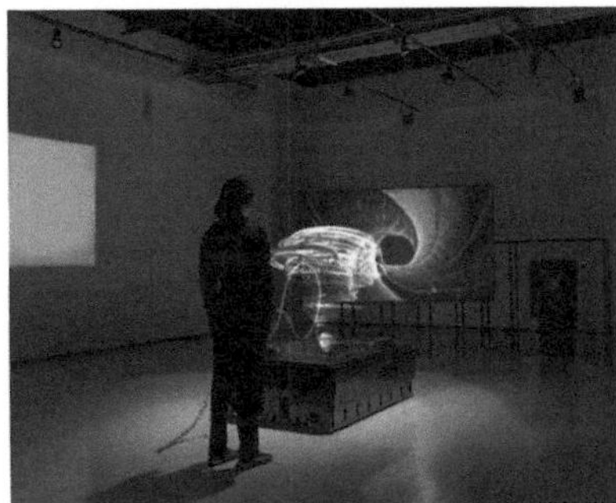

Fig. 4. 'SCHWEIGESPIRALE Spiral of Silence' Interactive Installation and Space.

This work explores the relationship between the spiral of silence on mass communication, human beings and society from a critical point of view. The designers chose different viewpoints from the fields of sociology, philosophy, and communication, and explored five long-standing controversial social hot topics from a shallow to a deeper level. When confronted with different views, the audience needs to make correct perception, judgement and action; when confronted with the convergence of views of the majority of the society, whether the audience should stick to themselves or go along with the majority's concept.

In the selection of topics, we start from the most life-like questions, such as 'What kind of qualities can attract you to a person', and select from appearance, inner, talent, economy, etc. In the popular view, traditional good virtues such as honesty and hard work, as well as talent are used as a standard to measure a person, but we don't rule out the fact that appearance and material are also used as the evaluation of a person, but we don't rule out the fact that appearance and material are also used as the evaluation of a person. In the initial research, most people would think that a person's superior material condition is a more attractive characteristic, but this is an answer that many people are ashamed to choose due to external factors, and therefore are reluctant to raise and discuss in public. Therefore, when people explore the viewpoints of an issue and make choices, they will always subconsciously think, 'What is the prevailing viewpoint of the society? Is the view I choose contrary to the mainstream?'. The design of the interactive part of this work is based on the idea of 'what is the current mainstream view?

In the design of the interactive section of this work, when the audience has not entered the exhibition area, the lights of the spiral and the button version of the platform are turned off, and the exhibition area presents a relatively dim environment (Fig. 5). When the audience stands on the selection platform, the infrared sensor senses the human body and slowly lights up the whole spiral device and the button plate (Fig. 6). Afterwards, the viewer makes a choice based on the question on the button plate and the corresponding answer (Figs. 7). When no audience enters the exhibition area, the dim lighting state is meant to simulate that a certain topic is in a hidden state when it is not discussed by people in the process of social mass communication; when people try to bring it up, the lights gradually light up the spiral, representing that the spiral of silence phenomenon starts to occur and gradually works, showing a spiral development, which not only creates a dramatic visual effect, but also symbolises that the spiral of silence phenomenon only becomes apparent when people start to pay attention to a certain topic. The design of the audience standing on the selection table to make a choice is intended to emphasise the importance and seriousness of this moment in the public space where the work is displayed (Fig. 8). The gaze of the crowd as it moves from side to side is also designed to be a social issue of discursive thinking (Fig. 9). In the gaze and scrutiny of the crowd, can the viewers still follow their own true thoughts at the moment, or do they go along with the thoughts of the public. It is a contradiction and conflict between following oneself and following the crowd.

The above is the overall expression of this installation, the designer allows the audience to participate in a simulation of the whole process of social mass communication, from the topic of thinking, to discussion, to express their views and dissemination, and ultimately the formation of the phenomenon of the 'spiral of silence' (Fig. 10).

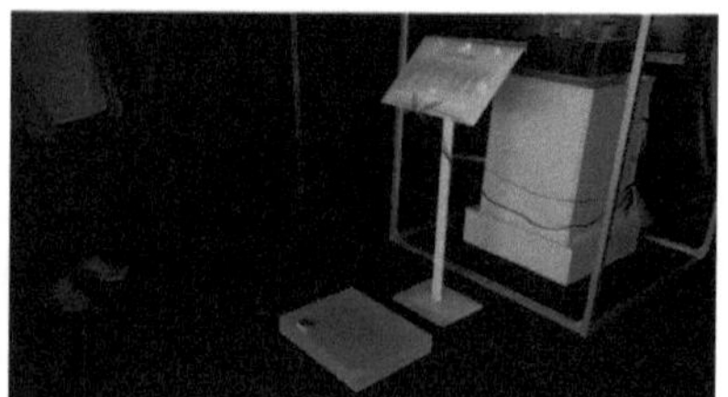

Fig. 5. Dark environment in the exhibition area.

Fig. 6. Sensor Body Illuminator.

The second part of the project is video interaction. The spiral of silence is a social phenomenon that makes the expanding viewpoints more and more diffuse and the niche viewpoints more and more submerged, which directly triggers a series of social problems, including information cocoon, digital out of control, false information, public opinion manipulation, etc. The designer adds the video interaction to allow the audience to immersively experience the echo chamber effect triggered by the spiral of silence, so that the audience can directly immerse themselves into the spiral within the vortex (Fig. 11), and feel the effect of the explosion of the information cocoon brought by the combination of audio-visual and audio-visual. The audio-visual combination of the

Fig. 7. Audience choice interaction.

Fig. 8. Experiencer Station Design

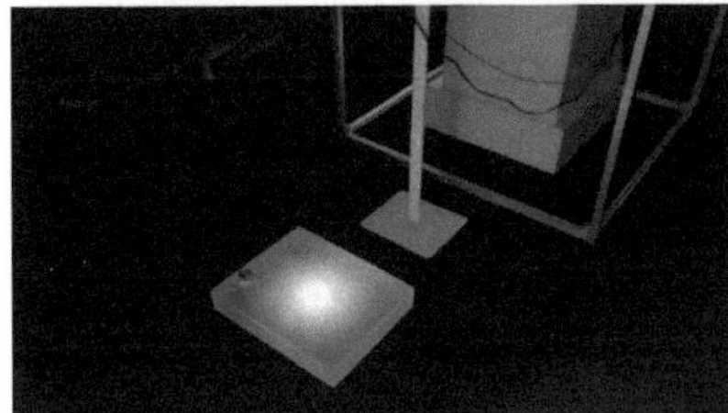

Fig. 9. Public environmental space.

Fig. 10. Photos of 'SCHWEIGESPIRALE The Spiral of Silence'

information cocoon brings a kind of sinking, indulgence, closure and the effect of the explosion of the information cocoon, creating an immersive experience space (Fig. 12).

During the primary research process, the designers interviewed and collected the views and opinions of people of different age groups and occupations on five long-standing controversial social hot topics (Fig. 13), and organised them into audio and text recordings, which were ultimately presented in the form of interactive text and sound in a video spiral (Fig. 14), visually and audibly amplifying and emphasising the mainstream viewpoints around the physical spiral device, creating an 'echo chamber effect' and a multi-sensory interactive space to enhance the audience's experience and immersion. It

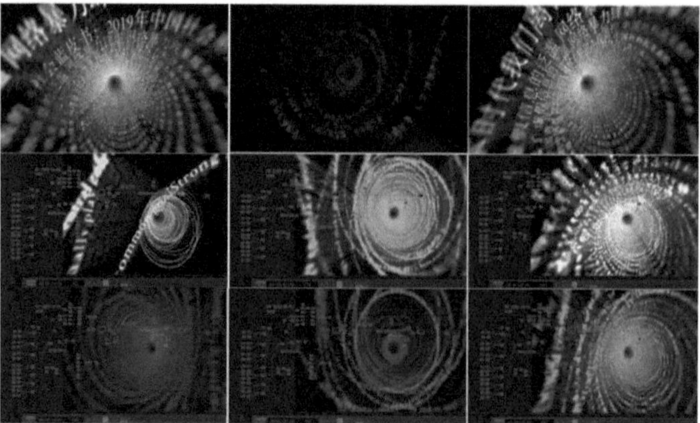

Fig. 11. Spiral, swirling visual interaction.

Fig. 12. Multi-sensory immersive experience space.

creates an 'echo chamber effect', and the multi-sensory interactive space enhances the audience's sense of experience and immersion.

The designers conducted a series of research on the choice of topic. The public discourse work needs to choose a hot social discussion topic to be thrown to the audience and let the audience make a discussion, public opinion trend and position choice. The topic chosen must be controversial and exploratory in nature. The designers asked the audience questions on five long-standing controversial topics, including human nature, gender opposition, self-identity, social relationships, etc., and changed the topic every hour to increase audience participation and discussion.

3.2 Innovative Nature of the Project

The innovation of 'SCHWEIGESPIRALE' lies in the fact that it is not only an art installation, but also a profound psycho-social experiment. By integrating a variety of technological means, such as Arduino sensors, TouchDesigner interactive image generation, cloud computing services, etc., the project successfully transforms abstract social

TOPIC SELECTION AND RESEARCH
调研采访 收集视频和观点立场 Research interviews Collect videos and opinions

Fig. 13. Primary Research Interviews.

Fig. 14. Interactive visual design—Text forming a spiral.

theories into a concrete and perceptible space. The audience is not just a spectator in this space, but becomes a co-creator of the whole experiential space, and every choice and action they make directly affects the content of the display and the outcome of the social opinion simulation. The following are some of the innovative aspects of the project:

1. The 'spiral of silence', a social phenomenon of mass communication, is visualised to show and amplify people's behaviour and psychology, and then prompt people to think.
2. The audience participates in the experience and interaction, so that the audience, as a member of the social mass communicators, can complete a discussion of the topic, judgement, and output of opinions, forming a complete mass communication chain of opinion climate and dissemination, and the self-feeling is more likely to cause reflection and resonance.
3. Cross-border and cross-discipline project, which is a high degree of integration of art design and computer technology, mass communication, sociology, political science and psychology.
4. Multi-modal interaction realises multi-sensory interactive experience, creating a contextual immersive interactive space, where physical interaction, visual interaction and sound interaction are combined to form a three-dimensional interaction.

3.3 User Experience Design

In the interactive art installation SCHWEIGESPIRALE, XR technology builds a unique contextual space beyond the traditional immersive experience. Unlike traditional art that mainly focuses on whether the information is received and understood, the artwork pays more attention to examining the user's emotional reaction, attitude change and behavioural intention after receiving the information. Through the application of new media technology and sensors, the work not only captures and responds to the audience's real physical environment, but also seamlessly integrates this information with virtual elements to create a multi-sensory and interactive immersive field. The audience is no longer a passive receiver of information, but becomes an active participant, whose behaviour, body movements and even emotional changes can instantly influence the presentation and trajectory of the work. This deep interactivity makes each viewer's experience unique, enhancing a sense of personal engagement and emotional resonance (Turk, 2014).

SCHWEIGESPIRALE THE SILENT SPIRALE skilfully employs XR technology, computer science and advanced HCI techniques to create an innovative immersive experiential environment that emphasises the autonomy of user participation and the psychological perception of multi-person synergy. The audience enjoys a high degree of autonomy and is able to freely choose the mode of interaction, which not only enhances the user's control and choice and promotes a personalised experience, but also avoids the operational constraints or sense of isolation associated with low autonomy. In addition, the work introduces a multi-person synergistic psychological perception mechanism, which makes the participants feel as if they are in a dynamically changing social collective opinion climate, where the audience's interactions are not independent and private, but rather group public synergistic interactions. Through real-time group-based interactive feedback, the installation captures individual responses while paying more attention to the impact of group dynamics on individual behaviours, reflecting the complex relationship between social pressure and individual expression. More importantly, the work also introduces an element of social networking, allowing people in different locations to synchronise their participation in the same virtual scenario, thus enabling a collective experience that transcends physical boundaries (Norris, 2004).

4 Design Principles and Technical Realisation Paths for Contextually Immersive Interactive Space

4.1 Technology-Enabled Immersive Experience

In the design and realisation of the interactive installation 'SCHWEIGESPIRALE', the designers used the integration of multimodal interaction technologies such as computer hardware construction, computer vision and natural language processing to create a highly simulated immersive experiential environment for the viewers, which makes the participants feel as if they are in a climate of constantly changing opinions. Being in a climate of ever-changing views.

Firstly, in terms of hardware, this project utilises the Arduino microcontroller platform, which consists of four Arduino boards: a Master board, responsible for overall control and coordination; an Interactive board, responsible for detecting button clicks and body sensing signals; and a Flow meter, used to monitor the flow of water, to record the amount of water corresponding to each viewpoint, which records the water level changes corresponding to each viewpoint; and finally a relay switch (Relay), which controls the switching on and off of pumps, solenoid valves and other equipment. These hardware components work together to achieve a complete closed loop from user input to system response.

Secondly, at the software level, the project is programmed to implement complex interaction logic. For example, when the audience presses the buttons representing different viewpoints, the corresponding pumps are activated to push the water up along the spiral structure, creating a visual and intuitive feedback. At the same time, if a viewpoint is not supported within five minutes, its corresponding water flow will gradually decrease until it disappears; the slower the water level decreases in the mainstream viewpoint channel with more choices, and the faster the water level decreases in the niche viewpoint channel with fewer choices, where a flow meter is used for variable speed code design. The design incorporates technology to cleverly simulate the process of climate change in the 'spiral of silence' theory. In addition, infrared sensors were used to detect the approach of an audience member, and once a person approached the installation, lights were slowly activated to create a sense of immersion into the discussion.

The visual interaction component is also crucial. Through Touchdesigner, a powerful interactive digital art tool, the designers transformed the collected audio and textual information on hot social topics into moving images, which were synchronised with the spiral installation. This not only enhances the visual impact, but also allows the audience to feel more deeply the sense of closure and oppression brought about by the information cocoon effect. The sound element synchronises the recording of the interview database of real-time mainstream viewpoints as an important part of the whole experience, aiming to enhance the sense of immersion and emotional resonance.

4.2 Interaction Design for Multi-Sensory Integration

In the SCHWEIGESPIRALE Silent Spiral project, multimodal interactions are used to enhance audience immersion from a multisensory perspective. From visual interactions with dynamic interactive video displays and ambient lighting, to auditory interactions with real sound effects that simulate crowd discussions, to haptic feedback mechanisms, the project creates an all-encompassing multisensory interactive experience (Figs. 15). The project successfully integrated three modes of physical interaction, visual interaction, and sound interaction to form a multi-dimensional interaction system. Through the synergistic effect of multiple senses, from vision, hearing, touch to environmental ambience, the audience obtains a deeper and more comprehensive emotional experience and cognitive perception. These different sensory inputs work together to help the audience better understand the complex psychosocial phenomenon of the 'spiral of silence'.

In addition, multimodal interaction includes the use of sensors, such as cameras to capture the user's movements, microphones to recognise voice commands, and touchscreens or gesture-recognition devices for direct manipulation of the interface. In SCHWEIGESPIRALE The Spiral of Silence, the designers utilised a depth camera to track the movements of the audience, as well as an infrared sensing ground to detect the position of the audience, allowing for a more precise interactive response.

Fig. 15. Ambient Light Sensor Interactive Experience

4.3   Application of Computer Technology

The powerful support of computer technology is indispensable behind SCHWEIGESPI-RALE Spiral of Silence. In order to realise the complex interactive functions mentioned above, the designers used a variety of information technology means including programming languages, interactive image generation technology, network communication. In particular, the flow meter has been designed with variable speed code, which represents that the heat of popular topics with high hotspots will not fall down much, while niche views chosen by a few people will spiral down and fall away quickly. Such technical implementation ensures that the device can accurately capture and reflect the changing trends of public opinion, and at the same time provides a reliable basis for subsequent data analysis.

4.4   The Central Role of Human-Computer Interaction

Last but not least, the success of SCHWEIGESPIRALE Spiral of Silence lies in its full utilisation of the power of human-computer interaction, which breaks the limitations of one-way communication in traditional media, encouraging everyone to make their voices heard and these voices will be recorded and displayed to other visitors. This form of two-way communication helps to break the deadlock caused by the spiral of silence, and makes people realise that even in front of the seemingly overwhelming mainstream public opinion, there is still room for the collision of diverse ideas. Multimodal interaction technology played a key role in this process, not only providing a visually realistic reproduction, but also strengthening the user's sense of presence through tactile, auditory and other multi-sensory feedback, realising the transition from pure viewing to an all-encompassing experience. SCHWEIGESPIRALE explores a new dimension of perceptual interaction through multimodal interaction, which is no longer limited to traditional narrative structure or physical interaction, but pays more attention to the changes in the user's inner perception, thus opening a new chapter of immersive artistic expression.

5   Interdisciplinary Research on 'SCHWEIGESPIRALE Spiral of Silence': A Field of Psychosocial Experimentation Constructed Through Contextually Immersive Interactive Spaces

5.1   From Viewing to Constructing: The Practice of Reconstructing Audience Identity

When the viewer steps into the exhibition space of Spiral of Silence, the trajectory of his/her body movement is transformed into a power source for the evolution of the installation—the pressure sensors triggered by his/her footsteps map the physical displacement into the rate of movement of the virtual water stream in the digital projection. This design echoes Nicolas Bourriaud's 'relational aesthetics', which transforms the experience of art into a temporary laboratory for social relations (Bourriaud, 1998). The viewer is no longer a passive aesthetic recipient, but a co-author who drives the meaning-making of the work, reshaping the material form and symbolic order of the installation with every choice.

From the viewer merely being a passive recipient of information, to being able to participate immersively in the real and imaginary environment, to interacting deeply with the media content, to the viewer becoming a part of the installation, the viewer's behaviour and choices influence the dynamic development of the installation. This in-depth participation and construction greatly enhances the audience's sense of immersion and participation, and also makes the audience no longer just 'the audience', leads the audience from the object to the subject, the audience becomes the constructor of the field, from passive viewing to active participation, from passive interaction to active construction, the audience as the construction and influence of the installation. The audience, as the main body of 'Spiral of Silence', brings them a deeper thinking from the first perspective.

5.2   Value of Psychosocial Experimentation: Deep Reflection on One's Own Behaviour and Social Phenomena

Norman proposed a hierarchical theory of users'emotional experience in Emotional Design, which divides users' emotional experience into three levels from bottom up: instinctive level, behavioural level and reflective level (Norman, 2007). The interactive experience of digital media art installation can be divided into sensory experience, exploration experience and thought experience accordingly. The 'Spiral of Silence' creates an immersive multi-sensory experience for the viewer through multi-modal interaction, and at the same time, it also serves as a tool to help the viewer understand complex social behaviours and psycho-social phenomena.

In seven sets of spiraling transparent tubes, the upward and downward movements of coloured liquids form a visualised climate of opinion that follows the metaphorical logic of social dynamics: the majority viewpoints continue to climb like energy-supplied water, while the minority voices quietly fade away under the force of gravity. This process of transformation reflects Wolfgang Welsch's idea of 'aestheticised cognition'—the transformation of abstract theory into an experiential perceptual event through art (Welsch, 1997).

The mirrored reflection area at the exit of the installation triggers the viewer to gaze at his/her own decision-making patterns through the real-time generation of data portraits. This design draws on Michel Foucault's notion of the 'technology of the self', in which the technological installation becomes a medium for the construction of the social subject (Foucault, 1988). The curatorial interviews revealed that 78% of the participants were critically aware of group polarisation in social media after experiencing the installation, confirming the potential efficacy of artistic interventions in reshaping public consciousness.

5.3   Interdisciplinary Integration: Opening New Paths for Artistic Inquiry and Social Science Research

Spiral of Silence marks the paradigm shift of digital art from object production to system construction. In the hybrid field constructed by the work, computer technology no longer remains a visual presentation tool, but becomes a converter connecting individual behaviour and collective consciousness. This practice echoes Roy Ascott's earlier prediction that 'interactive art will give rise to a new epistemology, blurring the boundaries between art, technology and society' (Ascott, 2003).

On a methodological level, the project has opened up a new path for 'art-driven social research': the behavioural data collected through the immersive experience (e.g. length of hesitation in choosing a place, hotspots in the space) provides a sample of embodied cognition that is not available through traditional questionnaires for communication research. In the future, this installation can be transformed as a prototype into a group decision-making laboratory, where research results show that haptic feedback in a physical space significantly enhances participants' ability to empathise with minority viewpoints (Picard, 2020).

This interdisciplinary practice foreshadows the future direction of digital art—the work is an aesthetic object, an active platform for social research, and a stimulus for public discussion. As viewers share videos of their experiences with the 'Spiral of Silence' hashtag on social media, the impact of art has broken through the limits of physical space and continues to ferment in the digital realm. This kind of online and offline linkage ecology is precisely the sharp response of contemporary 'post-network art' to the social and technological reality.

6 Conclusion and Outlook

6.1 The Important Role of Multimodal Interaction Technology in Constructing Contextually Immersive Interactive Spaces

Multimodal interaction technology, including the fusion of visual, auditory, tactile and other senses, has become an indispensable part of modern art installations and interactive design. In the 'SCHWEIGESPIRALE' project, a highly simulated social opinion field is created by combining multi-sensory stimuli such as high-definition impact interaction, surround sound system, touch selection mechanism and Arduino-controlled physical devices. This all-encompassing immersive experience not only enhances the user's sense of participation, but also enables them to more intuitively feel the actual operation of the 'spiral of silence' phenomenon.

In addition, with the support of the cloud computing platform, the system is able to predict the user's preferences based on their interactive behaviour and adjust the content accordingly, providing a personalised experience. Such personalisation not only enhances user engagement, but also facilitates the understanding of complex social phenomena. Thus, multimodal interaction technology not only provides users with a dynamic feedback system, but also helps them to better understand and reflect on their own social behaviour in a simulated social environment.

6.2 Trend of Integration of Interdisciplinary Explorations

As an interdisciplinary project, 'SCHWEIGESPIRALE' successfully combines various fields such as art creation, computer science, social psychology, mass communication, etc., demonstrating the great potential of combining science and technology with the humanities. Firstly, in terms of artistic expression, the project uses advanced digital technology and interactive media to create a new narrative, making abstract social theories tangible. This innovation not only enriches the expression of contemporary art, but also provides a new source of inspiration for future creations.

Secondly, in the field of social sciences, the project provides a unique experimental platform for studying group behaviour and social opinion. Traditional methods of investigation often rely on questionnaires or laboratory experiments, which make it difficult to fully capture dynamic changes in the real world. In 'SCHWEIGESPIRALE', participants interact in a highly simulated environment, and every choice they make is recorded, forming a valuable data resource. These data can not only be used to verify existing theoretical assumptions, but also to discover new research directions and promote the progress and development of related fields.

6.3 Limitations and Future Optimisation of the SCHWEIGESPIRALE Spiral of Silence

Although SCHWEIGESPIRALE has achieved significant success, there are still many areas that could be improved in future research. Firstly, the work relies heavily on physical devices and predetermined social hot topics for interaction, which limits its flexibility and immediate responsiveness. For example, when confronted with sudden social events or emerging topics, the current system may not be able to quickly adjust to reflect the latest public opinion dynamics. From a technological perspective, although current hardware configurations are capable of supporting basic interactive functions, there is still room for improvement in handling large-scale concurrent user requests and real-time data analysis. Artificial intelligence algorithms, especially natural language processing technology, can be introduced to help automatically analyse viewer input and generate more targeted feedback, which will further enhance the realism and depth of the user experience.

In order to further optimise the 'SCHWEIGESPIRALE' work, the following technological directions can be taken:

1. Application of Augmented Reality and Virtual Reality:

   The introduction of AR or VR technology can greatly enhance the audience's sense of immersion. By wearing specialised equipment, the audience can enter a completely digitally constructed space, where they can freely explore and interact with each other, and this immersive feeling will make the 'Spiral of Silence' phenomenon more intuitive and profound.
2. Artificial Intelligence and Machine Learning:

   Using AI to analyse the audience's behavioural patterns, emotional responses and opinion tendencies, it is possible to provide personalised feedback and suggestions to each participant. For example, predicting topics that may be of interest to the audience based on their historical choices and behavioural data, or adjusting the content of the display based on their reactions to promote deeper thinking.
3. Big data analysis:

   Collecting and analysing audience data from different regions, age groups and social backgrounds can help researchers understand more accurately how the 'spiral of silence' phenomenon manifests itself in different groups and the factors that influence it. This will not only help academic research, but also provide reference for policy makers.
4. Internet of Things (IoT) technology:

   By integrating more sensors and smart devices, such as environmental monitors for temperature, humidity, and air quality, as well as bio-signal detectors for heart rate and electrical skin response, we can capture changes in the physical state of the audience in real time, so as to better assess their mood fluctuations and psychological stress levels in specific contexts.

6.4 Conclusion

The creative practice of SCHWEIGESPIRALE's Spiral of Silence confirms Heidegger's philosophical insight into the nature of technology—that it is not only a tool, but also a way to 'uncloud' the world (Heidegger, 1994). Latour's theory of actor networks is materially interpreted in this study: Arduino sensors, hydraulics, group data, and participants weave dynamic networks of meaning that dissolve anthropocentric cognitive boundaries (Latour, 2005). This interdisciplinary practice not only validates the digital adaptation of the 'spiral of silence' theory, but also creates a new paradigm for art-driven social research, where technological artefacts are given an equal voice with humans.

Future research can be deepened in two directions: at the level of techno-philosophy, there is a need to construct a framework of interaction in line with Lévinas's 'ethics of the other', avoiding the erosion of individual autonomy by algorithmic power (Lévinas, 1961); and, at the level of social practice, there is a need to develop a Benjaminian 'mechanical reproduction' of art, transforming the prototype of the installation into a public platform of discussion for wide deployment (Benjamin, 1935). This kind of exploration is not only about the innovation of artistic language, but also a fundamental question about the way of human existence in the digital age—how can we safeguard the freedom of critical thinking when technology is deeply involved in the construction of cognition? This is perhaps the most challenging proposition of contemporary technopoetics.

References

Asch, S. E.: Studies of independence and conformity: I. A minority of one against a unanimous majority. Psychol. Monogr. General Appl. **70**(9), 1 (1956)

Ascott, R.: Telematic embrace: Visionary theories of art, technology, and consciousness. Univ of California Press (2003)

Benjamin, W.: The Work of Art in the Age of Mechanical Reproduction, 1936. New York (1935)

Bourriaud, N.: La mutuelle des formes. Anatomie des cultures électroniques», Art Press, hors série (1998)

Bovard, E.W., Jr.: Group structure and perception. Psychol. Sci. Public Interest **46**(3), 398 (1951)

Dourish, P.: Where the action is: the foundations of embodied interaction. MIT press (2001)

Foucault, M.: Technologies of the self. In Technologies of the self: A seminar with Michel Foucault (Vol. 18, p. 170) (1988)

Heidegger, M.: La pregunta por la técnica. Conferencias y artículos, **5**(2) (1994)

Holmqvist, K., Nyström, M., Andersson, R., Dewhurst, R., Jarodzka, H., Van de Weijer, J.: Eye tracking: A comprehensive guide to methods and measures. oup Oxford (2011)

Latour, B.: Reassembling the social: An introduction to actor-network-theory. Oxford university press (2005)

Levinas, E. Totalité et infini. Essai sur l'extériorité (1961)

Lewin, K. Frontiers in group dynamics: II. Channels of group life; social planning and action research. Hum. Relat. **1**(2), 143–153 (1947)

McDuff, D., Picard, R.W.: Physiological Synchrony in Affective Computing. Proceedings of the ACM on Interactive, Mobile, Wearable and Ubiquitous Technologies **4**(3), 1–22 (2020)

Noelle-Neumann, E.: The spiral of silence a theory of public opinion. J. Commun. **24**(2), 43–51 (1974)

Norman, D.: Emotional design: Why we love (or hate) everyday things. Basic books (2007)

Norris, S.: Analyzing multimodal interaction: A methodological framework. Routledge (2004)

Preece, J., Rogers, Y., Sharp, H., Benyon, D., Holland, S., & Carey, T.: Human-computer interaction. Addison-Wesley Longman Ltd. (1994)

Tajfel, H., Turner, J.C., Austin, W.G., Worchel, S.: An integrative theory of intergroup conflict. Organizational identity: A reader **56**(65), 9780203505984–16 (1979)

Turk, M.: Multimodal interaction: A review. Pattern Recogn. Lett. **36**, 189–195 (2014)

Welsch, W.: Undoing aesthetics (pp. x+-209) (1997)

Wang, Y.F., Petrina, S., Feng, F.: VILLAGE—V irtual I mmersive L anguage L earning and G aming E nvironment: Immersion and presence. Br. J. Edu. Technol. **48**(2), 431–450 (2017)

Research on the Influence Mechanism of Historical Architectural Elements of High-Density Urban Historic Neighborhoods on People's Pleasure and Historical Perception—The Case of Pantang Historic Neighborhood in Guangzhou, China

Hong Yun[1], Yifan Yang[2], and Zehao Hu[3]([envelope])

[1] Lecturer, School of Design, South China University of Technology, Guangzhou, China
[2] Master's Degree Candidate, School of Design, South China University of Technology, Guangzhou, China
[3] Assistant Professor, School of Architecture and Urban Planning, Shenzhen University, Shenzhen, China
zehaohu@szu.edu.cn

Abstract. With the development of urbanization, the protection and renewal of historic districts have become important issues. China has established a multi-level protection system, but still faces challenges such as inadequate mechanisms, excessive commercialization, and insufficient funding. Research indicates that in high-density urban areas, the alteration of the appearance of historic districts exacerbates psychological stress among residents, while excessive commercialization destroys the facade texture, weakens a sense of place, and impacts mental health.

VR technology shows significant potential in spatial perception research, enabling precise analysis of the influence of different elements. However, the impact of spatial elements in historical and cultural districts on mental and physical well-being remains unclear. Therefore, this study uses VR experiments to explore the influence of building facade elements on human spatial perception.

The study selected a typical street in the Pan tang Historic Neighborhood of Liwan District, Guangzhou, which retains its Qing Dynasty layout and appearance. Through field research and questionnaire surveys, key spatial elements were identified, and the confounding matrix theory was used to screen the elements to be reproduced in VR. A street model was constructed in Unreal Engine, and eye-tracking data were collected using HTC VIVE PRO EYE devices. The analysis of visitors' preferences for facade perceptions was conducted to precisely optimize historical architectural elements, exploring their effects on psychological perception and emotional relaxation, thereby enhancing historical and cultural identity and residents' physical and mental well-being.

Keywords: High-density city · Historic district renewal · Spatial elements · Spatial perception · Virtual reality technology

© The Author(s), under exclusive license to Springer Nature Switzerland AG 2026
J. Y. C. Chen et al. (Eds.): HCII 2025, LNCS 16338, pp. 236–257, 2026.
https://doi.org/10.1007/978-3-032-12808-9_15

1   Introduction

China, and even East Asian countries, have an urban development pattern of high-density dictated by the basic situation of a large number of people and a small amount of land, and historic districts are generally the most densely populated areas. On the one hand, the urban environment of high-density has a negative impact on people's physical and mental health [2–4], whereas the historic landscape and the inherent place dependence of historic districts contribute to people's perceptual restoration and other psychological well-being [5]; on the other hand, historic districts, as the material carriers of the city's history and memory, need to balance preservation and development in renewal. Therefore, how to simultaneous enhance the historical atmosphere and overall pleasantness of historic districts through precise adjustment of historical spatial elements is a key issue of great practical significance in urban construction, and needs an urgent solution.

In the identification of core historical spatial elements of historic districts, UNESCO's Historic Urban Landscape (HUL) method [6] emphasizes the "historical stratification" concept. Emphasizes the interpretation of urban landscape from the dimension of "historical layer", and controls the change of characters [7–8]. "Historical layer" refers to the understanding of urban history as interconnected 'layers' rather than exclusive "zones" [8] (Fig. 1). Historic Landscape Character (HLC) is an important method for identifying and interpreting the historical layers of urban landscape characters, which can be classified into different landscape character sub-areas with different historic characters [11–13], which helps to formulate a specific regeneration strategy that balances conservation and development [12–13]. Meanwhile, landscape gene theory can help to extract the core historical spatial elements of landscape characters.

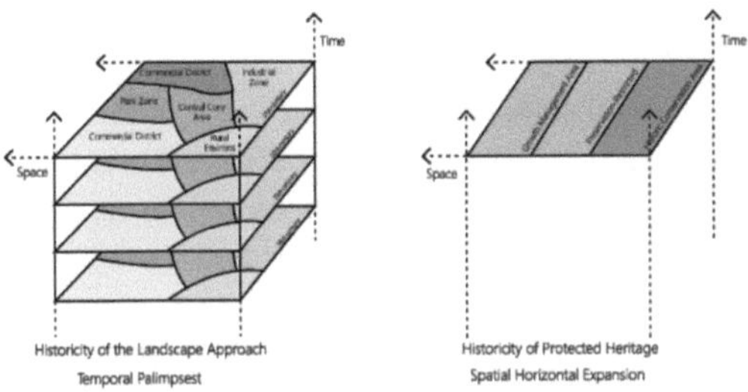

Fig. 1. Comparison of Historical Layering and Historical Spatial Zoning. [8]

In the analysis of people's spatial perception, the existing research methods are divided into quantitative and qualitative categories [14]: quantitative methods mainly use scales and social platform data to evaluate people's spatial perception imagery, and then analyze the evaluation of perceptual imagery through mathematical and statistical analysis; qualitative methods use textual analyze, in-depth interviews, and then apply the rootedness theory and other methods to analyze perceptual Imagery. However, the above research methods are highly subjective [15] and have limitations in analyzing the correlation of personal experience and spatial statue [16]. In recent years, cross-disciplinary research fields, such as urban human factors engineering [15] and neuroarchitecture

[17], have established quantitative description models of spatial perception and behavior through modern human factors technology, which provides a powerful technical method for extracting objective perception laws behind spatial experience, and helping to evaluate and optimize spatial design schemes [15–19]. Especially, the spatial perception experiments under VR environment have the advantages of high simulation [20], complete recording of the perception process [21], and the ability to accurately control the spatial variables [16–22], which can be used to accurately identify the perceptual effects of each spatial element through eye tracking and spatial-temporal localization. However, the analysis process of VR experiments is complicated, and it is necessary to debug the data transmission between multiple software. The existing VR analysis platforms are mainly aimed at data visualization, with limited functions of complex cross-analysis, so the vast majority of the studies still use two-dimensional environmental pictures or real-world environments [23], and fewer of them use VR environments [24].

Starting from the above urgent practical dilemmas and research trends, this study takes the Pantang Historic Neighborhood of Guangzhou City, China, as the research site, and utilizes spatial perception experiments combining VR environment with eye-tracking technology and subjective perceptual assessment, to quantitatively analyze the influence of the historical architectural elements on the people's historical perceptions and pleasure, then to reveal the influence mechanism of the "spatial elements—historical perceptions—pleasure". The study will provide an evidence-based design paradigm for the renewal of the historic district.

2 Identification of Historical Architectural Elements in Pantang Historic District, Guangzhou, China

2.1 Overview of the Study Area

The Pantang Historic Neighborhood, located in the Xiguan Historic Area of Liwan District, Guangzhou City, has a history of about 900 years, and is one of the most representative traditional settlements in Guangzhou, as well as an urban village with a high density of population and buildings. The Neighborhood retains a large number of historical architectural elements, such as grey brick wok house, oyster shell wall, Manchurian window, etc. At the same time, in the gradual process of adapting to urbanization, it has formed a low-rise and high-density layout, narrow street scale and dense living form. In recent years, Pantang Historic Neighborhood, as an outstanding sample in Guangzhou's urban renewal, has tried to repair damaged buildings and improve infrastructure through precise "micro-renovation" strategies, trying to strike a balance between the preservation of historical elements and the improvement of modern lives that enhance spatial vitality and community livability.

2.2 Identification of Historical Layers and Historical Architectural Elements

Based on the "Landscape Gene Theory—HLC—HUL" technical framework of historic district preservation and renewal [25] (Fig. 2), the research team identifies four typical historic layers/periods of the Pantang Historic Neighborhood, and extracts the core historical architectural elements of each historic layer (Fig. 3).

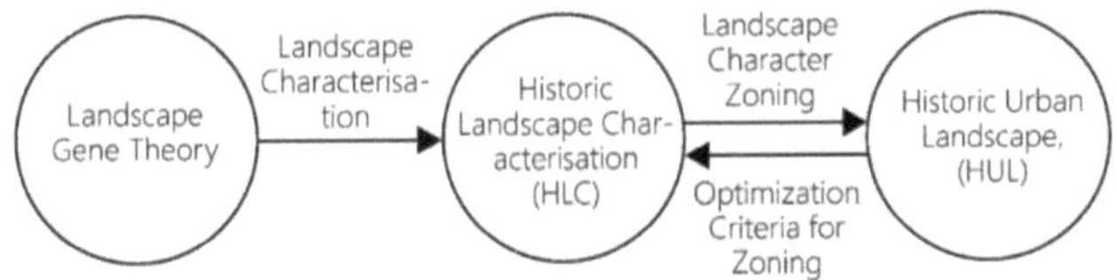

Fig. 2. Technical Framework of Historic District Preservation and Renewal. [25]

1. **Feudal Village Period (1100s–1840s)**

   Influenced by the southward migration of clans from the Central Plains of China, the Lingnan native dry-rail type residence evolved into a traditional "three-room, two-porch" house. The building layout was symmetrical, the primary and secondary are distinct, the roof is mostly Traditional pitched roof, the gables are mainly gable roof and wok-eared gable. The building materials are mainly wooden, Rubble stone footing and Grey brick. In terms of decoration, woodcarving, stone carving and brick carving were applied, and elements of architectural decoration began to increase. As this period is far from now-day and wooden structures are difficult to be preserved for a long period, very few historical architectural elements remain in current.

2. **Feudal Township Period (1841–1911)**

   The traditional "three-room, two-porch" houses developed into Xiguan grand house and Guangfu courtyard house. As the population increased dramatically, the three-bay Xiguan grand house was gradually "flattened" into a two-bay Mingzhi house and a one-bay bamboo house, and the architectural decorations became simpler. At this time, the architectural elements began to include western-style pediment, western-style columns, arch coupons, etc. Gable form still retains gable and wok-eared gable, and irregular rectangular gable began to emerge. In term of building materials, grey brick walls with white lime plaster were more common, along with some distinctive elements such as Tanglong door and Manchurian window.

3. **early Modern Urban Period (1912–1948)**

   The government of the Republic of China carried out top-down housing reforms and planned the construction of two kinds of imported architectural styles, namely, the arcade building and the Dongshan garden villa. The arcade building originated from the British colonies in Southeast Asia, and had many architectural decorations that combined Chinese and western elements in the porch of the house, door and window frame decorations, and the arcade corridor. The floors of the building increased, and 1–3 floors were more common. Gables were mainly Irregular rectangular gable, and red brick appears as wall materials. The spread of glass technology has promoted the popularization of Manchurian window. Modern metal processing technology shifted the material of door and window frame from wood to wrought iron.

4. **modern Urban Period (1949-Present)**

In the 1950s, rapid population growth led the government to construct cost-efficient house, primarily stairwell-access residence and galley-access houses, along with simple bungalows. Later, skywell courtyard house emerged. Then stairwell-access residence evolved into modern unit-type residence, while Dongshan Garden villa developed into detached courtyard house. Self-built rural dwelling style appeared in urban villages.

The roofs have various shapes, such as flat roofs and simple sloping roofs, and the gable are mainly irregular rectangles. The wall materials are various, including washed stone walls, cement plaster, ceramic tile surfaces, etc., and the doors and windows are mainly made of iron and aluminum alloy. This period was divided by 1979. The architectural elements before and including 1979 are considered historical, while those after 1979 are normal today.

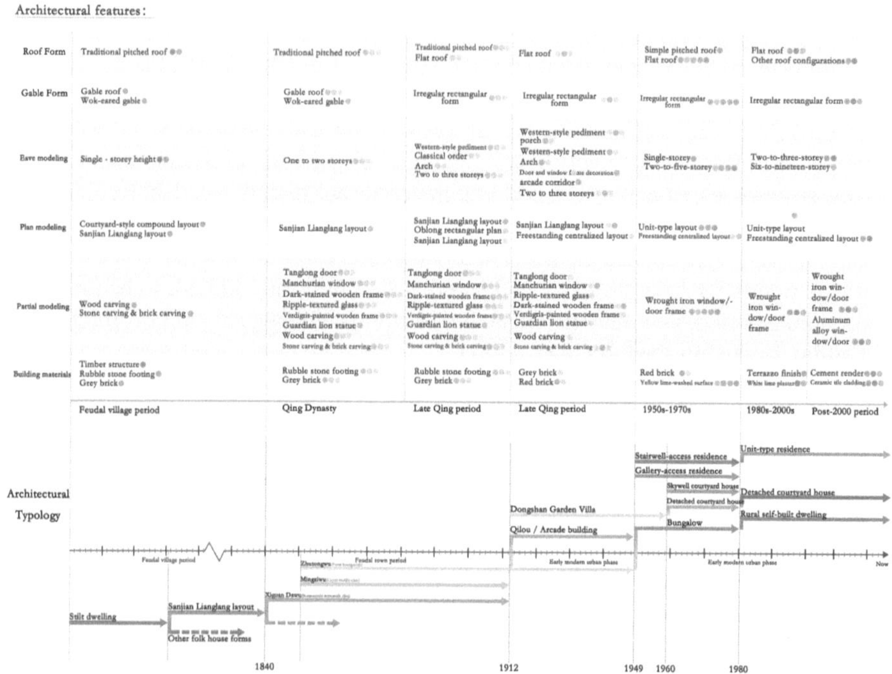

Fig. 3. Evolution of architectural form and related architectural elements. [25]

2.3 Screening of Historical Architectural Elements for the Spatial Perception Experiment

Since there are few historical architectural elements of the feudal village period remained today, there is no realistic basis for restoration of this period. The subsequent spatial perception experiments only focus on the historical architectural elements in the feudal township period (1841–1911), early modern urban period (1912–1948) and modern urban period (1949–1979). According to Fig. 3, there are 23 non-repeated historical architectural elements of the above three historical periods, and it is difficult to conduct a comparative experiments with so many variables. Therefore, the study made a preliminary compilation of the historical architectural elements:

1. According to the statistics of historical architectural elements in field investigation, verdigris-painted wooden frame, wok-eared gable gables, wood carvings, and stone lions with low cost performance in micro-renovation (the existing proportion is extremely low) are excluded.

2. In reality, ripple-textured glass coexists with Dark-stained wooden window and Manchurian window, so ripple-textured glass is classified into these two architectural elements, not as a separate architectural element.
3. Using the questionnaire, which shows the pictures of the historical architectural elements, let the local residents and tourists to assess the frequency of occurrence of the historical architectural elements in the Pantang Neighborhood as subjective memory intensity. A two-dimensional matrix (Table 1) was created with the subjective memory intensity and objective presence ratio of each historical architectural element, which divided architectural elements into high-perceived, medium-perceived and low-perceived. The elements that appeared after 1979 and were not visible from the human perspective were excluded from the high- perception and medium-perception architectural elements, and the remaining architectural elements of high or medium-perception were screened for the comparative experiments. Manchurian window, stone sculpture, and yellow lime surface, which are not available at present, are also included in comparative experiments because of their outstanding historical characters.

Table 1. Perceptibility Analysis Matrix of Historical Architectural Elements.

	High percentage of objective realities				Low percentage of objective realities			
	Architectural elements	Historical stratification	Subjective Memory Proportion	Objective Physical Proportion	Architectural Elements	Historical Layers	Subjective Memory Proportion	Objective Physical Proportion
High intensity of subjective memory	Gable roof	Feudal Village Period, Feudal Town Period	65.63%	31.66%	**Grey brick**	Feudal village period, feudal town period	84.38%	29.61%
	Simple pitched roof	Modern urban period	71.88%	32.59%	**Red brick**	Early modern town period, modern city period	60.94%	11.92%
	Flat roof	Feudal town period, modern city period	50.00%	43.02%	**Dark-stained wood window frames**	Feudal town period, early modern city period	65.62%	27.93%
	Rubble stone footing	Feudal village period, feudal town period	57.82%	33.71%	**Tanglong door**	Feudal town period, early modern city period	60.94%	5.40%
	Aluminum Doors	modern urban period (after 2000)	59.38%	38.55%	**Dark-stained wooden door**	Feudal town period, early modern city period	62.50%	20.48%
Low intensity of subjective memory	Irregular rectangular gable	Feudal town period, modern city period	37.50%	67.23%	Tin Roof	Modern urban period (after 1979)	43.76%	24.39%
	Aluminum alloy window frame	Modern urban period (after 2000)	34.38%	33.15%	Terrazzo finish	Modern urban period (1980s-2000s)	40.63%	15.64%
					Cement render	Modern urban period (after 2000)	42.19%	9.50%
					White lime plaster	Modern urban period (1980s-2000s)	42.19%	18.44%
					Ceramic tile cladding	Modern urban period (after 2000)	46.88%	29.42%
					Wrought iron window	Modern urban period (after 1949)	35.94%	15.64%
					Wrought iron door	Modern urban period (after 1949)	48.44%	19.74%

Note:

High-perception elements in orange, medium-perception elements in green, and low-perception elements in blue; bolded elements are control variables for spatial perception exeriments

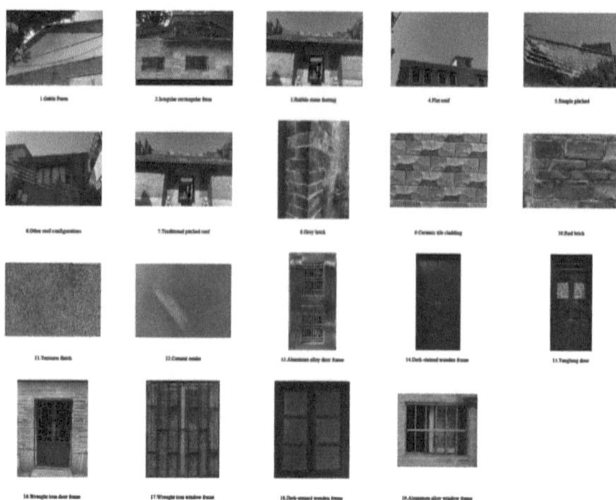

Fig. 4. Major Historical Architectural Elements.

3 Experimental Design

3.1 Research Objectives

The study constructs 4 comparative spatial models that reinforcing the characteristics of different historical periods by replacing historical architectural elements, and aims to demonstrate following research objectives by analyzing the correlation between the eye-tracking data of the historical architectural elements and of spatial perception evaluations of people:

1. Analyze the impact of perception levels of different historical periods on the pleasure of spatial experience;
2. Analyze the impact of perception levels of different historical periods on the overall historical sense of spatial experience;
3. Identify the historical architectural elements that affect the perception levels of each historical periods.

3.2 Research Framework

This study includes three parts: spatial models construction, comparative spatial perception experiment, and correlation analysis between historical architectural elements and people's spatial perception (Fig. 5).

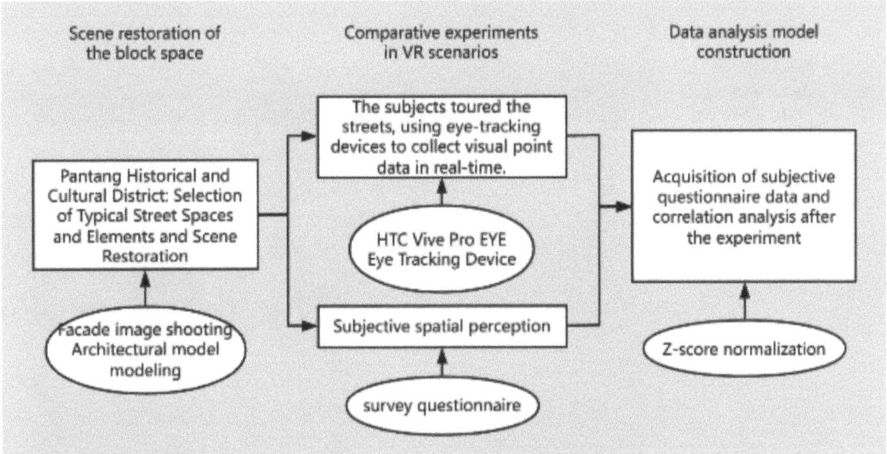

Fig. 5. Research framework.

3.3 Research Content and Method

The street selected for spatial perception experiments. Based on the historical architectural elements, the buildings in Pantang historic neighbourhood were clustered into 8 building types, and then whole Pantang area was clustered into 5 historical landscape character sub-areas by building types (Fig. 6). Sub-area B has the most mixed building types and overlays multiple historical layers (Table 2). The renewal of sub-area B is facing a practical problem of which historical layer's characteristic should be enhanced. Therefore, the study selects the main street of sub-area B for the spatial perception experiment.

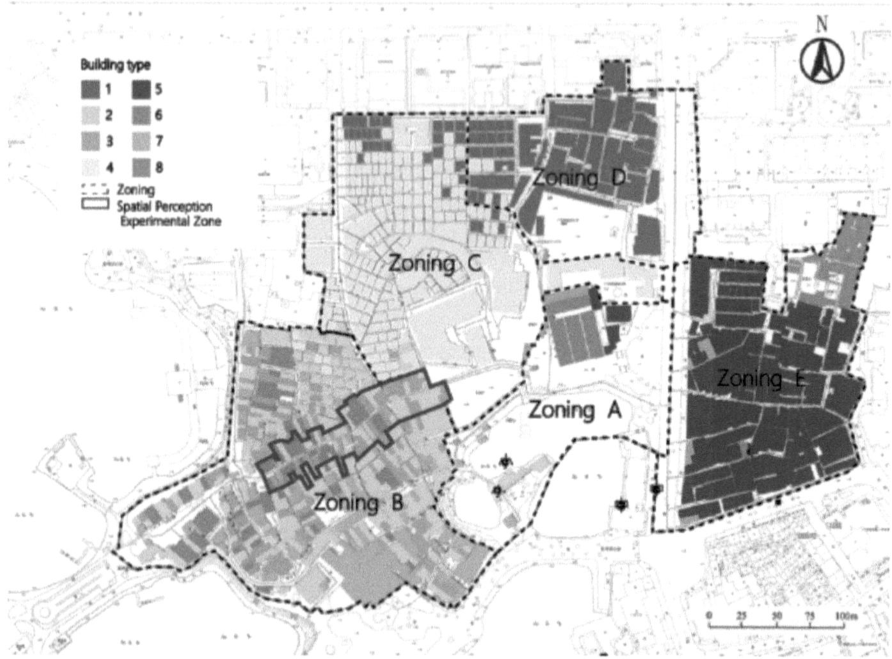

Fig. 6. Historical Landscape Character Zoning of Pantang Historic Neighbourbood. [25]

Table 2. Proportion of core historical architectural elements in each sub-area. [25]

Classification of building features	Specific characteristics	A	B	C	D	E
Gable Form	Gable roof	38.9*	32.8*	4.5	14.4	17.6
	Wok-eared gable	33.3*	0.2	0.0	0.0	0.0
	Irregular rectangular form	27.8	67.0*	95.5*	85.6*	82.4*
Building materials	Rubble stone footing	88.9*	34.2*	0.7	0.7	14.5
	Grey brick	88.9*	28.8*	1.0	19.2*	7.0
	Red brick	0.0	12.3	17.0	8.9	16.2*
	Yellow lime surface	0.0	0.6	24.7*	5.5	0.5
	Terrazzo finish	0.0	15.5	41.3*	15.1	17.4
	Cement render	0.0	8.9	39.6*	13.0	14.7
	White lime plaster	5.6	18.1	21.2	23.3*	29.0*
	Ceramic tile cladding	11.1	28.8*	25.7*	41.8*	27.3*
Partial modeling	Manchurian window	0.0	4.0	0.0	1.4	0.5

(continued)

Table 2. (*continued*)

Classification of building features	Specific characteristics	A	B	C	D	E
	Dark-stained wooden frame	33.3*	28.8*	19.8	8.2	9.7
	Verdigris-painted wooden frame	0.0	3.4	14.9*	6.8	5.6
	Wrought iron window/door frame	0.0	16.1	34.0*	16.4	24.2*
	Aluminum alloy window/door frame	61.1*	29.0	67.0*	84.9*	49.8*
	Ripple-textured glass	0.0	24.8*	11.6	18.2	6.7
	Traditional pitched roof	61.1*	32.4*	15.6	14.4	8.2
	Flat top	0.0	16.7	36.7*	29.4	47.6*
	Simple pitched roof	0.0	4.0	21.2*	15.1	17.4
	Other roof configurations	38.9	46.9	26.5	41.1	26.8

Note: * *represents the more significant architectural elements in each sub-district, and only shows the proportion of architectural elements with a relatively large number of extant buildings in Pantang*

Comparative Models that Reinforcing the Characteristics of Different historical Layers/Periods. The study captured the façade images of 63 buildings on the street, and corrected the orthographic projection of the façade images by using Adobe Photoshop, and then restored the current streetscape using the texture modeling technique in the Rhinoceros software, labeled as Model A (Fig. 7). Based on the model A, the model B, C and D replaced the historical architectural elements of the feudal township period, the early modern urban period and the modern urban period (1949–1979) respectively, in order to enhance different historical layers' characteristics (Table 3, Fig. 8).

Fig. 7. Rendering effect of model A.

Table 3. Proportion of historical architectural elements in each model.

Historic building elements		A model	B model	C model	D model
		Current Construction	Strengthen the characteristics of feudal cities and towns	Strengthen the characteristics of early modern urban period	Strengthen the characteristics of modern urban period
Wall surface (55.54%)	Grey brick	48.22%	54.54%	32.14%	0.00%
	Red brick	1.56%	0.00%	22.40%	44.41%
	Yellow lime wall	0.00%	0.00%	0.00%	10.13%
	Other types of walls	4.76%	0.00%	0.00%	0.00%
Window (8.35%)	Dark-stained wooden window	1.60%	5.50%	5.75%	0.00%
	Manchurian window	1.59%	2.85%	2.60%	0.00%
	Wrought iron window	5.16%	0.00%	0.00%	8.35%
	Other types of window frames	0.00%	0.00%	0.00%	0.00%
Door frame (19.35%)	Dark-stained wooden door	3.47%	11.36%	12.10%	0.00%
	Tanglong door	1.29%	7.99%	7.25%	0.00%

(continued)

Table 3. (continued)

Historic building elements		A model	B model	C model	D model
		Current Construction	Strengthen the characteristics of feudal cities and towns	Strengthen the characteristics of early modern urban period	Strengthen the characteristics of modern urban period
	Wrought iron door frame	5.16%	0.00%	0.00%	19.35%
	Other types of doors	9.43%	0.00%	0.00%	0.00%
Decoration	Rubble stone footing	7.31%	8.81%	5.76%	0.00%
	Stone Carving	0.06%	0.95%	0.71%	0.00%

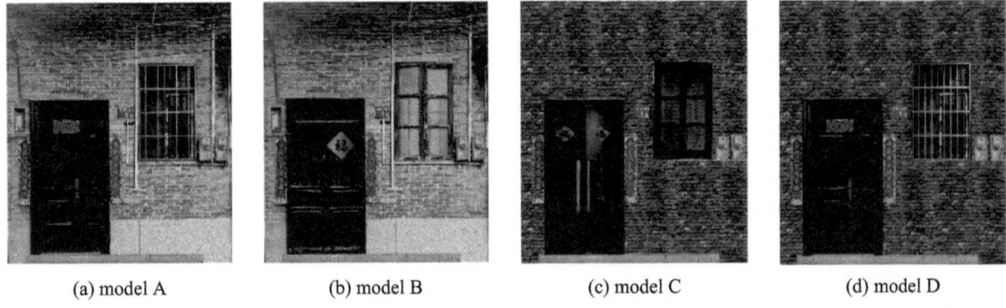

(a) model A (b) model B (c) model C (d) model D

Fig. 8. Comparison of the replacement of historical architectural elements on Building No. 20 facade in different models.

3.4 Variable Definition and Data Acquisition

This study involves four variables: the overall pleasure, the overall historical sense, the perception levels of three historical periods, and the eye-tracking data of each historical architectural element. The above data are used to demonstrate the impact of people's visual attention to each historical architectural element on the formation of perception of different historical, as well as the impact of perception of different historical periods on the overall historical sense and overall pleasure. The above data are obtained through the following two methods:

1. Eye-tracking technology

The eye tracker built into the VIVE Pro EYE VR headset is used to record real-time gaze points during the experiment. Gaze points are categorized into two types: visual points and fixation points:

- **Fixation points** refer to gaze points during the fixation process, representing conscious and slow observation. The fixation process is determined by a series of consecutive gaze points which the distance between adjacent points is less than 30 cm, and the total duration of these points exceeds 300 ms.
- **Visual points** are gaze points generated by saccadic movements between two fixation processes, representing unconscious and rapid observation, with a large distance between adjacent gaze points.

For each model, the proportion of fixation points (number of element's fixation points/total fixation points) and visual points (number of element visual points/total visual points) are statistic by historical architectural elements (Table 4). Both proportions are standardized using Z-scores before processing ordinal regression analysis in SPSS.

Table 4. Historical architectural elements included in each model.

Type	Model A		Model B		Model C		Model D	
	Variable Number	Element	Variable Number	Element	Variable Number	Element	Variable Number	Element
Eye tracking Indicator	A1	Grey brick	B1	Grey brick	C1	Grey brick	D1	Red brick
	A2	Dark-stained wooden window	B2	Dark-stained wooden window	C2	Dark-stained wooden window	D2	Yellow lime wall
	A3	Dark-stained wooden door	B3	Dark-stained wooden door	C3	Dark-stained wooden door	D3	Wrought iron door
	A4	Manchurian window	B4	Manchurian window	C4	Manchurian window	D4	Wrought iron window
	A5	Rubble stone footing	B5	Rubble stone footing	C5	Rubble stone footing		
	A6	Stone carving	B6	Stone carving	C6	Stone carving		
	A7	Tanglong door	B7	Tanglong door	C7	Tanglong door		
	A8	Red brick			C8	Red brick		
	A9	Wrought iron window						
	A10	Wrought iron door						

2. Questionnaire

After experiencing each model, participants are required to evaluate the overall pleasure, overall historical sense, and perception levels of the three historical periods through a questionnaire. The questions adopt a 5-point Likert scale (1 = Strongly Disagree, 5 = Strongly Agree).

3.5 Experimental Procedure

Before the experiment, an explanation of the experiment was given to each participant, and the participants were informed that the data of this experiment would only be used for scientific research. Then participants signed the "Informed Consent for Participants in Research Projects" if they agreed, and the participants' names, gender, age, place of domicile, and level of education were collected. Each participant will undergo four spatial models, without being informed of the modifications made to each model or which historical layers' characteristics be emphasized, so as to avoid psychological suggestion to participants' personal perception of each historical period. The spatial model's VR experiment as following:

1. The experimenter will explain to the participants the experimental equipment used in the experiment and its functions, and provide a detailed explanation of the operations that the participants need to perform when using the equipment.
2. Participants wore the VR equipment and adapted to the VR environment for 1–2 min, and the experiment was discontinued if there was any dizziness reaction. Thereafter, a spatial roaming task was carried out on a gimbaled treadmill, roaming from one end of the street to the other, and there were no fixed requirements for the elements and positions of the subjects' gaze in pursuit of a realistic process of touring the street.
3. After each spatial model, participants are required to fill out a questionnaire on the perception levels of three historical period, overall pleasure and historical sense. The entire experimental process takes approximately 40 min.

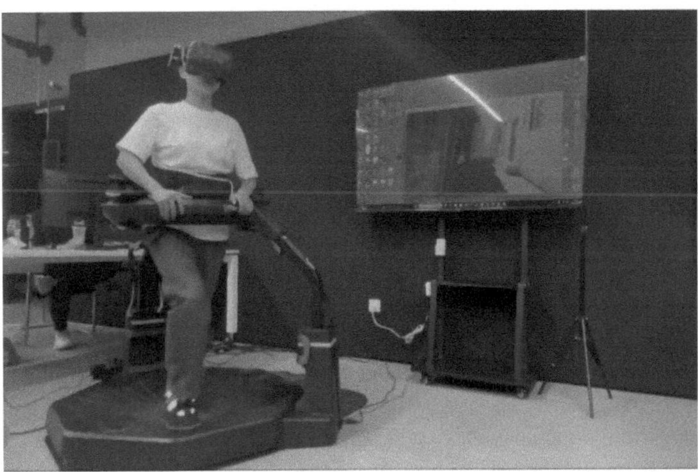

Fig. 9. Eye movement experiment process.

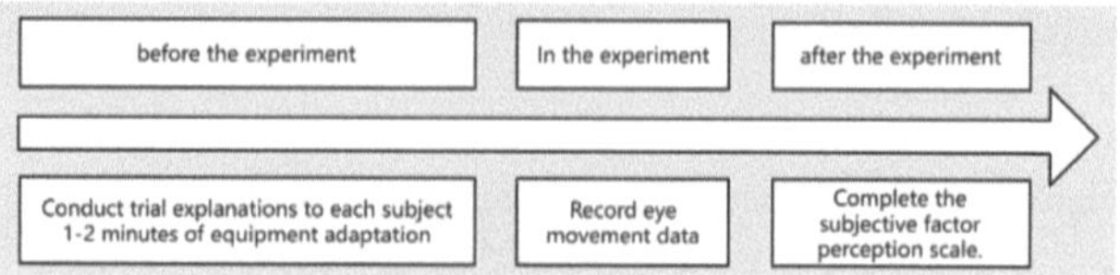

Fig. 10. Experiment flow chart.

4 Experimental Results and Analysis

A total of 60 participants were recruited in the study, and each participant had to go through 4 spatial models. After data cleaning, there were 41 valid samples, with an effective rate of 68.3%, and a total of 164 eye tracking data and questionnaires collected. All 41 participants are undergraduate students aged 19–23, with a male-to-female ratio of 17: 24, majoring in environmental design, product design, industrial design, journalism and communication, etc. Three progressive correlations were performed in this study (Fig. 11):

1. Taking all data of four spatial models as one group, Spearman is used to test the correlation between people's perception levels of three historical periods, overall pleasure and overall historical sense. In order to identify which historical periods will affect the sense of pleasure and history, as well as the degree of influence;
2. Taking each spatial model as one group, ordinal regression analysis is used to test the correlation between people's visual behavior of each historical architectural element and the perception levels of three historical periods, in order to clarify which historical architectural elements will affect the perception of which historical periods. Each spatial model is tested by 3 analysis models: analysis model M1 only takes the proportion of visual points of each historical architectural element as independent variable to verify whether unconscious visual behavior can independently affect people's historical stratification perception; The analysis model M2 only takes the proportion of fixation points of each historical architectural element as the independent variable to test whether conscious visual behavior can independently affect people's historical stratification perception; The analysis model M3 comprehensively considers the proportion of fixation points and visual points of each historical architectural element to demonstrate whether conscious and unconscious visual behaviors jointly affect people's perception of historical layers.
3. If a spatial model's all analysis model (M1,M2,M3) are not significant in second step, an additional ordinal regression analysis are conducted to test the correlation between people's visual behavior of each historical architectural element and the overall pleasure and the overall historical sense, so as to demonstrate whether the historical architectural elements may directly affect the overall pleasure and the overall historical sense in addition to the indirect mechanism of influencing the overall pleasure and the overall historical sense through perception of historical layers. Similar to the second step, 3 analysis models M1, M2 and M3 were used to test different visual behavior on the overall pleasure and overall sense of history.

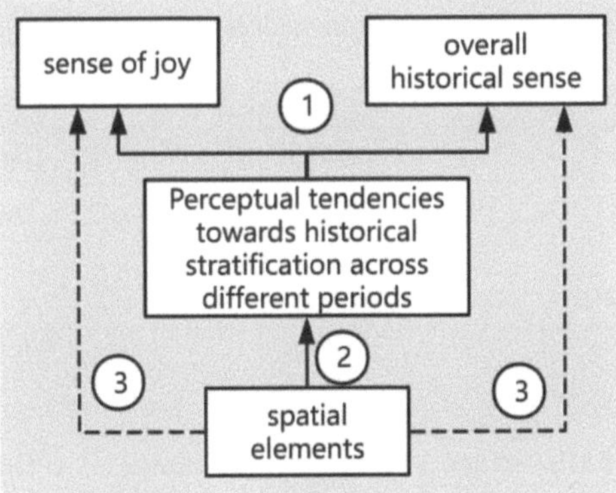

Fig. 11. Data analysis process.

4.1 The Influence of Perception Levels of Historical Periods on Overall Pleasure and Overall Historical Sense

Correlation between the perception levels of historical periods and the overall historical sense. As shown in Table 5, the perception level of the three historical periods is significantly and positively correlated with the overall historical sense, that is, historical layers analyze is meaningful on the historical sense. Meanwhile, the more distant the historical period imagery of the street from now-day, the higher the participants' perception of overall historical sense.

Table 5. Correlation analysis between the perception levels of historical periods and the overall historical sense.

	Feudal Township Period	early modern urban period	modern urban period (1949–1979)
Correlation coefficient	.413	.384	.257
Sig. (two-tailed)	< .001	< .001	< .001

Correlation between perception levels of historical periods and overall pleasure. As shown in Table 6, the perception levels of the three historical periods is significantly and highly positively correlated with the overall pleasure, that is, historical layers analyze is meaningful on pleasure. And similar to overall historical sense, the more distant the historical period imagery of the street from now-day, people can get a higher sense of pleasure.

Based on the correlation between the perception level of historical periods, the overall pleasure and the overall historical sense, the impact of historical architectural elements on the historical periods perception can further affect the overall pleasure and the overall historical sense.

Table 6. Correlation analysis between perception levels of historical period and overall pleasure.

	Feudal Township Period	early modern urban period	modern urban period (1949–1979)
Correlation coefficient	. 429	.382	.260
Sig. (two-tailed)	< .001	< .001	< .001

4.2 The Influence of Historical Architectural Elements on the Perception Level of Historical Periods

Model A (Current Status). Ordinal regression results show that the analysis model M1, M2 and M3 of model A are not significant, that is, the visual behavior of each historical architectural element has no effect on the forming of perception of any historical periods under model A. It is speculated that this street is the most mixed area in whole Pantang historical neighborhood, which leads to the unclear characteristics of historical layers, and the existing historical architectural elements cannot form a clear perception of any historical period. In the follow-up, the study will examine the influence of the visual behavior of historical architectural elements and the overall sense of history and pleasure under model A.

Model B (Characteristic Enhancement in Feudal Township Period).
The results of ordered regression show that analysis model M1, M2 and M3 of model B are not significant, that is, the visual behavior of each historical architectural element has no effect on the forming of perception of any historical periods under model B. It is speculated that due to the feudal township period is far from now-day, there are no examples of this period existing in Guangzhou, which leads to people's vague spatial imagery of this period. Therefore, even model B strengthens the characteristics of the feudal township period, it is difficult for participants to establish the corresponding relationship between the historical architectural elements and historical periods, but causes some confusion. In the follow-up, the study will examine the influence of the visual behavior of historical architectural elements and the overall historical sense and pleasure under model B.

Model C (Characteristic Enhancement in Early Modern Urban Period).
Table 7 shows that the participants' historical period perception of red brick is different from experts. Perhaps it is because red bricks appear very common in modern buildings, which leads the public to not think that red bricks are not elements in early modern urban periods. And the model C retains a large number of grey brick walls, makes the red brick walls appear more uncoordinated.

Table 7. Regression coefficient between environmental historical architectural elements in model C and perception level of early modern urban period (1949–1979).

Independent variable	M2 **
C1 fixation point	−.217
C2 fixation point	.235
C3 fixation point	.394
C4 fixation point	−.714
C5 fixation point	.644
C6 fixation point	.351
C7 fixation point	.097
C8 fixation point	−.938*

Note: ***, ** and * indicate $p < 0.01$, $p < 0.05$ and $p < 0.1$ respectively

Model D (Characteristic Enhancement in the Modern Urban Period, 1949–1979). In model D, analysis model M1, M2 and M3 for early modern urban period are all significant (Table 8), indicating that the visual behavior has a complex mechanism with the perception of early modern urban period. As far as the significant historical architectural elements in all analysis model are concerned, people's conscious visual process of wrought iron door, as well as comprehensive unconscious and conscious visual behaviors, will significantly reduce people's perception of early modern urban period. People's conscious gaze at the yellow-skin wall will also reduce people's feelings about the early modern urban period to a certain extent.

Table 8. Regression coefficient between historical architectural elements in model D and perception level of early modern urban period

Independent variable	M1 ***	M2 ***	M3**
D1 Visual Point	.299	–	.050
D2 Visual Point	–	–	–
D3 Visual Point	−.114	–	−.616
D4 Visual Point	−.591	–	.912
D1 fixation point	–	−.606	−.502
D2 fixation point	–	−.980	−.870
D3 fixation point	–	−.367	.106
D4 fixation point	–	−2.328***	−3.012***

Note: ***, ** and * indicate $p < 0.01$, $p < 0.05$ and $p < 0.1$ respectively

There are also a variety of influence mechanisms on people's perception of the modern urban period (1949–1979) (Table 9). Both the unconscious visual process and the conscious visual process can independently affect the perception of this historical period. However, most of the regression coefficients of historical architectural elements are not significant, and only the unconscious visual behavior of red brick walls will have a certain positive impact on the feelings of modern urban period (1949–1979) (Table 10).

Table 9. Regression coefficient of historical architectural elements and perception level of modern urban period (1949–1979) in model D.

Independent variable	M1**	M2**
D1 Visual Point	.360*	–
D2 Visual Point	0	–
D3 Visual Point	−.059	–
D4 Visual Point	−.386	–
D1 fixation point	–	−.227
D2 fixation point	–	.230
D3 fixation point	–	−.356
D4 fixation point	–	−.863

Note: ***, ** and * indicate $p < 0.01$, $p < 0.05$ and $p < 0.1$ respectively

Table 10. Regression coefficient of historical architectural elements and overall pleasure and overall historical sense in model B.

Independent variable	M2 (Pleasure)**	M3 (Historical Sense) **
B1 Visual Point	–	−5.863**
B2 Visual Point Proportion	–	−.817
B3 Visual Point Proportion	–	−2.194
B4 Visual Point Proportion	–	−1.225
B5 Visual Point Proportion	–	−1.837
B6 Visual Point Proportion	–	−2.602***
B7 Visual Point Proportion	–	−5.107***
B1 Fixation Point Proportion	.425	8.602**
B2 Fixation Point Proportion	−.367	2.018**
B3 Fixation Point Proportion	.095	2.789*
B4 Fixation Point Proportion	−1.060**	1.437
B5 Fixation Point Proportion	.333	.730
B6 Fixation Point Proportion	.924***	2.762***
B7 Fixation Point Proportion	.646*	4.968***

Note: * * *, * * and * represent p0.01, p0.05 and p0.1, respectively

4.3   The Influence of Historical Architectural Elements on Overall Historical Sense and Overall Pleasure

Model A (Current Status). After ordinal regression analysis, it was found that the visual behavior of model A were not significantly fitted to overall historical sense and overall pleasure. It can be inferred that under the state of mixed historical architectural elements, it is not only difficult to form a clear historical period perception, but also difficult to act on the formation of the overall historical sense and pleasure.

Model B (Characteristic Enhancement in Feudal Township Period). Although the historical architectural element in model B can't act on the formation of historical period perception, they can affect the overall pleasure through conscious visual behavior, and affect the overall historical sense through unconscious and conscious visual behavior. In terms of pleasure, it mainly depends on continuously looking at some elements with aesthetic tension—looking at stone carvings and Tanglong doors can significantly and directly produce pleasure, but paying attention to Manchurian windows will significantly reduce pleasure. It is speculated that Manchurian windows with brighter colors are inconsistent with other quaint architectural elements. For the overall historical sense, the process of looking at dark-stained wooden window and dark-stained wooden door can form a sense of history to a certain extent. However, the grey brick walls, stone carvings and Tanglong doors have opposite effects on the formation of historical sense between unconscious and conscious visual behavior. It may be that there are differences between the perceptual historical sense reflected and the internal historical connotation by these elements, so quick glancing and attentive observation give people a completely different historical imagery. It shows the complexity of the formation mechanism of historical sense.

5   Discussion

Taking Pantang Historic Neighborhood in Guangzhou as a case, this study reveals the influence mechanism of historical architectural elements on people's pleasure and historical perception in high-density urban historical districts through VR comparative experiments combining eye tracking and subjective perception evaluation, and mainly draws the following conclusions:

1. There is a significant correlation between people's perception of historical periods and the overall pleasure and the historical sense, and the influence degree of different historical periods' perception are different. When the elements of historical architectural elements are too mixed, it is difficult to form a clear perception of historical periods characteristic. As suggested by HUL, the preservation and renewal of historic districts should be comprehensively considered through the perspective of "historical stratification".

2. It is found that the perception level of three historical periods: feudal township period, early modern urban period and modern urban period (1949–1980) are highly positively correlated with the overall historical sense and pleasure of visiting a historic district. The more distant the historical period imagery of the street from now-day,

the higher the participants' perception of overall historical sense and pleasure. It indicates that the time span of historical period is an important factor affecting spatial perception;

3. The influence mechanism of historical architectural elements on the perception of historical periods is complex. Among the elements in the feudal town period, Manchurian window, Tanglong door and other elements are seen to significantly enhance the sense of pleasure and history through conscious visual behavior, while grey brick, stone carving, Tanglong door have a complex influence on the sense of history through conscious and unconscious observation behavior. Among the elements of modern urban period, red brick and wrought iron door will weaken the perception of modern urban period, but red brick will enhance the perception of modern urban period (1949–1979).

The research confirms the applicability of VR-based spatial perception experiment in the renewal of historic districts. The comparative model constructed by controlling variables, combined with eye tracking data and subjective questionnaire analysis, can accurately separate the perceptual effects of different spatial elements, which provides evidence-based design basis for the renewal of historic district. In the future, we will further optimize the VR experimental process, expand the sample size, and deeply explore the quantitative relationship between the proportion of architectural elements and historical perception, so as to provide more targeted strategies for the protection and renewal of historic district in high-density cities.

Acknowledgments. Acknowledgments. We gratefully acknowledge financial support from the General Project of the Humanities and Social Sciences Research Foundation of the Ministry of Education of China (Grant No. 24YJCZH404), the Discipline Co-construction of the Guangdong Provincial Philosophy and Social Sciences Planning (Grant No. GD23XLN31) and the Youth Project of Guangzhou Philosophy and Social Sciences Development Planning (Grant No. 2022GZQN48).

References

1. Xian, W., Leiqing, X.: Perceived density in the context of urban high density-connotation, value and important research questions[J]. Int Urban Plan. **39**(6), 62–70 (2024)
2. Bo, X., Yiling, Z., Li., Zhigang, et al.: Influence of high-density residential environment in urban China on stroke among residents–empirical study on Wuhan [J]. Urban Plan. **45**(5), 30–39 (2021)
3. Qiang, W., Chengyu, W., Hongyan, R., et al.: Urbanization environment and risk of schizophrenia [J]. Chin. J. Neuropsychiatric Dis. **39**(12), 758–763 (2013)
4. Li., Xin, Lin, Z., Tao, J., et al.: Analysis of Urban Spatial Risk Factors under the "New Crown" Epidemic-Taking Wuhan as an Example [J]. Urban Plan. **45**(8), 78–86 (2021)
5. Li, Jiaying, et al.: "Exploring perceived restoration, landscape perception, and place attachment in historical districts: insights from diverse visitors." Front. Psychol. 14.000(2023):13
6. Unesco.: Recommendation on the Historic Urban Landscape[R] (2011)
7. Wu, J., Hang, Ruoxi, Z.: Exploration of Historic Urban Landscape Approaches for the Renewal of Historic Neighborhoods[J]. Urban Des. **02**, 40–47 (2022)

8. Jianyun, Z., Dingzhe, J., Ziting, B., et al.: Historic Landscape Character Assessment – Linking Conservation Areas and Historic Urban Landscapes[J]. Int. Urban Plan. **38**(02), 124–132 (2023)

9. Whitrap.: The HUL Guidebook: Managing Heritage in Dynamic and Constantly Changing Urban Environments. A Practical Guide to UNESCO's Recommendation on Historic Urban Landscape[M]. Austria: Bad lschl (2016)

10. Li., Ji, Feng, J., Yong, S.: UNESCO's Historic Townscape (HUL) Global Practice–A 10th Anniversary Review and Implications for Urban Heritage Conservation in China[J]. Urban Plan. **46**(11), 90–98 (2022)

11. Carys, S.: Landscape Character Assessment Guidance for England and Scotland[R]. The Countryside Agency, Scottish Natural Heritage (2002)

12. Lun, W., Bin, Z.: Landscape Character Assessment – A Comparative Study and Implications of the LCA System and the HLC System[J]. Landscape Arch. **25**(05), 87–92 (2018)

13. Li., Heping, Ning, Y.: Management tools for urban historic landscapes-Research on character assessment methods for town historic landscapes[J]. China Garden **35**(05), 54–58 (2019)

14. Xie Tiexiang, Wu Jiaquan. Historical and Cultural Analysis Based on Web Text... -Taking Yongqingfang, Enning Road, Guangzhou as an Example_Xie Tiexiang [J]. Mod. Urban Res. (1), 64–71 (2023)

15. Li, Z., Huishu, D., Xiaohan, M.: Urban ergonomics: A design science for the quality of human spatial experience[J]. Sci. Bull. **67**(16), 1744–1756 (2022)

16. Wen, D., Donghui, D.: Progress and Trends of Digital Technology-Assisted Research on Urban Public Space Experience[J]. Southern Arch. **03**, 20–31 (2024)

17. Quanxiu, L., Yuan, Y., Linting, W., et al.: Emotional health impacts and planning strategies of urban micro-remodelling facades on female groups – an empirical study based on neuroscience experiments in Guangzhou[J]. World Arch. **6**, 35–40 (2024)

18. Li, Z.: Urban ergonomics: a new field of disciplinary intersection[J]. World Arch. **03**, 8–9 (2021)

19. Li, Z., FuGuang, S.: On urban ergonomics[J]. Urban Environ. Des. **3**, 10–15 (2021)

20. CHEN Y, CUI Z. An experimental methodology study on healthy lighting for the elderly with ad based on VR technology: 9th CJK Lighting Conference, Busan, Korea (2017)[C]

21. Wu Xia'an, Xu Leiqing. Perceived Density in the Context of Urban High Density – Connotation, Value and Important Research Issues[J]. Int. Urban Plan. **39**(06), 62–70 (2024)

22. Yuge, X., Wanting, H., Poli, M., et al.: Progress and perspectives of landscape cognition research incorporating the human factors perspective[J]. Landscape Arch. **29**(06), 63–69 (2022)

23. WU Chu Han, CHEN Zheng, ZHANG Jia Qi.: A meta-analysis of subjective and objective measures of health benefits of nature contact[J]. Gardening **40**(06), 21–27 (2023)

24. Ruoxi, Z., Li., Guangkai, Lemin, Z., et al.: Research on visual perception of crowd in historical area landscape under VR eye-tracking–taking Zhangzhou ancient city as an example[J]. New Arch. **6**, 58–63 (2023)

25. Hu., Yun Jian, Zehao, Z.H.: Optimisation of landscape feature identification and zoning method for urban historic districts[J]. Landscape Arch. **32**(01), 114–123 (2025)

Extended Reality in Healthcare and Medical Training

Advancing Clinical Care Through Virtual Reality: Lessons Learned and Future Directions

Brett T. Burrows[1]([✉]) [ID], Gianluca De Leo[1] [ID], Soonhyung Kwon[2] [ID],
and Rosalba Hernandez[3] [ID]

[1] Augusta University, Augusta, GA 30912, USA
bburrows@augusta.edu
[2] University of South Florida, Tampa, FL 33620, USA
[3] University of Illinois Chicago, Chicago, IL 60607, USA

Abstract. Virtual reality (VR) is increasingly being integrated into clinical health-care as a multifunctional technology, serving both as an advanced training plat-form for clinicians and nurses and as a non-pharmacological intervention for pain, phobias, and psychosocial conditions. Defined as an immersive, ultra-realistic, computer-generated environment, VR offers a unique combination of realism and customization, all within a controlled space. Its application in clinical training is rapidly expanding, often outperforming traditional instructional methods. In addi-tion to clinical training, VR has demonstrated potential as a non-pharmacological intervention across diverse patient populations, including individuals with severe burns, those with diagnosed psychological disorders, those undergoing hemodial-ysis and cancer treatment, and patients. Widespread clinical adoption has been hindered by small sample sizes, lack of rigorous, theory-driven frameworks, insuf-ficient user-centered designs, and the challenges posed by rapidly evolving tech-nology. The lack of high-quality evidence and large-scale clinical trials continue to limit the integration of VR into routine clinical care. This paper evaluates the current state of evidence supporting VR as a clinical tool, incorporating lessons from pilot trials conducted by our team and others, and aims to address ethical and equity-related considerations in patient care. We also examine the applications of VR in patient health education, emphasizing its potential to improve disease understanding, support self-management, and encourage healthy behaviors. The paper concludes with future directions, including the integration of artificial intel-ligence to enable personalized, patient-centered VR experiences and to support broader adoption in clinical practice.

Keywords: virtual reality · medical training · patient healthcare

1 Introduction

Virtual reality (VR) offers a computer-generated environment that simulates realistic sensory experiences and allows end-users to interact within lifelike digital spaces. Ini-tially adopted for simulation-based training and exposure therapy for military sectors [1, 2], VR has undergone rapid technological advancements over the past decade, becoming

© The Author(s), under exclusive license to Springer Nature Switzerland AG 2026
J. Y. C. Chen et al. (Eds.): HCII 2025, LNCS 16338, pp. 261–275, 2026.
https://doi.org/10.1007/978-3-032-12808-9_16

significantly more affordable and accessible to the broader public [3]. VR platforms are generally categorized into three formats: non-immersive (e.g., console-based systems like the Nintendo Wii), semi-immersive (e.g., flight simulators), and fully immersive systems that utilize head-mounted displays (HMDs) that largely occlude the end-user's visual field. For the purposes of this paper, VR refers specifically to fully immersive systems employing HMDs that enable visual and auditory immersion.

With the rapid advancement of technology and the development of immersive, lifelike experiences, VR has been widely adopted in gaming and entertainment. More recently, VR has been integrated into clinical healthcare, particularly as an advanced training platform for clinicians and nurses [4]. These technological innovations have positioned VR as a promising alternative to traditional training methods, increasingly becoming a standard in medical education. In parallel, VR has shown therapeutic potential as a non-pharmacological intervention for managing chronic pain, phobias, and psychosocial conditions [5–8]. However, despite the growing acceptance of VR in clinical education, its adoption as a non-pharmacological treatment for patients remains limited, and even fewer efforts have explored its application as an educational tool for patients themselves.

In this paper, we review the current state of evidence supporting VR as a clinical tool for healthcare training and education, and as a non-pharmacologic intervention for patients. We present lessons learned from our work and that of others to inform future research and development. Additionally, we explore ethical and equity-related considerations and provide recommendations to guide future VR design and clinical implementation. We conclude by outlining key priorities and future directions to advance the effectiveness and adoption of VR in clinical care.

2 Immersive Learning in Clinical Healthcare: The Role of VR

2.1 VR in Clinical Skills Training

In the medical field, rigorous training in complex procedures is vital to develop the technical skills required for optimal clinical outcomes while minimizing adverse events. As procedural complexity increases, the volume and quality of training become critical determinants of success. Traditional training pathways, however, may not always provide adequate procedural exposure. For example, a 2017 study reported that nearly 30% of US general surgery residents lacked the confidence and readiness to independently perform core procedures upon completion of their residency [9]. Medical use of VR and augmented reality is beginning to address some of these gaps by offering scalable, high-fidelity training environments that facilitate access and improve clinical preparedness.

Though not entirely integrated into the medical field, VR is currently being used for simulation training and is rapidly becoming the standard practice for clinical training and education over conventional methods [4, 10–13]. Due to its unlimited tailoring, VR can uniquely simulate complex medical scenarios that are realistic, hands-on, repeatable, and offer immediate feedback. Importantly, VR also provides a safe and controlled environment for clinicians to train, eliminating the risk of costly and possibly fatal mistakes. Recent evidence has shown that the advantages of VR help facilitate access to training, which improves the skillset and decision-making of many medical trainees. For example, a study from UCLA's School of Medicine found that VR training was 230%

more effective for learning orthopedic surgical techniques than traditional training for first and second-year medical students [14]. Though evidence supports the use of VR over traditional methods for medical training, VR should not replace but accompany traditional methods to foster the development of medical trainees.

The utility of VR in medical education extends well beyond surgical simulation. VR platforms support diverse applications, including anatomical exploration, procedural rehearsal, emergency response, patient communication, and interprofessional collaboration [15]. Integrating haptic feedback and artificial intelligence (AI) enhances realism, facilitates objective skill assessment, and enables adaptive, personalized learning [16]. Additionally, VR can enable multiple users for collaborative training scenarios and team-based skill development. The remote accessibility of VR eliminates geographic barriers, broadening access to high-quality training and fostering standardized, interdisciplinary education across institutions and borders [17]. Finally, VR has cultivated critical soft skills such as empathy and communication in simulated patient interactions when delivering bad news [18].

2.2 Revolutionizing Patient Education Through VR

Despite evidence supporting VR's overwhelming advantage for clinical training education, very few trials have investigated VR for patient education use (primarily as a treatment approach). While disease-related education is paramount for chronic disease management, traditional patient education materials are often filled with complex terminology, focus on disease vs a holistic behavioral approach (i.e., a healthy lifestyle), written above patients' reading level, and lack personalized and culturally relevant material [19]. These barriers often leave patients overwhelmed and uninformed, lowering their disease-related knowledge and reducing self-management practices [20]. VR may be a potential alternative modality to deliver disease-related patient educational content to improve their disease-related knowledge and self-management practices.

VR uniquely combines audio and visuals to deliver complex, personalized, and culturally tailored (e.g., language and ethnicity) content. However, according to Harvie [21], merely transitioning disease educational content onto a VR platform does not significantly improve knowledge. Self-management education must take advantage of VR's advanced technology, such as promoting immersion, presence, and engagement through interaction with the virtual environment and/or avatars. Literature suggests that higher levels of immersion and presence result in improved knowledge and recall of information [22, 23]. For example, cancer patients undergoing radiation therapy often report misconceptions of treatment leading to anxiety and non-compliance with treatment. In a recent study, educational sessions, via a VR HMD, immersed patients in a life-like virtual rendition of a radiation treatment room and helped patients understand what to expect during the radiation treatment. Participants reported significant improvements in their understanding of the treatment, which resulted in a significant reduction in their anxiety [24]. Additionally, theoretical models of behavior change should be considered to improve one's motivation and self-efficacy in performing self-management practices. VR HMDs may enhance patient knowledge and support self-management. Future research should examine how integrating behavioral change theories in VR affects motivation, self-efficacy, and disease management.

3   VR as a Non-Pharmacological Therapeutic Modality

3.1   Managing Chronic Disease: Innovative Use of VR

Healthcare providers are increasingly incorporating VR into patient care in various ways. For instance, gamifying physical therapy exercises into interactive VR games or delivering exposure therapy in a controlled setting for individuals suffering from severe phobias or post-traumatic stress disorder (PTSD). VR has shown several benefits as a non-pharmacological medical treatment option, including positive results in physical rehabilitation [25] and palliative care [26], and improved clinical outcomes such as blood pressure [27], pain management [6, 28], anxiety and stress disorders [7, 8], and depression [29, 30]. A recent study showed that among fibromyalgia patients, interactive balance and mobility VR games, when used as an adjunctive therapy with exercise, significantly improved pain, fatigue, and eased fear of being physically active compared to exercise alone [31]. Similar findings from a meta-analysis showed that VR significantly improved physical and cognitive function in patients suffering from stroke through interactive games and real-world simulations [32].

VR-based mindfulness and meditation therapy has predominantly used guided meditation by transporting the user to a desired virtual environment with calming sounds (e.g., meditation at the beach with ocean sounds) to effectively reduce anxiety and depression for patients with psychosocial conditions such as PTSD and depressive disorders [7, 8, 29, 30]. However, the use of AI-powered digital avatars is the latest advancement of VR for use in therapy and counseling. Avatar therapy, either as a virtual representation of the user, another patient or as a therapist/coach, has recently been used to treat mental and behavioral health conditions, such as depression and anxiety, as well as substance addiction and eating disorders [33, 34]. Additionally, with the evolution of movement, facial, and voice recognition technology, digital avatars have been successful in emotion regulation, verbal communication, and pain reduction [35–39]. Specifically, studies have shown that verbal and non-verbal interactions with digital avatars have improved social interactions in people with schizophrenia and autism [38, 39]. However, as AI and digital avatars become increasingly more intuitive and "real", ethical challenges such as the blending of realities become more problematic, especially for individuals with psychiatric illnesses such as psychosis [34, 40]. Though no solutions currently exist, it is clear that procedures must be in place to safeguard high-risk, vulnerable patient populations.

Though prior research has generally shown benefits associated with VR-specific use as a non-pharmacological treatment, a lack of significant difference compared to traditional methods is evident. The lack of significant differences may result from VR-related trials consisting mainly of underpowered pilot trials. Therefore, there is a critical need for more robust randomized controlled trials (RCTs) with greater statistical power to detect possible significant differences.

3.2   Enhancing Health and Well-Being in Older Adults Through VR

VR has also been increasingly investigated as a non-pharmacological treatment for the improvement of physical, cognitive, and mental health, specifically in older adult populations. Despite the social stigma that there is a digital divide among older adults, feasibility trials have concluded that older adults are willing and able to engage with VR technology. Specifically, a feasibility study found that older adults tolerated VR HMDs very well, and 76% wanted to try it again in the future [41]. Another pilot trial study found that older adults experienced enjoyment, relaxation, and happiness during the VR sessions [42]. Further, recent systematic reviews have highlighted that VR interventions through HMDs improved physical, mental, psychosocial, and cognitive health outcomes in older adults [43–45]. Specifically, a meta-analysis found that VR exergames showed moderate effects on overall cognitive function (g = 0.525) and memory (g = 0.507) and large effects on depressive symptoms (g = −0.977) with greater effectiveness observed in longer duration interventions (≥6 weeks) [46]. Clinical applications of VR have the potential to provide immersive and interactive experiences that screen, monitor, and train the cognitive abilities of older adults [43]. These findings suggest that gamified VR-based applications are not only feasible but also provide physical and cognitive benefits among older adult populations.

Despite its potential, VR-based interventions for older adults are early-stage and low-maturity [43, 45]. Additionally, the use of VR applications in healthcare settings still remains challenging for older adult populations because of the unknown risk of cybersickness (e.g., nausea, headaches, or dizziness), predominantly due to older adults' greater sensitivity to adverse side effects. Furthermore, a negative attitude toward VR technology for use among older adults is commonly reported by both older patients and healthcare providers [47, 48]. These challenges highlight the need for future refinement in VR hardware and software design to ensure user comfort, safety, and usability, specifically for older adults.

3.3 Use of VR in Pediatric Healthcare

VR has been widely applied in pediatric populations as a distraction-based tool during painful medical procedures. Immersive VR has been shown to significantly reduce pain and anxiety in children and adolescents undergoing burn wound care, venipuncture, and other medical procedures involving needle insertion [49]. Research suggests that VR distraction is more effective than standard distraction techniques, such as music or television, in reducing procedural distress and physiological markers of pain [50]. VR-related exposure therapy has also shown reductions in preoperative stress [51] and post-surgical side effects [52]; though few trials exist.

Beyond procedural distraction, VR is increasingly used in other pediatric contexts, including among children with physical and developmental disabilities. For example, VR-based rehabilitation programs have been shown to improve motor function, balance, and coordination in children with cerebral palsy through immersive simulation games that engage somatosensory and visual feedback pathways, such as virtual horseback riding or balance games [53]. VR has also demonstrated promise in addressing psychological conditions such as anxiety disorders and specific phobias, particularly by delivering graded exposure therapy and enhancing emotional regulation through interactive virtual environments [54].

Despite this growing evidence base, the adoption of VR in pediatric clinical settings remains limited. Concerns related to cost, integration into workflow, and lack of staff training continue to be a barrier [55]. Moreover, although early concerns about VR-induced cybersickness were common, current pediatric trials report minimal adverse effects, particularly when sessions are short and HMDs are appropriately calibrated [6]. Ensuring age-appropriate content, device sanitation, and individualized patient assessment are also critical for broader clinical integration.

4 Lessons Learned from Research and Practice

4.1 Addressing Patient-Centered Barries to VR Use

Although many clinical interventions report high patient satisfaction, VR's adoption, uptake, and clinical effectiveness in patient care have shown varied results. At the individual level, barriers include HMD discomfort (i.e., too tight or slipping down and not accommodating eyeglasses or hearing aids), usability (difficulty navigating the virtual environment), motivation (boring content), lack of personalization, physical impairments (poor vision, hearing, mobility, or chairbound), language and cultural barriers, and cognitive impairment [56]. Additionally, barriers at the macro-ecological level include: lack of buy-in, knowledge, and support from healthcare providers; time constraints restricting patients' ability to learn how to appropriately engage with the VR-specific program; limited technical support; wi-fi/connectivity issues; excessively loud clinical settings; VR-related trials not well integrated to accommodate healthcare staff workflow; and lack of progression or sustainability to enhance long-term adoption [56].

Notably, limited or no medical reimbursement by healthcare insurance providers, at the healthcare organization level, has also dramatically curbed VR's use in patient care. As of 2023, the Centers for Medicare and Medicaid Services (CMS) will only reimburse VR-related cognitive behavioral training when used strictly for pain management and only when using the RelieVRx (formerly EaseVRx) software. RelieVRx is currently the only VR-specific software to gain Food and Drug Administration (FDA) approval. The lack of insurance reimbursement has also constrained healthcare providers from adopting VR as an alternative non-pharmacological treatment option.

4.2 Potential Considerations

Much of the barriers associated with low use and performance and potentially inadequate effectiveness may be improved by including evidence-based frameworks and user-centered designs. Incorporating evidence-based frameworks and user-centered design approaches in the initial development phases will likely help identify barriers and better meet the needs of the user. By understanding the needs of the user, VR applications potentially could be more efficient and effective. For example, utilizing geriatric principles, such as the 5Ts Framework to support the inclusion of older adults, may help researchers overcome the unique challenges (e.g., cognitive impairment, polypharmacy, mobility limitations, etc.) associated with geriatric patients [57]. Additionally, we suggest the use of multidisciplinary teams (e.g., clinicians, digital engineers, patients, etc.) to collectively address the potential barriers and challenges specific patient populations may encounter while utilizing VR for medical care. Successfully addressing barriers and challenges may facilitate improved outcomes and lessen patient and staff burden.

4.3 Identifying When VR Adds Value: Lessons from Practice

Not all health behavior interventions are suitable for VR. Discerning when VR adds meaningful value is essential to its effective use. From our experience developing and testing Joviality™ [58], a VR-based positive psychological intervention, several conditions emerged as markers of VR readiness. First, the target health behavior must benefit from experiential, immersive learning, particularly when abstract concepts (e.g., mindfulness, gratitude) are more effectively conveyed through sensory and emotional engagement than didactic instruction. Second, the target population must be able to physically and cognitively interact with the technology. For instance, Joviality™ was implemented in a hemodialysis population, where patients often remain seated for several hours, making it possible, and even ideal, to incorporate VR modules during treatment sessions. Importantly, VR was not simply well-tolerated by patients but provided a welcome distraction, and an emotional uplift, within an otherwise distressing clinical environment.

Third, VR must offer apparent advantages over traditional delivery formats. In the case of Joviality™, patients previously struggled to navigate tablet-based interventions due to dexterity and literacy barriers. The transition to a VR HMD experience addressed these issues by enabling intuitive, hands-free eye-tracking navigation, verbal delivery of content, and multisensory environmental cues that deepened engagement. Rather than asking patients to read about mindfulness, VR allowed them to experience an immersive calming virtual forest while guiding them through mindful breathing. These design elements, tailored to the physical, emotional, and logistical needs of the population, highlight the importance of aligning the how of delivery with the who and what of intervention goals.

Finally, VR's value increases when paired with culturally resonant and inclusive content. Across multiple iterations of Joviality™, user feedback consistently emphasized the importance of personalized visuals, multilingual options, and emotionally relevant narratives. For instance, patients could choose whether to complete mindfulness exercises in a Japanese garden, on a tropical beach, or from atop a mountain, each curated to foster psychological safety and aesthetic appeal. We also found that participants valued the accessibility of their native language and experienced a strong sense of cultural affinity. This type of intentional and personalized design is not merely additive; it is fundamental to VR's success as a behavioral health tool. Lessons from Joviality™ suggest that VR is most effective when it fills a specific gap in delivery, addresses barriers to engagement, and personalizes the therapeutic experience in ways that traditional formats cannot.

5 Ethical Considerations in Integrating VR into Healthcare

When scaling VR applications for medical care, it is essential to examine ethical considerations to avoid harm. These concerns go beyond the individual to population-level implications, including the potential to exacerbate health disparities. Below, we outline key ethical considerations as VR technology increasingly integrates into healthcare delivery (see Table 1).

Given the emerging role of VR in medicine, a patient-centered design that considers patient limitations is critical. Cybersickness is a concern for patients with disease-related symptoms, such as those undergoing cancer treatment [59, 60], and it is essential to identify high-risk individuals, including those with a history of epilepsy or seizures. Clinical integration requires a clear understanding of risks to reduce harm [61]. VR sessions should be brief (15–20 min, max 30) to reduce cybersickness risk or adverse side effects [62, 63]. Additionally, VR content must protect vulnerable patients and avoid triggering adverse psychological reactions, such as reactivating traumas [64]. Thoughtful design and screening help prevent harm, such as sorrow from unreachable home country simulations or PTSD flashbacks in veterans and optimize therapeutic benefit [65]. Patients should not become overly reliant on VR as an escape from reality. In clinical settings, VR must not interfere with medical care or patient-provider interactions but should enhance real-world engagement and support health management. For example, our Joviality™ software used VR to promote gratitude, followed by a real-life task, bridging virtual and real experiences [66, 67].

There is a need for evidence-based VR software tailored to specific patient populations and treatment settings. Mobility limitations and restricted hand use of medical equipment must be carefully considered. Most psychosocial VR interventions use commercial meditation apps that overlook patient-specific limitations [68]. A user-centered design approach helps tailor VR experiences to patients' needs, enhancing safety and effectiveness [61]. For instance, our Joviality™ software for patients on hemodialysis was designed to accommodate seated use and control via head and eye movements, allowing for an improved user experience. Rigorous RCTs are needed to validate such interventions and assess their impact on health outcomes [69].

Addressing concerns over data security, sharing protocols, and equitable access for underserved communities is critical at the macro level. With major companies like Meta developing VR headsets, protecting sensitive health data from misuse is essential [59]. As VR devices collect sensitive health-related data, expanding Health Insurance Portability and Accountability Act (HIPAA) coverage and updating regulations may safeguard patient privacy and data protection [70]. Ensuring emerging health technologies, like VR, are accessible to vulnerable populations is crucial to reducing health disparities. With headsets costing $300 to $3,500, many may be excluded, limiting benefits to higher-income groups [61]. To promote equity, both affordability and access must be prioritized. Developers should prioritize solutions tailored to diverse needs while exploring low-cost options like smartphone-compatible VR viewers to broaden access to innovative, evidence-based care [56].

Table 1. Ethical considerations when integrating full-immersive virtual reality (VR) into patient healthcare.

Concern	Considerations
Cybersickness	• Limit individual VR sessions to < 30 min in duration • Evaluate patients' specific symptom burden and consider risks of VR • Identify high-risk, vulnerable patients (e.g., history of epilepsy, seizures, motion sickness, etc.)

(continued)

Table 1. (continued)

Concern	Considerations
Persuasive technology	• Safeguard vulnerable patients from triggering adverse reactions (e.g., veterans with PTSD in a combat-like scenario) • Clearly determine the need and use of VR (i.e., preventable risk of exposure) • VR should be an alternative/adjunctive therapy, not eliminate healthcare provider engagement (i.e., face-to-face interaction) and promote social isolation • User-centered designs that promote end-users as patients, not consumers • Clearly define outcomes of interest
Digital divide	• Promote low-cost options (e.g., smartphone-compatible VR) • Expand medical insurance coverage • User-centered designs to address physical, cognitive, sensory, and unique treatment limitations (e.g., hemodialysis patients have hand and mobility constraints during treatment) • Evidence-based frameworks to support inclusion (e.g., 5Ts Framework to support inclusion of older adults)
Privacy and security	• Improved encryption technology • Updating and enforcing privacy laws • Greater transparency in user data-sharing policies

6 Shaping the Future of VR in Clinical Practice

Despite significant advancements over the past two decades, substantial work remains to fully integrate VR into clinical practice. Future efforts should prioritize the development of VR interventions grounded in evidence-based frameworks and user-centered design principles, facilitated by multidisciplinary collaborations to meet the diverse needs of patient end-users and healthcare providers. Off-the-shelf software solutions are insufficient to meet the nuanced clinical and patient-specific demands of healthcare. Further, we must transition from pilot studies to large-scale RCTs with extended follow-up periods. Robust data from such studies will be critical in demonstrating the long-term benefits of VR on patient outcomes, thereby facilitating regulatory approvals and reimbursement pathways.

Incorporating AI into VR platforms offers a promising path toward personalized and adaptive clinical experiences. AI can dynamically tailor VR content based on patients' language preferences, cognitive abilities, and care settings, enhancing engagement and relevance. These capabilities may help increase the effectiveness, accessibility, and equity of VR interventions, particularly in diverse and underserved populations.

Moreover, the design of VR environments must account for patient safety, particularly for individuals with conditions that may predispose them to adverse effects such as cybersickness. Incorporating adaptive features that consider users' physical, cognitive, and sensory limitations is crucial for minimizing potential harm and enhancing user experience. As the FDA continues to evaluate and authorize medical devices incorporating VR technology, ongoing research and development efforts must align with regulatory standards to ensure the safe and effective integration of VR into healthcare.

For engineers and digital developers, sustained collaboration with clinicians and patients is key to ensuring that VR solutions are not only technologically sophisticated but also clinically relevant, usable, and aligned with real-world healthcare workflows. Early and continuous engagement with clinical stakeholders enables the identification of key operational needs, workflow constraints, and safety considerations that may be overlooked from a purely technical perspective [71]. Participatory design methods, including co-design workshops, iterative prototyping, and user-centered testing with healthcare professionals and patient end-users, yield essential insights into system usability, interface design, and functional requirements [72]. Moreover, developers should prioritize interoperability with existing electronic health record systems and adhere to healthcare data protection regulations, including HIPAA [73]. Establishing structured feedback mechanisms between technical and clinical teams can expedite the translational pathway from prototype to practice, facilitating the deployment of VR technologies that enhance both patient outcomes and provider experience.

7 Conclusion

VR holds significant promise as a clinical training tool, a non-pharmacological treatment modality, and a platform for patient education. However, its full integration into healthcare requires continued, rigorous development and validation. Future efforts must prioritize forming multidisciplinary teams with sustained collaborations between clinicians, developers, and patient end-users to embed evidence-based frameworks and user-centered design principles into the creation of VR applications. In parallel, research must shift toward large-scale, methodologically rigorous trials that include diverse populations and long-term follow-up to establish VR's effectiveness, safety, and cost-effectiveness in real-world clinical settings. Without consistent, high-quality evidence demonstrating improved outcomes and economic value, widespread FDA approval and insurance reimbursement will remain constrained. The innovation and investment long directed toward gaming should now be harnessed to transform healthcare delivery.

Disclosure of Interests..   The authors have no competing interests to declare that are relevant to the content of this article.

References

1. McCarty, W.D., Sheasby, S., Amburn, P., Stytz, M.R., Switzer, C.: A virtual cockpit for a distributed interactive simulation. IEEE Comput. Graphics Appl. **14**(1), 49–54 (1994). https://doi.org/10.1109/38.250919
2. Motraghi, T.E., Seim, R.W., Meyer, E.C., Morissette, S.B.: Virtual reality exposure therapy for the treatment of posttraumatic stress disorder: a methodological review using CONSORT guidelines. J. Clin. Psychol. **70**(3), 197–208 (2014). https://doi.org/10.1002/jclp.22051

3. Chang, S.N., Chen, W.L.: Does visualize industries matter? a technology foresight of global virtual reality and augmented reality industry. In: 2017 International Conference on Applied System Innovation (ICASI), pp. 382–385 (2017). https://doi.org/10.1109/ICASI.2017.7988432

4. Creutzfeldt, J., Hedman, L., Felländer-Tsai, L.: Cardiopulmonary resuscitation training by avatars: a qualitative study of medical students' experiences using a multiplayer virtual world. JMIR Serious Games 4(2), e22 (2016). https://doi.org/10.2196/games.6448

5. Dascal, J., Reid, M., IsHak, W.W., et al.: Virtual reality and medical inpatients: a systematic review of randomized, controlled trials. Innovations Clin. Neurosci. 14(1–2), 14–21 (2017)

6. Malloy, K.M., Milling, L.S.: The effectiveness of virtual reality distraction for pain reduction: a systematic review. Clin. Psychol. Rev. 30(8), 1011–1018 (2010). https://doi.org/10.1016/j.cpr.2010.07.001

7. Mishkind, M.C., Norr, A.M., Katz, A.C., Reger, G.M.: Review of virtual reality treatment in psychiatry: evidence versus current diffusion and use. Curr. Psychiatry Rep. 19(11), 80 (2017). https://doi.org/10.1007/s11920-017-0836-0

8. Meshkat, S., Edalatkhah, M., Di Luciano, C., et al.: Virtual reality and stress management: a systematic review. Cureus 16(7), e64573 (2024). https://doi.org/10.7759/cureus.64573

9. George, B.C., Bohnen, J.D., Williams, R.G., et al.: Readiness of US general surgery residents for independent practice. Ann. Surg. 266(4), 582–594 (2017). https://doi.org/10.1097/sla.0000000000002414

10. Maytin, M., Daily, T.P., Carillo, R.G.: Virtual reality lead extraction as a method for training new physicians: a pilot study. Pacing Clin. Electrophysiol. 38(3), 319–325 (2015). https://doi.org/10.1111/pace.12546

11. Khan, R., Plahouras, J., Johnston, B.C., Scaffidi, M.A., Grover, S.C., Walsh, C.M.: Virtual reality simulation training for health professions trainees in gastrointestinal endoscopy. Cochrane Database Syst. Rev. 8, CD008237 (2018). https://doi.org/10.1002/14651858.cd008237.pub3

12. Nagendran, M., Gurusamy, K.S., Aggarwal, R., Loizidou, M., Davidson, B.R.: Virtual reality training for surgical trainees in laparoscopic surgery. Cochrane Database Syst. Rev. 8, CD006575 (2013). https://doi.org/10.1002/14651858.cd006575.pub3

13. Jiang, H., Vimalesvaran, S., Wang, J.K., Lim, K.B., Mogali, S.R., Car, L.T.: Virtual reality in medical students' education: scoping review. JMIR Med. Educ. 8(1), e34860 (2022). https://doi.org/10.2196/34860

14. Blumstein, G., Zukotynski, B., Cevallos, N., et al.: Randomized trial of a virtual reality tool to teach surgical technique for tibial shaft fracture intramedullary nailing. J. Surg. Educ. 77(4), 969–977 (2020). https://doi.org/10.1016/j.jsurg.2020.01.002

15. Moro, C., Štromberga, Z., Raikos, A., Stirling, A.: The effectiveness of virtual and augmented reality in health sciences and medical anatomy. Anat. Sci. Educ. 10(6), 549–559 (2017). https://doi.org/10.1002/ase.1696

16. Tene, T., Vique López, D.F., Valverde Aguirre, P.E., Orna Puente, L.M., Vacacela, G.C.: Virtual reality and augmented reality in medical education: an umbrella review. Front. Digit. Health 6, 1365345 (2024). https://doi.org/10.3389/fdgth.2024.1365345

17. Kyaw, B.M., Saxena, N., Posadzki, P. et al.: Virtual reality for health professions education: systematic review and meta-analysis by the digital health education collaboration. J. Med. Internet Res. 21(1), e12959 (2019). https://doi.org/10.2196/12959

18. Dyer, E., Swartzlander, B.J., Gugliucci, M.R.: Using virtual reality in medical education to teach empathy. J. Med. Libr. Assoc. 106(4), 498–500 (2018). https://doi.org/10.5195/jmla.2018.518

19. Morony, S., Flynn, M., McCaffery, K.J., Jansen, J., Webster, A.C.: Readability of written materials for CKD patients: a systematic review. Am. J. Kidney Dis. 65(6), 842–850 (2015). https://doi.org/10.1053/j.ajkd.2014.11.025

20. Schrauben, S.J., Cavanaugh, K.L., Fagerlin, A., et al.: The relationship of disease-specific knowledge and health literacy with the uptake of self-care behaviors in CKD. Kidney Int. Rep. **5**(1), 48–57 (2020). https://doi.org/10.1016/j.ekir.2019.10.004

21. Harvie, D.S.: Immersive education for chronic condition self-management. mini review. Front. Virtual Real. **2** (2021). https://doi.org/10.3389/frvir.2021.657761

22. Pollard, K.A., Oiknine, A.H., Files, B.T., et al.: Level of immersion affects spatial learning in virtual environments: results of a three-condition within-subjects study with long intersession intervals. Virtual Real. **24**(4), 783–796 (2020). https://doi.org/10.1007/s10055-019-00411-y

23. Krokos, E., Plaisant, C., Varshney, A.: Virtual memory palaces: immersion aids recall. Virtual Real. **23**(1), 1–15 (2019). https://doi.org/10.1007/s10055-018-0346-3

24. Wang, L.J., Casto, B., Luh, J.Y., Wang, S.J.: Virtual reality-based education for patients undergoing radiation therapy. J. Cancer Educ. **37**(3), 694–700 (2022). https://doi.org/10.1007/s13187-020-01870-7

25. Gumaa, M., Rehan, Y.A.: Is Virtual reality effective in orthopedic rehabilitation? a systematic review and meta-analysis. Phys. Ther. **99**(10), 1304–1325 (2019). https://doi.org/10.1093/ptj/pzz093

26. Mo, J., Vickerstaff, V., Minton, O., et al.: How effective is virtual reality technology in palliative care? a systematic review and meta-analysis. Palliat. Med. **36**(7), 1047–1058 (2022). https://doi.org/10.1177/02692163221099584

27. Liu, K., Madrigal, E., Chung, J.S., et al.: Preliminary study of virtual-reality-guided meditation for veterans with stress and chronic pain. Altern. Ther. Health Med. **29**(6), 42–49 (2023)

28. Goudman, L., Jansen, J., Billot, M. et al.: Virtual reality applications in chronic pain management: systematic review and meta-analysis. JMIR Serious Games **10**(2), e34402 (2022). https://doi.org/10.2196/34402

29. Burrows, B.T., Morgan, A.M., King, A.C., Hernandez, R., Wilund, K.R.: Virtual reality mindfulness and personalized exercise for patients on hemodialysis with depressive symptoms: a feasibility study. Kidney Dial. **3**(3), 297–310 (2023). https://doi.org/10.3390/kidneydial3030026

30. Baghaei, N., Chitale, V., Hlasnik, A., Stemmet, L., Liang, H.-N., Porter, R.: Virtual reality for supporting the treatment of depression and anxiety: scoping review. JMIR Ment. Health **8**(9), e29681 (2021). https://doi.org/10.2196/29681

31. Gulsen Pt, M.C., SPTP, F., EPTM, K. et al.: Effect of fully immersive virtual reality treatment combined with exercise in fibromyalgia patients: a randomized controlled trial. Assist. Technol. **34**(3), 256–263 (2022). https://doi.org/10.1080/10400435.2020.1772900

32. Khan, A., Imam, Y.Z., Muneer, M., Al Jerdi, S., Gill, S.K.: Virtual reality in stroke recovery: a meta-review of systematic reviews. Bioelectron. Med. **10**(1), 23 (2024). https://doi.org/10.1186/s42234-024-00150-9

33. Franco, M., Monfort, C., Piñas-Mesa, A., Rincon, E.: Could avatar therapy enhance mental health in chronic patients? a systematic review. Electron. **10**(18) (2021). https://doi.org/10.3390/electronics10182212

34. Bell, I.H., Nicholas, J., Alvarez-Jimenez, M., Thompson, A., Valmaggia, L.: Virtual reality as a clinical tool in mental health research and practice
. Dialogues Clin. Neurosci. **22**(2), 169-177 (2020). https://doi.org/10.31887/DCNS.2020.22.2/lvalmaggia

35. Fernández-Sotos, P., García, A.S., Vicente-Querol, M.A., Lahera, G., Rodriguez-Jimenez, R., Fernández-Caballero, A.: Validation of dynamic virtual faces for facial affect recognition. PLoS ONE **16**(1), e0246001 (2021). https://doi.org/10.1371/journal.pone.0246001

36. Dang, M., Noreika, D., Ryu, S. et al.: Feasibility of delivering an avatar-facilitated life review intervention for patients with cancer. J. Palliat. Med. **24**(4), 520–526 (2021). https://doi.org/10.1089/jpm.2020.0020

37. Tong, X., Wang, X., Cai, Y., et al.: I dreamed of my hands and arms moving again: a case series investigating the effect of immersive virtual reality on phantom limb pain alleviation. Front. Neurol. **11**, 876 (2020). https://doi.org/10.3389/fneur.2020.00876

38. Muros, N.I., García, A.S., Forner, C., et al.: Facial affect recognition by patients with schizophrenia using human avatars. J. Clin. Med. **10**(9) (2021). https://doi.org/10.3390/jcm 10091904

39. Wang, X., Xing, W., Laffey, J.M.: Autistic youth in 3D game-based collaborative virtual learning: Associating avatar interaction patterns with embodied social presence. Brit. J. Educ. Technol. **49**(4), 742–760 (2018). https://doi.org/10.1111/bjet.12646

40. Rizzo, A.S., Schultheis, M.T., Rothbaum, B.O.: Ethical issues for the use of virtual reality in the psychological sciences. In: Bush, S.S., Drexler, M.L., Lisse, N.L.: Ethical issues in clinical neuropsychology, pp. 243–280. Swets & Zeitlinger Publishers (2003)

41. Appel, L., Appel, E., Bogler, O., et al.: Older adults with cognitive and/or physical impairments can benefit from immersive virtual reality experiences: a feasibility study. Front. Med. (Lausanne) **6**, 329 (2019). https://doi.org/10.3389/fmed.2019.00329

42. Chaze, F., Hayden, L., Azevedo, A., et al.: Virtual reality and well-being in older adults: results from a pilot implementation of virtual reality in long-term care. J. Rehabil Assist. Technol. Eng. **9**, 20556683211072384 (2022). https://doi.org/10.1177/20556683211072384

43. Skurla, M.D., Rahman, A.T., Salcone, S., et al.: Virtual reality and mental health in older adults: a systematic review. Int. Psychogeriatr. **34**(2), 143–155 (2022). https://doi.org/10. 1017/s104161022100017x

44. Dermody, G., Whitehead, L., Wilson, G., Glass, C.: The role of virtual reality in improving health outcomes for community-dwelling older adults: systematic review. J. Med. Internet Res. **22**(6), e17331 (2020). https://doi.org/10.2196/17331

45. Baragash, R.S., Aldowah, H., Ghazal, S.: Virtual and augmented reality applications to improve older adults' quality of life: a systematic mapping review and future directions. Digit. Health **8**, 20552076221132100 (2022). https://doi.org/10.1177/20552076221132099

46. Yen, H.Y., Chiu, H.L.: Virtual reality exergames for improving older adults' cognition and depression: a systematic review and meta-analysis of randomized control trials. J. Am. Med. Dir. Assoc. **22**(5), 995–1002 (2021). https://doi.org/10.1016/j.jamda.2021.03.009

47. Davis, S., Nesbitt, K., Nalivaiko, E.: A Systematic Review of Cybersickness. In: Proceedings of the 2014 Conference on Interactive Entertainment, Newcastle, NSW, Australia (2014). https://doi.org/10.1145/2677758.2677780

48. Weech, S., Kenny, S., Barnett-Cowan, M.: Presence and cybersickness in virtual reality are negatively related: A review. Front. Psychol. **10** (2019). https://doi.org/10.3389/fpsyg.2019. 00158

49. Tas, F.Q., van Eijk, C.A.M., Staals, L.M., Legerstee, J.S., Dierckx, B.: Virtual reality in pediatrics, effects on pain and anxiety: a systematic review and meta-analysis update. Paediatr. Anaesth. **32**(12), 1292–1304 (2022). https://doi.org/10.1111/pan.14546

50. Eijlers, R., Utens, E., Staals, L.M., et al.: Systematic review and meta-analysis of virtual reality in pediatrics: effects on pain and anxiety. Anesth. Analg. **129**(5), 1344–1353 (2019). https://doi.org/10.1213/ane.0000000000004165

51. Bekelis, K., Calnan, D., Simmons, N., MacKenzie, T.A., Kakoulides, G.: Effect of an immersive preoperative virtual reality experience on patient reported outcomes: a randomized controlled trial. Ann. Surg. **265**(6) (2017). https://doi.org/10.1097/SLA.0000000000002094

52. Eijlers, R., Dierckx, B., Staals, L.M., et al.: Virtual reality exposure before elective day care surgery to reduce anxiety and pain in children: a randomised controlled trial. Eur. J. Anaesthesiol. **36**(10), 728–737 (2019). https://doi.org/10.1097/eja.0000000000001059

53. Chang, H.J., Jung, Y.G., Park, Y.S., O, S.H., Kim, D.H., Kim, C.W.: Virtual reality-incorporated horse riding simulator to improve motor function and balance in children with cerebral palsy: a pilot study. Sens. (Basel). **21**(19) (2021). https://doi.org/10.3390/s21196394

54. Blanco, D., Roberts, R.M., Gannoni, A., Cook, S.: Assessment and treatment of mental health conditions in children and adolescents: a systematic scoping review of how virtual reality environments have been used. Clin. Child. Psychol. Psychiatry **29**(3), 1070–1086 (2024). https://doi.org/10.1177/13591045231204082
55. Vincent, C., Eberts, M., Naik, T., Gulick, V., O'Hayer, C.V.: Provider experiences of virtual reality in clinical treatment. PLoS ONE **16**(10), e0259364 (2021). https://doi.org/10.1371/journal.pone.0259364
56. Kouijzer, M.M.T.E., Kip, H., Bouman, Y.H.A., Kelders, S.M.: Implementation of virtual reality in healthcare: a scoping review on the implementation process of virtual reality in various healthcare settings. Implementation Sci. Commun. **4**(1), 67 (2023). https://doi.org/10.1186/s43058-023-00442-2
57. Bowling, C.B., Whitson, H.E., Johnson, T.M., 2nd.: The 5Ts: preliminary development of a framework to support inclusion of older adults in research. J. Am. Geriatr. Soc. **67**(2), 342–346 (2019). https://doi.org/10.1111/jgs.15785
58. Hernandez, R., Burrows, B., Browning, M.H.E.M. et al.: Mindfulness-based virtual reality intervention in hemodialysis patients: a pilot study on end-user perceptions and safety. Kidney360 **2**(3), 435–444 (2021). https://doi.org/10.34067/kid.0005522020
59. Yellowlees, P.M., Holloway, K.M., Parish, M.B.: Therapy in virtual environments—clinical and ethical issues. Telemed. e-Health **18**(7), 558–564 (2012). https://doi.org/10.1089/tmj.2011.0195
60. Marloth, M., Chandler, J., Vogeley, K.: Psychiatric interventions in virtual reality: why we need an ethical framework. Camb. Q. Healthc. Ethics **29**(4), 574–584 (2020). https://doi.org/10.1017/s0963180120000328
61. Zhou, S., Gromala, D., Wang, L.: Ethical challenges of virtual reality technology interventions for the vulnerabilities of patients with chronic pain: exploration of technician responsibility. J. Med. Internet Res. **25**, e49237 (2023). https://doi.org/10.2196/49237
62. Bruno, R.R., Wolff, G., Wernly, B., et al.: Virtual and augmented reality in critical care medicine: the patient's, clinician's, and researcher's perspective. Crit. Care **26**(1), 326 (2022). https://doi.org/10.1186/s13054-022-04202-x
63. Kennedy, R.S., Stanney, K.M., Dunlap, W.P.: Duration and exposure to virtual environments: sickness curves during and across sessions. Presence **9**(5), 10 (2000). https://doi.org/10.1162/105474600566952
64. Parsons, T.D.: Ethical challenges of using virtual environments in the assessment and treatment of psychopathological disorders. J. Clin. Med. **10**(3) (2021). https://doi.org/10.3390/jcm10030378
65. Kellmeyer, P., Biller-Andorno, N., Meynen, G.: Ethical tensions of virtual reality treatment in vulnerable patients. Nat. Med. **25**(8), 1185–1188 (2019). https://doi.org/10.1038/s41591-019-0543-y
66. Hernandez, R., Wilund, K., Solai, K. et al.: Positive psychological intervention delivered using virtual reality in patients on hemodialysis with comorbid depression: protocol and design for the joviality randomized controlled trial. JMIR Res. Protoc. **12**, e45100 (2023). https://doi.org/10.2196/45100
67. Kellmeyer, P.: Neurophilosophical and ethical aspects of virtual reality therapy in neurology and psychiatry. Camb. Q. Healthc. Ethics **27**(4), 610–627 (2018). https://doi.org/10.1017/S0963180118000129
68. Chung, O.S., Robinson, T., Johnson, A.M., et al.: Implementation of therapeutic virtual reality into psychiatric care: clinicians' and service managers' perspectives. Front. Psych. **12**, 791123 (2022). https://doi.org/10.3389/fpsyt.2021.791123
69. Javvaji, C.K., Reddy, H., Vagha, J.D., Taksande, A., Kommareddy, A., Reddy, N.S.: Immersive Innovations: exploring the diverse applications of Virtual Reality (VR) in healthcare. Cureus **16**(3), e56137 (2024). https://doi.org/10.7759/cureus.56137

70. Sombilon, E.V., Rahmanov, S.S., Jachecki, K., Rahmanov, Z., Peisachovich, E.: Ethical considerations when designing and implementing immersive realities in nursing education. Cureus **16**(7), e64333 (2024). https://doi.org/10.7759/cureus.64333
71. Molina Recio, G., García-Hernández, L., Molina Luque, R., Salas-Morera, L.: The role of interdisciplinary research team in the impact of health apps in health and computer science publications: a systematic review. Biomed. Eng. Online **15**(1), 77 (2016). https://doi.org/10.1186/s12938-016-0185-y
72. Duffy, A., Boroumandzad, N., Sherman, A.L., Christie, G., Riadi, I., Moreno, S.: Examining challenges to co-design digital health interventions with end users: systematic review. J. Med. Internet Res. **27**, e50178 (2025). https://doi.org/10.2196/50178
73. Olaronke, I., Soriyan, H., Gambo, I., Olaleke, J.: Interoperability in healthcare: benefits, challenges and resolutions. Int. J. Innov. Appl. Stud. **3**, 2028–9324 (2013)

Pulse of Learning: Complexity, Guidance, and Performance in VR-Based Serious Gaming for Medical Training

Dilan Cabuk-Colak[1]([⊠]) [iD], Mehmet Emin Aksoy[2,3] [iD], Dilek Kitapcioglu[3,4] [iD], Tuba Usseli[5] [iD], Arun Ekin Ozkan[6] [iD], Hayrettin Can Sudor[2] [iD], and Serhat Ilgaz Yoner[2,6] [iD]

[1] Department of Psychology, Faculty of Humanities and Social Sciences, Acibadem Mehmet Ali Aydinlar University, Istanbul, Turkey
dilan.colak@acibadem.edu.tr
[2] Department of Biomedical Device Technology, Acibadem Mehmet Ali Aydinlar University, Istanbul, Turkey
[3] CASE (Center of Advanced Simulation and Education), Acibadem Mehmet Ali Aydinlar University, Istanbul, Turkey
[4] Department of Medical Education, School of Medicine, Acibadem Mehmet Ali Aydinlar University, Istanbul, Turkey
[5] Program of Anesthesia, Vocational School of Health Services, Acibadem Mehmet Ali Aydinlar University, Istanbul, Turkey
[6] Institute of Biomedical Engineering, Bogazici University, Istanbul, Turkey

Abstract. Recent advances in virtual reality (VR) technology have opened new avenues for immersive, simulation-based training in medical education, offering learners realistic environments to practice critical procedures without risking patient safety. As VR becomes more prevalent in medical education, questions remain about how different instructional strategies and simulation designs affect learning outcomes. This study investigated the effects of simulation complexity—basic life support (BLS) versus advanced cardiac life support (ACLS)—and guidance modality—machine-guided (MG) versus instructor-guided (IG)—on performance in VR-based medical training. A total of 109 participants from Acıbadem Mehmet Ali Aydınlar University were assigned to one of four training conditions (BLS-MG, BLS-IG, ACLS-MG, or ACLS-IG). Following standardized VR training, participants' performance was assessed. The results of a 2x2 ANOVA revealed significant main effects for both simulation complexity and guidance type. Participants trained in the BLS condition outperformed those in ACLS, and those trained by an instructor scored higher than those trained via machine guidance. No significant interaction was found between the two factors, suggesting the benefits of instructor guidance hold across both simple and complex simulations. Greater performance variability in the BLS-MG group also indicated a stabilizing role of human instructors in foundational tasks. These findings underscore the importance of aligning guidance modality with task demands.

Keywords: Virtual Reality · Medical Training · Learning Outcomes

J. Y. C. Chen et al. (Eds.): HCII 2025, LNCS 16338, pp. 276–284, 2026.
https://doi.org/10.1007/978-3-032-12808-9_17

1 Introduction

Medical education has changed dramatically over the past few decades with rapid advances in technology, reshaping how healthcare professionals acquire and develop essential skills. Traditional methods—such as lectures, textbook learning, and training on physical mannequins— have long served as the foundation for medical education [1, 2]. While these approaches still hold value, they often fall short to fully replicate the fast-paced and high-pressure nature of clinical practice [3].

Given these limitations, simulation-based training has become increasingly important for teaching high-stakes interventions such as basic life support (BLS) and advanced cardiac life support (ACLS), where performance under pressure can directly impact patient outcomes [4, 5]. Mastering these high stakes interventions require accuracy, rapid decision-making, and the ability to adapt—skills that are difficult to cultivate through traditional instruction alone. Simulations offer a safe, controlled environment where learners can practice repeatedly, receive immediate feedback, and refine their techniques without any risk to patients [6, 7]. This vital role simulations play in developing clinical expertise highlights the importance of adopting innovative training strategies that can meet the demanding nature of modern medical care.

Virtual reality (VR) takes simulation training a step further by creating immersive, interactive environments that closely mimic clinical settings [8]. Unlike traditional simulations, VR allows for highly realistic practice—whether that's performing chest compressions during BLS or navigating the complex decision-making procedures required in ACLS scenarios [4, 5, 9]. Its ability to adjust simulation complexity—from foundational tasks in BLS to intricate decision-making in ACLS—makes VR a vital tool for learners at different expertise levels. By integrating advanced graphics, haptic feedback, and dynamic algorithms, VR not only enhances skill acquisition but also increases learner engagement and retention, positioning it as a transformative force in medical education [10].

Not all VR simulations are created equal, however. VR simulations used in medical training vary considerably in their design, particularly in terms of the cognitive and procedural demands they place on learners. Simulations for BLS, for example, emphasize fundamental skills such as chest compressions and airway management [11, 12]. In contrast, ACLS simulations involve more complex clinical scenarios. Trainees must interpret cardiac rhythms, decide on appropriate defibrillation protocols, and administer medications—often under significant time pressure [4, 9]. These higher-order tasks of the ACLS simulations demand rapid decision-making and the coordination of multiple skills simultaneously. Such differences in complexity likely influence the effectiveness of skill acquisition. For instance, while simpler tasks like BLS training may facilitate quicker mastery, more complex simulations like ACLS may require more time to master. Understanding how simulation complexity impacts performance, therefore, is crucial for optimizing VR training across different stages of medical education.

Equally important is the method of guidance embedded within VR simulations. Some platforms, for instance, may incorporate machine-guidance (MG), where instruction is standardized and delivered by software. Others may utilize instructor-guidance (IG), where experienced educators offer real-time teaching. Machine-led instruction offers consistency, precision, and scalability [9], which may enhance procedural learning by minimizing instructional variability. However, human instructors bring adaptive communication, emotional attunement, and the ability to respond empathetically to learners' needs [13], qualities that become especially valuable in high-stakes or stressful learning environments. This emotional scaffolding may help learners regulate stress and remain cognitively flexible, which is critical for retaining information and applying knowledge under pressure [14]. As VR-based education continues to expand, understanding how different instructor types influence cognitive and emotional engagement is essential for optimizing both performance and psychological readiness in complex learning scenarios. Prior research by Kitapcioglu, Aksoy [9] has shown that instructor guidance and machine guidance during VR-based ACLS training yields comparable learning outcomes. However, it remains unclear whether these benefits extend to simpler simulations like BLS, or how the effectiveness of guidance interacts with the overall complexity of the simulation.

Building on Kitapcioglu, Aksoy [9], the present study aims to address this gap by examining how simulation complexity and guidance type jointly influence learning outcomes in VR-based medical training by including an additional cohort trained on a BLS module either with a machine or human instructor. By combining the current study's data with Kitapcioglu's data, the present study investigated how the type of simulation—basic (BLS) versus advanced (ACLS)—and the mode of guidance—machine versus instructor—affect learners' performance on subsequent assessments.

2 Methods

2.1 Participants

This study included a total of 109 participants from the Vocational School for Anesthesiology at Acıbadem Mehmet Ali Aydınlar University in Istanbul, Turkey. All participants were second-year anesthesiology students, with foundational theoretical knowledge of BLS and ACLS protocols but no prior exposure to VR-based training. Inclusion criteria required participants to be actively enrolled in the anesthesiology curriculum, proficient in Turkish (the language of instruction and VR interface), and physically capable of using VR equipment. Exclusion criteria included previous VR-based BLS training experience, significant visual or motor impairments, a prior experience of motion sickness caused by virtual reality (VR), as well as medical conditions like vertigo or the use of medications that can produce vertigo-like effects.

The sample was composed of two distinct cohorts to allow for a meaningful comparison of simulation complexity and guidance modality. The first cohort consisted of 54 participants whose data were obtained from a previous study on VR-based Advanced Cardiac Life Support (ACLS) training [9], with 23 participants in the machine-guided (MG) group and 31 in the instructor-guided (IG) group.

The second cohort, newly recruited for the present study, comprised 55 participants who completed VR-based BLS training. Participants were recruited through announcements, and a total of 66 individuals volunteered. They were initially assigned to either the MG group (n = 32) or the IG group (n = 34). However, due to technical issues—such as file corruption and missing exam score recordings—only 30 participants in the MG group and 25 in the IG group were included in the final analysis. No participants were excluded based on predefined exclusion criteria.

Participants were randomly assigned to guidance groups (MG or IG) using university identification numbers, with allocation based on whether the ID number was odd or even. The integration of the prior ACLS data with the newly collected BLS data allowed for a robust total sample size of 109, enhancing the study's statistical power to detect differences in exam performance across simulation types and guidance conditions.

2.2 VR Simulation Modules

BLS Module. The BLS module was designed to train foundational life support skills, focusing on chest compressions, airway management, and rescue breathing. Developed by the Center of Advanced Simulation and Education (CASE) at Acıbadem Mehmet Ali Aydınlar University, the module utilized a simplified VR interface. The simulation presented a single-patient scenario, requiring participants to perform BLS according to American Heart Association (AHA) guidelines.

ACLS Module. The ACLS module, used in Kitapcioglu, Aksoy [9], was more complex, focusing on advanced resuscitation algorithms for cardiac arrest management. Also developed by CASE, the simulation involved a multi-step scenario requiring participants to follow AHA ACLS algorithms. The interface included dynamic patient monitors displaying vital signs, electrocardiograms, and oxygen saturation, increasing cognitive and decision-making demands.

2.3 Training Groups

Machine-Guided Group (MG Group). In the MG group, participants received automated feedback and prompts from the VR system, guiding them step by step through the simulation. The MG condition was fully automated, with no human intervention, and designed to standardize instructions across participants. The VR system logged performance out of 100 for later analyses.

Instructor-Guided Group (IG Group) In the IG group, participants were guided by an experienced instructor with over 10 years of expertise in medical education. The instructor provided real-time verbal feedback, observing participants' actions through a shared virtual interface. Instructors followed a standardized protocol to ensure consistency both across participants and MG and IG groups. The performance was also logged by the VR system, to ensure objectivity.

2.4 Data Analyses

Data was analyzed using a 2x2 ANOVA to examine the main effects of simulation complexity (BLS vs. ACLS) and guidance modality (MG vs. IG) on exam scores, as well as their interaction. Post-hoc t-tests with Bonferroni correction were planned for significant effects. Effect sizes were reported using partial eta-squared ($\eta^2 p$). All analyses were conducted using JASP (Version 0.19.3), with two tails and a significance threshold of $p < .05$.

2.5 Ethical Considerations

Participants provided written informed consent prior to enrollment. They were informed of their right to withdraw at any time without consequence. Participation was entirely voluntary. The study adhered to the Declaration of Helsinki, and data were anonymized to protect participant privacy. Potential risks, such as VR-induced motion sickness, were mitigated by screening for susceptibility during orientation and limiting session duration. Ethical approval for the data collection with the second cohort was obtained from the Scientific Ethics Committee of Acıbadem Mehmet Ali Aydınlar University (Approval Number: 2024–17/647).

2.6 Procedure

The study consisted of three phases: orientation, training, and assessment.

1. Orientation Phase: All participants underwent a VR orientation session with a separate module to familiarize themselves with the headset, controllers, and virtual environment.
2. Training Phase: Participants completed a training session either with a human instructor (IG group) or a software instructor (MG group). Both MG and IG groups received equivalent training scenario exposure, with the primary difference being the source of guidance. Training sessions were conducted in a dedicated VR lab at CASE, equipped with high-performance workstations and stable internet connectivity for the metaverse environment.
3. Assessment Phase: Right after training, participants completed a VR-based exam tailored to their simulation type. Exams were conducted in the same VR environment as training, using automated scoring algorithms to ensure objectivity. Scores were reported on a 100-point scale, with higher scores indicating better performance.

At the end of the study, all participants were thanked for their participation, and their questions regarding the study procedures or VR training were addressed by the research team.

3 Results

A 2x2 ANOVA showed significant main effects for both simulation type and training condition, with no significant interaction (see Fig. 1.). For simulation type, participants in the BLS training achieved significantly higher exam scores ($M = 85.80$, $SD = 13.56$) compared to ACLS ($M = 61.57$, $SD = 35.02$), $F(1, 105) = 26.62$, $p < .001$, $\eta^2_p = 0.20$. For training condition, the IG group outperformed the MG group, with mean scores of 78.45 ($SD = 29.11$) versus 68.89 ($SD = 28.36$), respectively, $F(1, 105) = 6.42$, $p = .01$, $\eta^2_p = 0.05$.

Importantly, the interaction between simulation type and training condition was not significant, $F(1, 105) = 0.22$, $p = .64$, $\eta^2_p = 0.002$, suggesting that the effect of guidance type on exam performance did not vary significantly between basic and advanced simulations. Notably, the BLS group showed greater variability in scores under

MG (SD = 15.79) compared to IG (SD = 7.19), suggesting that instructor guidance may help standardize performance, especially in simpler simulations.

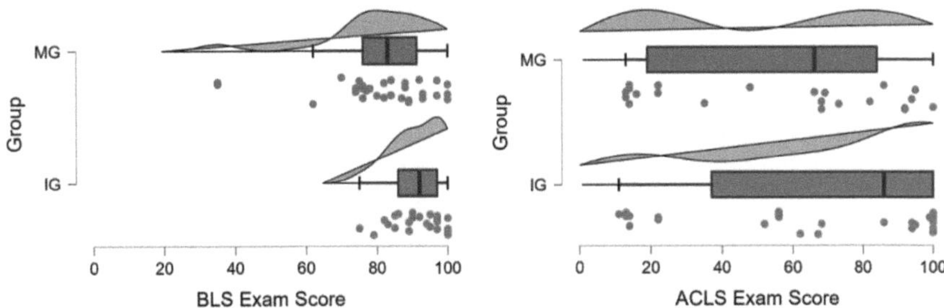

Fig. 1. BLS (on the left) and ACLS (on the right) exam scores of Machine Guidance and Instructor Guidance groups. The figure is created by using Jasp (2022). Dots indicate each participant's exam score. The boxes indicate interquartile ranges; the line in the middle indicates the median.

4   Discussion

The present study explored the effects of simulation complexity (BLS vs. ACLS) and guidance modality (MG vs. IG) on learning outcomes in VR-based medical training. Consistent with expectations, both simulation complexity and guidance modality significantly influenced exam performance, with no significant interaction between these variables. These findings align with and extend prior research, offering critical insights into optimizing VR-based training for medical education. Below, the implications of these results, their alignment with existing literature, and their relevance for designing effective training programs are discussed in further detail.

4.1   Influence of Simulation Complexity on Learning Outcomes

Participants who completed the VR-based BLS training outperformed those who completed the VR-based ACLS training, reflecting the impact of simulation complexity on performance. This aligns with existing literature emphasizing that simpler tasks are generally easier to master across various domains, such as linguistics [15]and mathematics [16], particularly when they require fewer simultaneous cognitive and procedural demands. BLS simulations focus on foundational skills such as chest compressions, airway management, and rescue breathing, which require repetitive practice of standardized procedures ([11]). In contrast, ACLS simulations demand higher-order cognitive skills, including rhythm interpretation, algorithm-based decision-making, and medication administration under time pressure [4, 9]. The stark performance gap suggests that this difference in simulation complexity strongly modulates learning outcomes.

The observed performance gap between BLS and ACLS groups underscores the need for structured scaffolding in advanced simulations. Advanced simulations may exacerbate individual differences in cognitive processing or preparedness, potentially requiring tailored instructional strategies to support novice learners. Therefore, it becomes pivotal to align simulation complexity with learners' strategies to optimize skill acquisition and performance.

4.2 Influence of Guidance Modality on Learning Outcomes

The findings revealed that instructor-guided training led to higher exam scores compared to machine-guided training, supporting prior research on the benefits of human instructors during education [13, 17]. Participants in the IG group may have benefited from subtle, human-driven cues—like timely encouragement or adaptive communication—that supported a clearer understanding of the task and reinforced a sense of personal capability. On the other hand, while offering consistency and scalability, machine-guidance appears to lack the flexibility needed to respond to learners' unique challenges during training. Lacking this type of interpersonal engagement, those in the MG group might have experienced the task as less predictable or more overwhelming. Therefore, the superior performance of the IG group across both BLS and ACLS simulations underscores the value of human instructors in providing nuanced guidance.

4.3 The Joint Role of Simulation Complexity and the Guidance Modality on Learning Outcomes

No significant interaction between simulation complexity and guidance modality was found. This suggests that the benefits of instructor guidance are consistent across both simple (BLS) and complex (ACLS) simulations, rather than being amplified in more cognitively demanding tasks. This finding partially diverges from Kitapcioglu, Aksoy [9], who reported comparable outcomes for MG and IG in ACLS training but did not explore simpler simulations like BLS. The lack of interaction may indicate that instructor guidance provides a universal benefit, regardless of task complexity, by fostering a supportive learning environment that enhances confidence and performance.

A closer examination of score variability, on the other hand, revealed a more nuanced picture. The BLS-MG group exhibited greater variability in exam scores compared to the BLS-IG group, suggesting that human instructors may play a stabilizing role in performance for simpler tasks. In contrast, the ACLS group showed similar variability across guidance types, possibly due to the inherent complexity of ACLS tasks overwhelming the stabilizing effect of instructor guidance. These findings warrant further research examining the stabilizing role of instructor types on learning outcomes.

4.4 Implications for VR-Based Simulations in Medical Education

The findings have several practical implications for designing VR-based medical training programs. First, they underscore the importance of tailoring simulation complexity to learners' expertise levels. Novice learners may benefit from starting with simpler BLS modules to build confidence and competence before progressing to ACLS. Beginning with relatively simpler simulations like BLS under guided instruction may serve as a valuable scaffold before progressing to more advanced modules like ACLS. Second, the superior performance of the IG group highlights the critical role of human instructors in VR training. While MG systems offer scalability and consistency, integrating human instructors—particularly for novice learners or complex tasks—can enhance learning outcomes by providing adaptive, empathetic support. Third, the study suggests that VR training programs should prioritize hybrid models that combine the strengths of MG and

IG. For example, MG could be used for initial skill acquisition in standardized tasks, while IG could be reserved for advanced scenarios requiring nuanced decision-making or emotional regulation. Such an approach could balance scalability with personalized instruction, addressing the limitations of both modalities.

4.5   Limitations and Future Directions

The study has several limitations. The sample consisted exclusively of students from a single institution, which may limit generalizability. Furthermore, only immediate post-training assessment scores were analyzed, leaving questions about long-term knowledge retention and skill transfer unanswered. Future research should consider longitudinal designs that assess the durability of learning over time and explore hybrid guidance models that combine the scalability of machine instruction with the adaptiveness of human feedback. Additionally, physiological and affective metrics (e.g., cognitive load, stress, engagement) could provide richer insights into why instructor guidance proves more effective, especially in high-pressure training contexts.

5   Conclusion

In sum, this study demonstrates that both simulation complexity and guidance modality are key determinants of learning outcomes in VR-based medical training. Instructor guidance enhances performance across simulation types, while simpler tasks are more readily mastered. These findings support the integration of instructor-led VR modules in foundational training and encourage the cautious use of machine guidance in more advanced scenarios. By strategically aligning guidance with simulation complexity, educators can better leverage VR technologies to cultivate competent, confident healthcare professionals.

Acknowledgments. The authors gratefully acknowledge the biomedical support team at the Center of Advanced Simulation and Education, Acibadem Mehmet Ali Aydinlar University, for their essential contributions to this study.

Disclosure of Interests.. The authors have no competing interests.

References

1. van der Vlugt, T.M., Harter, P.M.: Teaching procedural skills to medical students: One institution's experience with an emergency procedures course. Ann. Emerg. Med. **40**(1), 41–49 (2002)
2. Van Stralen, D.W., et al.: Retrograde intubation training using a mannequin. Am. J. Emerg. Med. **13**(1), 50–52 (1995)
3. Allen, M., et al.: The educational role of autonomy in medical training: a scoping review. J. Surg. Res. **240**, 1–16 (2019)
4. Kitapcioglu, D. et al.: Enhancing immersion in virtual reality-based advanced life support training: randomized controlled trial. JMIR Serious Games **13**, e68272 (2025)

5. Aksoy, M.E. et al.: Comparing the outcomes of virtual reality-based serious gaming and lecture-based training for advanced life support training: randomized controlled trial. JMIR Serious Games **11**, e46964 (2023)

6. Grant, D.J., Marriage, S.C.: Training using medical simulation. Arch. Dis. Child. **97**(3), 255 (2012)

7. Weller, J.M. et al.: Simulation in clinical teaching and learning. Med. J. Aust. **196**(9), 594 (2012)

8. Tudor Car, L. et al.: Outcomes, measurement instruments, and their validity evidence in randomized controlled trials on virtual, augmented, and mixed reality in undergraduate medical education: systematic mapping review. JMIR Serious Games **10**(2), e29594 (2022)

9. Kitapcioglu, D. et al.: Comparing learning outcomes of machine-guided virtual reality-based training with educator-guided training in a metaverse environment: randomized controlled trial. JMIR Serious Games **12**, e58654 (2024)

10. Sattar, M. et al.: Motivating medical students using virtual reality based education. Int. J. Emerg. Technol. Learn. (iJET) **15**(2), 160–174 (2020)

11. Aksoy, E. et al.: Performance monitoring via functional near infrared spectroscopy for virtual reality based basic life support training. Front. Neurosci. **13** (2019)

12. Aksoy, M.E.: Comparing basic life support serious gaming scores with hands-on training platform performance scores: pilot simulation study for basic life support training. JMIR Serious Games **8**(4), e24166 (2020)

13. Wang, J., Antonenko, P.D.: Instructor presence in instructional video: Effects on visual attention, recall, and perceived learning. Comput. Hum. Behav. **71**, 79–89 (2017)

14. Giacomino, K., Caliesch, R., Sattelmayer, K.M.: The effectiveness of the Peyton's 4-step teaching approach on skill acquisition of procedures in health professions education: a systematic review and meta-analysis with integrated meta-regression. PeerJ. **8** (2020)

15. Robinson, P.: Task complexity, task difficulty, and task production: exploring interactions in a componential framework. Appl. Linguis. **22**(1), 27–57 (2001)

16. Pavlov, A., Duhon, G., Dawes, J.: Examining the impact of task difficulty on student engagement and learning rates. J. Behav. Educ. **32**(3), 527–542 (2023)

17. Spence, P.R. et al.: Examining perceptions and outcomes of AI versus human course assistant discussions in the online classroom. Commun. Educ. **73**(2), 121–142 (2024)

Ishara: Virtual Sign Language Chatbot Proposal for an Interactive Learning Setting

Hoda Elsayed[1,2]([✉]), Danah Alharthi[1], Norah Aleisa[1], Haifa Alrabiah[1], and Nagham Naseeb[1]

[1] Software Engineering Department, Alfaisal University, Riyadh, Saudi Arabia
Helsayed1993@gmail.com
[2] Game Innovation Center, Alfaisal University, Riyadh, Saudi Arabia

Abstract. Virtual Reality (VR) technologies have transformed educational tools, particularly for communities requiring specialized learning solutions. Hearing-impaired individuals face significant challenges that impact their academic and social experiences. This project proposes the development of Ishara, a VR-based sign language chatbot designed to improve communication between deaf and hearing individuals, especially in educational settings, using Artificial Intelligence (AI). Integrating sign language into text translation and text-to-sign language conversion is crucial for fostering inclusion and equality in institutions such as schools, universities, and community centers. Ishara enables deaf students to conveniently share ideas with instructors, enhancing their academic performance and creating a more inclusive learning environment. It also assists teachers in understanding and addressing the needs of deaf students, reducing communication barriers. By leveraging machine learning and VR, Ishara provides an intuitive interface for seamless communication, bridging the accessibility gap. Its immersive VR environment enhances engagement, while AI algorithms adapt to users' needs, ensuring personalized and effective interactions. The short-term goal is to implement the technology using an Arabic Sign Language dataset in academic settings, while the long-term goal is to expand its application across various sectors, improving interactions between people with special needs and the broader community. This study explores the effectiveness of an AI-driven chatbot integrated with VR to eliminate communication barriers and enhance the learning experience for hearing-impaired students, ultimately contributing to a more inclusive society.

Keywords: Virtual Reality · 3D Unity · Machine Learning · Natural Processing Language · Deep Learning · Virtual Assistants · Sign Language Recognition (SLR) · Gesture Recognition · Neural Networks · Accessibility Solutions

1 Introduction

According to the General Authority for Statistics in KSA, 1,810,358 (or 7.1%) of Saudi residents suffer from disabilities, while the World Health Organization estimates that 360 million people worldwide suffer from disabilities [1]. To be more succinct, 70 million people globally use sign language, with about 1% of the world's population relying on it for primary communication. [2] The limited number of individuals proficient in sign language presents challenges that can hinder a hearing-impaired student's comprehension, as effective communication with deaf students requires elements such as body gestures, facial expressions, and hand signals. Teachers and hearing students who do not understand sign language may not fully grasp the conversation or effectively spread knowledge to deaf students. The deaf community often faces significant barriers when accessing digital services, primarily due to a lack of accessible content, such as captions and sign language interpretation. This exclusion is exacerbated in public spaces where the absence of sign language integration hinders effective communication, isolating deaf individuals from crucial information and services.

Virtual reality (VR) is a helpful tool that can be used as a treatment for a wide variety of people and even to enhance the different skills of normal individuals. For hearing individuals VR can help to create interactive environments that can benefit learners of new languages. For example, VR can be implemented to enable the person to hear and communicate with a native speaker, which will enhance his/her fluency in the language. However, VR can also be helpful for the deaf and hard-of-hearing communities. VR can enhance their communication accessibility by supporting sign-language interaction, which can be implemented using hand-tracking and additional AI-driven sign interpreters. Finally, VR can be used to help individuals with attention deficit hyperactivity disorder or autism by enabling them to go through environments that can be used to try different social and cognitive skills.

The VR oculus sign language chatbot provides an innovative tool to teach sign language, enhancing accessibility and spread awareness among both deaf and hearing users. In this way, VR allows learners to view signs which enhances understanding and will help promote familiarity with sign language [3]. We incorporated VR to create a unique interactive experience that traditional learning methods cannot offer, creating more effective and enjoyable learning. Utilizing Oculus VR can help bridge communication gaps with its impressive capabilities, allowing real-time interactive experiences. This creates a unique opportunity for deaf and hearing individuals to communicate in a virtual setting and adds more natural and effective learning that can significantly enhance communication between deaf and hearing individuals [4].

There have been tremendous advancements in the field of artificial intelligence and image processing, which has been transforming rapidly in recent years. This includes advanced image processing techniques that play a crucial role in interpreting sign language gestures within an Oculus VR. Convolutional Neural Networks (CNNs) are specialized neural networks designed for processing grid-like data; because of their ability to identify hand shapes and movements, they are widely used in gesture recognition. Moreover, edge detection and thresholding are fundamental techniques that detect sharp pixel contrasts to help isolate hand shapes from the background, which is essential for gesture recognition [5]. Additionally, feature extraction techniques, such as the Histogram of Gradients (HOG), are utilized to identify key characteristics in hand shapes, thereby providing accurate classification of each gesture [6]. These image processing techniques enable real-time gesture recognition, creating an interactive learning environment for the deaf community through Oculus VR technology.

2 Literature Review

Technology has rapidly advanced to meet clients' expectations. Currently, there are numerous platforms, startups, businesses, and projects focusing on chatbots that have seen continuous development over time, resulting in numerous versions. Fortune Business Insights (2021) predicts that the chatbot market will grow from \$400 million in 2019 to \$2 billion by 2027 [7].

Although previous studies have made valuable contributions in this regard, many were limited. We believe the proposed solution of a virtual sign language chatbot will improve the experience and challenges of communication and conversations between hearing individuals and hearing-impaired individuals and overcome these limitations. In this section, we will review the previous solutions and studies that have inspired the proposed approach.

One previous study in this area is by Pardasani et al. (2018), where they've developed a sign language chatbot by "creating a database of hand gestures using OpenCV," capturing "1200 grayscale images" of the American Sign Language alphabet, shown in Figs. 1 and 2. They trained a Convolutional Neural Network to recognize the gestures and integrated it with a chatbot using Artificial Intelligence Markup Language (AIML) to generate text and audio responses based on the input. While their study focused on "recognizing individual sign language gestures and translating them into English alphabets," the proposed approach expands on this by aiming to create more effective communication, facilitating real-time, natural conversations between hearing people and the hearing-impaired community in Saudi Sign Language [8].

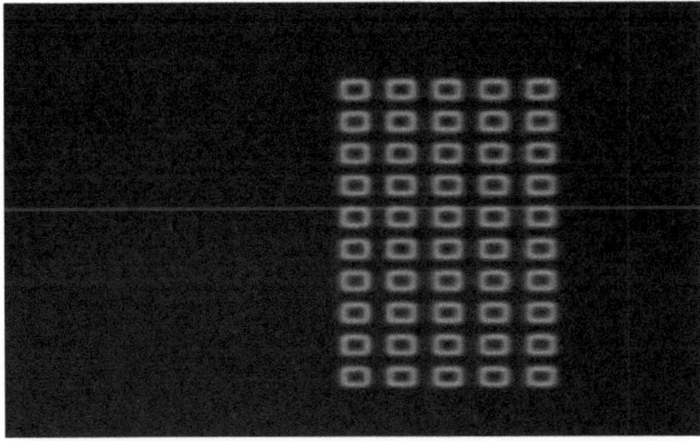

Fig. 1. The fields with green mark scan your hand and convert it into histogram data.

In 2024, Wyawahare, Adbale, and Jorvekar conducted a recent study. The research was about ListenBot, an augmented reality-based speech-to-sign language conversion application. This application uses CNN and RNN to accurately translate spoken language into expressive sign language animations [9].

Another notable recent research by Alsulaiman et al. (2024) focused on building the Saudi Sign Language (SSL) dataset. This dataset outlines the foundation for creating AI-powered tools customized to the specific requirements of the deaf community in Saudi

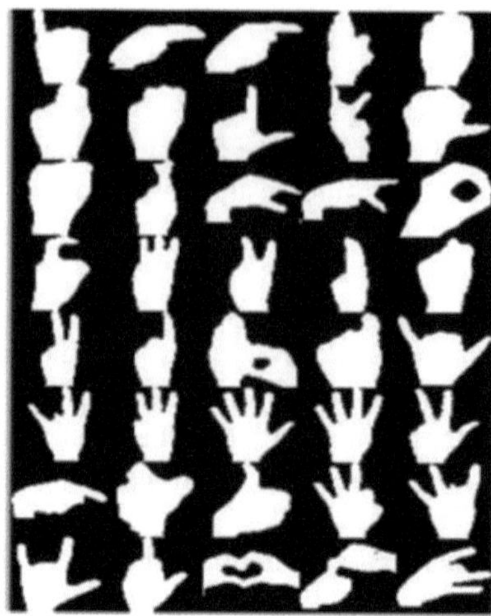

Fig. 2. Some accepted gestures featured in ASL.

Arabia. [1] The dataset development involved capturing 293 signs, covering various categories in the pre-recording phase, shown in Fig. 3.

List of the 293 selected signs.

Alphabets (37 Sign)						
ع	س	ذ	ا	ا	ن	ا
	b	al			e	i
ش	ز	ز	ذ	ع	غ	غ
ث	ز	ف	DH	d	KH	h
ض	ج	ش	ك	ط	ه	ه
ك	ق	ف	GH	ه	DH	ت
وY				ض	ز	ن
				y	w	h
Numbers (11 Sign)						
9	8	7	6	5	4	3
10						
Days (11 Sign)						
الجمعة	الخميس	الأربعاء	الثلاثاء	الاثنين	الأحد	السبت
Friday	Thursday	Wednesday	Tuesday	Monday	Sunday	Saturday
أمس/yesterday						
Family (8 Signs)						
زواج/marriage		ابن	بنت	ابن	اخت	اخ
		family	daughter	son	sister	brother
Pronouns and adverbs (18 Sign)						
ثم	تحت	بعد	بدون	انت	انا	امام
Then	Under	after	without	You	Me	ahead
منذ/since			قبل	قبل	قبل	قبل
			since	before		before

Fig. 3. The dataset development involved capturing 293 signs.

Furthermore, Khan et al.'s research was conducted in 2023. Their approach aims to create a robot-assisted system that utilizes deep learning models (Fig. 4) and Natural Language Processing (NLP) to recognize sign language and generate automated responses. As the authors explain, "This study's primary issue is identifying the best possible ways to detect sign language with the highest possible accuracy. It also focuses on the response a hearing-impaired person gets from a robot by utilizing NLP and then assessing the correctness of that answer." [10]. While this approach shows promising ad-vancements, this project takes a different direction by focusing on a virtual sign language chatbot that is accessible in Saudi Arabia without the need for specialized robotic equipment.

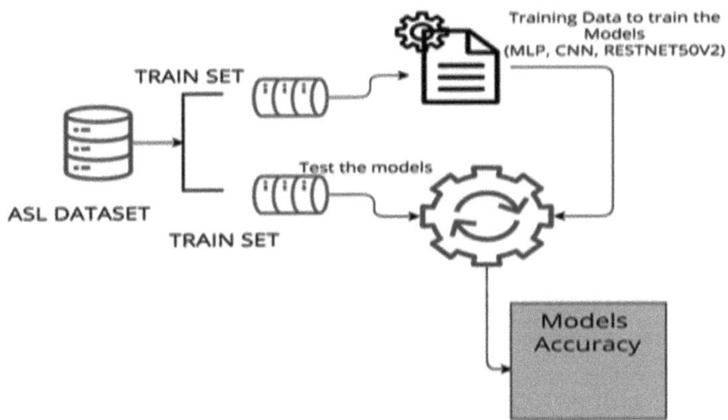

Fig. 4. Robot-assisted system that utilizes deep learning models.

In addition, a study was conducted by Chaix et al. (2020). The research was about "Vik: A Chatbot to Support Patients with Chronic Diseases." Wefight, a start-up committed to empowering patients with chronic diseases, designed the chatbot with the goal of empowering patients and their relatives through personalized text messages. The study used both machine learning and NLP to fully develop the chatbot. As the authors explained, "We build several Vik for each disease. Each Vik has its contents, its own NLP model, and interacts with the patient." [11] This research inspired the team to create a project that is specifically designed for the deaf community.

Finally, Papastratos et al. (2021) conducted research on AI-driven technologies for sign language recognition. Their study on a voice-enabled chatbot for chronic patients, utilizing natural language processing (NLP), showcases the application of AI for specific needs. [12] This study pertains to the proposed project to develop AI-driven communication tools for the deaf community.

Recent advancements in Human-Computer Interaction (HCI) have led to the integration of AI-powered digital avatars for real-time sign language interpretation, significantly enhancing accessibility for the Deaf and Hard-of-Hearing (DHH) community. For example, Sorenson Communications has recently acquired OmniBridge and Hand Talk to develop automated sign language translation technologies, enabling seamless bi-directional communication between American Sign Language (ASL) users and English speakers [16]. These systems utilize machine learning models and digital avatars to facilitate interactions, particularly in environments where human interpreters are unavailable. By leveraging gesture recognition and natural language processing (NLP), these AI-driven solutions improve translation accuracy and user experience in various settings, including education, workplaces, and customer service. Additionally, research institutions such as Gallaudet University's Artificial Intelligence, Accessibility, and Sign Language Center are actively working on developing AI-powered tools designed to enhance communication for the DHH community [17]. These initiatives highlight the synergy between AI and HCI, ensuring that these systems are adaptive, user-friendly, and capable of bridging communication gaps, ultimately fostering greater inclusivity in society.

Several existing projects and tools have contributed to sign language recognition and translation; however, Ishara presents a unique combination of features that enhance its effectiveness and relevance, particularly for the Saudi deaf community. For example, Pardasani et al. [8] developed a sign language chatbot using OpenCV to recognize grayscale images of American Sign Language (ASL) alphabets, which were then processed into text and audio responses. While this work demonstrated the potential of combining image recognition with chatbot technology, its focus was limited to the English alphabet and lacked real-time conversational capabilities in a specific cultural or linguistic context such as Saudi Sign Language (SSL). In contrast, Ishara expands upon this by supporting a full Saudi Sign Language dataset and enabling dynamic, real-time conversations through gesture-to-text and text-to-gesture translation within a virtual reality (VR) environment, providing a more immersive and contextually relevant solution for users in Saudi Arabia.

Similarly, ListenBot (2024) [9] introduced an augmented reality-based speech-to-sign language application, where spoken language was converted into animated sign gestures using CNN and RNN models. However, ListenBot focuses primarily on one-way translation (speech to sign), with limited emphasis on interactive, two-way communication between deaf and hearing users. Ishara addresses this gap by creating a bidirectional chatbot where deaf users can sign, and hearing users can text, fostering real-time interaction in both directions.

Another notable solution, the robot-assisted system by Khan et al. (2023), leverages deep learning and NLP to recognize sign language and generate automated responses [10]. While technically advanced, its reliance on specialized robotic hardware limits its accessibility and practicality for everyday users. In contrast, Ishara's VR-based approach makes it accessible on commercially available Oculus headsets, enabling flexible deployment in classrooms, community centers, and homes without requiring expensive or specialized hardware.

Lastly, existing text-based chatbots, such as Vik by Chaix et al. [11], demonstrated the effectiveness of AI-driven assistants for chronic patients through personalized text conversations. However, these systems do not support sign language input/output, which is essential for effective communication with the deaf community. Ishara bridges this gap by offering gesture-based interaction in VR, enhancing both usability and engagement for deaf users.

Overall, Ishara's unique contributions lie in its combination of Saudi Sign Language support, real-time bidirectional communication, immersive VR environment, and adaptability to individual signing styles, making it the first culturally and linguistically tailored VR chatbot of its kind for the Saudi deaf community.

3 Methodology

The project will adhere to the requirements gathering, design, implementation, and testing phases of the conventional software development life cycle (SDLC) methodology. In the requirements phase, information was gathered, and requirements were elicited using a survey in addition to the Saudi sign language dataset, virtual reality capabilities, and the necessary equipment.

During the design phase, technical and graphic designs for the virtual sign language chatbot and system architecture that connects all software and hardware components optimally to reduce errors and failures were produced. Furthermore, a detailed plan or high-level architectural design for the chat-bot and VR system, that demonstrates how the APIs will interact with each other and the user interface, was created. The system employs layered architecture, which streamlines development by segmenting the system into distinct layers, each handling a specific function. The system design is split into five layers, which are the presentation layer, application layer, data layer, external communication layer, and hardware layer, as shown in Fig. 5.

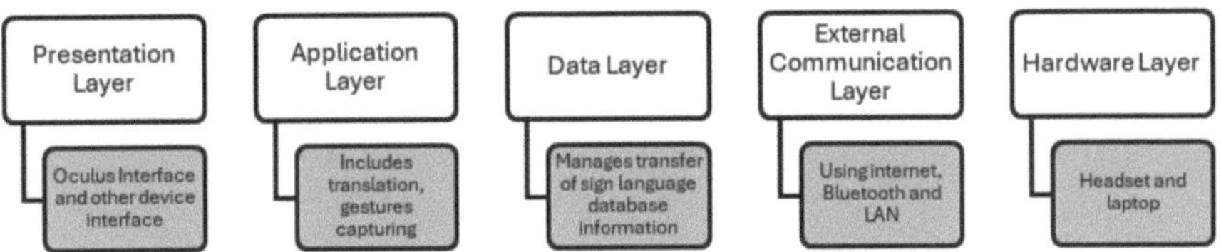

Fig. 5. Ishara's System Architecture.

In developing the AI-driven chatbot, integrated into a VR environment for individuals with hearing impairments, risk management was a critical component to ensure the system's reliability, security, and user accessibility. Thus, identifying potential risk factors was essential in the design phase. It outlines the key risks identified during the project and the corresponding mitigation strategies employed. This ensures that the project can address challenges proactively (Table 1).

To ensure uninterrupted chatbot services, the system is designed with redundancy measures, such as backup servers and failover mechanisms, minimizing the risk of downtime. Regular server maintenance schedules are implemented to identify and resolve potential hardware or software issues preemptively.

The system incorporates state-of-the-art encryption technologies, and secure authentication protocols to safeguard data and mitigate unauthorized access. Regular penetration testing is conducted to identify vulnerabilities and maintain compliance with data protection regulations. Moreover, recognizing the accessibility needs of the target audience, the user interface is developed iteratively, incorporating feedback from usability tests conducted with a sample of the deaf community. Human-Centered Design (HCD) principles guide the interface design to ensure it remains accessible for users relying on visual and gestural communication.

Ishara application interacts with external entities including: 1) users (deaf and hard-of-hearing individuals and hearing individuals and administrators)., 2) external devices (APIs, databases, cloud storage) and 3) devices (mobile and VR oculus) as shown in Fig. 6.

The system integrates a user interface (UI) with a VR headset and controllers to capture gestures or sign language from the user as shown in part a. It includes a text display area for showing recognized text, which is visible to both deaf and non-deaf

Table 1. Risk Assessment and mitigation strategies.

RAMS	Risk Assessment and Mitigation Strategies		
	Risk Factor	Identified risk	Mitigation strategies
1	Server Reliability	Server downtime disrupting the chatbot services	Designing high-availability (HA) architecture with failover mechanisms
2	Security issues	Breaches and data leaks	Deploying advanced encryption protocols (e.g., AES-256), secure authentication mechanisms, and conduct regular vulnerability assessments
3	System usability	interface complexity	Implementing human centered design approaches and conducting usability testing while actively acquiring user feedback

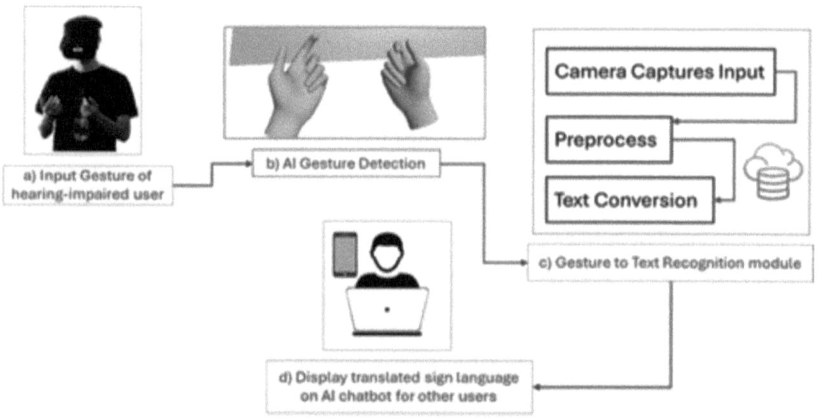

Fig. 6. Key interaction modules in Ishara VR app between users, services and devices.

users, and a chat window for user interaction. The AI Gesture Detection system uses machine learning models to interpret hands gestures as sign language or other gestures as in part B. These recognized gestures are processed by the Text Recognition Engine, which converts them into text format, reflected in part C. The text is displayed in the UI. The system also includes a backend with a database to store both deaf and non-deaf user data and external APIs for translation to render the text on AI chatbot for other users in the chat room, as shown in part D.

The VR sign language, Ishara chatbot, is implemented in accordance with the technical design Using the following: 1) C# and Python for design and machine learning respectively, 2) Unity IDE for development and VR support, 3) JSON database for establishing connection between front end and backend python processing of the Saudi Sign Language dataset.

The system undergoes extensive V-Model approach for testing to adhere to the set specifications and work well in real time use. To ensure the proper functionality of all components, the Unity test runner will be utilized for unit testing within the Unity environment, allowing for the testing of individual components such as NLP models and sign language recognition. A set of test cases will be developed to assess the expected functionalities of the project and identify potential failure scenarios. These tests will be executed regularly to ensure that the new code does not disrupt existing functionality. The testing process will be carried out in several phases, starting with unit testing, where individual components, like sign language recognition, are tested in isolation. Following this, integration testing will be conducted to ensure smooth interaction between all system modules.

Since the project involves participants testing the application to be impactful in the deaf and hearing communities, ethical considerations were addressed to ensure participant rights, data privacy, and responsible handling of information collected during the development and testing of the Ishara chatbot. All participants were informed of the purpose of the project, how their data would be used to improve the system, and their right to withdraw at any time without consequences. Informed consent was obtained prior to participation, ensuring participants understood all aspects of the study. To protect participant privacy, all collected data, including gesture recordings and user feedback, was anonymized and securely stored, accessible only to authorized research team members. Usability testing and feedback sessions followed human-centered design principles, with direct involvement from deaf participants to ensure the system meets their needs. While the project documents do not explicitly mention collaboration with an Institutional Review Board (IRB), the team ensured all ethical practices related to working with human subjects were followed, reflecting a strong commitment to responsible research and the protection of participants' rights.

4   Results and Discussion

This section summarizes insights from a survey of 50 participants, 20.5% males and the rest are females, on the effectiveness and potential of an AI virtual sign language chatbot. Participants shared their thoughts on how this chatbot can help to bridge the gaps in communication, features they would like to see added, and the challenges that might arise. Participants found Ishara chatbot very promising as it can contribute effectively to better communication between deaf and hearing individuals.

The majority confirmed that it would create a comfort zone to hold conversations 6.7% only, while 40% are unfamiliar with and cannot understand the sign language gestures. Respondents identified key factors to encourage the use of this chatbot. Ensuring high accuracy in sign language translation was a priority for 60.5%, while 42.1% wanted additional language support. Additionally, 39.5% expressed the need for a more engaging user experience. The responses show that while participants acknowledge the chatbot's potential, they'd like to see these improvements that would increase its usability and enjoyment. Real-time translation of signs to text was chosen by 40.7% of participants as the most valuable feature. Other features like the ability to connect with hearing individuals for personal usage (40.5%) and educational resources on sign language (56.8%) were also chosen by some of the respondents (Fig. 7).

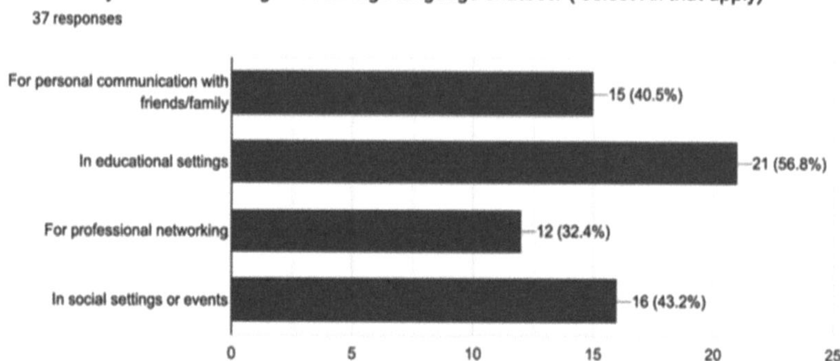

Fig. 7. A. Key Challenges in Developing Virtual Sign Language Chatbots.

The application was designed to bridge communication gaps by converting gestures into understandable text for both the user and the system. Following the demonstration of the application's features, we will share the results from User Acceptance Testing (UAT), which were gathered from a survey conducted with participants. The UAT feedback highlights the users' experiences with the application, providing insights into its effectiveness, efficiency, and overall usability. This section will offer an in-depth analysis of how the AI-driven translation and chatbot features were received by the users, revealing areas of strength and potential improvement based on real-world interaction.

As shown in Fig. 8 in scene A, the user will register within the system, saving their data to the database. Once registered, users can log in, join a chatroom, engage in conversations, and access chat history. Then in scene B, users who are already registered can log in to their account by entering their username and password in the required fields. An alert will be displayed if an incorrect username or password has been entered, and the user will have the option to try again or select "Forgot password?" to recover their password. Finally, in scene C, users can initiate a conversation and view a tutorial for a smooth onboarding experience. Following the tutorial will make users understand how the platform works, learn how to navigate themselves in the virtual environment, and feel comfortable in the interface.

As shown in Fig. 9 in scene A, the user can enable new users to view the translated chat, it also includes functionality to capture the user's hand movements, and users have the option to end the conversation at any point. Scene B shows the view of hands being captured.

Recognizing different sign languages and their variations presents several challenges, particularly due to the diversity in gestures, regional dialects, and contextual differences across languages like American Sign Language (ASL) and Saudi Sign Language (SSL). To ensure accuracy in translation, the Ishara chatbot employs deep learning algorithms,

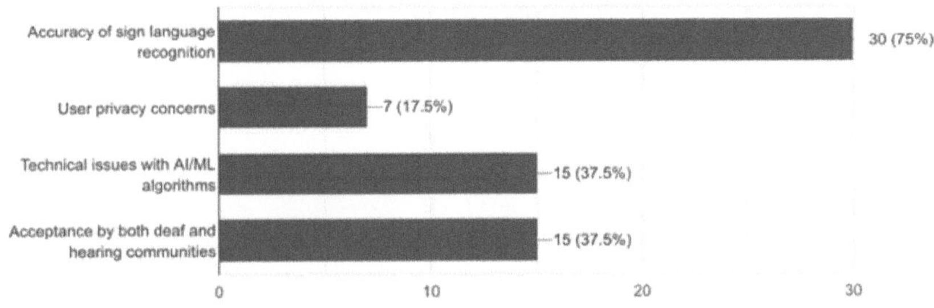

B. Chatbot Challenges Statistics

Fig. 8. Ishara chatbot Survey Statistics.

such as Convolutional Neural Networks (CNNs) for gesture recognition thereby refining real-time translation capabilities. The AI model continuously evaluates the accuracy of each recognized sign before processing it into the chat system. As shown in Fig. 10, if the translation accuracy is below 60%, the system discards the sign and does not process it in the chat. This threshold ensures reliable communication by preventing inaccurate or misleading translations. However, ensuring precision in sign language recognition remains a challenge due to potential errors in gesture interpretation, variations in user signing styles, and environmental factors such as lighting and occlusion. By incorporating a continuously learning AI model, user feedback, and an extensive SSL dataset, the system aims to enhance translation reliability while bridging communication gaps between the deaf and hearing communities.Ishara 's VR interactive chatroom environment was created using Unity, this enhances the user experience. The "Capture Hands" feature Enables real-time scanning and recognition of hand gestures. This allows the system to track the hand gestures instantly inside the VR oculus, ensuring smooth and natural interactions between users. Figure 11 shows the chatroom scene that opens the camera to capture hands.

In addition, a YOLO-based model (YOLO11) was trained to accurately recognize Saudi Sign Language gestures. The dataset was collected using a webcam with OpenCV and labeled with LabelImg to ensure accurate detection. After training on this data, the model achieved over 85% accuracy, with consistent improvements across metrics such as precision, recall, and loss values. These results confirm that the system's reliability in sign gesture interpretation. The performance of detected words is seen in Fig. 12.

Figure 13 illustrates the training and validation performance of the YOLOv11 model used for Saudi Sign Language gesture recognition. The top row displays training metrics, where the box loss, classification loss, exhibits a consistent downward trend, indicating effective learning and improved localization, classification, and object detection over time. Precision rapidly increases and stabilizes above 85%, reflecting a low false positive rate. The bottom row presents the corresponding validation metrics, with all loss

A. Ishara Registration Scene

B. Sign in Scene

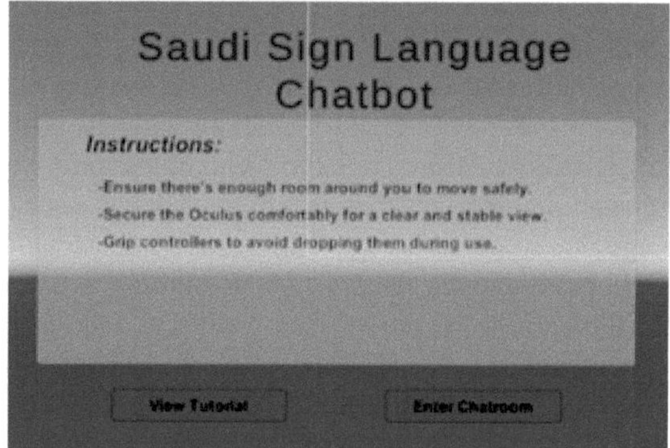

C. Ishara Hub Scene

Fig. 9. Ishara chatbot Oculus Scenes.

A. Chat Scene in Oculus

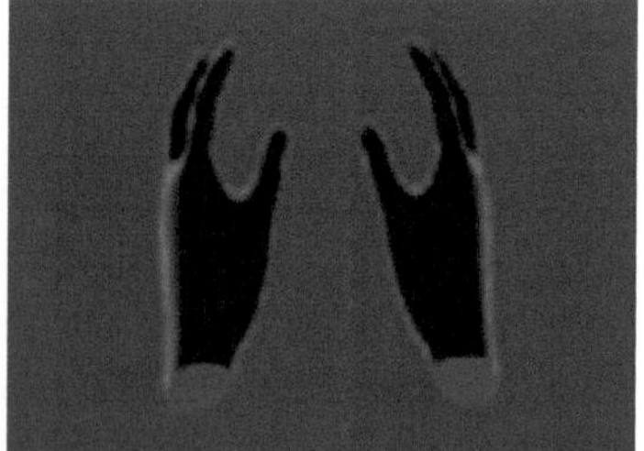

B. Hands view in Oculus

Fig. 10. Ishara chatbot Oculus Chatroom and gestures recognition Scenes.

A. Hello Word Recognition   B. Thank you Word Recognition

Fig. 11. Ishara AI Model Words Recognition and Accuracy percentage.

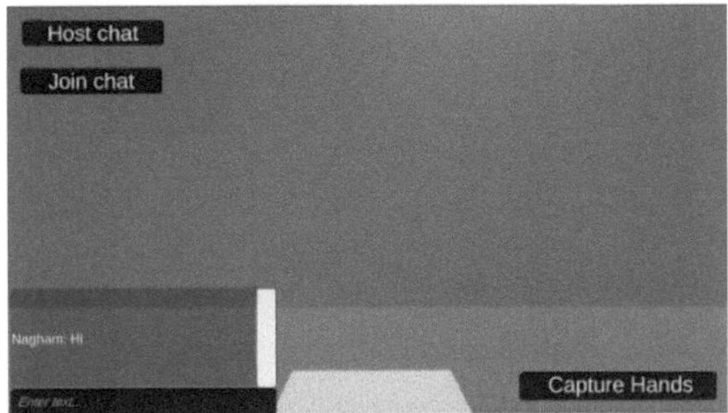

Fig. 12. Ishara Capture Hands in chatroom.

components, classification, showing steady decreases, suggesting that the model generalizes well to unseen data. Recall remains high throughout training, exceeding 80%, which implies strong true positive detection capability. Additionally, the model achieves impressive performance on the evaluation metrics, with mAP50 reaching nearly 100% and mAP50–95 approaching 85%, confirming the model's robustness and reliability in accurately interpreting sign language gestures (Fig. 14).

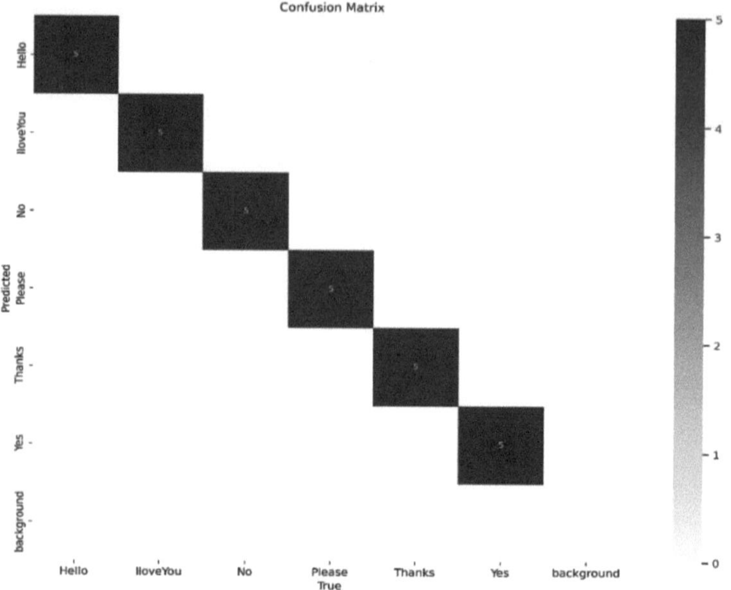

Fig. 13. Performance evaluation using confusion matrix of the sign detection model.

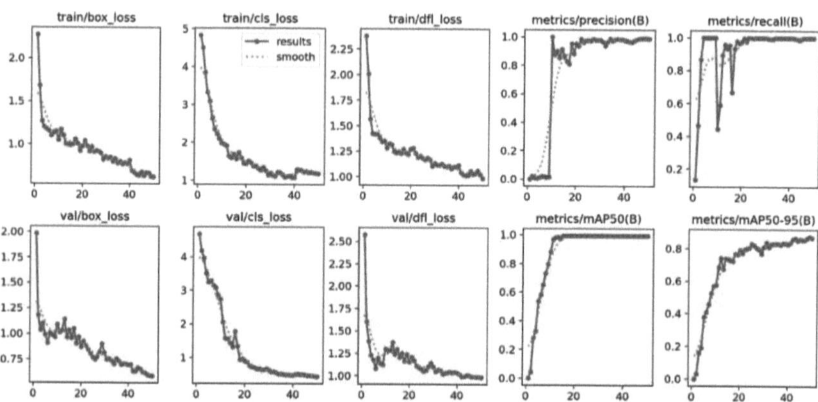

Fig. 14. YOLO11 model training using OpenCV and LabelImg.

5 Conclusion

In conclusion, the results show the effectiveness of the AI virtual sign language chatbot. Most of the survey respondents find it a useful tool for real-time translation and interactive learning. Suggestions include adding video call integration to draw attention to areas for improvements. This chatbot can significantly improve accessibility and inclusivity by providing innovative tools for the hearing-impaired community and opening the door for future advancements in sign language communication and education.

While Ishara is initially designed to support Saudi Sign Language (SSL), its scalable architecture allows for expansion beyond Saudi Arabia. By integrating additional sign language datasets, such as American Sign Language (ASL), British Sign Language (BSL), and International Sign (IS), Ishara can serve a global audience of Deaf and Hard-of-Hearing (DHH) users. The modular AI model can be retrained on region-specific sign languages, ensuring high accuracy in translation across different linguistic and cultural contexts. Furthermore, collaborations with international accessibility organizations and educational institutions can help integrate Ishara into global classrooms, workplaces, and healthcare settings, enhancing communication for diverse sign language users. By leveraging cloud-based AI processing and cross-platform compatibility, Ishara has the potential to become a universal sign language translation tool, fostering inclusivity worldwide.

Acknowledgments. This project was supported by Alfaisal University's Game Innovation Center, providing the tools, equipment and resources, used in AlfaVR development and College of Engineering and Advanced computing's Software Engineering Department.

Disclosure of Interests.. All authors have reviewed and approved the final version of this manuscript and agree to be accountable for its contents. The authors declare no competing financial or non-financial interests that could influence the work presented. The authors have no competing interests to declare that are relevant to the content of this article.

References

1. Alsubaie, K.H., Alqahtani, S.A., Alzahrani, A.I., Alzahrani, M.S., Alghamdi, A.O., Alqahtani, H.A.: Assessment of the impact of social media on the health and well-being of individuals: A cross-sectional study. J. King Saud Univ. Sci. **35**(6), 102035 (2023). https://www.scienc edirect.com/science/article/pii/S1319157823001969

2. Sharma, A.K.: The Rising Use of Sign Language in Modern Times. EarthWeb (2024). https://earthweb.com/blog/sign-language-users/

3. Shaw, A., et al.: JengASL: a gamified approach to sign language learning in vr. J. WSCG **31**(1–2), 33–40 (2023). https://doi.org/10.24132/JWSCG.2023.4

4. Serafin, S., Adjorlu, A., Percy-Smith, L.M.: A review of virtual reality for individuals with hearing impairments. Multimodal Technol. Inter. **7**(4), 1–13 (2023). https://doi.org/10.3390/mti7040036

5. Shivatare, A., Wagh, P., Pisal, M., Khedkar, V.: Hand gesture recognition system for Image Process (IP) Gaming. Int. J. Eng. Res. Technol. **2**(3) (2013). https://doi.org/10.17577/IJERTV 2IS3101

6. Sharma, A., Mittal, A., Singh, S., Awatramani, V.: Hand gesture recognition using image processing and feature extraction techniques. Procedia Comput. Sci. **173**, 181–190 (2020). https://doi.org/10.1016/j.procs.2020.06.022

7. Forecast Report 2021: HAL (2021). https://hal.science/hal-03230287/file/The%20Forecast%20report%202021%20%28May%2019%2008.28%29.pdf

8. Pardasani, A.: Enhancing the ability to communicate by synthesizing american sign language using image recognition in a chatbot for differently abled. In: 2019 International Conference on Reliability, Infocom Technologies and Optimization (ICRITO) (2019). https://doi.org/10.1109/ICRITO.2018.8748590

9. Qureshi, M.A.: Integration of sign language and machine learning for real-time communication. In: 2024 14th International Conference on Cloud Computing, Data Science & Engineering (Confluence), IEEE (2024). https://doi.org/10.1109/confluence60223.2024.10463363

10. Kumar, H.: A framework for real-time communication using sign language. J. VFAST Trans. Comput. Sci. **10**(2), 150–157 (2023). https://vfast.org/journals/index.php/VTCS/article/view/1491/1223

11. Smith, R.J.: Understanding the impact of sign language interpretation in healthcare. Health **12**(4), 567–574 (2020). https://www.scirp.org/pdf/health_2020071716101776.pdf

12. Williams, M.D.: Sign language recognition and translation in modern devices. PMC (2021). https://www.ncbi.nlm.nih.gov/pmc/articles/PMC8434597/

13. Ministry of Health, Saudi Arabia: With initiative. Ministry of Health Saudi Arabia. https://www.moh.gov.sa/en/Ministry/Projects/with-you/Pages/default.aspx. Accessed: 8 Sep 2024

14. Wu, X., Liu, H., Zhao, X., Wang, Y.: Artificial intelligence for sign language translation - a design science research study. ResearchGate (2023). https://www.researchgate.net/publication/370215194_Artificial_Intelligence_for_Sign_Language_Translation_-A_Design_Science_Research_Study

15. Consumer Electronics Show (CES): AI sign language translation service: hand sign talk talk. CES Tech Innovation Awards (2025). https://www.ces.tech/ces-innovation-awards/2025/ai-sign-language-translation-service-hand-sign-talk-talk

16. Sorenson: Sorenson acquires omnibridge and hand talk to develop automated sign language translation capabilities. Sorenson Newsroom (2025). https://sorenson.com/newsroom/enterprise/sorenson-acquires-omnibridge-and-hand-talk-to-develop-automated-sign-language-translation-capabilities/

17. Gallaudet University: Artificial intelligence, sign language, and accessibility center receives NSF EAGER research grant to build a panopticon studio. Gallaudet University Communications (2024). https://gallaudet.edu/university-communications/artificial-intelligence-sign-language-and-accessibility-center-receives-nsf-eager-research-grant-to-build-a-panopticon-studio/

Applications and Benefits of Augmented Reality in Medical Training

Eric Mera[1] , Kevin Castillo[1] , and Jorge Buele[2]( )

[1] Facultad de Ingenierías, Universidad Tecnológica Indoamérica, Ambato 180103, Ecuador
[2] Centro de Investigación en Mecatrónica y Sistemas Interactivos (MIST), Universidad Tecnológica Indoamérica, Ambato 180103, Ecuador
jorgebuele@uti.edu.ec

Abstract. Medical education faces challenges in teaching complex concepts and acquiring clinical skills. In this context, augmented reality has emerged as an innovative tool, enabling interactive visualization of anatomical structures and simulation of clinical procedures. However, its widespread implementation still faces barriers in terms of accessibility and costs, limiting its use in various educational institutions. This study presents a systematic literature review on the impact of augmented reality in medical education, analyzing experimental studies, systematic reviews, and empirical analyses published between 2010 and 2024. Articles from PubMed, Scopus, and IEEE Xplore were evaluated, selecting 11 studies that met the inclusion criteria. The results indicate that this technology significantly enhances knowledge retention (up to 75%), optimizes the understanding of human anatomy, and facilitates the teaching of clinical procedures without posing risks to patients. Applications such as Cranium and the use of Microsoft HoloLens have demonstrated benefits in the three-dimensional visualization of bone structures and surgical planning. Additionally, augmented reality has proven effective in nutritional education and cellular biology learning, expanding its applicability in health sciences. Augmented reality represents a significant advancement in medical training, although accessibility and costs remain challenges to be addressed. The integration of artificial intelligence and the development of open-source platforms are recommended to enhance its impact on global medical education.

Keywords: Augmented Reality · Medical Education · Clinical Simulation · Educational Innovation

1 Introduction

Traditional medical practice has historically relied on a trial-and-error approach, where professionals develop and refine their skills through experience [1–3]. However, with the implementation of advanced technologies such as extended reality (XR), this learning process can be significantly optimized [4–6]. Over the past two decades, XR has gained prominence in the educational field, offering immersive and interactive experiences that enhance knowledge acquisition and make learning more engaging [7, 8].

J. Y. C. Chen et al. (Eds.): HCII 2025, LNCS 16338, pp. 301–312, 2026.
https://doi.org/10.1007/978-3-032-12808-9_19

Among the technologies that comprise XR, augmented reality (AR) has emerged as a powerful tool with a growing impact across various sectors, including entertainment, marketing, advertising, and, most notably, education [9, 10]. AR integrates digital information with the physical environment in real time through devices such as tablets, smartphones, and specialized glasses, enabling enriched interaction with content [11].

In the medical field, AR is not only revolutionizing clinical practice but has also proven to be an essential tool in various specialties, such as surgery, rehabilitation, and diagnostic imaging [12–14]. Its application in the study of cardiovascular diseases, for instance, allows computer-generated images to be overlaid onto real anatomical structures, facilitating the understanding of complex medical conditions and improving procedural accuracy. These innovations have expanded AR's potential across multiple disciplines, including education and healthcare training [15, 16].

In this context, AR offers numerous benefits for medical education by providing students with a more interactive, immersive, and effective learning experience. Its ability to integrate detailed visual information with real clinical scenarios not only enhances knowledge retention but also better prepares students for professional practice. Therefore, its implementation in medical education represents a unique opportunity to optimize training and reduce the learning curve for future healthcare professionals.

Despite advancements in AR adoption within medical education, its widespread implementation still requires further exploration. Studies such as the RAFODIUN project (EDU2014–57446-P) [17] have demonstrated its acceptance in educational settings, yet key aspects regarding its impact and applicability in different contexts remain underexplored. A significant driver of AR development is artificial intelligence (AI), whose integration has enhanced the visualization and interactivity of virtual models through machine learning techniques [18]. However, further research is needed to determine how these technologies can maximize the potential of medical education and what strategies could expand their accessibility on a global scale.

To address these challenges, this article presents a comprehensive review of AR technologies applied in medical education, with a focus on their accessibility and scalability worldwide. Specifically, it aims to identify solutions that facilitate the development of open and adaptable applications for diverse educational contexts, promoting adoption in resource-limited countries. International collaboration in the development of these tools could enhance their impact, foster innovation, and improve medical training across various regions. By addressing these gaps, this review will not only contribute to understanding the current state of AR in medical education but also provide recommendations for large-scale implementation, promoting more inclusive and equitable learning opportunities.

2 Materials and Methods

This study was conducted through a systematic literature review with a qualitative-descriptive approach, aiming to analyze the impact of augmented reality (AR) in medical education. Relevant studies exploring the applicability of AR in health sciences education, its cognitive impact, and its benefits in the acquisition of knowledge and clinical skills were identified, selected, and synthesized.

2.1 Information Sources and Search Strategy

The literature search was conducted in the specialized databases PubMed, Scopus, and IEEE Xplore, considering publications from 2005 to 2024. Search terms were combined using Boolean operators, including:

- ("augmented reality" OR "realidad aumentada") AND ("medical education" OR "educación médica")
- ("AR" AND "clinical learning") OR ("augmented reality" AND "health sciences")
- ("augmented reality" AND "medicine" AND "teaching")

2.2 Inclusion Criteria

Studies were selected based on the following criteria:

- Experimental, descriptive, literature review, or empirical studies related to AR in medical education.
- Application of AR in health sciences learning, including medicine, biology, nutrition, and related fields.
- Assessment of cognitive, didactic, or technological interaction impacts of AR in the teaching-learning process.
- Publications in English or Spanish.
- Studies published in the last 20 years in indexed scientific journals or relevant academic conferences.

2.3 Exclusion Criteria

The following studies were excluded:

- Those not focused on the application of AR in medical education or health sciences.
- AR content without integration of physical elements.
- Studies centered on industrial, commercial, or entertainment applications unrelated to medical teaching.
- Studies without full-text access or lacking methodologically verifiable data.

2.4 Study Selection and Management

Search terms were adapted to each database according to its indexing criteria. Identified articles were stored and managed using Mendeley v2.128.0 (Mendeley Ltd., Elsevier, Netherlands), ensuring the removal of duplicates and facilitating organization.

3 Results

A manual review of titles and abstracts was conducted, applying inclusion and exclusion criteria. The selected studies were then analyzed in depth and classified based on the following:

1. Study type (experimental, descriptive, literature review, etc.).
2. AR technology used (mobile devices, specific applications, HoloLens, etc.).

3. Cognitive impact (benefits in learning, comprehension, and knowledge retention).
4. Key findings on AR implementation and reported limitations.

The information retrieved from each database, categorized according to the different search terms, is presented in Fig. 1.

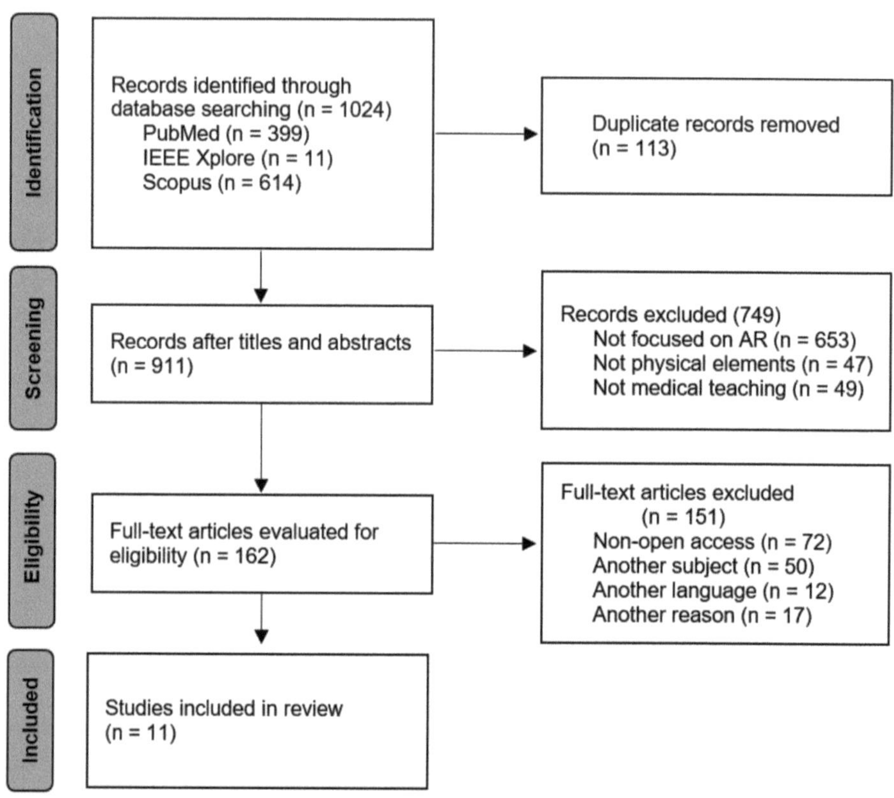

Fig. 1. PRISMA Flow Diagram.

3.1 Characteristics of the Selected Studies

The analyzed studies cover publications from 2010 to 2024 (Table 1), including diverse methodological designs. Most of them correspond to experimental studies (n = 4), followed by literature reviews (n = 3), descriptive studies (n = 1), empirical analyses with experimental evaluation (n = 1), and ex post facto studies (n = 1).

Table 1. Characteristics of the most relevant studies.

Reference	Article type	Technology	Cognitive	Key findings
Duriguez and Palaoag [19]	Experimental	Smartphones, mobile applications	Positive outcomes in nutrition trainees	AR technology enabled participants to make healthier food choices by highlighting relevant nutritional information
Pini et al. [20]	Literature Review	AR Orion	Development of AR potential in medical university studies	AR has the potential to transform the food industry in terms of safety, education, promotion, and consumer experience
Imre and Yikmis [21]	Descriptive	Medical advancements through AR technology	Cognitive and descriptive analysis of AR today	Review of AR applications at Universidad del Salvador
Poobrasert et al. [22]	Experimental	AR mobile application, QR codes	New AR application for studying cell biology	Implementation in schools showed a significant increase in spelling skills among students with learning disabilities
Cabero-Almenara al. [23]	Experimental	Industrialized AR application for medical studies	Analysis of industrialized mobile applications in universities	Study with 50 participants to assess the impact on information analysis
Elnaqlah, et al. [24]	Systematic Literature Review	AR	Potential of AR to enhance student engagement	AR can improve learning in higher education, although knowledge gaps still need to be addressed

(continued)

Table 1. (*continued*)

Reference	Article type	Technology	Cognitive	Key findings
Šulc et al. [25]	Empirical study with experimental evaluation	AR, enhanced workbooks	Improvement in studying neural schemes and medical education	AR applications contribute to understanding neural schemes and accelerate learning
Khan et al. [26]	Systematic review with analytical approach	Microsoft HoloLens	AR applicability in various fields	Immersive technologies have been crucial during the COVID-19 pandemic and have potential in education, training, and drug manufacturing
Cabero-Almenara et al. [27]	Ex post facto	AR learning objects	Assessment of impact on students	Study with 429 students in educational technology subjects, showing a positive impact on teaching strategies
Rodríguez and Montalván. [28]	Experimental	Mobile application "Cranium"	Study of bone structures in medicine	AR application for studying the skull, allowing detailed visualization and digital manipulation of bone models
Fernandez Nieto and Perez Timoteo [29]	Literature Review	AR applications in medicine	Case studies on cancer	AR applied in cancer diagnosis and study, facilitating university education through interactive digital models

3.2 Methodologies Used

The studies applied different methodologies to assess the effectiveness of AR in medical education. Experimental studies (n = 4) analyzed academic performance and improvements in understanding medical concepts in educational settings with and without AR technology.

Systematic reviews (n = 2) evaluated trends in AR implementation in higher education, identifying benefits and limitations in its adoption. One empirical study with experimental evaluation (n = 1) used AR-enhanced workbooks to improve the teaching of neural schemes in medicine.

The evaluation methods used in these studies included measuring the impact on knowledge acquisition (n = 5), assessments of the usability and accessibility of AR technologies (n = 3), and comparative analyses with traditional teaching methods (n = 2).

3.3 Main Findings

Experimental studies indicate that AR significantly contributes to the improvement of understanding complex anatomical structures (n = 3) and to immersive interaction in medical science learning (n = 4). AR mobile applications have been particularly effective in learning cell biology (n = 1) and in teaching bone structures in medicine (n = 1), allowing students to manipulate 3D models and enhance knowledge retention.

Studies also highlight the role of AR in interdisciplinary education, with applications improving nutritional education (n = 1), the teaching of neural schemes (n = 1), and the understanding of pathologies such as cancer through interactive models (n = 1). Research explored various AR applications in the educational field, with a particular focus on medical education. Among the technologies used, studies implemented AR mobile applications (n = 3), immersive AR devices like HoloLens (n = 1), QR codes in educational materials (n = 1), and AR-enhanced workbooks (n = 1).

The cognitive impact assessed focused on improving understanding and retention of medical information (n = 5), optimizing interactivity in the learning process (n = 4), and developing critical thinking and decision-making in clinical scenarios (n = 2). Experimental design studies included samples ranging from 50 participants in specific educational impact analyses (n = 2) to evaluations in larger cohorts of medical and health science students (n = 1, with 429 participants).

4 Discussion

AR represents a significant advancement in medical education, offering new teaching methods as technology evolves [30]. Its implementation has allowed medical students to access more dynamic and interactive learning environments, facilitating the understanding of complex concepts. Beyond anatomical visualization, AR has proven useful in teaching surgical procedures and other clinical applications. Human anatomy, due to its complexity, presents a challenge in medical education, especially when opportunities for hands-on learning are limited. In this context, AR has emerged as a key tool to enhance training without relying solely on physical models or laboratory practices.

4.1 Benefits of AR

AR offers multiple advantages in the cognitive development and learning of medical students, with studies reporting knowledge retention improvements of up to 75% due to its use in educational applications [31]. One of its primary advantages is the ability to explore biological content in an immersive way, allowing students to visualize physiological and anatomical processes from a more detailed and understandable perspective [32].

Another key benefit is the ability to simulate medical and surgical procedures in safe, controlled environments. These simulations enable students to practice clinical skills without risking patient safety, accelerating their learning curve and boosting their confidence in performing real-world procedures. Furthermore, AR fosters experiential learning, where students not only observe but interact with 3D models, reinforcing their ability to apply knowledge in real clinical scenarios [33].

In the realm of anatomy, AR has significantly improved the spatial understanding of body structures. Applications like Cranium have been successfully used for the identification of bone structures, demonstrating improvements in the academic performance of students who use these tools. This interactive approach overcomes the limitations of traditional physical models, offering customization in teaching and adapting to different learning styles [34].

AR also contributes to the development of essential technological competencies in an increasingly digitized medical environment. Students using AR devices and applications acquire digital skills that will be valuable in their future professional practice. Moreover, its flexibility and accessibility make it an inclusive tool, adaptable to different educational contexts and learning needs. Collectively, these benefits position AR not only as a technological complement but as a driving force of innovation in medical education, transforming the way future healthcare professionals acquire and apply knowledge.

4.2 Implications for Practice

AR has proven to be an effective tool in medical education and optimizing clinical training. In the teaching of anatomy, the use of applications like Cranium has facilitated the identification of bone structures, allowing for detailed visualization and better knowledge retention [28]. Similarly, the use of AR-based workbooks has improved the understanding of neural schematics, accelerated learning and promoted the development of spatial skills.

In the clinical realm, AR has been incorporated into surgical planning and the teaching of medical procedures. Technologies like Microsoft HoloLens have been successfully applied for real-time visualization of anatomical structures, optimizing diagnostic accuracy and facilitating surgical training in simulated environments [35]. Furthermore, the integration of AR into educational models has enhanced interactive learning in fields like cell biology, where mobile applications and QR codes have shown improvements in knowledge acquisition and performance among students with learning difficulties.

In higher education, AR has been key in increasing student engagement and improving the learning experience in various health-related disciplines. However, challenges remain in terms of accessibility and cost, limiting its widespread implementation. Continued exploration of strategies to ensure their integration into diverse educational contexts and clinics with limited resources is necessary.

4.3 Future Implementations

Future applications of AR in medical education are directed towards its integration with artificial intelligence (AI) and adaptive learning methodologies. The combination of these technologies will enhance the precision of 3D models and personalize teaching according to the individual needs of students [36].

Moreover, AR is projected as a viable alternative for advanced medical simulation, reducing the reliance on physical models in teaching clinical and surgical procedures. The development of interactive environments in which students can practice simulated physiological responses in real time represents one of the most promising innovations in medical education.

Another key aspect is the expansion of AR to various devices. Currently, its implementation in smartphones and tablets has improved access to educational materials in various disciplines, including preventive medicine and nutrition, where it has facilitated decision-making based on interactive visual information [37, 38]. This technological flexibility will allow its application in communities with limited resources, contributing to the reduction of the digital divide in medical education.

AR in biomedical research holds great potential for the development of new diagnostic and therapeutic tools [39]. Its integration with digital models in the study of diseases such as cancer has improved teaching in universities and the accuracy of medical image interpretation. These innovations will not only optimize the training of healthcare professionals but could also transform the design and evaluation of medical treatments in the future.

5 Conclusions

This review provides the most relevant current information on AR, along with various studies conducted on its applications and future interactions, and the necessary research for the implementation of new technologies in AR. From the analysis performed, it is concluded that AR helps to reduce the learning curve through interactive environments, fostering greater knowledge retention and application by medical students.

On the other hand, current practical applications of AR, such as its use in surgical simulations and assisted diagnostics, are already proving to be an efficient tool for improving accuracy and reducing risks in medical procedures. These implementations not only optimize learning and practice but also contribute to the development of personalized therapies, expanding the possibilities of precision medicine.

Acknowledgments. A special thanks to Universidad Tecnológica Indoamérica for its support through project IIDI-022–25 titled "Innovación en la Educación Superior a través de las Tecnologías Emergentes" and to the EDUTEM research network for assisting in the dissemination of results.

References

1. Chung, H.-Y., Yuasa, M., Chen, F.-S., Yukawa, K., Motoo, Y., Arai, I.: The status of education for integrative medicine in Japanese medical universities with special reference to Kampo medicines. Tradit. Kampo Med. **10**, 123–131 (2023). https://doi.org/10.1002/tkm2.1365
2. Jansen, C., et al.: Medicine in motion: opportunities, challenges and data analytics-based solutions for traditional medicine integration into western medical practice. J. Ethnopharmacol. **267**, 113477 (2021). https://doi.org/10.1016/j.jep.2020.113477
3. Aferu, T., et al.: Attitude and practice toward traditional medicine among hypertensive patients on follow-up at Mizan-Tepi University Teaching Hospital. Southwest Ethiopia. SAGE Open Med. **10**, 20503121221083210 (2022). https://doi.org/10.1177/20503121221083209
4. Buele, J., Palacios-Navarro, G.: Cognitive-motor interventions based on virtual reality and instrumental activities of daily living (iADL): an overview. Front. Aging Neurosci. **15** (2023). https://doi.org/10.3389/fnagi.2023.1191729
5. Taghian, A., Abo-Zahhad, M., Sayed, M.S., Abd El-Malek, A.H.: Virtual and augmented reality in biomedical engineering. Biomed. Eng. Online. **22**, 76 (2023). https://doi.org/10.1186/s12938-023-01138-3
6. Andrea Sánchez, Z., Santiago Alvarez, T., Roberto Segura, F., Tomás Núñez, C., Urrutia-Urrutia, P., Franklin Salazar, L., Altamirano, S., Buele, J.: Virtual rehabilitation system using electromyographic sensors for strengthening upper extremities. In: Rocha, Á., Pereira, R.P. (eds.) Developments and Advances in Defense and Security, pp. 231–241. Springer, Singapore (2020). https://doi.org/10.1007/978-981-13-9155-2_19
7. Avilés-Castillo, F., Buele, J., Palacios-Navarro, G.: Virtual reality and user experience: current trends and future challenges. IEEE Access. **13**, 55939–55956 (2025). https://doi.org/10.1109/ACCESS.2025.3554434
8. Pilatásig, M., Tigse, J., Chuquitarco, A., Pilatásig, P., Pruna, E., Acurio, A., Buele, J., Escobar, I.: Interactive system for hands and wrist rehabilitation. In: Rocha, Á., Guarda, T. (eds.) Proceedings of the International Conference on Information Technology & Systems (ICITS 2018), pp. 593–601. Springer International Publishing, Cham (2018). https://doi.org/10.1007/978-3-319-73450-7_56
9. Syed, T.A., et al.: In-depth review of augmented reality: tracking technologies, development tools, ar displays, collaborative ar, and security concerns. Sensors **23**, 146 (2023). https://doi.org/10.3390/s23010146
10. Devagiri, J.S., Paheding, S., Niyaz, Q., Yang, X., Smith, S.: Augmented reality and artificial intelligence in industry: trends, tools, and future challenges. Expert Syst. Appl. **207**, 118002 (2022). https://doi.org/10.1016/j.eswa.2022.118002
11. Buele, J., Espinoza, J., Ruales, B., Camino-Morejón, V.M., Ayala-Chauvin, M.: Augmented reality application with multimedia content to support primary education. In: Botto-Tobar, M., Gómez, O.S., Rosero Miranda, R., Díaz Cadena, A., Luna-Encalada, W. (eds.) Trends in Artificial Intelligence and Computer Engineering, pp. 299–310. Springer Nature Switzerland, Cham (2023). https://doi.org/10.1007/978-3-031-25942-5_24
12. Lastrucci, A., et al.: Exploring augmented reality integration in diagnostic imaging: myth or reality? Diagnostics **14**, 1333 (2024). https://doi.org/10.3390/diagnostics14131333
13. Negrillo-Cárdenas, J., Jiménez-Pérez, J.-R., Feito, F.R.: The role of virtual and augmented reality in orthopedic trauma surgery: From diagnosis to rehabilitation. Comput. Methods Programs Biomed. **191**, 105407 (2020). https://doi.org/10.1016/j.cmpb.2020.105407
14. Douglas, D.B., Wilke, C.A., Gibson, J.D., Boone, J.M., Wintermark, M.: Augmented reality: advances in diagnostic imaging. Multimodal Technol. Interact. **1**, 29 (2017). https://doi.org/10.3390/mti1040029

15. Ng, K.T., Thong, Y.L., Cyril, N., Durairaj, K., Assanarkutty, S.J., Sinniah, S.: Development of a road map for primary healthcare integrating ar-based technology: lessons learned and the way forward. In: Immersive Virtual and Augmented Reality in Healthcare. CRC Press (2023)
16. Khan, M.N.R., Lippert, K.J.: immersive technologies in healthcare education. In: Intelligent Systems and Machine Learning for Industry. CRC Press (2022)
17. Cabero Almenara, J., Puentes Puente, Á.: La Realidad Aumentada: Tecnología emergente para la sociedad del aprendizaje. AULA Rev. Humanidades Cienc. Soc. **66**, 35–51 (2020)
18. Khan, H.A., Jamil, S., Piran, M.J., Kwon, O.-J., Lee, J.-W.: A comprehensive survey on the investigation of machine-learning-powered augmented reality applications in education. Technol. **12**, 72 (2024). https://doi.org/10.3390/technologies12050072
19. Duriguez, H.S., Palaoag, T.D.: UX design of augmented reality-based at using design thinking approach. Int. J. Intell. Syst. Appl. Eng. **12**, 624–630 (2024)
20. Pini, V., Orso, V., Pluchino, P., Gamberini, L.: Augmented grocery shopping: fostering healthier food purchases through AR. Virtual Real. **27**, 2117–2128 (2023). https://doi.org/10.1007/s10055-023-00792-1
21. İmre, M., Yıkmış, S.: The use of augmented reality in the food industry: enhancing the dining experience. In: Impactful Technologies Transforming the Food Industry, pp. 135–155. IGI Global Scientific Publishing (2023). https://doi.org/10.4018/978-1-6684-9094-5.ch009
22. Poobrasert, O., Luxsameevanich, S., Meekanon, P.: Using the technique of Interaction Design (IxD) and Augmented Reality (AR) as assistive technology for students with disabilities. Int. J. Inf. Educ. Technol. **13**, 1199–1207 (2023). https://doi.org/10.18178/ijiet.2023.13.8.1921
23. Almenara, J.C., Osuna, J.B., Puente, Á.P., Pichardo, I.C.: The use of augmented reality in the medical teaching of anatomy: students' acceptance and motivation. Rev. Cuba. Educ. Médica Super. **32**, 56–69 (2018)
24. Elnaqlah, A., Jamiat, N., Madi, T.: Augmented reality in higher education: a 10-year systematic literature review. J. Theor. Appl. Inf. Technol. **101**, 6495–6511 (2023)
25. Šulc, J., Vidicki, P., Reljić, V., Milenković, I., Dudić, S.: Augmented reality as an aid to collaborative and autonomous learning in engineering education: augmented reality in engineering education. J. Sci. Ind. Res. JSIR. **82**, 736–744 (2023). https://doi.org/10.56042/jsir.v82i07.2150
26. Khan, H.U., Ali, Y., Khan, F., Al-antari, M.A.: A comprehensive study on unraveling the advances of immersive technologies (VR/AR/MR/XR) in the healthcare sector during the COVID-19: Challenges and solutions. Heliyon **10**, e35037 (2024). https://doi.org/10.1016/j.heliyon.2024.e35037
27. Cabero-Almenara, J., Llorente-Cejudo, C., Gutiérrez-Castillo, J.J.: Evaluación por y desde los usuarios: objetos de aprendizaje con Realidad aumentada. Rev. Educ. Distancia RED. (2017)
28. Rodríguez, J.P., Montalván, D.N.T.: Aplicación de realidad aumentada para el estudio de los huesos del cráneo utilizando dispositivos móviles. Espirales Rev. Multidiscip. Invesitgación Científica. **3** (2019)
29. Fernandez Nieto, J.C., Perez Timoteo, G.F.A.: Desarrollo de un simulador con realidad aumentada y realidad virtual para el aprendizaje del cáncer en estudiantes universitarios de medicina (2022). https://repositorio.ucv.edu.pe/handle/20.500.12692/93120
30. Ong, E.T., Pang, Y.J., Talib, C.A., Setiawan, R., Ng, J.H., Por, F.P.: Industrial Revolution (IR) and exemplary AR/VR-based technological tools in preventive health education: the past, present, and future. In: Immersive Virtual and Augmented Reality in Healthcare. CRC Press (2023)
31. Sutherland, J., et al.: Applying modern virtual and augmented reality technologies to medical images and models. J. Digit. Imaging **32**, 38–53 (2019). https://doi.org/10.1007/s10278-018-0122-7

32. Saritama, J.M.R., Almenara, J.C., Pérez, Ó.G.: Realidad Aumentada como recurso didáctico para el aprendizaje de Biología: un estudio exploratorio desde la percepción de los estudiantes universitarios. Edutec Rev. Electrónica Tecnol. Educ. 52–69 (2023). https://doi.org/10.21556/edutec.2023.84.2867

33. Crogman, H.T., Cano, V.D., Pacheco, E., Sonawane, R.B., Boroon, R.: Virtual reality, augmented reality, and mixed reality in experiential learning: transforming educational paradigms. Educ. Sci. **15**, 303 (2025). https://doi.org/10.3390/educsci15030303

34. Wu, H.-K., Lee, S.W.-Y., Chang, H.-Y., Liang, J.-C.: Current status, opportunities and challenges of augmented reality in education. Comput. Educ. **62**, 41–49 (2013). https://doi.org/10.1016/j.compedu.2012.10.024

35. Serrano Vergel, R., Morillo Tena, P., Casas Yrurzum, S., Cruz-Neira, C.: A comparative evaluation of a virtual reality table and a hololens-based augmented reality system for anatomy training. IEEE Trans. Hum. Mach. Syst. **50**, 337–348 (2020). https://doi.org/10.1109/THMS.2020.2984746

36. Qushem, U.B., Christopoulos, A., Oyelere, S.S., Ogata, H., Laakso, M.-J.: Multimodal technologies in precision education: providing new opportunities or adding more challenges? Educ. Sci. **11**, 338 (2021). https://doi.org/10.3390/educsci11070338

37. Saidani Neffati, O., et al.: An educational tool for enhanced mobile e-Learning for technical higher education using mobile devices for augmented reality. Microprocess. Microsyst. **83**, 104030 (2021). https://doi.org/10.1016/j.micpro.2021.104030

38. AlNajdi, S.M.: The effectiveness of using augmented reality (AR) to enhance student performance: using quick response (QR) codes in student textbooks in the Saudi education system. Educ. Technol. Res. Dev. **70**, 1105–1124 (2022). https://doi.org/10.1007/s11423-022-10100-4

39. Amara, K., Guerroudji, M.A., Kerdjidj, O., Zenati, N., Atalla, S., Ramzan, N.: Enhancing arrhythmia diagnosis through ecg deep learning classification deploying and augmented reality 3d heart visualisation and interaction. IEEE Access. 1–1 (2025). https://doi.org/10.1109/ACCESS.2025.3576243

Serious Games and Interactive Narratives

Towards Ambient Serious Games in Higher Education – Vision, Requirements and Technical Solutions

Lea C. Brandl[(✉)] and Andreas Schrader

Institute of Telematics, Universität zu Lübeck, 23562 Lübeck, Germany
{lea.brandl,andreas.schrader}@uni-luebeck.de
https://www.itm.uni-luebeck.de/home

Abstract. Serious games have shown educational benefits in various studies and case reports. In higher education, they support active learning and can align with the evolving concept of Education 4.0–an approach that leverages modern technologies to personalize learning. While virtual reality is one step in this direction, further opportunities arise through pervasive technologies such as IoT and natural user interfaces. These are central to the concept of smart universities, where smart, computing-enriched environments enhance learning experiences. This paper explores how serious games in higher education can integrate ambient computing concepts to create what we define as Ambient Serious Games (ASGs). A literature review identified key influencing factors, including digitalization, ethics, user needs, learning psychology, and smart environments. Based on these, a target scenario was developed using the human-centered design process to derive design requirements for ASGs. ASGs are serious games embedded in digitally smart environments. The surrounding smart space supports immersive, goal-oriented gameplay. In higher education, ASGs are characterized by an integration with learning management systems for adaptive content delivery, full coverage of educational material through game progression, immersive, multimedia environments to boost engagement, usable interfaces avoiding interaction barriers, physical activity tailored to individual abilities and many other aspects, shown in the paper.

Keywords: Ambient Serious Games · Requirements · Pervasive Computing · Ubiquitous Computing

1   Introduction

According to the concept of Education 4.0, we are in a new phase of shaping education [47]. In higher education, this has led to the use of Learning Management Systems (LMS) over the past few decades, which typically leverage web technologies to provide learning content via a graphical user interface [13,45]. Another trend is the use of serious games in education, which are often, but not

J. Y. C. Chen et al. (Eds.): HCII 2025, LNCS 16338, pp. 315–331, 2026.
https://doi.org/10.1007/978-3-032-12808-9_20

exclusively, digital. Serious Games aim to achieve a serious goal in addition to entertainment [35]–in the case of educational games, the goal is knowledge transfer. These games have been shown motivating effects and positively effects on adherence [8,23,53]. According to the Cognitive Theory of Multimedia [34], it makes sense to develop serious games that offer multiple channels for processing learning content. This aligns with the concept of ambient intelligence in LMS, which aims to create adaptive learning spaces that adjust to learners and present content in a multi-modal way. From this idea, the concept of Ambient Serious Games emerged. Ambient Games belong to the category of Pervasive Games. These games are not clearly limited in terms of time, space, or social interaction [38]. Ambient games leverage the concept of ubiquitous computing, which envisions computers embedded in the physical environment, making them unobtrusively available to users and, thus, effectively invisible [67]. Ambient games create an atmosphere where players can engage in various activities, some of which may not be game-related. Players can use information from their environment, provided by the surroundings, without being forced to interact [22].

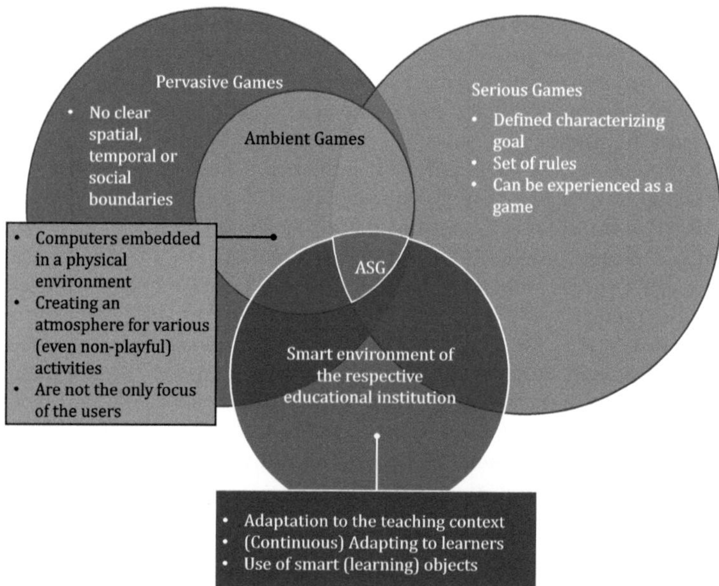

Fig. 1. Ambient serious games as distinct from the overlapping topics of pervasive games, ambient games, serious games and the smart environment of the educational institution.

As a result, the term Ambient Serious Games refers to games with a serious purpose, embedded in a computer-enriched environment that could be mentally invisible to the players. Despite this, the game itself remains the focus, with its rules and defined goals (cf. [9]). Additionally they are integrated in the learning context and the smart environments of the educational institutions - in case of this paper the universities. The overlap with the areas mentioned can be seen in Fig. 1.

The goal of this publication is to identify the influencing factors from various disciplines on concepts for designing ambient serious games for higher education. The factors are illustrated in a user scenario and result in requirements on Ambient Serious Games in Higher Education.

The term Serious Games is defined in various ways by different authors. For example, Abt coined the term, describing Serious Games as those that combine the seriousness which is needed in thought and problem-solving with the experimental and emotional freedom of play [1]. Michel et al. [35] define Serious Games as games whose main purpose is not fun, entertainment, or enjoyment. Serious Games are not limited to educational contexts but are also used in healthcare, politics, and employee recruitment, for example [12,51]. They are often, but not exclusively, defined as computer games [60].

There is evidence in the literature suggesting that Serious Games have a positive learning effect. Wouters et al. [69] report that Serious Games are more effective for conveying knowledge and cognitive skills than traditional teaching methods. Key factors include repeated game play, the combination with other methods, and group play. Narrative elements and realism play a minor role [69]. Regarding motivation, the intuitive integration of serious games into other teaching units is important. However, the authors note that, in line with self-determination theory, even good integration may not lead to increased motivation if players do not have control over whether they participate in the game [69]. Self-determination theory links motivation to autonomy and control, with autonomous motivation benefiting performance as well as physical and mental health [19]. A balance between teaching methods and serious games is crucial [69]. However, barriers remain to the widespread use of games in education, including issues of acceptance and technological challenges. Ullah et al. [66] note both positive and negative effects of serious games, depending on the game's difficulty. A challenging game can increase cognitive workload, thus impairing learning performance [66]. Based on these findings, serious games can have positive effects if they are appropriately designed for users and well-integrated into the context.

In the context of the digitization of higher education, serious games appear to be a flexible method that allows adaptation to learners and the use of various interaction technologies. Technologically, the games are typically designed for use on standard computers. Motivational mechanisms and game design are diverse and seem to be more aligned with the game or teaching content rather than the preferences of students or player types among them. [10]

2   Methods

To address the question of which factors influence serious game concepts, a requirements analysis based on the human centered design process [21] was conducted. This was realized through both systematic and unsystematic literature reviews, user surveys, and a structured examination of the university context and processes. This analysis covers not only the previously discussed research on serious games and their use in higher education but also ambient learning management systems, pervasive university environments, human learning processes, the structure and organization of learning content in academic contexts, as well as user/player characteristics and ethical considerations. All identified factors result in a user scenario, which shows an example of the vision of Ambient Serious Games. As a consequence requirements are presented, derived from parts of the presented scenario. At last possible technical solutions are discussed. In the research field of smart environments, technologies are examined to determine whether they represent a way of addressing the requirements.

3   Results

This section presents the results. First, the results of the literature research are presented, followed by the user scenario and the resulting requirements.

3.1   Factors Influencing Ambient Serious Games

The examined fields are (a) Ambient Learning Management Systems and Pervasive Universities, (b) Learning Processes and Flow Theory, (c) Structure and Organization of Learning Content in the University Context, (d) User and Player Characteristics, and (e) Ethical Considerations. Therefore the results of the literature reviews are presented in the corresponding structure.

Ambient Learning Management Systems and Pervasive Universities. There are already publications that explore the idea of using ambient technologies in universities and learning management systems [41,42,46,56]. For example, Tavangarian and Lucke [56] describe the concept of the Pervasive University, which involves context-sensitive systems supporting users without requiring explicit instructions. These systems are integrated into the environment so that they only capture users' attention when needed [56]. In a university setting, this implies supporting teaching with technology in such a way that intelligent spaces become effectively usable. A similar concept, known as ambient Learning Management Systems (aLMS), aims to design intelligent environments that recognize students and present learning content in multimedia and adaptive formats [46]. Both in the context of the Pervasive University and aLMS, authors have published requirements for such systems. Caserman et al. [12] have also published quality criteria for serious games, which will be combined with the requirements for intelligent environments in universities to derive the requirements for an adaptive serious game. In the context of aLMS, user profiles are required to adapt the displayed learning content to individual students [41]. After identification, the profile should be loaded by the aLMS, and the environment should be adjusted accordingly [42]. The focus should always be on the learner [46]. Further requirements for aLMS include context-based services, user adaptation, personalization, and ubiquitous monitoring [42,46], all aimed at continuously optimizing user support. Personalization is also a key requirement for serious games [12], ensuring (a) an engaging experience for different player types, (b) adaptation to players to enhance effectiveness, and (c) the use of appropriate methods for each application area and target audience [12]. User profiles could contain information about the player type and current knowledge level, enabling adaptation in both educational games and aLMS. To achieve this, new algorithms will be necessary, which will also be relevant for aLMS.

Learning Processes and Flow Theory. Learning theories play a crucial role in designing educational games. One widely discussed theory is Cognitive Load Theory (CLT) [14,31]. It divides memory into working memory and long-term memory. Working memory is limited in capacity, while long-term memory appears limitless [31,55]. According to Miller, working memory can handle 7 ± 2 chunks of information, while more recent studies suggest 4 ± 1 chunks [16,31,37]. Chunks represent units of information to be processed [31]. As learning content is processed in working memory, these chunks are transformed into schemas and stored in long-term memory. Whether all chunks are processed correctly depends on cognitive load, which can be intrinsic or extrinsic [31]. Intrinsic load is influenced by the complexity of the chunks being processed. The so called element interactivity describes the difficulty and complexity of the chunks: the more interconnected the elements, the higher the element interactivity. For instance, element interactivity is lower when learning individual vocabulary compared to learning a grammar rule. Extrinsic load is influenced by the way the learning material is presented. Poorly prepared learning materials can increase extrinsic load [31]. The modality principle suggests that learning with auditory text and an accompanying image is more effective than an image with written description, which could result in higher extrinsic load [25,31]. Also interesting in this context is Dale's cone of experience [17], as it shows that people remember more when they learn through active engagement, with retention rates of 90% for what they do compared to 10% for what they read and 20% for what they hear [18]. Another factor for learning could be physical activity. Studies show a positive correlation between physical activity and academic performance. Keating et al. [30] found that weekly strength training can improve academic grades. Winter et al. [68] demonstrated that intense physical exercise can enhance vocabulary learning by 20% compared to moderate exercise or sedentary behavior, while also improving long-term retention.

Emotions also play a significant role in memory and learning. Numerous studies have reported that brain regions activated during emotional processing strengthen memory connections, meaning emotional content is remembered better than neutral content [65].

A concept connected to both learning and gaming is the *flow state*, which refers to a balanced relationship between challenge and skill, leading to deep immersion in an activity [20,54]. Csikszentmihalyi developed the flow concept, which applies to gaming as players become fully engaged and focused [54]. To foster flow, games should be challenging enough to motivate the player but not so difficult as to cause frustration. Additionally, clear goals and immediate feedback are essential [54]. Flow measurement is complex because asking about flow or extensive measurements can disrupt the state. However, flow correlates with physiological parameters, making it measurable through electroencephalograms (EEG), heart rate variability, or electrodermal activity [27,44]. EEG-based flow measurements have shown that flow positively impacts learning during gameplay [27].

Structure and Organization of Learning Content in the University Context. As already mentioned, LMS organize and support the delivery of university courses by providing platforms for making lecture content available to students and instructors through various media. LMS offer additional interactive learning tools such as whiteboards, calendars, or quizzes. The latter of which can be graded by instructors. Across different LMS providers, common quiz formats include multiple-choice, single-choice, and free-text questions, followed by true/false and gap-fill questions in frequency [7,26,29,32,36,49,52,63]. To enable easy integration of learning materials into adaptive serious games, interfaces should exist between LMS and ASG to transfer course materials to the game.

User and Player Characteristics. Students, as potential users of such systems, tend to share certain characteristics: most are between 20 and 25 years old [64]. Considering the age and education level of students, it's likely they are also involved in volunteer activities. Among 14 to 29-year-olds, 42% engage in volunteer work, with 52% of volunteers having a higher education degree. Most are active in sports, culture, and social causes [50]. Students are also likely to engage with video games, as over 85% of those aged 16 to 29 play games [59], with nearly a quarter having an academic degree [58]. Popular genres among at least 60% of players include casual games, strategy, management, and simulation games, as well as fitness and movement games, with 46% occasionally playing educational games [57]. The preferred game genres and motivational mechanisms - often referred to as mechanics - depend on players' personality traits, known as player types. Since students in this system take on the role of players, understanding the distribution of player types in this group is relevant. Various studies have explored the distribution of player types among students. Gaalen et al. [24] conducted a study among medical and dental students, asking participants to rank 49 statements about gaming preferences. Of the 109 participants, 30 were categorized into Social Achiever (n=12), Explorer (n=7), Competitor (n=4), Socializer (n=5), and Troll (n=2). Social Achievers are motivated by achieving goals together, Explorers enjoy discovering and altering the game, Competitors seek competition, Socializers use games to connect with others, and Trolls try to break game rules or annoy others [24]. Barata et al. [5] analyzed the behavior of students in a gamified engineering course, using clustering to identify four groups: (1) Achievers, who collect all in-game achievements;

(2) Regular Students, who avoid difficult tasks but perform well overall; (3) Half-hearted Students, who show little interest and achieve below-average results; and (4) Underachievers, who do the minimum to pass the course [5]. Trojanek et al. [62], on the other hand, used the User Types Hexad Framework and a validated questionnaire to identify player types among students at TU Dresden. Participants were assigned to the player type with the highest score. If there was a tie, another type was also considered. Among the users, Philanthropists were the most common type, followed by Free Spirits and Socializers. As observed in analyses by Marczewski et al., the most frequent combination was Philanthropist and Socializer [62]. We also studied students using the Hexad-Framework and proposed classifying player types based on varying degrees of certain traits. Their analysis resulted in three user classes among students, each corresponding to a player profile. These were labeled as Social-Achiever, Player, and Socializer [11]

Ethical Considerations. In the context of Serious Games, ethical aspects of game design should also be considered. Video games not only reflect culture and society but also influence them, especially through their participatory nature [6,40]. Design decisions regarding narratives and motivational mechanisms often portray a reflection of our culture. However, the majority of popular games tend to depict white male characters in positive and influential roles, while women and minorities are over represented in insignificant, stereotypical, or - in the case of women - sexualized roles [15,39,40,43]. Although these representations are not explicitly racist, hero characters are usually depicted as white. Female characters appeared as often in leading roles as male characters but were portrayed stereo-typically, with feminine features emphasized by sexualized clothing and slim bodies [39]. Black men often appear as athletes [39], while black women are largely ignored [43]. Criticism has already been voiced regarding these portrayals, but it seems to have little impact on the design decisions of major game companies [61]. From an ethical standpoint, this contradicts ethical guidelines for software development. For example, the IEEE Code of Ethics outlines the fair and respectful treatment of individuals and the avoidance of discrimination in its second clause [28]. In the context of higher education, the avoidance of discriminatory content and depictions is particularly important, as universities are responsible for protecting against discrimination [2]. Therefore, games used in academic settings should avoid stereotypical or racist depictions.

4   User Scenario and Requirements

The following section illustrates the vision of Ambient Serious Games in education through a practical scenario. It centers on a learning game set in a multimedia-enhanced environment, which students can freely use for learning and practicing exercises in the form of a game. After that user stories and requirements are presented.

4.1   Scenario: Ambient Learning Environment

Tobias is a third-semester Media Informatics student at the University of Lübeck. As part of his studies, he is required to take the "Fundamentals of Multimedia Technology" course. Alongside the lectures, he can access related exercises through the university's LMS to review and test his knowledge. Since Tobias finds it hard to stay motivated, he chooses to complete the exercises in a playful way. For that, he visits the university's ambient learning space.

At the entrance, he logs into the LMS and selects the course and topic he wants to review. After a brief recap, the actual exercise begins. He is offered several game-based versions of the same exercise. Because he enjoys solving puzzles in his free time, Tobias selects a single-player escape game. Although he has played this game before, it never gets boring - the puzzles and tasks change each time. The LMS shows that he can still play the game eight more times before completing all levels.

He starts the game, and the room responds immediately. The lighting shifts, and projectors transform the walls so that he is immersed in a different environment. He now stands in a lab filled with various electrical measurement devices. On one side, he notices a door and a Kundt's tube used to visualize sound. He also sees a table with several physical cubes and a projected oscilloscope that he hadn't noticed before. The cubes display six different microphones on their respective screens - devices he's already encountered in lectures. One of the screens shows a diagram with axes labeled in kilohertz and decibels.

As he explores the room, he finds more interactive displays - tablets, smartphones, and cubes - all showing graphics related to the topic. At first, he feels unsure of what to do. Then, a silhouette appears on a screen mounted on the right wall. A virtual guide explains that he must solve ten puzzles in the next 20 min to discover a password that unlocks the door.

The first puzzle appears on the screen, accompanied by calm background music. It's a multiple-choice question. To answer it, he must find the letter corresponding to the correct option, hidden somewhere in the room. He discovers an A on a tablet, a B on a smartphone, a C on another device, and a D on a large screen. He's torn between answers A and C. After thinking for a while, he still can't decide. His motivation begins to ease. Before he considers quitting, the letter C disappears from the smartphone and the answer option vanishes from the screen. Now confident that A is correct, he inspects the image more closely. A graphic in the back of the smartphone screen prompts him to zoom in. In the background of the image, he spots a chalkboard. When he zooms in, he sees a new task.

Now he must match the microphones to specific statements. To do so, he needs to find another board containing the statements. A clue leads him to a table with a touchscreen surface. He swipes away the displayed tablecloth and finds the statements underneath. By placing the microphone cubes in the correct positions, he solves the task. The lighting above the table briefly turns green and a confirmation sound plays. The cubes' surfaces change, revealing the next task.

Tobias instantly realizes he needs the diagram he found earlier. He becomes fully immersed in the experience, forgetting that he's simply completing an exercise. After 15 min and 10 s, he has solved all the puzzles. The final task reveals the pin, which unlocks the door. Behind it, a brightly lit area appears and spreads across the entire room. Once the room is fully illuminated, the original environment - where the game began - rebuilds itself.

On the screen at his current position, Tobias sees the results of his exercise. He didn't answer all questions correctly. Two tasks were incorrect, and he can review them right there. As he's about to start, a message appears recommending a short break. He reflects for a moment and realizes he's no longer able to concentrate. He logs out and leaves the room.

After a break, he opens the LMS at home and reviews his mistakes. He's relieved that he completed the exercise in under 20 min and now feels more confident about passing the course.

4.2   User Stories and Requirements

This section summarizes all requirements derived from the first part of the result. Each user story is followed by core requirements. The scenario is set within the context of higher education. The games should either be integrated into self-study time or embedded within the lecture to avoid requiring additional time. Furthermore, enough available rooms must be provided where such games can be conducted.

To allow instructors to offer their content in game format, it must be possible to convert traditional exercises into games with minimal effort. In the scenario Ambient Learning Environment, the room where Tobias plays the game adapts to his and the selected subject upon login. This information is retrieved from his user profile in the LMS.

1. User profiles should describe individual characteristics and allow the system to adapt accordingly
2. The system should analyze the user during gameplay and adapt dynamically
3. User profiles should update after each game session
4. Profiles should include knowledge level and player type

Tobias completes an exercise through gameplay. By answering all questions, he unlocks the final door's code. The game thus fulfills both the gameplay objective and the characterizing goal.

1. The game should pursue a clear characterizing goal

At first, Tobias doesn't know how to interact with the environment. However, the game provides video guidance and in-game tutorials that explain the interaction process without requiring him to read a manual.

1. The game should include in-game tutorials
2. Interactive objects should explain how to use them

Tobias uses smart cubes representing microphones to interact with the game. In another game, the same cubes could represent different objects.

1. New types of learning objects should be introduced
2. Learning content should be presented in a multimodal and adaptive manner

Tobias discovers answer options on different devices. The interfaces are clearly designed and easy to use.

1. User interfaces should be intuitive and free from unnecessary information

As Tobias's motivation drops, the system detects it and removes confusing options from the screen. This helps him regain focus and stay engaged in reaching the characterizing goal. The game captures his uncertainty and emotional state to adjust difficulty accordingly.

1. The game should support the user in reaching the characterizing goal
2. Learning content should be adapted to avoid both under- and over-challenging the user and support flow
2. The system should recognize and respond to user emotions

As the game progresses, Tobias forgets he's completing an exercise. He becomes fully immersed in the game, following its rules to solve all puzzles within the time limit.

1. The game itself should be the user's focus, not just a gamified exercise
2. It should be perceived as a genuine game, not merely a gamified task

This level of immersion results from tailored adaptations to both the subject Multimedia Technology and Tobias's player type. Elements like the Kundt's tube and microphone cubes simulate real-world experiments.

1. Appropriate methods should be used based on the application context and target group
2. The game should offer an engaging experience for various player types
3. The game should connect theoretical and practical knowledge
4. Learning and training tasks should be integrated into the gameplay

Tobias receives immediate feedback on each answer, and the overall result is shown at the end. Even with some incorrect answers, he completes the game.

1. Learning content should not hinder gameplay or progression
2. In-game feedback should help users understand whether their answers are correct and how to improve
3. Feedback should be immediate and multimodal

The game presents itself with a simulated environment. Background music enhances the atmosphere. When he answers a question or completes the game, both lighting and music shift briefly. Subtle effects help his stay focused on the tasks.

1. Appropriate background music and audio effects should enhance the experience
2. Learning content should be segmented according to the Cognitive Load Theory (ideally 4 ± 1 chunks)
3. The game should foster an emotional connection with the user

To answer all questions, Tobias needs to move around the room. The time-limited format prevents long sitting periods. This physical activity keeps his alert and engaged.

1. The learning pace should adapt to the player
2. Integrated movement elements should promote well-being and better focus

Additionally, several ethical aspects must be considered when designing and implementing ambient learning games:

1. Avoid political or religious content, unless it is directly related to the educational material
2. Avoid stereotypical or racist depictions to ensure cultural neutrality
3. Ensure language is not a barrier to understanding the content
4. Avoid excluding users with physical or cognitive impairments, provided they meet the academic requirements

5   Discussion

First we discuss possible technical solutions to address the requirements. After that the limitations and a conclusion are presented.

5.1   Technical Solutions

To meet the outlined requirements for Ambient Serious Games, it is necessary to identify which aspects can be fulfilled or supported by technical tools. Some context-related requirements, such as the availability of physical rooms, cannot be addressed by tools directly. However, tools can support room utilization by integrating presence detection and shared occupancy schedules. For example, Mahendran et al. [33] propose infrared sensor-based systems that notify users about available rooms. Tools that support various input/output devices can also increase room usability by enabling gameplay across heterogeneous environments.

University classrooms are typically not equipped with ready-to-use smart objects. Devices and people may also dynamically enter or leave the space. Tools must therefore support dynamic environments by preparing games compatible with diverse hardware and changing conditions [9].

Another major requirement is the effortless conversion of existing exercises into games. Tools can address this by importing digital LMS exercises via defined interfaces, allowing instructors to avoid additional manual work. Similarly, tools should support user profiles from LMS systems, which may include player types and subject proficiency levels, enabling adaptive gameplay.

The diversity of content and design options in educational contexts poses a significant technical challenge. Tools must generate games automatically based on user profiles or parameters to ensure a strong connection between exercise content and game mechanics. While tools can structurally represent exercises, didactic quality depends on instructors.

Ambient technologies can help guide players toward learning goals by adapting difficulty, recognizing emotions, and continuously personalizing content presentation. Rahimi [46] and others describe how systems can monitor mental states and adapt in real-time. Tools should also support immersive presentation through adaptive lighting, ambient music, and consistent chunking of content

Room-based interactions support movement and engagement. Game mechanics should consider timing, spatial layout, and physical activity. Tools must also adapt to physical impairments and avoid delays that disrupt immersion or induce cognitive overload.

Interaction design remains critical. Players and instructors need clear in-game guidance. According to Baalsrud et al. [4], instructors must understand both the game and the underlying technologies. Usability of all components is essential, especially given the current lack of smart devices in classrooms. Instructors may need to bring additional equipment, increasing system complexity [9].

Games should run across interchangeable smart learning objects. Components must be able to detect their status, connections, and effects of interactions. Ideally, each device can explain itself or is represented by an avatar to support emotional connection.

Ethical considerations remain critical. Tools that design or generate games must respect cultural, religious, and accessibility constraints. These aspects must be integrated into the design process or verified by the system. Otherwise, they cannot be addressed by technical means alone.

5.2   Conclusion

Pervasive or ubiquitous games have already been explored in research and practical applications [3]. Pervasive serious games with explicit learning objectives exist, such as those designed for older adults [48]. However, within the vision of a pervasive university, no known contributions focus on learning games in the context of ASGs. This paper provides researchers and game designers with a set of requirements to guide ASG development. Additionally, it outlines solution approaches leveraging pervasive technologies to facilitate their implementation. The authors identified the examined areas as the most relevant in the context of higher education. However, additional aspects may emerge, leading to further requirements for ASGs. While this study focuses on higher education, ASGs could be adapted to other educational contexts, such as primary schools, by modifying the identified requirements accordingly. Thus, the results are transferable to other domains, providing a foundation for future research on ASGs as an alternative to augmented or virtual reality games.

Disclosure of Interests. The authors have no competing interests to declare that are relevant to the content of this article.

References

1. Abt, C.C.: Ernste Spiele: Lernen durch gespielte Wirklichkeit. Kiepenheuer & Witsch, Köln, Germany (1971)
2. Antidiskriminierungsstelle des Bundes: Diskriminierung an Hochschulen (2023). https://www.antidiskriminierungsstelle.de/DE/ueber-diskriminierung/lebensbereiche/bildungsbereiche/hochschule/hochschule.html. Accessed 13 June 2025
3. Arango-López, J., Gallardo, J., Gutiérrez, F.L., Cerezo, E., Amengual, E., Valera, R.: Pervasive games: giving a meaning based on the player experience. In: Proceedings of the XVIII International Conference on Human Computer Interaction, Interacción '17, pp. 1–4. Association for Computing Machinery, New York (2017). https://doi.org/10.1145/3123818.3123832
4. Baalsrud Hauge, J., et al.: Current competencies of game facilitators and their potential optimization in higher education: multimethod study. JMIR Serious Games **9**(2), e25481 (2021). https://doi.org/10.2196/25481
5. Barata, G., Gama, S., Jorge, J.A., Gonçalves, D.J.: Relating gaming habits with student performance in a gamified learning experience. In: Proceedings of the first ACM SIGCHI annual symposium on Computer-human interaction in play, CHI PLAY '14, pp. 17–25. Association for Computing Machinery, New York, (2014). https://doi.org/10.1145/2658537.2658692
6. Billingslea II, S.: It's just a game, or is it?: A study of racism in game and character design. In: Engaging with Videogames, pp. 91 – 100. Brill, Leiden (2014). https://doi.org/10.1163/9781848882959_009
7. Blackboard Inc.: Fragentypen — Blackboard-Hilfe (2018). https://help.blackboard.com/de-de/Learn/Instructor/Ultra/Tests_Pools_Surveys/Question_Types. Accessed 16 Nov 2021
8. Boeker, M., Andel, P., Vach, W., Frankenschmidt, A.: Game-based e-learning is more effective than a conventional instructional method: a randomized controlled trial with third-year medical students. PLoS ONE **8**(12), e82328 (2013). https://doi.org/10.1371/journal.pone.0082328
9. Brandl, L.C., Kordts, B., Schrader, A.: Technological challenges of ambient serious games in higher education. In: Kriglstein, S., Wintersberger, P. (eds.) Proceedings of the MuM'23 Workshops on Making a Real Connection and Interruptions and Attention Management. CEUR Workshop Proceedings, vol. 3712. CEUR, Vienna (2023)
10. Brandl, L.C., Schrader, A.: Serious games in higher education in the transforming process to education 4.0—systematized review. Educ. Sci. **14**(3), 281 (2024). https://doi.org/10.3390/educsci14030281
11. Brandl, L.C., Schrader, A.: Student player types in higher education-trial and clustering analyses. Educ. Sci. **14**(4), 352 (2024). https://doi.org/10.3390/educsci14040352

12. Caserman, P., et al.: Quality criteria for serious games: serious part, game part, and balance. JMIR Serious Games **8**(3), e19037 (2020). https://doi.org/10.2196/19037
13. Cavus, N.: Distance learning and learning management systems. Procedia. Soc. Behav. Sci. **191**, 872–877 (2015). https://doi.org/10.1016/j.sbspro.2015.04.611
14. Chandler, P., Sweller, J.: Cognitive load theory and the format of instruction. Cogn. Instr. **8**(4), 293–332 (1991). https://doi.org/10.1207/s1532690xci0804_2
15. Cote, A.C.: Tits, tokenism, and trash-talk: overt sexism in game culture. In: Cote, A.C. (ed.) Gaming Sexism: Gender and Identity in the Era of Casual Video Games, p. 0. NYU Press, New York, USA (2020). https://doi.org/10.18574/nyu/9781479838523.003.0003
16. Cowan, N.: The magical number 4 in short-term memory: a reconsideration of mental storage capacity. Behav. Brain Sci. **24**(1), 87–114; discussion 114–185 (2001). https://doi.org/10.1017/s0140525x01003922
17. Dale, E.: Audiovisual Methods in Teaching, 3rd edn. Holt, Rinehart and Winston Inc, New York 0128(1969)
18. Davis, B., Summers, M.: Applying dale's cone of experience to increase learning and retention: a study of student learning in a foundational leadership course. Hamad bin Khalifa University Press (HBKU Press), Abu Dhabi (2015). https://doi.org/10.5339/qproc.2015.elc2014.6
19. Deci, E.L., Ryan, R.M.: Facilitating optimal motivation and psychological well-being across life's domains. Can. Psychol./Psychologie canadienne **49**(1), 14–23 (2008). https://doi.org/10.1037/0708-5591.49.1.14
20. Engeser, S., Rheinberg, F., Vollmeyer, R., Bischoff, J.: Motivation, Flow-Erleben und Lernleistung in universitären Lernsettings. Zeitschrift für Pädagogische Psychologie **19**(3), 159–172 (2005). https://doi.org/10.1024/1010-0652.19.3.159
21. Ergonomie, N.: DIN EN ISO 9241–210: Ergonomie der Mensch-System-Interaktion-Teil 210: Prozess zur Gestaltung gebrauchstauglicher interaktiver Systeme (ISO 9241–210: 2010); Deutsche Fassung EN ISO 9241–210: 2010. DIN Deutsches Institut für Normung e. V, Berlin (2011)
22. Eyles, M., Eglin, R.: Ambient games, revealing a route to a world where work is play? Int. J. Comput. Games Technol. **2008**, e176056 (2008). https://doi.org/10.1155/2008/176056
23. Faiella, F., Ricciardi, M.: Gamification and learning: a review of issues and research. J. e-Learn. Knowl. Soc. **11**(3) (2015). https://doi.org/10.20368/1971-8829/1072
24. Gaalen, A.E.J.V., Schönrock-Adema, J., Renken, R.J., Jaarsma, A.D.C., Georgiadis, J.R.: Identifying player types to tailor game-based learning design to learners: cross-sectional survey using Q methodology. JMIR Serious Games **10**(2), 1–15 (2022). https://doi.org/10.2196/30464
25. Ginns, P.: Meta-analysis of the modality effect. Learn. Instr. **15**(4), 313–331 (2005). https://doi.org/10.1016/j.learninstruc.2005.07.001
26. GmbH, F.: Test Fragetypen - OpenOlat 16.0 Benutzerhandbuch - OpenOlat Confluence (2021). https://docs.openolat.org/manual_user/learningresources/Test_question_types/#sc. Accessed 13 June 2025
27. Hugentobler, U.: Messen von Flow MIT EEG in Computerspielen. PhD Thesis, University of Zurich (2011). https://doi.org/10.5167/uzh-61078
28. IEEE: IEEE Code of Ethics (2023). https://www.ieee.org/about/corporate/governance/p7-8.html. Accessed 13 June 2025
29. Ilias: DOCU: Dokumentation für Autoren (2021). https://docu.ilias.de/ilias.php?baseClass=illmpresentationgui&cmd=layout&ref_id=15428&obj_id=208450. Accessed 13 June 2025

30. Keating, X.D., Castelli, D., Ayers, S.F.: Association of weekly strength exercise frequency and academic performance among students at a large university in the United States. J. Strength Cond. Res. **27**(7), 1988–1993 (2013). https://doi.org/10.1519/JSC.0b013e318276bb4c

31. Klepsch, M.: Differenzierte Messung kognitiver Belastung beim Lernen im Rahmen von Instruktionsdesignfragestellungen. PhD Thesis, Universität Ulm (2020). https://doi.org/10.18725/OPARU-33554

32. LTD, M.P.: Fragetypen – MoodleDocs (2018). https://docs.moodle.org/311/de/Fragetypen. Accessed 13 June 2025

33. Mahendran, S., Nallathambi, B., Mahalakshmi, T., Saravanan, K., Viswanth, M.: Intelligent room allocation using smart IoT devices. In: 2024 4th International Conference on Pervasive Computing and Social Networking, ICPCSN '24, pp. 724–729 (2024). https://doi.org/10.1109/ICPCSN62568.2024.00121

34. Mayer, R.E.: Cognitive theory of multimedia learning. In: Mayer, R. (ed.) The Cambridge Handbook of Multimedia Learning, Cambridge Handbooks in Psychology, pp. 31–48. Cambridge University Press, Cambridge (2005). https://doi.org/10.1017/CBO9780511816819.004

35. Michael, D.R., Chen, S.L.: Serious Games: Games That Educate, Train, and Inform. Muska & Lipman/Premier-Trade (2005)

36. Milius, F.: CLIX - learning-management-system für Unternehmen, Bildungsdienstleister und Hochschulen. Wirtschaftsinformatik **44**(2), 163–170 (2002). https://doi.org/10.1007/BF03250834

37. Miller, G.A.: The magical number seven, plus or minus two: some limits on our capacity for processing information. Psychol. Rev. **63**(2), 81–97 (1956). https://doi.org/10.1037/h0043158

38. Montola, M.: Exploring the edge of the magic circle: Defining pervasive games. In: Proceedings of the Digital Arts & Culture 2005 Conference: Digital Experience: Design, Aesthetics, Practice, DAC '05, pp. 103–106. IT University of Copenhagen KBH (2005)

39. Mou, Y., Peng, W.: Gender and racial stereotypes in popular video games. In: Ferdig, R.E. (ed.) Handbook of Research on Effective Electronic Gaming in Education, pp. 922–937. IGI Global, Hershey (2009). https://doi.org/10.4018/978-1-59904-808-6.ch053

40. Muriel, D., Crawford, G.: Video Games as Culture: Considering the Role and Importance of Video Games in Contemporary Society. Routledge, London (2018)

41. Olsevicova, K., Mikulecky, P.: University education as an ambient intelligence scenario. In: Proceedings of the 4th European Conference on e-Learning, ECEL '05, pp. 275–280. Academic Conferences Limited (2005)

42. Olsevicova, K., Mikulecky, P.: Learning management systems as an ambient intelligence playground. Int. J. Web Communities **4**, 348–358 (2008). https://doi.org/10.1504/IJWBC.2008.019194

43. Peck, B.M., Ketchum, P.R., Embrick, D.G.: Racism and sexism in the gaming world: reinforcing or changing stereotypes in computer games? J. Media Commun. Stud. **3**(6), 212–220 (2011)

44. Peifer, C., Tan, J.: The psychophysiology of flow experience. In: Peifer, C., Engeser, S. (eds.) Advances in Flow Research, pp. 191–230. Springer International Publishing, Cham (2021). https://doi.org/10.1007/978-3-030-53468-4_8

45. Popplow, A.: Auswahl einer Lernplattform für wissenschaftliche Weiterbildung. Zeitschrift Hochschule und Weiterbildung (ZHWB), pp. 60–67 (2018). https://doi.org/10.4119/zhwb-134

46. Rahimi, I.D.: Ambient intelligence in learning management system (LMS). In: Intelligent Computing, SAI '22, pp. 379–387. Springer International Publishing, Cham (2022). https://doi.org/10.1007/978-3-031-10467-1_24

47. Ramírez-Montoya, M.S., Castillo-Martínez, I.M., Sanabria-Z, J., Miranda, J.: Complex thinking in the framework of education 4.0 and open innovation—a systematic literature review. J. Open Innov.: Technol., Market, Complex. **8**(1), 4 (2022). https://doi.org/10.3390/joitmc8010004. Accessed 02 Jan 2024

48. Salazar Cardona, J.A., Arango López, J., Gutiérrez Vela, F.L.: Pervasiveness for learning in serious games applied to older adults. In: García-Peñalvo, F.J., García-Holgado, A. (eds.) Proceedings TEEM 2022: Tenth International Conference on Technological Ecosystems for Enhancing Multiculturality, pp. 624–632. Springer Nature, Singapore (2023). https://doi.org/10.1007/978-981-99-0942-1_65

49. 2i2L Sar: Adding questions to the test (2021). https://docs.chamilo.org/teacher-guide/interactivity_tests/adding_questions_to_the_test. Accessed 13 June 2025

50. Simonson, J., Kelle, N., Kausmann, C., Karnick, N., Arriagada, C., Hagen, C., Hameister, N., Huxhold, O., Tesch-Römer, C.: Freiwilliges Engagement in Deutschland. Fünftes Deutsches Freiwilligensurvey des Bundesministeriums für Familie, Senioren, Frauen und Jugend **1**, 1–57 (2021)

51. SPEC, DIN: 91380: 2018-06, serious games metadata format. https://www.beuth.de/de/technische-regel/din-spec-91380/289947896,   https://doi.org/10.31030/2853739. Accessed 13 June 2025

52. Stud.IP e.V. und die Autor/-innen der Stud.IP-Dokumentation: Stud.IP-Nutzerdokumentation (deutsch): Gestaltung Anlage (2008). https://hilfe.studip.de/help/4.2/de/Vips/GestaltungAnlage. Accessed 13 June 2025

53. Susi, T., Johannesson, M., Backlund, P.: Serious games – an overview (2007). https://urn.kb.se/resolve?urn=urn:nbn:se:his:diva-1279. Accessed 06 June 2025

54. Sweetser, P., Wyeth, P.: GameFlow: a model for evaluating player enjoyment in games. Comput. Entertain. **3**(3), 3 (2005). https://doi.org/10.1145/1077246.1077253

55. Sweller, J., van Merrienboer, J.J.G., Paas, F.G.W.C.: Cognitive architecture and instructional design. Educ. Psychol. Rev. **10**(3), 251–296 (1998). https://doi.org/10.1023/A:1022193728205

56. Tavangarian, D., Lucke, U.: Pervasive University – A Technical Perspective Die Pervasive University aus technischer Perspektive. IT - Inf. Technol. **51**, 6–13 (2009). https://doi.org/10.1524/itit.2009.0517

57. Tenzer, F.: Computerspiele - bevorzugte Gaming-Genres in Deutschland 2022 (2022). https://de.statista.com/statistik/daten/studie/315938/umfrage/umfrage-zu-den-bevorzugten-gaming-genres-in-deutschland/. Accessed 13 June 2025

58. Tenzer, F.: Computerspieler - Verteilung nach Bildungsgrad Deutschland 2021 (2022). https://de.statista.com/statistik/daten/studie/418967/umfrage/verteilung-der-computerspieler-in-deutschland-nach-bildungsgrad/. Accessed 13 June 2025

59. Tenzer, F.: Themenseite gaming (2022). https://de.statista.com/themen/1095/gaming/. Accessed 13 June 2025

60. Tolks, D., Lampert, C., Dadaczynski, K., Maslon, E., Paulus, P., Sailer, M.: Bundesgesundheitsblatt - Gesundheitsforschung - Gesundheitsschutz **63**(6), 698–707 (2020). https://doi.org/10.1007/s00103-020-03156-1

61. Tompkins, J., Martins, N.: Masculine pleasures as normalized practices: character design in the video game industry. Games Cult. **17**, e25481 (2021). https://doi.org/10.1177/15554120211034760

62. Trojanek, A., Fischer, H., Heinz, M.: Auf die Typen kommt es an. Eine empirische Analyse studentischer Spielertypen. In: Workshop Gemeinschaften in Neuen Medien, GeNeMe '17, pp. 137–144. TUDpress, Dresden (2017)
63. Turnbull, D., Luck, J., Chugh, R.: Learning content management systems. In: Tatnall, A. (ed.) Encyclopedia of Education and Information Technologies, pp. 1051–1051. Springer International Publishing, Cham (2020). https://doi.org/10.1007/978-3-030-10576-1_300397
64. Turulski, A.S.: Studierende in Deutschland nach Alter 2021/2022 (2023). https://de.statista.com/statistik/daten/studie/1166109/umfrage/anzahl-der-studenten-an-deutschen-hochschulen-nach-alter/. Accessed 13 June 2025
65. Tyng, C.M., Amin, H.U., Saad, M.N.M., Malik, A.S.: The influences of emotion on learning and memory. Front. Psychol. **8** (2017)
66. Ullah, M., et al.: Serious games in science education. a systematic literature review. Virtual Reality Intell. Hardware **4**(3), 189–209 (2022). https://doi.org/10.1016/j.vrih.2022.02.001
67. Weiser, M.: The computer for the 21st century. ACM SIGMOBILE Mob. Comput. Commun. Rev. **3**(3), 3–11 (1999)
68. Winter, B., et al.: High impact running improves learning. Neurobiol. Learn. Mem. **87**(4), 597–609 (2007). https://doi.org/10.1016/j.nlm.2006.11.003
69. Wouters, P., Nimwegen, C., Oostendorp, H., Spek, E.: A meta-analysis of the cognitive and motivational effects of serious games. J. Educ. Psychol. **105**, 249 (2013). https://doi.org/10.1037/a0031311

A Biofeedback-Based Integrated Game Intervention for Adolescent Stress Management

Qihui Zhou[✉], Wanyue Wang, Hongjie Ge, Yuqing Chen, and Shiguang Ni

Tsinghua University, Shenzhen Guangdong 518000, China
Lenox_Chou@163.com

Abstract. As adolescents face increasing academic, familial, and social pressures, their stress levels rise, leading to persistent emotional distress and loss of interest in activities. This issue is exacerbated by immature psychological development and poor self-regulation, resulting in higher rates of hospitalizations and dropouts. Traditional stress management interventions, such as therapist-guided techniques, often lack engagement and fail to capture the interest of adolescents. This study introduces Soul Gate, a serious game designed for adolescents aged 11–17, which integrates biofeedback technology and Self-Efficacy Theory. Utilizing the Experience, Dynamics, and Artifacts (EDA) game design framework, the game incorporates engaging mechanics and is structured around Cognitive Behavioral Stress Management (CBSM), featuring four key stages: breathing exercises, heart rate training, attention bias training, and heart rate variability regulation. By leveraging these principles, it offers an interactive self-help tool to enhance stress regulation and emotional resilience. Soul Gate employs a dual-system biofeedback approach, monitoring physiological indicators such as heart rate and brainwaves, and providing real-time adaptive feedback in games that improves player awareness and emotional management. A randomized controlled trial will assess its effectiveness, with expected outcomes demonstrating its potential as a viable intervention for reducing adolescent stress and enhancing emotional self-regulation. This study highlights the value of integrating biofeedback with gamification in mental health therapy and outlines future research directions to improve cultural adaptability and device portability.

Keywords: Biofeedback · Serious Game · Stress Management · Adolescent Mental Health

1 Introduction

As adolescents navigate growing academic, familial, and social pressures, their stress levels continue to rise. Adolescent stress involves persistent emotional distress and loss of interest in activities, exacerbated by immature psychological development, poor self-regulation, and academic pressure, rising stress level among students have led to increased hospitalizations and dropouts.

Emotional and stress management plays a crucial role in the prevention of adolescent mental health problems. Stress management aims to help adolescents identify, regulate,

J. Y. C. Chen et al. (Eds.): HCII 2025, LNCS 16338, pp. 332–350, 2026.
https://doi.org/10.1007/978-3-032-12808-9_21

and cope with various external stressors, thereby enhancing their self-regulation abilities and resilience, traditionally relying on school therapist-guided techniques like breathing exercises and muscle relaxation. There have also been attempts to present stress management through videos and animations for home-based self-practice, but often fail to engage adolescents, highlighting the need for more interactive solutions. Thus, developing more engaging and personalized therapeutic interventions has become a critical task [1].

In the design of online emotional training and stress management systems, many studies have adopted multi-modal interactive feedback methods, such as eye-tracking [2] and biofeedback. Biofeedback refers to a mechanism that detects and provides real-time feedback on various physiological data through sensors. It is commonly used in serious games to train self-awareness and emotional regulation abilities [3]. Physiological signals are more accurate and real-time compared to subjective experiences, making them widely used in physiological training processes and prognostic assessments. In systems designed to create immersive interactive experiences [4], feedback signals include galvanic skin response (GSR), electroencephalographic (EEG) activity, respiration rate, and heart rate.[5]. The integration of real-time biofeedback enhances the interactivity and immersion of training, thereby improving the quality of user experience and therapeutic outcomes [6][7].

This study addresses the limitations of traditional intervention by proposing an innovative solution that integrates serious game approaches with biofeedback technology. Soul Gate, a serious game for stress management in adolescents aged 11–17. By integrating psychological theories with game design principles, it offers an interactive self-help tool to foster stress regulation, relax skills, and positive psychological change. By leveraging the entertaining nature of video games, this approach enhances accessibility and appeal among young users.

2   Literature Review

2.1   Previous Research on Biofeedback-Game

Biofeedback is a technology that collects users' physiological signals through sensors and provides real-time feedback to the user [8]. Biofeedback has numerous therapeutic applications in helping individuals learn to achieve and regulate positive mental states, such as focused attention or relaxation [9], and has been utilized for patients with anxiety, depression, and attention-related issues. Furthermore, evidence suggests that game-based biofeedback can effectively aid in treating anxiety and depressive symptoms in children and adolescents [10].

To date, research and game product involving biofeedback-assisted relaxation training for adolescents have been growing [11]. Numerous previous studies have demonstrated that biofeedback technology can effectively reduce anxiety and stress levels in adolescents by monitoring and providing feedback on physiological indicators such as heart rate variability (HRV) and GSR. For example, Dojo (see Fig. 1), a game that integrates HRV biofeedback with emotion regulation training, has been shown to effectively help adolescents recognize and manage anxiety. Research findings indicate that Dojo is particularly effective in controlling heart rate and enhancing emotion regulation skills [12].

Fig. 1. Dojo's screenshot.

Relax to Win (see Fig. 2) is a biofeedback-enhanced video game developed by the MindGames team using the aforementioned approach. In the game, relaxation is measured by placing electrodes on the player's middle and index fingers. When the player relaxes, their dragon begins to walk, then run, and eventually take flight. If the player experiences excessive stress at any point, the dragon will descend within the cycle. Through this mechanism, players can "compete with themselves" and learn to improve their relaxation levels over time [13].

Fig. 2. Relax to Win's screenshot.

Heart Rate Variability Biofeedback (HRV-BF) is a relatively new respiratory biofeedback modality [14], designed to train heart rate oscillations to align with respiratory patterns, which can restore dysfunctional autonomic responses. Single sessions of HRV-BF have been shown to reduce anxiety levels and promote relaxation. In a study assessing the efficacy of a computer-based physiological feedback game, Journey to Wild [15], 24 children diagnosed with attention deficit hyperactivity disorder (ADHD) were included, and 35 children were taught breathing techniques from the game to control their heart rates. The experimental group exhibited a significant reduction in ADHD symptoms. Additionally, the game DEEP (see Fig. 3) promotes diaphragmatic breathing through biofeedback to provide personalized breathing and meditation support [16]. Players wear a sensor-equipped elastic band around their waist to gather respiratory data based on abdominal expansion: when a player inhales correctly, their diaphragm expands, and the sensor's resistance decreases. A microcontroller interprets the sensor readings and transmits the data to the game, which utilizes this information in various ways. Players receive real-time feedback on their breathing status through a circle that continuously expands and contracts in front of them.

Fig. 3. DEEP's screenshot.

EEG have been identified as quantifiable indicators of relaxation levels. In a neurofeedback game designed to prevent anxiety in children, MindLight [17], children use a single-channel dry sensor EEG headset to convert raw EEG values, which are then represented in the game as light emitted from their avatars' heads. The more relaxed the player becomes, the brighter the light source in the maze, using this neurofeedback mechanism to train, recognize, and alter the player's mental state (see Fig. 4).

Fig. 4. MindLight's screenshot.

In the RelaWorld system designed by Kosunen, EEG also serves as a primary biofeedback signal [18]. This system monitors users' levels of concentration and relaxation by analyzing EEG signals: as users' concentration increases, the viewpoint shifts upward, creating a sensation of floating; as users' relaxation levels rise, the energy bubbles decorating the surrounding scene become more transparent.

2.2 Theory Behind Biofeedback-Game

Biofeedback games integrate physiological feedback with interactive gaming mechanisms, providing users with a personalized and dynamically adjustable experience [19]. Currently, there is limited research on the design frameworks for biofeedback games.

Scholar Nan Chao, based on the psychological engineering paradigm of biofeedback and the framework of serious games, proposed design strategies for biofeedback games [20]. This approach maps game objectives, interactions, rules, and challenges to the five elements of the biofeedback psychological paradigm: motivational game objectives, autonomous game interactions, real-time game feedback, learnable game rules, and manageable game challenges. Each of these elements is extended into key design strategies for the games (see Fig. 5).

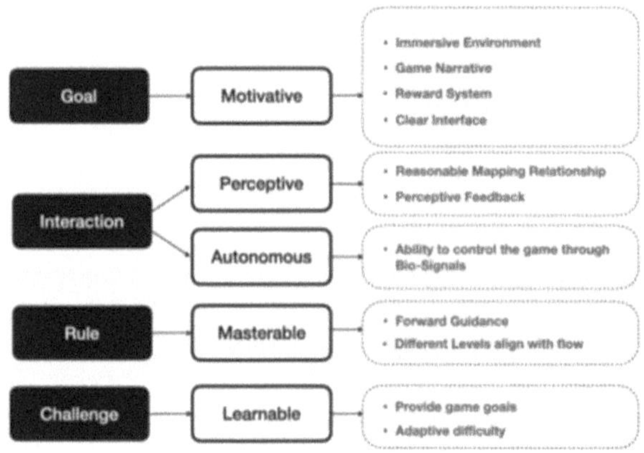

Fig. 5. Game design framework based on biofeedback psychological engineering paradigm.

Additionally, Forstner proposed a new framework from the perspective of intervention roles [21], suggesting that integrating Dynamic Difficulty Adjustment (DDA) within games can significantly enhance user experience. He developed a design framework for biofeedback games that emphasizes dynamic difficulty adjustment (see Fig. 6).

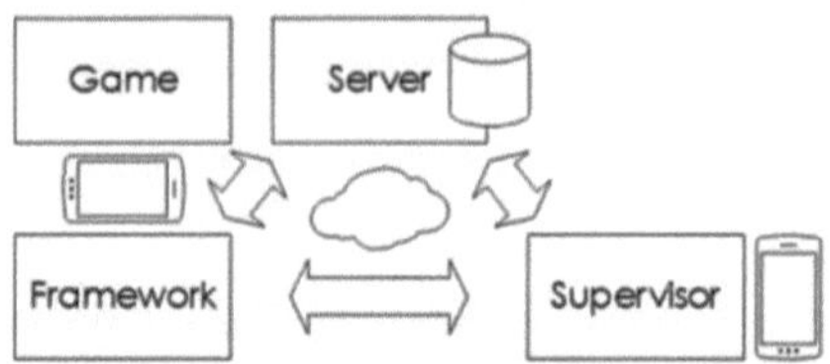

Fig. 6. Simplified architecture for biofeedback games.

This system comprises four distinct roles: the framework, the game, the manager, and the server. It is designed to adapt to various biofeedback sources. The "supervisor" role can simultaneously monitor multiple players and intervene to modify the next difficulty level in the game.

Overall, biofeedback games, as a combination of psychological regulation and entertainment experience, demonstrate significant application potential. Guided by the psychological engineering paradigm, biofeedback games not only offer users a personalized and immersive experience but also effectively promote mental health management. In the future, biofeedback games hold broad application prospects in healthcare, psychological therapy, and educational training, aiding individuals in enhancing their self-regulation abilities and mental well-being.

2.3 Self-Efficacy Theory

Self-Efficacy Theory, initially proposed by American psychologist Albert Bandura in 1977, is a core component of social cognitive theory. This theory emphasizes individuals' beliefs and expectations regarding their abilities to complete specific tasks or achieve certain goals, a belief known as self-efficacy [22]. Self-efficacy not only influences individuals' choices, effort levels, and persistence but also affects their attitudes and resilience in the face of difficulties. Bandura conducted extensive research on the factors influencing self-efficacy, identifying four pathways through which self-efficacy can be cultivated: direct experience, vicarious experience, social persuasion, and physiological and emotional states (see Fig. 7).

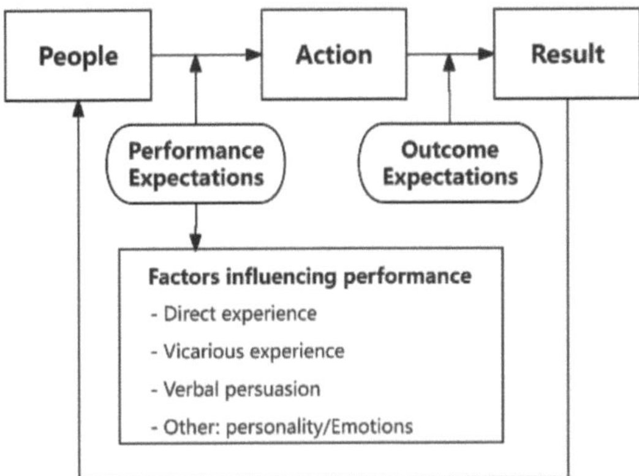

Fig. 7. The main component of self-efficacy theory.

In recent years, with the continuous development of biofeedback technology and the rise of gamification design, the application of self-efficacy in biofeedback games has gradually attracted the attention of researchers [23]. Biofeedback games assist individuals in learning to regulate and control their physiological states (such as heart rate, respiration, and galvanic skin response) through real-time monitoring and feedback, thereby achieving goals such as relaxation, stress reduction, or improved attention [24]. In this process, self-efficacy plays a crucial role [25].

In the study conducted by Weerdmeester, the application of self-efficacy in the biofeedback video game DEEP was explored [26]. AS mentioned above, DEEP is a virtual reality-based biofeedback game in which players navigate a mysterious underwater world through deep breathing. The research found that players with higher self-efficacy were better able to control their emotions and physiological responses. This indicates that self-efficacy in biofeedback games not only predicts players' physiological regulation abilities but may also further enhance the effects of physiological regulation by boosting players' confidence and sense of control. Self-Efficacy Theory may influence biofeedback games through the following mechanisms:

Predicting Biofeedback Regulation Effects. Self-efficacy predicts therapeutic outcomes in biofeedback games, where players use strategies to improve their physiological states. Those with high self-efficacy are more confident in mastering skills and achieving goals, maintaining motivation and effectively utilizing biofeedback for self-regulation.

Enhancing Perception of Control. Self-efficacy is linked to locus of control [27]. In biofeedback games, players receive real-time physiological feedback, helping them assess their ability to control their physiological states. Successful regulation, such as transitioning from tension to relaxation, enhances their internal locus of control and boosts self-efficacy.

Improving Self-Regulation Abilities. Self-regulation abilities are strongly related to self-efficacy. Biofeedback games provide real-time data (e.g., heart rate), allowing players to monitor and reflect on their physiological states. Feedback that connects effort and ability to performance boosts self-efficacy and motivation, improving self-regulation abilities. Studies show that regulating physiological indicators, such as lowering heart rates, significantly enhances self-efficacy, leading to increased motivation and behavioral change [28].

In summary, the application of Self-Efficacy Theory in biofeedback games not only reveals the psychological mechanisms underlying players' self-regulation abilities but also provides important insights for game design. Future biofeedback game designs should fully consider players' self-efficacy, enhancing their confidence and sense of control by optimizing game difficulty, providing timely feedback, and encouraging players, thereby further improving the therapeutic efficacy and user experience of the games.

2.4 EDA Theory

The EDA (Experience, Dynamics, Artifacts) model, proposed by scholar Natucci, aims to provide a comprehensive framework for serious games designed for educational purposes [29], emphasizing the integration of learning and entertainment to enhance players' learning and enjoyment experiences. This model integrates learning theories and game mechanics to propose a design process centered around the game loop (see Fig. 8). The core idea of the EDA model is to provide feedback mechanisms through dynamic interactions in the game, while incorporating learning elements into the player experience, effectively combining the entertainment and educational functions of the game.

In the EDA loop, players interact with artifacts, which triggers emergent behaviors in the dynamics, and then players interpret these dynamics within their experience, forming a complete game loop. Compared to the traditional MDA (Mechanics, Dynamics, Aesthetics) model [30], the EDA model incorporates stronger learning elements and continuously optimizes player feedback through the game loop. This integrative design not only enhances player engagement but also effectively supports the conveyance of educational content, thereby advancing the practical development of serious game design.

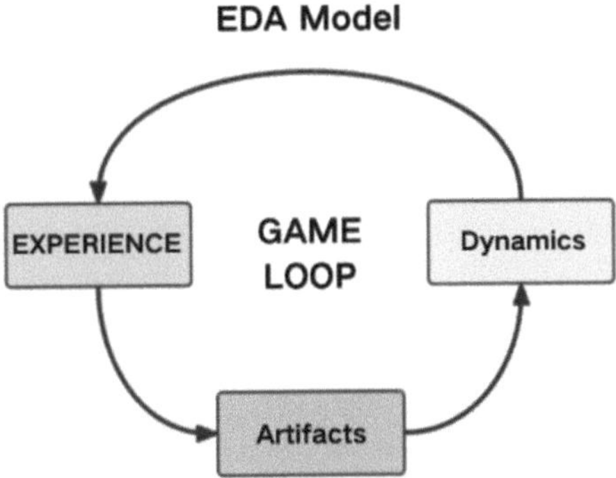

Fig. 8. The EDA Model.

3 Related Work

Creating user personas based on target users before game development is crucial, as it provides numerous benefits for the game development team [31]. User personas help the team clearly define the target audience for the game, including information about their age, gender, interests, gaming experience, and more, ensuring that the game's design, content, and features align with the needs and preferences of the intended audience.

In the early design phase of Soul Gate, a comprehensive survey was conducted focusing on adolescents as the core target player group to better understand their preferences and guide the game's design direction. The survey covered multiple aspects, including basic information about adolescents, stress levels, sources of stress, preferred game genres, artistic style preferences, scene preferences, music preferences, and their understanding of emotions and stress. This series of questions aimed to help the team outline the target user persona, ensuring that the game content, visual style, and interactive experience meet the needs of adolescents.

The survey was conducted offline, visiting two junior high schools in Longgang District, Shenzhen, where a class of students was randomly selected for game testing. After the testing, feedback collection questionnaires were distributed to them. A total of 88 valid questionnaires were collected after screening, with most respondents aged between 12 and 15 years, the following Table 1 gives a summary of user's basic information.

Table 1. Summary of Demographic characteristics of the sample (N = 88).

Age	Male	Female	Total
12	48.57% (17)	51.42% (18)	5.45% (35)
13	50.00% (5)	50.00% (5)	58.18% (10)
14	59.26% (16)	40.74% (11)	15.45% (27)
15	75.00% (12)	25.00% (4)	20.91% (16)
Total	50	38	88

3.1   Results on Game

Statistical analysis results indicate that the target users show a strong preference for "building" gameplay types, which received the highest proportion of responses. This suggests that adolescent users are more inclined towards creative and personalized gaming experiences, enjoying the sense of achievement that comes from constructing their own virtual worlds. Following this, "puzzle" and "collection" gameplay types were also popular, indicating their interest in exploratory and challenging content, as they seek the joy of discovery within games.

In terms of art style, adolescent users preferred the "flat 2D" visual style, which is well-received for its clean and vibrant presentation, outpacing options like "3D low-poly" or "pixel art." Additionally, there was a strong preference for game environments, with the most popular choice being "fantasy space." This demonstrates that adolescents are inclined to immerse themselves in fantastical, surreal virtual worlds, seeking experiences that are fun and novel, distinct from real life. Moreover, the analysis of music style preferences revealed that adolescents have significant needs regarding their gaming experience. They expect the background music of games to align with emotional expression and emotional regulation functions, helping them immerse themselves better in the game atmosphere.

These insights provide strong design rationale for "Soul Gate," allowing the team to optimize aspects such as emotional regulation, atmosphere creation, and immersive experiences. Overall, this survey offers data support for the game's overall design direction, ensuring that the developed game aligns with the preferences and expectations of adolescent users.

3.2   Results on Stress

In addition, the questionnaire also surveyed players' stress levels. According to the statistics (see Fig. 9), 66% of adolescents reported feeling stressed "once or twice a day," while 27% indicated that they "often feel stressed throughout the day." Only 7% of players stated that they "never feel stressed at all." These data suggest that the vast majority of adolescents experience varying degrees of stress in their daily lives, and the frequency of this stress is relatively high.

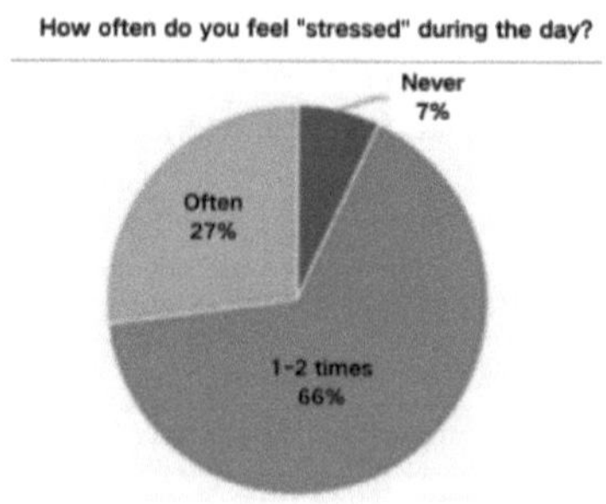

Fig. 9. Results of user stress situations.

The survey also explored the causes of stress among adolescents and their common stress-relief methods. Results showed nearly 40% of users cited "school exams" as their primary stress source, followed by "subject assignments" (13%). For stress relief, 25% of participants preferred "playing games," with "sleeping" (24%), "eating" (23%), and "watching TV" (16%) also popular choices, highlighting video games as a key stress-relief method for adolescents.

Lastly, the survey assessed players' attitudes toward "biofeedback" and "stress management." Results revealed that 93% of adolescents wanted "Soul Gate" to include emotional soothing and relaxation exercises, 99% were willing to try stress-relief games, and 98% supported incorporating physiological monitoring in the game.

This small-scale survey reveals that adolescents frequently experience stress, primarily from "school work". To cope, they often turn to games for emotional relief, highlighting their role in stress reduction. The survey also shows strong interest in integrating emotional regulation and stress management features into games, with a positive attitude toward incorporating biofeedback, offering clear support and design guidance for developing biofeedback-based stress management game.

4   Game Design and Technology

4.1   Construction of the Serious Game Design Framework

Based on theoretical research and analysis of successful cases, this study proposes a construction approach for a serious game design framework focused on stress management using biofeedback technology (see Fig. 10). First, the main theoretical systems applied are identified: biofeedback technology, self-efficacy theory, and the EDA serious game design theory. Additionally, a user profile targeting domestic adolescents is described to provide reference for gameplay design, game narrative design, and game process design. Second, from a practical perspective, an in-depth analysis of multiple successful cases of serious games based on biofeedback is conducted, summarizing their strengths and deficiencies, as well as the guidelines and authoritative frameworks to be followed in subsequent designs. Finally, the game process design is established based on the standards of cognitive-behavioral stress management manuals and methods used in actual therapeutic processes.

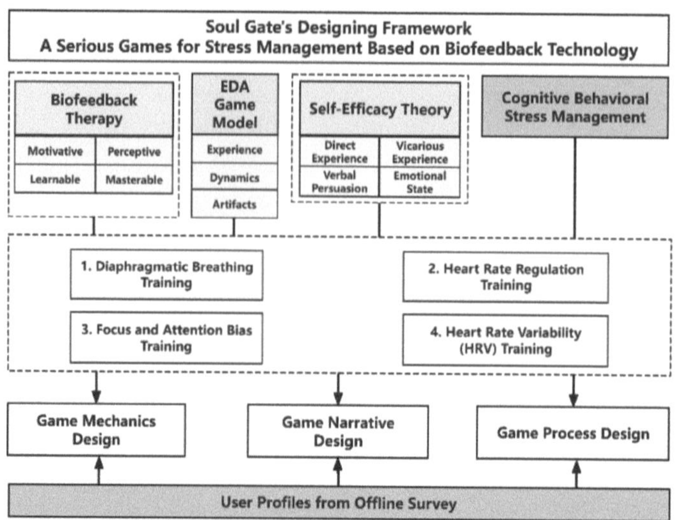

Fig. 10. Soul Gate's Designing Framework.

4.2 Biofeedback Mechanism Design

Signal Acquisition and Processing. The overall architecture of the system's data channel is shown in Fig. 11, where respiratory and heart rate data are obtained through serial communication. The communication format is set according to the technical documents of the sensor devices, sending a signal to the sensor to start transmission and setting the data amplitude. Once transmission begins, raw data is collected in byte array format, and the second data bit is checked according to the communication protocol in the document. In order to ensure both the accuracy of the sensors and the comfort of the players wearing them [32][33][34], this study uses a stretchable band as the tool for collecting respiratory signals. The HKH-11C model respiratory sensor and the HKX-08C model digital heart rate sensor produced by the Hefei Huake Electronic Technology Research Institute were selected, along with the BrianLink Pro headband produced by Shenzhen Hongzhili Technology Co., Ltd.

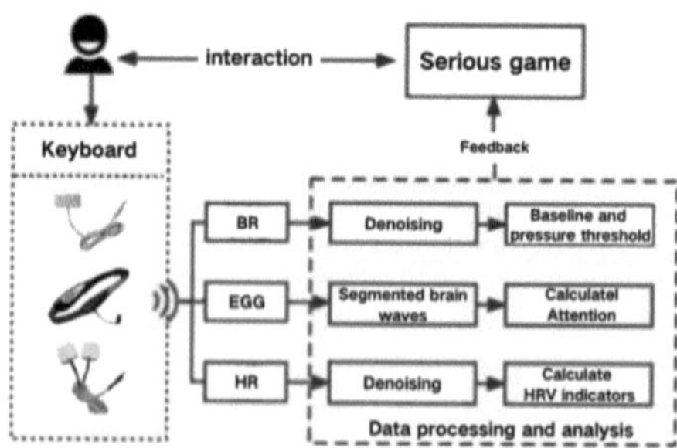

Fig. 11. The overall architecture of the system's data channel.

Signal and Game Interaction Design Strategies. This study draws on strategies for biofeedback and game interaction mentioned in previous research [35], including direct control and indirect control [36].

Direct Interaction Strategy. The direct interaction strategy focuses on directly mapping players' physiological signals to game mechanics, allowing for intuitive and immediate feedback on player control. The specific approach is as follows: Physiological responses are captured in real-time through physiological sensors, and these responses are directly translated into actions or effects in the game. For example, players can adjust their breathing rhythm to change the size of targets in the game or control jump height through leg muscle activity. This mapping enables players to intuitively feel the impact of their physiological state on the game, enhancing interactivity and immersion.

In this level, when adolescents face tense or stressful situations, their heart rate typically exceeds 100 BPM, sometimes reaching 120–150 BPM, indicating that the body is in a "fight or flight" response state. In the design of the second level of Soul Gate, the player is placed in a desert where the player's 'moisture value' is depleted over time, and the player will die when the 'moisture value' reaches 0 (see Fig. 12). "Dew" is the only source of moisture in this scene, and when the player's heart rate exceeds 20% of the baseline heart rate, the rate of 'moisture value' consumption increases. At this point, the player has two options: move quickly across the terrain in search of more "Dew", or force themselves to stabilize their heart rate to reduce the consumption rate of their " moisture value". This design enhances the immediate experience while training the player to self-regulate under pressure.

Fig. 12. Soul Gate's screenshot: player's moisture value and dew.

Indirect Interaction Strategy. Compared to the direct interaction strategy, the indirect interaction strategy relies more on the player's physiological state to dynamically adjust the game environment or mechanics, rather than directly mapping physiological signals to game actions. Physiological sensors monitor the player's physiological status, and the visual representation of physiological data or the game environment is dynamically adjusted based on these states. For example, in Soul Gate, the player is defined as having the ability to control the changes of this game world within their body. The breathing is represented by the particle effects in the game, and players can immediately understand their breathing status through the size of the particle. As shown in Fig. 13, in implementation, the size and color of the particle are determined by the backend, which identifies the "starting point" and "ending point" of the breath.

Fig. 13. Soul Gate's screenshot: the particle change represents the player's breathing state.

4.3 Game Narrative Design

Based on the preliminary player research and self-efficacy theory, several guidelines should be established for the narrative before officially beginning the scriptwriting.

Use Relatable Daily Scenarios as the Foundation of the Storyline. To foster immersion and lasting appeal, the game narrative design is key. In player research, 40% emphasized the importance of "narrative immersion." Flow theory in game design also highlights the link between player challenges and emotions [37]. Soul Gate avoids fixed "character settings," allowing players to uncover the truth and rebuild their self-identity through personal experiences and exploration. It also incorporates everyday school scenarios, enhancing relatability and immersing players in their characters' internal struggles and growth. This approach not only boosts immersion but also keeps the narrative full of surprises, encouraging continued exploration [32].

The Game Guide Will Assume the Role of "Verbal Persuasion". Self-efficacy theory highlights "verbal persuasion" as a key factor in improving self-efficacy, where guidance, suggestions, and encouragement from others help individuals build confidence. Receiving consistent care and support, especially from authoritative figures, strengthens self-efficacy [28]. In the game, players' self-perceptions are shaped by the evaluations of other characters. Thus, the role of guide in game, "Spirit Cat", plays a crucial role in the narrative (see Fig. 14). Before challenges, it provides clear explanations and suggestions; during challenges, it offers regular encouragement and feedback. After success, it emphasizes rewards and praise, and after failure, it helps players make positive "attributions," subtly enhancing their self-efficacy.

Fig. 14. "Spirit Cat" of Soul Gate.

Integrate clear game rules and biofeedback guidance into the narrative. Nan Chao's design strategy for biofeedback games emphasizes "progressive guidance," allowing players to learn through gameplay. The rules should be clear and concise, enabling quick understanding and application. To achieve this, each "trial arena" level starts with comprehensive materials, including text instructions and animated references. These materials explain biofeedback concepts, methods, and their application within the game, ensuring players can effectively learn and practice. This creates a seamless learning path from theory to practice, fostering deep engagement and experiential learning.

4.4 Game Process Design

As shown in Table 2, this study selected four typical practices suitable for gamified biofeedback from the actual processes outlined in the "Cognitive Behavioral Stress Management Manual (CBSM)" and common biofeedback training content: diaphragmatic breathing, stabilizing heart rate, enhancing focus, and HRV. These practices serve as the foundational content for the game, comprising the four main levels, which are ultimately connected into a complete game flow through narrative design.

The game process is divided into five levels. The level 1 starts with the storyline, introducing the characters, worldview, and challenge settings. The aim is to allow players to quickly engage with the narrative of the first phase while establishing the tone for ongoing exploration throughout the game, enhancing the intrinsic motivation for players to play this game while reduces players' perceptions of the game as a therapeutic tool. Levels 2–5 are designed based on the corresponding training content and narrative dialogues outlined in the CBSM, incorporating content that combines biofeedback technology with gameplay and clearing objectives. Moreover, Soul Gate treats levels 2–5 as mutually independent levels, allowing players to choose to repeatedly experience one relaxation training or to progress through the game levels in the recommended sequence.

Table 2. The game process of Soul Gate.

Level	Scene	Goal	Content	Signal	Time
1	Lost Place	Establish Basic Settings	Character Setting, Basic Concepts of Biofeedback	-	3 min
2	Nest of Demon	Breathing Training	Basic Techniques of Diaphragmatic Breathing	BR	8-10 min
3	Wasteland	Heart Rate Training	Perceive the Relationship Between Heartbeat and Relaxation	HR	8-10 min
4	Yellow Tomb	Focus Training	Observe the Changes in Objects Caused by Attention	EGG	6-8 min

(*continued*)

Table 2. (continued)

Level	Scene	Goal	Content	Signal	Time
5	Underwater	HRV-BF Training	Breathe at an Appropriate Frequency and Speed	HR	10-12 min

4.5 Technical Details

The game was developed using Unity, with the specific logic scripts being written in C#. Unity is a cross-platform game engine that can be used to develop 2D and 3D games, AR and VR applications, and more. It provides an easy-to-use development environment, including a visual editor, scripting tools, and plugins, enabling developers to easily create complex games and applications.

During the project development process, Notion was used for information synchronization, project management, and meeting records. Github was utilized for storing and managing the project's source code. GitHub is a hosting platform for open-source and private software projects, offering advantages such as being free, easy to use, and supporting content recording and version rollback for each uploaded version. The development process employed an agile iteration methodology, and some of the artistic and musical assets in the game were selected from commercially available resources.

Additionally, Fig. 15 presents the system mechanism framework of this study, referencing the framework proposed by Forstner. During gameplay, physiological data such as HR, breathing, and EGG are collected in real-time through different sensors and transmitted to the framework (in this game, the game controller) via wireless or wired methods. Once the program receives the data, it transmits the data to the mobile device held by the supervisor for storage. At the same time, the program processes and calculates the raw signals, assessing the player's current physiological state and making further adjustments to the game difficulty. In addition to real-time monitoring of various physiological data on the mobile device, the supervisor can also perform basic processing of this data to obtain reports on the player's emotional and stress state, as well as intervention guidance based on data analysis. If necessary, the supervisor can decide to pause or restart the game, creating a dynamic game loop.

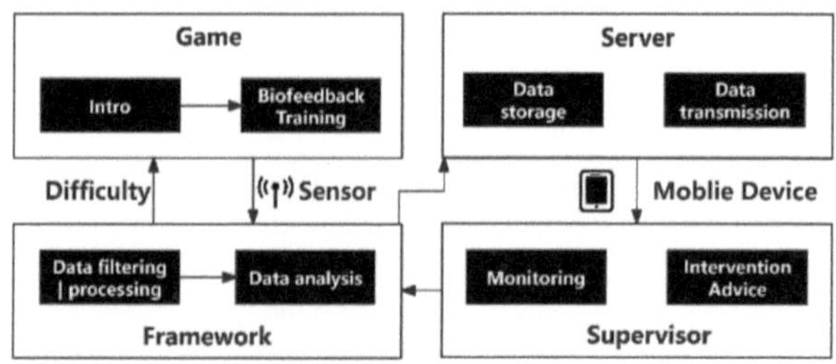

Fig. 15. Framework of biofeedback mechanics of Soul Gate.

5 User Study and Discussion

To evaluate the effectiveness of Soul Gate, a randomized controlled trial (RCT) will be conducted. We will recruit 30–50 adolescent participants from a High School in China, randomly assigned to either an experimental or control group. During the RCT, we'll divide participants into three control groups: The biofeedback game group (subjects need to play the game completely, for about 40 min), the non-biofeedback game group (subjects need to play the game completely without all biofeedback mechanisms, for about 40 min), and the traditional video group (subjects need to perform stress management training according to the video, and the content and order of the exercises are consistent with the game. The whole course is about 40 min), each of them will intervene, and the results will be analyzed and discussed from the following three perspectives:

RQ1: How effective are the game's interaction strategies and the quality of the game's dimensions? What's the player experience like?

RQ2: Does the game have a significant effect on increasing stress levels and improving emotional state? How does it compare to traditional interventions?

RQ3: Does the addition of biofeedback affect the intervention effect? What is the influencing mechanism?

Assessments will be conducted using standardized measures like Brief Resilience Scale (BRS) [38], General Self-Efficacy Scale (GSES) [39], and The Positive and Negative Affect Scale, PANAS (PANAS-C) [40]. Game quality will be evaluated using the System Usability Scale (SUS) [41] and the Game Engagement Questionnaire (GEQ) [42]. Participants will complete pre- and post-intervention assessments to measure their resilience, self-efficacy, and emotional state, alongside tracking their game experience. Expected outcomes include demonstrating the game's potential as a viable intervention for reducing adolescent stress and enhancing emotional self-regulation. We expect that the biofeedback game group will show a more significant improvement in stress management ability and emotional regulation compared to both the non-biofeedback game and traditional video groups, meanwhile we can prove that compared with traditional intervention, the form of games is more appealing to adolescent.

6 Conclusion

This study integrates biofeedback and serious game research into a practical intervention for adolescent stress management. By providing an engaging, accessible tool for emotional regulation, it advances mental health therapy and underscores the potential of biofeedback and gamification in building resilience and well-being, highlight insights for further development in both serious game design and therapeutic applications.

While valuable, this study has several limitations that provide important directions for future research. One key area for improvement is the enhancement of cultural adaptability, ensuring that the design of biofeedback games is responsive to diverse cultural contexts and aligns with the specific needs and preferences of various adolescent populations across the globe. Additionally, future research should focus on improving the portability and accessibility of biofeedback devices, making them more user-friendly and suitable for widespread use in everyday settings, as well as ensuring they can be easily integrated into a variety of technological platforms. Furthermore, there is a need for the development of standardized frameworks for the implementation and evaluation of serious games in the context of mental health, which will allow for more robust comparisons across studies and improve the overall effectiveness of these interventions.

By expanding the application of serious games in adolescent psychological interventions, this research aspires to make a significant contribution to the academic discourse, offering innovative insights into the potential of serious games not only as tools for stress management and emotional regulation but also as a promising approach to advancing human psychological well-being. Ultimately, these efforts aim to support the integration of serious games into broader mental health strategies, thereby creating more accessible and engaging solutions to improve psychological health.

References

1. Bischke, C., Debnath, N.: Biofeedback implementation in a video game environment. In: International Conference on Information Technology: New Generations, IEEE Computer Society (2014)
2. 李玖菊: 心智化家庭治疗对青少年抑郁障碍的疗效评估及神经机制研究. 华北理工大学 (2020)
3. Fernandez, J.A., Maes, P., Richer, A.: Deep reality: An underwater VR experience to promote relaxation by unconscious HR, EDA, and brain activity biofeedback. In: ACM SIGGRAPH 2019 Virtual, Augmented, and Mixed Reality. ACM (2019)
4. Tozzi, F., Nicolaidou, I., Galani, A., Antoniades, A.: EHealth interventions for anxiety management targeting young children and adolescents. JMIR Pediatr Parent. 1(1), e5 (2018)
5. 张玲, 胡华: 儿童青少年情绪障碍与家庭关系的研究进展. 神经疾病与精神卫生. 18(11), 806–809 (2018)
6. Jnox, M., Lentini, J., Cummings, T.S., et al.: Game-based biofeedback for paediatric anxiety and depression. Mental Health Family Medicine. 8(3), 195–203 (2011)
7. Dillon, A., Kelly, M., Robertson, I.H., et al.: Smartphone applications utilizing biofeedback can aid stress reduction. Front. Psychol. 7, 832 (2016)
8. Lehrer, P.M., Vaschillo, E., Vaschillo, B.: Resonant frequency biofeedback training to increase cardiac variability: Rationale and manual for training. Appl. Psychophysiol. Biofeedback 25(3), 177–191 (2000)
9. Zafar, M.A., Ahmed, B., Rihawi, R.A.: Gaming away stress: Using biofeedback games to learn paced breathing. IEEE Transactions on Affective Computing (2020)
10. Alexandra, K., Mirjana, P., Riecke, B.E.: Immersive interactive technologies for positive change: A scoping review and design considerations. Front. Psychol. 9, 1354 (2018)
11. Huang, Y.-C., Luk, C.-H.: Heartbeat Jenga: A biofeedback board game to improve coordination and emotional control. In: Interacción (2015)
12. Schuurmans, A.A.T., Nijhof, K.S., Vermaes, I.P.R., et al.: A pilot study evaluating 'Dojo', a videogame intervention for youths with externalizing and anxiety problems. Games for Health Journal. 4(5), 1–8 (2015)
13. Sharry, J., Mcdermott, M., Condron, J.: 'Relax to Win' - Treating children with anxiety problems with a biofeedback video game. Eisteach (2003)
14. Rockstroh, J.G.A.S.: Virtual reality in the application of heart rate variability biofeedback. Int. J. Hum. Comput. Stud. 130 (2019)
15. Mattulich, L., Paperny, D. M.: Biofeedback. Encyclopedia of Quality of Life and Well-Being Research, 401–405 (2014)

16. Rooij, M. et al.: DEEP: A biofeedback virtual reality game for children at-risk for anxiety. ACM (2016)
17. Schoneveld, E.A., Malmberg, M., Lichtwarck-Aschoff, A., et al.: A neurofeedback video game (MindLight) to prevent anxiety in children: A randomized controlled trial. Comput. Hum. Behav. **63**(10), 321–333 (2016)
18. Kosunen, I. et al.: RelaWorld: Neuroadaptive and Immersive Virtual Reality Meditation System. IUI (2016)
19. Gaume, A., Vialatte, A., Mora-Sánchez, A., et al.: A psychoengineering paradigm for the neurocognitive mechanisms of biofeedback and neurofeedback. Neurosci. Biobehav. Rev. **68**, 891–910 (2016)
20. Chao, N., Huang, W., Wang, X.: Design of a respiratory biofeedback serious game for stress management based on HRV analysis. HCII 2023. CCIS. **9**(7), 16–24 (2023)
21. Forstner, B., et al.: A general framework for innovative mobile biofeedback based educational games. In: IEEE 4th International Conference on Cognitive Infocommunications (CogInfoCom), 775–778 (2013)
22. Bandura, A.: Self-efficacy: toward a unifying theory of behavioral change. Adv. Behav. Res. Ther. **1**(4), 139–161 (1977)
23. Hofmann, S.G., Smits, J.A.J.: Cognitive-behavioral therapy for adult anxiety disorders: A meta-analysis of randomized placebo-controlled trials. J. Clin. Psychiatry **69**(4), 621–632 (2008)
24. Diclemente, C.C., Fairhurst, S.K., Piotrowski, N.A.: Self-Efficacy and Addictive Behaviors. Springer, US (1995)
25. Benight, C.C., Bandura, A.: Social cognitive theory of posttraumatic recovery: The role of perceived self-efficacy. Behav. Res. Ther. **42**(10), 1129–1148 (2004)
26. Weerdmeester, J. et al.: Exploring the role of self-efficacy in biofeedback video games. In: Annual Symposium on Computer-Human Interaction in Play. ACM (2017)
27. van Rooij, M.M.J.W., Granic, I.: Visualization, Self-Efficacy, and Locus of Control in a Virtual Reality Biofeedback Video Game for Anxiety Regulation. Cyberpsychol. Behav. Soc. Netw. **25**(6), 360–368 (2022)
28. Doménech, P., Tur-Porcar, A.M., Mestre-Escrivá, V.: Emotion regulation and self-efficacy: The mediating role of emotional stability and extraversion in adolescence. Behav. Sci. **14**(3), 206 (2024)
29. Natucci, G.C., Borges, M.A.F.: The experience, dynamics and artifacts framework: Towards a holistic model for designing serious and entertainment games. In: IEEE Conference on Games (CoG), Copenhagen, Denmark, pp. 1–8 (2021)
30. Hunicke, R., Leblanc, M.G., Zubek, R.: MDA: A Formal Approach to Game Design and Game Research (2004)
31. Kaistinen, J.: User Experience in Digital Games: Differences between laboratory and home. Simulation & Gaming. **42** (2011)
32. Price, S.: The screenplay: Authorship, theory and criticism. Palgrave (2010)
33. Shaw, C.D., Gromala, D., Seay, A.F.: The meditation chamber: Enacting autonomic senses. In: Proceedings of ENACTIVE 7, 405–408 (2007)
34. Patibanda, R. et al.: Life tree: Understanding the design of breathing exercise games. In: Proceedings of the Annual Symposium on Computer-Human Interaction in Play, pp. 19–31 (2017)
35. Wu, D. et al.: Optimal Arousal Identification and Classification for Affective Computing Using Physiological Signals: Virtual Reality Stroop Task. IEEE Transactions on Affective Computing 2 (2010)
36. Zafar, M.A. et al.: Gaming Away Stress: Using Biofeedback Games to Learn Paced Breathing. IEEE Transactions on Affective Computing 1–1 (2018)

37. Csikszentmihalyi, M.: 心流: 最优体验心理学. 中信出版社 (2017)
38. Smith, B.W., Dalen, J., Wiggins, K., et al.: The Brief Resilience Scale: Assessing the Ability to Bounce Back. Int. J. Behav. Med. **15**(3), 194–200 (2008)
39. Schwarzer, R., Jerusalem, M.: General Self-Efficacy Scale (GSE). Outcomes Measurement Tool: Attitudes & Feelings - Self-Efficacy (1995)
40. Watson, D., Clark, L.A., Tellegen, A.: Development and validation of brief measures of positive and negative affect: The PANAS scales. J. Pers. Soc. Psychol. **54**(6), 1063–1070 (1988)
41. Brooke, J.: SUS: A retrospective. J. Usability Stud. **8**(2), 29–40 (2013)
42. Brockmyer, J.H., Fox, C.M., Curtiss, K.A., McBroom, E., Burkhart, K.M., Pidruzny, J.N.: The development of the game engagement questionnaire: A measure of engagement in video game-playing. J. Exp. Soc. Psychol. **45**(4), 624–634 (2009)

"To Feel, Not to Tell": Using Experiential Metaphors in Game Narrative as a Method for Cognitive Enhancement

Yishan Duan, Jialu Ni$^{(\boxtimes)}$, Xuezhu Wang, Yao Lu, and Xiaohan Dong

Tsinghua University, Beijing 100084, China
2362843204@qq.com

Abstract. Metaphor plays a crucial role in how humans understand abstract concepts by mapping concrete experiences from a source domain onto a target domain. As an interactive and multimodal medium, digital games offer unique potential for conveying metaphor through procedural rules and immersive experience. However, many existing games rely heavily on narrative rather than embodied interaction, limiting their ability to stimulate cognitive reflection. This study proposes a design framework for experiential metaphor in games, grounded in situated cognition theory. Based on this framework, we developed Subway Migration, an immersive prototype that explores themes such as social structure, identity, and control through spatial loops and role transitions. A small-scale user study was conducted with participants from design and psychology backgrounds, using a mixed-methods approach that included pre-/post-questionnaires and semi-structured interviews. Results suggest that the game enhances players' cognitive awareness, enriches their sensory experience, and encourages reflective engagement. This work provides practical guidance for integrating metaphor into game design and demonstrates the potential of experiential metaphor to support deeper player meaning-making and critical thinking within interactive environments.

Keywords: experiential metaphor · game design · situated cognition · cognitive reflection · metaphor mapping

1 Introduction

In the field of cognitive science, metaphor has long been recognized as a core mechanism through which humans understand abstract concepts. [1] By mapping concrete experiences from a source domain onto a target domain, metaphors not only reduce cognitive load but also evokes cross-modal emotional resonance. Metaphor, therefore, is not merely a rhetorical device, but a fundamental cognitive tool that shapes human thinking, perception, and communication. It enables the effective expression of complex and serious issues across cognitive, emotional, and communicative dimensions.

Y. Duan and J. Ni—Equal contribution.

J. Y. C. Chen et al. (Eds.): HCII 2025, LNCS 16338, pp. 351–367, 2026.
https://doi.org/10.1007/978-3-032-12808-9_22

As an interactive medium, games have increasingly become a means for simulating reality, exploring internal states, and constructing systems of meaning. At their core, games convey meaning through procedural rhetoric—that is, the use of rules and mechanics to express arguments and ideologies [2]. Examples such as SimCity, which simulates urban systems, or Foldit, which transforms protein folding into gameplay, show that when metaphorical design aligns with cognitive principles, players' behavior within the "magic circle" [3] can translate into meaningful cognitive reconstruction. This transformation has been shown to outperform traditional methods in educational and training contexts [4].

Despite the proven value of metaphor in game-based learning, several challenges remain:Many games still rely heavily on narrative telling rather than embodied experience, which undermines the multimodal cognitive potential of games and often limits players to surface-level understanding.There is a lack of systematic frameworks for mapping metaphorical elements, classifying metaphor types, and aligning them with cognitive mechanisms, which hinders the effective application of metaphor in gameplay.

These issues not only impact the design of meaningful gameplay experiences but also constrain the player's ability to engage in deeper reflective thinking and symbolic reasoning.

To address these challenges, and building on existing research in metaphor, game design, and situated cognition, we propose a design framework for experiential metaphor in games. Based on this framework, we developed an immersive interactive prototype.

The main contributions of this paper are as follows:

(1) Design Methodology: We propose a metaphorical game design framework grounded in situated cognition theory, identifying three primary types of metaphorical mappings. The framework supports designers in constructing experiential metaphors that prompt players to engage in reflective thought.
(2) Implementation: We applied this framework in the development of Subway Migration, an immersive metaphorical game exploring social structure, identity, and control dynamics.
(3) Evaluation: We conducted a small-scale user study using a mixed-methods approach (pre-/post-questionnaires and semi-structured interviews). Results indicate that the game effectively enhances players' cognitive awareness, enriches the sensory experience, and fosters reflective engagement.

This paper first reviews relevant theoretical foundations. It then introduces the experiential metaphor game design framework, followed by a detailed explanation of the design and development of Subway Migration. We then describe the evaluation methods and results, and conclude with a discussion of the findings and potential directions for future research.

2   Theoretical Background and Related Work

2.1   Metaphor Theory and Game Narratives

In the increasingly diverse context of digital media, metaphors are no longer understood merely as a rhetorical ornament of language, but rather as a fundamental tool for cognition and world understanding. Lakoff and Johnson famously argued that "metaphor is the essence of our thought," emphasizing that metaphor exists not only in language but is deeply embedded in our conceptual system. It shapes how we perceive, comprehend, and construct reality [1].

Building upon this perspective, Forceville introduced the concept of multimodal metaphor, highlighting that metaphor can be constructed not only through language, but also via the integration of various modalities such as visuals, gestures, and sound. [5] Within this framework, digital games—due to their inherent capacity for multimodal integration—are particularly well-suited for metaphorical representation and construction. Incorporating metaphor into game design is therefore not merely an artistic choice for narrative expression, but also an effective pathway for cognitive construction and psychological processing. Games, in this light, are not just entertainment media, but ideal arenas for metaphor-based cognition [6].

2.2   Situated Cognition Theory

Situated cognition theory emphasizes that individual cognitive activity does not occur in isolation from the environment but is deeply embedded within specific social, cultural, and physical contexts. [7] Knowledge is not a static, transferable internal content, but a capacity that is generated and applied through continuous interaction with the environment. This theoretical perspective provides crucial support for understanding experiential metaphors in gameplay: players construct meaning dynamically through engagement with virtual environments, embodied actions, social cues, and visual symbols. [8,9] As a highly contextualized and interactive medium, games naturally align with key tenets of situated cognition theory, such as learning by doing and the integration of knowing and acting. They offer a dynamic, concrete, and immersive cognitive pathway for comprehending complex concepts and facilitating cognitive transformation [10].

3   Game Design: Theoretical Framework

3.1   Three Primary Mapping Strategies in Metaphor Design

In metaphor cognition theory, Lakoff and Johnson (1980) proposed the concept of structural metaphor, which emphasizes that humans understand complex phenomena by mapping the structure of a familiar conceptual domain onto a more abstract one (see Fig. 1).

Building on this foundation, the present study categorizes metaphor design in games into three primary mapping pathways: audiovisual mapping, interactional mapping, and narrative mapping. Based on these three metaphorical mapping approaches, we constructed a design framework for immersive gameplay and applied it in practice [1].

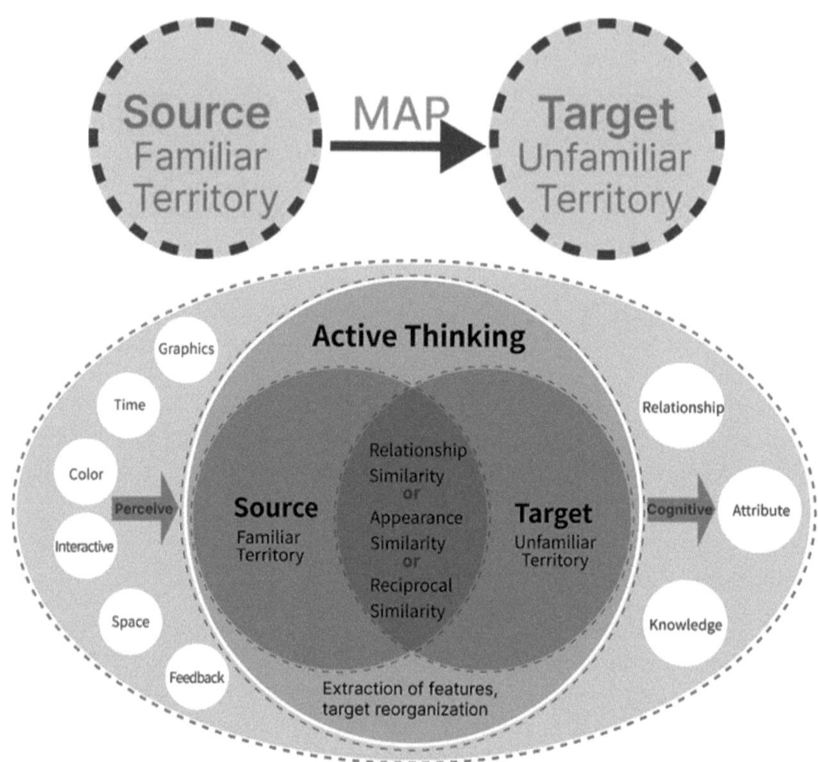

Fig. 1. How people understand new things through structural metaphors.

(1) audiovisual mapping: As the most immediate and foundational mapping tool, audiovisual metaphor enables players to form concrete metaphorical associations through their perception of color, sound, imagery, and other sensory symbols. This mapping facilitates the linkage between emotional perception and narrative concepts. Games enriched with audiovisual elements are more likely to attract players and enhance their overall gameplay experience. [11,12] The cognitive basis for audiovisual metaphor design in games lies in the embodied nature of human cognition, which posits that abstract concepts originate from concrete bodily experiences. This perspective provides a solid theoretical foundation for designing perceptual metaphors in gameplay. Through elements such as color schemes, spatial arrangements, and auditory cues, designers can evoke symbolic meanings grounded in players' bodily experiences—enabling players to feel the meaning rather than merely know the concept [6,13,14].

(2) interactional mapping: Compared to static audiovisual metaphors, interactive metaphors link players' embodied experiences with game mechanics, allowing players to construct metaphorical meanings through actions such as triggering events, exploration, and trial-and-error. This mapping depends on player agency and the interactive feedback loop, characterized by its procedural, individualized, and generative nature. [13,15] Interactive mapping not only serves as a medium for metaphorical transmission but also constitutes a core pathway for meaning construction. [16] In immersive narrative games, interactive mapping stimulates players' internal cognitive processing through behavioral experience, enhancing their embodied understanding and reflection on abstract social issues. Consequently, game metaphors shift from being "images to be viewed" to "cognition in action" [17].

(3) narrative mapping: In the generation mechanism of narrative metaphors, the degree of player engagement and the distribution of narrative control across different game types significantly influence the paths of metaphor construction. We broadly categorize narrative mapping into two mechanisms:

(a) Designer-driven. Common in linear or branching narrative structures, where players mostly act as passive recipients. Metaphors are primarily conveyed through pre-designed visual elements, linguistic narration, or symbolic events, forming a relatively closed "textual metaphor" system. In this mode, players effectively "read" a fable or allegorical story, with metaphors representing the author's intended meanings.

(b) Player-driven. In player-driven narratives, players actively co-construct the story through free exploration and interaction with the environment. Consequently, metaphors become more open-ended, polysemous, and experiential, manifesting features of "processual metaphors" or "generative narratives." This narrative mode constitutes a cognitive construction process of "understanding by doing." [18–20]

The theoretical framework proposed in this paper aligns more closely with the second, player-driven type of experiential metaphor expression. Game narrative metaphors tend to be jointly driven by audiovisual and interactive mappings.

The three mapping types—audiovisual mapping, interactive mapping, and narrative mapping—are not simply parallel; rather, they form a progressive, nested structure that can be understood as a cognitive depth hierarchy in the construction of game metaphors. These mapping pathways correspond to multiple dimensions of cognitive generation—perception, action, and meaning construction—thereby realizing a contextualized and experiential metaphorical framework. This layered structure supports players in activating deeper levels of thought and understanding during immersive gameplay.

3.2   Metaphor-Driven Game Design Framework

Grounded in situated cognition theory and integrating structural metaphor with three metaphor mapping pathways commonly found in game design, along with their progressive interrelationships, we developed a metaphor design framework for immersive games. This framework emphasizes that metaphor functions not only as a form of artistic expression but also as a tool for cognitive construction. By embedding thematic content into immersive, interactive experiences in a gamified manner, designers can guide players to actively generate meaning through a continuous cycle of perception–action–reflection.

4   Game Design in Practice

Based on the three metaphorical mapping pathways and the constructed immersive metaphor design framework, we conducted a design practice.We developed an immersive RPG puzzle game titled Metro Migration, which integrates elements of walking simulation and puzzle-solving mechanics. Players engage in a walking experience by freely exploring a looping metro tunnel. Through interactive engagement, they gradually become aware of shifts in their identity and progressively construct an understanding of the full narrative and its underlying social metaphors.

4.1   Input Perception: An Audiovisual Metaphor System

In the design of Metro Migration, we systematically employed multimodal perceptual elements to construct a metaphor system that is both "visible" and "audible" through the layered integration of visual and auditory cues. Within this immersive environment, players are no longer merely seeing the scene—they are acting within a perceptional structure shaped by social mechanisms.

Specifically, visual mapping is achieved through the deliberate use of color, form, spatial structure, and even camera framing techniques. These design choices transform abstract emotions and sociopolitical structures into perceivable elements within the game environment, allowing players to intuitively sense meaning as they navigate the space.

In terms of visual mapping, the "sheep" serves as a recurring visual symbol throughout the game.(see Fig. 2) Depicted in white, motionless, and scattered across the corridor space, the sheep metaphorically represent the standardized and de-individualized masses within a structured society. The overall design of the metro corridor adopts a cool-toned color palette and a looping architectural layout, evoking a sense of a programmed, enclosed system—subtly suggesting that the player is trapped in an inescapable cycle of social order.

Above the corridor, "exit signs" direct the player toward the supposed way out. Within this confined space, advertisement billboards are designed as critical metaphorical nodes. These high-frequency visual elements form a persistent "information landscape" along the player's journey, serving as a critique of ideological indoctrination and consumerist logic in real-world society. Some of these

Fig. 2. "The sheep" as a recurring visual motif throughout the experience.

billboards mimic iconic visual media such as Time magazine covers or Leonardo da Vinci's Mona Lisa, symbolizing the unbreachable status of elite classes. Others imitate entertainment program posters, satirizing mechanisms of attention economy and infotainment culture.

Advertisements for consumer goods—such as lamb meat, wool products, and goat milk—construct a complete consumption chain centered around the sheep. In this context, sheep are reduced to commodified products, generating a profound sense of identity displacement and systemic alienation. These metaphorical constructs reflect broader institutional narratives, mechanisms of consumer manipulation, and the objectification of identity, thereby amplifying the metaphorical intensity of the metro corridor as a symbolic space of modern society.(see Fig. 3)

Additional visual elements—such as haystacks piled in corners, scattered documents on the ground, and surveillance cameras symbolizing constant monitoring—further reinforce themes of survival pressure and surveillance awareness. Together, these components create a visual tension that guides players toward a state of awakening and the pursuit of escape, stimulating cognitive dissonance and critical reflection.

Fig. 3. Visual metaphors in the game environment.

On the auditory level, high-frequency alert sounds triggered during interactions with the sheep are repetitive and short, creating a sensation of "information overload" that immerses players in a tense sensory environment. Interspersed advertisement voice-overs, characterized by their repetitive, cold tone and commercial logic, subtly position the player as an exploited subject within a discourse shaped by capital and power structures. Meanwhile, faint and concealed sounds such as chewing, footsteps, and bells subtly enhance the atmosphere and hint at a transformation in the player's identity.

These design elements do not exist in isolation but operate synergistically to form a perceptual system that frames the subway corridor as a "social metaphor space." Through continuously "hearing prompts," "seeing the sheep," and seemingly "progressing forward," players are gradually immersed as participants within a systematized order rather than as external observers. This immersive metaphorical mapping reinforces the design framework proposed in this study, which emphasizes cognitive transformation driven by spatial experience.

4.2   Experiential Construction: Mechanism of Interactive Metaphor

In the design of Metro Migration, the dynamic interaction between audiovisual cues and player behaviors forms the narrative foundation of the game. This narrative does not rely on linear text or explicit task prompts; instead, it emerges through the player's operations, feedback, and perceptual pathways within the system, gradually constructing an experiential metaphorical structure. Within this structure, meaning is not externally imposed on the game's surface but is "performed"—activated through players' continuous actions such as migrating, approaching, guiding, turning back, and waiting. These actions trigger symbolic feedback embedded in the system, thereby facilitating a process of "understanding through experience."

The player's act of herding sheep forward within the subway corridor serves as an explicit metaphorical mechanism, symbolizing the social psychological phenomenon known as the "herd effect"—where individuals tend to imitate the majority rather than exercise independent judgment under conditions of incomplete information. Simultaneously, the audiovisual feedback embedded in the system—such as sudden red lights at corners, fog filling the passageway, rolling haystacks, and advertisement billboards repeatedly broadcasting promotional phrases like "freshly slaughtered lamb"—constitutes strong cues of alienation. (see Fig. 4) These seemingly random events occur precisely when players have gained a sense of mastery, disrupting rhythm and disorienting direction. This design evokes players' cognitive associations with real-world systemic dilemmas where order equates to control and guidance amounts to domestication.

Within this mechanism, players' behavioral decisions not only determine the pace and trajectory of progression but also activate the symbolic tension controlled by the system. The game thus shifts from being a medium that shows players certain elements to one that enables players to trigger meaning through action. This process embeds the social metaphor into the players' cultural cognitive framework, completing a metaphorical experiential loop that moves from perception, through behavior, to meaning construction.

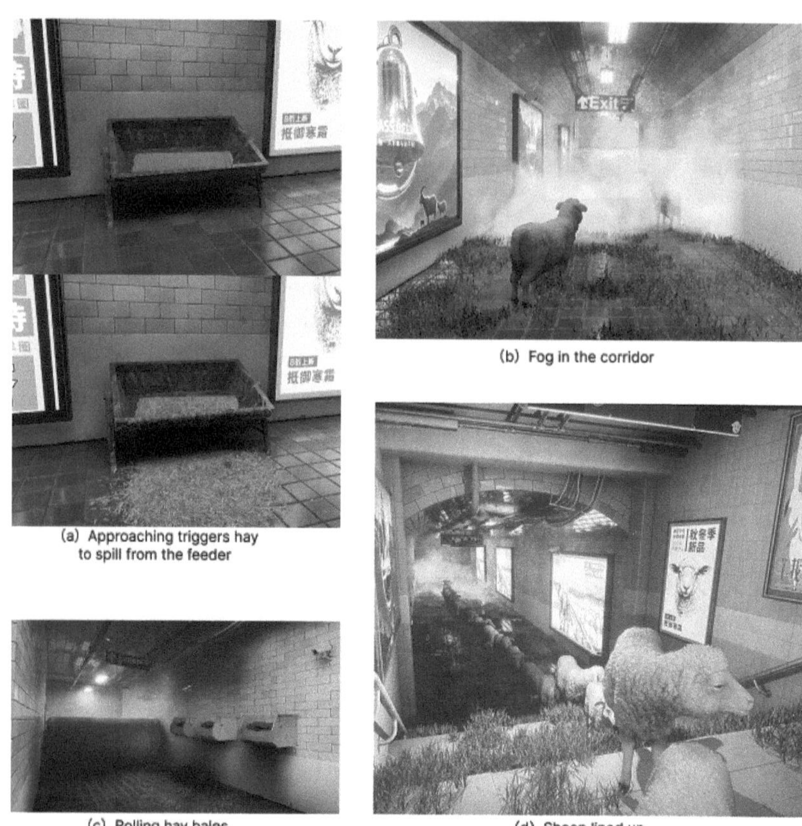

(a) Approaching triggers hay
to spill from the feeder

(b) Fog in the corridor

(c) Rolling hay bales

(d) Sheep lined up

Fig. 4. Interactive metaphor in the game environment.

4.3   Cognitive Integration: Narrative Metaphors in Games

Narrative mapping, at a macro level, revolves around identity cognition and action logic. Players, situated in a first-person perspective aboard a stationary train, engage in self-exploration through visually reconstructed real-world scenes and the design of a procedural path aligned with daily habits. This metaphorically reflects the routine urban commute, characterized by highly procedural rhythms and mechanized action logic. The subway functions not only as a spatial backdrop but also serves as a container metaphor within the symbolic system, implying the individual's enclosed and guided existence within institutional tracks.

Upon entering the metro corridor, players gradually realize that the space is not an extension of a real subway station but a looping maze-like environment. Throughout the corridor, players repeatedly encounter lost sheep, and by approaching and confirming guidance, they lead the sheep to follow and form a procession.

Simultaneously, this process inversely shapes the player's identity cognition: the game does not explicitly define a moment of identity transition but guides players to discover their evolving identity during gameplay. The balance of identity cognition shifts from the shepherd watching behind the flock to the lead sheep guiding at the front. The player's identity transforms progressively from an "individual" to a "group leader," and eventually to a "lost one."

This progression aligns with the ritual structure consisting of three stages: separation, liminality (transition), and incorporation. The liminal space refers to the ambiguous middle state during which the participant no longer holds their pre-ritual identity but has not yet assumed their post-ritual identity [21] (see Fig. 5).

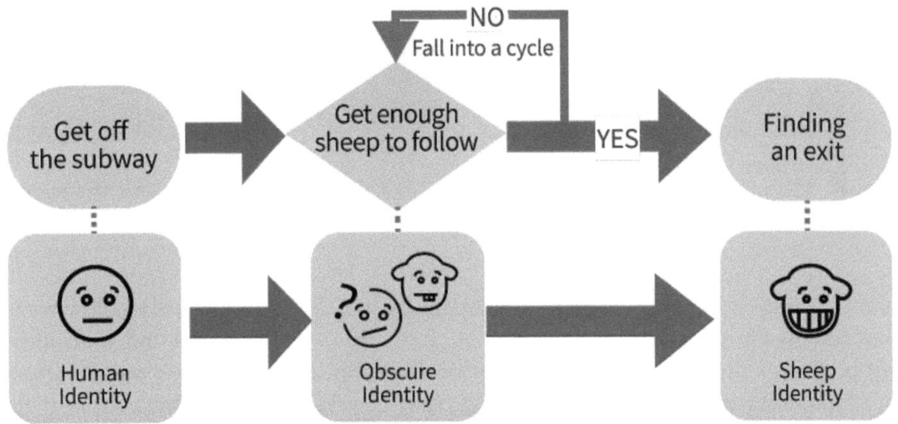

Fig. 5. The transformation of player identity.

As players engage in interactions, their viewpoint gradually lowers until, upon finally looking into a mirror, they discover their identity as the lead sheep reflected back at them. (see Fig. 6) The player's actions not only drive the interactions within the corridor but also metaphorically represent the fluidity of their social role and state of consciousness. This constitutes a typical narrative mapping based on structural metaphor.

4.4   Development and Operational Environment

In the development of this project, Unreal Engine was selected as the primary game development platform. Its powerful real-time rendering capabilities enable the detailed reproduction of subway environments and visual metaphor elements with high-quality lighting and complex material effects. Furthermore, both interaction mechanics and gameplay were implemented using Unreal Engine's Blueprint visual scripting system, significantly lowering the prototyping barrier

Fig. 6. The mirrors in the game, the subway exit behind the mirrors, and the ending of the game.

and allowing designers to rapidly realize interactive logic and narrative flow without relying on complex coding. The engine's robust physics system and audio support also provide a stable foundation for interactive feedback and auditory metaphors within the game. Benefiting from Unreal Engine's strong support for immersive experiences and atmosphere construction, this project successfully balances technical feasibility with artistic expressiveness in conveying serious themes (see Fig. 7).

5   User Study

5.1   Research Objectives

This study aims to investigate whether experiential metaphors embedded in immersive game narratives are more effective than direct information delivery in eliciting players' cognitive reflection, symbolic thinking, and transformative potential. To explore this, we conducted a mixed-method experiment that combined gameplay sessions with pre- and post-test questionnaires and tasks. The evaluation instruments included the Reflection Tendency Questionnaire (RTQ) and the Torrance Tests of Creative Thinking (TTCT). Both quantitative and qualitative approaches were employed to analyze the collected data. The game was developed for both PC and VR platforms. To minimize motion sickness commonly associated with VR experiences and to lower the participation threshold for individuals without prior VR gaming experience, the user study was conducted using the PC version of the game.

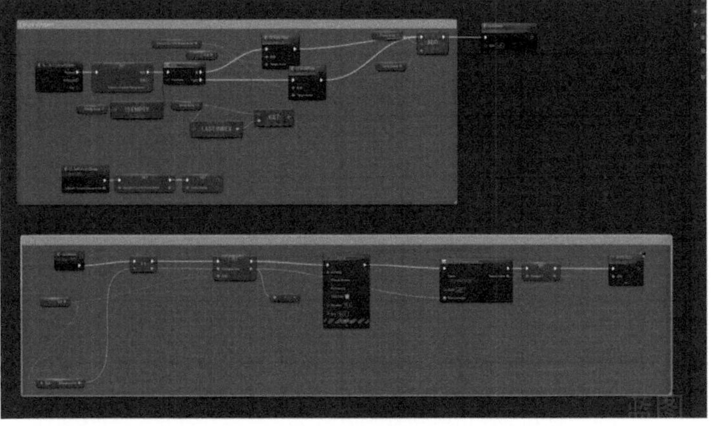

Fig. 7. Unreal Engine and visual scripting with blueprints.

5.2 Experimental Instruments

We designed a pre-post structured questionnaire based on the Reflection Tendency Questionnaire (RTQ), ensuring consistency across both stages. The questionnaire was constructed around four dimensions: Habitual Action, Understanding, Reflection, and Critical Reflection, with two items for each dimension. Responses were rated on a 7-point Likert scale.

The Habitual Action dimension focuses on individuals' roles and positions within a collective, exploring the unconscious influences exerted by social contexts. The Understanding dimension shifts attention to the relationship between individuals' thinking and everyday social structures, investigating both their effects and reciprocal impacts. Reflectionemphasizes self-directed exploration, highlighting autonomous reasoning and feedback toward the surrounding world. Critical Reflection further addresses individuals' capacity for active agency, involving deeper structural analysis and a movement from surface-level observation to the essence of phenomena.

A total of 21 valid participants were recruited for this study, ranging in age from 18 to 40 years. Most participants came from disciplines related to design, human factors engineering, and psychology. Prior to the experiment, all participants signed an informed consent form and confirmed the absence of visual or auditory impairments. Basic demographic information was collected, including age, gender, educational background, field of study, and gaming experience.

Ethical Statement. Due to the game's 3D and first-person perspective design, all participants were thoroughly informed of the experimental procedures and any potential discomfort prior to the study. All procedures were conducted based on informed consent. All data were collected anonymously and used solely for academic research purposes. This study was approved by the Ethics Review Committee of the affiliated research institution.

5.3   Method

The experiment was structured into three sequential phases:

Phase 1: Pre-test. Participants completed the Reflection Tendency Questionnaire (RTQ pre-test), which consists of 8 items across four dimensions: Habitual Action, Understanding, Reflection, and Critical Reflection. Each item was rated on a 7-point Likert scale. The pre-test was designed to assess participants' baseline level of cognitive reflection prior to the game experience.

Phase 2: Game Experience. Participants engaged with the prototype game Subway Migration for approximately 20–30 min. The game integrates metaphorical elements such as subway environments, shepherding behaviors, and the herd effect to construct an immersive narrative. Through recursive spatial design and identity transitions, players are guided through a psychological and behavioral shift—from the role of the "controller" to that of the "controlled." This experiential journey aims to evoke reflection on social structures and group mechanisms (see Fig. 8)

Fig. 8. User game experience.

Phase 3: Post-test. Upon completion of the gameplay session, participants were asked to fill out the RTQ post-test, containing the same 8 items as the pre-test. Responses were again measured on a 7-point Likert scale, allowing for comparative analysis.

Statistical Analysis. A paired-sample t-test was conducted to compare pre- and post-test scores across the four RTQ dimensions: Habitual Action, Understanding, Reflection, and Critical Reflection. In addition, the mean scores of each dimension were analyzed to examine potential differences before and after gameplay. Statistical significance was evaluated using a threshold of $p < 0.05$.

6   Conclusion

6.1   Quantitative Results and Interpretation

The reliability of the questionnaire was verified using Cronbach's alpha, yielding a value of 0.733, which indicates good internal consistency and confirms its suitability for subsequent analysis.

The questionnaire results showed that the game had the most significant impact on players' perception of spatial and social metaphors ($p = .001$). This suggests that the spatial layout, visual cues, and contextual feedback effectively prompted players to associate the game environment with real-world structural dilemmas and metaphorical representations. In the dimension of identity cognition and role transformation, the post-test scores also exhibited a significant increase ($p = .047$), indicating that the game mechanics successfully triggered players' reflection on their own roles—particularly fostering an understanding of the fluidity between being a "controller" and being "controlled."

Although the dimension of reflective and transformative potential did not reach statistical significance ($p = .091$), the results showed a positive trend, suggesting that the game holds potential to encourage players to extend their reflection to real-life behaviors. The general reflection dimension did not show a significant difference, which may indicate that the game primarily functions as a tool for mapping social contexts and structural awareness, rather than for stimulating broad-based critical reasoning.

6.2   Participant Feedback and Qualitative Insights

Participants generally responded positively to the gameplay experience of Subway Migration, highlighting its strong emotional guidance and immersive quality in terms of narrative style, spatial expression, and symbolic representation of group dynamics. Most participants reported that the game prompted reflections and associations related to real-world social structures, identity roles, and behavioral patterns, describing it as an "experience beyond entertainment." Some users also offered constructive suggestions, primarily concerning the clarity of interaction feedback and visual cues, noting that such design details significantly affect the fluidity and depth of immersion.

User feedback focused on the following aspects:

(1) Narrative Expression and Metaphorical Perception: Many users felt the overall pacing of the game was natural and that the metaphorical expression through spatial and mechanic design was "thought-provoking." The transition of role identities was described as "gradual yet impactful." However, some users noted that the symbolic relationship between "the herd" and "the sense of control" was understood rather late in the experience, suggesting a need for clearer narrative foreshadowing or metaphorical cues.

(2) Interaction Rhythm and Behavioral Guidance: Several participants commented that the game had a "weak sense of task but a strong sense of experience," emphasizing that it felt more like a simulation of social behavior than a goal-driven process. Some suggested incorporating more actionable character choices or branching behavioral paths to enhance player agency and strategic engagement.

(3) Visual-Spatial Design: Most users were impressed by the game's sense of enclosure, cyclical structure, and visual coherence, considering it effective in conveying systemic constraints and institutional repetition. However, some participants pointed out that the visual rhythm was relatively even, with certain scenes lacking dramatic tension. They recommended introducing more visual disturbances or moments of contrast to intensify the emotional and psychological experience.

In summary, the interview findings indicate that Subway Migration effectively elicited cognitive engagement, emotional response, and metaphor comprehension. Players resonated with the design concept of being "gradually absorbed into the system" and suggested that further refinement of narrative cues, interaction prompts, and pacing structure would enhance the game's overall tension and cognitive depth.

Acknowledgments. This research was supported by the Key Research and Development Program of Xinjiang Uygur Autonomous Region, under the project "Digital Restoration and Immersive Demonstration of Key Murals in the Kizil Caves" (Project No. 2022B03035-3).

References

1. Lakoff, G., Johnson, M.: Metaphors We Live By. University of Chicago Press, Chicago (2008)
2. Swink, S.: Game Feel: A Game Designer's Guide to Virtual Sensation. CRC Press, Boca Raton, FL (2008)
3. Ferreira, E., Falcão, T.: Through the looking glass: weavings between the magic circle and immersive processes in video games. In: Proceedings of DiGRA Conference (2009)
4. Gendron, G.: Innovating training through immersive environments: generation Y, exploratory learning, and serious games. In: MODSIM World 2011 Conference and Expo, Selected Papers (2012)
5. de Rosa, F., Marfisi Schottman, I., Baalsrud Hauge, J., Bellotti, F., Dondio, P., Romero, M. (eds.): GALA 2021. LNCS, vol. 13134. Springer, Cham (2021). https://doi.org/10.1007/978-3-030-92182-8
6. Rusch, D.C., Weise, M.J.: Games about love and trust?: Harnessing the power of metaphors for experience design. In: Proceedings of the 2008 ACM SIGGRAPH Symposium on Video Games (Sandbox '08), New York, NY: ACM, pp. 89–97 (2008)

7. Brown, J.S., Collins, A., Duguid, P.: Situated cognition and the culture of learning. Educ. Res. **18**(1), 32–42 (1989)

8. Sanford, K., Hopper, T.: Videogames and complexity theory: learning through gameplay (2009). *Unpublished manuscript*

9. Adcock, A.B., et al.: Effective knowledge development in game-based learning environments: considering research in cognitive processes and simulation design. In: Van Eck, R. (ed.) Gaming and Cognition: Theories and Practice from the Learning Sciences, pp. 152–168. Hershey, PA, IGI Global (2010)

10. Squire, K.: From content to context: videogames as designed experience. Educ. Res. **35**, 19–29 (2006)

11. Meiners, A.L., Reich, D., Hicks, K., et al.: Lushness in game design: the role of non-interactive visual embellishments in player experience. In: Proceedings of the 20th International Conference on the Foundations of Digital Games, pp. 1–11 (2025)

12. Hicks, K., Rogers, K., Gerling, K., et al.: Juicy audio: audio designers' conceptualization of the term in video games. Proc. ACM Hum.-Comput. Interact. **8**(CHI PLAY), 1–28 (2024)

13. Antle, A.N., Corness, G., Droumeva, M., et al.: What the body knows: exploring the benefits of embodied metaphors in hybrid physical-digital environments. Interact. Comput. **21**, 66–75 (2009)

14. Fahlenbrach, K.: Embodied metaphors in film, television, and video games: cognitive approaches (2015). *Journal name if available*

15. Gibbs, R.W. Jr.: Metaphor interpretation as embodied simulation. Mind Lang. **21**(3), 434–458 (2006)

16. Bauer, R., Suter, B.: Game mechanics (2021). *Publisher/journal name if available*

17. Calleja, G.: In-Game: From Immersion to Incorporation. MIT Press, Cambridge, MA (2011)

18. Frasca, G.: Rethinking agency and immersion: video games as a means of consciousness-raising. Digit. Creat. **12**, 167–174 (2001)

19. Calleja, G.: Experiential narrative in game environments. In: DiGRA Digital Library (2009)

20. Toh, W.: The player experience and design implications of narrative games. Int. J. Hum.–Comput. Interact. **39**, 2742–2769 (2022)

21. Rothem, N., Fischer, S.: Reclaiming Arnold Van Gennep's Les rites de passage (1909): the structure of openness and the openness of structure. J. Class. Sociol. **18**(4), 255–265 (2018)

Creating Agency Through Comics: "Tierschutz-Erleben" E-Learning Platform

Akshatha Hariharan[✉], Ido Iurgel, Anja Waldmann, Denis Malinko, Isabelle Decher, Jana Mariella Kalb, Mateo Covic, Maren Weller, Anabela Parente, and Steffi Wiedemann

Rhine-Waal University of Applied Sciences, Faculty of Life Sciences and Faculty of Communication and Environment, Marie Curie-Street. 1, 47533 Kleve, Germany
`akshatha.hariharan@hsrw.org, Ido.Iurgel@hochschule-rhein-waal.de`

Abstract. Tierschutz-erLeben – Animal Welfare Experience is an educational platform that introduces a gamified, story-driven approach to learning, specifically designed for agriculture students. Traditional teaching strategies often fall short in communicating the complexity of decision-making and its practical implications, resulting in a disconnect between academic theory and real-world practice. To address this gap, the project offers an innovative platform that leverages storytelling through interactive comics and a creative tool called the comic automaton, available in both English and German.

The platform promotes a "learning by doing" philosophy by combining engaging narratives with hands-on digital tools. It covers key topics in cattle, sheep, and beef production, structured into clear subtopics that guide students through their learning journey. These interactive comics are illustrated in a distinctive comic style that adds visual engagement and contextual depth. Realistic characters—such as farmers, veterinarians, and animals—are featured throughout, making the learning experience more relatable and grounded in real-world agricultural settings.

At the heart of the platform is the comic automaton, which enables students to create their own comics using a rich library of characters and farm-related elements. This encourages active learning by allowing users to reflect on various scenarios, express empathy, and engage with complex concepts from different viewpoints. Student participation has been central to the platform's ongoing development, with feedback from multiple testing stages shaping its usability and content. Tierschutz-erLeben represents a fresh and impactful educational approach that connects theoretical instruction with practical, experience-based learning in agriculture.

Keywords: Gamified learning · interactive comics · comic creation · educational games

© The Author(s), under exclusive license to Springer Nature Switzerland AG 2026
J. Y. C. Chen et al. (Eds.): HCII 2025, LNCS 16338, pp. 368–387, 2026.
https://doi.org/10.1007/978-3-032-12808-9_23

1 Introduction

The maintenance of livestock such as cattle and sheep plays in food security and maintaining cultural landscapes. This management of livestock is under heavy public scrutiny often marked by emotionally charged debates and a declining appreciation for animal agriculture (Boehm et al., 2010). In light of these developments, improving animal welfare has become a key ethical and legal priority (Spiller et al., 2015). Meeting this responsibility requires well-trained farmers, educators, and veterinary professionals who possess current and practice-relevant knowledge of animal needs, species-specific husbandry systems, and early indicators of illness or distress.

The field however is riddled with the gap in knowledge transfer between scientific findings and the connection to practices on the field as it fails to reach the major stakeholders. This gap in the educational contexts is persistently cited as a major barrier hindering the advancement in the field (Jansen et al., 2009; Merle et al., 2024; Shiels et al., 2021). This disconnect is further exacerbated by traditional teaching methods that prioritize passive, lecture-based instruction over active and experiential learning.

This underscores the need for training and policy initiatives that effectively bridge the gap between scientific knowledge and practical, on-the-ground expertise. Contemporary learning theory, however, highlights that lasting learning outcomes are most effectively achieved when learners are empowered to take ownership of their education and engage with content in self-directed, contextually grounded, and socially meaningful ways (Ragland et al., 2023).

A major challenge in animal welfare education is presenting the consequences of poor decision-making in a way that is both understandable and pedagogically sound. These outcomes are difficult if not impossible to demonstrate realistically or ethically in hands-on training. Digital tools, however, present a promising alternative. Simulated digital environments can illustrate the significance of care and responsibility while also evoking the kind of tacit knowledge that is often essential for practitioners such as farmers. Despite its importance, this dimension is often overlooked or poorly understood in terms of how it can be effectively taught or transferred.

Building on interdisciplinary collaboration between animal scientists, media designers, educators, and developers, we have developed an educational platform (Tierschutz erleben) that integrates narrative learning and user participation. In this context, we introduce the concept of an integrated comic creation tool (Comic Automaton), which serves as an authoring environment enabling learners to engage with animal welfare issues creatively and reflectively. This paper outlines the process from conception to the development of a platform designed to empower users with agency through creative engagement. It documents the exploratory journey undertaken to identify and address the gaps in knowledge transfer within the field of animal welfare. By combining digital media with comic creation, the project introduces a pedagogical approach that bridges the divide between theoretical understanding and practical knowledge offering an engaging, harm-free alternative to traditional learning methods involving animals (Veenema et al., 2024).

2 Fostering User Agency

Our analysis revealed the need for a more engaging, experience-based approach to animal welfare education one that moves beyond text-heavy materials and top-down instruction to better capture the field's practical and emotional realities. With the goal of conveying factual knowledge in animal agriculture while also fostering empathy, the project explored non-traditional, technology-based methods of education. Initial efforts focused on 3D simulated environments designed to replicate real-life scenarios for students in animal husbandry or agriculture. However, these simulations often place the users in passive roles, limiting their ability to make decisions or engage critically with the material, an approach that proved less effective for deep learning and meaningful knowledge transfer. To promote a more participatory form of pedagogy, alternative approaches were actively explored and developed to enhance learner involvement and educational impact.

Narrowing down from the concept of intelligent systems through which the users have full autonomy over their learning, the platform draws from this approach and fits in the technically achievable and ethical framework given the topic of animal husbandry. Although being an intellectually compelling concept, it would be a complex challenge and recognising constraints would allow both agency and to learn in a guided path as being more effective.

The project evolved towards a model of learning through active creation, achieved primarily through storytelling and narrative engagement. In *Tierschutz-erleben*, we interpret agency not as total freedom, but as guided creation a space where users shape their own narratives within carefully crafted boundaries. This balance enables self-expression while preserving ethical and educational integrity.

3 Supporting Pedagogical Theories

In response to the limitations of conventional materials, we adopted a design approach grounded in constructivist learning theory, which emphasizes active engagement, self-directed learning, and contextualized meaning-making. The learning platform is closely aligned with Self-Deterministic Theory - Deci, E. L., & Ryan, R. M. (2000). It aims to strike a balance between autonomy, competence, and relatedness by integrating these core psychological needs into its two main features. The platform is designed to foster intrinsic motivation and empathetic engagement, while also incorporating structured boundaries that guide learners within a defined narrative and set of learning goals ensuring both meaningful and effective learning experiences.

A key platform feature is the Comic Automaton (Comic4Welfare), which enables learners to create their own stories and explore individual perspectives on animal welfare practices. Comic4Welfare integrates narrative elements, role-playing, and decision-making with factual content and is intended to create immersive and experience-oriented learning environments. This learner-centred strategy may support personal meaning-making and enhance knowledge transfer through active participation. This process is expected to foster deeper engagement and may support cognitive strategies such as active recall, potentially strengthening memory and comprehension through creative expression. The Comic4Welfare consists of a repository of familiar characters and scenes from the field which facilitates active role-playing and building narratives. The output of the Comic4Welfare are Learner-generated comics that can be shared and discussed with peers, which might promote the exchange of diverse viewpoints and collaborative reflection. Using comics supports socio-emotional learning by encouraging empathy and ethical reflection through expressive visuals of animals in vulnerable situations.

Comic4Welfare is one key feature of the learning platform, complemented by another important element: interactive comics that follow the learning modules. These comics are structured around specific processes and are designed to serve as decision-making tools, guiding learners through story-driven narratives.

However, integrating such interactive narratives into educational contexts presents certain challenges. As Goodbrey (2015) points out, interactive or "game" comics represent an emerging narrative medium with underdeveloped design frameworks and theoretical foundations. These limitations become particularly evident when attempting to implement branching narratives in educational contexts. Neo and Mitchell (2016) similarly describe a conceptual tension between interactivity and narrative coherence, which can hinder the effectiveness of learning experiences.

Considering these challenges, we opted against the use of a drama management system. Instead, we implemented a simplified "string of pearls" structure, which maintains authorial control while allowing for limited narrative flexibility. This design is intended to balance learner agency with a clear and coherent storyline, thereby offering a potentially engaging and pedagogically sound alternative to traditional self-directed learning tasks. It may also lower the threshold for content creation, both for educators and learners.

4 Workshop and User Feedback

Four workshops with agriculture students, guided by a human-centered design approach, were key to shaping the platform's direction. Insights from these sessions informed the concept, content, and interactive features, helping evolve the platform into a more immersive and learner-driven experience through ongoing feedback and reflection.

The first workshop introduced students to the different concepts that were being planned for the learning platform, with a focus on key topics such as cattle and sheep. As early adopters and primary users, students participated in an initial brainstorming session where preliminary prototypes were presented. This session aimed to elicit their impressions, emotional responses, and expectations regarding the proposed learning environment. Demonstrations included early 3D simulations, paper prototypes, and potential learning strategies. The feedback and discussions served to understand how learners in this domain acquire knowledge and what resources they typically rely on. The feedback highlighted a need for engaging, visually appealing tools. This input led to a shift in development priorities, favoring the use of narrative storytelling and 2D comic-based formats. These were found to be more effective in maintaining motivation and clarifying learning objectives, while 3D simulations, despite initial interest, were seen as time consuming and less efficient at emphasizing key visual features.

The second workshop focused on A/B testing between interactive prototypes to evaluate the role of storytelling in the learning process. An interactive dot-voting technique encouraged active participation, while the User Experience Questionnaire (UEQ) was employed to gather quantitative data on users' impressions, attitudes, and emotional responses. This session marked a shift from purely exploratory, qualitative feedback to include data-driven evaluations of design decisions. The results underscored the value of storytelling in increasing learner engagement and directly influenced the structure and design of the interactive comics. The participants were split into two groups where one group was exposed to the comic automaton first and the other to the learning platform. This approach was used to observe how users responded to the specific learning journey they experienced. Figure 1, Fig. 2, Fig. 3

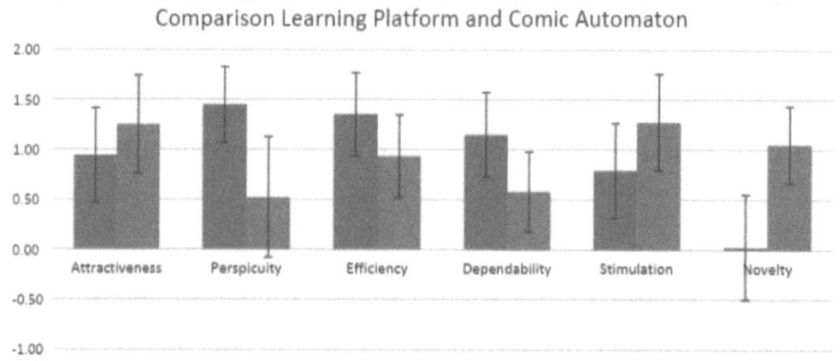

Fig. 1. Blue represents Group A, who were first exposed to the learning platform, while orange represents Group B, who interacted with the Comic Automaton as their initial experience. The figure represents a comparison between experiences of the two groups for the parameters listed.

Participants appreciated both tools for different strengths: the Learning Platform was seen as clear, reliable, and helpful for exam preparation, while the Comic Automation was valued for its creativity, novelty, and ability to keep users engaged. Group feedback confirmed this contrast between practical usefulness and motivational impact.

The third workshop tested early developments of the Comic4Welfare feature, initially conceived as a creative playground for learners. Students explored narrative creation using paper prototypes as a form of active learning. The session assessed how participants approached storytelling tasks, revealing both enthusiasm and challenges. Some students struggled with generating narrative ideas or maintaining focus on learning objectives. These insights prompted the development of an additional mode within the Comic Automaton designed to serve as a structured guide that supports learners during the comic creation process while helping ensure alignment with the intended educational objectives. The workshop focused on introducing the platform's characters particularly those featured in Comic4Welfare and exploring their relevance, as well as gathering feedback from participants to understand perceived connections and impact.

The fourth workshop assessed the usability and effectiveness of the near-complete platform. Participants engaged in a think-aloud protocol, during which they explored the system's main features while verbalizing their thoughts and actions. This real-time observation offered critical insights into the intuitiveness of the interface and revealed some usability challenges and technical pain points, prompting final refinements. The

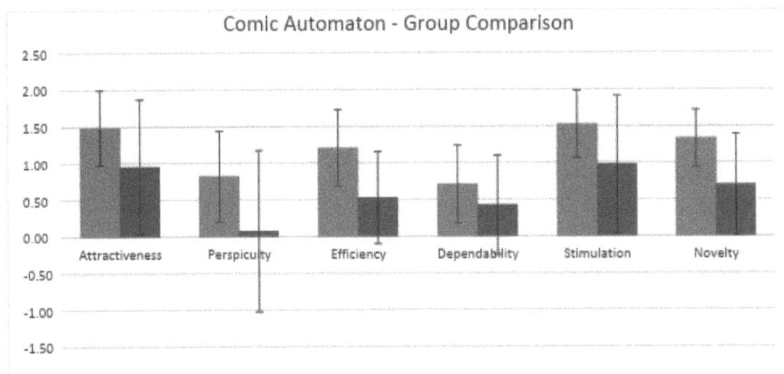

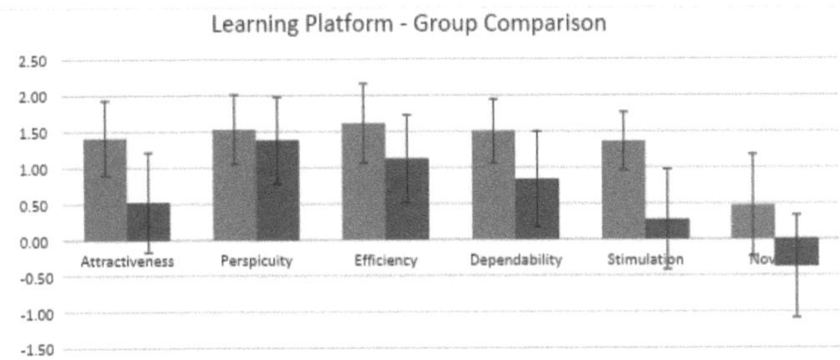

Fig. 2. a and b Green represents Group A and red represents Group B. The table displays the ratings given by both groups for the Learning platform in Fig. 2a and Comic Automaton in Fig. 2b for the specified parameters, within the defined rating scale. The figures represent the responses provided by participants after engaging with all the features of the learning platform.

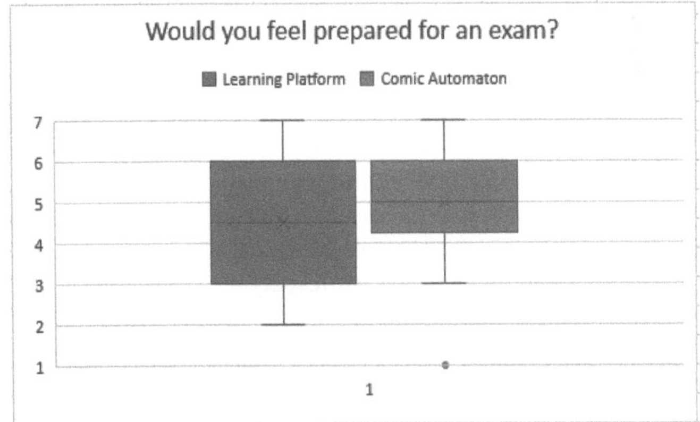

Fig. 3. The table presents a key question that helped us understand how each group perceived the two different starting points beginning with the learning platform versus the Comic Automaton. On average, both groups rated the effectiveness of the platform within the range of 3–6, indicating a moderate to positive reception.

overall response was positive, and the workshop indicated both the relevance of the design choices and the platform's potential to engage its intended audience. Collectively, these workshops helped keep the discovery of essential user needs at the core of the development process. They not only informed the design of individual features but also contributed to shaping Comic4Welfare into a coherent learning environment, supporting both structured step-by-step learning and creative exploration.

4.1 Ethical Framework for User Testing and Workshops

Workshops with Animal Husbandry and Agriculture students at Rhine-Waal University were integrated into regular coursework as practical or credit-bearing activities. Led by professors, they provided an initial classroom-based introduction to the learning platform.

Verbal consent was obtained from participants for feedback and internal documentation, including photos taken during the sessions. As part of regular classes and facilitated by professors one involved in the project's inception ethical concerns were minimal and aligned with institutional guidelines. These sessions served as early trials for exploring new teaching methods in agricultural education. With students preparing for real-world agricultural roles, the potential impact is significant. The learning platform remains the key outcome offered to stakeholders in the agricultural sector.

5 Design Rationale

The rationale for adopting a comical visual language across the platform is deeply rooted in the conceptual foundations of Comic4Welfare, wherein narrative construction, storytelling mechanics, and user agency converge to empower learners as co-authors of their educational journey. The inherent structure of comics characterized by sequential paneling and cohesive visual storytelling served as the skeleton for the platform's design logic.

To ensure narrative continuity and immersive engagement, this aesthetic framework was deliberately extended throughout the platform's interface and content. The platform is illustrated and made interactive through a distinctive comical visual style that defines its overall aesthetic and user experience. Recurring archetypal characters such as the farmer, the veterinarian, cattle, and sheep act as narrative anchors, appearing consistently across learning modules and reinforcing the connective tissue between the Comic Automaton, interactive comics, and the broader pedagogical architecture. This stylistic and conceptual coherence cultivates a unified visual narrative that does more than entertain; it scaffolds the user's immersion in role-play and perspective-taking. The comic-inspired modality thus becomes a strategic vehicle for fostering empathetic engagement, enhancing cognitive involvement, and embedding the learning objectives within a richly contextualized and experientially meaningful environment.

Visualization was one of the key design pillars of the platform, playing a central role in unifying the user journey. The learning modules were selected to elicit emotional resonance while remaining within ethically appropriate boundaries, acknowledging the delicate nature of animal welfare education. User agency is gradually introduced throughout the platform, with varying levels of freedom designed in alignment with expected learning outcomes. The linear narratives of the interactive comics and the flexible modes within the Comic Automaton work in tandem to balance structured learning with creative exploration. Minimal interactions are required to navigate the platform effectively, while the Comic Automaton serves as a primarily exploratory medium, allowing learners to express understanding through storytelling and role-play within a visually coherent and emotionally engaging environment.

6 System Architecture

The learning platform is a full-stack educational web application that supports a multimodal blend of text, images, videos, and interactive content, including interactive comics and a comic creation tool. Its system architecture follows a modular client–server model. The front end was implemented using Angular and Ionic, with WebGL employed to render interactive elements and Apollo Client facilitating communication with the back end via GraphQL. Unity (version 2021) was selected to develop both the Comic Automaton and the interactive comics, based on the development team's expertise and Unity's flexibility in accommodating evolving creative concepts during the innovation process. Figma prototypes were created and iteratively refined to guide and streamline the design phase. This technical foundation enables the implementation of the platform's key interactive elements, particularly the interactive comics and the Comic Automaton, which are described in the following section.

7 Project Execution

This section focuses on detailing the core features at the heart of the platform namely, the decision-based interactive comics and Comic4Welfare and how they function within the overall learning platform. The interactive comics present decision-based scenarios in which users actively apply their knowledge and experience the consequences of their choices in a safe, simulated environment. These narrative sequences are embedded in thematic modules and can be repeated with different outcomes, encouraging exploration and critical thinking.

In a subsequent phase, learners use the Comic Automaton to create their own comics, drawing on characters, scenes, and events introduced in earlier stages. This creative process supports reflective learning, emotional engagement, and value-based reasoning. It also allows learners to reframe and express their understanding of animal welfare topics through personal storytelling. Optional sharing features encourage peer feedback and dialogue, supporting collaborative reflection and exposure to diverse viewpoints.

7.1 The Learning Platform

Following the introduction of the two core components interactive comics and the comic automaton that defines the learning platform positions itself as a comprehensive guide and provides supportive modules thus seamlessly combining all the components (Fig. 6). The platform addresses key topics such as Diary, Cattle, sheep and beef that are subdivided further (Fig. 4). These topics are outlined by explicit learning goals communicated to the users clearly, allowing the users to prepare themselves and to know the intended outcome of the learning exercises. The modules are accompanied by illustrations and visuals, which help in better understanding the processes and reinforcing the content described. Feedback loop for learning is well established in the platform through note taking after every exercise and also acts as the space where the comics gets saved. This collective space is termed the 'learning diary' This diary fosters active, experiential learning; integrates assessment and strategy; and includes gamified elements that provide both structure and motivation (Fig. 5).

The platform thus fosters learning by trying and doing, (b) it integrates learning assessment and a learning strategy, (c) it contains game elements for additional structure and motivation, (d) it is visually attractive and easy to understand, (e) the experience is overall inviting and encouraging, rather than dry and "traditional", (f) it represents and simulates correctly farm situations and animal behaviour, and shows consequences of correct and wrong decisions, (g) it is not only a platform for trying and testing, but also for learning for examinations, integrating text and visual explanation rendering a textbook superfluous, in principle, (h) it allows for the easy integration of storytelling, for identification, structure, and other engagement.

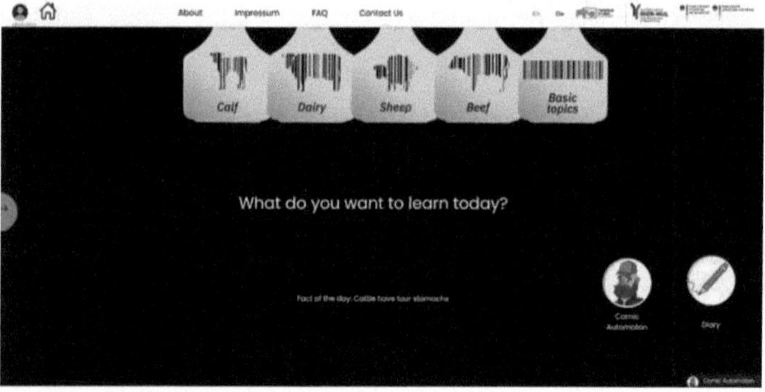

Fig. 4. Screenshot of the landing page that greets every user. The main features - the Comic automaton, the basic study modules and the learning diary are clearly defined.

Fig. 5. Screenshot of the learning diary. The diary acts as a collection of notes entered automatically from interactive comics and manually by the user.

Fig. 6. Screenshot of the playground screen that greets the User as they click on the Comic Automaton feature where they can access the interactive comics or the comic creator.

7.2 Interactive Comics

The Platform includes three comics aligned with core learning modules: Colostrum and Milking, both interactive, and a linear sheep-focused story designed to explore more emotionally driven storytelling and narrative structure. The interactive comics exemplify the principle of learning through decision-making and acting, where users encounter branching points that illustrate the consequences of their choices in subsequent panels. As the branching structures are intentionally limited to a few key decision points or simple equivalent tasks, all narrative paths ultimately converge back to the main storyline. Typically, one path represents an optimal outcome, while alternative paths reveal the potential negative consequences of poor decisions. If a potentially negative outcome is reached, the decision simply redirects the user back to the main storyline of the comic.

Animals like cows and sheep are featured as central characters, with expressive visual cues to enhance emotional resonance. Their interactions with human figures, farmers, veterinarians, and trainees serve to guide learners through complex processes related to animal welfare. These comics are designed as dialogic experiences, interspersed with instructional slides, and delivered through interactive speech bubbles that simulate a guided conversation between the learner and the system.

For instance, the Colostrum comic follows the decision-making process surrounding administering first milk to newborn calves. The users are greeted by a relatable character (Fig. 7) as the narrator and alongside storytelling elements, the comic characters provide information on the tools, techniques, and timing required for effective care. The correct path in the narrative results in healthy calves, while poor decisions, such as neglecting hygiene or mismanaging storage time, alerts the user of the adverse outcomes (Fig. 8). In addition to decision-based interaction, the comic includes informational slides that appear throughout the experience. These slides provide immediate, context-specific knowledge to support the user's understanding. By integrating factual content into these segmented knowledge and decision-making slides, the comic simplifies complex processes and enhances knowledge transfer within an engaging, interactive format. (Fig. 9).

Fig. 7. Screenshot of a slide where a friendly character guides the user through making choices to move the comic forward.

Fig. 8. Screenshot of the screen where the user realizes the impact of their hygiene-related choice, shown through a clear and engaging visual outcome.

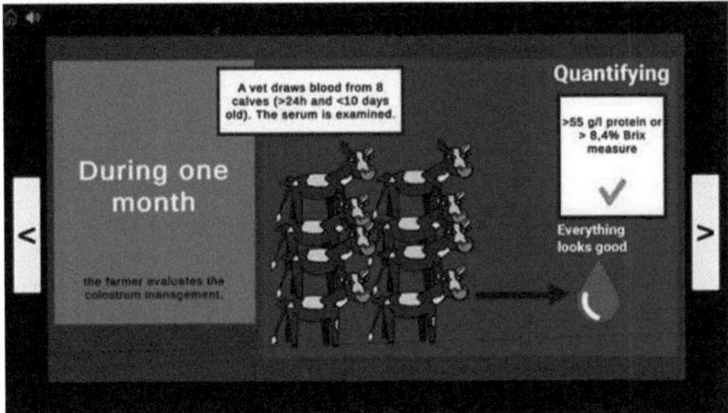

Fig. 9. Screenshot of the screen where the user gains knowledge by encountering various facts shared throughout the comic journey.

Similarly, the Milking comic places the user in the role alongside a new trainee on the field, experiencing the common challenges and stress of managing milking for the first time (Fig. 10). The storyline highlights the correct milking procedures, emphasizing key aspects such as hygiene, proper equipment uses, and effective techniques (Figs. 11 and 12). At the same time, it illustrates the potential health risks cattle may face from even minor errors or oversights.

A central aim of this comic is also to cultivate the user's sensitivity in recognizing signs of distress in animals, promoting both technical knowledge and empathetic awareness.

Fig. 10. Screenshot of the screen where the user takes on the role of supporting a new trainee on the field in the milking procedures.

Fig. 11. Screenshot of the screen as the user steps into the milking parlor about to inspect the available instruments to successfully complete milking the cows.

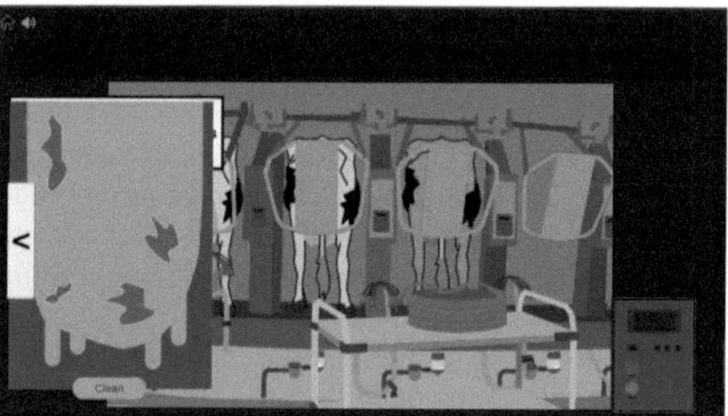

Fig. 12. Screenshot highlighting a step that emphasizes the importance of cleaning and maintaining hygiene among cattle, serving as a visual reminder to draw the user's attention to this critical practice.

7.3   Comic Automaton

The Comic Automaton is designed as a creative editor for constructing stories, granting learner's significant agency to visualize and articulate their understanding of animal welfare. Once the user enters the creation space navigating through the playground of choices between the interactive comics and the Comic Automaton they are greeted with a welcome screen that functions like a user manual, introducing the platform's key features and guiding them through the initial steps (Fig. 13). While many learners welcomed the creative freedom, some found it challenging to generate narratives independently and maintain alignment with learning objectives. To support such users, the Comic Automaton includes two modes of use: a Free Mode, allowing unrestricted storytelling; and a Task Mode, which provides narrative scaffolding via a set of four randomly drawn 'task cards.'

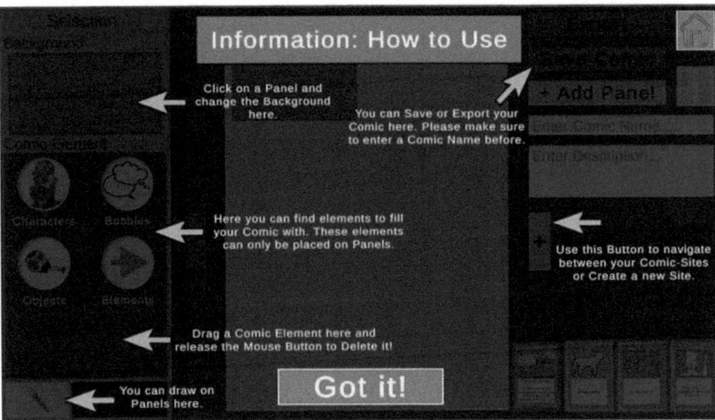

Fig. 13. Screenshot of the initial screen displaying basic guidelines, where the comic automaton introduces itself and explains the different features available to the user.

Each card represents one of four categories: a learning goal, a main character, a tool, and an out-of-context element. Inspired by the metaphor of a deck of cards, this structure stimulates imaginative storytelling while keeping the narrative anchored in educational objectives. (Fig. 14).

Users begin by adding empty panels that serve as a canvas for story development. The tool offers a rich asset library that includes characters frequently encountered in prior modules, such as farmers, veterinarians, and trainees, as well as imaginative additions like an alien or a rubber duck, intended to foster creativity and engagement. The asset pool also includes objects ranging from brix scales (a tool to measure colostrum quality) to fences and animals depicted with varied emotional expressions, broadening the tool's applicability across diverse learning scenarios.

Fig. 14. Screenshot of the task cards mode, which prompts a combination of four play cards that acts as a foundation for the student's narrative.

Completed comics can be saved, retrieved, and exported as PDF files, enabling learners to present their work in classroom settings, share with peers, or use as a personal record of learning progress. An example of a comic created shows the usage of various components of the comic automaton. This combination of creative freedom and structured guidance makes the Comic Automaton a powerful tool for reflective and expressive learning. (Fig. 15).

Fig. 15. Screenshot of a comic sequence generated using the comic automaton, illustrating the story of a perceptive farmer who consults a veterinarian in a timely manner to ensure his calf's well-being.

8   Usability

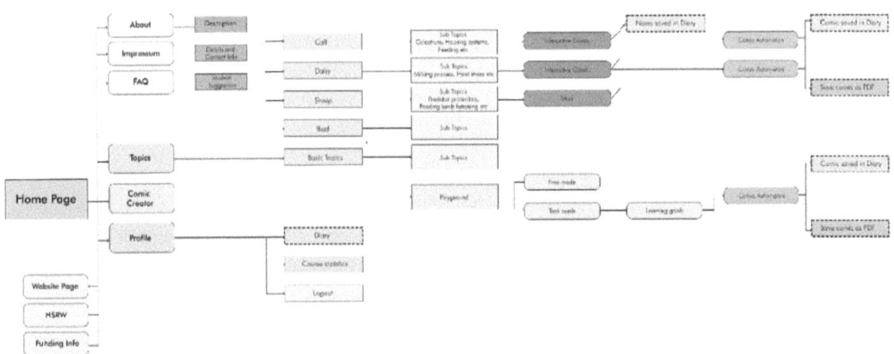

Fig. 16. User journey diagram mapping out seamless navigation across the learning platform.

Fig. 16 Usability played a key role in determining the engagement with the platform. Grounding in User experience research, the design was refined using established According to Nielsen and Molich (1990), heuristic principles and usability guidelines to ensure the platform is intuitive, effective and user-friendly. Throughout the development process, careful attention was paid to the visual composition and color choices. A dark mode was adopted for the overall aesthetics and background for the website to reduce visual strain on the users. Whereas the screens for reading are on a lighter grey tone, which enhances reading experience. The platform's visual identity aligns with the comical style of the illustrations, characters and background to streamline the overall design of the platform.

A simplified and clear user journey has been laid out making the most effective path for the users to easily navigate and access all features. The main features of the platform such as the interactive comics and comic automaton are consistently accessible, ensuring users can easily reach and utilize its primary features at any time. e. A clear distinction is made between structured learning and creation modes, allowing users to switch effortlessly between guided instruction and creative exploration. Furthermore, in creation mode, the comics and learning modules are designed to interact seamlessly with one another, all of which are ultimately integrated into the learning diary, creating a cohesive and continuous learning experience. The platform's flexible backend enables instructors to easily add and customize content, increasing both its adaptability to different contexts and its relevance to specific learning objectives. The goal was to make the platform self-sufficient, thus rendering traditional methods superfluous.

To ensure consistent development of usability throughout the development, a team member conducted regular checks on new features. Additional insights were obtained during workshops and user testing sessions. The presence of an external perspective proved invaluable for identifying usability issues and refining the user experience.

9 Findings or Reflections

At its inception, the Comic4Welfare project was conceived in response to a growing need for innovative, user-centered pedagogical approaches in agricultural education (Boehm et al., 2010; McGrath et al., 2024). Traditional methods often struggle to engage learners with the ethical complexity and emotional dimensions of animal husbandry. The project was therefore designed to integrate established pedagogical strategies, such as narrative framing, visual communication, and the didactic potential of comics, with the principle of learning by doing, in order to address the challenge of creating immersive and engaging educational experiences appropriate to the domain of animal husbandry. This approach aims to foster not only knowledge acquisition but also critical thinking, empathy, and reflective decision-making within playful, but realistic scenarios.

The current version of Comic4Welfare is designed to guide learners through interactive, branching storylines and ultimately enable them to create their own comics. This fosters a dual learning role as both recipient and creator of knowledge, an approach grounded in participatory culture and learner agency (Jenkins et al., 2015). While the present narrative structure relies on largely predefined story paths and simplified interaction logic, the platform's underlying architecture is intentionally modular and scalable, laying the groundwork for future expansion and technical sophistication. Unity was selected as the development environment due to its robust multimedia capabilities and flexibility in rapid prototyping. This choice aligned with available development expertise and the ambition to create a visually rich user experience. In retrospect, however, frameworks dedicated to 2D interactive storytelling, such as Ink or Twine, might have proven more efficient for handling complex branching logic and deploying lightweight, text-driven applications (Letonsaari, 2019).

Artificial intelligence (AI) is not yet integrated into the system but is envisioned as a transformative element in subsequent development phases. Its implementation could support subject-matter experts in generating content more efficiently and expand the Comic Automaton's capacity for adaptive, user-driven narratives. For example, AI could dynamically adjust storylines based on learner choices or offer intelligent feedback during comic creation, thereby enriching both the creative and reflective dimensions of learning. Currently, narrative progression is constrained by technical and design considerations to maintain feasibility and focus. As a result, the full potential of emergent, non-linear storytelling where user decisions dynamically shape multiple, meaningful plot outcomes remains untapped. Nonetheless, the system architecture and authoring model are intentionally open to such future enhancements, reinforcing the project's long-term vision of fostering individualized, emotionally engaging, and pedagogically grounded learning experiences.

Initial evaluations of Comic4Welfare focused on user engagement and perceived relevance. Formative feedback from workshops with students in agricultural and animal welfare programs revealed high levels of motivation, curiosity, and a sense of personal relevance. Participants highlighted the value of combining visual storytelling with ethically complex situations and expressed a strong interest in further developing their own comics.

10 Post Evaluation Protocol

As part of a post-evaluation exercise conducted during classroom session, the platform was introduced by the professor as a component of the practical coursework. Since the session was self-moderated, feedback was gathered through PDF submissions and online survey forms. The survey included both qualitative and quantitative questions, offering valuable follow-up insights into user experience and platform effectiveness. Quantitative items focused on rating the platform's usability, engagement, and the likelihood of using it for future learning (Figs. 17, 18, and 19).

These findings form the basis of our evaluation - The survey results across all three charts indicate moderate user engagement and usability, with most participants rated their experience around the midpoint. While the Comic Automaton showed potential, user willingness to continue using it was mixed. The platform overall was seen as somewhat engaging and reasonably easy to use, but the feedback highlights areas for improvement particularly in increasing interactivity, emotional engagement, and clarity of value to enhance learning outcomes. The qualitative questions explored aspects such as the preference between task mode and free mode, the ease of continuing with choices, and how well students perceived the connection between the learning platform and the comics.

The responses provided valuable insight: despite some technical issues, many students made effective use of the task mode. However, a few expressed confusions regarding how to use the comic creator. Nonetheless, the majority of responses reflected that students enjoyed the process and found it fun, even when the purpose or functionality was not fully clear.

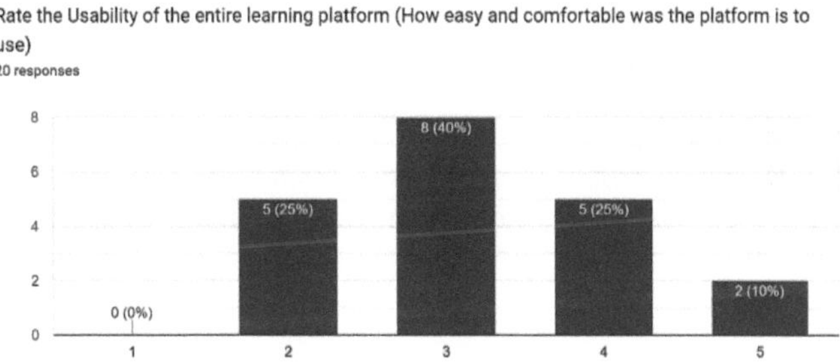

Fig. 17. XXXXX

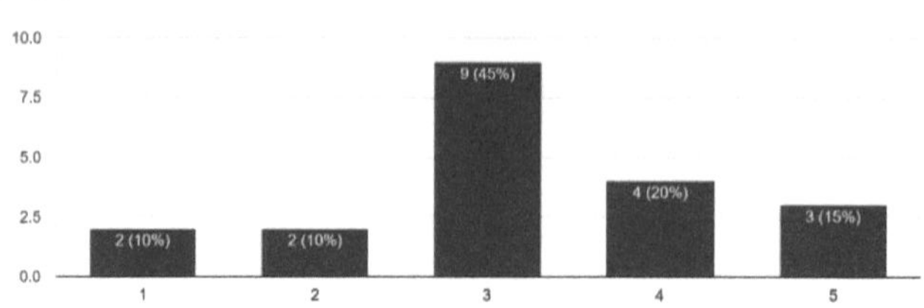

Fig. 18. XXXXXX

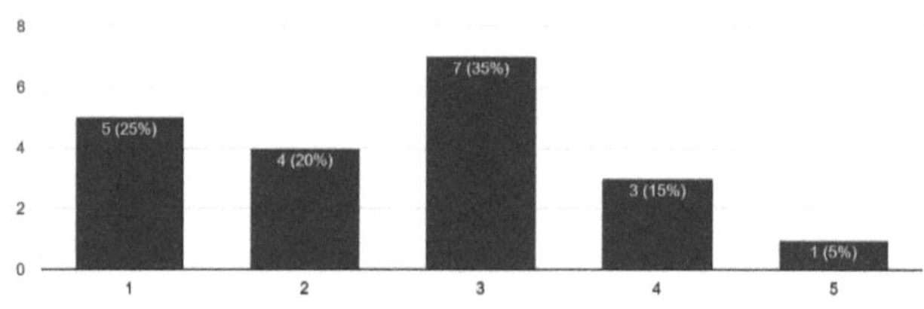

Fig. 19. XXXXXX

These findings suggest that the platform effectively lowers entry barriers, enhances emotional involvement, and supports contextualized understanding. However, the long-term educational effects remain to be systematically evaluated. Future research will need to assess learning outcomes, user retention, and transferability to other subject areas. Moreover, the scalability of the platform and its adaptability to diverse user groups, ranging from vocational trainees to university students and even practitioners, will be critical factors for its sustainable implementation. Comic4Welfare thus represents a promising, but still evolving, approach to transforming agricultural education through creative digital pedagogy.

Acknowledgements. Funding: This work (Model- and Demonstration Project for animal welfare) is financially supported by the Federal Ministry of Food and Agriculture based on a decision of the Parliament of the Federal Republic of Germany, granted by the Federal Office for Agriculture and Food.

Declaration of AI Assistance.. This paper was linguistically refined with the assistance of ChatGPT-4o (OpenAI, 2024). All ideas, interpretations, analyses, and conclusions are entirely the authors' own.

Ethics Declaration.. The authors declare that this work is original and has not been published elsewhere. All sources and references have been appropriately acknowledged. No part of this paper involves plagiarism, data fabrication, or unethical research practices. Where applicable, all necessary ethical approvals have been obtained, and there are no conflicts of interest to declare.

References

Boehm, J., Kayser, M., & Spiller, A.: Two Sides of the Same Coin? International Journal on Food System Dynamics. **1**(3), 264–278 (2010). https://doi.org/10.18461/ijfsd.v1i3.139

Goodbrey, D.M.: Game comics: An analysis of an emergent hybrid form. Journal of Graphic Novels and Comics. **6**(1), 3–14 (2015). https://doi.org/10.1080/21504857.2014.943411

Jansen, J., van den Borne, B.H.P., Renes, R.J., van Schaik, G., Lam, T.J.G.M., Leeuwis, C.: Explaining mastitis incidence in Dutch dairy farming: The influence of farmers' attitudes and behaviour. Prev. Vet. Med. **92**(3), 210–223 (2009). https://doi.org/10.1016/j.prevetmed.2009.08.015

Jenkins, H., Ito, M., & boyd, D.: Participatory Culture in a Networked Era: A Conversation on Youth, Learning, Commerce, and Politics. John Wiley & Sons (2015)

Letonsaari, M.: Nonlinear storytelling method and tools for low-Threshold game development. Seminar. Net. **15**(1), 1–17 (2019). https://doi.org/10.7577/seminar.3074

McGrath, K., Regan, Á., Russell, T.: A user-centred future for agricultural digital innovation: demonstrating the value of design thinking in an animal health context. The Journal of Agricultural Education and Extension, 1–19 (2024). https://doi.org/10.1080/1389224X.2024.2397968

Merle, R. et al.: Application of Epidemiological Methods in a Large-Scale Cross-Sectional Study in 765 German Dairy Herds-Lessons Learned. Animals: An Open Access Journal from MDPI. **14**(9) (2024). https://doi.org/10.3390/ani14091385

Neo, T., Mitchell, A.: Beyond the Gutter. In: Nack, F., Gordon, A.S. (eds.) Lecture Notes in Computer Science: Vol. 10045, Interactive storytelling: 9th International Conference on Interactive Digital Storytelling, ICIDS 2016, Los Angeles, CA, USA, November 15–18, 2016: Proceedings (pp. 375–387). Springer (2016). https://doi.org/10.1007/978-3-319-48279-8_33

Ragland, E.C., Radcliffe, S., Karcher, E.L.: A review of the application of active learning pedagogies in undergraduate animal science curricula. Journal of Animal Science. **101** (2023). https://doi.org/10.1093/jas/skac352

Shiels, D. et al.: A Survey of Farm Management Practices Relating to the Risk Factors, Prevalence, and Causes of Lamb Mortality in Ireland. Animals: An Open Access Journal from MDPI. **12**(1) (2021). https://doi.org/10.3390/ani12010030

Spiller, A. et al.: Wege zu einer gesellschaftlich akzeptierten Nutztierhaltung. Advance online publication (2015) (Berichte über Landwirtschaft - Zeitschrift für Agrarpolitik und Landwirtschaft, Sonderheft 221, März 2015). https://doi.org/10.12767/buel.v0i221.82

Veenema, N.J., Hierck, B.P., Bok, H.G.J., Salvatori, D.C.F.: Links between learning goals, learning activities, and learning outcomes in simulation-based clinical skills training: A systematic review of the veterinary literature. Frontiers in Veterinary Science **11.**, 1463642 (2024). https://doi.org/10.3389/fvets.2024.1463642

Deci, E.L., Ryan, R.M.: The "what" and "why" of goal pursuits: Human needs and the self-determination of behavior. Psychol. Inq. **11**(4), 227–268 (2000). https://doi.org/10.1207/S15327965PLI1104_01

Exploring the Design of Portable Devices in Science Fiction Video Games

Tommi Kiianmies$^{(\boxtimes)}$ ⓘ, Ashley Colley ⓘ, and Jonna Häkkilä ⓘ

University of Lapland, Rovaniemi, Finland
{tommi.kiianmies,ashley.colley,jonna.hakkila}@ulapland.fi

Abstract. The design of handheld interactive devices in science fiction video games often prioritizes visual impact over usability, limiting their plausibility as future technology visions. To investigate the topic, we used physical prototyping and user evaluation to critically examine how such fictional devices might function if realized. We selected 20 devices from popular science fiction games and conducted a visual thematic analysis. Focus groups evaluated both device images and full-scale physical prototypes of one device and redesigned variants. The findings show that many in-game devices suffer from poor ergonomics and unclear interfaces, but small design adjustments, such as relocating buttons or reshaping grips, can improve perceived usability without breaking narrative immersion. This work introduces a user-centered approach to evaluating speculative virtual objects and offers Human Computer Interaction (HCI) researchers and game designers a method for grounding future technology visions in practical interaction concerns.

Keywords: Design fictions · Video games · World building · Imaginary Futures · Design · Ergonomics

1 Introduction

Design fictions and science fictioninspired technology visions are increasingly acknowledged for their role in shaping how future technological trends are imagined and communicated. Design fictions have been used in various domains to present possible technology trends, to manifest how technologies can shape society and user behavior, and to present speculative futures. Design fictions have taken various forms, including physical artifacts such as handheld [7] and wearable devices [11], short films [30], fiction writing and pastiche scenarios [4], as well as fictional research papers [20] and 'imaginary abstracts' for non-existent prototypes [3]. Despite the diverse forms design fiction can take, science fiction remains an underused resource in Human Computer Interaction (HCI) research [14], leaving many opportunities yet to be explored.

Our research focuses on science fiction in video games, specifically analyzing the design of interactive gadgets featured within them. Science fiction games reach a vast user base and serve as a prominent medium for conveying imaginative visions of technology-rich futures. Through gameplay, millions of players are

J. Y. C. Chen et al. (Eds.): HCII 2025, LNCS 16338, pp. 388–401, 2026.
https://doi.org/10.1007/978-3-032-12808-9_24

exposed to designers' creative interpretations of future technologies, which are visualized and articulated as part of the game world. Prior research on video games is vast and has investigated them from many different angles, including both positive and negative effects [26], from improvements in cognitive skills and decision making [27] to concerns about gaming addiction [8]. However, outside of game UIs and player interaction, there is relatively little research on the HCI aspects of game worlds and the design solutions they present. As early as 2009, Bruce Sterling noted that futuristic objects depicted in science fiction were often badly designed [29]. Still, in many science fiction games, portable devices serve as central tools for exploration, communication, and gameplay progression. Understanding how these elements affect user engagement can lead to improved design practices that enhance both usability and narrative coherence. With the increasing sophistication of object design in games, the integration of futuristic technology into interactive storytelling plays a significant role in shaping the player experience [9].

In this study, we first analyzed a sample of interactive devices from science fiction video games, then selected one for redesign and constructed full-size physical prototypes. These, along with the broader sample of devices, were evaluated in a focus group. The findings aim to support game designers and developers in creating intuitive and plausible in-game device interfaces and gadget designs. While many of these devices are visually compelling, our study reveals that they often exhibit ergonomic and usability shortcomings. Through thematic analysis and user evaluation of physical prototypes, we demonstrate that small design adjustments can improve usability without undermining narrative coherence.

2   Related Work

The speculative design of fictional technologies has been used as a tool for exploring future possibilities, both in academic research and in popular media. In design research and HCI, this takes the form of design fiction, diegetic prototypes, and technologies embedded in interactive environments such as video games.

2.1   Design Fictions and Imaginary Technologies

The term *Design Fiction* was first coined by Bruce Sterling [29] and extended in design research to describe speculative artifacts situated in plausible futures. Bleecker describes design fiction as "a conflation of design, science fact, and science fiction" that leverages narrative contexts to raise questions about emerging technologies [2]. Lindley et al. have linked design fiction to research-through-design methodologies [18,19], while others have emphasized its value in world-building, where speculative designs are embedded within broader socio-technical contexts [10].

Diegetic prototypes are a form of design fiction where fictional technologies are portrayed as real within a cinematic narrative [15]. By embedding these prototypes in routine actions and familiar environments, the film creates an impression of technological feasibility and societal acceptance. They have been used in HCI research to explore speculative concepts in areas such as future funerals [30] or wearable technologies [31]. Diegetic prototypes can be used to demonstrate to large audiences a technology's need, viability, and benevolence [15]. Video games extend this narrative approach into interactive spaces. Game players not only view the fictional technologies, but actively interact with them. Video games create fictional experiences that are simultaneously narrative, spatial, and procedural [23], allowing players to interact with speculative devices in ways that are not possible in films.

2.2 Diegetic Interfaces in Video Games

Prior research has explored how user interfaces can be integrated into video game worlds as diegetic elements. These are interfaces that exist within the fictional space and are visible to the character, not just the player. Examples include the RIG suit in *Dead Space*, which displays health and ammo directly on the character model, or the Pip-Boy in *Fallout*, a wearable terminal to manage inventory and missions. Bowers categorized game interfaces into non-diegetic, diegetic, spatial, and meta types, highlighting how UI elements may or may not be grounded in the game's world and story [5]. Diegetic interfaces are often praised for increasing immersion, although they introduce trade-offs in usability and development complexity [22]. Andersson examined the trade-off between immersion and usability by comparing a non-diegetic inventory UI to a diegetic version embedded as an in-world object [1]. While the diegetic interface was found to enhance immersion, participants preferred the non-diegetic version for its simplicity and ease of use. Similar findings have been reported from other sources, diegetic interfaces often promote engagement and realism but can compromise efficiency and player performance [17,22,25]. For example, Rosyid et al. [28] observed improved immersion in role-playing games when using diegetic interfaces, though their impact on usability was unclear. Similarly, Iacovides et al. [13] found that replacing traditional head-up display (HUD) elements with diegetic alternatives increased players' sense of control and involvement, but introduced usability challenges, particularly during high-intensity gameplay.

Portable in-game devices, such as the Omni-Tool in *Mass Effect*, the Focus in *Horizon Zero Dawn*, and the OmniWrench and Holo-guise in the *Ratchet & Clank* series [12], are examples of diegetic interfaces that double as speculative technologies. These devices typically serve both gameplay and narrative functions, enabling scanning, hacking, or tactical management. They embody the intersection of interaction design and storytelling, simulating how wearable or handheld tech might shape future human-computer interaction.

Building on the prior work, this paper focuses specifically on portable diegetic interfaces in science fiction games, examining how they are designed, embedded in gameplay, and used to speculate on technological futures.

3   Object Analysis and Redesign

To investigate the design qualities of interactive gadgets in science fiction games, we first conducted a visual analysis of 20 selected devices. This analysis informed the redesign of one object, which was then fabricated as a full-scale physical prototype for further study. The following sections describe the analytical process, selection rationale, and construction of the models.

3.1   Selecting Game Objects

To examine common patterns in the design of portable in-game devices, we selected 20 examples from popular science fiction video games and related media. The selection prioritized titles using first-person or third-person perspectives with photorealistic or semi-photorealistic visual styles, while excluding stylized or cartoon-like aesthetics such as *Ratchet & Clank* [12]. First-person games typically support more direct diegetic interaction, but third-person titles were included where the character in-world visibly handles devices. The focus was specifically on interactive devices, as these serve functional roles within the gameplay and are not merely background props. For example, the Pip-Boy in *Fallout 4* is strapped to the character's arm and functions as an interactive in-game menu through which the player can manage inventory, check stats, and navigate the world. All the selected games fall within the science fiction genre and include narrative or environmental elements that support speculative technology. The titles were selected based on commercial success, critical recognition, or cultural prominence, and include widely known examples such as *Half-Life 2*, *Cyberpunk 2077*, and *Alien: Isolation*. Devices were identified through gameplay footage, fan documentation, and concept art, and filtered to include only handheld or body-worn objects integrated into the diegesis, e.g. for scanning, communication, hacking, or mission-related tasks (Table 1 and Fig. 1).

3.2   Object Analysis

To investigate the design qualities of the selected interactive devices, a visual thematic analysis was conducted using an affinity wall approach [21]. Images of the objects were arranged and iteratively grouped into emergent categories based on their visual or functional characteristics. The clustering process was carried out using an online whiteboard tool, enabling images to be duplicated and included in multiple groups where appropriate. Each device was first examined independently, then compared with others to identify recurring patterns. The analysis focused on visual form, perceived usability, clarity of function, and ergonomic plausibility as represented in the images, aiming to identify recurring design issues across the selected objects based on visual cues rather than gameplay.

The coding process resulted in seven problem categories: unwieldiness, difficulty of use, unclear interface, awkward operation, clumsy appearance, fragile construction, and heavy or burdensome form (Table 2). Several devices exhibited

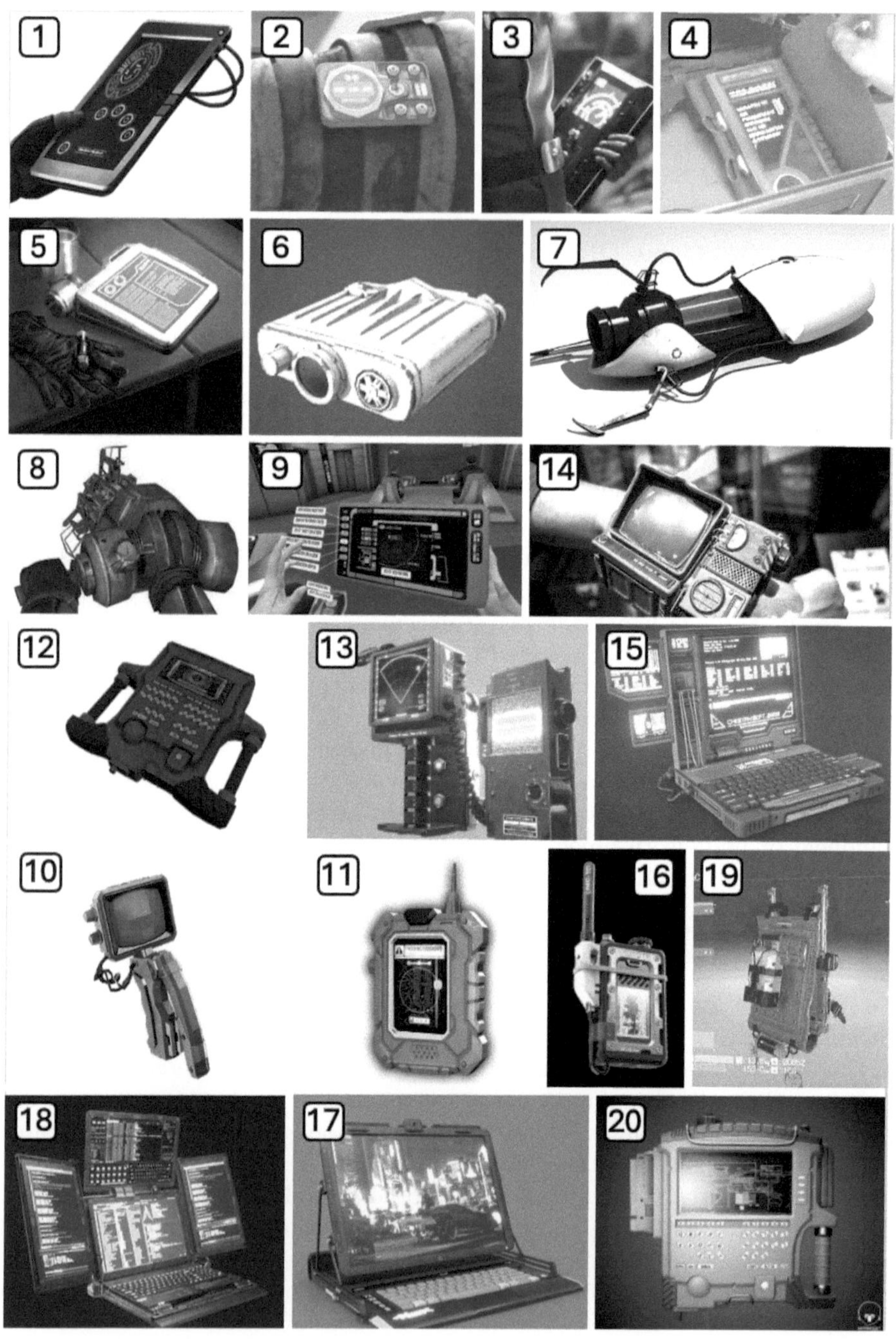

Fig. 1. Selected game objects

Table 1. Selected portable devices from science fiction video games.

	Game or Media	Device	Function
1	Star Wars: Episode III – Revenge of the Sith	Data pad	Mission data access
2	Star Wars: The Old Republic	Chronometer	Timekeeping/interface lore
3	Star Wars: The Force Unleashed II	Data pad	Mission objectives
4	Battlefront: Twilight Company	Data pad	Tactical command
5	Star Wars: Battlefront (2004)	Recon Intel	Map & targeting
6	Star Wars Jedi: Fallen Order	Binoculars	Environment scanning
7	Portal 2	Portal gun	Mobility/puzzle
8	Half-Life 2	Gravity Gun	Object manipulation
9	Star Trek: Bridge Crew	PADD	System control & commands
10	Deep Rock Galactic	Laser pointer	Ping/mark/navigate
11	Deep Rock Galactic	Hacking pad	Objective interaction
12	Aliens vs. Predator 3	Hacking tool computer	Minigame/access
13	Alien Isolation	Tracker	Motion detection
14	Fallout 4	Pip-Boy	Stats/inventory/map
15	Cyberpunk 2077	Laptop	Access/hacking/browsing
16	Cyberpunk 2077	Walkie-talkie	Comm with NPCs
17	Cyberpunk 2077	Laptop	Hacking
18	Cyberpunk 2077	Laptop	Story delivery
19	Death Stranding	Backpack	Equipment carrying/gameplay mod
20	Alien Isolation	Hacking device	Security access

multiple overlapping problems, e.g. objects 7 and 8 were each associated with four distinct negative traits, including clumsiness, perceived awkwardness during use, and excessive bulk. In contrast, object 6 did not appear in any problem categories and was perceived as visually clean and functionally sound. Based on the combined analysis of form and perceived usability, objects 1, 6, 9, and 17 were considered well-designed. Objects 2, 5, 10, 11, 16, and 19 were average in design quality, while the remaining half of the devices were judged to be poorly designed due to multiple visual or ergonomic problems.

The in-game use context of each device was also taken into consideration. Eight of the twenty devices played a central role and were consistently visible during gameplay (e.g., the Portal gun in *Portal 2*), ten were used intermittently for specific tasks, and two served as non-interactive background elements.

This usage context informed the evaluation of how effectively each device's visual design supported or hindered its perceived usability. The analysis also identified several cases where stylistic choices appeared to compromise the ergonomic function. For example, the handles on the hacking tool computer in *Aliens vs. Predator* (object 12) were noted to obstruct access to key buttons, potentially hindering the device's intended use. Such cases illustrate the trade-off between visual style and functional clarity in the design of speculative in-game technologies.

Table 2. Summary of common design issues identified during visual affinity wall analysis.

Defect Category	Objects
Unwieldy	3, 7, 8, 13
Difficult to use	2, 3, 12, 19
Unclear interface	1, 2, 5, 9, 11, 16
Awkward to operate	7, 8
Clumsy appearance	3, 5, 7, 8, 11, 13, 14
Fragile-looking	15, 17, 18
Heavy-looking	7, 8, 12, 13, 14

3.3   Game Object Redesign

To provide further insights into the trade-offs in game object design, a redesign task was included in the study. This enabled critical reflection on how speculative interfaces from digital games communicate function, support interaction, and reflect design values when translated into physical form. This process involved creating full-size physical models of the original and redesigned objects, allowing participants to physically handle previously virtual devices. This hands-on interaction provided a more concrete basis for evaluating ergonomics and usability, increasing the validity of the user feedback collected during focus group sessions.

Based on the findings from the visual evaluation, the hacking tool computer from Aliens vs. Predator (object 12) was selected for redesign. Thematic analysis linked it to several design issues, such as clumsy appearance, awkward use, and obstructive handles, showing clear room for ergonomic improvement. In the game, the device is used to hack into secure areas and is represented as a handheld unit weighing 4.2 kg with dimensions of approximately $25 \times 20 \times 6$ cm [32]. The redesign focused solely on the object's physical characteristics, aiming to improve form and usability without altering its fictional software functions. A full-scale physical model was created to match the in-game representation, enabling hands-on evaluation of proposed improvements and their potential to enhance immersion.

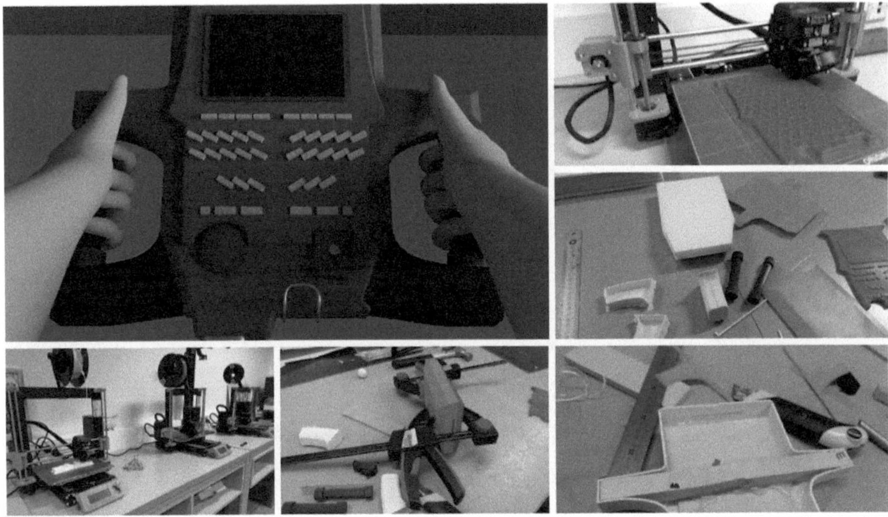

Fig. 2. 3-D modeling and construction of the hacking computer (object 12).

The object redesign process included the following steps, (1) mapping of the original design's shortcomings, (2) benchmarking similar devices, (3) 3D modeling the original object, (4) ideation and modeling of redesign alternatives, (5) 3D printing of both versions, (6) focus group evaluation, and (7) final refinement and synthesis of results. The original hacking tool presented several ergonomic issues, which contributed to a broader usability issue. Most critically, the device's handles were poorly placed, too low and far from the center of gravity, resulting in a front-heavy object that was difficult to hold and operate. Additionally, the device's buttons were positioned such that they could not be operated without removing one hand from the handle, disrupting use.

Two alternative designs were developed to improve the object's ergonomics while maintaining visual consistency with the game, based on insights from the defect mapping and benchmarking. Full-size physical prototypes were then created using 3D modeling and printing (Fig. 2). Although the original in-game object was specified as weighing 4.2 kg, the printed models were made lighter (approximately half that weight) to support ease of evaluation. The models were printed at a 1:1 scale with hollow interiors. The original version included wooden reinforcement due to its fragility. All models were painted to look accurate, but realistic materials were not used as the prototypes were made for testing ergonomics, not as exact replicas (Fig. 3).

4   Evaluation of the Designs

Focus groups were used to explore the topic and evaluate the physical prototypes, offering a structured yet flexible format for gathering diverse perspectives on open-ended questions [16].

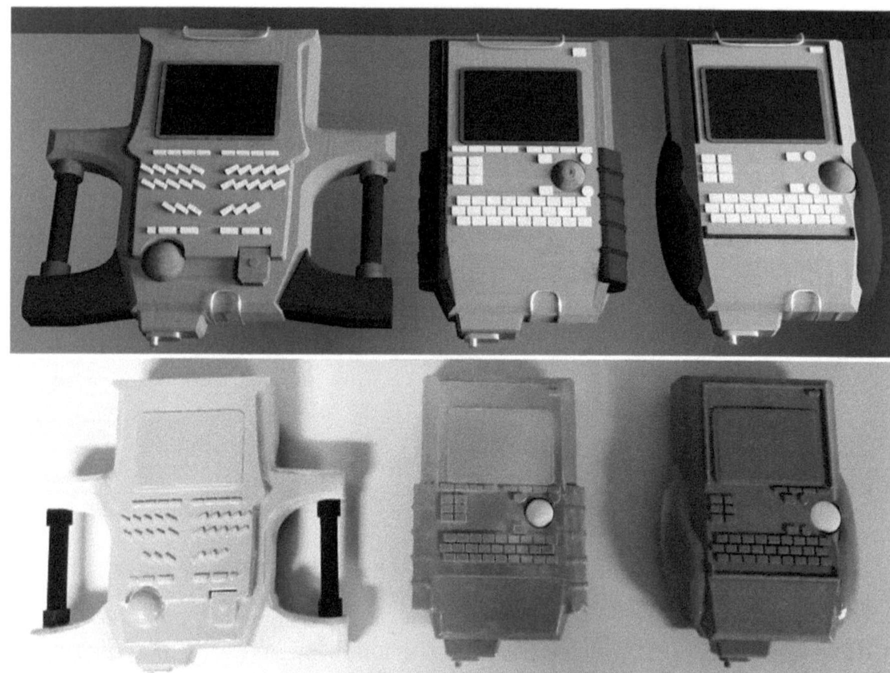

Fig. 3. 3D-models and 3D-prints of the original hacking device (object 12) and the two redesigned prototypes.

4.1   Focus Group

Method. To explore opinions of portable diegetic interface devices in video games, a focus group was invited. The session started with participants providing informed consent, background information, and completing a warm-up task. Participants then shared their opinions by placing post-it notes on 20 images of diegetic interface devices from video games (Fig. 1), which were displayed around the room. Following this, an open discussion was facilitated, based on the comments and observations recorded on the post-it notes. During this discussion, participants were free to add additional post-its and comments. Finally, participants handled the physical 3D models of the hacking tool computer and provided feedback on their overall impressions, as well as on the perceived ergonomics and usability of the devices. The focus groups were conducted by a facilitator and an observer who documented the proceedings. The sessions were audio recorded, and participants were encouraged to think aloud [24].

Two focus group sessions were held, including a total of 7 participants. Participants' ages ranged from 21 to 38 years, with a mean of 24 years. Three participants self-identified as men, three as women, and one as other. All participants reported playing video games at least occasionally, with more than half playing weekly or more frequently. All participants stated that they had noticed the design of artifacts used in video games.

Results. Participants attached a total of 52 post-it note comments to the probe images. Three images received no comments at all. The data were analyzed using open coding thematic analysis following Braun and Clarke's framework [6]. One researcher developed an initial codebook through inductive coding. Two researchers then independently coded all 52 comments using the codebook. Coding discrepancies were reviewed and resolved through discussion, leading to agreement on the final thematic structure. Themes were further organized into sub-themes to better capture the nuances in participant feedback. In cases where comments related to multiple aspects, they were assigned to more than one sub-theme. Table 3 presents an overview of the resulting categories and associated frequencies.

Overall, 72% of comments had a negative sentiment. Perceived problems with *Comfort and Handling* was the most mentioned sub-theme (24% of comments), e.g., "Might be hard to use and hold at the same time" (item 12) and "Looks heavy" (item 14). *Interface clarity and learnability* received a large number of comments, which were evenly divided in polarity, e.g., positively "Easy to use/simple appearance" (object 1) and negatively "Lots of small buttons, somewhat messy" (object 20). Participants noted *perceived build and durability* problems with some objects, e.g., "Exposed circuit board breaks on impact" (item 20) and "Looks cheap" (item 1).

Participants noted that some objects (items 3, 9, and 18) lacked *Futururistic appeal* or *Visual coherence with the game world*. On the other hand, 5 items were criticized for poor narrative fit (1, 7, 9, 10, 20), e.g., "Coloring makes it look like a toy" (item 10).

When handling the 3 physical probe items, based on image item 12, most participants considered the original model's handles to be useless or even actually hindering its operation. The placement of the unit's power button was also criticized as awkward or unintuitive. One participant stated, "Commodore [64] style

Table 3. Thematic analysis of participant feedback on selected objects from video games (Fig. 1), showing the number of mentions for each subtheme. The reference number of the objects referred to is shown in parentheses.

	Positive Mentions	Negative Mentions
Usability and Ergonomics		
Build and Durability	**3** (3, 11, 16)	**7** (1, 7, 7, 8, 8, 15, 20)
Comfort and Handling	**1** (2)	**16** (3, 6, 7, 8, 8, 10, 11, 11, 12, 13, 14, 14, 14, 14, 14, 20)
Interface Clarity and Learnability	**10** (1, 3, 6, 9, 10, 15, 15, 17, 17, 20)	**14** (1, 6, 7, 7, 7, 8, 9, 10, 10, 12, 13, 13, 20, 20)
Narrative Fit and Immersive Coherence		
Futuristic Appeal	**2** (9, 18)	**6** (1, 9, 9, 9, 10, 20)
Visual Coherence with Game World	**3** (3, 18, 18)	**6** (1, 1, 7, 10, 10, 10)

keyboards are no longer used", an issue that was considered during the redesign process. Both redesigned models received mainly positive reactions. The first version was generally preferred, as participants felt it better reflected the game's visual style. One participant proposed relocating the ball mouse to the center of the device to accommodate both left- and right-handed users. However, the group was unable to identify a layout that would still allow the mouse to be operated with the thumb of the hand holding the device. The second redesigned prototype was described by six out of seven participants as more comfortable to handle and ergonomically improved, although less aligned with the visual style of the game.

5   Discussion

This study examined how players perceive and evaluate the design of interactive, handheld devices in science fiction video games through the physical prototyping of a redesigned in-game object and focus group evaluation. Our findings from the focus group evaluations align with earlier research that highlights the importance of diegetic elements for player immersion [1,17,25]. Participants valued devices that felt native to the game world and offered clear functional cues, consistent with Andersson's findings on inventory UIs [1] and Peacocke et al.'s observation that strong narrative fit enhances engagement, while poor interaction design may reduce performance [25]. Our results also confirm reports by Köhle et al. that physical plausibility shapes the credibility of in-world tools [17].

Where our study differs from prior work is in its emphasis on tangible ergonomics. Whereas earlier research has relied on on-screen prototypes or VR mock-ups, we created full-scale physical models, enabling direct perception of factors such as weight, balance, and grip. This provided insights into physical usability that cannot be identified by screen-based evaluations. This physical prototyping is not typical in design fiction methods, and demonstrates how speculative interfaces can be assessed not only for narrative plausibility but also for ergonomic viability. This hybrid approach offers a contribution to both game asset design and design fiction practice, connecting imagined digital artifacts and real-world interaction.

The redesign of the *Aliens vs. Predator* hacking tool focused on addressing the key ergonomic issues identified in the visual analysis, such as the placement of handles and button reachability. The focus group participants responded positively to these changes, reporting improved comfort and handling. While the study did not measure presence directly, participants' comments suggest that greater physical plausibility and coherence with expected use may enhance perceived realism. This supports prior observations by Marre et al. that natural interaction in diegetic interfaces can contribute to a sense of presence [22], and extends the discussion by exploring how tangible design changes can shape user perceptions of virtual tools. This work also connects to the findings by Rosyid et al. [28], who examined whether diegetic interfaces enhance immersion in role-playing games. While their focus was on immersive potential, our results suggest that improved physical plausibility and usability need not come at the cost of narrative coherence, pointing to design strategies that balance both.

A key limitation of this study is that the focus group evaluation was based on static images of the in-game objects, which may have constrained participants' ability to assess in-game contextual immersion. Additionally, while the physical models offered insight into ergonomic perception, the study did not measure long-term usability or performance during interactive tasks.

6   Conclusion

This study explored the design of portable interactive devices in science fiction video games by combining visual analysis, thematic analysis, and physical device prototyping. While these virtual devices often support the game narrative and contribute to world-building, our analysis revealed they often suffer from shortcomings in ergonomics, clarity of use, and physical plausibility. Despite their futuristic appearance, analyzed objects exhibited design flaws such as poor weight distribution, awkward control placement, or ambiguous interface logic.

This study demonstrates how translating virtual diegetic objects into full-size physical prototypes can uncover design insights that are otherwise overlooked in screen-based analysis. By allowing users to handle and evaluate speculative devices, we were able to examine ergonomic factors such as balance, grip, and button placement, key elements often neglected in fictional interfaces. The findings show that narrative coherence and usability are not mutually exclusive, and small physical refinements can improve perceived functionality. Although the study was conducted outside of gameplay, the method offers a promising way to assess fictional design through user-centered principles, contributing to both interaction design research and the development of more believable game worlds.

Acknowledgments. The research has been supported by the MOCAPPE project, co-funded by ERDF/Regional Council of Lapland, and the Research Council of Finland as part of the Human Augmentation through Aware Extended Reality (AWARE) project (decision 355694).

Disclosure of Interests. The authors have no competing interests to declare that are relevant to the content of this article.

References

1. Andersson, R.: Effects of diegetic user interface on immersion and user experience in video games (2024). https://www.theseus.fi/handle/10024/862563
2. Bleecker, J.: Design fiction: a short essay on design, science, fact, and fiction. In: Machine Learning and the City: Applications in Architecture and Urban Design, pp. 561–578 (2022)
3. Blythe, M.: Research through design fiction: narrative in real and imaginary abstracts. In: Proceedings of the SIGCHI Conference on Human Factors in Computing Systems, pp. 703–712. ACM (2014)

4. Blythe, M.A., Wright, P.C.: Pastiche scenarios: fiction as a resource for user centred design. Interact. Comput. **18**(5), 1139–1164 (2006)
5. Bowers, M.: Level up: a guide to game UI. Toptal Design Blog (2019). https://www.toptal.com/designers/ui/game-ui
6. Braun, V., Clarke, V.: Using thematic analysis in psychology. Qual. Res. Psychol. **3**(2), 77–101 (2006)
7. Brun, D., Jordan, P., Häkkilä, J.: Demonstrating a memory orb—cylindrical device inspired by science fiction. In: Proceedings of the 20th International Conference on Mobile and Ubiquitous Multimedia, pp. 239–241. ACM (2021)
8. Brunborg, G.S., Mentzoni, R.A., Frøyland, L.R.: Is video gaming, or video game addiction, associated with depression, academic achievement, heavy episodic drinking, or conduct problems? J. Behav. Addict. **3**(1), 27–32 (2014)
9. Christou, G.: The interplay between immersion and appeal in video games. Comput. Hum. Behav. **32**, 92–100 (2014)
10. Coulton, P., Lindley, J., Sturdee, M., Stead, M.: Design fiction as world building. In: Proceedings of the 3rd Biennial Research Through Design Conference, pp. 1–16 (2017)
11. Etto, J., Kirjavainen, E., Kalving, M., Häkkilä, J.: Aware eye-wearable provotype as a playful design on sensing environments. In: Proceedings of the International Conference on Mobile and Ubiquitous Multimedia, pp. 442–444. ACM (2024)
12. Games, I.: Ratchet & clank: Rift apart. PlayStation 5 Game (2021). Sony Interactive Entertainment
13. Iacovides, I., Cox, A., Kennedy, R., Cairns, P., Jennett, C.: Removing the HUD: the impact of non-diegetic game elements and expertise on player involvement. In: Proceedings of the 2015 Annual Symposium on Computer-Human Interaction in Play, pp. 13–22. ACM (2015)
14. Jordan, P., Silva, P.A.: Science fiction—an untapped opportunity in HCI research and education. In: Soares, M.M., Rosenzweig, E., Marcus, A. (eds.) HCII 2021. LNCS, vol. 12779, pp. 34–47. Springer, Cham (2021). https://doi.org/10.1007/978-3-030-78221-4_3
15. Kirby, D.: The future is now: diegetic prototypes and the role of popular films in generating real-world technological development. Soc. Stud. Sci. **40**(1), 41–70 (2010)
16. Krueger, R.A.: Focus Groups: A Practical Guide for Applied Research. Sage Publications (2014)
17. Köhle, K., Hoppe, M., Schmidt, A., Mäkelä, V.: Diegetic and non-diegetic health interfaces in VR shooter games. In: Ardito, C., et al. (eds.) INTERACT 2021. LNCS, vol. 12934, pp. 3–11. Springer, Cham (2021). https://doi.org/10.1007/978-3-030-85613-7_1
18. Lindley, J.: Researching design fiction with design fiction. In: Proceedings of the 2015 ACM SIGCHI Conference on Creativity and Cognition, pp. 325–326. ACM (2015)
19. Lindley, J., Coulton, P.: Back to the future: 10 years of design fiction. In: Proceedings of the 2015 British HCI Conference, pp. 210–211 (2015)
20. Lindley, J., Coulton, P.: Pushing the limits of design fiction: the case for fictional research papers. In: proceedings of the 2016 CHI Conference on Human Factors in Computing Systems, pp. 4032–4043. ACM (2016)
21. Lucero, A.: Using affinity diagrams to evaluate interactive prototypes. In: Abascal, J., Barbosa, S., Fetter, M., Gross, T., Palanque, P., Winckler, M. (eds.) INTERACT 2015, Part II. LNCS, vol. 9297, pp. 231–248. Springer, Cham (2015). https://doi.org/10.1007/978-3-319-22668-2_19

22. Marre, Q., Caroux, L., Sakdavong, J.C.: Video game interfaces and diegesis: the impact on experts and novices' performance and experience in virtual reality. Int. J. Hum.-Comput. Interact. **37**(12), 1089–1103 (2021)
23. Meskin, A., Robson, J.: Fiction and fictional worlds in videogames. In: Sageng, J., Fossheim, H., Mandt Larsen, T. (eds.) The Philosophy of Computer Games. Philosophy of Engineering and Technology, vol. 7, pp. 201–217. Springer, Dordrecht (2012). https://doi.org/10.1007/978-94-007-4249-9_14
24. Nielsen, J.: Usability Engineering. Morgan Kaufmann (1993)
25. Peacocke, M., Teather, R.J., Carette, J., MacKenzie, I.S., McArthur, V.: An empirical comparison of first-person shooter information displays: HUDs, diegetic displays, and spatial representations. Entertain. Comput. **26**, 41–58 (2018). https://doi.org/10.1016/j.entcom.2018.01.003
26. Prot, S., Anderson, C.A., Gentile, D.A., Brown, S.C., Swing, E.L.: The positive and negative effects of video game play. Media Well-being Child. Adolescents **109**, 2010–2014 (2014)
27. Reynaldo, C., Christian, R., Hosea, H., Gunawan, A.A.: Using video games to improve capabilities in decision making and cognitive skill: a literature review. Procedia Comput. Sci. **179**, 211–221 (2021)
28. Rosyid, H.A., Pangestu, A.Y., Akbar, M.I.: Can diegetic user interface improve immersion in role-playing games? In: 2021 7th International Conference on Electrical, Electronics and Information Engineering (ICEEIE), pp. 200–204. IEEE (2021)
29. Sterling, B.: Cover story design fiction. Interactions **16**(3), 20–24 (2009)
30. Uriu, D., Arima, S.: Designing virtual funerals as a design fiction: a film-based exploration of near-future memorial rituals. In: Proceedings of the 2025 CHI Conference on Human Factors in Computing Systems, pp. 1–19. ACM (2025)
31. Wang, J., Juhlin, O., Hughes, N.: Fashion film as design fiction for wearable concepts. In: Proceedings of the 2017 CHI Conference Extended Abstracts on Human Factors in Computing Systems, pp. 461–461. ACM (2017)
32. Weyland Fandom Wiki: Hacking device (2014). https://weyland.fandom.com/wiki/Hacking_Device. Accessed June 2025

Critical Sound Identification for Children with Autism Spectrum Disorder: Toward Personalized Serious Games for Auditory Desensitization

Hanan Makki Zakai[(✉)] [ID]

Qindeel Studio, Riyadh, Saudi Arabia
hananmakki@gmail.com

Abstract. Children with Autism Spectrum Disorder (ASD) frequently experience auditory hypersensitivity, which can significantly impact their daily lives. While serious games (SGs) have shown promise in addressing sensory challenges, limited research exists on identifying the specific sounds most distressing to this population. This study aimed to determine the critical auditory stimuli for children with ASD and assess whether sound intensity influences their perceived discomfort. An Audio Interactive Questionnaire alike digital questionnaire was developed, incorporating 30 sounds across categories (low-frequency, high-frequency, sudden) with varying intensities. Participants (n = 12 males aged 8–11 with ASD) rated sounds using a Likert-scale emoji interface. Results identified seven sounds as most aversive: high-intensity fire engine sirens, traffic noise, baby crying, drilling, school bells, and trains. While higher-intensity sounds generally elicited stronger negative responses, exceptions (e.g., checkout till sounds) suggested individual variability. These findings highlight the need for personalized SG interventions to desensitize children with ASD to distressing auditory stimuli, emphasizing the role of sound characteristics in therapeutic design.

Keywords: Serious Games · Game-Based Therapy · Autism Spectrum Disorder · Moderating Sensory Hypersensitivity · Auditory Hypersensitivity · Hyperacusis

1 Introduction

Many children with Autism Spectrum Disorder often struggle with Moderating Sensory Hypersensitivity (MSH) in one or multiple sensory modalities, including those involving tactile, visual, vestibular and auditory contexts [1] and [2]. SGs have shown a certain degree of effectiveness in helping children with ASD and hypersensitivity. Several studies have suggested the effectiveness of therapeutic games for children with ASD [3] and [4]. Despite increasing research in the field, there is still a lack of understanding concerning the functioning of SGs when used in the context of ASD with MSH [5] and [6]. Nevertheless, to the best of our knowledge, there is little number of published studies in

J. Y. C. Chen et al. (Eds.): HCII 2025, LNCS 16338, pp. 402–413, 2026.
https://doi.org/10.1007/978-3-032-12808-9_25

this area, and particularly when focusing on auditory hypersensitivity. The game EASe Funhouse Treasure Hun[1] uses 3D game technology to help ASD children and all other children diagnosed with auditory hypersensitivity, and sensory integration disorder to cope with noise and improve their sensory processing [7].

2   Rational and Objective

Although such hypersensitivity is the most commonly reported by parents of autistic children [8] and many autistic children are thought to suffer from this sensitivity [9], a few studies have discussed what the most relevant noises are [6], since there are large individual differences [10]. This an experimental approach aims to determine the major characteristics of the sounds that are related to sound sensitivity among children with ASD and address the following research questions through an Audio Interactive Questionnaire (AIQ) alike digital questionnaire:

- Research question: What are the most critical sounds for children with ASD?
- Sub-research question: Does the intensity of sounds affect the degree to which children with ASD tend to consider these sounds?

Building upon an exhaustive literature review [6] and discussions with experts in the field, ten types of sounds were selected among those proposed by [11]. These sounds represented most disturbing sounds according to people with auditory hypersensitivity, and classified in three categories; low-frequency sounds (drilling, traffic noise, dog barking); high frequency sounds (rattling of dishes, child crying, rustling of paper, applause, birdsong); and sudden sounds (hammering and door slamming). In addition, five other sounds proposed by [12] were added to the selection. These sounds consisted of school bell, supermarket till, train, fire engine siren, and fireworks banging. The outcomes of the proposed experiment will assist in the design and development of an SG strategy that will effectively familiarize autistic children with auditory hypersensitivity to those critical sounds.

3   Methods

3.1   Recruitment of Participants

The strategy for recruiting participants followed a three-stage approach: (1) send an invitation letter; (2) arrange meetings for individual groups; and (3) conduct the preliminary experiment. Invitations were sent by e-mail to parents with children with ASD as well as to institutions for children with special needs, including Scottish Autism, The Scottish, Autism Research Group, Strathclyde Autistic Society Club (SASC) and Kindred Scotland, targeting at ASD children. Additionally, recruitment of participants was assisted by psychologists from Creatovators CIC in Glasgow. Although the study was advertised at schools, parent-led organizations, psychologists and various groups on social media (Call for Participants, Facebook, Twitter), the number of participants was

---

[1] www.vision-play.com/product/ease-funhouse-tresure-hunt

lower than expected. However, recruitment appeared to be was challenging and lengthy, requiring approximately one year to enroll a relatively small cohort of participants. After six months of repeated attempts, it seemed that many parents with ASD children often assume that their children do not live with sound hypersensitivity.

3.2 Materials

Different software was used for developing the AIQ alike digital questionnaire, for various purposes such as editing audios, designing graphics, and developing the AIQ application.

Audio Design. Most of the audio resources were collected from the audio library of the Glasgow School of Art, while a few audio samples were taken from the Freesound website[2] (Table 1). In terms of ensuring auditor level safety, I used Reaper 2016 software to measure all 30 sound levels to be no more than 80 dB [15], whilst Adobe Audition CC 2016 was utilized for editing, such as duplicating some audio samples (doors and school bells).

Table 1. Sounds used for audio experiments.

No	Sounds	Intensity	Description	Time (S)
1	Applause 1	Low	A few claps in small room	10
2	Applause 2	High	Many audience claps in a hall	10
3	Baby Crying 1	Low	Sound of a crying new-born baby (3 weeks)	9
4	Baby Crying 2	High	Sound of a crying baby (5 months)	9
5	Bell 1	Low	Close sound of school bell ringing once	6
6	Bell 2	High	Distant sound of school bell ringing twice	10
7	Bird 1	Low	Sound of a seagull repeated 3 times	11
8	Bird 2	High	Sound of small bird chirping 3 times	4
9	Checkout Till 1	Low	Sounds of one scanner beeping 7 times	8
10	Checkout Till 2	High	Sounds of 3 scanners beeping in different timing	10
11	Dog 1	Low	Sound of Labrador puppy barking	5
12	Dog 2	High	Sound of old Rottweiler dog barking	10
13	Door slamming 1	Low	Sound of car door slamming 3 times	7
14	Door slamming 2	High	Sound of wooden door slamming 3 times	8
15	Drill 1	Low	Sound of drilling wood once	8
16	Door slamming 2	High	Sound of small drill (tooth drill) twice	12

(continued)

<hr>

2 https://freesound.org/home/login/

Table 1. (continued)

No	Sounds	Intensity	Description	Time (S)
17	Fire engine 1	Low	Sound of 2 fire engine sirens	10
18	Fire engine 2	High	Sound of 2 fire engine sirens	10
19	Fireworks 1	Low	Sounds of hissing and banging fireworks on floor	9
20	Fireworks 2	High	Sound of banging fireworks in sky 3 times	4
21	Hammering 1	Low	Sound of one hammer hammering 7 times	10
22	Hammering 2	High	Sounds of 3 hammers hitting wood and metal	10
23	Rattling dishes 1	High	Sound of tidying dishes and cutlery in a drawer	10
24	Rattling dishes 2	Low	Sound of tidying dishes and cutlery in a drawer	11
25	Rustling paper 1	Low	Sound of turning 3 pages	11
26	Rustling paper 2	High	Sound of fast rustling a bunch of papers	6
27	Traffic noise 1	High	Sounds of crowded cars and horns in traffic	10
28	Traffic noise 2	Low	Sounds of 3 cars passing by	10
29	Train 1	Low	Sound of a steam train passing by a platform	9
30	Train 2	High	Sound of a moving train and horn passing by a platform	12

Graphic Design. A series of emoji and buttons (Fig. 1) were designed using Adobe Illustrator CS6 and Photoshop CS6, in order to translate the Likert scale items into graphical information that children could easily understand.

Fig. 1. Designs of Emoji and buttons in the AIQ application.

Application Development. The AIQ alike digital questionnaire application was developed using the Unity3D5.6 game engine (Fig. 2) on Apple and Windows compatible computers. Unity 3D is a well-known piece of software for game engine design which has been used by artists, designers and developers. It is utilized for 2D and 3D scene design tools, storytelling, lighting, audio, sprite management tools, particle effects and animation. Participants were asked to rate all sounds using the smiley like emoji described in the previous section and data were collected on real time in an external text file. Audio files were randomized before reproduction in order to avoid any possible order effect.

Fig. 2. Designs of Emoji and buttons in the AIQ application.

4   Experimental Procedure

Based on the participants' and their gatekeepers' preferences, the experimental study was conducted in different places, including at the GSA, Creatovators CIC, Strathclyde Autistic Society Club and participants' homes. The experimental procedure consisted of three stages: (1) a pilot test; and (2) and a formal testing throughout which ratings of sounds were collected as experimental data.

4.1   Pilot Testing

The AIQ was tested on typical healthy children (n = 3) with the same age range (8–11) as the target audience; two participants at The Glasgow School of Art and one at their home. THE AUTHOR observed the children and took notes during the course of each of the assessment steps required during the experimental study. The objectives of the pilot-test are to:

- Measure the duration of the experiment
- Explore any difficulties or issues of using the AIQ on a computer
- Understand how accessible it is for children

- Test the functionality of emojis and other buttons in the AIQ
- Test the sounds' volume • Ensure that the system is collecting data properly into an external file (Appendix I-5)
- Ensure that the sound order is randomized from one participant to another

Prior to conducting the pilot-test, the author ensured that the volume for every participant was suitable by testing a sound. Additionally, the participant was asked whether they prefer to wear headphones or earphones. Lastly, the participant was shown how to interact with the AIQ; as illustrated in Figure xx, there are three steps required to answer the questions on the AIQ interface: 1) in the right top box the tester is required to enter their initials – this is important in order to link each participant's answers to the AQ-Children questionnaire (Auyeung et al., 2007), (Appendix H) by their gate-keepers; 2) the participant is asked to play the button and rate the sounds they heard based on their feelings by clicking one of the emojis in a typical Likert scale (Very Happy = 1, Somewhat Happy = 2, OK = 3, Somewhat Unhappy = 4 and Not Happy at All = 5); and 3) once the participant has rated all sounds the system transfers them to the thanking scene. At the end of the test, the testers were handed a gift (rubber animal eraser). The testing was successful, with no technical issues or complications. However, there was one common comment from the testers which was that the volume was too low and needed to be increased.

4.2 Experiment 1

Consent Forms (3 min). Before the experiment day, gatekeepers of children with ASD were e-mailed the Project Information Sheet. They were informed about the objectives of the experiment, their right as participants to leave the study at any point, their participation being anonymous, confidentiality of experimental data being ensured by assigning a unique numerical identification to each participant, and policies of publication for scientific purposes through informative documentation provided to them before their performing the experiment. Gatekeepers were then asked to fill out a consent form. On the experiment day, gatekeepers and children signed the consent form after fully reading it, and which was tailored specifically for their understanding.

Visual Illustration (2 min). Before performing the experiment, participants were handed a Visual Illustration Sheet (Fig. 3) providing step-by-step instructions on how to use the material presented to them. As mentioned in Section 4.2.1, under supervision of the participant's gatekeepers, the participants received verbal and written instructions about the purpose of the task and were explained using a laptop how to use the AIQ, play, stop, and rate sounds.

State Mood. Children were asked how they felt prior to answering the AIQ (Fig. 4). This step was crucial for the rest of the study as it would ensure that participants' answers were not biased by a 'bad day'.

Tasks (10 min). The author was present at the agreed premises (at SimVis, Creatovators CIC, SASC, and at the participants' home) and along with the gatekeepers observed the children during the experiment. First, gatekeepers were requested to fill out AQ-10 for children aged 4–11, which has already been validated through several research works

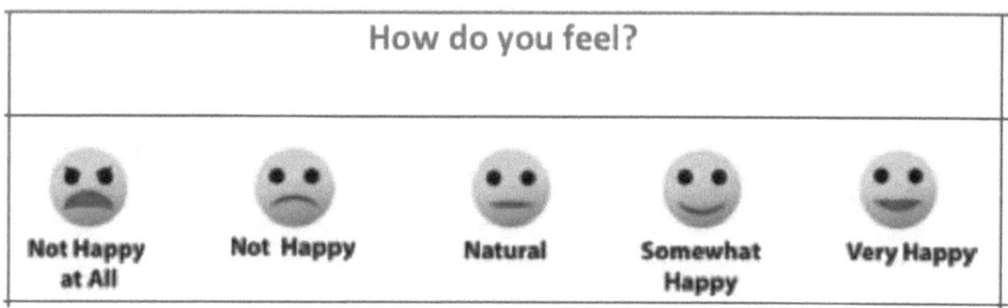

Fig. 3. Illustration of how to use the Auditory Interactive Questionnaire.

Fig. 4. Sate mood question prior starting the Audio Interactive Questionnaire.

(Autism Research Centre, 1992). The purpose of this questionnaire was to ensure that the participants were appropriate subject for the experiment. Children were then required to complete the AIQ in which they were asked about their degree of tolerance to sounds (Fig. 5). The question about the type and intensity of sound was answered using a computer interface presented in Section 6.4.1 because it was deemed to be difficult to describe in textual form. According to the participants' comfort, they were asked whether they wanted to wear headphones or [13, 14] and use a mouse. As introduced earlier, for health and safety reasons, the volume of the reproduced sounds was previously (Section 3.2.1) tested using a sound level meter to ensure that it did not exceed safe recommended audio levels [15].

4.3　Data Analysis

A typical Likert scale (Very Happy = 1, Somewhat Happy = 2, OK = 3, Not Happy = 4, and Not Happy at All = 5) using iconic faces was employed to rate the statements proposed through the questionnaires (Fig. 6). Data analysis involved averaging questionnaire statement outcomes. Thus, due to the limited number of participants, no statistical analysis was performed at this stage. Data management was performed using Microsoft Excel for calculating means and standard deviation values (Table 6).

Fig. 5. Photos of AIQ on the laptop along with the headphones and earphones

Fig.6. Typical Likert scale in the Audio Interactive Questionnaire.

5 Results

Seven out of 30 sounds were identified to be more critical (Table 6).

Table 2. Sounds used for audio experiments.

Sounds	Mean Rating (1–5)	σ
Applause 1	2.2	1.14
Applause 2	2.4	0.7
Baby Crying 1	3.2	1.32
Baby Crying 2	3.7	1.64
Bell 1	2.8	0.79
Bell 2	3.4	0.84
Bird 1	1.4	0.7
Bird 2	2.3	1.16
Checkout Till 1	3.0	0.94
Checkout Till 2	2.3	1.06

(continued)

Table 2. (*continued*)

Sounds	Mean Rating (1–5)	σ
Dog 1	2.2	1.32
Dog 2	2.4	1.07
Door slamming 1	2.6	1.07
Door slamming 2	2.6	1.07
Drilling 1	3.5	0.97
Drilling 2	3.4	1.58
Fire engine 1	3.2	1.32
Fire engine 2	4.1	1.29
Fireworks 1	3.0	1.63
Fireworks 2	2.2	1.75
Hammering 1	3.1	1.29
Hammering 2	2.7	1.34
Rattling of dishes 1	2.8	1.03
Rattling of dishes 2	2.8	1.4
Rustling paper 1	2.0	0.94
Rustling paper 2	2.5	0.97
Traffic noise 1	3.9	0.99
Traffic noise 2	2.5	1.72
Train 1	3.4	1.07
Train 2	2.6	1.65

From Table 2, it can be observed that the Fire Engine 2 sound was rated highest in terms of dislike ($M = 4.1 \pm 1.29$), followed by Traffic Noise 1 ($M = 3.9 \pm 0.99$) and Baby Crying 2 ($M = 3.7 \pm 1.64$), whereas Bell 2, Drilling 1, Drilling 2, and Train 1 were rated lowest ($M = 3.5 \pm 0.97$ to $M = 3.4 \pm 1.07$) of the seven sounds. Most higher intensity sounds were rated higher than those sounds of lower intensity.

Surprisingly, however, only the intensity of the sound Supermarket Check Out Till 1 (two sounds of check out tills) had a lower rating ($M = 2.3 \pm 1.06$) than Check Out Till 2 ($M = 3 \pm 0.94$). Also, Drilling sounds 1 and 2 were repeatedly rated similarly ($M = 3.5 \pm 0.97$ and $M = 3.4 \pm 1.58$ respectively). The seven most disliked audio samples will be implemented in the following serious game experimental study in the next chapter. Therefore, these sounds will be considered for the design of an SG that aims to familiarize children with ASD and auditory hypersensitivity are:

- Baby crying 2: sound of a crying new-born baby
- Bell 2: sound of school bell ringing twice
- Drilling 1: sound of drilling teeth
- Drilling 2: sound of drilling wood
- Fire engine 2: sound of three fire engine alarms

- Traffic noise 1: sound of three cars passing on a highway
- Train 1: sound of a moving train from right to left direction

6 Discussion

This study has illustrated the most irritating sounds for children with ASD aged between 8 and 11. Twelve male participants aged from 8 to 11 (M = 9.5), were recruited for the experiment. Only males attended the experiment, which was not surprising considering that statistics show that more males than females are diagnosed with autism [16–18]. All participants were diagnosed with ASD. However, the data from two (out of 12) participants had to be excluded; this is because participant 10 was very happy with all 30 sounds, and participant 7 had responded with 'Very Happy to OK' to the questions (Appendix I-5). The type of sounds in the AIQ were inspired from an earlier study (see Section 1.1). Then, the AIQ application was refined to be consistent with expert reviews in the internal testing (Section 1.4.1) and tester feedback in the pilot testing (see Section 1.4.2). Later, in the experiment (Section 1.4.3) allowed highlighting seven sounds that appeared to be particularly critical for children with ASD, these sounds were rated from M = 3.4 and above consider as closer in the Likert scale to Not Happy = 4 and Not Happy at All = 5 than the sounds rated with M = 3.2 and below. These sounds are the following; Baby Crying 2, Bell 2, Drilling 1, Drilling 2, Fire Engine 2, Traffic Noise 1, and Train 1 and therefore allow addressing the research question - What are the most critical sounds for children with ASD?.

Moreover, the results addressed the second sub-research question- Does the intensity of sounds affects the degree to which children with ASD tend to consider these sounds? - with 13 sounds of high intensity out of a total of 15 being recognized as the most disliked.

Overall, all participating children completed the AIQ successfully. None of the participants reported to experience anxiety before the experiment and therefore it can be assumed that experimental outcomes were not bias by a particular participant altered mood.

Although each participant was clearly explained the aim of this experiment; one participant stated to feel very happy with all sounds. Later analysis of the gatekeeper AQ-Children revealed that the participant was somehow sensitive to certain sounds but did not tend to feel uncomfortable when the participant was in control of the sound reproduction. In this case, the gatekeeper and the main researcher asked the participant for further explanation concerning the possible effect of these sound when reproduced unexpectedly in an everyday environment. As result, participant answered ranging from 'Very Angry' to 'Very Happy'.

In addition, it was observed that two participants were not listening to each sound entirely. For instance, when the author realized that participants 8 and 11 were avoiding listening to some sounds, the author asked them why this was occurring, to which they responded that 'I already listened to the same sounds earlier' and 'it's looping the same sounds again' – so the author then explained that every type of sound has two different audio samples. However, in this instance, it may be that participants 8 and 11 were very irritated by the sounds they tried to skip. Similarly, another participant stopped answering the AIQ, saying 'I finished' as he thought that he had completed rating all sounds; therefore, he was shown the visual illustration sheet again and informed that he must see the final scene (once it had finished. Certain sounds (fireworks 1, rustling of paper 1 and 2) were also confused by participants 1 and 12, and the author therefore had to explain what they were. This would suggest a possible participatory design approach for further development of this study, where an individual participating autistic child acknowledges irritating sounds in order for the results to be more accurate.

7 Conclusion

This study identified seven critical sounds—fire engine sirens, traffic noise, baby crying, drilling, school bells, and trains—that evoke significant discomfort in children with ASD, with higher-intensity sounds generally being more aversive. The use of an emoji-based digital questionnaire effectively captured children's responses, demonstrating the feasibility of child-friendly tools in sensory research. However, the small, male-only sample and challenges in participant recruitment limit generalizability. Notably, individual differences in sound perception, such as variability in responses to intensity, underscore the need for personalized approaches in therapeutic SG design. Future work should incorporate participatory design methods to refine sound selection and address potential ambiguities in auditory stimuli recognition. Expanding recruitment to include diverse demographics and larger cohorts will enhance robustness. These insights provide a foundation for developing targeted SGs to improve sensory coping strategies, ultimately enhancing quality of life for children with ASD and auditory hypersensitivity.

Acknowledgments. This work was funded by the King Abdullah Scholarship Program (2014–2018). We thank the participating children, parents, and educators. We are grateful to Dr. Mathieu Poyade (The Glasgow School of Art) and Dr. David Simmons (University of Glasgow) for their supervision, as well as June Grindley, Neelam Jhakra, Dr. Sandy Louchart, and Brian Loranger for their critical feedback. Institutional support was provided by the depute head teacher, school staff, Creatovators CIC, Strathclyde Autistic Society Club, Glasgow Science Centre, and the Glasgow School of Art's School of Simulation and Visualisation. Special thanks to Victor Portela Romero, Louise Dolan, Hajara Alfa, Akash Angral, Dr. Polina Zioga, Dr. Jessica Argo, and Sawitree Wisetchat.

References

1. Case-Smith, J., Weaver, L.L., Fristad, M.A.: A systematic review of sensory processing interventions for children with autism spectrum disorders. Autism **19**(2), 133–148 (2014)
2. Tomchek, S.D., Dunn, W.: Sensory processing in children with and without autism: A comparative study using the short sensory profile. Am. J. Occup. Ther. **61**(2), 190–200 (2007)
3. Dawson, G., Watling, R.: Interventions to facilitate auditory, visual, and motor integration in autism: A review of the evidence. J. Autism Dev. Disord. **30**(5), 415–421 (2000)
4. Rogers, S.J., Ozonoff, S.: Annotation: what do we know about sensory dysfunction in autism? A critical review of the empirical evidence. J. Child Psychol. Psychiatry. **46**(12), 1255–1268 (2005)

5. Zakari, H.M., Poyade, M., Simmons, D.: Sinbad and the Magic Cure: A Serious Game for Children with ASD and Auditory Hypersensitivity. In: Dias, J., Santos, P., Veltkamp, R. (eds.) Games and Learning Alliance. GALA 2017. Lecture Notes in Computer Science, vol. 10653. Springer, Cham (2017)

6. Zakari, H.M., Ma, M., Simmons, D.: A review of serious games for children with autism spectrum disorders (ASD), Lecture Notes in Computer Science (including subseries Lecture Notes in Artificial Intelligence and Lecture Notes in Bioinformatics), Vol. 8778 (2014)

7. 'EASe Funhouse Tresure Hunt - Vision Play' (2017). https://visionplay.com/product/ease-funhouse-tresure-hunt/. Accessed 21 Feb 2017

8. Rimland, B., Edelson, S.M.: Brief report: A pilot study of auditory integration training in autism. J. Autism Dev. Disord. **25**(1), 61–70 (1995)

9. Gomes, E. et al.: Auditory hypersensitivity in children and teenagers with autistic spectrum disorder. A quivos de Neuro-Psiquiatria. **62**(3B), 797–801 (2004)

10. Ben-Sasson, A., Hen, L., Fluss, R., Cermak, S.A., Engel-Yeger, B., Gal, E.: A meta-analysis of sensory modulation symptoms in individuals with autism spectrum disorders. J. Autism Dev. Disord. **39**(1), 1–11 (2009)

11. Anari, M., Axelsson, A., Eliasson, A., Magnusson, L.: Hypersensitivity to sound Questionnaire data, audiometry and classification. Scand. Audiol. **28**, 219–230 (1999)

12. Robertson, A.E.: Sensory experiences of Individuals with Autism Spectrum Disorder and Autistic Traits: A mixed Methods Approach (2012)

13. Beers, A.N., McBoyle, M., Kakande, E., Dar Santos, R.C., Kozak, F.K.: Autism and peripheral hearing loss: A systematic review. Int. J. Pediatr. Otorhinolaryngol. **78**(1), 96–101 (2013)

14. Nordahl, C.W., Simon, T.J., Zierhut, C., Solomon, M., Rogers, S.J., Amaral, D.G.: Brief report: Methods for acquiring structural MRI data in very young children with autism without the use of sedation. J. Autism Dev. Disord. **38**(8), 1581–1590 (2008)

15. LexisNexis, B.: Headphones and the Noise at Work Regulations (1992). http://www.isvr.co.uk/reprints/Headphones. Accessed 14 Feb 2017

16. Arking, D.E. et al.: A Common Genetic Variant in the Neurexin Superfamily Member CNTNAP2 Increases Familial Risk of Autism. Am. J. Hum. Genet. **82**(1), 160–164 (2008)

17. Baron-Cohen, S.: The extreme male brain theory of autism. Trends Cogn. Sci. **6**(6), 248–254 (2002)

18. Goin-Kochel, R.P., Abbacchi, A., Constantino, J.N.: Lack of evidence of increased genetic loading for autism among families of affected females: Replication from family history data in two large samples. Autism. **11**(3), 279–86 (2007)

Author Index

MIX
Papier aus verantwortungsvollen Quellen
Paper from responsible sources
FSC® C105338

If you have any concerns about our products,
you can contact us on
ProductSafety@springernature.com

In case Publisher is established outside the EU,
the EU authorized representative is:
Springer Nature Customer Service Center GmbH
Europaplatz 3, 69115 Heidelberg, Germany

Printed by Libri Plureos GmbH
in Hamburg, Germany